THE ILLUSTRATED ENCYCLOPEDIA OF
WITCHCRAFT &
PRACTICAL MAGIC

THE ILLUSTRATED ENCYCLOPEDIA OF
WITCHCRAFT & PRACTICAL MAGIC

A visual guide to the history and practice of magic through the ages – its
origins, ancient traditions, language, learning, rituals and great practitioners.

Susan Greenwood and Raje Airey

LORENZ BOOKS

This edition is published by Lorenz Books, an imprint of Anness Publishing Ltd, Hermes House, 88–89 Blackfriars Road, London SE1 8HA tel. 020 7401 2077; fax 020 7633 9499 www.lorenzbooks.com; www.annesspublishing.com

UK agent: The Manning Partnership Ltd, tel. 01225 478444; fax 01225 478440; sales@manning-partnership.co.uk

UK distributor: Grantham Book Services Ltd, tel. 01476 541080; fax 01476 541061; orders@gbs.tbs-ltd.co.uk

North American agent/distributor: National Book Network, tel. 301 459 3366; fax 301 429 5746; www.nbnbooks.com

Australian agent/distributor: Pan Macmillan Australia, tel. 1300 135 113; fax 1300 135 103; customer.service@macmillan.com.au

New Zealand agent/distributor: David Bateman Ltd, tel. (09) 415 7664; fax (09) 415 8892

© Anness Publishing Ltd 2006, 2007

Publisher: Joanna Lorenz
Editorial Director: Helen Sudell
Executive Editor: Joanne Rippin
Designers: Lesley Betts, Tony Cohen
Jacket Design: Jonathan Davidson

ETHICAL TRADING POLICY
Because of our ongoing ecological investment program, you, as our customer, can have the pleasure and reassurance of knowing that a tree is being cultivated on your behalf to naturally replace the materials used to make the book you are holding. For further information about this scheme, go to www.annesspublishing.com/trees

Previously published in two separate volumes, *The Encyclopedia of Magic and Witchcraft* and *Natural Magic*

The author and publishers have made every effort to ensure that all instructions contained within this book are accurate and safe, and cannot accept liability for any resulting injury, damage or loss to persons or property, however it may arise. If you do have any special needs or problems, consult your doctor or a physiotherapist. This book cannot replace medical consultation and should be used in conjunction with professional advice.

CONTENTS

FOREWORD

White sage smoke has cleansing properties.

We all share a common humanity, as a species we emerged from Africa and spread across all continents of the earth, and we are remarkably similar in having a human need to explain and shape the world around us. In this book we range across cultures and time – from informed speculation about humanity's earliest forms of spirituality to specific practices of magic across the globe. We examine ideas about witchcraft in non-Western and Western societies and, with one eye on the past, we also look at present Western magical practices, from Western Mysteries, druidry and the New Age to the most contemporary of all – chaos magic. One cannot help but be left with a feeling of amazement at the variety of ideas and practices which people all over the world use to communicate with other worlds, in the hope they could explain the realm of spirit. The human ability to create meaning is seemingly inexhaustible and ever-creative.

However, the similarities underlying all the different approaches to magic are also striking: the belief in an interconnecting realm of spirit, often termed the Otherworld in Western cultures, and explained as sympathetic magic by the early anthropologist James Frazer, is a constant thread running through the multiplicities of difference that separate societies and cultures in time and place. This connects us all in terms of physiology – all human beings have the ability to experience sympathetic magic through what have been called alternate forms of consciousness. There is what may be seen as an underlying shamanic dimension to human experience. Shamanism can be viewed very broadly as a form of consciousness which all human beings are capable of sharing but, in order to avoid what anthropologists call Eurocentrism, shamanic consciousness must also be viewed according to its specific cultural context. It is also important that Western cultures do not romanticize or "exoticize" the non-Western shamanic cultures that remain – seeing them in ways that deny their full humanity by projecting qualities on to them that have more to do with an imagined way of life than day-to-day reality. Shamanic consciousness is a source of human creativity and spirituality. Human consciousness has been explained by reference to a two-hemisphere model of the brain: the left being concerned with analytical thought processes, the right having an analogical or synthesizing function. Analytical thought and analogical thought have been seen as opposed, as two essentially unconnected modes of operation or as two orientations to reality. More recent work is seeking to overcome this dichotomy of consciousness, seeing the two as biologically, intimately connected and as two sides of a unitary process of thinking.

At a time when we as a species are in danger of destroying our planet, it is important to recognize our common humanity, as well as our connection to other forms of life. This does not mean that we must forget our differences or what makes us individuals; neither does it undervalue cultural variation. Magic today offers a view of the world that sees relationships between things – there is a connection shared between mountains, trees, animals, the moon, sun and stars, as well as the person next door. This book explores these relationships and the way that traditional, international, and modern forms of magic have been used in different ways to harness the powers of the natural world, and define human experience. The first part of the book will inform you, the second will inspire and teach you how to practise your own personal magic, and fulfil your potential in working in harmony with the natural magical world.

SUSAN GREENWOOD AND RAJE AIREY

The powerfully magical spiral shape.

Trees have enormous symbolic and magical power, and are also vital for the sustenance of life on our planet.

Some of the signs used in magic work.

The basic tools of magic include the chalice, or cup, the wand, the knife and the pentacle.

Crystals have magical properties.

THE HISTORY OF MAGIC

Although human societies have developed in extremely diverse ways, they have all shared a perception of the world that includes a spiritual dimension. Religious and magical traditions seek to explain the ordering of the universe and to understand our origins on earth and our eventual destination in some kind of afterlife. They also attempt to engage the energies of the natural world, to support human endeavour and to procure protection from the elemental violence of a universe in which our survival can sometimes seem fragile and uncertain.

Communication with the world of spirit has traditionally been channelled through individuals: shamans, priests, witches and magicians who have developed, or were born with, the ability to cross the divide. Their skill has often set them apart from other people, placing them in an ambiguous position where they are both revered for their power and reviled for their strangeness, sought out for help yet excluded from society. Meanwhile, our fundamental yearning to fathom the mysteries of magic and the unseen sustains our fascination with their practices.

INTRODUCTION

Shamanic or magic trances are depicted in these Palaeolithic rock paintings from Tanzania.

Our earliest forebears would have possessed an intimate knowledge of the features of the world around them: the rising and setting of the sun, the movement of the moon through the sky, the changing seasons and minute details about plants and animals. They depended on this knowledge for their survival – as a matter of life or death. We do not know the answers to questions about the early beliefs of humanity. All we can do is examine the evidence left in cultural artefacts, such as cave rock paintings, to imagine what life would have been like, and then make educated guesses. The first forms of spirituality probably arose through human interaction within the social group and through relationships with the wider surroundings; perhaps rituals were performed to find the whereabouts of animals to hunt or to heal a sick person. We can imagine that rites may have developed out of sharing wonder at the birth of a child, or expressing grief in the face of death.

Modern human beings, or *Homo sapiens*, were not the first hominids to have complex social groups: the Neanderthals were a sophisticated parallel species, who buried their dead with flowers, decorations or grave goods, possibly in readiness for the next life. What we both share is the ability to create order out of our experiences. Our large brains are able to question, experiment and search for answers to essential questions about life and death. The ability to question, to reflect, to represent experiences symbolically – in cave art and in language – is part of a process of creating meaning. Spiritual beliefs and magic all play a part in this process.

Spirituality for early humans was probably associated with keeping a social group or band together, curing the sick and controlling the natural world. It concerned much that we would describe as magical today. Only later did it come to be formalized with sacred texts and called religion. However, magic and religion are categories that are difficult to maintain, and for most of human history, and across the world in various cultures, there is no absolute separation.

In the first section of the book we will look at the rich variety of magico-religious beliefs around the world. We will explore how different cultures, varying in both place and time, have created meaning through worlds of spirits. Starting with what has been termed shamanism, humanity's oldest spiritual practice, we will see that although it has occurred in many different places, there is an underlying essence that involves specialist communication with spirits.

Belief in a spiritual realm is also the foundation of ideas about witchcraft – witches inhabit a universe in which powers and forces may be directed for good or ill. Definitions of witchcraft, like those of magic and religion, change from society to society and through the passage of time. What is called witchcraft in Africa is very different to that of European societies.

As the chapters of this section unfold, the fascinating variety of differences will become apparent. We will meet the Azande of central Africa to see how life is ordered through ideas about witchcraft and divination, and how oracles are used to determine important events. In Europe we will see how the Christian Church played a central part in the creation of the stereotype of the evil witch, and how ordinary women, and to a lesser extent men, were tried and executed as witches during the period 1450–1750. Magic is currently undergoing a revival in the West, and more and more people are turning to alternative magico-religious traditions such as druidry, the New Age, Western forms of shamanism, heathenism, and chaos magic as ways of creating meaning and of expressing their spiritual lives.

The earliest human civilizations used magic and religion to explain natural manifestations.

An Indian priest performs a ceremony to capture spirits, which has its roots in prehistory.

Modern pagans in Europe celebrate rituals that mark the passing of the seasons, with symbolism and practices that they claim go back to the days before Christianity.

MAGIC IN MYTH, RELIGION AND SCIENCE

Throughout the world, human beings have engaged in a multitude of beliefs and practices to express, explain and give meaning to the cosmos. In the past magic and religion and also science, which often overlaps the two, are categories that have been difficult to distinguish between, but today we tend to see magic and religion as entirely different from each other. Although sometimes dismissed as merely fantasy, magic is also sometimes seen as manipulation of the divine, even to the extent of being evil. Religion, on the other hand, is regarded as involving the worship of an essentially good deity. Through history, the word magic has been a term of abuse for what is thought to be antisocial and immoral forms of spirituality; it has become a scapegoat for everything that an established religion disapproves of. This chapter will explore the differences and similarities between the way creation mythologies, religious beliefs, scientific endeavour, and magical practices are linked.

WHAT IS MAGIC?

The dictionary definition of magic is that it is the art of using spells to invoke supernatural powers to influence events. This is a very general description and it is important to consider in greater detail what these supernatural powers are and which events are to be influenced. This book advocates that magic is a word that describes the inner nature of the beings that make up the universe – the spiritual part of all things. The spirit forms a hidden dimension to the ordinary, everyday world that we inhabit. Most of the time we are unaware of it (hence magic often being called "the occult" – literally "concealed") and when something uncanny happens, we tend to put it down to coincidence. What we call coincidence today would be interpreted very differently by people of cultures other than our own, or by people from varying times in the past. Unfortunately, magic is often used as a derogatory term used to encompass all that orthodox religion disapproves of or prohibits and is therefore frequently viewed in negative terms.

To many peoples throughout the world there are spirits in nature.

Stop for a moment and imagine what it would be like to live in the world of our ancestors, where everything was perceived as alive and permeated with vibrant force and energy, both good and bad. This included not only mountains, rocks, rivers, oceans, plants, algae, fungi and insects, but also human ailments, such as toothache or the common cold. How differently would we perceive the world around us? Would we feel linked to everything – from the chair we sit in to the trees in the fields, the sun, moon and stars? Spirits were part of everyday life for our ancestors and it is likely that these ancestors performed rituals to create meaning, balance and a feeling of connection between them and the spirit world. These ceremonies would have integrated the group and the cosmos into the world, providing security on physical, psychological and social levels. This spirit world that co-exists with the physical world could be called a "magical" world. Today's focus in the Western world on rationality and the development of a view of science that does not take spirits into account has meant that this magical connection between humankind and the spirit world has been lost.

In many cultures around the world, the everyday world co-exists and overlaps with a spirit dimension. Living in touch with spirits can bring anxiety. The way in which spirits are manipulated can be a constant source of speculation and concern in such societies, and problems such as illness, death or misfortune are frequently put down to witchcraft or sorcery. When people practise magic they attempt to control, communicate or influence spirits. Magical specialists explore, modify or move the borders between the ordinary world and the spirit

The importance of the sun to human life has given it a special place in many belief systems around the world.

The highest mountains were often seen as the kingdom of the gods; their inaccessibility and their nearness to heaven ensured their special status.

world – the known and the unknown. These technicians of magic, who may be called shamans, sorcerers, magicians, witches, witch doctors or medicine men and women, all share a relationship with the spiritual realm.

Magic involves an animistic worldview. Anima means "the soul", the innermost part or essence of a being and its animating principle. Animism is the belief that the world is profoundly alive and that all natural objects and phenomena – the trees and rocks, wind, rain, snow, birds, insects and fish, as well as humans – are alive and have vital essence; everything that exists lives and has consciousness. The consciousness of spirits can merge into human consciousness, and the soul of a living human is believed to become spirit when it dies, dead people becoming either ancestor spirits or part of a larger elemental spirit. For the Native Americans, each wind is the breath of some being that lives in the direction from which the wind blows. The wind talks with the voice of its spirit as it roars, moans, sighs or whistles.

The nineteenth-century anthropologist Edward Tylor (1832–1917) claimed that the origins of religion lay in animism, which he defined as a "belief in spirit beings". Tylor saw the origin of religion in individual psychology. He thought that in primitive humans the idea of religion arose from the notion of a soul which came from dreams. The soul was transformed into a spirit being after death, leading to the development of ancestor and spirit cults.

Tylor was an evolutionary thinker: he reflected the ideas of his time by seeing animism as a lower form of religion than polytheism (a belief in many gods) and monotheism (a belief in one creator god). He saw a natural progression from animism through polytheism to monotheism, with Christianity as a higher revealed religion that is characterized by intercessionary worship and prayer.

SACRED GEOGRAPHY

The ancient native religions of Central and South America – including the Aztecs, the Maya and the Inca – had elaborate rituals that linked the people and the land in a sacred relationship. The Mayans conceived the earth as a square – flat and four-cornered – with an elaborate colour symbolism that placed red in the east, white in the north, black in the west, yellow in the south, and green in the centre. This pattern formed the back of a monstrous crocodile that lurked in a pool of waterlilies. For the Mayans the sky was multi-tiered, supported on the four corners by gods, and formed a double-headed serpent; the 13 layers of the heavens had their own gods. The underworld had nine layers and the sun and the moon passed through it after they had disappeared below the horizon.

For the Inca a supreme creator called Viracocha, a white-bearded god who created the sun, moon and stars after a flood that destroyed the world, was a controller of the various spheres of the cosmos. Inca religion emphasized harmony with the land and the ceremonial at Cuzco (which means navel in Quechua, the Incan language) integrated the life of the people with the wider cosmos.

SHAMANISM

Human beings have often turned to a spirit world for help and advice in times of trouble. In early groups of people it is likely that a shaman would have undertaken trance journeys to mediate between the human and the spirit worlds; it was the shaman who perhaps helped to resolve problems as to why someone was ill, or to find out why the animals had not returned from a particular migration and there was nothing to hunt. Even today in small-scale societies – from Siberia to the Amazonian region to Africa – shamanism is still practised, albeit under increasingly difficult conditions.

A Stone Age rock painting that records a shamanic trance, known as simbo, in which dancers somersault above hallucinated animals.

PREHISTORIC SHAMANS

The discovery of prehistoric cave paintings around the world has led to many speculations that the earliest people to practise magic were shamans. These cave paintings may represent the shaman linking the spirit world to the real world – for example, by painting scenes of certain wounded or dead animals, he was communicating his wish for a successful hunt.

Some cave paintings are 30,000 years old, others may be older, while some are much more recent. Rock art has been found throughout the world – in Africa, Australia, Europe and South America. Made with flint blades and coloured with iron ochre or black manganese dioxide, the paintings are detailed and delicate portrayals of prey animals such as wild cattle, mammoths, deer, horses and bison and, more rarely, predator species such as lion, wolf and bear. Some of these paintings show hunting scenes with animals carrying spear-inflicted wounds or dead carcasses; representations of human beings are much less common.

What did these paintings mean for the people who created them? We will never know for sure, but we do know that the peoples who painted them were culturally sophisticated and that the paintings in all probability contributed to relationships of reciprocity between humans in their everyday social interactions, and between humans and animals. What made modern human beings so successful was the ability to create a web of social alliances in kinship links and trading associations, as well as passing on information about animals to hunt. People thought about the animals that they hunted. The visual images of the animals may have involved a form of sympathetic magic whereby a hunter, or a group of hunters, in a state of altered consciousness or trance, would dance the animal that they wanted to capture, creating a powerful link between themselves and their prey.

Art may have had a part in creating and maintaining these links. It seems likely that it had a role to play in rituals to communicate clan or tribal values and important information regarding adulthood – perhaps the secrets of menstruation or hunting techniques.

A shaman of the Huli tribe from Papua New Guinea stands at an altar in a sacred place that is decorated with painted skulls.

A LIFE OF SPIRIT

Sometimes it is helpful to look at contemporary modern humans who have gathering and hunting lifestyles to gain some sort of idea about what the spiritual beliefs of our ancestors might have been. Modern hunter-gatherers, such as the !Kung of the Kalahari Desert in southern Africa, practised a semi-nomadic lifestyle until comparatively recently. According to anthropologist Richard Katz, there was much emphasis on sharing, and all resources were circulated among band members, and also between bands. Neither was religion a separate enterprise for the !Kung – the life of the spirit was an inextricable aspect of everyday life. The god Gao Na sent good and bad fortune through the spirits and to Kauha, a lesser god, and Gao Na was human in his follies and pleasures. The gods lived in the sky and were attended by the spirits

A Siberian shaman at a sacred site, wearing clothes that are made from animal hides.

of the dead; they were god-like in their powers but were a part of everyday life as well as being apart from it.

The !Kung practised healing dances, which they performed at night. These dances were an integrating and enhancing force central to group solidarity. The dances may have cured an ill person by "pulling out" a sickness, but the healing was also synergistic – bringing people together and thereby creating a whole society from separate individuals.

!Kung healers are what we might call shamans and they were able to see what was troubling everyone. By getting into a trance they could 'see' inside people's bodies, or travel to the realm where the gods and the spirits of dead ancestors lived. A struggle would ensue between the spirits of the dead and the healer, who would attempt to bring back the soul of a sick person to the realm of the living.

Men and women of the San "Bushman" Tribe from the Kalahari, Botswana, dancing a traditional dance at night.

THE SHAMAN'S ROLE

The historian Mircea Eliade defined a shaman as a man or woman who "journeys" in an ecstatic trance, usually induced by rhythmic drumming or, in some cases, by the use of psychoactive drugs. In its widest sense a shaman is someone who has specialist techniques for communicating with spirits through entering a trance or alternative state of consciousness. It is the shaman's task to make sure that relationships between the human world and the spirit world are kept harmonious.

A shaman is often "called" by the spirits. He or she is one who is set apart from others by a special sign such as being born with a caul (the membrane that encloses the fetus in the womb), a deformity or a tendency to be dreamy, or through some life crisis such as serious disease or mental breakdown. A shaman's initiation usually takes the form of a psycho-spiritual disintegration, which leads to a death of the former self and a rebirth into a shamanic life with the spirits.

Shamanic initiation involves visiting the underworld, a place where the initiate shaman has to undergo dismemberment. The initiate has to "die" in everyday reality and enter a special relationship with spirit beings, a process whereby knowledge and teachings about the spirit world are communicated.

Petroglyphs on a sandstone slab in Johns Canyon, Cedar Mesa. The triangular figure is thought to be a bird shaman, illustrating the belief that a shaman could take on the characteristics of a chosen animal.

Eliade tells of how each Yakut Siberian shaman has a Bird-of-Prey Mother with an iron beak, hooked claws and a long tail. This mythical bird, which shows itself only at the shaman's spiritual birth and death, takes his soul and carries it to the underworld, where it is left to ripen on a branch of pitch pine. When the soul has reached maturity the bird carries it back to earth, cuts the candidate's body into bits and distributes them among the evil spirits of disease and death. Each spirit devours the part of the body that is his share, and this is seen to give the future shaman power to cure corresponding diseases. After devouring the whole body, the evil spirits depart, the Bird Mother restores the bones to their places, and the candidate wakes as from a deep sleep.

JOURNEYING BETWEEN WORLDS

Shamanic cosmologies are frequently formed from three regions: a middle world corresponding to the everyday world on earth, an upper world related to the sky and celestial realms, and a lower or underworld, which reaches deep down into the earth. These three regions are often connected by a central axis – an opening through which the shaman travels on his

An Inuit carving showing a shaman in a trance, helped by two animal spirits and a drum.

An Inuit carving representing a shaman associated with a spirit called Taqhisim.

or her journey, which may be represented as a tree. The tree connects the three regions – the branches touch the sky, while the roots go into the underworld. The axis may also be likened to a pillar or a mountain, but all the variations of shamanic cosmologies function like spiritual road maps.

When a shaman journeys to spiritual realms, she or he seeks to understand the relationships between different realities and to mediate any breakdown in communications that affect the social group. Knud Rasmussen, an authority on Inuit (Eskimo) shamans, describes how the shaman makes a journey to the bottom of the sea to find out why the sea spirit is withholding animals for the Inuit people to hunt. As the shaman journeys, the household sits waiting and singing songs to help the shaman as he descends on his perilous journey. After overcoming many obstacles, he enters the house of the sea spirit. She sits with her back to the seals, walrus and whales, who are puffing and blowing. The sea spirit is angry with humans because they have broken taboos. Her hair hangs down in a tangled, untidy mess hiding her eyes so she cannot see. Human

An important element of shamanic belief was the link that the shaman had with the animal world. It was thought that while in a trance, a shaman could become one with the spirit of an animal such as a wolf, and benefit from its wisdom.

misdeeds and offences gather as dirt and impurity over her body. The shaman must turn the sea spirit's face to the animals and comb her hair to appease her anger so that she will clear the way for the animals and rich hunting will return. When the shaman returns to the community the breaches of taboo must be confessed so that harmony between the human and spirit worlds can return. In this way the shaman heals discord within the social group.

A Tibetan shaman wearing a special "ringer" hat, which for centuries has been worn for aiding trances.

A modern day shaman from Kenya, wearing a ceremonial headdress.

MAGIC AND RELIGION

Although most religions differentiate themselves clearly from magic, what is meant by "magic" and "religion" changes over time. When we look at spiritual beliefs and behaviour cross-culturally and at different periods in time, it is almost impossible to make clear demarcations between what is magic and what is religion. It is likely that our earliest human ancestors practised what we would now call magic, and only later did spiritual beliefs and practices become more formalized and written down to found the basis of what we refer to as religion today, such as Hinduism, Buddhism, Judaism, Christianity and Islam. In the pages that follow we will look at the cultures of antiquity: those of the Egyptians, Greeks, Romans, Celts and North European peoples. We will also study the ideas of India, Africa and Australia, and then explore the relationship between science and magic, and the role that astrology and alchemy have played in the development of Western thought.

A bronze portal in San Zeno Cathedral, Verona, showing a magical battle between Israel and Egypt. Aaron's staff is being transformed into a serpent and is attacking an Egyptian.

Most cultures have, or have had in their past, some form of magical tradition that recognizes a shamanistic inter-connectedness of spirit. This may have been long ago, as a folk tradition that died out with the establishment of a major world religion, such as Judaism, Christianity, Islam or Buddhism, or it may still co-exist with that world religion. Some small societies still retain the remnants of shamanistic practices, such as in Siberia, India or Africa, although because of the pressures of the modern world they are becoming fewer. Many, such as the Native Americans and Native Australians, have been persecuted by European settlers, who have taken their land and annihilated their people. For these peoples, "magic" is an integral aspect of their culture, and one that has survived persecution, and it cannot be neatly separated from religion. However, magic to Westerners became associated with "primitive" peoples who were represented as uncivilized natives with exotic and strange customs.

CONTROLLING HIDDEN FORCES

Magic is similar to religion in its focus on the spiritual dimension and the worship of a supernatural authority, but it differs in its attempt to control hidden forces. It may include an aspect of worship but it is also associated with the coercion and command of hidden (occult) or spiritual forces. This control may be achieved through divination, spells or the making of amulets.

Divination is the art and practice of discovering the past or the future by spirit communication. Spells are all-powerful spoken formulae, words or phrases, which provoke a desired chain of events: these may be destructive, protective or medicinal, or may be used to break other spells or to obtain something, such as love or money. Amulets are protective charms that are worn to ward off evil.

This nineteenth-century picture of a medicine mask dance shows how native peoples have been portrayed as an "exotic other", having more to do with Westerners' ideas about Native Americans than the actual reality of their lives.

THE ORIGINS OF MAGIC

The word "magic" comes from the Greek *mageia*, which derives from *magoi*. The *magoi* were a Persian caste of priests who studied astrology and divination. During the Hellenistic period the new words *mageuein* and *magikos* took on a negative meaning. This negative view of magic was adopted by the Romans. Their officials and intellectuals pointed to its fraudulent character, seeing it as a mixture of medicine, astrology and religion. Practitioners of magic during this period made a distinction between lower (*goetia*) and higher (*theourgia*) forms. In practice, the division between lower and higher magic is flexible and, like the distinction between magic and religion, it tends to vary from place to place and from society to society. There are no hard and fast rules, and what may be termed bad and associated with the manipulation of spirits in one setting may be deemed positively beneficial in another.

Divination is the art of discovering the past or the future. Here, in a fresco painting from Pompeii, a Roman traveller consults a sorceress.

FROM SHAMAN TO PRIEST

Originally, in the earliest human societies, it was the shaman who took on the specific role of mediator between the everyday world and the spiritual dimensions, although the rest of the community was also involved in the process. Increasingly, as societies became larger and more complex, religious specialists took over this task. This created a more distinct specialist area, which later came to be governed by the interpretation of religious texts such as the Bible or the Koran. Spontaneous trance or possession by spirits began to be viewed as unorthodox practice and was relegated to marginal cults.

THE USE OF RITUAL

Both magic and religion often depend on ritual to maintain cosmic order, either through communication with a variety of sentient beings or through the worship of a divine creator god. Ritual creates a "space between the worlds" for communication with otherworldly beings or supernatural powers.

Rituals demarcate the ordinary from the extraordinary; they focus attention on cosmic processes, and thus often help maintain social solidarity and identity. This helps to define common values and affiliations and marks out those who contravene social rules. So the distinction between magic and religion often depends on the approval and disapproval of different kinds of spiritual practice. Magical elements exist in most religions, and most religions have their roots in some form of shamanic practice.

Fresco from Tepantitla Teotihuacan, Mexico, of an Aztec priest praying.

Three Nepalese shamans, known as Jhankaris, wear traditional clothes and perform an all-night ceremony for a boy with abdominal pains.

EGYPTIAN MAGIC

Both magic and religion depend on ritual to maintain cosmic order. The power of magico-religious names, spells, pictures, figures, amulets and the performance of rituals, which were seen to produce supernatural results, formed an important part of early Egyptian life. What ancient Egyptians believed to be their religion is today more commonly referred to as magical practice. Egyptian magic dates from a time when the predynastic and prehistoric inhabitants of Egypt believed that the earth, the underworld, the air and the sky were populated by countless beings, some of whom affirmed life and were friendly, while others caused death and destruction. The magical basis of early Egyptian thought is shown through its creation myths.

For early Egyptians, all life orginated from the waters of the Nile. Egyptian myth tells how a hill called Atum, "the Complete One", rose up out of the primordial waters of the abyss at the first

The River Nile in the mystical evening light.

The air god Shu is here depicted separating the sky goddess Nut from the earth god Geb. Detail from the coffin of Nespawershepi, chief scribe of the Temple of Amun c.984 BC.

time of light. Every day this was repeated in the birth of the sun from the abyss of the night, and also every year when the waters of the Nile flooded the surrounding land, bringing it to life. Atum, the risen land and light, generated the male Shu and the female Tefnut who gave birth to Nut (the sky goddess who gave birth to the stars) and to Geb (the earth god).

ISIS AND OSIRIS

Nut and Geb gave birth to Osiris and to Isis, and their brother Seth and sister, Nephthys. Osiris became the first king of Egypt and the creator of civilization, and his sister-wife Isis ruled in his absence. However, their brother Seth was jealous and conspired to kill Osiris. He constructed a chest and tricked Osiris into lying inside it, whereupon the lid was nailed shut and it was thrown into the Nile. The chest floated to the coast of Byblos and lodged itself in the branches of a tree, which grew up around it and enclosed it. The tree was so beautiful that the king and queen of Byblos had it made into a pillar for their palace.

Isis was stricken with grief and started to search for the chest. Disguising her divinity, she waited by a well in the city of Byblos. She befriended some of Queen Astarte's maidens and braided and perfumed their hair. When the maidens returned to the palace the queen sent for the person who had created such a wonderful fragrance, and made her the nurse to her child. Isis gave the child her finger to suck instead of her breast, and each night placed him in a fire to remove all his mortality. Meanwhile, she transformed herself into a swallow and flew around the pillar. One night the queen entered the room and was horrified to see her son lying in the fire. At this, Isis revealed her true identity and asked to be given the pillar. The king and queen agreed.

Taking the chest containing the body of Osiris, Isis set out for Egypt. While she was in the boat she took the form of a kite, hovered over her husband, and conceived their son Horus. Then she hid the chest and went to Buto to raise her child. However, Seth discovered the

chest one night while he was out hunting; he tore the body into 14 pieces and scattered them around the country. When Isis discovered what Seth had done she searched for the pieces, aided by their sister Nephthys and her son, the jackal-headed Anubis. Isis found every part of Osiris's body except his penis, for which she made a replica. When she fanned the reassembled body with her wings Osiris came to life again, to become the ruler of Eternity judging the souls of the dead.

COSMIC UNITY

This myth shows the interconnections between the human world, the realm of the gods and nature. Osiris dies with the parched land, the withering grain, the waning moon and all that is destructive. He returns to life in the rising waters of the Nile, the growing grain, the waxing moon and the affirmative nature of human beings. Osiris is brought to life by Isis. The creative force of Osiris, as the flooding of the Nile, and Isis, as the earth, is interrupted by the necessary element of death and destruction,

A wall painting of Osiris c.1300 BC from Sennutem's tomb, Thebes.

represented by Seth: from death comes life, and in life there is death. Both are part of the same cosmic unity. This primal Egyptian myth demonstrates the human connection with both the natural world and the spiritual realm of the gods; all are interlinked in the magical processes of life and death.

The cyclical nature of Egyptian mythology is shown here by the goddess Nut swallowing the sun at night to give birth to it again the following morning. The wall painting is from the ceiling of the tomb of Ramses VI in the Valley of the Kings.

GRAECO-ROMAN MAGIC

Greek religion originally consisted of simple rituals, later developing into complex systems of science and philosophy. It shifted from the veneration of local deities, in the forms of satyrs, shades, furies, nymphs, sibyls and muses, to the worship of an Olympian pantheon, headed by the god Zeus and his consort, the goddess Hera. Magic was a central part of this early Graeco-Roman culture.

ORACULAR MAGIC

Within the Graeco-Roman world, magic formed a common tradition and although each cultural region had its own specialization, there was an enormous amount of overlap and similarity; an abundance of material on magic was brought together and combined in

A detail from a vase painting of Aegeus, King of Athens, consulting the Delphic Oracle.

varying ways. Magic was a common theme in literary works, and Homer's *Iliad* and *Odyssey* contained many descriptions of it. The *Odyssey* in particular was recognized primarily as a book of magic, and Homeric verses were used as magical formulas. Magicians wrote handbooks that brought together spells, ritual procedures, instructions for using and making amulets, curse tablets and magical tools.

The Greeks were polytheists: they believed in many gods. Unpopulated areas of the country were dedicated to the gods, and oracular temples for divination and prophecy were frequently built near volcanic chasms or caverns, where misty vapours arose from underground waters. The oracles were a means by which humans could commune with gods. The best known of these was the Delphic oracle on Mount Parnassus, where people journeyed to learn about the future from the Pythia or priestess of Apollo who would pronounce their fate in an intoxicated frenzy. Attendant priests and priestesses assisted questioners by interpreting the Pythia's speech and sometimes by asking questions about the supplicants' dreams.

CLASSICAL WITCHES AND GODDESSES

Three witches were prominent in Graeco-Roman myth and literature and all presided over the mysteries of darkness: they were Circe, the enchantress visited by Odysseus; Medea, the niece of Circe, who helped Jason achieve his quest for the Golden Fleece; and Hecate, who was a goddess of the underworld.

The Greeks practised a form of rites called "Mysteries", which were known only to those who had been initiated. The most famous were the Eleusinian Mysteries. After a preparatory purifying stage that led the neophyte to a state of readiness, sacred objects were shown and it is thought likely that the myth of

Demeter, the goddess who represents life, welcomes her daughter Persephone, the goddess of the dead, back from the land of Hades.

A nineteenth-century portrayal of Circe, one of the three witches of the Graeco-Roman tradition.

Medea mixing one of her infamous potions.

Demeter and Persephone was performed as a form of initiation into the process of life and death. Demeter is the great mother of life and death and she contains within herself the upper and lower worlds. Demeter and her daughter Persephone are two aspects of the goddess and represent the living and the dead, the upperworld and the lower. Demeter searches for Persephone who has been abducted by Hades the ruler of the underworld. Because she has eaten the food of the dead, in the form of pomegranate seeds, she must spend one third of the year underground with him and two thirds above the ground with her mother. Upper and lower worlds are separated and reunited in a continuous regeneration as Demeter repeatedly loses and finds Persephone.

The practice of magic was seen to bring power, but it also had its pitfalls, as told in *The Golden Ass*, written by a Roman citizen, Lucius Apuleius in the second century AD. In the story, Apuleius is a naive young man who is accidentally transformed into an ass while trying to imitate a witch who is able to change herself into an owl at night. As an ass, Apuleius undergoes many trials and is mistreated by various masters. After a series of exuberant acts

of seduction and apparent murders, he escapes in desperation to a beach in the moonlight and prays to the goddess Ceres. She tells Apuleius that the next day there will be a festival in her honour, and that if he eats a garland of roses carried by a high priest he will be transformed back into his human form. Apuleius follows her instructions and in gratitude becomes an initiate.

ROMAN RELIGION

This was very eclectic and adopted the Greek pantheon, albeit with Romanized names. In addition, several cults taken from other traditions arose during the period: of particular note were those of Isis, Mithras (the Persian god of mediation beteen light and dark), and Christianity, which eventually became the state religion of the Roman Empire.

Hecate, goddess of the dark phase of the moon sits facing outwards, Artemis and Selene sit on either side of her, representing the new and full moon respectively.

CELTIC MAGIC

The word "Celtic" has become a convenient label for the indigenous peoples of north-west Europe, who occupied a vast territory from the Pyrenees to the Rhine, and from Ireland to Romania. By about 600BC, most of western Europe was occupied by tribes that were thought to be culturally one people. The Greeks named these peoples of central Europe *Keltoi*. The Celts were despised by the Greeks and Romans, who thought them barbarians, viewing their nomadic lifestyle as lacking the arts of civilization.

Who were the Celts? They left no written records and so no direct information is known about them. All that we have found out comes from archaeological discoveries or through the writings of classical Mediterranean authors such as Caesar, Pliny, Tacitus and Lucian. These accounts are probably biased but they are useful when their descriptions match archaeological evidence. We do not know what the magico-religious beliefs of these peoples were, but classical accounts and archaeological descriptions demonstrate the existence of human sacrifice and head-collection.

CELTIC SPIRITUAL BELIEFS

Archaeologists have excavated a number of sites where votive deposits – including axes, swords, daggers, corn grinding stones and coins – show evidence of ritual activity, and many interpretations have been made, but we have no definite answers to questions about Celtic spiritual beliefs. These peoples did not construct permanent roofed temples but probably created sacred enclosures as a focus for ritually damaged votive deposits to be offered to the gods. Many rites may have been performed at sites of natural, religious significance – by the side of rivers, springs, in woods, and on mountains. In other words, places endowed with sanctity, a central component of Celtic magico-religious practices.

Castlerigg in Cumbria is one of the many stone circles in Britain and northern Europe that are believed to be ancient sites of Celtic worship.

The Druids were Celtic priests, prophets, soothsayers and magicians, and were written about by a number of Graeco-Roman authors, who derived their information from Posidonius. Caesar says that the Druids officiated in the worship of the gods, regulated sacrifices and ruled on religious questions.

An ancient carved head at a natural spring, in Clwyd, Wales, probably once a shrine to a water spirit or god.

It appears that these tribal peoples had a wide variety of deities, which were focused on appropriate tribal gods and the locality. Weird-shaped rocks, gnarled trees, springs and bogs were all places where the gods could be contacted. Female deities may have had some association with fertility; they could also have been endowed with healing attributes. However, their greatest powers were likely to have been associated with their relationship with a magical otherworld.

MYTHS AND LEGENDS

The Celts had an oral tradition and so the only information we have about their beliefs comes from early Christian monastic scribes who collected accounts of pre-Christian beliefs in the eighth and ninth centuries. One such Irish story concerns a vengeful goddess called the Mórrigan. When the hero Cú Chulainn ignores her sexual advances she gets her revenge by trying to distract him while he is engaged in battle with Lóch:

So the Mórrigan came there in the guise of a white red-eared heifer accompanied by 50 heifers … Cú Chulainn made a cast at the Mórrigan and shattered one of her eyes. Then the Mórrigan appeared in the form of a slippery, black eel swimming downstream and went into the pool and coiled herself around Cú Chulainn's legs ... Then the Mórrigan came in the guise of a shaggy russet-coloured she-wolf. While Cú Chulainn was warding her off, Lóch wounded him. Thereupon Cú Chulainn was filled with rage and wounded him ... and pierced his heart in his breast.

A great weariness fell on Cú Chulainn. The Mórrigan appeared to him in the shape of a squint-eyed old woman milking a cow with three teats. He asked her for a drink and she gave him milk from the first teat. "Good health to the giver!" Cú Chulainn said. "The blessing of God and man on you." And her head was healed and made whole. She gave him milk from the second teat and her eye was made whole. She gave him milk from the third teat and her legs were made whole. "You said you would never heal me," the Mórrigan said. "If I'd known it was you I wouldn't have," Cú Chulainn said.

This story illustrates an essential magical world view – that there is no permanent boundary between the human and the animal worlds. The tale demonstrates the Mórrigan's powers to change her shape or "shape-shift" into a red-eared heifer, a black eel and a she-wolf; and by her metamorphosis into an old woman she tricks Cú Chulainn into healing her from the wounds that he has inflicted upon her.

THE CELTIC CHARACTER

Much romance has been built up around the Celts and they have, in modern times, become the focus of a particular nostalgic view of the past. They have been portrayed as a distinct cultural group displaying characteristics such as chivalry, courage and dauntless bravery. The Celts have also been viewed as posessing a sensitivity to music and poetry, and are thought of as being prone to philosophizing. However, recently some archaeologists are now questioning how far it is possible to see the Celtic people as originating from a single common source possessing a uniform culture. Other scholars are pointing to

A highly imaginative artist's impression from the 1700s of a Druidic ritual.

the fact that "the Celts" have been romanticized as an "imagined community" based on a certain shared identity that has more to do with the concerns of modern life than of peoples who existed more than 2,000 years ago.

SHAMANIC ELEMENTS

A story concerning Taliesin the Bard, which comes from the Welsh *Mabinogion*, is widely held to offer a profound insight into the deeper mysteries of the Celts, and is popular among modern-day witches. This myth,

A romantic portrayal of a Celtic bard.

which also comes from an oral tradition that was recorded by Christian scribes, demonstrates the same magical technique of shape-shifting utilized by the Mórrigan.

During the reign of Arthur, there lived Tegid Voel of Penllyn and he had a wife called Ceridwen who was a witch and a sorceress. They had a son named Avagddu who was ugly, and so Ceridwen decided to compensate him for his looks by giving him wisdom. Casting the necessary accompanying spells and uttering incantations, she brewed a concoction in a magical cauldron. The potent mixture had to be kept boiling for a year and a day and was watched over by Gwion Bach, Ceridwen's second son, and Morda, a blind man, who was charged with keeping the fire going. One day, towards the end of the alloted brewing time, a drop of the mixture flew out of the cauldron and landed on the finger of Gwion Bach, who tasted the liquid and became gifted with supernatural sight. Realizing that this was not intended for him, Gwion Bach took flight but was hotly pursued by his mother. Gwion Bach saw Ceridwen chasing him and turned himself into a hare. Ceridwen changed into a greyhound, whereupon Gwion Bach became a fish. Ceridwen turned into an otter and the chase continued. He became a bird and she a hawk. Eventually Gwion Bach turned himself into a grain of wheat but Ceridwen became a black hen and ate him. Nine months later Ceridwen gave birth to a beautiful baby son whom she wrapped up in a leather bag and cast to sea in a coracle. The baby was found by Gwyddno, named Taliesin, and raised as his own. Taliesin became a wizard and a bard and had the skill of prophecy.

In this story Ceridwen and Gwion Bach change shape in a chase that is characterized by its interchange of shamanic-type metamorphoses, or shape-shifting. Ceridwen, as a sorceress mother, by accident confers wisdom and inspiration upon her second son, Gwion Bach, who then has to undergo initiation – through gestation in the womb – and rebirth, before he can realize his magical inheritance as the legendary Taliesin.

NORTHERN EUROPEAN MAGIC

It is difficult to be specific about the magico-religious beliefs of the Germanic and Norse peoples. Historians and archaeologists are now coming to the conclusion that rather than there being a clear contrast between the religions of the Celts and the Germanic peoples, there was, in fact, a wider spectrum of beliefs in existence.

GERMANIC TRIBES

During the years of empire, the Romans called the tribes living east of the Rhine the "Germani". The culture that grew up in the region of Copenhagen was described by the Roman, Tacitus, writing in the last decade of the first century AD. Tacitus describes German society as being "heroic". The leading characters were the kings and chiefs and their companions, élite warriors who were bound to their lords through honour, courage and generosity.

Tacitus divided the peoples of this area into western Germani, who he said had a cult of symbolic atonement, and eastern Germani, who had a religion that seems to have had much more of a shamanic nature, as it involved trance and possession. All the Germani believed in women's prophetic powers, and the prophetesses of their society were sometimes thought of as divine. Divination was apparently carried out through the use of strips of wood, cut from a nut-bearing tree and carved with special signs that were called sigils. The sigils were spread out at random on a piece of white cloth. Later, a similar procedure was adopted using strips of wood with special symbols called runes carved on them.

ENGLISH TRIBES

According to Tacitus, the English were a separate tribe conforming to the general Germanic pattern, apart from the fact that they worshipped an earth mother, Nerthus. The English believed that she intervened in human affairs.

The god Odin, who had a central role in Nordic mythology, and was also called Wotan or Wodin, astride his horse and accompanied by his hunting dog.

VIKING MYTHOLOGY

During the period AD780–1070 the Danes, Norwegians and Swedes, because of a system of primogeniture that forced

A Viking memorial picture stone showing the god Thor, son of Odin.

younger sons into looking for fortune abroad, mounted Viking raids and invaded the coasts of Britain and France. They settled in Iceland in about AD870 and the Icelandic sagas reveal this Norse influence. The word "saga" is related to the English "say" and in Icelandic it refers to something said in a narrative. The Icelandic sagas concern human dilemmas and conflicts that arise out of everyday life – robberies, thoughtless words, loves and jealousies, arguments about property – things that set people against each other before there is reconciliation. Based on aristocratic and chivalric conceptions of honour, they often told of strength and courage in battle. Heroes could perform magical curses and cures through their poetry, and their inspiration was gained from the one-eyed god Odin, who had given his other eye away in order to gain wisdom by drinking from the underworld well of the wise god Mimir.

Norse cosmology tells that life was created though the union of ice from Niflheim in the north and fire from Muspellheim in the south when they met in the chasm of Ginnungagap. The first creatures made were a frost giant called Ymir and a cow called Audumla. The cow licked a man, Buri, out the ice. His three grandsons, the gods Odin, Vili and Ve, killed the giant Ymir and created nine worlds from his body.

In mythology, the nine worlds are organized on three different levels. On the top is Asgard, the realm of the Aesir or warrior gods. Here the gods and goddesses have their halls, and one can also find Valhalla, the hall of warriors who had died valiant deaths and now feast each evening while they await the final battle. Vanaheim, where the fertility gods live, and Alfheim, the land of the light elves are also on this level.

Midgard forms the middle level and is inhabited by humans. Jotunheim, the citadel of the giants, Nidavellir, where dwarfs live, and Svartalfheim, the land of the dark elves, are also located here. Asgard and Midgard are connected by Bifrost, a rainbow bridge.

Alberich curses Wotan (Odin) and Loge in an illustration for Wagner's opera Das Rheingold.

The third level comprises Niflheim, the world of the dead, which is always dark and bitterly cold and has a citadel called Hel. It is nine days' ride northwards and downwards from Midgard.

The ninth world may have been Muspellheim, the land of fire and the first world to exist, according to the thirteenth-century writer Snorri Sturluson, but it is not given a position in the cosmology.

Yggdrasill, a mighty ash tree, stands at the axis of the three levels and has branches that spread out over the whole world and reach up to heaven. Its roots spread under the three levels: one is linked to Asgard and is guarded by three Norns or goddesses of destiny; another connects to Jotunheim, and the Spring of Mimir, whose waters are a source of wisdom; and a third goes into Niflheim and the Spring of Hvergelmir.

ANGLO-SAXON BELIEFS

Literature from the Anglo-Saxon era tells of the notion of "Wyrd", an all-powerful sense of destiny that shapes the world, which may be visualized as a web in which all of life is interconnected. Wyrd means "destiny" and also "power" and "prophetic knowledge" in Anglo-Saxon. It is a term used to express the magical interconnectedness of all life.

Hermod, son of Odin, at the barred gates of Hel, pleading for the return of his brother.

MAGIC AND THE JUDAEO-CHRISTIAN TRADITION

Judaism and Christianity are monotheistic: they both focus on a belief in one creator God and both condemn magic and sorcery. Magic was seen to be a way of manipulating supernatural power for human ends, and was often described as *maleficium* ("evildoing").

Darius I of Persia and Ahura Mazda, flying above the chariot, hunting.

ZOROASTRIANISM:
This monotheistic faith was developed around 1200BC by the Persian religious reformer Zoroaster, who saw the world as a battleground between the principle of good, embodied in the creator god Ahura Mazda, and the force of evil represented by Angra Mainyu.

GNOSTICISM:
This Palestininan cult of the first century AD held that salvation was possible through the secret knowledge of the true nature of things, or gnosis, and the corrupt nature of the physical world. A transcendent and hidden God is opposed to an ignorant demiurge. All matter is part of satanic darkness and it is necessary to rise above evil matter to transcendent light.

NEOPLATONISM
Plotinus (c.205–c.270), a Roman born in Egypt, viewed divinity as a transcendental spirit and the source of all things. His philosophy taught that all existence emanated from the one and the aim was to become one with divinity.

The spirit of Samuel appearing to Saul at the house of the Witch of Endor.

The early religious philosophies of Zoroastrianism, Gnosticism and Neo-platonism all had an influence on the development of Christianity as a world religion. Magic has co-existed in an uneasy and tenuous relationship with both Judaism and Christianity, despite being at odds with scriptural orthodoxies. Magic was generally condemned in the Old Testament: God was averse to divination, augury, necromancy (the art of predicting by means of communication with the dead), mediums and wizards, and all forms of enchantment and shape-shifting.

The Old Testament includes an account of the witch of Endor who gives Saul advice, gained through her familiar spirit, as to why God has deserted him and why the Philistines are successful in battle against him. Despite Saul having punished wizards and "those that had familiar spirits", he seeks out the witch, and she conducts a seance to conjure the spirit of Samuel:

*Then said the woman, "Whom shall I bring
up unto thee?"
And he said, "Bring me up Samuel."
And when the woman saw Samuel, she cried
with a loud voice: and the woman spake to
Saul, saying, "Why hast thou deceived me?
for thou art Saul."
And the king said unto her,
"Be not afraid: for what sawest thou?"
And the woman said unto Saul,
"I saw gods ascending out of the earth."
And he said unto her, "What form is he of?"
And she said, "An old man cometh up; and
he is covered with a mantle."
And Saul perceived that it was Samuel, and
he stooped with his face to the ground, and
bowed himself.*

Zoroaster, the founder of a cult that was formative in developing Christian ideas about good and evil.

Samuel told Saul he had not obeyed the voice of the Lord and Israel would therefore be delivered into the hands of the Philistines.

Monotheistic religions and philosophies tend to see a gap between humanity and divinity, and in its most extreme form it is usually seen to be a religious duty for humans to reach out to God, and to rise from the earthly material world to God's realm of transcendent spirit.

THE CABBALA

In Genesis, primordial humans disobeyed God and were driven from Paradise for eating the fruit of the Tree of Knowledge. This disobedience led to the human fall from a state of divine grace. In order to overcome the radical separation from God, the Cabbala (also spelt Kabbalah and Qabalah), a form of Jewish mysticism, was developed to reunite human beings with divinity. Mystics have tried to describe levels of awareness beyond the ordinary and everyday world of the senses. Sometimes they have used myth to articulate what seems like indescribable religious experience.

The Cabbala is said by some to have been taught to Adam and Eve by God, while others say that it was given orally by God to Moses. It is a secret doctrine

handed on to initiates and concerns the "mysteries" that were not explained in Genesis. The Cabbala consists of numerous writings by various anonymous authors. The most important are the *Sepher Yetzirah* (Book of Formation), probably written in Babylonia around 2,000 years ago, and the *Zohar* (Book of Splendour) written in Spain in the thirteenth century.

In the Cabbala the universe is seen as encompassing different levels of reality at the same time. In the symbolism of the "Tree of Life" the ten "sephiroth", or spheres, are emanations from En Sof, or the will of God and impersonal ground of Being, through which the infinite relates with the finite. By meditating on the sephiroth a person is said to be able to link up with the greater plan of the universe and so become closer to God.

Adam and Eve in Paradise. Eve is shown handing the fruit of the Tree of Knowledge to Adam.

The study of the Cabbala encourages a direct and unmediated relationship with God and may be seen to be heretical because it may challenge religious interpretations based on a study of texts.

Hermetism is the term used to describe a collection of beliefs, doctrines and practices that derive from a set of Greek texts written in Alexandria between the first and third centuries, setting out the teachings attributed to Hermes Trismegistus, a Greek name for an Egyptian priest identified with the god Thoth. Called the *Corpus Hermeticum*, many of these treatises describe the soul's ascension through the celestial spheres. In essence, much

A sixteenth-century engraving showing a Jewish Cabbalist holding the Tree of Life.

The Cabbalistic Tree of Life, representing the relationship between the microcosm (all the cosmic forces within the individual) and the wider macrocosm as an all embracing totality.

of Hermetism seeks to unite the the microcosm of the human being with divinity and the macrocosm.

During the Renaissance the writings of the Cabbala were interpreted by Christians and magic was used as a means to bring higher angelic forces down to the ordinary world. This changed the status of the magician from evildoer to agent of God and good. Three important

magicians of the Renaissance were Marsilio Ficino (1433–99), Giovanni Pico Della Mirandola (1463–94) and Giordano Bruno (1548–1600). Ficino, who was a priest and a physician, developed a system of "natural magic" concerned with drawing down the natural powers of the cosmos. His theory of magic was based on the guiding of spirit from the stars using the natural sympathies running through nature. Pico was influenced by Ficino's natural magic but, in an attempt to increase its power, he incorporated the Cabbala to tap the higher powers of angels and archangels. Bruno sought to return magic to what he saw as its purer pagan source in Egypt. He also used the Cabbala but in contrast to Pico, who wanted to work only with angelic forces, Bruno attempted to unlock demonic forces.

The Renaissance magi Pico Della Mirandola (centre) and Marsilio Ficino (right).

The corruption of nature after the Fall and humanity's supreme position within the created world became central to Christian teachings, but not all Christians agreed with this view. St Francis of Assisi (c.1181–1226) taught that all life formed part of the fellowship of God; all creatures were equal and interrelated and there was no dualism between God and his creation but a seamless web of life. While St Francis cannot be called a magician in the strict sense of the word, he reintroduced a spiritual view of the world which is magical, where God and creation are not separated:

Most High, omnipotent, good Lord,
All praise, glory, honour, and
blessing are yours.
To you alone, Most High, do they belong,
And no man is worthy to
pronounce your name.
Be praised, my Lord, with all
your creatures,
Especially Sir Brother Sun,
Who brings the day, and you give
light to us through him.
How handsome he is, how radiant,
with great splendour!
Of you, Most High, he bears the likeness.
Be praised, my Lord, for Sister
Moon and the Stars.
In heaven you have formed them, bright,
and precious, and beautiful.
Be praised, my Lord, for Brother Wind,
And for Air, for Cloud, and Clear,
and all weather,
By which you give your creatures
nourishment.
Be praised, my Lord, for Sister Water,
She is very useful, and humble,
and precious, and pure.
Be praised, my Lord, for Brother Fire,
By whom you light up the night.
How handsome he is, how happy,
how powerful and strong!
Be praised, my Lord, for our Sister,
Mother Earth.
Who nourishes and governs us,
And produces various fruits with
many-coloured flowers and herbs.
Praise and bless the Lord,
And give thanks and serve him with
great humility.

St Francis of Assisi, a Christian monk with a unique spiritual view of the world, who preached of a seamless web of life.

Divine nature

Some writers have blamed the Judaeo-Christian Bible for encouraging an anti-ecological position. By denying a magical world view, nature ceases to be regarded as divine. In addition, it is sometimes argued, the Bible is strongly anthropocentric, or human-centred – human beings are divinely ordained to rule over and dominate all other species, in contrast to an animistic view, which sees nature as permeated by spirits that inhabit natural phenomena such as trees, rivers, animals, mountains and planets.

Adam and Eve are banished from Paradise after eating the forbidden fruit.

ISLAM AND MAGIC

Magic in Islam forms part of the occult sciences, which include divination, astrology and prophecy. It is seen as a fragment of the celestial knowledge that was given to humans by fallen angels who revealed secrets. Thus humans have come to know what they should not know, and divinatory magic uses these secrets. Spells and incantations are also used to compel the spirits and demons called *jinn*, or *djin*. Two types of conjuring are distinguished. The first is bad and involves directing the mind toward an object rather than God, thus being unfaithful and acting in a manner that is wicked and harmful to others. The second concerns the conjuring of spirits with piety and lawfulness and in surrender to God, the spirits acting like angels: this is viewed in more positive terms.

A healer tapes up the toes and fingers of a person possessed by a jinn spirit to "lock it in".

RELIGIOUS VALUES

Islam was instituted as a recall to monotheism, from which Jews and Christians had drifted away; it was not a new religion but a call to Muslims to return to a strict path. It recognizes Jewish and Christian prophets but believes that their messages have been tampered with and are thus based on the work of humans rather than God.

There is one God, Allah, who is separate from humans: he has no likeness and no divine Son; he is transcendent but present everywhere.

A herbalists' souq in Marrakesh. Herbal remedies have been in use for centuries.

A Moghul prince speaking to a Dervish.

Allah is seen to preside over two worlds: the visible *al shahada*, which is accessible to humans; and the unseen *al ghaib*, which is accessible only to humans through special revelation. In the visible world, the earth, moon, stars and animals are not autonomous but are evidence of the unseen creative force – the signs by which Allah reveals himself. The reality of the unseen world is unknowable and mysterious and can be revealed by miracles, which show the unseen but true form of what is beneath. Miracles are a sign of God's power.

THE SUFIS

In Islam there has been a strong emphasis on the difference between human beings and God, but Sufism, so-called because the earliest followers of the movement wore woollen garments (*suf* means wool), developed as a form of personal mystical training that aimed at overcoming this distinction. The Sufis brought an inner spirituality into Islam. By the purification of consciousness, the self and God could merge. The mystical poet Jalal ad-Din ar-Rumi was born in what is now Afganistan in 1207 and was the founder of the sect known as the Dancing Dervishes. Its members were adherents of a form of Sufism that was developed around AD800–900 as a way of attaining union with God:

I died a mineral and
became a plant.
I died a plant and rose an animal.
I died an animal and I was a man.
Why should I fear? When was
I less by dying?
Yet once more I shall die as
man, to soar
with the blessed angels; but
even from angelhood
I must pass on. All except
God perishes.
When I have sacrificed my angel soul,
I shall become that which no
mind ever conceived.
O, let me not exist! for Non-
Existence proclaims,
"To Him we shall return".

The founder of the Dancing Dervishes, Jalal ad-Din ar-Rumi.

The Sufi mystical tradition claimed descent by a chain of grace that linked the holy men to the family of the Prophet. The Sufi saint, who acts as a spiritual teacher and master, is said to have the ability to foresee the future, control spirits and know what is in human hearts. The saint's knowledge is a concrete manifestation of divine grace demonstrated by his power over nature, and he uses his mystical powers to perform miracles.

From about the twelfth to the nineteenth centuries, Sufi brotherhoods, under the direction of a shaikh, were widespread. The aim of the ascetic practices of the Sufis is not to earn themselves credits in the next world by the mortification of the flesh, but rather to liberate the spirit for improved communication with the divine. The idea of union with God is seen by some as blasphemous, and the idea that the individual could in some sense become God is resisted by more orthodox Muslims.

Members of the Whirling Dervish sect, performing the dance that they believe helps them to find union with God.

CHINESE MAGIC

Magic was very important in the Chinese royal ancestral religion of the Shang and early Chou (between the sixteenth and eighth centuries BC). The wu was a shaman or sorcerer who sacrificed to and invoked the spirits, and effected cures by means of medicinal plants and spells. The wu tradition is connected with individuals known as fangshi – "persons of techniques". These were outsiders, marginal or peripheral from the point of view of official Confucianist doctrine. They specialized in astrology, medicine and geomancy, as well as methods for achieving a long life. They were usually solitary seekers who tried to find the laws behind natural phenomena.

Increasingly, a differentiation evolved between magic, as archaic religion dealing with spirits, and a developed theory of symbolic correspondences.

Lao Tzu, the legendary founder of Taoism, is presented with the baby Confucius.

Some rulers, such as Liu Chíe (140–87BC), favoured shamans and established shamanic cults, and the court became a gathering place for those who claimed to possess magical powers and the secrets of immortality. Li Shaoweng, a psychopomp (a conductor of souls to the place of the dead), gained Liu Chíe's favour by conjuring the ghost of the ruler's recently deceased concubine, but was executed after he was exposed as a fabricator of portents. Near the end of Liu Chíe's reign the court was paralysed by an outbreak of shamanic witchcraft known as *ku*, a type of demonic affliction which attacked its victim as the result of witchcraft. Sometimes shamans were hired to work black magic, and accusations of charlatanism and fear of witchcraft were widespread during the Han period.

During the periods of the Warring States (403–221BC), Chíin (221–207BC), and Han (206BC–AD220) there was a decline in the prestige of shamanism and the practice became associated with witchcraft.

TAOISM

Chinese religion is said to be a mixture of Taoism, Confucianism and the later arrival of Buddhism from India. Taoism and Confucianism share the same system of divination called the *I Ching* (Book of Change). This consists of 64 six-line figures, which represent every possible combination of hexagrams, and eight three-line figures, or trigrams. In order to consult the I Ching, a hexagram is constructed by determining each line (which may be either yin or yang) with the tossing of coins. Explanations attached to each hexagram advise on how to cope with a particular situation.

The *Pa Kua*, the symbolic arrangement of the eight trigrams, is said to have been developed around 3100BC from the inscriptions on oracular shells and bones from an earlier age. Today, the Pa Kua appears on flags, plaques and porcelain and is used as a charm to bring

A belief in spirits is widespread in China and here a pilgrim burns spirit money at the temple of the spirits' retreat.

good luck. It is hung up in Chinese homes to ward off unfriendly spirits and other evils. Often a mirror is placed in the centre to reflect evil influences.

The most harmonious hexagram combinations balance the two elements of yin and yang. Yin and yang are opposites: yin is dark, female, cold, solid and wet, while yang is light, male, fiery, ethereal and dry, but they are inseparable and each is dependent on the other. Each carries the other within it: they are not opposed in a fixed dualism, but combine polarity and ambiguity to produce the dynamic energy of life.

Everything is interconnected, as the interaction of the seasons shows. Autumn and winter are yin, but at the moment when yin triumphs in the heart of the cold dark winter, it also begins its inevitable decline and yang forces begin to arise, leading to the yang times of spring and summer. When summer reaches its high point, the seasons begin to change and yin is once more in the ascendant.

The altar of the Yap Kongsi temple in Penang showing the eight-sided Pa Kua, *the symbolic hexagrams and trigrams of the* I Ching.

Heaven has four seasons, to allow cultivation, growth, harvesting and storing, and five elements: wood, fire, earth, metal and water. It produces cold, heat, drought, humidity and wind. Humans have five vital organs that transform the five influences of the elements to engender happiness, anger, vexation, sadness and fear. The five elements represent forces that react against each other. Wood brings forth fire, fire produces ashes, earth brings forth metal, metal produces steam when heated and water produces trees. On the other hand, earth is broken by wood, water is contained by earth, fire is extinguished by water, metal is melted by fire and wood is shaped by metal. The five elements are linked to nature and to humans by a whole series of connections. For example, wood corresponds to spring, germination and wind, and to the liver, gall bladder and mouth, as well as to anger.

NATURAL TRANSFORMATION

The Taoist system inspires a sense of confidence in the normal course of nature, and a mistrust of human intervention. This is expressed in the Taoist notion of wuwei – meaning a positive non-intervention with the Tao. The Tao is not a deity but simply the innateness of life. From the Tao comes the One, which is the primal essence of being, the core of innateness. The One splits and forms the two – yin and yang. Lao Tzu, the legendary founder of Taoism, explains the meaning of Taoism to Confucius:

Human life between Heaven and Earth is like a white colt glimpsed through a crack in the wall, quickly past.
It pours forth, it overwhelms, yet there is nothing that does not emerge.
It drifts, it swirls, yet there is nothing that does not return.
Life is transformation, death is also transformation.
All living creatures are saddened, all humanity mourns.
However, it is simply the releasing of the Heavenly bowstring, or the emptying of the Heavenly satchel, a yielding and a changing which release the soul, as the body follows, back at long last to the great Returning.
That without shape comes from shape, that with shape returns to the shapeless ...

This philosophy reflects one of the great magical themes of transformation: of life and death and a constant interplay between form and formlessness as part

A Taoist weather manual depicting fire (yang) and cloud (yin) from the nineteenth-century Qing dynasty.

of a universal pattern of energies. The similarities between this strand of Chinese wisdom and the Egyptian myth of Osiris and Isis, the Greek underworld versus overworld rhythm of Demeter and Persephone, and the Celtic death and rebirth theme of Gwion Bach/Taliesin are apparent.

An Immortal plays a flute in the Tao paradise.

JAPANESE AND KOREAN MAGIC

The magico-religious thought of these countries cannot be viewed in isolation from China. Japanese spiritual beliefs are a combination of indigenous Shinto, Confucianism and Buddhism, with Taoism as a secondary Chinese import.

JAPANESE SHINTO

In the early centuries AD, Japan was organized into clans, each with its own mythology and *kami* – gods or spirits of nature. Gradually a central core of myths centred on Amaterasu, the great goddess of the sun, and ancestress of the royal family. The kami of mountains, streams and the sea blended with tutelary kami who were associated with particular clans. Only gradually did Shinto emerge as a self-conscious religion. Shinto means the "way of the spirits" and is the name for a collection of myths and rites that are rooted in conceptions of kami. Kami are associated with natural phenomena, deified heroes, or anything that may inspire awe; worship is designed to please the gods. Purity is central – the *mago koro* or "true heart" is sincere and pure, and the divine light that illuminates the kami is also found within the human heart.

A Shinto priest from Northern Honshu, Japan.

There are two categories of religious leaders who deal with spirits: the *miko*, who are female shamans and mediums through whom the spirits descend and who are associated with witchcraft; and the *kannushi*, spirit controllers or priests who oversee the worship of the spirits and officiate in the state cults. Buddhism was introduced into Japan in the sixth century and it blended with Shintoism as part of the fabric of Japanese life with kami being viewed as manifestations of Buddhas and Bodhisattvas.

KOREAN SHAMANISM

Chinese religion, as well as Chinese magic and occultism, was part of the general flow of Chinese culture into Korea. The Korean religious culture includes Confucianism, Buddhism, Protestant Christianity and cults formed around female shamans who were a source of native Korean magic that was known as *Mu-sok* ("shamanic customs"). All religions co-exist and a Korean Buddhist may consult a shaman. People tend to participate in the rites of several of these religions for different purposes.

Korean shamanism is centred around the individual shaman or *mansin* and her household gods. Men are not generally shamans but they do conduct formal rites of ancestor worship. The few men who are shamans perform in women's clothing, including long silken pantaloons. It is the role of the shaman to seek out the gods, communicate with them, lure them into houses and bargain with them. The mansin is one who invokes gods and ancestors, speaks with their voice, uses their power to interpret dreams and visions, and deals with potentially dangerous spirits or ghosts.

The mansin purifies the dwelling and invites the gods and the ancestors inside to possess her. They vent their grievances and give divinations, exorcise the sick and banish lingering ghosts. The gods receive tribute, while the ancestors are given sustenance. The anthropologist Laurel Kendall describes the role of a shaman called Yongsu's Mother:

Garbed in the red robes of an antique general or wielding the Spirit Warrior's halbard as she drives malevolent forces from her path, Yongsu's Mother claims an imposing presence. Even in everday dress and sprawling comfortably on the heated floor of her own home, she speaks with authority. By virtue of the powerful gods who possess her, she can summon up divination visions and probe the source of a client's misfortunes, exorcise the sick and chronically unlucky, remove ill humors

A South Korean shamanic ritual held on a boat.

Wooden good luck charms hung in a Shinto temple in Kyoto, Japan.

from those who have difficulty finding mates, and coax a reluctant birth spirit into an infertile womb. The professional shaman makes the gods and ancestors a vivid presence in the home; she spots them in her visions and gives them voice in trance. In kut, *her most elaborate ritual, she garbs herself in their costumes and in their person scolds, banters, advises and commiserates with the mortal members of household and community.*

Korean shamans use horoscopes to link individual afflictions to the household. They believe that when the gods are angry the household's defences are lowered, and the individual who will suffer at this time is the person whose horoscope indicates vulnerability. The goal of many shamanic rituals is to discover which household god has been offended and to make amends in order to restore harmonious relations between humans and spirits.

In this photograph, taken in 1919, a Korean shaman (lower right) tries to drive evil spirits out of an old man (lying on floor).

A present day female Korean shaman performing a rite involving the gods of a household.

MAGIC AND RITUAL IN INDIA

What has been called the Vedic phase of Indian history began with the influx of Aryans, a tribe of pastoral nomads from central Asia, who settled on the plains of the Ganges around 2000BC. They had an agrarian culture that was dependent on the forces of nature and this was reflected in the canonical body of texts called the Vedas (*veda* is Sanskrit for "what is known"). The Vedas praised and appeased the forces of nature as well as higher beings depicted as gods. In Indian tradition, the human being is a part of incarnation where everything has the power of sense perception, and where the highest good is identified with the total harmony of the cosmic order.

The Vedas are a rich source of magical ideas; no fundamental distinction is made between substances or beings and their qualities. Reality is built up from various networks of affinities or connections, which can be evoked and controlled by human beings. The Vedas

Indra, the Aryan god of war, seated on an elephant.

seen as healthy, a point of incentive for the growth of the natural world to overcome malignant spirits.

The aim of ritual was to keep the life processes of the universe moving and to maintain good relations with the powers of the unseen. Rituals were held on special occasions, such as festivals, and for specific ends, such as the curing of disease or the exorcism of malevolent spirits. The ritual might include divination, witch-finding and the manipulation of spirits or deities. There was a sacred power implicit in the action of sacrifice, and the sacrifice itself was supposed to have a beneficial effect on the person on whose behalf it was made; it was thought to have within it a power that the priest manipulated, and which was also in the priest himself.

VEDIC SPELLS

The Atharva-Veda, one of the oldest collections of Hindu scriptures, contains a rich collection of spells and magical

show the unity of creation as a mysterious interconnectedness and co-dependence of everything. Each bio-organism, element or species has a purpose in a larger scheme and is sacred.

GODS AND RITUAL

Like the Greeks and Romans, the Aryans were polytheistic – they believed in many gods, as well as spirits and demons. They had four main gods: Indra, a weather and warrior god; Varuna, who maintained order; Agni, a fire god; and Soma, a plant god who is also concerned with the visible and invisible world, and the different aspects of experience.

Rituals, which were performed by the Brahmin class, were conducted not to control nature but to restore equilibrium. Competition, struggle and tension were

Varuna, keeper of moral order, as portrayed on a stone carving on the Konark Sun Temple, Orissa.

Agni, a fire god associated with sacrifice. Fire was of central importance in Vedic ritual: it was through the consuming flames that sacrifices were sent to the heavens.

A modern day Hindu ascetic chanting a mantra.

A coin holding an impression of the goddess Kali.

The god Varuna.

rites. These were later divided into those that were concerned with positive welfare or the pacification of evil influences, and those directed against hostile powers or individuals. The Hindu goddess Maya, who is an aspect of Kali, refers to a creative capacity for magic or transformation that may be turned to good as well as evil purposes, and may be used to beguile or subjugate a victim.

A key to hidden reality is the realm of sound, which can be manipulated by the power of the sacred, ceremonially uttered word or mantra. Usually such spells contain invocations of deities who are ordered to carry out the magician's commands. Some mantras can be obtained only under the guidance of a guru and may involve preparation, astrological readings, long recitations and the regulation of breath.

A Pakhandi ritual showing participants using the plant soma.

Pakhandi

The magico-religious use of the plant soma shows that great importance was given to the use of drugs and intoxicants to induce experiences that were beyond those of the everyday and that were seen to have a sacred quality. Juice was prepared from the soma plant and drunk during ritual, and a hymn extols its beauty.

Men beautify him in the vats, him
worthily to be beautiful,
Him who brings forth abundant food.
Him, even him, the fingers ten and the
seven songs make beautiful,
Well weaponed, best of
gladdeners.

HINDUISM, BUDDHISM AND MAGIC

What is now called Hinduism developed out of Vedism. Towards the end of the Vedic period there was an increased interest in ascetic practices concerned with self-discipline and yoga techniques aimed at individual spiritual development.

THE BRAHMAN

In Hinduism, there is one and only one being in existence: the absolute Brahman, who is without form and is both immanent (within) and transcendent (beyond), and creates the world out of himself. The individual soul, or *atman*, is a part of this reality. Hinduism developed a number of orthodox systems of philosophy concerned with salvation and attaining oneness with God. In the post-Vedic Hindu tradition, supernatural powers are seen to derive from Brahman and the whole world is understood as divine action welling forth from this mysterious supreme power.

ASCETICISM AND DESIRE

The *Upanishads* were composed between 800 and 400BC and were a synthesis of Vedic and contemplative ideas and yoga practices aimed at training the mind and

A Hindu woman practising Padmasana yoga meditation.

dangerous amount of magical "heat", which might cause fires, droughts or earthquakes. In Indian folklore, water is associated with sexuality and opposed to heat and asceticism. On occasion, sacred temple prostitutes called *devadasis* would be called on to seduce an ascetic and thereby dispel the heat.

SALVATION

Buddhism is a religious tradition associated with the teachings of Siddhartha Gautama, the Buddha, who was born around 563BC. The Buddha's world-view and teaching is concerned with a practical path to salvation. This is

The god Brahma (right) looks on as Siddhartha Gautama, the Buddha, cuts off his hair as a sign of his asceticism. He later came to abandon asceticism and developed his own path to enlightenment.

A devadasis or sacred temple prostitute.

body. The Upanishads led to the development of Buddhism and Jainism, as well as a more devotional form of Hindu religion expressed in the *Bhagavadgita*, a sacred text composed around 200BC and incorporated in the epic *Mahabharata*.

Hinduism embraces asceticism (*tapas*) and desire (*kama*) and these are not necessarily opposed but are frequently seen as interchangeable forms of energy. Asceticism is viewed as beneficial but in certain circumstances may generate a

based on the assumption that the world is suffering and that liberation comes from the elimination of desire or craving by following the Noble Eightfold Path, a set of moral and ethical teachings leading to Nirvana, an enhanced state of awareness and enlightenment.

SPIRIT CULTS

In Hinduism and Buddhism the manipulation of superhuman powers motivated by worldly ends is seen to detract people from their proper purpose, which is the release from ordinary existence. In practice, Hinduism and Buddhism have co-existed with many spirit cults and folk religions and are often concerned with the problems and trials of everyday life. One example of how spirit cults exist alongside orthodox Buddhism is given by the anthropologist Stanley Tambiah. In *Buddhism and the Spirit Cults in North-East Thailand* (1970) he writes that the orthodox Buddhism of the monastic order concerns the withdrawal from the world, and a concentration on following an individual path that leads to Nirvana and the release from reincarnation. However, among lay people Nirvana is not a goal, for they cannot hope for salvation, only a better rebirth.

Ordinary people are involved with Buddhist practices but they also engage with spirit cults. At village level, spirit cults are concerned with the family, household and community; they involve the animistic, pre-Buddhist cult of guardian spirits who are concerned with good crops and healing.

There are a large number of specialists in the village who cure disease and communicate with spirits. Most are

A spirit priest prays before a sacrificial post during a funeral ceremony at the village of Pa Bu.

called by names that have the prefix *mau*. There is mau song, who acts as a diviner or diagnostician; a mau du, or mau lek, who is an astrologer or fortune-teller; a mau mau, who is a discoverer of lost property; a mau ya, a physician or herbal doctor; mau ram, a spirit medium; and mau tham, who acts as an exorcist. Spirit mediums officiate in rituals to appease the spirits; they have to be chosen by the spirits and undergo repeated possessions by them. Assistant mediums deal with individual cases of illness. Many of these mediums are female and serve as oracles of the guardian spirit. They inform the victim whether the spirit is responsible for the illness and what offerings it requires.

Prayers performed in the shade of the Bodhi Tree which grows at the site of the tree under which Buddha sat.

TANTRIC RITES AND BELIEFS

Magic in Hinduism and Buddhism is most prominent in the esoteric practices of Tantrism. The mystic combination of Hinduism and Buddhism, Tantrism originated in India around 700BC. Tantric goddesses are particularly highly valued and are seen as divine forces from which the universe emerged. The coming together of god and goddess in sexual union is central to Tantric rites, and men and women took on the qualities of the deities in the pursuit of enlightenment. *Tantra* represents the magical generation of life in the material and spiritual dimension. It is a Sanskrit word meaning "web" or "weaving" and can be interpreted as a practice that expands understanding; Hinduism and Buddhism each have their own versions. There are Tantric elements in the *Vedas*, and the Upanishads include descriptions of Tantric ritual sex.

Tantra developed in India in small cult groups centred around a particular set of deities and practices that were based

The Hindu god Shiva.

on either private meditation aimed at self-development, or public ritual performance. A central practice was the evocation of a Tantric deity through which the practitioner learnt to replace

their ordinary view of the world with a different "pure" vision. Enlightenment was not achieved by denying the world or the self but by merging with a transcendental reality.

Everything in both the ordinary and the transcendental world is seen to be generated by the interaction of the goddess Shakti and the god Shiva, and the universe is seen to be born of their desire. Tantrists, unlike orthodox Hindu Brahmins, do not moderate their desire but redirect its energy. The cosmos and the human body are intimately linked and, by a process of training, the Tantric practitioner can attune his or her body to progressively higher levels of cosmic awareness until she or he becomes one with the deity. The process involves activating the energy of the opposite sex in the individual body. In some traditions this is effected by meditation,

A linga, or phallus, symbol of the god Lord Shiva. The linga is the main object of worship in Saivite temples and family shrines. This example shows one of the five faces of Shiva carved on its top.

Shiva and Shakti in sexual embrace. In Tantrism, the Universe is born of their union.

the recitation of spells and words of power; in other traditions it is pursued through ritual sexual intercourse.

MAITHUNA

A form of ritual sex, Maithuna forms the last part of a ceremony known as the "five Ms". The preliminary stage involves taking wine, fish, meat (all forbidden to Hindus) and parched grain for their aphrodisiac properties. Maithuna is said to be a ritual during which Shakti and Shiva are united in the practitioner and this is believed to cause a transformation of consciousness. The ritual is usually carried out in a circle of initiates guided by a guru and it may incorporate meditation, yogic postures, the recitation of mantras, visualizations of diagrammatic representations of energy fields called yantras, and the invocation of many deities.

The basic theory is common to Buddhist and Hindu yogic traditions and involves *prana*, a flow of psychic energy through the body via the *chakras* (or energy centres) and channels. This forms a psychic model of the body, which relates the person to the wider spiritual world. Hindu Tantra identifies chakras at the base of the spine, the genitals, the navel, the heart, the throat, between the eyes and at the crown of the head. Buddhist Tantra locates chakras at the base of the spine, the navel, the

Padmasambhava (AD721–c.790), a Buddhist monk who spread the Tantric belief system to Tibet when he visited as a missionary in AD777.

throat and the crown of the head. Enlightenment is achieved when the energy located at the base chakra rises to progressively higher states of awareness. In Hindu terms, the female *kundalini*, represented by a serpent manifestation of Shakti, shoots up through the body to the crown of the head where it finds union with Shiva.

The seven chakras shown in an illustration from the nineteenth century.

Tantrists carrying out a ritual with corpses.

Tantrikas

Tantric practices can be concerned with the breaking of social taboos, which is believed to liberate much power. Some Tantrists have made their homes in graveyards, and some have meditated inside rotting corpses. This practice is intended to demonstrate the impermanence of the world, and to help the Tantrists to conquer their fear or disgust of death; it also openly flouts the caste divisions of Hindu society (the work of handling corpses is carried out by members of the lowest caste).

AFRICAN RELIGION AND MAGIC

African religions have complex cosmologies and display a strong sense of connection with a spiritual force that permeates the universe, as we have already seen with the !Kung of the Kalahari Desert. Early missionary zeal led to the mistaken view that African religion was primitive and undeveloped. In fact, the first missionaries erroneously described the magical practices they saw as a form of deception.

THE SPIRITUAL AND PHYSICAL WORLD

There is no body of beliefs and practices common throughout Africa and it is therefore very difficult to generalize, but in most African societies the spiritual world is seen to be a part of the everyday world. Many societies hold a pantheistic world-view that expresses life as an on-going process that includes living and dead ancestors. Pantheism is a view whereby everything in the natural world has a unity and is seen to be divine.

African cultures are very diverse, but they are all similar in the way they connect human beings (both living and as ancestors) and the natural world with a strong magical power.

This power is viewed as a kind of vital force, which flows through the universe and permeates all aspects of life. Some societies see it as originating from a creator spirit, and in Tanzania and Kenya, for example, the notion of a supreme named god is well established. The Janjero of Ethiopia believe in a supreme being that they call Hao. The Swahili word for God is Mungu or Mulungu, whereas the Kikuyus and the Masai of Kenya call him Ngai. The Nuer in the Sudan pray to Kwoth and the Nupe in Nigeria say that their god Soko is in the sky.

There is often a hierarchy of spirits: from the nature spirits of rivers, rocks, trees and animals, through ancestor spirits, to divinities who derive their power from the creator spirit. The Lugbara have a cult centred on the

The pastoralist Masai of Kenya depend on cows for their subsistence. Here a cow is ritually killed.

spirits of the dead, in which the living are seen to belong to the "outside" world and the dead belong "in the earth". If they are neglected, the dead punish their descendants by inflicting misfortune and sickness.

A Zulu diviner.

A female witch doctor of the Usumbura, 1929.

THE EARTH GODDESS

In African thought, complex systems of magico-religious beliefs, myths and cosmologies are interlinked with moral rules of behaviour. This is illustrated here by the myth of the great earth goddess Dzivaguru, who was once worshipped by the Korekore people of Zimbabwe. Dzivaguru lived in a palace by a lake, wore goatskins and possessed a long horn filled with magical substances that gave her everything she wanted. Nosenga, the son of the sky-god Chikara, became jealous of Dzivaguru's wealth and decided to drive her away. He descended into her valley but Dzivaguru surrounded herself with fog so Nosenga could not see her. Nosenga tied a magic red ribbon around his head so that he could see Dzivaguru's palace and he entered it to search for her. However, Dzivaguru had taken to the hills with all the light of the earth. Nosenga was surrounded by darkness. He cut fibres from a plant and made a snare, which he set up by the lake to catch sunbirds. As dawn came Nosenga could see Dzivaguru standing on the hill. She said that she would take the lake with her and told Nosenga that as he had brought the sun out it would soon become so hot that the forest would dry out. Dzivaguru warned that if any of Nosenga's sons commited incest she would withhold the rain from the land, and that if they wanted to pray to her they would have to slaughter a sheep first.

SPIRITUAL POWER

Most African societies believe that spiritual power can be manipulated by humans for good or bad. Positive mystical power is productive, can cure illnesses, and is protective, while negative power eats the health and souls of its victims and causes misfortune. Witches and sorcerers employ this power for antisocial ends.

An Igbo, a Nigerian goddess figure made from wood.

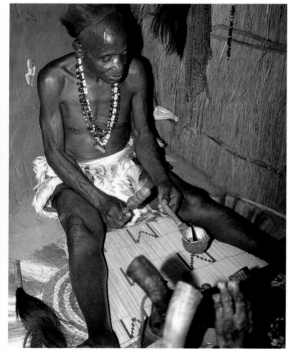

A witch doctor from Zimbabwe.

MAGIC AND MEDICINE

It is generally acknowledged that words can be powerful. They can "cause" good fortune, success or blessing, or they can curse and bring sorrow. It is usually specialists such as witch doctors, medicine men, diviners or rain-makers who use their knowledge of this magical power. The words are seen to work through the actual herbs of the medicine and are thought to cure or prevent misfortune. Medicines may be used to prevent rain from falling, to delay sunset, to aid hunting – by making a hunter invisible or preventing a wounded animal from escaping – for success in love affairs, or to find stolen property.

Medicines may also be used for treating illnesses. The diviner or medicine man may protect people by using spiritual power in amulets or charms. Magic involves rites using medicines made from trees and plants, and the magician addresses the medicines and tells them what he wants them to do: they are commissioned to carry out the task. Success is not seen to be due to magic but unusual success is.

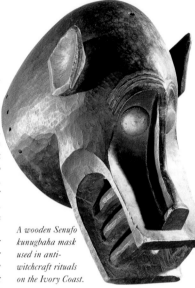

A wooden Senufo kunugbaha mask used in anti-witchcraft rituals on the Ivory Coast.

Nganga is the term used in most Bantu languages to refer to a medicine man, magician, herbalist or shaman. In Zimbabwe, a young man becomes a nganga if his father or some other male relative will train him, and a young woman will become a nganga if some female relative will teach her the art of recognizing diseases and their cures. The nganga goes into the forest to collect herbs, roots, bark, flowers and leaves needed for the practice.

Knowledge about plants is wide spread, but what is secret is their magical properties and uses, and this information is inherited from nganga to nganga. Some nganga families have a tradition of healing going back many generations and the living members receive guidance from their ancestors, who speak to them in dreams. For example, the spirit of a grandfather may tell his grandson where to find the herbs that will cure an illness, and which spirit has caused it. The spirits tell the nganga how to prepare the herbs, and also reveal the person responsible for the disease. This information is important because healing may involve not just one person but sometimes the whole village or clan. The authority of the ancestors is necessary in order to make the medicines effective.

A Kikuyu witch doctor from Kenya.

A witch doctor with fetishes, Zimbabwe.

A traditional healer's medicines, as used in Zimbabwe.

THE MORALITY OF MAGIC

Magical power is seen to come either from the creator spirit, or through the spirits of the ancestors, or as part of the invisible force of nature in the universe. When spiritual power is used in antisocial or bad ways it is termed "sorcery" or "black magic". This type of magic may be used, for example, to send animals, such as lions, flies or snakes, to attack a person or carry disease; it might be used to send spittle laced with secret incantations; or to possess a person's spirit. Many misfortunes are the result of this type of magic. Sorcery is bad not because it can destroy health and property, but because it is immoral and flouts the law. Good magic may also be destructive but it strikes only at those who have commited a crime, it cannot be used for evil purposes. Oracles may be used to determine witchcraft, illness or misfortune.

A healer casting out devils during a ceremony in Zimbabwe.

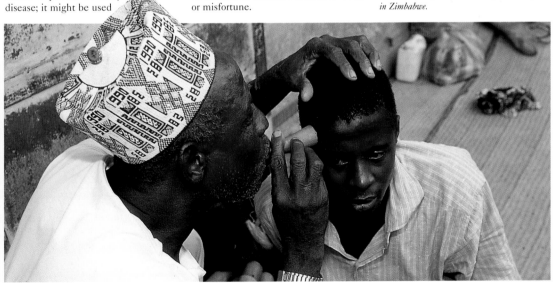

A healer treating a man for migraine in Mali.

VOODOO RITUALS AND BELIEFS

Voodoo (sometimes also spelt vodu or vodou) is the word for the gods in the Fon language of Dahomey (now Benin). The Fon people differentiate between three regions for the gods: the sky, the earth and the clouds in between. The first god, the Creator, lives in the sky and created twin gods: Lisa, the sun god of day, strength and endurance, and his sister, Mawu, a moon goddess of night, peace, joy, fertility, motherhood and rain. The two eldest children of Lisa and Mawu were Sagbata and his twin sister who were sent to earth to populate it with their children.

The younger brother, Sogbo, was sent to the clouds to become the ruler of thunder and lightning, but in spite of his power, he was jealous of his elder brother who was the ruler of the earth, and withdrew rain. Nothing could grow and the people were starving. The prayers of the people moved Mawu to send Lega, a god of fate and the youngest son of Lisa and Mawu, to earth. He took the Otutu, a songbird, with him and told it to sing as soon as fire broke out. Soon the angry Sogbo caused a fire on earth with his lightning, but Otutu began to sing and this informed Mawu who sent rain and saved the earth.

COLLECTIVE SPIRITUAL CREATION

Voodoo, vodu or vodou is also the name for the religion of former slaves from West Africa imported into Haiti in the West Indies. The diverse magico-spiritual beliefs of peoples from the African states of Dahomey, Loango, Ashanti, Yoruba and Mandingo, whose cultures were deliberately broken up and scattered through Haiti, have been brought together to form a sense of religious identity and continuity out of fragmentation. Voodoo is a collective spiritual creation born out of the inhumanity of the slave system, and it brings together ancestor worship, spirit possession, dance, song and drumming.

A Fon bocio figure, which is believed to embody a potent magical power.

HAITIAN VOODOO

Today, voodoo is a peasant religion practised by 90 per cent of Haitians but regarded with contempt by the small Westernized ruling class. It is a fusion of African spirit beliefs and Catholic Christianity. The Christian God (called Bondye in Haitian Creole) presides over the ritual and sends down his angels in a variety of performances, which range from the lighting of candles to animal sacrifice. Much of the ritual and liturgy is of Chrisitan origin and the *loa*, who are also called "saints" or "angels", are seen to be a part of Christian cosmology. Santeria is a Caribbean practice similar to voodoo, and is also centred on the worship of African gods within a Christian religious framework.

The human being is seen to consist of a material body animated by spirit, and may achieve the status of divinity or loa, which possesses the body. When a loa possesses a new devotee it has to be baptized and take holy communion. The loa moves into the head of an individual and displaces his or her *gros bon ange* or "good angel" soul, one of the two souls

An ancestor-worshipping ceremony in Ghana, West Africa.

Haystack-like mounds that will become spiritual village guardians when worn by Voodoo worshippers at a festival. The guardians, called zangbetos, are said to contain the spirits of the village.

that a person carries, causing trembling and convulsions. The spirit incarnates into its earthly host and rides it like a horse (like the Greek Pythia at Delphi who were mounted by Apollo, who rode on the nape of their necks). This spirit union may be marked by a celestial marriage whereby the possessed person may seek the permanent protection of the loa. When the god and his or her mortal partner have undergone a wedding, they then share a common destiny. The spirit's duty is to protect its spouse, but it must be given presents in return.

The spirits help to deal with the ordinary problems of life and maintain African roots and identity. They help to heal relationships, putting problematic human relationships into an external form where they can be worked out.

Voodoo initiates in "kapame", a secret ritual enclosure, near Lomé, Togo.

Fetishes for sale at Lomé Voodoo market, Togo.

THE MAGIC OF ABORIGINAL DREAMING

The religious life of the Native Australian peoples is focused on what Europeans term the "Dreaming" or the "Dreamtime", and what Aborigines call *jukurrpa*. The Dreaming relates to a state of reality beyond the everyday in which ancestral creators – such as the Wauwalak Sisters and the Wandjina – travelled across the unshaped world in human and non-human form, classifying it as they went and bringing laws of social and religious behaviour.

THE WAUWALAK SISTERS

Myths about the Dreaming show how humans are related to the land. The myth of the Wauwalak Sisters shows how the spiritual heritage of the Dreaming is passed on through rituals and ceremonies.

A bark painting depicting a Wandjina, one of a group of ancestral beings from the sea and sky that bring rain and control the fertility of the animals and the land.

A Churinga, a sacred disc believed to be a transformation of the ancestors of the Dreamtime and their weapons. They represent each person's spirit, while the design is a totemic pattern of the associated sacred site. They could only be viewed by initiated men and had to be handled with the correct ritual songs.

Two sisters left their homeland after the elder of the two became pregnant through an incestuous relationship. They travelled to the sacred waterhole of Muruwul and on the way named all the animals, birds and plants. As they walked along they killed lizards, possums, bushrats and kangaroos, and dug yams. They placed the animals and plants in their dilly bags.

When they stopped to rest at Gruawona, the elder sister gave birth to a baby girl. They made a fire and attempted to cook the food from the dilly bag. They put the animals on the fire but as soon as the creatures warmed they came back to life, escaped to the sacred waterhole and in the process became sacred themselves. In the waterhole lived the great rock python Julungul, the rainbow serpent. Julungul slowly emerged from the waterhole smelling the birth blood of the eldest sister. The sisters danced to keep the snake at bay, and this dance caused the younger sister to start menstruating. Attracted by the blood, the snake swallowed both of the sisters and returned to the waterhole. Later the snake vomited up the sisters, saw that they were still alive, beat them with her song-stick, and swallowed them again.

Julungul then returned to all the other snakes in the sacred waterhole and the spirits of the Wauwalak Sisters spoke to them through Julungul. In this way the snake delivered to her people the spiritual heritage of the Dreaming: the sacred law, ritual, dance and song. When this was done she retired to a cave and never emerged again.

A WEB OF DREAMINGS

Australia is covered by an intricate web of Dreamings. Some relate to a particular place, while others reside within individuals. On one level, the Dreaming is shrouded in the mists of time; people claim to be descended from a particular region without actually tracing the links through specific ancestors, and exact names and dates add little to their perceptions of the past. What is stressed, however, is the relationship to others, their Dreaming affiliations and ritual associations, and this is a way of focusing on relationships with the land and with the people. Individuals derive their

An Aboriginal shaman of today. The patterns of the body painting across his chest represent the Oruncha, the mythical creature from whom his shaman's powers are derived.

identity from the land. Relationships are stated and affirmed in terms of rights and responsibilities in the country of their ancestors. During the Dreamtime an all-encompassing law bound people, flora, fauna and the natural world together. One native Australian elder has described the Dreaming in the following manner:

Dreaming,
The first ones lived, those of long ago.
They were the Wandjinas –
Like this one here, Namalee.
The first ones, those days,
Shifted from place to place,
In the Dreaming before the floods came.
Bird Wandjinas, crab Wandjinas
Carried the big rocks.
They threw them into deep water,
Then piled them on the land.

All kinds –
She the rock python,
He the kangaroo,
They changed it.
They struggled with the rocks,
They dug the rivers.
They were the Wandjinas. They talk
With us at some places
they have marked.

Where the sun climbs, over the hills
And the river they came,
And they are with us in the land.
We remember how they fought
Each other at those places they marked.
It is Dreaming there.
Some Wandjinas went under the land,
They came to stay in the caves
And there we can see them.
Grown men listen to their Wandjinas.
Long ago, at another time,
These Wandjinas changed the bad ones
Into rocks
And the spring we always drink from.
These places hold our spirits,
These Ungud places of the Wandjinas.
There a man learns
Who his child really is:
Its spirit comes when he is dreaming
And tells him its name.
Then the man has been given his child:
It has its own name
Beside the land-name of its father ...

A petroglyph incised in the rock at an Aboriginal sacred site. These designs are believed to have been made by clan ancestral beings during the Dreamtime.

A bark painting depicting three spirit figures, legendary supernatural beings of the Dreamtime.

An Aboriginal bark painting of two crocodiles appearing as a shaman might see them.

SCIENCE AND MAGIC

Human beings have always tried to make sense of the world around them. In modern times we often look to science to give us explanations for the way things are. Way back, in the distant past, our ancestors probably would have turned to the spirits and what we would now call magic as a source of information. Today, in Western societies, this way of seeking knowledge has been devalued. Magic has often been contrasted with both science and religion. However, magic is similar to science in the way that it offers an explanation of the world, although it uses the medium of spiritual connection, which cannot be observed or measured in a laboratory; the cause-and-effect relationship between an act and its consequence is spiritual, rather than scientifically validated and observable. More recently, there has been a shift from comparing magic and science to looking at different ways of thinking. All human beings are capable of exercising two ways of thinking: these are logical, analytical thought, the thought required to work out a complex mathematical formula, for example, and analogical or magical thinking, the state of mind required to enter a trance, such as a shamanic journey. Both can be examined and understood through a scientific world-view.

Alchemists in the middle ages believed they used scientific methods to control natural magic.

Sir James George Frazer, Scottish social anthropologist, classicist, folklorist and author.

JAMES FRAZER (1854–1941)

An early anthropologist and the author of *The Golden Bough* (1890), James Frazer saw the relationship between magic, science and religion in evolutionary terms. Frazer thought that magic was the first stage in the evolution of the human mind, and that both magic and religion, which grew from the mistakes of magical thinking, would eventually be superseded by science. As people came to realize that magical techniques were ineffective, they created omnipotent gods that controlled nature and needed to be supplicated. Finally, as humans began to recognize the existence of empirical natural laws, religion would join magic as superstition.

A depiction of a witch doctor discovering an unfavourable sign, c.1870.

Frazer thought that magic was formed from the association of ideas, and developed the notion of sympathetic magic – the belief that everything is connected in a state of sympathy or antipathy. Magical rites were based upon the idea of "homeopathic magic", founded on a "law of similarity" that "like produces like"; and "contagious magic", based on a "law of contact", which holds that things that have been in physical contact continue to act upon each other at a distance.

LUCIEN LÉVY-BRUHL (1857–1939)

The French philosopher Lucien Lévy-Bruhl thought that while modern Western societies were scientifically orientated, what he termed "primitive" societies were mystically oriented, and he used the supernatural as an explanatory framework. Lévy-Bruhl saw pre-scientific or magical thinking as "pre-logical" (a term he later abandoned). He said that "primitive" societies were "pre-scientific" because their collective representations inhibited the development of a scientific world-view. Lévy-Bruhl thought that there was a special primitive way of thinking that explained collective life, and which every individual unconsciously accepted as a result of the influence of society. He was interested in how collective beliefs explained what seemed to be irrational religious views such as witchcraft.

EDWARD EVANS-PRITCHARD (1902–73)

The anthropologist Edward Evans-Pritchard, in his study of the African society of the Azande in the 1920s, was interested in Lévy-Bruhl's ideas but questioned his view that "primitive" people had a special way of thinking that was "pre-logical". He asked why the Azande still believed in magic despite its frequent failure and came to the conclusion that they attributed failure to a particular magician's performance and not to the magical world-view itself. This led him to speculate that the Azande had a closed system of thought, which inhibited scientific verification. He saw the Azande magical system as rational in itself, but ultimately inferior to science.

The Polish-born British anthropologist, Bronislaw Malinowski, working among the people of the Trobriand Islands, 1914–18.

BRONISLAW MALINOWSKI (1884–1942)

An anthropologist who conducted fieldwork among the inhabitants of the Trobriand Islands (now part of Papua New Guinea), Malinowski emphasized that magic was both material and spiritual and was similar to both science and religion. He claimed that magic was used in high-risk situations, such as when fishing in the open sea, but not in the safe waters of the shallow lagoon. He argued that the Trobrianders used both magical and scientific knowledge in the way that they planted yams: they grew yams with a great deal of technical expertise but also employed magical spells to protect them.

In a painting from 1913, a witch doctor in Swaziland goes round the village "smelling" for the sorcerer who is using magic against his client.

ASTROLOGICAL KNOWLEDGE

Astrology derives from the magical practice of linking the individual human being with the wider universe, as microcosm to macrocosm. Astrology is said to have its origins in Egyptian and Chaldean astral lore, and in the revelations of the Egyptian god Thoth, a scribe of the gods and divinity of wisdom who was identified by the Greeks with Hermes. It has also been attributed to the mythical Egyptian pharaoh Nechepsos and the priest Petosiris. Eudoxus of Cnidus (c.408–353BC), said to be the father of Greek astronomy, was also versed in the principles of astrology. The astronomer Hipparchus (second century BC) studied the correspondences of planetary signs with the people and the geographical features of the earth.

THE DEVELOPMENT OF ASTROLOGY

According to the historian Frances Yates, astrology developed from a collection of Greek writings called the *Corpus Hermeticum*. During the Renaissance, these writings were believed to be by an Egyptian priest known as Hermes

Hipparchus in his observatory in Alexandria.

Trismegistus, but have since been identified as largely Greek and dated between the first and third centuries BC or AD. This large body of magical writings concerned astrology and the occult sciences; it involved the drawing down of the powers of the stars, and the understanding of the secret virtues of plants and stones. A form of sympathetic magic, it was a way of connecting the material everyday world with the influence of the stars and planets.

An understanding of the astrological pattern in the cosmos enabled the positive influences of the stars pouring down on to the earth to be captured in talismans and used by a magician with the right knowledge. The magician who wished to capture the power of the planet Venus must know what plants belonged to Venus, what stones, metals and animals to use when addressing Venus; images inscribed on talismans had to be made of the right materials, and used at precisely the right astrological moment. Talismans were believed to capture the spirit of the star and to hold or store it for use.

THE SIGNS OF THE ZODIAC

The cosmos was divided into 12 signs of the zodiac, each with its own complicated correspondences and associated animals, plants and other attributes. The magician was the person who knew how to operate this complex system of links

The Ibis-headed Egyptian god Thoth is associated with the beginnings of astrology. Thoth is depicted here with the pharaoh Seti I.

between the celestial and the earthly realms. The powers so derived could be used to obtain material benefits, or to gain insight into the worship of the divine forces in nature. Knowledge gained from the celestial realms could be used to predict a person's future based on a cosmological analysis of their past, or it could indicate the future of whole societies or nations.

WORLD ASTROLOGY

Greek ideas about astrology spread around the world, reaching India between AD100 and 300. Chinese astrology may have derived from Indian astrology. Astrologers predicted cultural and political events, and connected every important moment in history with the movements of the planets, comets or eclipses. The discipline had a prominent place in Renaissance science, but it gradually lost this position after the Christian church disassociated itself from astrology during the Reformation of the sixteenth century. Today, many people read their "stars" in popular newspapers and magazines, but such horoscopes constitute a form of entertainment rather than a serious study of a person's connections with the planetary

A representation of the heavens: the northern and southern hemispheres with the star signs. A copper engraving of c.1700.

sphere. The link uniting the individual with the wider connections of the cosmos has largely been lost.

Signs of the Chinese zodiac surrounding the symbol of yin and yang.

A Christian allegorical depiction of the planetary system.

THE SCIENCE OF ALCHEMY

Alchemy is an esoteric technique and has spiritual goals similar to many magical traditions. Appearing as a term of reference in the West from the twelfth century, it referred to a quest for either an "elixir of immortality", a universal cure, or for a means of transmuting base metals into gold. It has been seen as a speculative precursor of chemistry, but it is very different to chemistry: chemistry deals with the scientifically verifiable while alchemy, as a magical practice, is concerned with a hidden reality underlying ordinary perception.

Through an alteration of consciousness, the ordinary way of seeing the world (which is likened to the metal lead) is changed to a more subtle perception, which is thought to penetrate the secrets of nature, life, death, eternity and infinity (associated with the sacred metal gold).

The bible of the alchemists, *The Emerald Table*, is attributed to Hermes Trismegistus. It states that "that which is above is like what is below", and that all things come from the infinite, eternal

The legendary Hermes Trismegistus, the alleged author of The Emerald Table.

A portrait of Paracelsus who sought to found a medical science based on a relationship between human beings and the cosmos.

One, symbolized by Ouroboros, a snake or dragon eating its own tail, which represents the cycle of the universe and the infinite eternal.

PARACELSUS

A dominant figure of sixteenth-century medicine and philosophy, Paracelsus (1493–1541) was an alchemist. He argued against the position of seeing reason as the basis of medicine and sought to found a new medical science based on the spiritual relationship between humans and the cosmos. He believed that he could convert base metals into gold by "curing" them of their impurities. Paracelsus compared alchemy to medicine and the baseness of metals to disease. Alchemy was a way of perfecting what nature had left in an imperfect state. Paracelsus saw humanity as the crown of creation and believed in personal free will and power to the extent that it could influence the stars. He wrote that:

Medicine must be understood and classified internally ... The physician should know how to bring about a conjunction between the astral Mars and the grown Mars [i.e. the herbal remedy]. In this sense the remedy should be prepared in the star and should become a star, for the stars above make us ill and die, they make us healthy ... The physician must therefore ... understand medicine in the light of the heavens, namely that there are stars both above and below. As a remedy cannot act without the heavens, it must be directed by them. Thus you must make a remedy volatile, that is to say, remove what is earthly in it, for only then will the heavens direct it. What should act in the brain will be directed to it by the Moon; what on the spleen by Saturn; what belongs to the heart will be guided to it by the Sun, and to the kidneys by Venus, by Jupiter to the liver, by Mars to the gall-bladder ...

ALCHEMY AND SPIRITUALITY

In every culture where it is practised, alchemy is related to esoteric traditions. In China it is associated with Taoism. The alchemical view of the self in this tradition is associated with practices

An early sixteenth-century woodcut of two alchemists at work.

An early sixteenth-century diagram of the alchemical processes for the production of the philosopher's stone (the elixir).

of a whole, and the aim of the elixir was to preserve the spirit.

In Hinduism, alchemy is concerned with techniques of bodily perfection, invigoration and rejuvenation, whereas in Buddhism there is a greater emphasis on internal yogic processes, and prolonging life is seen only as a means towards realizing total liberation. Islamic alchemy is concerned with the transmutation of the material and the spiritual with the highest form of perfection. The prophet Muhammad is said to have endorsed alchemy, and its origins are traced back to Adam, the major prophets and masters from the ancient world, including Aristotle, Galen, Socrates and Plato.

An alchemist surrounded by his equipment.

that aim at perfection of the spirit and refining the body to encompass the Way, a mystic path in which the individual is integrated with society and the cosmos.

The Chinese were interested in prolonging life and an "elixir of immortality" appears to have been developed in the fourth century BC. Chinese alchemists were single-minded in their quest and, unlike Indian, Greek or Western alchemists, did not make a distinction between this world and the next, nor did they seek liberation from the cosmos. By contrast, matter and spirit were part

The four elements, zodiac signs and alchemical symbols in conjunction.

WITCHES AND SUPERNATURAL BEINGS

Nearly all societies have some conception of witchcraft in which individuals are thought to possess a form of extraordinary power. A belief in witchcraft is part of a magical worldview that sees powers and forces inherent in the universe, which may be directed by certain people. These people have been called witches but are also known by other names such as sorceror, shaman or witch doctor. Having all manner of special abilities, these people are often frightening figures that are thought to have the ability to change their shape, fly and sometimes trick and deceive, and they have been the subject of folklore in numerous countries. They have also been used as scapegoats for the unexplained or the unexpected elements of everyday life.

WHAT IS WITCHCRAFT?

If you look up "witchcraft" in a dictionary, you will read that it is the art of bringing magical power to bear, or at least of trying to do so. This magical power can be used to both harmful and beneficial effect, but it is the former quality that is most often thought of in the context of witches. The idea that it is possible for human beings to cause harm to their fellows through the exercise of a special power not possessed by others is widespread throughout the world. Nearly all societies have some concept of witchcraft, in that certain individuals are thought to have supernatural or occult powers, which may be used to do harm or, in some cases, to heal.

A Ndebele shaman, wearing an "isiba" headdress, which features porcupine quills, divines the setting sun to foresee the future.

Various forms of witchcraft beliefs appear from India to the Pacific, but they are most widespread in Africa. In Europe between the fifteenth and eighteenth centuries, witchcraft was seen to be an organized heretical sect, which was opposed to Christianity. Witches during this time were considered to be possessed of an evil power as a consequence of being the Devil's agents. Large numbers of Europeans of all social classes believed in the existence of witches, and witchcraft was defined as a crime: people were prosecuted and executed. The European witch hunts spread to the American colonies in the seventeenth century.

The word "witch" comes from the Old English *wician*, meaning "to cast a spell". The meaning of witch and witchcraft changes from society to society and there is no neat and precise definition with which everyone agrees. A witch is often female, frequently old, although she may also be especially beautiful and lure unsuspecting men by her charms; she may shift between different guises to trick and deceive. In Africa, she may be thought to be fattened on human flesh. She almost always has the ability to change shape or cause others to be turned into other beings. By changing her form or substance she can appear in human form, as an animal or as a feeling of anxiety or horror; she also has the capacity to become invisible and to fly, often on a broom.

A witch is often believed to be capable of being in two places at once: she can act at night while her physical body lies sleeping at home. In Nigeria, the Yoruba believe that witches are generally women who fly about at night and meet in secret places. They are associated with birds, especially the nightjar, and they suck the blood of their victims until they die. For the Ibo, also of Nigeria, witches fly as balls of fire or as night-birds to their meetings. Witches are not entirely human.

They are associated with the dark, with night and with the reversal of normal human lives. A witch could be an envious neighbour who wished ill will or could be envy itself, as a powerful force for evil might take on any particular shape or guise. Witchcraft frequently

A witch doctor in Bulawayo, Zimbabwe.

represents greed, depravity, corruption or unrequited love, and it is also associated with sexuality. Witches turn against their neighbours and delight in "unnatural" practices such as incest or bestiality; they may eat their own children or dig up corpses. In short, they are immoral.

Witches have supernatural power or strength, and frequently have a knowledge of herbs and plants. A witch is a human being who incorporates a non-human power. How a witch's power is acquired varies: to Christian intellectuals at the period of the witch hunts it was derived from a pact with the Devil; in other places the power is acquired through an association with carnivorous predators, or it is gained through a skill that can be learnt; sometimes it is thought to be inherited, as in the African society of the Azande. The evil power of witches may work on their victims immediately or it may take some time to take effect. Witches can be recognized by particular signs such as a red eye or some kind of devil's mark, or they may have a snake in their belly or a special witchcraft substance.

One of the marks of witches around the world is that they are able to fly; their flight takes place at night-time.

A fifteenth-century English engraving of witches making a spell to brew up a hailstorm.

A sharp distinction between witchcraft and sorcery is impossible to maintain. Sorcery is also associated with maleficent magic, evil spells and injury. Some scholars and writers on witchcraft do not make a distinction between witchcraft and sorcery, while others differentiate between conscious harming, which they call sorcery, and unconscious harming, which they term witchcraft. Others have used the word "wizard", which comes from Middle English "wis", meaning "wise woman or man". The choice of terms is arbitrary.

A popular portrayal of witches in the seventeenth century. Here they are associated with the darkness, death, cannibalism and nakedness.

THE CLASSICAL WORLD

From writers such as Homer, Apuleius and Ovid, we learn that magic was a central and necessary part of Graeco-Roman society. It was commonly practised by a variety of people, including doctors and priests of specific deities. The state employed diviners to predict the future, and political and military decisions often depended on what the diviners foretold. Although magic was accepted as a part of everyday life, any spells that were intended to cause harm were actually illegal, and it was considered a serious, punishable offence to engage in maleficent occult acts.

The gods of the Greeks and the Romans were held to be largely subject to the same physical and spiritual laws as humans. Ideas about good and evil were related to physical feelings and experiences, which were common to gods and humans. There was no strict division between divinity and humanity, unlike the monotheistic religions of Judaism, Christianity and Islam.

ANCIENT NATURE GODS

Early Greek religion was based on the power of nature. Peoples' lives were subject to external powers – of which some could protect and some cause harm – which made up a universe of order and harmony. Greek religion was polytheistic – many gods and goddesses were worshipped – and the powers of nature were personalized. The gods dwelt in the fields, woods, rivers and springs, and later in the sea. Rivers were few and sacred: each had its deity in the form of a bull or a horse. Spirits peopled the countryside in semi-animal and semi-human form. The centaurs had the bodies of horses and the heads and torsos of men, and were probably tutelary spirits of the mountain torrents.

A nature spirit, or nymph, in the form of a beautiful young woman.

Nymphs were spirits in the form of young women: they were enchanting but they might also become threatening.

The centaur Chiron, half man and half horse, and one of the archetypal nature gods of the classical world. Chiron was renowned for his musical gifts, which were so seductive he could even bewitch the Sirens themselves.

ROMAN WITCHCRAFT

Acceptable magic acts took place in daylight; the night was considered to be the time when evil magic was practised. Roman literature is full of references to a creature called a *strix* (a word of Greek origin meaning "to screech"), which flew about at night uttering its ear-piercing screams, and feeding on the flesh and blood of human beings. The strix was usually thought of as an owl and had feathers and laid eggs, but it was more than a bird as, according to popular belief, it was able to suckle its young, and one of its evil acts was to offer its teats for human babies to suck its poisoned milk. When a *strix* found an unprotected baby it dragged it from its cradle and tore it out and ate its entrails.

Witchcraft was portrayed in works such as *The Golden Ass*, in which the writer, Lucius Apuleius, writing in the first person, was transformed into an ass when he tried to imitate a witch. He describes how he observes her change herself into a bird so that she is able to fly into her lover's bedroom at twilight:

An illustration from an edition of The Golden Ass *in which Lucius Apuleius has succeeded in changing himself into an Ass.*

I ... watched Pamphil' first undress completely and then open a small cabinet containing several little boxes, one of which she opened. It contained an ointment which she worked about with her fingers and then smeared all over her body from the soles of her feet to the crown of her head. After this she muttered a long charm to her lamp, and shook herself; and, as I watched, her limbs became gradually fledged with feathers, her arms changed into sturdy wings, her nose grew crooked and horny, her nails turned into talons, and soon there was no longer any doubt about it: Pamphil' had become an owl. She gave a querulous hoot and made a few little hopping flights until she was sure enough of her wings to glide off, away over the rooftops.

Lucius cannot believe his eyes: he thinks he was dreaming, or perhaps going mad, but he nevertheless wants to try the ointment himself. However, instead of becoming transformed into a witch he metamorphoses into a donkey, a lesson to those who might experiment with forces they can't control.

In an illustration from an Italian edition of The Golden Ass *from the early 1800s, Lucius watches the transformation of the witch into an owl.*

THE CLASSICAL WITCHES

The three most famous witches in the classical world are Hecate, Circe and Medea. They are witch-goddesses that are also associated with darkness and the night. These magical beings were not the completely evil hags that witches later became under the influence of the Christian Inquisition, but represented a necessary component of the life/death interaction that went back to much earlier times. Witches were believed to be able to call down the moon from the sky with chanting, to make waxen figures move, to invoke the spirits of the dead and to make love philtres.

Among the Romans it was thought that men were more prone to thieving, while women were more inclined to witchcraft and poisoning. However, in their original form witches represented part of a wider totality, before dark became totally separated from light.

Hecate (right) and Persephone, two classical goddesses associated with darkness and the underworld, as depicted in the fifth century BC.

HECATE

The witch-goddess Hecate was associated with the night and the moon. Hecate was called the "Queen of Night" by the poet Sappho in the sixth century BC. She was the goddess of the dark phase of the moon (while Artemis, the huntress virgin goddess, represented the new moon, and Selene, or Demeter, the full moon). Hecate was looked upon as queen of the spirits of the dead; she lived in tombs, although she might also sit by the hearth. She was believed to be

The witch-goddess Medea with one of her murdered children beside her.

Hecate, witch-goddess of darkness and the queen of the spirits of the dead.

Odysseus lands on the island of Aeaea, the home of Circe. A group of Odysseus' men enter Circe's palace. They are invited in and Circe gives them a drug that changes them into pigs, though their minds remain human. She drives them into pigsties. Odysseus sets off to rescue the men, and on the way meets the god Hermes, who gives him a drug that will make him immune to Circe's magic. When Circe finds that she cannot enchant him, Odysseus persuades her to release his men, and she uses an ointment to restore them.

They stay in Circe's palace for a year until Odysseus is reminded by his men that they must go home. Circe tells Odysseus that he must first make a journey to Hades, the world of the dead, and consult Teiresias, a blind prophet from Thebes, who will reveal his future

A sixteenth-century depiction of Circe as a sorceress, sitting in a magic circle, wand in hand, a flaming chalice at her side.

present at a person's birth and death – when the spirit entered and left the human body.

Hecate appeared at crossroads on clear nights with a following of spirits and dogs, who were sacred to her and barked at the moon. Her power was threefold and extended to heaven, earth and the underworld. Witches were said to gather at crossroads and invoke Hecate, and offerings of the remains of purifying sacrifices were placed each month at crossroads to appease her. The women who were believed to invoke Hecate in this manner were held to be experts in the manufacture of poisons.

CIRCE

Witches feature in the works of the Greek poet Homer, to whom the *Iliad* and the *Odyssey* are attributed. These two epic poems, composed in the eighth century BC, were based on the legends surrounding the Trojan War. The former describes part of the war and the latter tells how Odysseus struggled to find his way home. The *Odyssey* is a tale of the hero Odysseus' mastery of nature. It is an inner quest for illumination in which the journey to reach "home" works as a metaphor for finding the treasures of the soul.

The sorceress Circe with the companions of Odysseus that have been transformed into animals.

to him. The north wind will carry his ship to the ends of the world, across the river of the ocean where he can enter Hades. Odysseus must dig a trench and pour in honey, milk, sweet wine and water as offerings to the dead. He must also sacrifice two sheep, being careful not to let any ghost near the blood until he has consulted the prophet. Odysseus follows Circe's instructions and meets various spirits, including the fallen heroes of the Trojan War and his dead parents, as well as Teiresias.

On his return to the witch's palace, Odysseus is warned by Circe of the dangers that he and his men will meet on their journey. The first of these is

Odysseus tied to the mast of his ship so that he can hear the song of the Sirens but is unable to answer their call.

the Sirens, nymphs who attract and enchant. The voices of the Sirens are divine, but the land where they sing is strewn with human bones. Circe tells Odysseus to instruct his men to put beeswax into their ears so they will not hear the Sirens' song, and if Odysseus wishes to hear their singing, she says that he must get his men to tie him to the ship's mast. Circe also warns him of the wandering rocks where he must pass between the monstrous Scylla, who has twelve feet and six heads at the end of long necks and will snatch any sailors whose ship comes within her reach, and Charybdis, a whirlpool that sucks in passing ships.

Medea helps Jason to flee with the stolen fleece as they are pursued.

Circe symbolizes the woman who seduces men by enchanting or bewitching as well as by her skill. She is the gateway to the dark and she instructs Odysseus to journey to Hades, to enter the underworld. This has been interpreted as an inner quest to find the "treasures of the soul". Circe gives Odysseus advice about how to deal with magical pitfalls in the shape of the Sirens, Scylla and Charybdis. She is a witch in the sense that she is mistress of the dark, but she will assist those whom she favours to find illumination or enlightenment through an encounter with the underworld.

MEDEA

Medea, like Circe, has a knowledge of spells, potent brews and concoctions for causing sleep or changes in consciousness. She is the dark power that is uncontained and that, in the stories told about her, eventually creates chaos and destruction.

In Ovid's *Metamorphoses*, Medea invokes the night at the point of committing an evil action: "O night, most faithful guardian of my secrets, and golden stars, who, with the moon, succeed the brightness of day …". At other times she also calls on Hecate, the "night-wandering queen of the world below".

Medea's most famous role in legend is in the expedition of Jason and the Argonauts, when she falls in love with Jason and helps him to gain, and then keep, the Golden Fleece:

The monster in his sheath of horny scales rolled forward his interminable coils, like the eddies of black smoke that spring from smouldering logs and chase each other from below in endless convolutions. But as he writhed he saw the maiden take her stand, and heard her in her sweet voice invoking Sleep, the conqueror of the Gods, to charm him. She also called on the night-wandering queen of the world below to countenance her efforts. Jason from behind looked on in terror. But the giant snake, enchanted by her song, was soon relaxing the whole length of his serrated spine and smoothing out his multitudinous undulation, like a dark and

Medea after the dreadful murder of her own children, the darkest evil imaginable.

silent swell rolling across a sluggish sea. Yet his grim head still hovered over them and the cruel jaws threatened to snap them up. But Medea, chanting a spell, dipped a fresh sprig of juniper in her brew and sprinkled his eyes with her most potent drug; as the all-pervading magic scent spread round his head, sleep fell on him. Stirring no more, he let his jaw sink to the ground, and his innumerable coils lay stretched out far behind, spanning the deep wood. Medea called to Jason and he snatched the Golden Fleece from the oak.

When Jason beds the daughter of Creon, King of Corinth, Medea is full of vengence. She invokes Hecate and is filled with magical power, which she uses to torture the woman. Medea sends her children with a rich enchanted wedding robe that is steeped in poison and will cling to the princess's flesh and kill her. Then, in the madness of jealousy, Medea kills her own sons before she is borne away through the air in a chariot drawn by dragons.

Circe pouring poison into a vase and awaiting the arrival of Odysseus, whose ships can be seen in the background.

THE EUROPEAN TRADITION

In Europe, as elsewhere, people believed in witches. Witches were a normal part of everyday life for most people. If something went wrong, such as a cow dying or the butter failing to churn, it was due to witchcraft. People looked to their immediate neighbours to see who might be responsible. During the fifteenth to the seventeenth centuries the Christian church claimed that witches were members of a devil-worshipping cult who flew to night Sabbaths to feast on the bodies of children and indulge in orgies. Witches were said to be responsible for all types of misfortune, and they were tried and condemned to death for their supposed evil ways. Ideas about witches are still deeply embedded in folklore, literature and fairy stories.

Kit's Coty, one of the sites in England that bear witness to the folkloric prevalence of witches.

FOLK BELIEFS

Witchcraft beliefs form part of a magical world-view in which powers and forces inherent in the universe may be directed for good or ill. This is a world where everything is seen in terms of spirits and where certain persons specialize in their control. This was the case until the eighteenth century in Europe, when the Enlightenment – an intellectual movement that cast aside what it saw as the dark mysteries of religion in the pursuit of scientific research based on reason – changed the way that people thought. The process was aided by the development of rationalism, a particular way of thinking that sees all knowledge of the world as based on reason and logic. Magical beliefs came to be seen as superstition based on ignorance.

Ideas about witches, witchcraft, wizards, magic and sorcery are deeply embedded in European culture in the classical world and also in fairy tales and folk beliefs, and the countryside.

In Kent, England, for example, a megalithic chamber tomb was for centuries said to have been raised by four witches, and was known as Kit's Coty. Likewise, at the Rollright Stones in Oxfordshire, England, legend tells of a local king and his knights who were going to war. It was prophesied that if he reached a place called Long Compton he would be king of all England. However, as he was making his way up a big hill he met an old witch who turned him and all his men to stones. It is still said

A portrayal of the three witches of Shakespeare's Macbeth *as they work their magic.*

that ill-luck will fall on anyone who tries to move them. This folk tale holds echoes of the witches' role in the play *Macbeth*.

Shakespeare wrote *Macbeth* at the beginning of the seventeenth century, and in it he describes the role that three witches play in Macbeth's ambition to be king. The portrayal of the "weird sisters" is how most Europeans at that time would have viewed witches. The three women were isolated from society, living outside the community, and they were strange, both physically and behaviourally, taking on almost unhuman aspects. The witches exercised a certain amount of power and prophecy, but were only potent on their own ground – it is Macbeth that comes to them rather than the other way round: their territory is the wasted heath. Their activities are also typical of contemporary thought. They work in the dead of night, around a fire, they make plans for future meetings, and they cook a spell in a huge cauldron that is the receptacle for all kinds of unlikely ingredients. They also invoke Hecate, a Roman witch from classical times whose reputation as the witches' queen had lasted until this time:

3rd Witch: *Scale of dragon, tooth of wolf;*
Witches' mummy; maw, and gulf,
Of the ravin'd salt-sea shark;
Root of hemlock, digg'd i' th' dark;
Liver of blaspheming Jew;
Gall of goat, and slips of yew;
Sliver'd in the moon's eclipse;
Nose of Turk, and Tartar's lips;
Finger of birth-strangled babe,
Ditch-deliver'd by a drab,
Make the gruel thick and slab:
Add thereto a tiger's chaudron,
For th' ingredients of our cauldron.

2nd Witch: *Cool it with a baboon's blood.*
Then the charm is firm and good.

ENTER HECATE

Hecate: *O, well done!*
I commend your pains,
And every one shall share i' th' gains.
And now about the cauldron sing,
Like elves and fairies in a ring,
Enchanting all that you put in.

Hansel and Gretel outside the witch's house made of bread, cake and sugar.

As queen of witches, Hecate was the epitome of evil in the classical world, invoked in rites of black magic. Here she is the antithesis of good and plays a central part in Macbeth's downfall.

FAIRY STORIES

Tales of witches abound in fairy stories. They are almost always portrayed as evil old women who must be defeated by the innocent heroes or heroines. The German folk tale of Hansel and Gretel typically expresses these kinds of popular ideas about the witch. In this story Hansel and Gretel are the children

of a poor woodcutter. When famine strikes, their stepmother persuades their father to take the two children into the wood and abandon them. The children wander in the wood for three days until they come to a clearing where there is a house made of bread, cake and sugar. The children begin to eat the house and an old woman comes out and invites them in for a meal and shelter. The following morning, however, she locks Hansel in a cage and forces Gretel to work for her. She feeds Hansel to fatten him up to eat but she starves Gretel. Each day she makes Hansel hold out his finger to see how fat he has got, but he holds out a bone instead. The witch decides to eat him anyway and she orders Gretel to stoke the oven, however, Gretel tricks the witch into climbing into the oven herself. The two children return home to find that their stepmother has died and they are welcomed home by their father.

This fairy tale shows how in folklore the witch is associated with the female and with evil; she can be seen at one and the same time as the stepmother in the home who is trying to get rid of the children and as the outsider, a sinister inhabitant of a dark and frightening wood. One is a threat from within, the other represents a world of anxiety, chaos, darkness and terror.

Macbeth encountering the three witches who foretell his rise and fall as King of Scotland.

ORIGINS OF EUROPEAN WITCHCRAFT

W here did the idea of a witch come from? Scholars have seen witchcraft in terms of superstition, peasant credulity or female hysteria. They have focused on the persecution of witches without looking for the origin of such beliefs. The historian Carlo Ginzburg has criticized this approach and has looked to folklore to find the origins. He studied the *benandanti*, men and women in sixteenth- and seventeenth-century Italy who claimed that in their dreams they were wizards who fought against witches in order to protect their community. Other examples supported Ginzburg's belief – the *kresniks* of Slovenia and the *táltos* of Hungary. Together with the benandanti, he described these peoples as the surviving elements of shamanism – those who use their spiritual powers for protective purposes.

Carlo Ginzburg discovered documents of the Inquisition relating to these persons known as benandanti of the region of Friuli in north-east Italy, ranging from 1575 to the second half of the seventeenth century. Originally writing in 1966, Ginzburg described how the benandanti fought against the harmful activities of witches. They identified witches, cured the bewitched and used counter-magic against witches' spells. Four times a year they went into a trance while their souls left their bodies and, armed with fennel stalks, fought for the fertility of the fields against male and female witches armed with canes of sorghum. The spirits of the benandanti left their inanimate bodies and took the shapes of mice or butterflies. Sometimes they rode hares, cats or other animals to battle against witches or to join a procession of the dead.

A person had to be born a benandanti, and the sign of their vocation was a caul, or portion of the amniotic sac, covering their head at birth. The parents generally had the caul baptized with the child, and either preserved it until the child grew up, or made the child carry it around the neck or shoulder. When they were around twenty years old they were initiated during a visionary soul journey, during which another benandanti or an

angel of God appeared to them, beating a drum, and called their soul to an assembly of the benandanti.

The inquisitors were baffled by the strange beliefs of the benandanti,

A popular stereotype of witches, showing scenes of sacrifice, orgy and night-flying to sabbaths to worship the Devil and his countless demons

Witches and their familiars, according to a seventeenth-century view.

An erotic seventeenth-century portrayal of a witches' Sabbath, which became stereotyped by the inquisitors as a meeting for female witches who renounced their Christian faith and indulged in sexual orgies.

THE KRESNIKS

In later works, Ginzburg attempted to find other folk beliefs like those of the benandanti, and found that the beliefs of the kresniks in Slovenia and Istria were closely related. Yugoslavian and Hungarian folklorists have collected much data on the beliefs associated with the kresniks. They were people who acquired the power to confront witches because they, like the benandanti, had been born with a caul. During the night the kresniks fought witches in the shape of dogs, horses or giants. In another version, the kresnik fell into a sleep, and a big black fly flew out of his throat to fight the witches. Yet another version states that kresniks fought witches with sticks in the air near a crossroads, or they crossed the sea in eggshells to fight in Venice above St Mark's Square.

Every clan had two kresniks, one who did good, and one who did harm. They could take the shape of any animal, although they mostly fought in the form of goats, bullocks or horses. A natural opponent of the kresnik was the *vucodlak* or werewolf. The vucodlaks were also capable of soul journeys during which they transformed into wolves. It has been suggested that the fights of the kresniks and the vucodlaks were not, in fact, encounters between positive and negative forces, but the clash of "sorcerers" who represented different communities or regions.

especially the fact that they claimed that they were fighting for God and Christ. The inquisitors tried to shape the beliefs of the benandanti into what they knew about demonology. They likened their assemblies to the witches' Sabbath. The Sabbath became stereotyped as a night meeting of witches, who were usually female, and flew to the nocturnal gathering astride broomsticks, or on the backs of animals. This spirit flight was seen to be aided by the application of unguents made from children's fat. The first time a witch went to the Sabbath she had to renounce the Christian faith, desecrate the sacrament and pay homage to the Devil. They had banquets with dancing and sexual orgies.

A much less erotic image of a witch was the old crone. Here the Lancashire witch Mother Chattox rides to Pendle Hill, England, a notorious meeting place for witches, according to folklore.

The shamanic basis of ideas about witchcraft lies in the concept of the soul leaving the body and transforming into animals.
In this Scandanavian illustration from 1555, men are transformed into wolves in a ferocious flying hunt.

THE TALTOS

The Hungarian táltos were, like the kresniks, rivals of witches, and they fought for the fertility of their own village or region with adversaries from neighbouring regions, diverting drought, hail or animal plague from their own locality to that of their adversary. These fights are mentioned in accounts of witch trials. In 1741, a female táltos said that the ability to transform into animals was not necessarily related to the fights. She described how sometimes she looked into a plate filled with water and turned into a fish, disappearing for three days. On other occasions she could become a dove or a fox if she wished.

SHAMANIC LINKS

Ginzburg makes the connection between the benandanti and shamans, and a case can be made for seeing the benandanti, kresnik and táltos as various surviving elements of shamanism in central and southern Europe. Shamans use their power to communicate with the spirit world for the benefit of their social group. They are protectors of their community from magical aggression and natural calamities. They can also heal sick people, communicate with the spirits of the dead, find lost objects and predict the future. They do this by entering into a trance during which their soul leaves

Witches were said to have a close association with animals. Here three witches are shown with their familiars in a seventeenth-century woodcut.

their body and changes into spirit forms such as various animals, to battle with spirits or forces or to gain information.

The soul of a witch was said to leave the apparently lifeless body of the witch through the mouth and take the form of a butterfly, a fly or other small animal, returning some time later. Ginzburg argues that it is shamanic folk beliefs that were reinterpreted by the Inquisition as witchcraft, because the Christian church took a hostile approach to any form of magical activity. There emerged an image of a heretical witch sect, which was identified with evil and maleficence. The witches' Sabbath had two cultural aspects. The first, which was the view of the inquisitors and lay judges, was that there was a hostile social group conspiring against the Church and the forces of good. The second was that elements of shamanic origin were rooted in a folk culture of magic flight and animal metamorphosis. The result was a conflict between folk beliefs and the learned culture of the inquisitors. The belief that a witch could fly through the air and transform into various animals has its roots in an earlier magical world-view. Perhaps these ideas go back to societies where shamans engaged, through trance, with spiritual other worlds to protect the community from harm, to resolve problems like the whereabouts of animals to hunt, or to heal. These shamanic activities were reinterpreted by the Inquisition as the work of witches and labelled as harmful rather than beneficial to society.

MAGIC AND FLIGHT

How did these shamanic beliefs change into ideas about witches? The cannibalistic night witch was a part of traditional European folk beliefs. The notion of cannibalistic witches or *strigae* flying at night was familiar to many Germanic peoples of the early Middle Ages. At this time there was also a cult of the night-flying goddesses Diana, Herodias and Holda. These goddesses were beneficent female protective spirits who were sometimes associated with the souls of the dead and had no association with witchcraft or evil.

Diana was worshipped as goddess of the moon, lover of the night and associate of Hecate. She rode out at night followed by a train of souls disguised as women. These were souls of the prematurely dead, those who had died by violence, or of those that had never been buried.

Diana is equated with Herodias, the wife of Herod the tetrarch and the instigator of the murder of John the Baptist. According to a twelfth-century Latin poet Reinardus, Herod's daughter, who is referred to as Herodias rather than Salome, falls in love with John the Baptist. Unfortunately, her love is not returned and when his head is brought to her on a platter she kisses it, but it shrinks away. Herodias is blown into outer space where she must hover for ever. From midnight until cockcrow she is permitted to rest from her eternal travelling through the air by sitting on oak trees and hazel bushes.

Holda, or Hulda, is a fertility goddess who circles the earth and is particularly active in the depths of winter. She travels in the 12 days between Christmas and Epiphany bringing fertility to the land for the coming year. The historian Norman Cohn suggests that originally Holda was a pagan goddess who was associated with the winter solstice and the rebirth of the year. She is a patroness of husbandry, assisting with the crops, and the plough is sacred to her; she is also interested in spinning, weaving and childbirth. She can become terrifying if angered, but will reward hard work. When she rides out on nocturnal journeys she takes with her a train of the souls of the dead, including those who have died without being baptized.

Holda's cult followers imagined that their souls were joining this night flight, not for destructive purposes but rather for positive and sustaining ends. However, according to the *Canon Episcopi*, written in the tenth century, the women who sent their souls to ride in such a train were wicked; they had been seduced and deluded by Satan, and by the illusions and phantoms of demons, into believing that they really were riding with Diana:

… [they] openly avow that in the hours of the night they ride on certain animals, together with Diana, the goddess of the pagans, with a numberless multitude of women; and in the silence of the dead of night cross many great lands; and obey [Diana's] orders as though she were their mistress, and on particular nights are summoned to her service.

The canon reminds priests to warn their congregations that this is an illusion inspired by Satan. Thus folk beliefs of the night-flying goddesses Diana, Herodias and Holda were equated with those of cannibalistic strigae, and the wicked stereotype of the witch flying to the sabbath was created.

The cult of the night-flying goddess Diana was one manifestation of a social preoccupation with the possibility of human flight, and its association with the divine or the magical.

THE WORLD OF FAIRIES

Ideas about witches are sometimes associated with those concerning fairies. European folklore tells of worlds inhabited by little people called by various names such as elves, fairies, pixies or goblins. The land of faery is a magical place and special human beings were intermediaries between this enchanted realm and the ordinary, everyday world. In other cultures these people may have had a shamanic role to play in their communities. These fairy tales have often become mingled with tales of witches and sorcery, and at times the two have become indistinguishable.

As we have discussed, the origins of European witchcraft beliefs may lie in the shamanic elements of folklore. According to Carlo Ginzburg, the benandanti of northern Italy told their inquisitors that they were good wizards who fought against witches. In Romania, the historian of religion, Mircea Eliade, found information on another group of healers who cured diseases caused by fairies. The folklore of certain areas of Europe shows fairy cults in which special individuals

Fairies take possession of the human world at night, and their flickering, unearthly lights would act as a warning to humans to keep away.

served as intermediaries between the world of the fairies and the human world. They had elaborate rituals for curing people and animals stricken by illness because they had offended the fairies.

THE FAIRY KINGDOM

The words "faerie" and "fey" are of French derivation, and started to replace the Old English *elf* during the fourteenth century, so the words "faerie" and "elf" are interchangeable. The world of faery is said to be a world of enchantment, captivating beauty, humour, mischief, laughter and love; it is also a world of darkness, ugliness, callous superficiality, terror and tragedy. Faery is an otherworld, a place of magical power that can reveal itself to certain people. Many fairies were said to live inside hollow hills or barrows of the dead and

Fairy kingdoms were said to be places of beauty, mischief and love, ruled over by the fairy king and queen. Note the interesting depiction of the god Pan in the top right hand corner of this painting of Titania and Oberon.

The fairy kingdom was inhabited by weird and wonderful creatures, as this procession of curious sprites and goblins illustrates.

these were thought to be entrances to the otherworld. There are many types of fairy, including pixie, elf, goblin, lubberkin and hobgoblin; banshee, sidhe and leprechaun in Ireland; fynodere on the Isle of Man, gruagach, urisk, brollachan and fuath in Scotland. They range in height from the size of a human to minute proportions, and their appearance varies from extreme beauty to grotesque ugliness.

ROYAL FAIRIES

The fairies have kings and queens. Gwyn ap Nudd is a fairy king and lord of the underworld. In Celtic folklore Gwyn ap Nudd is a wild huntsman who rides a demon horse and hunts in waste places at night with a pack of white-bodied and red-eared dogs of hell. The Wild Hunt is the generic name given to numerous folk myths associated with such "soul-ravening" chases. There are many

The goddess Diana in her hunting role, with her bow and arrows, horn and dog.

leaders of the Wild Hunt in folklore, including Woden (Odin or Wotan) and Herne the Hunter. The leader of this ghastly rout is sometimes female and associated with the goddess Diana.

A later derivative of Diana is Titania, queen of the fairies in Shakespeare's *A Midsummer Night's Dream*. Also known as Mab, she probably derived from the Celtic Medb, or Maeve, queen of Connaght, who fought against Cú Chulainn. In sixteenth- and seventeenth-century literature Medb was the fairy queen who gave birth to dreams in humans. Oberon, a king of the fairies, also features in *A Midsummer Night's Dream* in which he is the estranged, and later reconciled, husband of Titania . His first appearance is in a medieval French romance called *Huan de Bordeaux* where he is called Alberon, a dwarf-king, the son of Julius Caesar and the witch queen Morgan le Fay, who helps the hero in an impossible task. His origins probably derive from Alberich, the king of Teutonic dwarfs.

Human beings – usually men – were said to be lured into the otherworld by irresistibly beautiful female fairies, and were often never seen again.

Morgan le Fay, sometimes called a witch, sometimes a dark fairy, whose lust for power brought about the end of King Arthur's reign.

FAIRY CAPTIVES

Humans may be lured to the otherworld, as in the Scottish ballad of Thomas the Rhymer. One day as he lay down on a bank, the Queen of Elfland rode past on a horse whose mane was plaited with silver bells:

True Thomas lay o'er yond grassy bank,
And he beheld a ladie gay,
A ladie that was brisk and bold,
Come riding o'er the fernie brae
Her skirt was of the grass-green silk,
Her mantel of the velvet fine,
At ilka tett of her horse's mane
Hung fifty silver bells and nine.

True Thomas he took off his hat,
And bowed him low down till his knee:
'All hail, thou mighty Queen of Heaven!
For your peer on earth I never did see.'

'O no, O no, true Thomas,' she says,
'That name does not belong to me;
I am but the queen of fair Elfland,
And I'm come here for to visit thee.
But ye maun go wi' me now, Thomas,
True Thomas, ye maun go wi' me,
For ye maun serve me seven years,
Thro' weel or wae as may chance to be.'
She turned about her milk-white steed,
And took True Thomas up behind,
And aye whene'er her bridle rang,
The steed flew swifter in the wind.

Thomas dwelt underground for seven years before returning to the ordinary world where he wrote poetry and made prophecies.

The fairies of Ireland are called sidhe (pronounced "shee") and are thought to be the descendants of the Tuatha dé Danaan, the original Irish. Their music is said to be a joy to listen to and their Queen Maeve is so beautiful that it is dangerous to look at her. The sidhe live happily if left undisturbed, but if they are molested or have any of their taboos broken, they can be very dangerous.

Their touch can sicken or madden a human being and their elf-arrows can cause instant paralysis or death. Contact with the sidhe should be avoided on 1 May and Hallowe'en when they are moving homes, at twilight, before sunrise and at noon. It is wise never to walk inside sidhe circles or over sidhe hills. Cutting down a thorn bush or leaving something on their path also invites disaster. If angered they will sometimes kidnap people and make them their slaves inside their hills. Even a short stay with the sidhe can change a person completely and they may not return. If they do, they are likely to be either mad, or come back as seers, healers or prophets.

In one story a girl heard music and was enticed into fairyland by the song – it made her think of things far away and of rivers flowing slowly to the sea. Her encounter with the sidhe was to have serious consequences for her.

As she was gathering nuts in the forest, a girl heard music of a kind different from any she had ever known. It warmed her heart and made her forget the half-gathered nuts lying beneath the tree. The soft whisper of the wind was loud in comparison with this music, and she thought of things far away and of the neighbours came to the wake, they found a hag with long teeth in her place. She was so old and so wrinkled that she could have been 100. That night the music was heard again. The mother saw flashing coloured lights outside every window and heard for the last time the music of the pipers who had taken her daughter away.

In this story, the music drew the girl into the magical land of fairy, her place in the ordinary world being taken by an old hag. Did she die as the hag or did she go to live with the sidhe in a different place and time? We do not know, we can only imagine. Such is the enduring magic of these tales.

FAIRIES AND HUMANS

Fairies were said to be fond of dancing in circles, and if a person took a walk outside at night they might actually see the fairies enjoying themselves, feasting and dancing. Fairies could be mischievous or even cruel, capable of stealing human children for their own breeding purposes and leaving substitutes or changelings in their place. If anything angered them, they could use their magical powers to inflict disease, but they could be kept friendly by offerings of food or drink. Iron objects were said to repel them. They were sometimes said to live in a fireplace and help with housework, if the fireplace was kept clean for them. They could lend farmers cattle that yielded unending milk. Fairy women were said to marry mortal men and bring much happiness, and they could also bestow good luck, beauty and talent on children.

The fairies were associated with nature; they were said to inhabit wilderness, heaths and forests. They were akin to the "wild men and women" who combined human, animal and spirit, and were believed to roam the forests in medieval times. Elements of the wild woman, who was often portrayed as a childeater and bloodsucker, lingered in the folk tales of the lonely witch who dwelt in the forest. Gradually, the characteristics of wild women were transferred to witches.

Fairies were said to be able to entice humans into their magical realms, and children were warned never to step into a fairy ring by superstitious parents.

rivers flowing slowly to the sea, until twilight darkened around her and she could hear no more.

She told her mother of the music and left even earlier the next day for the woods. She stood there beneath the nut tree, listening until the last echoes of the song had faded and the stars glittered in the night. She went again the next day to listen and the music overwhelmed

her and followed her home, filling her room with its magic. Then suddenly it stopped. When the girl emerged from her room, her mother asked her about the strange sounds. 'There was no music, mother. You must have imagined it.' With a doubtful shake of her head, her mother turned back to her work and said no more about it. The next day she found her daughter dead in bed. When

Faires and witches were often interchangeable. This is a painting of a fairy tale witch from the early 1900s.

FAIRIES AND WITCHES

It is often difficult to make distinctions beween fairies and witches, and ideas about both have merged at certain periods and changed over time. Eliade discovered that the Romanian healers, who cured diseases caused by the fairies, met in night gatherings ruled over by Doamna Zónelor, the "Queen of the Fairies", a Romanian version of Diana or Aradia, both of whom have connections with Western European beliefs in witch-craft and the Wild Hunt. Satanic ele-ments of these beliefs about night-flying goddesses may have been forcibly imposed during the trials, when they were associated with maleficent witchcraft.

The historian Gustav Henningsen studied Sicilian fairy cults. In the archives of the Spanish Inquisition he found accounts of trials of Sicilian witches between 1579 and 1651 documenting beliefs about the *donna di fuora*, who was a mixture of fairy and witch. The Inquisition material reveals that the Sicilians had two meanings for the term *donna di fuora*. The first was as a supernatural fairy-like creature of either sex who accompanied witches on their night-time excursions, and the second was associated with accused witches who adopted the name.

FAIRY CULTS

According to the Inquisition trial records, fairy cults were organized in companies. Those who attended were described as beautiful women dressed in black or white with cats' paws, horses' hooves, or "round feet". Some also had pigs' tails. Sometimes one of the group was a male fairy, who played the lute or the guitar while the others danced with linked hands.

In 1588 a fisherman's wife from Palermo confessed to the Inquisition that in a dream she and her company rode on billy goats through the air to a country called Benevento, which belonged to the Pope. They worshipped a king and a queen who, they were told, would give them wealth, beauty and young men to make love with. After the worship there was feasting, drinking and lovemaking. She also told about another witches' assembly called "The Seven Fairies". These witches had the habit of transforming themselves into dogs, cats and other animals, before going out to kill boys and commit other misdeeds. The fisherman's wife confessed the error of her ways and said that at the time she did not know that it was devilment. However, in spite of this she went on doing it because of the pleasure it gave her and because the king and queen gave her remedies for curing the sick.

In 1627 a 36-year-old wise woman related how she was taken by her "company of the Romans" to many places, including Rome, Messina and a "vast plain with a big walnut tree in the centre". The "Romans" were the "wise Sybil's people" (Sibil was King Solomon's sister) who came from a cave in the tower of Babylon. The woman talked about her experience and this was recorded by the inquisitors:

She had instructed the others together with the bliss-crowned Virgin Mary, and had received the impression that she herself must be the Mother of God. But when she saw that it was not to be her, but the bliss-crowned Virgin, she threw all her books on the fire. But Mary kept hers under her arm.

The company toured around the houses of the town each Tuesday, Thursday and Saturday night. The "Matron" leading the procession carried a torch to light the way, which was visible only to members.

Members of these secret assemblies were poor: they were farm labourers and their wives, workmen and their wives, fishermen's wives, a tailor, a shoemaker and his wife, a deacon, two Franciscan begging nuns, a charismatic healer, a washerwoman, two prostitutes, two gypsy women, some widows and various other people. There were more women involved than men.

The majority of the accused were practising wise women who were skilled in sorcery and magical healing rituals and who were known to cure misfortune brought about by the fairies. *Tocadura de brujas*, or "witch-touching", was the term for these illnesses, which could take every possible form, from indis-position to epilepsy, and which were caused by offending the fairies. For example, a young man who suffered an attack of cramp while playing the guitar was told by a wise woman in Noto that he had pushed some fairies with his arm who had gathered around him to listen to the music. The wise woman would explain the cause of the illness or misfortune to the patient and explain that she would attend a nocturnal meeting and persuade the fairies to make the sick person well. In the meantime the fairies could be mollified with offerings of a ritual meal. The wise woman would decorate the sick person's room, covering the bed with a red cloth and perfuming the whole room. On a table she would put water, wine, sweetmeats, loaves and a honey-cake. The fairies would usually visit at night when everyone was asleep, but the wise woman, or *donas*, would come when the family was present. She would walk up

Fairies carried out their work invisibly, and one talent of the wise women was to be able to "see" or sense their presence.

Fairies were not just ephemeral, lacy-winged beings, they were often grotesque and hostile too, such as these hobgoblins up to no good.

and down near the sick person playing her tambourine, and picking up food from the plates as if to feed the fairies. She told the family that she was being instructed in how to make the sick person better. The tocadura de brujas could also strike horses and donkeys, and rituals would be carried out in the stable. Sometimes rituals would be performed to bless the fields.

SHAMANIC LINKS

We can see from this that ideas about fairies have become intermingled with those about witches. Both fairies and witches were thought to have an association with a magical otherworld – the fairies as otherworldly beings and witches as gaining power from a supernatural realm. In reality, these ideas were probably a particularly European interpretation of an older shamanic pattern, whereby a specialist in dealing with spirits would go into trance to visit these otherworlds for information, advice or knowledge.

AFRICAN WITCHCRAFT

In most African societies witches are described as morose, unsociable people; they eat alone so as not to share their food, but are dangerous if food is not shared with them. They are arrogant and pass people without greeting, but are also easily offended if the same is done to them. Witches are often said to have the evil eye. Explanations of witchcraft rest on the boundless possibilities of human misdeeds and antisocial acts due to rivalry, jealousy, prejudice or any personal grievance of which you can think. Magical charms, spells and objects, such as fetishes, are often employed as protection. Witchcraft is seen as evil and it is often motivated by ill feelings generated by a quarrel, which may be remembered when someone becomes ill or suffers some misfortune. Witchcraft is always unjustified – a person may have good cause for anger, but anger should not be expressed as witchcraft.

Fetishes, magical objects used as protection against witchcraft, in Akodessewa market in Lomé, Africa.

Many African peoples believe that certain relatives might, if provoked, curse, and this inevitably has dire consequences. Relatives must accordingly be treated with respect. In Ghana, some peoples think that the power of witchcraft is inherited, and witchcraft is thought to flow along the recognized line of inheritance of property, succession to office etc; it can pass through the mother's or the father's line. Other societies believe that witchcraft power is transmitted by the parent other than that from whom property is inherited. The Tallensi of Northern Ghana believe that witchcraft powers are transmitted to persons of both sexes by their mothers.

PROTECTIVE SHRINES

In the Akan-speaking parts of Ghana, people go to shrines for protection against witchcraft. Shrine deities possess those persons who act as their priests and mediums. Talisman or fetish shrines are common in western Africa where medicines of protection are dispensed in rituals. A person thought to be bewitched is taken with the suspected witch to the shrine, where the witch is forced into making a confession. A new medium for the spirits is created when a person becomes possessed and runs wild in the bush, and is then taken to a priest of a shrine where the name of the possessing spirit is revealed. The objects in which the spirit power is embodied are thought to fall from the sky and they are captured by a diviner in a brass pan before the new medium enters the priesthood. A temple is built to the responsible spirit and people who are victims of witchcraft come for protection. The shrine is the focus of a village, and people bring offerings with requests for protection and help.

Medicines may be used as protection against witchcraft.

Night witches and animals

The night witches of the African tradition were witches who worked only in the hours of darkness. Their night time activities meant that they were associated particularly with the nocturnal owl. The hooting of owls was said to warn the night witches of someone approaching, and owls were therefore feared by the people, who saw them as bad omens. Night witches were also associated with hyenas, which they were said to ride on to distant places. When riding the hyena the witch would keep one leg on the ground and put the other on the animal's back, this had the effect of progress at great speed. Some people said that the witches were even capable of making their own hyenas by creating the body from porridge and bringing it to life with special medicines.

Potent magical symbols of the Azande people, of Sudan.

MAGIC AS A SOCIAL RULER

Witches, fairies and other spirit beings abound in European folklore; they are a central part of a magical view where a spirit world co-exists with ordinary, everyday reality. In African beliefs about witches and magic, similar ideas can be found. Magic and beliefs about witchcraft regulate many African societies. They allow grudges to be brought out in the open and provide a formula for action in misfortune. Accusations appear where tensions between neighbouring rivals could not otherwise be resolved.

NIGHT WITCHES

The Tswana of Botswana, studied by the anthropologist Isaac Schapera in the 1930s, believed in "night witches" and "day sorcerers". The night witches were mainly elderly women who bewitched people. By day they went about their everyday activities but at night they gathered in small groups, visiting one homestead after another carrying out wicked practices. They were naked and smeared their bodies with white ashes or the blood of dead people. Before a woman was admitted to the group she had to prove that she had caused the death of a close relative, preferably her own first-born child. Once initiated, she was given an ointment to smear on her

A stool shrine of the Omanhene of Anomabu, Ghana, which is associated with the spirit of the tree. Such shrines are seen as sources of spiritual power, and are often used as protection against the presence of witchcraft.

A shrine of an Ashanti spirit medium. Here, a witch and those thought to have been bewitched are brought together and a confession is extracted from the witch. Shrines are also spiritual centres of the village and offer help and protection to people.

body, which would make her wake up immediately when her fellow witches came to call. In some tribes, it was said that a special medicine was injected into a witch's thumb to make it itch when she was required to attend a night gathering.

Night witches were said to dig up newly buried corpses with the aid of a special magic that made the grave open by itself and caused the corpse to float to the surface. The witches would then take parts of it to use in their medicines. It was said that they had special medicines that would put the inhabitants of a homestead into a deep sleep so that the witches could enter and find a victim. They inserted small stones and fragments of flesh into the victim's body that would make him or her fall ill and ultimately die unless counter-magic was applied in time.

DAY SORCERERS

Not everyone believed in the night witches but day sorcerers, on the other hand, were taken very seriously. Sorcerers did not belong to bands but they did use magic to harm and bewitch specific people. They might sprinkle the blood of their enemy's sacred totem animal over their courtyard. If the victim stepped on the blood it was said to affect their feet, leading to death or the loss of a limb. The sorcerer might hide rags containing special roots in the eaves of a victim's hut, or bury them at the entrance of their homestead. The sorcerer might take some dust from his victim's footprint to work magic upon it with medicines, or he might blow special powder in the direction of the victim, calling their name; he might send an animal such as a lion, snake, ox or leopard to cause bodily injury; or put special medicines in food to poison them. By using the appropriate medicines, the sorcerer was said to direct lightning so that it struck its victim, or their hut or cattle. Some sorcerers were believed to be able to fly through the air and then descend on their victims in the guise of lightning.

NIGHTWATCHMEN

Many African peoples have chiefs or village headmen whose duty is to watch over the community by day and by night. The night watch is sometimes described as a war against witches. Among the Nyakyusa witches, power is thought to derive from the python in their entrails, and so the chiefs or headmen must also have pythons in theirs. A part of the accession ritual for chiefs and headmen involves them drinking medicines made from the flesh of a python, this is thought to give the power to see and to fight witches.

A shaman of Botswana with a small animal skin, about to perform a divination, perhaps to detect the presence of witchcraft.

A divining instrument for the detection of witches, used in Zaire. The instrument is held in a diviner's lap and springs forward when a witch's name is mentioned.

THE AZANDE – A CASE STUDY

African studies of witchcraft have been influenced by the work of the anthropologist Edward Evans-Pritchard (1902–73), who carried out research among the Azande of central Africa in the late 1920s. Evans-Pritchard's book *Witchcraft, Oracles and Magic Among the Azande* is a study of Sudanese tribal kingdoms ruled by the Avongara and indirectly ruled by the British colonial administration. Evans-Pritchard showed how witchcraft played a major part in all parts of Azande life, from agriculture, fishing, hunting and domestic life to law, morality, technology and language. He wrote that witchcraft, which he likened to bad luck, was ever-present in Azande life: there was no niche or corner of Azande culture where it was not apparent. If blight seized the groundnut crop it was witchcraft; if there was no game in the bush it was witchcraft; if there were only a few small fish to catch it was witchcraft; if a wife was unresponsive to her husband it was witchcraft; if a prince was cold and distant with his subject it was witchcraft; if a magical rite failed to achieve its purpose it was witchcraft. Any failure or misfortune that could befall anybody at any time in relation to any activity might be because of witchcraft. Witchcraft was intertwined with everyday happenings and was a part of the ordinary world.

There was nothing remarkable about a witch – you might be one yourself, as might your neighbour.

Evans-Pritchard took witchcraft beliefs seriously and described how they structured Azande thinking; they provided a philosophy by which relations between humans and unfortunate events were explained. For example, a granary collapsed because termites had eaten the supports; it crushed the people sitting underneath. Rather than blame the rotten wood this was said to have happened because of witchcraft. The Azande knew that termites had undermined the supports of the granary and did not call this disaster witchcraft in its own right; they also knew that people were sheltering from the heat of the sun and that they were not there due to witchcraft. But they then asked why the two events happened at once: and the answer to this was witchcraft. Witchcraft explained the coincidence that the granary collapsed at the time when people were sitting under it sheltering from the sun. To the Western way of thinking these would be two independent factors.

An Azande ritual of cleansing a baby after birth by passing it through the smoke of a fire to banish evil spirits.

An Azande shaman and diviner holding a rodent's skull in his mouth as part of a ritual.

The Azande used common sense as well as magical explanations. For example, where there was a clear law or moral code witchcraft was not involved, and witchcraft could not make someone lie or commit adultery.

Witchcraft explained what we would call coincidence. Evans-Pritchard described how a boy knocked his foot against a small stump of wood in the centre of a path and suffered pain and inconvenience as a result. The boy declared that witchcraft had made him knock his foot in this way. Evans-Pritchard argued with the boy, saying that it was his own carelessness that had made him knock his foot and that witchcraft had not placed the stump in the path – it had grown there naturally. The boy agreed that witchcraft had nothing to do with the stump of wood being in the path, but argued that because he had been bewitched he had not been able to see it. He added that the cut had festered and not healed quickly and this was proof of witchcraft.

An Azande chief pictured here with members of his family.

Another example was provided when he noticed that a hut had been burnt to the ground. Evans-Pritchard spoke to the owner, who was overcome with grief because it had contained beer he was preparing for a mortuary feast. He explained that he had gone to examine the beer the previous night, lighting a handful of straw to cast light, and this had ignited the thatch. He was convinced that the disaster had been caused by witchcraft.

Likewise, a woodcarver explained the splitting of wooden utensils he was carving as due to the witchcraft created by his jealous neighbours. Similarly, a potter would attribute the cracking of his pots during firing to witchcraft. As an experienced potter, he knew that his pots would not crack as a result of error because he selected the proper clay, kneaded it thoroughly to extract grit and pebbles, and built it up slowly and carefully. On the night before digging the clay he abstained from sexual intercourse, so he should have had nothing to fear, and yet the pots cracked.

WITCHCRAFT AND THE SOUL

Evans-Pritchard claimed that the Azande made the distinction between witchcraft as a hereditary quality within a person, which might be unconscious and remain inoperative, and sorcery, the conscious and deliberate perform-ance of a magical rite to cause injury. *Mbisimo mangu*, or the soul of witchcraft, might leave the body at any time, but especially at night when the victim was asleep. The Azande thought of a witch sending his soul on errands at night when his victim was asleep. It sailed through the air, sending out a bright light. During the daytime this light could only be seen by witches and witch doctors who were primed with medicines, but anyone might be unfortunate enough to see it at night. It was said to be like the gleam of firefly beetles but larger and brighter. If a person happened to see the light they picked up a piece of charcoal and threw it under their bed so that they would not suffer misfortune from the sight.

Only once did Evans-Pritchard say that he had seen witchcraft on its path. Around midnight, before retiring to bed, he went for a stroll in the garden at the back of his hut. He noticed a bright light passing at the back of his servants' huts towards the homestead of a man called Tupoi. He followed the light, running through his hut in order to see where the light was going, but he lost sight of it. On the following morning he learnt that an old relative of Tupoi had died. This event fully explained the light he had seen in terms of witchcraft: the light was coming from the body of the witch. The witch remained on his bed while the soul of his witchcraft was dispatched to remove the psychical part of his victim's organs – the *mbisimo pasio*, the soul of his flesh – which he and his fellow witches would devour. Evans-Pritchard never discovered the real origin of the light but speculated that it was possibly a handful of burning grass lit by someone on their way to defecate.

The soul of witchcraft, the mbisimo mangu, which was said to devour its victim's organs slowly, needed conscious direction to determine its route or else it

The Shilluk of Sudan constructing the thatched roof for a mud hut.

would return. The witch could not send out his witchcraft and leave it to find its victim for itself, he had to define its objective and determine its route. A sick man could elude its ravages by with-drawing to the shelter of a grass hut in the bush, unknown to all but his close relatives. The witchcraft would search at his homestead in vain and return to its owner. Sometimes a person would leave a homestead before dawn to escape witchcraft when witches were asleep and

The Pende of Zaire, dancing at a festival.

Oracles, like this divination board, are consulted to determine who is responsible for witchcraft.

would therefore not see his departure. Witchcraft worked only at close range. If a person fell sick visiting relatives then the source of the witchcraft would be sought there.

A witch destroyed his victim slowly. It was only when a witch had completely eaten the soul of a vital organ that death resulted. A witch made frequent visits over a long period and consumed only a little of the soul of the organ on each visit. Alternatively, he might remove a large portion, but he hid it in the thatch of his hut or in a hole in a tree and ate it slowly. Witches also shot objects called *ahu mangu* into the bodies of those they wished to injure. This led to pain in the place where the missile was lodged and a witch doctor would be summoned to extract it. The missiles might be material objects or living organisms such as worms or grubs.

GROUP WITCHCRAFT

Witches cooperated in destructive activities: a witch might not kill a man entirely on his own initiative but would present proposals to a witch meeting presided over by a witch leader. They assisted each other in their crimes and were called to congress by the beating of drums. They possessed a special kind of ointment that they rubbed into the skin to render them invisible on night-time excursions. Knowledge had to be gained from the experience of elder witches before a man was qualified to kill his neighbours. When a witch died he became an evil ghost and showed a hatred of humanity by bedevilling travellers in the bush, causing them to become confused.

ORACLES

In order to combat more serious cases of witchcraft, or to find out about possible misfortunes in the future, the Azande consulted oracles. If the oracles told of inauspicious circumstances or said that witchcraft hung over them, their plans were abandoned or postponed until the oracles had been consulted again. An oracle would be asked about suitable sites for a homestead or land for particular crops. If the oracle decided against one site it was asked again until it announced that one was auspicious and that there was no danger associated with it. An Azande man would ask the oracle if particular witches were threatening a future marriage and if they were he would try to persuade them to withdraw their ill will. He would leave things for a time before asking the oracle again if there was still danger ahead.

The main oracles used by the Azande were the poison oracle, the rubbing board oracle, the termite oracle, and the stick oracle. The poison oracle was by far the most important and the Azande relied on its decisions, which had the force of law when obtained on the orders of a prince. It was important in collective understanding, serious legal disputes and all life crises. A poisonous liquid, similar to strychnine and made from a forest creeper mixed with water, was given to small domestic fowls. The doses sometimes proved fatal but often the fowls recovered. In some cases, the birds were completely unaffected by the poison. From the behaviour of the birds the Azande received answers to the questions they placed before the oracle.

The rubbing board was the most frequently used oracle and it might be consulted when a man was on a visit to a friend's homestead. When the visit was finished he asked the oracle whether he should leave openly during the day or secretly at night, so that any witch wishing to send witchcraft or cause misfortune on the journey would be unaware that he had left. The rubbing board, although considered inferior to the poison oracle, had the advantage of being portable, and some were carried around in a leather or plaited-grass bag. It consisted of a miniature table-like construction in two parts – the flat surface of the table and a lid that fitted over it. The oracle answered questions

Belief in witchcraft is part of a rich oral tradition, here a Dinka storyteller tells a tale.

put to it by either allowing the lid to slide freely on the surface or by causing it to stick and not move.

When making a rubbing board, a man was subject to taboos. He must not have sexual relations for two days before he started to make it. He cut the wood, shaped it and blackened it with a red-hot spear. The rubbing board was then given its magical potency: it was anointed with medicine derived from boiled roots, whose juices were mixed with oil and boiled again while the following words were said over the pot:

This is my rubbing-board oracle,
which I am going to doctor.
When I consult it on a man's behalf may
it speak the truth, may it foretell the
[threatened] death of a man.
May it reveal things to me,
may it not hide things from me.
May it not lose its potency.
If a man eats tabooed food, such as
elephant [and comes near my oracle],
may it not lose its potency.

He then took the mixture off the fire and rubbed some of it into cuts in the table of the oracle. The remainder of the oil and juices were mixed with the ashes of various plants and rubbed on to the face of the table. The oracle was then buried to give the medicines time to sink in. It was wrapped in a piece of new barkcloth or the skin of a small animal and placed in a hole dug in the centre of a path where people would walk over it to remove all the "coldness" from the rubbing board.

The termite oracle came second only to the poison oracle. Often, preliminary verdicts were obtained from it before consulting the poison oracle. A termite mound was found and two sticks from two different trees were pushed into two holes. When the questioner returned to the mound the next day he or she received an answer according to whether the termites had eaten one stick or both. If both were left untouched, this meant that the termites had refused to answer. The Azande said that the termites did not listen to all the talk that was going

A group of Himba widows in Namibia in a healing trance, being exorcised of a lion spirit by a healer.

on in the homesteads and heard only the questions put to them.

The stick oracle consisted of three small pieces of wood or three sticks. Two pieces of stick were placed side by side on the ground and a third was placed on top of them. They were generally arranged just before nightfall in a clearing at the edge of a garden or at the back of a hut. When asking about a new homestead they were arranged in a small clearing at the proposed site. The oracle gave its answer by either remaining in position – generally an auspicious sign – or by falling, which was frequently seen as inauspicious.

Oracles are consulted to determine the site of a new homestead.

WITCH DOCTORS

Witchcraft is an activity that cannot be detected by everyday means, and so the actions of witches have to be discovered by divination. Some divination is revealed to men or women who are thought to have special powers and who speak as the mediums of the spirits.

These people are often called "witch doctors", although the term can be misleading. In many African societies the same word is used for a person who professes to cure sickness by physical means and one who claims to detect and counter the activities of witches. Many such people say that they are called to the service of the spirits; others simply receive the appropriate training from an already qualified practitioner.

A witch doctor among the Ashanti in western Africa is typical of many in the role that he performs in detecting witches. Possessed by a monster who is believed to be in league with the witches and the enemy of the good spirits, the witch doctor could discover who was responsible for committing an act of witchcraft.

The Azande witch doctor was a diviner and a magician who exposed witches and cleared areas of witchcraft. The Azande believed that witches brought sickness and death at any time and they sought to control their evil powers. A witch doctor was one who knew what medicines to use to be able to see witchcraft with his own eyes and how to drive it away.

Witch doctors held public seances at which they danced and divined, usually at the request of someone who was suffering or feared misfortune. Members of the audience would pose questions to a particular witchdoctor who responded by dancing alone. When he had become exhausted he signalled to the drummers to stop drumming at which point he began his revelations. After he had finished one question he would take another question and the whole process would start again

Azande witch doctors wore hats that were decorated with feathers and carried

A traditional healer is often called a witch doctor. This is a Pedi healer from Transvaal, South Africa.

Ideas about witchcraft shape much African thought. They form part of a moral order which inititates learn about during rituals. Here boys take part in the circumcision dance, part of a puberty ritual in Tanzania.

large bags containing skins, horns, magic whistles, belts, leglets and armlets made from various wild fruits and seeds. They often worked together and the seances were led by the eldest, most experienced magician, who may have initiated the others into the practice. Edward Evans-Pritchard notes that it was not usual for women to become witch doctors, but a few, usually older and widowed, were qualifed to act as leeches, and some gained a considerable reputation as healers.

Evans-Pritchard called witchcraft accusations an all-purpose social device for restraining uncharitable behaviour and bringing grudges out into the open. He explained how witchcraft acted as a stabilizing influence on the social and moral systems of the society, insulating its beliefs from social conflict. Only commoners could be accused, and a son could not accuse his father without accusing himself, so authority remained unchallenged. Evans-Pritchard was keen to show the meaning of witchcraft as a way of seeing the world, as well as describing the way it worked to order and regulate society.

Sociological explanations of witchcraft are concerned with how witches represent immoral forces and how these ideas work to order society. Some scholars have seen witchcraft beliefs only in terms of ordering social relations. Others are critical of this approach and say that comparisons between European and African witchcraft are limited and that witchcraft must be studied within its own environment; witchcraft should be analysed as part of a larger cultural scheme particular to each case.

Right: Witchcraft beliefs structure everyday life in African societies.

A fetish priest, believed to have special powers to cure sickness, makes a libation at a shrine in the Volta region of Ghana.

NATIVE AMERICAN WITCHCRAFT

As in other parts of the world, witches among the Native Americans are viewed as antisocial people who can inflict harm and cause injury to people. A witch is someone who uses magical powers for their own ends rather than working in harmony with the good powers of the universe and helping their community. North American shamans had to know about working with the helpful and benign spirits of the universe; they also had to know about those spirits that could bring harm and illness. A good shaman would harness beneficial spirits and control those who had ill will. In some cases though, a shaman could turn his or her knowledge of such matters to antisocial ends. This was viewed as witchcraft and as such was considered to be illegal.

A portrait of the famous Black Elk, a shaman of the Oglala Sioux.

To the Native American Indians, the links that the tribe had with the spirit world was a central part of their culture. Not only did it link them with their past and the wisdom of their ancestors, it also provided them with a means of communication with the animal spirits and the spirits of nature on whom their survival depended. It was the tribal shaman who, through trances and vision quests, was responsible for maintaining these links between the community and the spirit world.

Various rituals and artefacts were used as tools by the shaman to aid trances. In the following extract Black Elk, a

A traditional medicine pipe used by a shaman.

shaman of the Oglala Sioux, who dictated his life story to John G. Neihardt in the 1930s, used the ritual smoking of a pipe used in the propitiation of the spirits to send an offering to the Spirit of the World and to call on all the good spirits of the universe:

... I will first make an offering and send a voice to the Spirit of the World, that I may help me to be true. See, I fill this sacred pipe with the bark of the red willow; but before we smoke it, you must see how it is made and what it means. These four ribbons hanging here on the stem are the four quarters of the universe. The black one is for the west where the thunder beings live to send us rain; the white one for the north, whence comes the great white cleansing wind; the red one for the east, whence springs the light and where the morning star lives to give men wisdom; the yellow for the south, whence come the summer and the power to grow.

But these four spirits are only one Spirit after all, and this eagle feather here is for that One, which is like a father, and also it is for the thoughts of men that should rise high as eagles do. Is not the sky a father and the earth a mother, and are not all living things with feet or wings or roots their children? And this hide upon the mouth-

The shamans of the tribes of North America would use a drum to help induce a trance.

piece here, which should be bison hide, is for the earth, from whence we came and at whose breast we suck as babies all our lives, along with all the animals and birds and trees and grasses. And because it means all this, and more than any man can understand, the pipe is holy.

Smoking the pipe put Black Elk in touch with all the spirits; these are all a manifestation of the Great Spirit. The Oglala Sioux, like many other North American peoples, share a belief in a great controlling power that is made up of a hierarchy of a series of lesser powers that pervade the universe. This power is frequently called Wakan-Tanka, the "sacred ones". Native American peoples believe in a multitude of spirits who inhabit all natural phenomena – plants, animals, rocks, wind, rain, the stars and so on. Although many aspects of the spirit world have benign features, the world is seen to be full of spirits that can also do great harm. Each individual possesses a guardian spirit that was originally found in a vision quest or a dream, and protects a person through their life. Among the Ojibwa of the north-east, the spirit world is loosely divided into an upper world inhabited by benign spirits represented by the sun, moon and thunderbirds (spirit beings that are half human and half turkey cocks, representing the spirit of rain, thunder and lightning), and an underworld inhabited by underwater

A shaman of the Assiniboin, placating the spirit of a slain eagle.

panthers, and a cannibal giant called Windigo, who searches for people to eat in the winter. These malign spirits are connected to ideas about witchcraft, and witches are thought to know how to use them to cause misfortune.

WITCHES' POWER

It is witches who use these dangerous spirits to cause disease. Evil witches are usually medicine men or healers who called upon the spirit world for help in curing the sick but have come to use

A Sun Dance effigy doll used by the Crow people. These were used in Sun Dance rituals to assist a pledger in obtaining a vision that would lead to the defeat of an opponent. A witch might acquire such a doll to represent a person's spirit.

their power for their own ends, rather than for the benefit of others. They may have become diverted from their previous task of healer, or perhaps they have become mentally unstable by their association with evil guardian spirits. Witches may turn upon people making them suffer from starvation and disease. They may inflict hunger on them by destroying their hunting luck, and they might cause disease by creating an image of their victim on the ground and placing poison over the organ to be damaged. Alternatively, they might tie a carved wooden image of the person they want to destroy to a tree, believing that when the thread breaks the person will die.

A witch will try to obtain an object connected with the person they want to harm, such as hair, spittle or nails. Then he or she goes to a burial place and puts the object into a grave where there is a body, or the ashes of a body, and curses it. The witch may make an effigy of the victim's body, making it as thin as a skeleton or deforming its hands.

It is said that over 100 years ago one Plains Indian witch carried a doll wrapped in buckskin attached to his

The interior of the Medicine Lodge of the Mandan people, during an O-kee-pa ceremony.

A mid-nineteenth-century depiction of a North American Indian medicine man in a wigwam preparing medicine while holding a gourd rattle and chanting an invocation.

necklace. It represented his guardian spirit, a mountain ogre, and was acquired intentionally to injure people, and he was said to steal people's souls during the Sun Dance ceremonies, which honoured the sun. The witch was finally killed by the stronger magic of a Ute Indian medicine man.

Some witches are said to shoot disease-ridden or pathogenic objects into a person. Among the Coast Salish of the north-west coast, diseases are seen to be due to a malevolent shaman or witch shooting an object imbued with their power into a patient. The object has to be removed, in this case by a medicine man. Witches may inject a piece of flesh from a corpse, a shred of funeral cloth or a splinter of bone, or any sharp or pointed thing such as a cactus point or a shard of glass. It is often the job of the shaman to remove the object that has caused the disease. This is done by sucking it out through a hollow bone or by putting their mouth on the affected part of the ill person's body to suck out the sickness. The disease may also be

pulled out by the shaman using his or her hands, or just by rubbing or touching. Sometimes the shaman may bleed the bad blood out or order the person to bathe the disease away.

Witches might also use soul-stealing procedures to destroy their victims, and then it is the task of the shaman to venture into the spirit worlds to find the soul or parts of the soul and return them to the sick person. Insects are controlled by witches. They can send caterpillars or grasshoppers to destroy crops, and they may send insects into the body of a victim to destroy it. Witches may also attack through the ghosts of members of the family they are persecuting. Witches can also control the weather – they can keep the rain away or cause wind.

According to anthropologist Åke Hultkrantz, the Zuni of the north bank of the Upper Zuni river close to the western border of New Mexico, are likely to have witchcraft societies. Zuni society is horticultural. Since early times they have cultivated corn, squash and beans, and they have elaborate maize

ceremonies. Frequent allegations of witchcraft reveal a strictly ordered social system in which curing societies heal the sick. All members of curing societies have been close to death due to illness, accident, or the effects of breaking taboos. The "beast gods" are the patrons of the curing societies and live in the place where once, at the beginning of time, people emerged from underground. Witches are said to have imitated these curing societies, but instead of curing people they are thought to project disease objects into them. Organized like any other society, the members have to obey the orders of their officers and go out and make people sick. To be initiated, the candidate must bewitch a member of their household to death. In the initiation the candidate allegedly has to go under an arch or bow with a member of the society to metamorphose into spirit animal form. If the initiate wishes to be a witch cat, for example, then he or she must choose a member of the society whose spirit animal is a witch cat. Alternatively, a candidate can put on the skin of the animal that she or he wishes to be transformed into.

In the past, witchcraft was a very dangerous activity, and until the middle of the nineteenth century was punished by death. The witch's own relatives could kill him or her when the shaman

The anthropologist Lewis H Morgan.

had identified the correct person. However, witches of high social rank were not attacked because of their position, and were asked to heal the person they had bewitched in secret. Among the Iroquois, according to the anthropologist Lewis Henry Morgan (1818–1881), any person could take the life of a witch when discovered performing witchcraft. If this was not done, a council was called, and the witch was called before it in the presence of the accuser. If the witch confessed fully and promised to amend his or her ways, a discharge was made. However, if the accusation was denied, witnesses were called and the circumstances of the case were heard. If the charge was established, death was sentenced. After the decision of the council, the relatives of the witch gave him up without protest.

WITCHES AND MYTHOLOGY

Like many other Native American peoples, the Tlingit of the north-west coast of Canada say that all dangerous disease is caused by witchcraft. Witches are said to have learnt their art from Raven. Raven features in North American mythology and is a trickster, rearranger and transformer of the world. Tricksters are beings that deliberately upset order or a certain train of circumstances. Their role in mythology is to cause disruption, and out of the ensuing chaos comes a different understanding. Tricksters have an ambiguous part to play, often they are difficult characters with good and bad qualities, but they are seen to be essential to the overall pattern of life. For example, Raven steals things being hoarded by people and redistributes them. He is associated with origin stories in which he takes the sun, moon, stars and daylight from one person who is unwilling to share them and gives them out to others, and in the process other features of the world, such as rivers, lakes and animals, are created. However, in some stories, Raven is driven entirely by ego, hunger and greed, with no evident good motives. Small birds are lucky to go away hungry but alive

Witches are said to have learned their art from Raven, the trickster.

after Raven cheats them out of their share of the king Salmon, Bear loses the fat from his thighs in one story and his genitals in another, Cormorant loses his tongue.

Coyote, another trickster, is said to be responsible for the introduction of witchcraft. Coyote assumes a dual personality

in most Native American mythologies. Like Raven, he is sometimes seen as having a positive involvement in creation, but he is also a thief and a coward. He bestowed fire but also introduced death. The negative aspects of his image may be attributed to his habit of eating nearly anything and stealing other animals' prey. He is widely regarded as envious, greedy, and easily duped; he is also a bungler and a coward. A powerful spiritual entity, he is associated with illness and witchcraft. Eating a melon that a coyote has previously bitten, or killing a coyote, can trigger an illness. The cure often consists of waving a coyote tail over the ailing person and singing songs. He is believed to cause several diseases, which can only be treated by a shaman.

Native Americans inhabited a world that was alive with spirit powers – theirs was a cosmos that was made up of good and bad entities. Witches were those individuals who worked against the harmonious ordering of the universe by using their powers to disrupt in a wholly negative way.

A shaman of the Zuni Pueblo people blows pollen over a village shrine in a ritual to invoke a spirit.

EARLY MODERN WITCHCRAFT

The years 1450–1750 cover a time that is referred to as the early modern period, and in Europe it was a time in which the Christian Church attempted to introduce new ideas about witchcraft. The witch had always been portrayed as an anti-social creature but now she was – according to certain theologians – in league with the Devil and responsible for many atrocious acts previously attributed to heretics. In fact, those persecuted were probably just ordinary women and men – but maybe some of them were practising folk medicine, and it might have been this that set them apart. The distinction between healers and witches was not always clear: in theory – the authorities felt – a person who knew how to heal also knew how to harm.

[I]

HOW WITCHCRAFT DEVELOPED

In Europe between the fifteenth and eighteenth centuries, a time known as the early modern period, the figure of the witch known in the pagan Greek and Roman worlds took on a different character, as a particularly Christian interpretation was superimposed on older beliefs. For many Christians the world was seen to be divided between good and evil: God represented the good, and an evil realm was ruled over by the Devil, or Satan. Devilish powers were attributed to witches, sorcerers and all those who were thought to follow Satan. Thus Christianity shaped ideas about witchcraft in early modern Europe.

Witches were often associated with lewd behaviour, and were said by their accused to gather in groups with no clothes on.

Witches were thought to be in contact with Satan through their familiars, who would do their bidding and carry out tasks.

From the Saxon period onwards, most of Europe held the same sort of reasonably tolerant beliefs about magic, sorcery and witchcraft, but by the fifteenth century a widespread and popular fear of witchcraft had been fostered by the Church.

Ordinary people were concerned about the practical effects of witchcraft on their daily lives, not where the power of witchcraft came from: this was the preoccupation of the Church authorities. During the early modern period in England, most people lived in rural villages and hamlets and were mainly concerned with the production of food. Society was highly stratified and between a third and half the population lived at subsistence level. Consequently, poverty, sickness and sudden disasters, such as plague or starvation due to crop failure, were familiar events.

Some anthropologists and historians have suggested a comparison between European beliefs in witchcraft and those in Africa. The anthropologist Edward Evans-Pritchard and the historians Keith Thomas and Alan Macfarlane have argued for a dialogue between anthropological and historical approaches. In his study of witchcraft beliefs in Tudor and Stuart Essex in England, Macfarlane discovered that witchcraft allegations were a normal part of village life. Accusations reflected the concerns of yeomen and husbandmen who felt they had been harmed by witchcraft. Witchcraft explained misfortune, so that when a new baby refused to drink its mother's milk, or a child became ill, or farm animals died, the people looked to their social relationships rather than blaming their economic state, to see who might be responsible.

The victims of witchcraft were generally neighbours of the so-called witches. The accused were usually poor women living alone, and accusations tended to follow quarrels that were centred on a refusal to give charity. In a typical case brought on 31 December 1646, Henry Cockcrofte, a member of a yeoman family living in Heptonstall in the West Riding of Yorkshire, gave evidence to two Justices of the Peace about a woman called Elizabeth Crossley. When Crossley had come begging for alms at his door, Cockcrofte's wife had given her something, but she was not pleased with what she had been given.

That night, Cockcrofte's baby son fell ill, partially recovered, but later died. Cockcrofte accused another woman called Mary Midgely of witchcraft. Midgely confessed to being a witch but denied harming his son and blamed Elizabeth Crossley, her daughter and another woman. Cockcrofte's decision to take the affair to the courts prompted his neighbours to make formal accusations against Midgely. In one of these, Richard Wood told how Midgely had begged for wool at his door. His wife had refused her, telling Midgely that she had given her wool three weeks before and would give her no more, but she had given her alms of milk. Midgely

The Devil would summon witches to Sabbaths and would visit their meetings.

Witches were said to have familiars, animals that acted as tools and servants.

had left in an obviously angry mood. After this Richard Wood's cattle had sickened mysteriously.

Such village beliefs about witchcraft would appear to be similar to those of the African Azande studied by Evans-Pritchard. In both cases, witchcraft explained what at that time was the inexplicable, and was a way of under-standing social relationships. Thomas argued that witchcraft beliefs helped to uphold traditional obligations of charity and neighbourliness at a time of change, when social and economic forces were weakening communities.

Other scholars have questioned how far it is possible to compare cultures as different in time and place as the Azande and the inhabitants of Tudor and Stuart England. Links can be made between European and African witch-craft if a belief in spirits – a magical or animistic world-view – is accepted as being common to both cultures.

WITCHCRAFT IN POPULAR CULTURE

To ordinary people living during the early modern period, magic and witchcraft were a way of life and witches were a part of European culture. But the Christian church began to construct the image of a diabolical witch, and gradually a stereotype of an anti-Christian follower of Satan emerged. This view of witches infiltrated and merged with older Greek and Roman ones. Magical objects were thought to ward off a witch's attack, and people learnt how to live and deal with those they suspected of witchcraft. Magical practitioners – "cunning folk", wizards and conjurers – were found in every village, and their services were used to identify witches, find lost or stolen goods, tell fortunes and give remedies for a whole host of diseases in both humans and animals.

In early modern Europe, witchcraft beliefs were a part of everyday life for ordinary people and they co-existed and intermingled with Christian beliefs. According to the historian Keith Thomas, in a study of popular beliefs in sixteenth- and seventeenth-century England, the hold of orthodox Christianity on the English people was never complete. Although few avoided baptism, matrimony or holy burial, there is evidence to suggest that the poorest classes never became regular church-goers at any time. Thomas notes that even when they did put in a reluctant appearance, "Members of the congregation jostled for pews, nudged their neighbours, hawked and spat, knitted, made coarse remarks, told jokes, fell asleep and even let off guns".

An eighteenth-century illustration in which a witch is performing a ritual surrounded by herbs, magical grimoires, skulls and bones.

The poorest people in the sixteenth and seventeenth centuries never became regular churchgoers, and when they did attend were not as orderly as this nineteenth century congregation.

However, even if they did not attend church or have a religious belief, ordinary people had a view of the world in which the belief in witches was an everyday reality; and they used magical means against the power of witches.

PRECAUTIONS AGAINST WITCHES

Before a witch attacked, precautions could be taken to safeguard a likely victim. Once witchcraft was believed to have been used, cures could be sought. Finally, attempts could be made to locate the witch and either force her to withdraw her power or have her punished.

Precautions to avoid being bewitched included a person regulating his or her life so that a witch was unlikely or unable to attack. This often involved moving out of a "witch-infested" area, or refusing to allow those thought to be witches to live nearby. Sometimes kindness to witches was advocated, and humouring them was thought to ward off an attack.

A witch-doll with an attached written curse, from the late eighteenth century.

SOCIAL SANCTION

Fear of witches acted as a sanction enforcing neighbourly conduct. Alternatively, cutting all contact and avoiding the borrowing or lending of objects through which witches might work magic was another option. It was considered dangerous to receive a gift from a witch as this might cause misfortune. In 1617, the Puritan, Thomas Cooper, in *The Mystery of Witch-Craft*, warned his readers to avoid witches and not give alms:

Be wise in our Liberalitie, and Almesdeedes, not distributing to each sort of poore, because many times Witches go under this habite ... especially, to take heed if any such suspected seeke unto us; to bee straight-handed towards them, not to entertaine them in our houses, not to relieve them with our morsels.

If a witch was seen loitering near a person's house she should be warned off in case she was burying magic under the bedstraw or under the threshold.

Thus, for ordinary people, ideas and beliefs about witchcraft were a part of everyday life. The established church tried to impose a certain view of diabolical witchcraft, which was then incorporated with existing folk beliefs in popular culture.

A modern version of the holed stones that were used as charms against witchcraft.

Magical objects

Charms, objects and gestures were used by most people as protection from witches and evil. Hanging a copy of the first chapter of John's Gospel around the neck was particularly popular, and a woman said to be 'haunted with a fairy' was rumoured to wear such an amulet. Certain plants, roots, stones or holy objects were used as amulets against evil. Holed stones, salt, communion wafers, holy water and the sign of the Cross were also used to prevent or cure the effects of witchcraft.

Witches were commonly thought to be able to perform supposedly supernatural feats, such as drawing milk from an axe handle, as shown in this woodcut from 1517.

CUNNING FOLK

Ordinary people relied on the services of "cunning men and women", wizards, wise folk, sorcerers, conjurers or "white witches". These magical practitioners were to be found in every village, and it was common for them to be consulted for help in identifying witches, fortune-telling, finding lost or stolen goods and identifying those who had taken them, and for providing remedies for a wide range of illnesses, both human and animal.

Cunning folk often wore strange costumes, for example dressing in scarlet or, in the case of a well-known cunning man in Essex, wearing "terrifying goggles". They were aided by magical spells and oracles. It was common for people to consult cunning men and women about witchcraft: cunning folk battled against witches – they were "unbewitchers". However, to unbewitch entailed knowing enough about magic to bewitch, and cunning folk were feared as well as respected for their magical powers.

Cunning folk were often quite ordinary members of the community.

The costumes that cunning folk adopted marked them out, such as this outfit shown in a seventeenth-century manuscript.

SOCIAL SERVICE

The distinction between cunning folk and witches is not always altogether clear. Some have called cunning folk "white witches" because they used their magical powers for the good of their community.

If someone was possessed by a spirit they would consult the cunning folk. If the pigs were not doing well, someone might be bewitching them. Practical options were tried first, such as buying another lot of pigs in another name, or nailing a stallion's shoe to the pigsty. Only if the problem persisted would the services of a cunning man or woman be sought. In his study of Essex witch-craft, Alan Macfarlane shows how cunning folk helped people locate their enemies in intimate situations, which prohibited open or immediate accusations. The secret wrongs of neighbours, relatives or supposed friends called for secret detection.

The cunning folk provided an outside, apparently objective and impartial analysis of a person's relationships. They provided a remedy for physical pain and could also explain why the suffering had occurred; they could confirm that the misfortune was due to witchcraft. Macfarlane quotes an account of how, in 1582, a cunning man was believed to have given more satisfaction than an ordinary doctor:

A sailor, landing in Ipswich, found that his daughter was very ill and therefore took a sample of her urine to a local physician. The sailor asked the doctor "if that his daughter were not bewitched", but the latter replied "that hee woulde not deale so farre to tell him", so "not satisfied to his minde", the sick child's father went to a local cunning man, who confirmed that the child was bewitched.

Cunning folk used various techniques in their work, but one practice was common. When a client first arrived to ask for help, they were told that they had come only just in time. The Ipswich sailor referred to above was told that "if hee had not commen with some great hast to seeke helpe, hee had come too late". This created a let-out if the remedies failed.

COUNSELLING AND COMMUNICATION

The cunning folk enquired about the nature of the trouble and sought information about social relationships surrounding the issue, especially who was suspected of inflicting misfortune and whether a particular neighbour was mistrusted. The cunning person's aim was to bring out all information, and if the person was unsure who was the suspect then it was their task to raise suspicions. The Essex writer George Gifford, an Elizabethan clergyman, has given many insights into the workings of popular magic. According to his account, a cunning woman told a client that he was:

Village brawls and feuds were often at the root of accusations of witchcraft, and the cunning man or woman would make it their business to know all such gossip.

... plagued by a witch, adding moreover, that there were three women witches in that towne, and one man witch: willing him to look whom he most suspected: he suspected one old woman, and caused her to be carried before a Justice of the Peace.

Macfarlane says that cunning folk acted as information centres, allocated blame and distributed antidotes to witchcraft. Cunning folk would have gained much information about local witches from gossip, rumour and previous consultations. They divulged this information to their clients, putting them in touch with suspicions circulating in their own village. When the client first arrived at the cunning man or woman's home, they were warned of the difficulties in the task and then told to go away for nine days. In the meantime the cunning man or woman, if they had decided to help, would make enquiries and find out about local gossip. On return, the client would look into a magic mirror and be instructed to see the face of the witch.

The final decision was the client's: cunning folk would not identify the witch themselves, they only provided the situation for the client to discover the witch. Once again, they had created an effective get-out clause.

DIVINATION AND FORSEEING

Oracles were also consulted by cunning folk to determine the location of stolen goods. A common method was to employ a sieve and a pair of shears:

Stick a pair of shears in the rind of a sieve and let two persons set the top of each of their forefingers upon the upper part of the shears holding it with the sieve up from the ground steadily; and ask Peter and Paul whether A, B, or C hath stolen the thing lost; and at the nomination of the guilty person the sieve will turn round.

Subtle questioning and sleight of hand could be used to influence an apparently objective test. Hidden thoughts could be brought into the open and made to appear as if they were dictated by an external power.

Another oracle used was a mirror, basin of water or other reflective surface. One Essex woman went to a conjurer on

A witch, accompanied by a beggar and a fool, curses two terrified sergeants-at-arms in an illustration from the late fifteenth century.

London Bridge to help her to find some lost money. He showed "her in a glass a boye in a sherte gleninge Corne resemblinge the countenance of John Hayes that had her monye". In another account a cunning man took his client out into the hall and:

... browghte with him a looking glasse, (about vii or viii inches square), and did bange the said glasse up over the benche in his said hawle, upon a nayle, and bad the said examinate look in yt, and said as farr as he could gesse, he shulde see the face of him that had the said lynnen.

In several of the cases of theft it was the suspect himself who went to the cunning man to clear his name of suspicion, the cunning man giving him a note vouching for him.

HEALING AND CHRISTIAN ELEMENTS

The remedies for bewitching included using the Christian religion. When Robert Booker informed his patient in 1622 that he had been bewitched by three sources of witchcraft – concealed malevolence ("heart"), bitter words ("tongue") and ocular fascination ("eye") – the cunning man anointed his patient with oil and uttered the following charm: "Three biters have bit him – heart, tongue and eye; three better shall help him presently – God the Father, God the Son, and God the Holy Spirit."

Much healing was conducted with the aid of Catholic prayers. Prescriptions of Paternosters, Aves and the Creed in honour of the Holy Ghost and the Virgin Mary were common. Some cunning folk used debased versions of Christian prayers or bits and pieces of semi-religious

verse, describing supposed episodes in the life of Christ or the saints. These reflected the belief that mythical events could be a source of magical power:

There was a man born in Bethlem of Judaea whose name was called Christ. Baptized in the River Jordan in the water of the flood; and the Child also was meek and good; and as the water stood so I desire thee the blood of [such a person or beast] to stand in their body, in the name of the Father, Son and Holy Ghost.

Religious language possessed a magical power, which could be used for practical purposes. This corresponded with the idea that disease was a foreign presence in the body that needed to be conjured or exorcised out. A fever could be drawn out if the following formula was repeated:

> Two angels came from the West,
> The one brought fire,
> the other brought frost,
> Out fire! In frost!
> In the name of the Father, Son
> and Holy Ghost.

There were also charms for women in labour, mad dogs, sick horses and all aches and pains. The churchwardens of Barnsley, Gloucestershire, reported on a parishioner in 1563:

> There is one Alice Prabury in our parish that useth herself suspiciously in the likelihood of a witch, taking upon her not only to help Christian people of diseases strangely happened, but also horses and all other beasts. She taketh upon her to help by the way of charming, and in such ways that she will have nobody privy of her sayings.

HAUNTINGS AND SPIRITS

The cunning man or woman frequently diagnosed bewitching or "overlooking" as the cause of a patient's illness. The patient might have been haunted by an evil spirit, a ghost or a fairy. If a person suspected that they had been bewitched they would go to a cunning person in the next village. The methods used by cunning folk to diagnose witchcraft were diverse. They might use a technique such as boiling the victim's urine, or burning a piece of thatch from the suspected witch's house to see whether this brought her running to the scene. Alternatively, they would use a mirror, crystal ball, sieve and shears, or a familiar spirit. Sometimes cunning folk said that the fairies told them the answers to their questions.

Keith Thomas gave an account of the cunning woman Elizabeth Page who, in 1555, was asked to cure a sick child who had been bewitched. The cunning woman explained to the child's mother that the cure involved the mother making herself as ill as the child: "… she must cause herself to be in as ill a case as the said child then was [who was then likely to die] ere that she could help her …". This shows that disease was seen to be a

A seventeenth-century depiction of a witch working inside a magic circle, familiars at hand.

foreign element which could be transferred from one person to another, the second person completely relieving the first one of the illness.

Cunning folk were the specialists in magic that ordinary people turned to in times of distress or illness, and their role in society was an important one.

The wise woman of a French village uses her powers to discover who has cast a spell on her client. This is an illustration from a book published in 1853, showing that folk beliefs endured for several centuries.

WITCHES, SPIRITS AND FAMILIARS

Witches were said to have special spirit animals or familiars that performed services for them. In return, the familiars demanded milk, or sometimes to suck a witch's blood. Cunning folk were also said to have familiars and these often helped them to diagnose illnesses or find lost objects. The origin of ideas about familiars may lie in a belief in nature spirits – dwarves, elves, fairies etc – and, going farther back in time to our common shamanic heritage, to when shamans communicated with the spirits of the animals that their community was to hunt.

The idea that witches were aided by spirit familiars occurred again and again in pamphlets. In the first pamphlet account of an English trial describing witchcraft, one of the accused, Elizabeth Francis, allegedly confessed to having been given a cat familiar by her grandmother when she was 12 years old. The cat, which she called Sathan (Satan), spoke to her, brought her sheep and also a lover. She began to use the familiar for maleficent purposes when her lover refused to marry her and the cat supposedly killed him. Another pamphlet, published in Essex in 1582, portrayed familiars as domestic pets, which had names such as Jack, Robin and Tyffin. One eight-year-old girl described how her stepmother kept her familiars in an earthenware pot lined with wood, and fed them on milk from a black dish.

One sixteenth-century Essex woman accused of witchcraft said that she had three mouse familiars: Littleman, Prettyman and Daynty. Another woman had four mice named Prickeare, James, Robyn and Sparrow. Yet another woman admitted having five familiars: Holt, a kitten; Jamara, a fat, legless spaniel; Sack-and-Sugar, a black rabbit; Newes, a polecat; and Vinegar Tom, a long-legged, greyhound-like creature with an "ox's head and broad eyes, which could turn itself into a headless four-year-old child". Witches were said to take great care of their familiars: they might, for example, baptize toads, dress them, put little bells on their feet and make them

dance. They were also said to allow familiars to suck their blood.

Familiars were said to help cunning men and women by assisting in the diagnosis of illnesses and the sources of bewitchment; they were also used for divining and finding lost objects.

The witch Jennet urges her familiar, the cat Tib, to attack her victim in The Lancashire Witches, *1612*

Sometimes they were locked into bottles, rings and stones, and these were often sold as charms.

A black cat, a newt and a snake, animals that were often linked to witches and thought to be their familiars.

FAIRY FAMILIARS

Some familiars were said to be fairies. A cunning man said in 1566 that there were three types of fairies: the white, the green and the black. The black were the worst and he found them indistinguishable from malignant devils.

Beliefs about fairies varied, and many traditions give alternative accounts of their origins, including ancestral spirits, ghosts and fertility spirits, as well as pagan gods. Fairies were frequently thought of as malevolent, and were often associated with malignant disease of a spiritual origin, which could only be cured by charming or exorcism. The Anglo-Saxons described a person smitten with such a malady as "elf-shot". It was during the Shakespearean period in England that a view of fairies as a dwarf race of mischievous but fundamentally friendly beings became popular.

SHAMANIC ORIGINS OF FAMILIARS

The origins of witches' familiars lies with dwarves, fairies, trolls and spirits of nature. Robin, one of the first named witch familiars, was probably a version of an Irish folk spirit who appeared as a cat, a shaggy dog or a black man. Going further back in time, the roots of beliefs in spirit beings such as fairies and familiars may lie in the shamanic heritage. Human beings have always had a close association with animals, and in early times everything in the world was seen to possess spirit. Early humans used their knowledge of animals in order to trap and hunt them for food and skins, and it is likely that shamans in these early societies had a particular function as communicators and negotiators with the spirits of the animals. A shaman might have been able to locate or lure game because he or she had been that animal in spirit, or may have been taken and dismembered by that spirit animal at initiation. This relationship between shamans and the animal spirit world may have been behind the folk beliefs about witches' familiars. Later, during the early modern period in Europe, these beliefs were interpreted by the Christian church as relationships with demonic spirits.

A "magic scene" from the seventeenth century showing the familiars that were associated with witchcraft: a goat, bats, snakes and an owl are all part of this illustration of sorcery and the dark arts.

Fairies and elves on their nightly ritual dance in a sixteenth-century "history" of Scandinavia.

OLD WIVES' TALES

Today, so-called old wives' tales are often seen as trivial nonsense, but they have their origins in popular medical lore and reflect the domestic medicine practised by the cunning folk. Some old wives' remedies sound bizarre but they often have a sound medicinal base. By combining remedies with spells or charms, important psychological aspects of curing were included. In our time this is called the "placebo effect" – if a patient believes in the power of the cure, and imagines they are getting better, they often do.

A French village wise woman uses her secret herbal cures to treat a patient.

In early modern Europe the spirit world was at one with the material, everyday world; the two were interconnected. Healers such as cunning folk, wizards and witches used fingernails, hair, amniotic membranes (cauls) and such like, to heal, protect from harm or cause harm, bring luck or cause some sort of magical transformation. Discarded or stolen pieces of a person's body or clothing were seen to be invested with their owner's spiritual essence and might be used in a magical way to identify that person in the spirit world for beneficial or malign purposes. Magical power was gained from a number of different sources to make up a potpourri. Many spells relied on the unauthorized use of Christian prayers, which were thought to give magical potency.

This magical way of healing was often dismissed as old wives' tales. "Old wives", according to modern popular definition, are old women who tell trivial stories and give advice that cannot be relied upon. A more sympathetic view is that old wives' tales have their origins in the popular medical lore and domestic medicine of the cunning folk – the unofficial healers who dispensed their remedies alongside magical lore. It was knowledgeable, outspoken women who were most likely to be accused of witchcraft, and in the witch trials such a woman was often described as a "busy woman of her tongue" or "devilshe of her tonge"; they "scolded" and "railed".

CUNNING CURES

Old wives had many remedies for ordinary complaints. For a headache, for example, cures included fixing "around the head a halter with which one had been hanged"; the application of moss found growing on a human skull, dried and powdered and taken as snuff; bathing the forehead and temples with hot water to which mint or sage had

Witches were often called in to heal an apparently hopeless case, as in this illustration from King Arthur's Knights, *depicting a healing from the earlier medieval period.*

sides, out of the knees, out
of the thies.
*Free the points of the fingers
to the nebs of the toes. Out sail
the fevers, go some to the ill,
some to the hope, some to the
stone, some to the stock.
In St. Peter's name, St. Paul's name,
and all the saints of heaven.
In the name
of the Father, Son and Holy Ghost.*

For epilepsy, the prescription was one ounce each of mistletoe, valerian root, pellitory and black horehound boiled in three pints of water, to which one ounce of tincture of scullop was added. This mixture was to be taken in a wine glass four times a day.

An alternative cure was the powder made from crushing a man's bones, preferably a skull that had been found in the earth. This was accompanied by the chanting of the following charm about the three wise men who attended the baby Jesus:

*Gasper with his myrrh beganne
The presents to unfold
Then Melchior brought frankincense
And Balthasar brought gold,
Now he that of these holie kings
The names about shall beare
The fallyng ill by Grace of Christ
Shall never need to feare.*

been added; soaking the feet in a hot mustard bath; nutmeg in a little water; inhaled pipe tobacco smoke; woodlice "taken as a pill"; and vinegar and brown paper applied to the head. A "thimble-full of whisky rubbed sharply in the hands and held to the nose, cures headache at once, or mix one drachm of sweet nitre, one drachm of sal volatile and two drachms of carbonate soda, in a teacupful of cold water; two tablespoons to be taken three times a day".

The remedies were combined with spells designed to instruct the spiritual agents of disease verbally and symbolically. For example, to cure fever a concoction of four ounces nitre, one drachm camphor, 30 grains saffron, four grains cochineal, all powdered and well mixed together, were to be administered in a small teaspoon each night with the following charm:

*I forbid the quacking fevers,
the sea fevers, the land fevers
and all the fevers that ever
God ordained;
out of the head, out of the
heart, out of the back, out of the*

Three witches at the beside of a sick woman. An engraving from the Compendium Maleficarum, *published in 1626.*

HEALING AND SYMPATHETIC MAGIC

During the early modern period the process of healing was based upon what is now called "sympathetic magic", a different way of seeing the world to that of our modern scientific one. Sympathetic magic works on the principle that everything in the universe is in connection with everything else, and that each part has an influence on the whole. Therefore, things could be associated by their colours as well as their physical properties, for example certain metals, such as silver and mercury, were thought to have a special affinity with the moon through their hue, shine, changeability and other characteristics. Healing also had an important social and psychological dimension, one that is frequently ignored today in Western societies.

In 1589 an old woman called Maria Marquart was arrested in Augsburg, Germany. She identified herself as a white witch and gave a full account of her magical powers to her interrogators. Maria Marquart claimed that she used the "natural arts" and these consisted

An early fifteenth-century herbal illustrating the properties and associations of fennel.

of spells that used devotional prayers and rituals. Using needles and thread designed for sewing corpses into shrouds for strengthening spells, as well as herbs and crystal balls, her spells imitated and invoked Jesus's sufferings. She proudly described her art as working with the gift granted to her by God. The city council had previously ordered her to stop her healing, and the barber-surgeons' trade had tried to ban her from practising, but to little avail. Finally, however, she was banished from the city for life.

LIKE HEALING LIKE

Healing during the early modern period was based on sympathetic magic, or the notion that like attracts like. Thus, for example, a red flannel was used to draw out a fever, red flowers were used for disorders of the blood and yellow objects were used to cure jaundice. Numbers were seen to have a strong potency, with the numbers three and seven being especially important. The moon and the sun were thought to direct the course of the illness and marked the correct times for gathering herbs as well as for administering treatment. For example, club moss, which was believed to be effective for eye diseases, had to be gathered on the third day of the moon's cycle. The person gathering the moss was instructed to take the knife, show it to the moon and say:

A sixteenth-century Polish woodcut showing the administration of medicinal herbs.

> *As Christ healed the issue of blood*
> *Do thou cut what thou cuttest for good.*

When the moon was setting, the gatherer had to kneel to wash the club moss and their hands, and then wrap it in a white cloth. Afterwards, the moss had to be boiled in water from a nearby spring and the decoction used as a treatment for the eyes, or made into an ointment by mixing it with butter made from the milk of a new cow.

A popular cure for juvenile rickets and hernias involved passing a child three times through a young ash tree that had been split down the middle, with the child facing the rising sun as it passed between the two sides of the trunk. The tree would then be bound up and it was believed that as it healed so would the patient.

CONTROLLING THE SPIRITS

Spells gave precise magical directions. For example, a spell for a "tetter" (a kind of skin disease) contained the following instructions:

Tetter, tetter, thou hast nine brothers
God bless the flesh and preserve the bone;
Perish thou tetter and be thou gone
In the name of Father, Son
and Holy Ghost.

Tetter, tetter, thou hast eight brothers
God bless the flesh and preserve the bone;
Perish thou tetter and be thou gone
In the name of Father, Son
and Holy Ghost.

And so on, until the last verse:

Tetter, tetter, thou hast no brothers
God bless the flesh and
preserve the bone ...

The spell instructs the invading spirits of disease to depart. Invading spirits were often given orders, but sometimes they had to be tricked into leaving their victim, have their attention distracted or be transferrred on to some other person or object. Sometimes disease spirits were sent into animals such as worms, slugs, shrews, mice or cats, the animal being contained until it died. A spell for removing a wart follows this principle: "Steal a piece of meat, rub it over the warts, bury it in the ground, and as the meat decays, so the warts will go."

SYMBOLIC HEALING

Some spells involved a symbolic acting out of sickness as a form of initiation from death into life, a passing on of the sickness into something else. This was often enacted symbolically, with a patient passing through an arch, aperture or hole in a stone. Some healing rituals involved symbolic death, as in this remedy for a cough: "Lay the child face downwards on the turf of a meadow. Cut round the child in the shape of a coffin. Remove the child and turn the turf root upwards. As the turf withers so the cough disappears."

This symbolic acting out of sickness is a common method of healing in other parts of the world, especially in small-scale or tribal societies, and it recognizes important and psychological dimensions of healing.

A patient visits an apothecary (left), and the insides of a dispensary (right). From a twelfth-century manuscript.

The zodiacal signs around a herbal dispensary from a 1550 manuscript, showing how connections were made between things in a way that later became known as sympathetic magic.

Collecting plants from a herb garden. Ordinary people would have collected herbs from the countryside.

FAMOUS WITCHES

Dame Alice Kyteler, Mother Shipton and Isobel Gowdie all gained notoriety during their time for being witches, although for different reasons. Dame Alice Kyteler was a wealthy and respected woman who was accused of poisoning. She allegedly headed a band of heretical sorcerers in Kilkenny, Ireland. Mother Shipton apparently had a much humbler background – being orphaned at birth she was brought up by a local woman – and married a Yorkshire carpenter. Having inherited her mother's magical powers, Mother Shipton was famed for her prophecy. It is not certain that she ever existed; the stories surrounding her prophecies may have just been legend, we do not know for sure. The case of Isobel Gowdie is interesting because it is not known why she suddenly confessed to acts of witchcraft. She graphically described attending witches' Sabbaths in which she had sexual relations with the Devil. This demonstrates that ordinary people as well as the witch-hunters had powerful imaginations where witchcraft was concerned.

A fifteenth-century woodcut of the Devil and a witch. It was at this time that Satanic links with witchcraft began.

DAME ALICE KYTELER

Dame Alice was the first person to be tried for witchcraft and heresy in Ireland. In the fourteenth century there were growing ideas about demonic magic and its connection with upper-class sorcery, and the case demonstrates the coming together of witchcraft accusations and demonological heresy. It illustrates a mixture of popular beliefs about witchcraft and magic among the educated elite.

An illustration from the Compendium Maleficarum, *1626, of sorcerers and witches at a Sabbath dancing to the violin.*

Dame Alice married four times. Her first husband was William Outlawe, a wealthy banker; the second was Adam le Blond; the third was Richard de Valle. Her fourth husband, who was very ill with a wasting disease when Dame Alice was charged, was Sir John le Poer. Sir John's children thought that she might be poisoning him and allegedly found hidden in their home some potions and powders, which could have been used in black magic. Sir John and his children accused Dame Alice of bewitching her first three husbands to death and of depriving her current husband of his "natural senses" by her use of magic. Through sorcery she was said to seek advice from demons during nightly meetings in which she blasphemed the Church. Causing death and disease by ointments made of the entrails of cocks sacrificed to demons and unbaptized boys' brains, amongst other things, she supposedly used sorcery to bewitch to death three husbands, and poisoned her husband of the time.

In 1324 Richard de Ledrede, the Bishop of Ossory, made an inquisition that alleged that Dame Alice was the head of a band of heretical sorcerers in Kilkenny. He indicted them on the following counts:

1 The denial of the faith of Christ.
2 The sacrifices of living animals – allegedly nine red cocks and the eyes of nine peacocks – to various demons, including a low-ranking one named Robin, or Son of Art. The animals had been dismembered and left at crossroads.
3 Using sorcery to seek advice from demons.
4 The holding of nightly meetings during which they blasphemed the church and excommunicated themselves with lighted candles by naming each part of their bodies and shouting "Fi! Fi! Fi! Amen".
5 Causing disease and death and arousing love and hatred by using evil powders, unguents, ointments and candles. The ingredients of these potions included worms, dead men's nails, entrails of cocks sacrificed to demons, the hair, brains and shreds of shrouds of boys who had been buried unbaptized, various herbs and "other abominations". These had been cooked in a cauldron made out of a thief's skull.
6 That Dame Alice has used sorcery to cause the children of her four husbands to bequeathe all their wealth to her and her favourite son William Outlawe. She has bewitched Sir John le Poer until his hair and nails fell out.
7 That Robin, or Son of Art, or a black man, was Dame Alice's incubus and the source of her wealth.

It was also alleged that Dame Alice swept the streets of Kilkenny with a broom, raking the filth towards the home of her favourite son, muttering, "To the house of William my sonne Hie all the wealth of Kilkennie towne". Bishop de Ledrede tried to arrest Dame Alice, her son William and the other unnamed sorcerers, but because of the family's status the arrest was blocked. Ledrede excommunicated Dame Alice

A witches' kitchen as portrayed in the late 1500s.

A fifteenth-century woodcut of a demon carrying off a child promised to the Devil.

and cited her to appear before him, but she fled to Dublin. The bishop charged William with heresy. Dame Alice brought pressure to bear on influential contacts and had Ledrede arrested and jailed. He was released after 17 days.

He tried several times to get Dame Alice arrested on charges of sorcery but was unsuccessful. Dame Alice fled to England, although in Kilkenny she was condemned as a sorceress, magician and a heretic. Her son William was arrested and spent nine weeks in jail. He decided to confess to all the charges but was let off with a penance of a pilgrimage to the shrine of St Thomas at Canterbury. He was also made to pay for the re-roofing of the Cathedral.

Dame Alice's maid, Petronilla, was then arrested and flogged until she confessed to deeds of sorcery and orgies that involved her mistress. She was excommunicated, condemned and burned alive on 3 November 1324. The others were sentenced to be whipped in the marketplace and through the streets of Kilkenny. Dame Alice was also sentenced in her absence and presumably her lands were forfeited. Ledrede was subsequently accused of heresy and had all his lands seized by the Crown. He was later acquitted, but ten years later he was again accused and deprived of his land and possessions.

MOTHER SHIPTON

It is not known whether the English witch Mother Shipton was a real person or a legend, but her predictions are well known. She was said to have been born Ursula Southeil or Sonthiel and, according to different accounts, was born in Yorkshire in either 1448, 1486 or 1488. She married a carpenter called Toby Shipton and lived in the village of Skipton in North Yorkshire. Her mother, who was supposed to have possessed powers of healing, clairvoyance, storm-raising and hexing, had died giving birth to her. Ursula, who was raised by a local townswoman, was said to have inherited her mother's powers, and it was said that strange things happened around her and strange forces were noticed. Furniture apparently moved around on its own; food disappeared from dinner plates; a woman was hung by her toes from a staff floating in the air; men were yoked to the same staff; women found themselves dancing in circles and, if they tried to stop, an imp, in the form of a monkey, pinched them to keep them going.

In a book on her life and predictions, published in 1684, Richard Head described her as having:

Mother Shipton with her cartoon-like nose and chin.

... very great goggling, but sharp and fiery eyes; her nose of incredible and unproportionable length, having in it many crooks and turnings, adorned with many strange pimples of divers colours, as red and blue mixed, which, like vapours of brimstone, gave such a lustre to the affrighted spectators in the dead time of the night, that one of them confessed that her nurse needed no other light to assist her in the performance of her duty.

In a later book of her prophecies, published in 1797 by one S. Baker, she is described thus: "Her stature was larger than common, her body crooked, her face frightful; but her understanding extraordinary ...".

Mother Shipton was summoned to court for taking revenge on a group of prying neighbours by bewitching them at a breakfast party. The guests were made to break out in hysterical laughter; they ran out of the house and were pursued by goblins. Mother Shipton threatened the court that if she was prosecuted she would do worse. She is said to have said "Updraxi, call Stygician Helleuei", and soared off on a winged dragon.

Her predictions, published in doggerel verse form, included motor cars, aeroplanes, submarines, iron ships

Mother Shipton depicted with a familiar, 1804.

and gold in California, the Yukon or South Africa:

> *Carriages without horses shall go*
> *And accidents fill the world with woe.*
> *Around the earth thought shall fly*
> *In the twinkling of an eye.*
> *The world upside down shall be*
> *And gold found at the root of a tree.*
> *Through hills man shall ride*
> *And no horse be at his side.*
> *Under water men shall walk*
> *Shall ride, shall sleep, shall talk.*
> *In the air men shall be seen*
> *In white, in black, in green.*
> *Iron in the water shall float,*
> *As easily as a wooden boat.*
> *Gold shall be found and shown*
> *In a land that's now not known.*
> *Fire and water shall wonders do,*
> *England shall at last admit a foe.*
> *The world to an end shall come*
> *In eighteen hundred and eighty one.*

One famous story tells how she predicted that Cardinal Wolsey would never reach York. The Cardinal sent three lords incognito, one of whom was

Mother Shipton casting a horoscope, from a late sixteenth-century pamphlet.

Thomas Cromwell, to check on Mother Shipton. However, she knew who they were and told them that the Cardinal would see but never arrive in York. One of the lords allegedly said that when Cardinal Wolsey reached York he would have her burnt as a witch. Mother Shipton tossed her handkerchief in the fire and said that if it burnt so would she. It was said that the handkerchief remained unburnt.

Thomas Cromwell asked her about his own future and she replied that in time he would be as low as she was; Cromwell was later beheaded. Her prediction about Wolsey proved correct too. He arrived at Cawood, eight miles from York, and viewed the city from the top of the castle tower. While he was at the top of the tower he received a message saying that the king wished to see him. He turned back towards London but never arrived, having fallen ill and died at Leicester.

Mother Shipton admonishes Cardinal Wolsey, in a fifteenth-century woodcut.

A fanciful depiction of Mother Shipton's favourite mode of transport.

ISOBEL GOWDIE

Not much is known about Isobel Gowdie as a person, but she is famous for confessing to witchcraft on four occasions in April and May 1662. She is described as an attractive red-headed girl who married a Scottish farmer and lived on a remote farm in Morayshire. Life on the farm was dull, she had no children and her husband was said to be an unimaginative boor. According to her confessions, Isobel began her involvement with the Devil in 1647, when she encountered him in the shape of a man in grey and promised to meet him in the local church. The Devil stood in the pulpit with a black book in his hand and made her renounce Jesus. He baptized her with her own blood, which he sucked from her in the church, renamed her Janet, and gave her a mark on her shoulder. She described him as a big, black, hairy man, who visited her a couple of days later and copulated with

At her trial in 1662, Isobel Gowdie tells how since 1647 she and her companions were visited by "Black John" who chastised disobedient witches.

A scene of sorcery from 1632, in which a gathering of witches with their demon familiars is depicted.

A typical fifteenth-century depiction of a chaotic witches' Sabbath.

her. Isobel Gowdie described witches' Sabbaths with covens of 13 witches. The witches flew to the Sabbaths on corn straws, beanstalks and rushes, which they charmed into flight by shouting "Horse and Hattock, in the Devil's name!". If someone should see them and not cross themselves, the witches would shoot them with elf arrows. She described how she had intercourse with the Devil and other demons, and how she transformed herself into a cat. She said she had had intercourse with one of her demons while lying in bed beside her husband, that the Devil's enormous, scaly penis had caused her great pain but also pleasure, and that his semen was as cold as ice. He was said to have had sexual relations with all the female witches, sometimes changing himself into an animal such as a deer or a bull. The coven met regularly and when she was away attending the Sabbath she said that she put a broom-stick in the bed so that her husband would think that she was still there. Apparently he never knew about her night-time activities.

She told about how she and her coven tormented their neighbours by raising storms; beating wet rags upon stones while reciting incantations; making farmland sterile by ploughing it with a miniature plough drawn by toads; hexing children by sticking pins in dolls; blasting a farmer's crops by digging up

the body of an unchristened child and burying it in a manure heap; and shooting elf arrows to kill and injure people. Gowdie seemed to welcome punishment and allegedly said, "I do not deserve to be seated here at ease and unharmed, but rather to be stretched on an iron rack: nor can my crimes be atoned for, were I to be drawn asunder by wild horses."

Isobel Gowdie confessed to witchcraft after 15 years and it remains unclear why she should suddenly do so. It has been suggested that she was a highly sexed masochistic woman with a vivid imagination, and that she turned to her fantasies to alleviate her boredom. In making these fantasies public she increased the excitement by shocking the stolid Scottish community and reinforcing their fears about the evils of witchcraft. It is not known what happened to Isobel Gowdie, or to the other witches that were implicated by her confession.

The case is interesting because it demonstrates the importance of the imagination and sexual desire in the

creation of fantasy, and how this is connected with popular ideas about witchcraft. However, to reduce all ideas and beliefs about witchcraft to fantasy would be a simplification that ignores the reality of a magical world-view that sees the universe as consisting of various energies and powers that can be harnessed.

FEMALE STEREOTYPING

Images of women as sorcerers, foretelling the future and attending witches' Sabbaths, were all part and parcel of the popular stereotype of the witch in early modern Europe, and these women's alleged activities represent the dominant ideas about witches of the time.

Dame Alice, Mother Shipton and Isobel Gowdie all conform, in one way or another, to stereotypes of the witch. This standardized idea of a witch had the effect of controlling and shaping the lives of these women, and in later centuries some would say that this was an effect of the patriarchal times in which they lived.

This artist's depiction of a witches' gathering from 1607 is a perfect illustration of how the anti-witchcraft factions fuelled their own fantasies with lurid descriptions, culminating in accusations that demonic influences were leading ordinary women astray.

THE ARISTOCRACY AND MAGIC

Magic was not just the preserve of the common people or the basis of peasant credulity. Magic also formed part of the world-view of kings and queens and those occupying high-status positions in society. Queen Elizabeth I of England took very seriously the astrological advice of her astrologer royal, John Dee, and he was a formidable influence at court throughout and beyond her reign. Her successor, James VI of Scotland, was also affected by witchcraft when a plot against him was declared to have been instigated by witches, but he was eager to introduce a new rationalism to the higher echelons of society and declared himself anxious to establish the unlawfulness of witchcraft. This hostility to magic was partly self protection, as he viewed magicians as a threat to the divine right of kings.

The integration achieved by the completed alchemical work – the hermaphrodite, a mixture of feminine and masculine attributes.

Magical beliefs concerning an inter-connected universe formed part of a complex body of knowledge in early modern times. A magical world-view included what today would be called the irrational or the superstitious, but magic was a part of ordinary reality for most people of all social classes. It was not simply a part of folk belief or the "primitive" thinking of common people. Those in the highest positions in society, well-educated scholars and the pioneers of contemporary thought, used this magical world-view as a way of attempting to understand the universe.

Astrology, alchemy and the importance of the spiritual realms were central to the mental world of early modern Europe. The influence of classical culture, elements of Christian thought including demonological tracts, as well as folklore and pamphlets of witch trials, all helped to ensure that magic was a part of everyday life.

NEOPLATONISM

The popularity of Neoplatonism as a quest for the ultimate realities and a universal knowledge was widespread among educated people. Neoplatonism is a spiritual philosophy that envisions a universe full of powers whose secrets can be unlocked by those who seek the answers to life's eternal questions. It formed a body of contradictory elements, most of which were brought together in the *Corpus Hermeticum*, a collection of Greek texts that were written in the early centuries AD. The *Corpus Hermeticum* placed humans in the centre of the universe, acting as the link between the physical and spiritual worlds.

JOHN DEE (1527–1608)

A good example of a scholar, astrologer and early scientist, John Dee published *The Hieroglyphic Monad* in 1564. His scientific interests included navigation, geography, mathematics and astronomy. In 1553 when Mary Tudor came to the

The alchemical macrocosm showing a magical world-view through which all is related.

English throne, Dee was invited by her to draw up her horoscope, and when Mary's sister Elizabeth succeeded Mary in 1558, she chose the astrologically auspicious date of 14 January 1559 for her coronation on the advice of Dee. He acted as astrologer royal and also advised the queen on medical matters. From 1584 he was involved in alchemical experiments and also those designed to raise angels. In 1581 he met Edward Kelly who professed to receive visions from a heavenly stone, which Dee wrote down. In November 1582, Dee claimed to have been visited by an angel in the form of a boy who gave him a stone that was like black crystal. The angels taught Dee the

"language of Enoch", which was supposedly spoken by Adam before the Fall. Kelly, in a trance, dictated to Dee *The Book of Enoch*, which revealed the mysteries of creation. Dee was consulted on matters as diverse as assisting in providing a geographical description of the lands to which Elizabeth I had the right to be sovereign in 1580, giving advice to the government on calendar reforms in 1584–5, and helping to cure Elizabeth I when she was ill in 1571.

The historian James Sharpe has observed that there were sporadic accusations of witchcraft among persons of high social class (similar to those made against Dame Alice Kyteler), and that these sometimes

Queen Elizabeth I, a portrait by Isaac Oliver.

involved treason against a monarch. John Dee's life at court was not an easy one in this respect. As early as 1553 his connection with the then Princess Elizabeth was being investigated by the Star Chamber, and he was suspected of trying to kill Queen Mary by poison or magic. In the 1580s his house was attacked by a mob when rumours spread that he was using witchcraft.

In 1604 he petitioned James I asking that he might be cleared of accusations of being a "conjurer, or caller, or invocator of devils".

COURTLY ACCUSATIONS

Beliefs about witchcraft were held by those in the highest social positions, and the case of the 5th Earl of Sussex demonstrates what James Sharpe has described as a magical dimension to aristocratic infighting. A suit that was examined by the Star Chamber involved the marital problems of Robert Radcliffe, the 5th Earl of Sussex. The earl's marriage to Bridget, the daughter of Sir Charles Morison, was problematic. After Bridget was given substantial lands, she allegedly committed adultery and

A portrait of John Dee, the sixteenth-century English scholar and astrologer.

attempted to kill her husband. The couple separated in 1612 and the earl took up with Frances Shute, a woman supposedly of bad reputation. Allegations were made against her that she had tried to injure three of the earl's kinsfolk by magic and that she had used witchcraft to turn the earl against his wife. She was said to have been aided by a magician named Matthew Evans, who, it was alleged, had been involved in her attempts to damage the earl's relatives to favour Shute's children. Evans confessed to helping her by the use of astrology and by casting a horoscope for one of her daughters. He had also been asked to help her gain the affections of the Duke of Buckingham, one of the most powerful men in England.

Another case involving members of the aristocracy and village witchcraft was that against Joan Flower and her daughters Margaret and Phillipa, who were executed at Lincoln on 22 March 1618 for killing Henry Lord Roos and "damnable practises against others the Children of the Right Honourable Francis Earle of Rutland".

Astrological chart with signs of the zodiac from the sixteenth-century Portolan map.

The three women were charwomen at Belvoir Castle in Rutland. Joan Flower was described as "a monstrous malicious woman, full of oaths, curses, and imprecations irreligious … her very countenance was estranged; her eyes were fiery and hollow, her speech fell and envious, her demeanour strange and exotic, and her conversation sequestered, so that the whole course of her life gave great suspicion that she was a notorious witch".

One of her daughters, Margaret, it was maintained, kept "debauched and base company", while the other daughter, Phillipa, was said to have bewitched her lover. After Margaret's dismissal for neglecting her business and indecency Joan cursed all that were the "source of her discontentment". As the court records read:

At last, as malice increased in these damnable women, so his family felt the smart of their revenge and inficious disposition, for his eldest son Henry Lord Roos, sickened very strangely and after a while died. His next, named Francis, Lord Roos accordingly, was severely tormented by them and most barbarously and inhumanly

Above: The crystal ball of Dr John Dee, the best known magician of the Elizabethan era.

Right: An Aztec obsidian mirror, which once belonged to Dr John Dee. It was thought to have been part of the treasure brought back from Mexico by Cortes. It was used as a tool for divination.

tortured by a strange sickness; not long after, the Lady Katherine was set upon by their dangerous and devilish practices and many times in great danger of life thorough extreme maladies and unusual fits; nay (as it should seem and they afterwards confessed) both the Earl and his Countess were brought into their snares as they imagined, and indeed [they] determined to keep them from having any more children. Oh unheard-of-wickedness and mischievous damnation!

THE PRIVY COUNCIL

This body of men acted as England's central governing body and its councillors were aristocrats and high churchmen who were alert to threats of witchcraft, especially any prophesying against the monarch. The Privy Council was often the arbiter in difficult criminal cases and in 1579 ordered the interrogation of a group of witches from Windsor, who, it was claimed, had used image magic, through the use of a bewitched puppet, in an attempt on Elizabeth I's life.

James VI

In 1597 James VI of Scotland published a tract against witches called *Daemonologie*. It consisted of a debate between Philomathus and Epistemon on issues concerning witchcraft, and was concerned to establish the unlawfulness of both natural magic and witchcraft. James executed the work in response to a plot against him by alleged witches, which led to mass trials and executions from 1590–1. During and since his reign, James was held to be a witch hunting fanatic by many, and he did indeed see witches,
– thought of as anti-Catholic heretics –
as a natural threat to the divine right of monarchs, but evidence shows that he was also interested in the fair examination of women who were accused of the crime.

King James VI of Scotland, later also James I of England.

The High Commission Court and the Star Chamber of the sixteenth and seventeenth centuries. It was all-male bodies such as this, both secular and ecclesiastical, that sat in judgement over witchcraft and magic.

REGINALD SCOT AND WITCHCRAFT

Not everyone believed in witchcraft. Reginald Scot, the first English writer to publish a major theoretical work on witchcraft, thought that there were no reasons to believe in witchcraft. Scot, who was probably born in 1538 of Kentish Protestant gentry stock, thought witchcraft was a conjuring art that profaned the name of God. He generally attacked popular beliefs about witchcraft, and said that witches were only able to perform the feats that were attributed to them by trickery and fooling the credulous. He thought that witch hunters were wrong in what they thought about witches, and that the notion that any kind of demonic pact could be established between Satan and witches was absurd.

Reginald Scot set out to demonstrate in *The Discoverie of Witchcraft* (1584) that beliefs in witchcraft were superstition and were a sign of an imperfect faith in God. He dismissed descriptions of the Sabbath, shape-shifting and the demonic pact with the Devil. He was concerned with the reality of divine providence and believed that ascribing misfortune to witchcraft was denying the existence of God's master plan. Whatever his views, the book has been influential as a source of magical lore and gives descriptions of rituals, charms and spells, as well as literary references. Shakespeare and King James, among others, used it. The book provides authenticated stories of contemporary village witchcraft. Scot describes witchcraft as:

… a cozening [defrauding] art, wherein the name of God is abused, profaned and blasphemed, and His power attributed to a vile creature. In estimation of the vulgar people it is a supernatural work contrived between a corporal old woman and a spiritual devil.

An illustration from Reginald Scot's The Discoverie of Witchcraft, "the names written within the five circles doo signifie the five infernall kings".

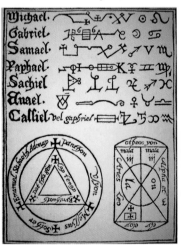

A page of symbols called "the seales of the earth" from Reginald Scot's The Discoverie of Witchcraft.

The Devil is conjured up from a magic circle, an illustration from the Compendium Maleficarum, *1608.*

"Trick bodkins" used in torture, an illustration from The Discoverie of Witchcraft.

Witches, according to Scot, are commonly "old, lame, blear-eyed, pale, foul, and full of wrinkles; poor, sullen, superstitious". They are either papists or those in whose minds the Devil "hath gotten a fine seat"; as mad or devilish they "do not differ much from those possessed with spirits". These miserable wretches go from house to house and from door to door for milk, yeast, drink or pottage, and they are feared by their neighbours who feel "they are capable of doing things beyond the ability of human nature".

A whole family of witches, including children, are initiated into a Sabbath overseen by two demons. From the Compendium Maleficarum.

ALL IN THE MIND

Scot tried to show that the threat of witchcraft superstition could be avoided:

One Ada Davie, the wife of Simon Davie, husbandman, being reputed a right honest body and being of good parentage, grew suddenly ... to be somewhat pensive and more sad than in times past .... But when she grew from pensiveness to some perturbation of mind ... he could not but demand the cause of her conceit [fancy, fantasy] and mourning. But although at that time she covered the same, acknowledging nothing to be amiss with her, soon after, notwithstanding, she fell down before him on her knees, desiring him to forgive her for she had grievously offended ... both God and him. Her poor husband, being abashed at this her behaviour, comforted her as he could, asking her the cause of her trouble and grief, who told him that she had, contrary to God's law and to the offence of all good Christians, to the injury of him and specially to the loss of her own soul, bargained and given her soul to the Devil, to be delivered unto him within short space.

Whereunto her husband answered, saying, "Wife, be of good cheer, this thy bargain is void and of none effect, for thou hast sold that which is none of thine to sell; since it belongeth to Christ who hath bought it and dearly paid for it, even with His blood which He shed upon the cross, so the Devil hath no interest in thee". After this, with like submission, tears and penitence, she said to him, "Oh husband, I have committed another fault and done you
more injury, for I have bewitched you and your children". "Be content", quoth he, "by the grace of God, Jesus Christ shall unwitch us; for no evil can happen to them that fear God ...".*

This was a recurrent theme, although sometimes hidden, that those accused of witchcraft only had to turn back to the Church, and to God, for their misdeeds to be forgiven and expunged.

People's precarious existence meant they were susceptible to superstition and irrational fears.

WITCH HUNTS

In early modern Europe, thousands of people were tried for witchcraft; most were poor and elderly women. The Christian Church created the stereotype of a witch as someone who killed babies and engaged in sexual orgies during night-time Sabbats (or Sabbaths) in honour of the Devil, the force of evil that was opposed to the Christian God. The prosecutions, convictions and executions of witches varied in form and number in different parts of Europe but all of them had similarities in the way they were carried out, who they were directed against, and the kinds of people who propagated them. An examination of witch hunts in this period gives a particular insight into a time of significant cultural and religious change.

HOW WITCH HUNTS BEGAN

During the twelfth century, the Christian Church's ideas about witches began to change. Up until that time, women who joined cults of the night-flying goddesses Holda, Diana and Herodias were thought to have been seduced by Satan into believing that they were riding at the dead of night across many lands. This was seen to be an illusion. However, in the twelfth-century the Church became particularly worried about secret organizations plotting its overthrow, and beliefs that had previously been ascribed to vivid imagination inspired by the Devil now came to be seen as having actually occurred in reality. The Church had always been suspicious of dissident sects – such as the Montanists and the Paulicians – but religious dissent had spread and the Church was beset with alternative religious groups claiming their own version of spiritual truth. These groups were branded heretics because their views did not accord with those of the Church. A number were accused of conducting sexual orgies and eating children; their members were persecuted and put to death.

A sixteenth-century illustration of a man who is suspected of sorcery being tortured by the "strappado", a German torture aparatus.

Ideas about witches are found in most cultures all over the world, and a belief in people who had the ability to harm using spiritual forces is probably as old as humanity itself. These ideas can be traced back to societies that relied on a shaman as a specialist who communicated between the everyday world and the spiritual realm. The shaman's special powers could be used for good and helpful purposes – such as finding the whereabouts of food sources – but sometimes, in certain circumstances, these special powers could be manipulated for anti-social or destructive ends; perhaps when they were used to bolster the shaman for his or her personal gain rather than for the good of the group. Thus a shaman who ceased to work for the good of the community was probably the proto-type of the witch.

In general terms, a witch is someone who performs antisocial and terrifying deeds, frequently at night. What is different about early modern European witch beliefs is that they became Christianized: witches were not just individuals who were responsible for misfortune and bad things happening, but part of an anti-Christian heretical sect, which worshipped the Devil. They gained their power not through their own wickedness but through a pact with the Devil, the leader of the forces of evil against the Christian God of good.

Ideas about witchcraft and magic were a part of European culture before witchcraft became specifically anti-Christian. Ideas about witches had come from the classical world of Greek and Roman mythology, folk beliefs and fairy stories. In the seventh and eighth centuries there was a widespread belief in the figure of a night-flying cannibalistic female witch called *striga* or *stria* in Italy, *sorcière* in France and *bruja* in Spain. At this early stage, the Christian Church had less emphatic views about witches and witchcraft: St Boniface declared that a belief in witches was not Christian, while Charlemagne ordered the death penalty for those who burnt witches. By the ninth century, Christian authorities had refused to recognize

A sixteenth-century woodcut showing witches being burnt in the market place in Guernsey.

ideas about night-flying witches or beliefs that they could metamorphose into different beings.

The Church's position began to change during the twelfth century with the arrival of popular heresies, according to which Jews, lepers and homosexuals were thought to form secret organizations to plot the overthrow of Christian society. A Western myth of a company of witches that flew to Sabbaths or Sabbats – said to be nocturnal meetings to worship the Devil – was created out of existing folklore.

In early modern Europe, thousands of people – it is not known exactly how many but the estimates of nine million are greatly exaggerated – were tried for witchcraft. The majority were women, usually poor and elderly. About half of those convicted were executed, mostly by burning. Some of the convicts were let off with a warning. The witch hunts represented a very large judicial operation. Some trials took place in ecclesiastical courts while others, especially after 1550, were held in secular courts.

Poor women being hanged as witches. From a seventeenth-century English engraving.

The geographical distribution of witch trials was uneven. In some areas there were few prosecutions while in others thousands may have been tried over a period of 300 years. The witch trials increased in numbers during the fifteenth century, reduced in the sixteenth, increased dramatically in the late sixteenth and early seventeenth, and declined in the late seventeenth and early eighteenth centuries. The historian Norman Cohn suggests that the fully developed stereotype of the witch, as someone who flew at night to Sabbaths, where she engaged in sexual origies and ritually consumed children, was a by-product of the fierce persecution of Waldensian heretics, who were themselves members of a small reform movement.

Three sorceresses being burnt at the stake in Derneburg in October 1555. Taken from a contemporary leaflet.

THE DEVIL'S ROLE

According to the witch-trial judges there were two main parts to the crime of witchcraft. The first was the practice of harmful magic, or *maleficium* – the practical working of evil or malign magic against other people, which is found worldwide. The second, which marks the difference between beliefs in European witchcraft and that in other cultures, and which became more and more emphasized, was diabolism – the connection with the Devil, the creator and lord of evil in opposition to God, the lord of all good.

The origins of the concept of the Devil may lie in *The Epic of Gilgamesh*, composed in Sumeria during the third millennium BC. This is the first narrative to record the combat between good and evil. Gilgamesh seeks to free the land from the evil inflicted on it by the monster Huwawa, whose roaring is the flood-storm, whose mouth is fire and whose breath is death. Gilgamesh goes with his companion Enkidu to a cedar forest, which is guarded by Huwawa. When Gilgamesh and his companions start felling trees, Huwawa defends his domain by putting Gilgamesh into a deep sleep. Later, when Gilgamesh awakes, he finds Huwawa and kills him. In the poem the underworld is viewed in negative terms, not as part and parcel of the rhythm of life:

Satan gives images to witches to use as charms. A fifteenth-century woodcut.

There is the house whose people sit in darkness; dust is their food and clay their meat. They are clothed like birds with wings for covering, they see no light, they sit in darkness.

This vision ruptures the continuity with the past seen in earlier myths, such as that of Isis and Osiris. It marks a separation between the living and the dead, light and dark, and eventually good and evil. God becomes identified with good, while the Devil becomes associated with evil.

THE DEVIL OF JUDAISM

The idea of the Devil is vague in the Old Testament. To the early Jews, God was omnipotent and there was no conspiracy of human beings under the command of the Devil. Yahweh was a tribal god who originally combined light and darkness, good and evil. However, as religious consciousness changed it

Gilgamesh stands between two demigods on this carving from the ninth century BC.

The Sumerian hero, Gilgamesh, holding a captured lion. From an Assyrian stone relief of c.725 BC at the Palace of Sargon II, Iraq.

was thought incongruous that God should be responsible for evil. Influenced by the dualistic Persian religion of Zoroastrianism, in which the world is seen in terms of a cosmic warfare between the good god of light and the evil god of darkness, some areas of Jewish religion became more concerned with the Devil. Successive invasions, enslavement and persecution by the Egyptians, Assyrians, Babylonians, Persians, Greeks and Romans led the Jews to view themselves as a people suffering from the gentiles and their associated evil spirits. The Essenes, a Jewish sect, saw the world in apocalyptic terms as a cosmic battle between the

Gradually, Jewish religion became more concerned with the Devil. Here Satan is pictured binding the eyes of the Jews.

Satan and the birth of sin, as portrayed in an eighteenth-century painting illustrating Milton's Paradise Lost.

lord of light and the prince of darkness which would ultimately be won by God who would triumph eternally. However, after the destruction of Jerusalem by the Romans in AD 70, which involved the diaspora of the Jews, the Pharisees, as the leading Jewish group, downplayed the Devil's power and influence.

Christianity as a religion was born from a culture of which such dualistic views were a part. In particular, the Gnostic sects combined Iranian and Greek dualism. Unlike the Zoroastrian dualism, which opposed the spirit of

light with a spirit of darkness, the Greeks posited a struggle between good spirit and evil matter. The Devil became creator and lord of evil matter. The early Christians saw life as a struggle against the Devil. Jesus himself was tempted in the wilderness, and the desert in particular became a symbol of evil and the haunt of demons.

SATAN AND WITCHES

By the fifth century, a theology of the Devil was well established. The Devil was increasingly thought to be active everywhere, and was accompanied by demons who were fallen angels. St Augustine wrote that God created intelligent creatures who were given a free choice between good and evil. Adam and Eve were created pure, he declared, but yielded to Satan and so were banished from Paradise.

Up until the thirteenth century, however, although practising magic was seen to be a sin, it was not linked with the Devil. After this time, magic came to be seen as inevitably demonic. Due to the influence of Aristotelian theology, the distinction between the natural and the supernatural was made, and

magic, which was seen to be aided by the work of demons, was placed on the supernatural side. The period from the fourteenth to the sixteenth centuries saw European societies undergoing an enormous amount of social and economic change, and the idea of a widespread conspiracy of witches in league with the Devil took hold.

Satan was reputed to have a voracious sexual appetite and is pictured here having sex with a sleeping woman.

HERETICS

During the third century AD, Christianity ceased to be a militant sub-group and became integrated into Graeco-Roman society. By the fourth century it had become adopted as the official religion of the Roman Empire and was changing its position accordingly to become a part of the establishment. Part of its evolution into a state religion was to extend its authority over its congregation, and as a result it began increasingly to view dissident sects with suspicion and to see them as a threat to its supremacy. All those who deviated from the Church's orthodoxy in any way became labelled as heretics.

Members of a religious sect called the Turlupins being burnt in Paris in the fourteenth century.

MONTANISTS AND PAULICIANS

One such group of dissidents was a Christian group called the Montanists, founded by a man called Montanus. This sect had turned against what it saw as the relaxed, easy-going Christianity of the Greek towns. Accusations were brought against Montanists and it was claimed that they practised cannibalism. At Easter they were said to mix the blood of a child with their offering, sending pieces of it to their supporters. Augustine reported that:

People say that they have most lamentable sacraments. It is said that they take the blood of a one-year-old child, drawing it off through tiny cuts all over his body, and at the same time produce their Eucharist, by mixing this blood with meal and making bread out of it. If the boy dies, they treat him as a martyr; but if he lives, they treat him as a great priest.

Likewise, the Paulicians, an eighth-century sect in Armenia, were condemned as the "sons of Satan" for allegedly coming together under cover of darkness in hidden meetings to commit incest with their own mothers. If a child was born, it was said to be thrown from one to the other until it died, and the person in whose hands it died was promoted to leader of the sect. The blood of such infants was mixed with

Heretics being tortured and taken to execution in the fifteenth century.

Torture being used to obtain a confession in the sixteenth century.

As religious dissent spread from the late twelfth century onwards, legislation was introduced to combat it. At the Synod of Verona in 1184, Pope Lucius III and Empereror Frederick I decreed the excommunication of heretics. In 1215 the death penalty was introduced for impenitent heretics. Inquisitional procedures were established by Pope Innocent III as a way by which the ecclesiastical authorities could take action against any wayward behaviour of clerics. The Inquisition took its name from the inquisitional procedure and adapted it to eradicate heresy, becoming fully organized by the late thirteenth century.

THE WALDENSIANS

In 1173, a rich merchant of Lyon named Peter Waldo gave all his wealth away in a bid to gain salvation. He attracted a group of followers, known as the Waldensians, who were keen to follow a path of poverty. They pledged themselves to observe the law of Christ by renouncing the world, modelling their way of life upon the apostles, being chaste and owning nothing that was not absolutely necessary. The Pope imposed restrictions on their preaching in 1179, and when they failed to stop they were excommunicated in 1181, finally being condemned as heretics in 1184. This

flour to make the Eucharist. The Paulicians were said to worship the Devil by bowing low while foaming at the mouth.

These tales of cannibalism and the workings of the enemies of God were applied to various religious out-groups and became part of a body of Christian demonology. Later, the Devil, or one of his subordinate demons, presided over the nocturnal orgies of heretics, usually in the form of an animal, often a cat. These night meetings were called "Sabbats". The term derives from Judaism, which was regarded as anti-Christianity.

Waldensians fleeing from their burning village.

Illustration of an early Papal crusade against the Waldensians.

failed to stop people being drawn to the sect. Even persecution and the threat of being burnt at the stake did not deter the most persistent, and the movement spread from France into Spain, Italy, Germany and Austria. The members devoted themselves to an intensive study of the Scriptures, and although many were totally illiterate peasants and artisans, they were often able to recite the four Gospels and the Book of Job by heart.

The Waldensians were persecuted for their heresy, and accusations were brought against them. According to one account by a Franciscan monk, they met in an assembly presided over by three strikingly handsome men, wearing shining robes, who were identified as the Father, Son and Holy Spirit. However, when the Franciscan held up the Eucharist, the spirits vanished leaving an evil stink.

THE CATHARS

For the Cathars, all matter was evil and the human body was a container that held a soul struggling to free itself. The Cathars believed that the material world was created by an evil spirit who dominated it. They practised vegetarianism and fasting, and evinced a total revulsion of the material world. Souls, who they saw as angels created by God, had fallen from heaven and

Cathar heretics, stripped and without any possessions being expelled from Cerlesonne by military forces.

A Christian expedition embarking on a crusade. From a fourteenth-century miniature.

were imprisoned in human bodies. As heavenly beings, souls yearned to escape from the material demonic world and re-enter the world of pure spirit. Thus, for the Cathars, procreation was to be avoided and preventing souls from being brought into the world was seen to be very important. Like the Waldensians, the Cathars were branded as heretics and accused of conducting sexual orgies and worshipping the Devil. Accusations against heretics tended to follow a stereotype of orgies and child-eating, which had originated in the second century.

THE KNIGHTS TEMPLAR

Jerusalem was captured in 1099 during the First Crusade and it became a sacred place, which many pilgrims visited. In 1118 a fellowship was founded for the military protection of the pilgrims from attack by Moslems. It was based on the Order of the Hospital of St John of Jerusalem, which provided alms and medical care to pilgrims. The new military monastic order vowed chastity, obedience and self-denial as a fraternity of warriors pledged to fight for the King of Heaven. They were first called the "Poor Fellow-Soldiers of Christ of the Temple of Solomon" because their headquarters were a wing of a palace that had once been Solomon's Temple, but soon they became known simply as the Knights Templar.

The Knights Templar, who were backed by the Pope, were committed to struggling against the forces of Islam for the reward of valour in war and salvation. They also, however, entered into financial transactions and cultivated secrecy; their headquarters were used as safe deposits for crown jewels and public monies, as well as for banking and trade.

In 1187 the Templars were massacred by Saladin, but those remaining soon regained their power and wealth, and in 1244 they regained Jerusalem by negotiation. However, the same year they were almost wiped out by the Egyptian army. The Mongols under Genghis Khan and the Egyptians under Baybars kept up the pressure on the

The looting of Jerusalem after it was captured by the Christians in 1099.

King Philip IV accuses the Knights Templar of heresy. From a fourteenth-century illustration.

Knights Templar and by 1303 they had been driven out of the Holy Land. They were finally branded as heretics by King Philip IV of France, who sought to remove them altogether so that he could

become Roman emperor and reconquer the Holy Land to establish a federation of nations. This was the beginning of the end for the Templars.

It was held by their accusers that the Knights conducted secret rituals during which an initiate was taken behind an altar and shown a crucifix. The initiate had to deny Christ three times and spit three times on the crucifix. After stripping naked, he was kissed three times by the leader, once on the base of the spine, once on the navel, and once on the mouth, and he was told that he must agree to commit sodomy if requested. These were the charges by which the Knights Templar were tried and with which the fellowship was suppressed. However, like the charges of heresy that were brought against the Waldensians and the Cathars, they had absolutely no foundation.

THE LEGALITIES OF WITCH HUNTING

The stereotype of a witch as a human being who was usually a woman, but could sometimes be a man, or even a child, bound to the Devil by a pact as his assistant, developed as a by-product of the campaign of the Inquisition against heretics. The fully developed stereotype of the witch as someone who specialized in the cannibalistic killing of babies to gain supernatural power, and who attended Sabbaths, was first officially sanctioned by the Church in the fifteenth century. Trial records show accounts of Sabbaths and nocturnal flying from 1420 onwards.

A judge interrogating prisoners. From a fifteenth-century manuscript.

Witchcraft was not just an ordinary crime, it was thought to be the most noxious of all crimes because it represented those who were working against God and good society. This very essence of false religion had to be eradicated, and it was the judge's or magistrate's responsibility to act on the authority of God and the monarch, who ruled by divine right, to put witches to death. To this end, judges and magistrates were seen to have great power over the Devil and his assistant

demons, as James VI of Scotland wrote in his *Daemonologie*: "For where God beginnes justlie to strike by his lawfull Lieutennentes, it is not in the Devilles power to defraude or bereave him of the office, or effect of his powerfull and revenging Scepter".

The Devil was seen to lose his power in the presence of judges, as in the case of Jean de Bonnevaux, who in 1599 was tried for witchcraft at Montmorillon in Poitou. While in court, it is reported that de Bonnevaux:

... called on the Devil, who, in the presence of the judges ... seized him and lifted him four to five feet from the ground, and let him drop onto the tiled floor like a bag of wool ...; whereupon, being picked up by two guards he was found to be black and blue all over, frothing at the mouth and suffering grievously in his body. Questioned as to the cause of his levitation and the sudden illness or change in him, he replied that it was the Devil on whom he had called to remove him from the hands of Justice, who having made an effort to do this, could not do it, because he had taken the judiciall oath, and the Devil had no more power over him.

Thus, the primary task of the judge was to maintain true religion and this entailed the destruction of magic and witchcraft. The defeat of witches represented a victory for the authority and the supernatural power of God. People were formally and legally tried for crimes of witchcraft and they were frequently sentenced to death. Between the thirteenth and the sixteenth centuries in Europe there were changes to the legal system that had a direct effect on the people who were accused of witchcraft.

The secular and ecclesiastical courts of continental Europe adopted a new system of criminal procedure called the "inquisitional" legal system, which was different from the "accusatorial" system of trying a suspected criminal. The latter arrangement involved a judge presiding over a contest between two private parties, the outcome of which was left to God to decide. By contrast, under the inquisitional system the judge and court actively investigated whether or not the defendant was guilty from the evidence and facts given.

TORTURE OF SUSPECTS

By the time witch hunting began, England was the only country in Europe that had not adopted at least some of the features of the inquisitional procedure into its legal system. Torture was often used as a means to get an accused person to confess to crimes of witchcraft, and it greatly increased the numbers convicted. Various methods were used, ranging from sleep deprivation to the use of certain instruments of torture. The instruments comprised two types: those of distension – such as the strappado, a pulley that raised the person off the floor by his or her arms, and the rack – and instruments of compression – thumb screws, leg screws and head clamps.

In Germany many courts used a "witches' chair", which was heated by a fire below. In Scotland, according to a pamphlet called Newes from Scotland published in 1591, a witch suspected of treason against the king, "was put to the most severe and cruell paine in the world, called the bootes", and "his legges were crushte and beaten together as small as might bee, and the bones and flesh so bruised, that the bloud and marrowe sputed forth in great abundance".

There were strict rules in existence governing the use of torture, but in practice they were relaxed, flouted or

A suspected witch being ducked into the river in a witches' chair.

completely disregarded by the accusers. The effect of torture was to help spread the concept of witchcraft; the inevitable production of confessions under torture

confirmed the inquisitors' most bizarre fantasies, and it also gave the inquisitors names of alleged accomplices of witches.

TRIAL BY ORDEAL

Suspected witches often had to undergo other ordeals that were intended to provide additional evidence of guilt. "Swimming the witch" was widely practised in England and other parts of Europe; it involved tying the witch's wrists to her ankles and throwing her into water. If she sank she was innocent, but if she floated it was confirmation that she was a witch.

The commonest ordeal in Scotland was pricking for the Devil's mark to find a spot where the witch didn't feel pain – this marked the place where the Devil had consummated their pact. In cases of possession the possessed person was taken into the presence of the accused witch and if they had a fit the witch was guilty. Thus ordinary people, mostly old, poor women, were put through a legal system fuelled by fantasies created by the Christian Church and were cruelly persecuted and tortured by "tests" that were manifestly absurd.

Mary Sutton was suspected of witchcraft in 1612, and is here being "swum" to establish her innocence or guilt.

WITCH HUNTERS

In the early modern period, the legal system of witch hunting led to the rise of professional people who dedicated themselves to the persecution of women they saw as a threat to society. Witches were seen as real and not imaginary, and published works helped to synthesize ideas about diabolic witchcraft into the recognizable, sexualized and cannibalistic stereotype. Heinrich Kramer and Jacob Sprenger, authors of the witch hunting manual the *Malleus Maleficarum*, Jean Bodin, author of *De la démonomanie des sorciers*, and the self-styled Witchfinder General, Matthew Hopkins, were all well known for their zealous campaigns against witches. Kramer and Sprenger were inquisitors from the Dominican monastic order who were determined to eradicate heretics, who they claimed were most often women. Bodin, a French philosopher and judge, saw the universe as an organic unity ruled over by God. This natural order was broken by witches with their evil ways, and they therefore had to be eradicated to secure social and spiritual harmony. Why Matthew Hopkins felt called to engage in a personal crusade to elimate witches in his native East Anglia is unclear.

judicial proceedings against witches, and when they met resistance from local ecclesiastical and secular authorities, they obtained a papal bull from Pope Innocent VIII which allowed them to continue. The bull accused witches of all manner of abominations:

It has indeed lately come to Our ears, not without afflicting Us with bitter sorrow, that in some parts of Northern Germany, as well as in the provinces, townships, territories, districts, and dioceses of Mainz, Cologne, Trèves, Salzburg, and Bremen, many persons of both sexes, unmindful of their own salvation and straying from the Catholic Faith, have abandoned themselves to devils, incubi and succubi, and by their incantations, spells, conjurations, and other accursed charms and crafts, enormities and horrid offences, have slain infants yet in the mother's womb, as also the offspring of cattle, have blasted the produce of the earth, the grapes of the vine, the fruits of trees, nay, men and women, beasts of burthen, herd-beasts, as well as animals of other

KRAMER AND SPRENGER

These two Dominican inquisitors are well known for publishing a manual for inquisitors called the *Malleus Maleficarum* (sometimes known as "The Witches' Hammer"), which became a seminal text at the time, and a valuable source on contemporary thought ever since.

Heinrich Kramer was a trained theologian and was appointed inquisitor for southern Germany in 1474, while Jacob Sprenger, a professor of theology at the University of Cologne, became an inquisitor for Rhineland in 1470. Together they agreed that women were more likely to be heretical than men because they were more subject to superstition and credulity, more impressionable than men, and were also insatiable with carnal lust, unlike men. The two inquisitors were involved in

"Women are naturally more impressionable", an idea that has continued through the years, as can be seen in this painting from 1832, which perpetuates early modern ideas of women and their susceptibility to Satan, in the supposedly more enlightened nineteenth century.

kinds, with terrible and piteous pains and sore diseases, both internal and external; they hinder men from performing the sexual act and women from conceiving, whence husbands cannot know their wives nor wives receive their husbands; over and above this, they blasphemously renounce that Faith which is theirs by the Sacrament of Baptism, and at the instigation of the Enemy of Mankind they do not shrink from committing the foulest abominations and filthiest excesses to the deadly peril of their own souls, whereby they outrage the Divine Majesty and are a cause of scandal and danger to very many.

THE MALLEUS MALEFICARUM

First published in 1486, the *Malleus Maleficarum* was not the first manual giving advice for those involved in judging witches. It was similar to the *Directorium Inquisitorum* by Nicholas Eymerich, which was published a century earlier in 1376, but it was significant because it played a major role in bringing together many ideas about witchcraft and presenting them as a single concept. *Malleus Maleficarum* educated the population about witches and introduced the idea of diabolic witchcraft to a large audience: it was this that played a vital part in witch hunting.

Before the *Malleus Maleficarum* ordinary people did not share the same world view as the educated elite; their beliefs concerned magic, maleficence, night-flying witches and metamorphosis, but in general they did not feature the Devil. Nevertheless, notions of diabolic witchcraft did filter through from time to time.

Kramer and Sprenger's *Malleus Maleficarum* contributed to the creation of a composite stereotype of diabolic witchcraft; it synthesized ideas about witchcraft and gave them theological support, even though it referred to the Sabbath only in passing, and did not discuss the obscene kiss or the Devil's mark. Perhaps its greatest contribution was the introduction of a sexual element into the stereotype of the witch by strengthening the association of women with witchcraft. It has much to say about wicked women – "All wickedness is but little to the

The Malleus Maleficarum *increased the association of women with witchcraft. After all, it was Eve who had tempted Adam with the apple from the tree of knowledge and caused their expulsion from the Garden of Eden.*

wickedness of a woman" – and it states that the word "woman" is used to mean the "lust of the flesh", and that women are subject to superstition and credulity. Because Eve, the first temptress, was formed from the rib of a man, women are defective, imperfect and always deceive. Having "defective intelligence" they are more prone to renounce the faith and:

... through their second defect of inordinate affections and passions they search for, brood over, and inflict various vengeances, either by witchcraft, or by some other means. Wherefore it is no wonder that so great a number of witches exist in this sex.

Women are "quicker to waver in their faith", "naturally more impressionable", "more ready to receive the influence of

a disembodied spirit". They possess weak memories, are undisciplined, have slippery tongues that make them unable to conceal their knowledge of evil arts, and they vindicate themselves by witchcraft. Women are naturally more carnal than men, and "All witchcraft comes from carnal lust, which is in women insatiable".

The *Malleus Maleficarum* was a practical handbook offering legal advice on how to bring witches to trial. To start the trial proceedings, a notice was to be fixed to the walls of the parish church or town hall and instructions were given as to the wording,

WHEREAS we, the Vicar of such and such Ordinary (or the Judge of such and such county), do endeavour with all our might

*and strive with our whole heart to preserve
the Christian people entrusted to us in unity
and the happiness of the Catholic faith and
to keep them far removed from every plague
of abominable heresy ...*

*Therefore we the aforesaid Judge to whose
office it belongs, to the glory and honour
of the worshipful name of JESUS Christ
and for the exaltation of the Holy
Orthodox Faith, and for the putting
down of the abomination of heresy,
especially in all witches in general and
in each one severally of whatever
condition ...*

Malleus Maleficarum gave information
on the initiation of proceedings against
an alleged witch, the arrest, treatment of
witnesses, defence, use of torture and

*A nineteenth-century depiction of the torture of a
suspected witch. The conflict between the male
world of authority and the female is obvious,
as is the artistic addition of female nakedness.*

sentencing. It gave a presiding judge
specific advice on how to treat the
accused, for example he was warned not
to touch a witch, especially not with his
bare hands, and always to carry salt that
had been consecrated on Palm Sunday
together with some Blessed Herbs
enclosed in Blessed Wax and worn
around the neck. A witch should be led
backwards into the presence of the
judge and his assessors, and he must
cross himself and approach her manfully
and "with God's help the power of that
old Serpent will be broken".

The aim of the *Malleus Maleficarum*
was to seek out and punish heretics –
those who, while professing the Catholic
faith, still held to their error. One sure
way of detecting a heretic was if they
practised any kind of witchcraft, even
people who denied the reality of witchcraft were seen to be heretics. Witchcraft
was not imaginary or unreal but a bodily
contract with the Devil; women who
thought they were riding at night with a
goddess were really, so said the inquisitors, riding with the Devil.

It appears that the impact of the
Malleus Maleficarum was limited: the
Spanish Inquisition, for example, was

The frontispiece from the Compendium Malificarum *printed by Francesco Guazzo.*

sceptical about its value. Pope Innocent VIII did not sanction the work, even though he did encourage Kramer and Sprenger to hunt witches (they attached the papal bull to the front of the book to make it look as if it had official approval).

JEAN BODIN

In 1580 the French philosopher and judge Jean Bodin published *De la démonomanie des sorciers*, which was to become the *Malleus Maleficarum* of the next 100 years. It was a very influential work which fused the judge's or inquisitor's fantasies and obsessions with charges against the accused: Bodin based his belief in the reality of a witch cult on the uniformity of witches' confessions. By extracting confessions, usually under torture, to the activities that he believed the witch had engaged in, the inquisitor received confirmation of his suspicions, and so the beliefs acquired validity.

THEOLOGICAL JUSTIFICATION

Bodin believed in the mystical authority of the divine right of monarchs. He saw the universe as an organic unity regulated by harmonious laws and ruled over by God. The monarch was God's divine representative on earth; those who spoke evil against the monarch spoke evil against God. Bodin saw the magistrate as a person responsible for the creation of harmonic justice in a godly society. Witches broke natural and divine laws – by infanticide, cannibalism, killing by poisoning or charms, blighting crops, slaughtering animals, creating sterility and famine – and had to be punished to appease divine anger.

His condemnation of witches was anchored in the Jewish tradition, and their punishment was supported by texts in the Old Testament: the first rationale for punishments is to appease divine anger (*Numbers* 25); but it is also to obtain God's blessing on a land (*Deuteronomy* 13), to deter other malefactors (*Deuteronomy* 13), to prevent the "infection" of the good (*Deuteronomy* 15,19), to diminish the number of the evil (*Leviticus* 12,14), and to punish the actual crime (*Deuteronomy* 19).

Jean Bodin, French philosopher, judge and witch hunter.

Bodin claimed that the most powerful magic in the world would not work against the officials of the law, and that it was impossible to kill judges. He asserted that witchcraft utilized evil spirits, though these were not evil of themselves but ultimately vehicles for the good because they served God's design; like sewers and cesspools that are necessary even in a palace. Humans have free will and the harmony of the world is sustained by the friendly rivalry between good and evil. His call for the eradication of witches stemmed from his belief that French society was dangerously out of harmony: the bad was much stronger than the good, and he therefore wrote *De la démonomanie des sorciers* to deal with the situation.

Various instruments of torture from a woodcut of c.1513.

MATTHEW HOPKINS

This man is a mysterious figure, and not much is known about his early life except that his family came from East Anglia and that he lived in the village of Manningtree in Essex, England. It appears that he may have gained some of his education in Holland, and worked as a clerk for a shipowner in Mistley, Essex. He must have been aware of local witch legends and traditions, among them those of sea witches, and it is possible that he was affected by a fear of witches through his work.

SEA WITCHES

There was a widespread fear of witches among seafarers and those connected with the sea. Astrologers were consulted by insurance brokers in cases of mysterious disappearances of ships. In a number of witch trials evidence was taken concerning the bewitchment of ships and captains. One account tells of a woman who lent an old woman some money, taking a brass kettle for security, while awaiting passage from Amsterdam to England. The old woman was unable to repay the debt but demanded the return of the kettle. When the request was refused, the old woman cursed the ship. A bad storm hit the ship and the crew saw an old woman sitting on top of the mainmast. The captain urged the woman to let him throw the kettle into the sea. When this was done, "the witch dismount her selfe from the mast, goes aboord the brasse kettle, and in a moment sails out of sight". After this, the air cleared, the wind grew calm, and the storm came to a stop.

WITCHFINDER GENERAL

For nearly three years – from the beginning of 1645 to August 1647, when he

Two witches, one female and one male, use their powers to create a storm at sea, and succeed in wrecking a ship.

Matthew Hopkins, the self-styled Witchfinder General, shown with two of his accused together with their familiars, or "imps", all of whom have names. From a seventeenth-century engraving.

died – there is documented proof of Hopkins' activities as the self-styled Witchfinder General. His witch hunting extended all over East Anglia, but Essex was the centre of his campaign to eliminate witches. From 1645, Essex witch trials bore an increasing resemblance to the more sensational descriptions of legal proceedings in France or Germany. Hopkins started his campaign on his own but later employed searchers. John Stearne, a Puritan "given to declamatory speeches full of the horrors of hell-fire and brimstone", and Mary "Goodwife" Phillips, a midwife, joined his team.

IMPS AND FAMILIARS

Witches in Essex were not generally thought to fly to Sabbaths, or to have sexual perversions. Instead, the focus of the witch-hunting process was on witches' marks and familiars or imps. The body of

A witch sits surrounded by devils. The witch hunters would search for the marks left by devils such as these. This illustration is from the title page of the seventeenth-century Daemonolatria *by Nicholas Remy.*

a quarter of an hour, after which it was wiped off with a cloth. This woman was more fortunate: she was aquitted.

Hopkins himself allegedly had an encounter with a familiar. He wrote a pamphlet called *The Discovery of Witches: in Answer to Severall Queries, lately Delivered to the Judges of Assize for Norfolk county*, printed in 1647. In it he described how the familiar came into his yard at night, "a black thing, proportioned like a cat oneley it was thrice as big, sitting on

a strawberry bed, and fixing the eyes on this Informant; and when he [Hopkins] went towards it, it leapt over the pale ... but ran quite through the yard, with his greyhound after it ... and the said greyhound returned again to this Informant, shaking and trembling exceedingly".

Thus the witch hunters Kramer, Sprenger, Bodin and Hopkins carried out their crusade against ordinary people. Their misogynistic legacy remains in popular stereotyped images of witches as old evil hags. The Christian Church, therefore, played a part in the persecution of many innocent people in the name of a battle against an evil that had never existed except in the often perverse minds of the persecutors.

The Essex witch Joan Prentis sits with her familiars. In the background is a reminder of the penalty of witchcraft.

an accused person was searched for the Devil's marks, which were usually found. The woman was then "watched" or kept awake for a minimum of 24 hours, strapped naked and cross-legged to a stool or table, while her accusers waited for the appearance of her familiars or imps. A woman called Joyce Bonds confessed to having "two imps in the likeness of mice, which came into her bed and sucked her body". Apparently, she used these imps to kill a neighbour's lambs, and she was hanged for the crime. Another woman, who was named Binkes and lived in Haverhill, was reported by Stearne as having a fly for an imp. She denied being a witch and requested to see the rector of her parish, saying that "the Lord would shew an example upon her and that if she had any imps, that they would come out whilst he was there". Apparently the imp appeared while the rector was there, and Stearne claimed that it fastened itself on her body for about

THE REFORMATION

The years between 1520 and 1650, a period later known as the Reformation, divided Christian Europe into Catholics and Protestants. A series of individual movements rather than one coherent organization, it was to have a profound effect on European religious life. The Reformation intensified witchcraft prosecutions and both Catholic and Protestant churches were determined to impose their views and practices in campaigns that were aimed at discrediting folk beliefs in magic. By doing this, the Church would take its rightful place as the sole spiritual and moral influence in the lives of ordinary men and women.

John Wyclif denied that the Eucharist actually transformed into the body and blood of Christ.

Beliefs about witchcraft took on a specific character during the Reformation, and they were an important part of the reformers' thought. The Reformation, which lasted from 1520 to 1650, divided European Christianity into Catholic and Protestant traditions, and led to many wars and conflicts, most notably the Thirty Years War (1618–48). It was a series of parallel movements that sought to purify society and promote individual morality, rather than a single movement with a coherent organization or a clearly defined set of objectives.

JOHN WYCLIF AND THE LOLLARDS

There had been attacks on the Catholic Church before the Reformation when John Wyclif (c.1330–84), one-time master of Balliol College, Oxford, England, had rejected the notion of papal supremacy, and denounced the wealth of the Church, and denied that the Eucharist bread and wine actually transformed into the body and blood of Christ.

In 1395 the Lollards, Wyclif's followers, were also bitterly critical of what they saw as the Church's involvement with magic in the Eucharist. In their *Twelve Conclusions* they stated:

John Wyclif appearing before the Prelates at St Paul's to answer the charge of heresy in 1377.

That exorcisms and hallowings, made in the Church, of wine, bread, and wax, water, salt and oil and incense, the stone of the altar, upon vestments, mitre, cross, and pilgrims' staves, be the very practice of necromancy, rather than of the holy theology. This conclusion is proved thus. For by such exorcisms creatures be charged to be of higher virtue than their own kind, and we see nothing of change in no such creature that is so charmed, but by false belief, the which is the principle of the devil's craft.

In short, false belief was the work of the Devil.

In the fifteenth century many people suffered deep religious unease owing to the hardships that they had had to endure through famine, war and disease. An obsession with death and sin had intensified Christian religious fervour, and more and more people turned to the Virgin Mary and the saints to save their souls. Many placed great faith in the power of relics and indulgences to gain them salvation.

The Pope selling indulgences so that people could be absolved of their sins. From a sixteenth-century woodcut.

The Protestant reformer Martin Luther, who described the Church's sale of indulgences as scandalous.

MARTIN LUTHER

The Reformation began because the Protestant reformers saw the Church as full of false beliefs. Reformers such as Martin Luther (1483–1546) and John Calvin (1509–64) broke with Rome and the papacy in a bid to restore the Church to what they saw as its earlier Christian purity. The dispute was provoked by the sale of indulgences, whereby people could pay to be absolved of their sins. On 31 October 1517 Luther posted up on the church door at Wittenberg, where he was a member of the university, 95 theses in which he contested the worth of indulgences and described their sale as scandalous. Luther, an Augustinian monk, believed that only faith could make people righteous, and that the Holy Scripture was the only source of true faith. He was against the cult of the Virgin Mary and the saints and thought that they should not be worshipped. Luther called for a change in the role of the clergy, relaxing the rule on celibacy and allowing priests to marry. Above all, he stressed the role of the individual conscience in the formation of a direct relationship with God.

The Protestant Reformation led to a reform movement within Catholicism known as the Counter-Reformation, which had the aim of reforming the Church from its worst excesses and eliminating corruption without changing its main structure. These changes, which were authorized by the Council of Trent from 1545 to 1563, claimed that tradition as well as Holy Scripture was a source of revelation.

A portrait of Jean Calvin, a Protestant reformer who broke with Rome in a bid to restore Christian purity.

Doctor Martinar Argentinen. Doctor bock Emfer Lipfii Leo papa.r. Antichuft Doctor Eckius. Ingelftatenfis Doctor Lemp. Tubingenfis.

A sixteenth-century woodcut caricature of Luther's opponents.

WITCH HUNTS INTENSIFY

Did the Reformation cause witch hunting? It has been claimed that the Reformation was a catalyst for witch hunting, but there is no direct relationship between the ideas and events that caused the break-up of European Christianity and the persecution of witches. However, the Reformation did intensify witchcraft prosecutions. The incidence and severity of campaigns mounted against witches depended on a complex mixture of social and political circumstances, which cut across different religious beliefs. According to the historian Brian Levack, witch hunting was most severe in countries or regions where there were large religious minorities, or where the people of one state were of one religion and those nearby were of another. Witch hunting took place in Protestant and Catholic lands but was at its most intense in regions that had a mixed population of Protestants and Catholics, such as Germany, Switzerland, France, Poland and Scotland. Spain and Italy, although they did not avoid witch hunts completely, had fewer "witch panics" because they remained largely

Ego fum Papa.

A Protestant caricature of Pope Alexander VI as the Devil. From a sixteenth-century woodcut.

Catholic. The historian Stuart Clark has claimed that beliefs in witchcraft were at the heart of the reforming process. He has argued that although there were differences between witch hunting in Protestant and Catholic regions, both Catholic and Protestant Churches were determined to impose the fundamentals of Christian belief on ordinary people; they vigorously campaigned to discredit popular beliefs in magic, calling them superstition. A Christian was forbidden to observe magical practices, such as:

... casting holy water upon his bed ... bearing about him holy bread, or St John's Gospel ... ringing of holy bells; or blessing with the holy candle, to the intent thereby to be discharged of the burden of sin, or to drive away devils, or to put away dreams and fantasies; or ... putting trust and confidence of health and salvation in the same ceremonies.

How were beliefs in witches part of Reformation thought? During the Reformation there was an increased awareness of the Devil. Protestant reformers, especially Luther and Calvin, adopted the traditional late medieval view of the Devil, and a war was waged against Satan, both internally (by resisting temptation) and externally (by the prosecution of witches and other heretics). The importance of leading a moral life was seen to be an absolute priority: the individual was considered responsible for his or her own salvation. This had a psychological effect. Feelings of guilt could be transferred to another person in the shape of a witch who personified evil. Many witchcraft accusations were made against those who had come asking for charity. To refuse charity caused guilt, but by branding the person a witch, and therefore morally unworthy, the action was justified. It has also been suggested that when priests felt guilty about lapses in their sexual chastity they projected their guilt on to women, and so the witch also came to represent women's uncontrollable sexuality.

PROTESTANT ATTITUDES

Stuart Clark argues that the nature of everyday misfortunes lies at the very heart of Protestant attitudes to

A sixteenth-century anti-Catholic caricature of monks and nuns feasting in the mouth of the Devil, who is sitting on a letter of indulgence.

witchcraft. Protestant theologians argued that to blame afflictions only on witches was a kind of hypocrisy, which undervalued misfortune as a punishment for sin, or as a test of faith. To apply counter-

witchcraft, or to seek the services of cunning men or women – so-called "white witches" – was equally bad and was viewed as a form of idolatry, which ignored the need for repentance; it also attributed the power that was rightfully God's to magicians. Protestant demonologists concentrated their attack against superstition on cunning men and women and frequently saw them as more harmful than maleficent witches. According to an account in a book called *A Discourse of the Damned Art of Witchcraft* by William Perkins, published in 1608:

by Witches we understand not those onely which kill and torment: but all Diviners, Charmers, Juglers, all Wizzards, commonly called wise men and wise women; yea, whosoever doe any thing (knowing what they doe) which cannot be effected by nature or art; and in the same number we reckon all good Witches, which doe no hurt, but good, which doe not spoile and destroy, but save and deliver.

The attack against magic and witches served to unite the different factions of Christianity.

Luther writes his 95 theses against indulgences on the church door at Wittenberg in this contemporary allegorical woodcut.

THE GEOGRAPHY OF WITCH HUNTS

Witch hunting varied in intensity, not only in different countries and regions but also at different periods of time. It started, grew, peaked and then declined at varying times in diverse places. The ways and methods of prosecution, conviction and execution of witches also varied greatly in different regions but it is possible to see broad patterns. The majority of witchcraft prosecutions took place in Germany, France, Switzerland and the Low Countries. In the early years, most prosecutions occurred in France, especially in the east, while in later years more people were taken to court in Germany, particularly in the south and west of the country.

The period from 1580 to 1650 was when witch hunting was at its peak. From the 1550s to the 1570s there was an increase in individual witch-trials and small hunts, while in the 1580s and 1590s there was a period of mass trials and large hunts. The process reached its high point between 1610 and 1630. The 1580s were particularly bad in Switzerland and the Low Countries; the 1590s in France, the Low Countries and Scotland; the 1600s in the Jura region

A condemned witch is taken to be burnt during the Bamberg witch trials in Bavaria.

and in parts of Germany; the 1610s in Spain; the 1620s and 1630s in Germany; the 1640s in England; the 1660s in Scotland; and the late 1660s and early 1670s in Sweden and Finland. Western and southern European countries (except Portugal) were the first to adopt the ideas of a diabolic witch as constructed by the demonologists. Persecution was only possible where there was a definite image of a witch who was a threat to good Christian society. Thus the spread of the witch hunt depended on the rise of demonology. The areas that were the first to take up the prosecution of witches were also the first to end such trials, with the emergence of ideas that were sceptical about such beliefs.

Early explanations for witch persecutions saw magic and superstition as part of the backwardness and primitivism of

La Murqui, the noted witchfinder of the French Basque country, indicates marks that prove a pact with Satan.

rural folk. The historian Hugh Trevor-Roper thought that the mountains were the home of sorcery, witchcraft and primitive religious forms, which had to be won back to "sound religion". His explanation for what he called the "witch craze" was in terms of the superstition of mountain peasants and concerned what he saw as "disturbances of a psychotic nature" and the "mental rubbish of peasant credulity and feminine hysteria". How could an advanced and civilized society like Europe, which was undergoing a scientific revolution at the same time, unleash a persecution based on the delirious notion of witchcraft?

POLITICAL OR RELIGIOUS PERSECUTION?

The witch persecutions were a single, unified phenomenon that coincided not only with the Reformation and the Counter-Reformation, but also with the growth of the modern nation state, and with new attitudes to science. They occurred at a dynamic time during which the educated elite of the cities and towns came to impose their beliefs on the ordinary people of rural areas.

Village beliefs about ordinary maleficent magic and witchcraft that concerned conflict between neighbours became diabolized by those who controlled the churches, schools and law courts of the emerging nation states. It has been said by some that witch hunting was a political rather than a religious activity, whereby the views of the educated elite, developed in the towns and cities, were imposed on the people who lived in the countryside. European witch trials had two main themes: popular beliefs in malevolent and harmful magic, and elite ideas about a diabolical Christian conspiracy. A precondition for the spread of witch persecutions was that elite ideas filtered down to the lower strata of society.

In rural areas, legal prosecutions reflected the inevitable social tensions of village life, while in urban centres it was sorcery inspired by political life. People such as plague-spreaders, who were thought to be capable of distilling the essence of the plague and infecting parts of the community, were accused of

The alleged activities of witches from the North Berwick coven in England in 1591. One of their number takes down the words of the Devil, while others boil a cauldron to create a storm and sink a ship at sea.

collectively worshipping the Devil and were prosecuted as witches.

The Reformation and the Counter-Reformation encouraged witchcraft prosecutions in the late sixteenth and early seventeenth centuries but during the earlier years, with the disintegration of medieval Christianity and the theological controversy involved, there were distractions from witch hunting. Also, the task of developing a specifically Protestant demonology took time to work out. After much work, finally the Protestants rejected the work of the Catholic Inquisition and drastically changed the legal procedure by moving witchcraft trials to secular courts. Therefore, coinciding as they did with a period of political and religious upheaval in the Reformation, the Counter-Reformation and the rise of the modern nation state, the witch hunts and the way they were prosecuted, represent a response to considerable social change.

The inside of the Justice Chamber at Valenciennes, northern France, during the period of the witchcraft trials.

WITCH HUNTS IN SWITZERLAND AND FRANCE

The first witch trials occurred in the French and Swiss Alps in the fifteenth century. According to the historian Norman Cohn, the early accounts of the witch trials in France in the thirteenth and fourteenth centuries were forgeries. The stereotype of the witch as someone who flew at night to Sabbaths was not sanctioned by the Church until the fifteenth century when trials occurred in the mountainous areas of the French and Swiss Alps as a result of the persecution of a group of Waldensian heretics. In 1428 the peasant communities of the Swiss canton of Valais, under the guidance of the Bishop of Sion, declared that anyone accused of witchcraft by more than two people should be arrested and made to confess. On the basis of their confession they were condemned to the flames. A witch hunt began at the same time in the Val d'Anniviers and the Val d'Hèrens, two valleys south of the Rhône. This was the first time that the stereotype of the witch that would come to inspire the great witch hunt appeared.

In 1453 a sensational witch trial took place in Evreux, Normandy. Guillaume

The witch Guillemette Babin in front of the inquisitors. Jean Bodin was responsible for her capture and trial in 1564, at which she was condemned and burned to death.

Adeline, a doctor of theology and former Paris professor, was accused of writing a compact with Satan binding him to preach sermons against the reality of the Sabbaths. This was allegedly supposed

to have the effect that judges would be discouraged from prosecuting those who went to Sabbaths, thus allowing more members to frequent such gatherings. Adeline confessed to a compact with Satan. He said that he had flown on a broomstick to the Sabbaths and had found there a demon called Monseigneur, who changed himself into a he-goat, and whom Adeline kissed under his tail as homage. Perhaps because of his position, Adeline was sentenced to perpetual imprisonment rather than death. Adeline was supposed to have belonged to a sect of Waldensians, but Cohn notes that by this time the term was generally used as a synonym for "witches".

The northern and eastern regions and parts of the south-west of France – the peripheral areas – were the most heavily affected by witchcraft. The prosecution of witches may have been part of a general disciplinary programme for controlling rebellious outlying regions. Courts in these far-flung places had great independence from central government, but when a central monarchy was

Joan of Arc, convicted of heresy and sorcery rather than witchcraft, was burnt at the stake in Rouen in 1431. From a contemporary manuscript.

The burning of witches in Paris.

established in the sixteenth and seventeenth centuries, there were fewer witch executions.

JOAN OF ARC

One famous case was that of Joan of Arc, who was tried for heresy and sorcery and burnt at Rouen in 1431. In 1429 this young peasant girl introduced herself to Charles, the Dauphin of France, as his God-given saviour, telling him that she could change his fortune in the war against the English. She said that a voice from God had told her to raise the siege of Orléans to help Charles recover his kingdom and drive the English out of France. From the age of 12, Joan had seen visions, heard the voices of the Archangel Michael, Catherine of Alexandria and Margaret of Antioch, and made prophecies according to what they had to say. The Duke of Bedford, who commanded the English forces at the siege of Orléans, attributed English losses to the unlawful supernatural forces deployed by Joan of Arc, and called her a "disciple of the Fiend" who used false enchantment and sorcery.

Shakespeare described the two views of Joan in *Henry VI*, part 1 – as a French patron saint:

> *No longer on St Denis will we cry,*
> *But Joan la Pucelle shall be*
> *Franceís saint.*

And as a heretic:

> *Coward of France! how much he*
> *[the Dauphin] wrongs his fame...*
> *To join with witches and the help of hell.*

Joan was brought before the Inquisition by the English for heresy and for her idolatry and the "cult and veneration" of her saints, which was said to be part of a pact with the Devil. The tribunal was composed mainly of ecclesiastics and lawyers, sometimes numbering more than 70 men. She was taken to the cemetery of St Ouen in Rouen and placed on a scaffold, surrounded by cardinals, bishops and various earls, dukes and officials, while passages from John's Gospel, including

A nineteenth-century portrayal of Joan of Arc being led to her death in Rouen in 1431.

the saying that "the withered branch must be thrown in the fire else the tree cannot flourish", were shouted. There is much controversy surrounding what happened, but Joan signed a document of recantation and was condemned to lifelong imprisonment, on bread and water and in solitary confinement, because the Inquisition could not condemn to death a heretic, only a relapsed heretic. When Joan withdrew her declaration, saying that she was still hearing voices, the way was open for her inquisitors to put an end to what they saw as her communication with evil spirits. When she went to the stake she wore over her shaven head a tall mitre that was inscribed with her crimes and the names of her malign spirits – Belial, Satan and Behemoth.

Gilles de Rais

Some years after Joan of Arc's exploits and execution, one of her comrades in arms, Gilles de Rais, was accused by the state of, among other things, being 'possessed by the Evil One', and of killing 140 children under this satanic influence. Gilles admitted to the children's murders but insisted that he acted in accordance with his own imagination and was not inspired by the Devil, an important distinction in those times.

Gilles confessed to killing the children and begged the mercy of the court and the forgiveness of their parents. In 1440 he was found guilty of both crimes, that of murder and also of diabolical inspiration, and was sentenced to be hanged and then burnt. His execution took place nine years after Joan's death.

The notorious Gilles de Rais, whose story remains somewhat of a mystery. He was one of the most famous people to be accused of working under Satanic influences.

WITCH HUNTS IN GERMANY

The first major witch hunt in Germany was the Ravensburger persecution of 1484 which inspired Heinrich Kramer and Jacob Sprenger to compose the *Malleus Maleficarum*, the infamous witch hunters' manual.

The main areas of witch hunting were in the south and west of the country, and Würzburg, Bamberg, Eichstött, Württemberg and Ellwangen were all the sites of famous witch hunts. A large witchcraft persecution occurred in 1563, in the small Lutheran territory of Wiesensteig: it claimed the lives of 63 women. Local German courts exercised a great deal of autonomy in the trials of witches and in Ellwangen, a small Catholic region in south-west Germany, almost 400 individuals were condemned to death between 1611 and 1618 without any appeal to a higher court. However, although local German courts did not

The notorious German witchfinder Konrad von Marburg sends another victim to the torture chamber and the stake.

The "Malefitz Haus" constructed at Bamberg specifically for the interrogation and torture of suspected witches.

usually have dealings with imperial tribunals or with supervision by imperial judicial authorities, they were required to consult with the universities for help with the complexities of criminal procedure in witchcraft cases. Before sentencing was carried out, reports were sent to the law faculty of the nearest university so that the advice of academics could be sought. As the universities were the centres for the development

and spread of demonological theory, this process usually resulted in more prosecutions.

THE CASE OF ANNA EBELER

In Augsburg in January 1669, a lying-in maid called Anna Ebeler was accused of murdering her employer by giving her a bowl of soup. Instead of restoring her strength after childbirth the soup had allegedly increased her fever, and she had become delirious and died. As news of the death spread, other women accused Ebeler of poisoning their young children. One child had lost its baby flesh and had become thin and dried out. A second had been unable to suckle from its mother (although it could suck from other women) and had died in agony. Another had died after becoming covered in pustules and blisters, and its seven-year-old brother had suffered from aches and pains and had visions caused by sorcery. His mother had had headaches and all the household had suffered from strange growths on their bodies. One woman had found her baby covered with blisters

and red patches and the mother's menstruation had stopped. Anna Ebeler confessed at the end of the second of her six interrogations, when torture was threatened. She was executed and her body was burnt on 23 March 1669.

Augsburg did not have a witch craze and did not execute a witch before 1625. According to the historian Lyndal Roper, cases came singly, with one or two every few years after 1650. Anna Ebeler was one of 18 witches executed in Augsburg, and Roper says that a dominant theme of the witch trials in this part of Germany was their connection with motherhood: relations between mothers formed the basis of most of the witchcraft accusations in the town. Accusations were typically brought by mothers soon after giving birth against lying-in maids, not midwives. The food the witch gave the mother was said to be sprinkled with white or black diabolic powders, or she administered poisoned soups, and these influenced the mother's milk. The witch perverted the mother's capacity to nourish.

One grandmother was interrogated three times and tortured because her young grandson suspected witchcraft when he felt ill after drinking an aniseed water tonic she had given him. In another case a woman was accused of reversing the flow of maternal fluids by sucking the infant dry and feeding on it. Its mother described how "its little breasts had been sucked out so that milk had been pressed out from the child's little teats … and from this time on the child had lost weight so that it looked as if hardly a pound of flesh remained on it".

Roper is interested in viewing witchcraft accusations as reflecting psychic tensions of maternal depression, anger or envy, or invoking deeply ambivalent emotions from the mother's early life, which might be projected on to the lying-in maid during the six-week period of convalescence after childbirth. However, it was dangerous to antagonize a lying-in maid, and one woman is said to have repeated the following threatening rhyme on her departure:

My dear little treasure, now
you are well recovered
Look master and mistress
Now I depart from the child
Whatever may happen to him now
I will not be held to blame.

A midwife assisting a woman in labour. In the background, astrologers are predicting the future of the child.

The frontispiece for a tract against witchcraft in 1591 shows an affair with the Devil, flying witches and a child being used to make a potion.

Despite 24 hours of torture, Herr Lirtzen, Burgomaster of Rheinbach in 1631, refused to confess to witchcraft but was burnt anyway.

WITCH HUNTS IN BRITAIN AND IRELAND

Compared with other parts of Europe, witch hunting in Britain was restrained and mild, although in Scotland it was more intense and illegal torture was used. In England there was a belated and incomplete reception of the stereotype of the witch, and courts were more lenient, using torture only sparingly. At first witchcraft was seen to be a hostile act rather than heresy, and no reference was made to a diabolical contract with the Devil. A distinction between maleficent witchcraft and less harmful forms, such as divination, was made, and penalties for the latter were much lighter. Few British hunts could be compared in size or intensity with those that occurred in Germany. The total number of British trials probably did not exceed 5,000, and the number of executions has been estimated as less than 2,500.

The main difference between Britain and Ireland and continental Europe was that the notion of diabolic Sabbath meetings of witches and the Devil was largely absent in England and Ireland, although towards the end of the sixteenth century continental demonology and Devil-related evidence did start to make an appearance in British courts. Many English cases centred on the witch's use of familiars, as in the well-known trial of the Chelmsford witches.

THE CHELMSFORD WITCHES

The Witchcraft Bill was passed under Queen Elizabeth I in 1563, and at Chelmsford three women were charged with acts of witchcraft in 1566. Two of these were Elizabeth Francis and Agnes Waterhouse. Elizabeth Francis was accused of bewitching a child and making it ill. She admitted to learning witchcraft from her grandmother, who was named Mother Eve, at the age of 12, and to having a "familiar", a white spotted cat called Sathan, which bewitched people for her. The cat had helped her to become rich by obtaining goods and sheep; it had also helped her obtain a lover, but when he refused to marry her

The English witch Anne Turner who was executed at Tyburn, London, in 1615. From a contemporary print.

the cat had killed him by witchcraft. On the advice of the cat she had become pregnant by a man called Christopher Francis, whom she had later married. She was sentenced to a year in prison for these offences, but she appeared before the same court on two further occasions. When questioned, she confessed to allowing Sathan to kill three of Father Kersey's hogs, to drown Widow Goodday's cow and to kill three geese owned by a neighbour.

Agnes Waterhouse was the first woman to be hanged for witchcraft in Chelmsford, England, in 1566.

Christian Bowman being burned at the stake in the Old Bailey in the eighteenth century.

... [she] willed him to kill a hog of her own, which he did; and she gave him for his labour a chicken, which he first required of her, and a drop of her blood, and this she gave him at all times when he did anything for her, by pricking her hand or face and putting the blood to his mouth, which he sucked, and forthwith would lie down in his pot again, wherein she kept him ...

She also admitted attempting to bewitch another neighbour and to kill her husband.

It was also said that Agnes Waterhouse turned her familiar into a toad, which she kept in a pot. Agnes was charged, alongside Elizabeth Francis, with acts of witchcraft and was hanged in 1566. Elizabeth was hanged soon afterwards.

Agnes's daughter Joan, aged 18, also confessed to witchcraft. When her mother was out, she had gone to a neighbour's child and asked for bread and cheese. When denied the food, she called on the familiar Sathan, who had emerged from her mother's shoe under the bed in the likeness of a great dog. It was alleged that Joan made the dog haunt the child, but officials found her not guilty of bewitching the child.

SCOTLAND

In Scotland the officially appointed witch pricker was a key figure in gathering evidence against a witch. His role was to examine the suspect for any unusual bodily marks and then test them by pricking to find out whether she could feel it. The idea behind this practice was that the Devil would consummate a pact by nipping the witch, and that this left a permanent mark, which did not bleed and did not feel pain. John Kincaid, the most famous pricker, tested Jonet Paiston and reported that:

She did nather find the preins [pin] when it was put into any of the said marks nor did they blood when they were taken out again: and when shoe was asked quhair shoe thocht the preins were put in, schoe pointed at a pairt of hir body distant from the place quhair the priens were put in, they being lang priens of thrie inches or theirabouts in length.

IRELAND

European ideas did not penetrate Ireland either, and witchcraft in Ireland was primarily a crime of maleficium rather than Devil-worship. Even so, there were few witch trials, and those that were held were carried out by English or Scottish Protestant settlers. The best-known case happened in 1661 and concerns Florence Newton, "the witch of Youghal", who, when refused a piece of beef from the household of John Pyne, went away cursing. A short while afterwards she kissed one of Pyne's female servants, and when the servant started having fits and vomiting, she accused Newton of witchcraft. Newton was arrested and while in prison supposedly kissed a man through a gate and caused his death. What happened to Florence Newton after her arrest is not known,

Judith Philips, a cunning woman, fortune-teller and swindler, who was sentenced to be whipped through the City of London on 14 February 1594.

but the witchcraft of which she was accused bore very little relation to European ideas of collective diabolical gatherings of witches.

The execution of Catherine Cawches and her two daughters at St Peter's Port, Guernsey, in 1700.

WITCH HUNTS IN SCANDINAVIA

Witch hunting in Scandinavia was more intense than in Britain; in the same period of activity, the total number of prosecutions was approximately 5,000, resulting in between 1,700 and 2,000 executions. Although the figures are similar to those of Britain, the population of Scandinavian countries was only about 40 per cent of Britain's.

Scandinavian witch hunting was not based on a complete concept of witchcraft, and even when the demonological aspects of collective Devil-worship do appear, they lack the distinctive features of those in German, French and Swiss cases. In addition, there was a reluctance in Scandinavia to use torture on the accused witches to obtain confessions or the names of their accomplices.

Nevertheless, large witch hunts did take place in certain areas. Denmark was the first Scandinavian country to engage in witch hunting, and here the

A Norwegian "huldre" who appears to be an innocent milkmaid but is in reality a witch who can lead the unwary into all kinds of trouble.

Lutheran clergy took the initiative in spreading the idea of witchcraft. In the 1540s the Lutheran bishop of Sealand urged the prosecution of witches, claiming that those with Catholic tendencies were to blame.

NORWAY

The most famous case of Norwegian witchcraft also concerned Lutherans and was focused on Anna Pedersdotter Absalon, the wife of Lutheran minister Absalon Pedersen Beyer, a humanist scholar. A group opposing the Lutheran destruction of holy images attacked the minister's wife, since she made an easier target than the clergy themselves. This followed a pattern common in Germany, where political factions used charges of witchcraft against their opponents' wives to advance their own political careers.

Anna was cleared in 1575 but the case was reopened in 1590 when additional

A sixteenth-century Scandinavian depiction of witches calling up monsters while ordinary people lie asleep.

charges were made. In the second trial she was accused of putting a man into a coma because he had refused to pay for a weaving frame, inflicting sickness on a man who had refused her wine, beer and vinegar, and of causing the death of a four-year-old boy by giving him a bewitched biscuit.

In addition to these accusations came others that included aspects of diabolism: Anna's servant testified that she had turned her into a horse and had ridden her to a Sabbath that was taking place on a mountain called Lyderhorn, where a number of witches plotted to summon up a storm that would wreck all ships arriving in Bergen. On subsequent occasions, they had schemed to burn the town and cause flooding. This Sabbath had been dispersed by a man in white who forbade it in God's name. This time Anna was not so lucky and she was burnt as a witch. Hans Wiers-Jenssen wrote a play about the case (*Anne Pedersdotter*), and a film, called *Day of Wrath*, was made in Denmark in 1943.

SWEDEN

Witch hunting in Sweden was similar to that in Norway. There was an increase in the intensity of persecutions in the three towns of Stockholm, Jønkøping and Vadstena during the period 1490–1614, and there was also a large panic in the late seventeenth century. During the 1600s, isolated but specific references were made to the witches' Sabbaths and they were connected with the Blåkulla or "Blue Hill". A writer of the time claimed that the Blåkulla was used by Nordic witches for their meetings to practise the Devil's arts. Between 1520 and 1699 more than 1,000 people were accused of sorcery and witchcraft: the exact number is unknown because some of the court records were destroyed by fire. In the 1670s the number of cases reached a peak, and during the year 1675/76, at least 157 witches were accused, 41 of whom were sentenced to death.

Swedish witches gather for a Sabbath on the Blokula in a seventeenth-century portrayal.

FINLAND

In Finland, unlike other parts of Europe, witchcraft was not primarily associated with women. Out of 641 people known to have been accused, only around half were female. As late as the sixteenth century, 60 per cent of those accused and 75 per cent of those found guilty were men. However, as soon as the number of trials increased, the percentage of women also went up, surpassing that of men in the 1650s. As soon as the witch hunt had peaked the number of women began to decrease again and the number of men accused increased. The reason for this is that in Finland a sorcerer tended to be a man and, in Finnish folk traditions and religion, supernatural powers were associated with men rather than women.

It is thought that the European stereotype of the diabolical witch as female broke down the Finnish male stereotype. In Iceland too, the typical witch was male, and of the 120 witch trials that took place only ten involved women; out of 22 burnt, only one of them was a woman.

Finnish witches were usually men rather than women, and here some male witches sell favourable winds to sailors. From a woodcut of 1555.

WITCH HUNTS IN EASTERN EUROPE

Witch hunting in Eastern Europe was similar to that in other parts of Europe in the manner in which it relieved social, psychological and religious tensions but, like Scandanavia, it was also different because its foundations were not based so securely on demonological theory. As elsewhere, in order to extend and consolidate its control on ordinary people, the Christian Church in Eastern Europe launched an attack on pagan folk beliefs and versions of Christianity that did not meet with its approval.

HUNGARY

Hungarian witch persecution records show that legal measures against maleficium started with the legislation of the Hungarian kings István (St Stephen) (1000–38), Ladislas I (1077–95) and Kálman (1095–1116). Over the following four centuries, witchcraft charges were dealt with by hot-iron ordeals, at feudal courts and by town juries. A regular prosecution of witches started only in the sixteenth century, intensifying by the end of that century and becoming a mass witch hunt in the final part of the seventeenth century. It peaked in the first half of the eighteenth century, but was finally stopped by the intervention of Empress Maria Theresa and prohibited in 1768.

The historian Gábor Klaniczay points out that the foundation of demonological theory, which was seen to be so important to the explosion of witch hunting in sixteenth- and seventeenth-century Europe, was "almost completely lacking in Hungary". Witchcraft accusations relieved social, psychological and religious tensions through the process of magical revenge, which was practised both among nobles and in the village. The possibility of accusing and denouncing someone as a witch gave power to all members of the community. Klaniczay notes that in 1728 a poor wise woman accused an ex-judge of being the head of a coven; he was arrested, tortured and condemned to death by burning.

The Empress Maria Theresa (1717–80) – a merciful monarch who intervened and stopped witch persecutions in Hungary.

Children of nine to eleven years old, and many kitchen maids from 14 to 16 years old, also accused people of being witches.

TRANSYLVANIA

Transylvania was already notorious in Europe as a dark and sinister country, ruled by psychopathically cruel princes such as Vlad the Impaler, also known as the notorious Dracula. These kings had fierce military reputations but were also associated with the occult, and the kind of inspired wickedness so out of the ordinary that it is associated with extra-human forces. In later years, Transylvanian princes of the sixteenth and seventeenth centuries accused the families of their defeated political enemies of witchcraft. Sigismund Báthory blamed the mother of Boldizsár Báthory, whom he had murdered, for his impotence. After Gábor Bethlen had taken power from Gábor Báthory, who was murdered in 1612, he accused Anna Báthory, the sister of the dead man, of witchcraft with two other noble women of her entourage. Between 1679 and 1686 Prince Mihály Apafy accused about 20 people of witchcraft in the large trial of the wife of his exiled rival Pál Béldi. She was accused of causing the prince's wife to suffer serious illnesses as revenge for their defeat.

ESTONIA

According to the historian Maia Madar, the earliest records of how many witches and heretics were burnt in Estonia date from the fourteenth century, but it is difficult to tell how many witch trials were held because of the lack of documentation and the loss of court records. At the provincial Synod of Riga, the clergy of Livonia threatened all soothsayers, sorcerers, and practitioners of the "Jewish superstition" with excommunication in 1428.

In 1519 witchcraft was defined as a capital crime, and people were ordered to watch out for sorcerers, witches or heretics and "those who were not true Christians but worshipped at sacred groves, stones and trees". Those who used the services of soothsayers and sorcerers regarding illnesses or misfortune, or followed their advice about cattle, or worshipped thunderstorms, were to be burned as heretics. The majority of those sentenced to death were burnt at the stake, but execution by sword was considered a lighter punishment where a person confessed voluntarily or there was no evidence of a pact with the Devil. In one case, a court ordered that a person named Tattra Santi Michel should have his head cut off before being burned:

... on the basis of his testimony, [that] it cannot be positively established that he entered into an agreement with the Devil. However, in his youth, his father gave him

Like witches, Dracula came to hold a particular fascination for many people in later centuries.

to an evil spirit, and he has twice met the Devil in the guise of a dog. He has learned formulas to bewitch and to heal ... The hangman is ordered to cut off his head and then burn him to ashes.

The bewitching of a person's lord carried a death penalty, and a particularly barbaric execution was carried out in 1642 when Willakasz Jürgen was convicted for having murdered the Count of Audru with the Devil's help.

Below: Vlad the Impaler, Prince of Wallachia 1431-1476. Associated with evil and the occult, he was the inspiration for Bram Stoker's novel about Dracula.

WITCH HUNTS IN NEW ENGLAND

The first New England colonists crossed the Atlantic in 1620 and founded the settlement of Plymouth. Their exodus from England was prompted by Puritan religious zeal and the hope of founding a new society based on their spiritual ideals; their flight was an escape from what they saw as the corrupt religious culture of their country of origin.

Life in New England was similar to that in Europe: Protestant religion co-existed with magical beliefs and practices. However, one important difference was the absence of a general organizing structure like the Church of England; instead, small autonomous self-governing bodies of clergy and con-gregations worked together co-operatively, if not always harmoniously. Magic was condemned by Puritan ministers as blasphemous and diabolical but the courts were ill-equipped to deal with cases of witchcraft. This was because a witch was defined, according to the Bible, as "any man or woman [who] hath or consulteth with a familiar spirit", and most cases brought to court concerned maleficium – cursing or causing harm – rather than communication with familiars. Evidence rarely resulted in a conviction, and out of 61 prosecutions in the seventeenth century only 15 resulted in conviction and execution.

THE SALEM WITCH TRIALS

The one exception was the Salem witch hunt, which erupted in 1692, when formal charges of witchcraft were brought against 156 people from 24 towns and villages in the County of Essex, Massachusetts. A special court was set up to deal with the crisis, and the final toll was 19 deaths by hanging and one fatality that occurred under interro-gation. Salem acquired the nickname of "Witch City".

The witch panic started when several girls in Salem Village experienced "fits" and "distempers". Samuel Parris, the minister at Salem Village and the father and uncle of two of the girls, instructed

The pilgrims land at Plymouth in the new land of America on 11 December 1620. Their arrival is watched by hidden Native American Indians.

A suspected witch is arrested in Salem by zealous pilgrims in traditional dress.

them to name their tormentors. The girls accused three women: Tituba, a Caribbean slave in the Parris household; a homeless and destitute woman named Sarah Good; and Sarah Osborne, a resident of a nearby village. Some time later, the girls denounced others. John Hale, an observer of the time, wrote the following account:

These Children were bitten and pinched by invisible agents: their arms, necks and backs turned this way and that way, and returned back again, so as it was impossible for them to do of themselves, and beyond the power of any Epileptick Fits, or natural Disease to effect. Sometimes they were taken dumb, their mouths stopped, their throats choaked, their limbs wracked and tormented so as might move a heart of stone to sympathise with them.

Accused witches were brought to a specially appointed court, which was allowed to administer torture to obtain confessions. Hundreds of people became accusers in the 1690s but the girls were the focus of public interest, and they were brought to the courtroom to see if they would be attacked by the accused. The court assumed the guilt of the accused until it was convinced otherwise, and leading questions and bullying were common, as demonstrated by John Hathorne's examination of Sarah Good:

Hathorne: *Sarah Good, what evil spirit have you familiarity with?*
Good: *None.*
Hathorne: *Have you made no contract with the Devil?*
Good: *No.*
Hathorne: *Why doe you hurt these children?*
Good: *I doe not hurt them. I scorn it.*
Hathorne: *Who doe you imploy then to doe it?*
Good: *I imploy nobody.*
Hathorne: *What creature do you imploy then?*
Good: *No creature but I am falsely accused.*

A view of Salem, the town in which a frenzy of witch hunting erupted in 1692.

is the descent of the Devil at this day upon our selves, that I may truly tell you, the Walls of the whole World are broken down!". Many confessions were made, which suggests that there was religious anxiety among the New Englanders. Several claimed that the fear of damnation played a role in their recruitment to the Devil's service; one woman

confessed to signing a covenant with the Devil after he promised to pardon her sins; another thought that she would be saved if she became a witch. However, there was hardly any evidence and the whole episode may have been a reaction to the threat of Quaker evangelism, which had started in 1656 with the arrival of missionaries.

Cotton Mather, Puritan minister involved in the Salem witch trials and founder of Yale College.

Cotton Mather argued in *The Wonders of the Invisible World*, published in 1693, that the threat that faced the New Englanders was an assault by a witch conspiracy, just one part of a diabolical offensive against New England: "... such

Accused witches were brought to court to face their accusers. Here a girl is bewitched, thus proving the accused guilty.

THE ENDING OF WITCH HUNTS

Eventually the witch hunts came to an end and witchcraft ceased to be a crime. People still believed in witches and magic but they were no longer prosecuted and put to death for supposedly practising it. The emergence of modern rationalism and the rise of science, dispelling so called superstition, has been held to be responsible for a different and "rational" way of viewing the world. However, ideas about magic did not disappear, they just went underground and would emerge in secret societies such as the Rosicrucians and Freemasons.

During the seventeenth and eighteenth centuries there was an increasing reluctance to prosecute witches; many who were tried were acquitted and many convictions were reversed on appeal. Prosecutions and executions for the crime of witchcraft declined and eventually came to an end with the repeal of the witchcraft laws. In 1782 the last officially sanctioned execution was carried out, after which witchcraft ceased to be a crime. This did not stop people naming family members and neighbours as witches, but they could no longer be prosecuted and the accusers had to be careful to avoid prosecution themselves.

The reduction and eventual end of witch hunting occurred at different times in the various regions of Europe. In some areas, such as the Dutch Republic, it declined well before the sixteenth century, while in Poland, for example, it did not finish until the middle of the eighteenth century. In Scotland an initial reduction in the number of prosecutions was followed by more than 50 years of trials. By contrast, in colonial Massachusetts the witch hunts came to a complete end a few years after the courts discouraged prosecutions. Legislation declaring that witchcraft was no longer a crime was passed at different stages. In Hungary and Prussia the decriminalization of witchcraft was responsible for the ending of witch hunting, but in Britain and Denmark legislation was not passed until the witch trials had stopped.

Why did the witch hunts end? It has

often been suggested that the reason was human progress: the emergence of modern rationalism during the period known as the Enlightenment, the rise of science and the accompanying dispelling of ignorance and superstition.

Even though witchcraft was no longer a crime, magic was still a preoccupation in society, and was reflected in its literature. Here Faustus makes his pact with the Devil.

Jane Wenham, who, in 1712, was the last person in England to be convicted of witchcraft.

However, more recent studies of the witch hunts have pointed to the fact that long after the end of the witch-trials people continued to think in terms of witchcraft, since it formed a useful means of dealing with problems and explaining any misfortune. Witchcraft was also a means of power by which it was possible to damage the position of another person by accusations and counter-threats of bewitchment.

In 1895 in the Irish village of Ballyvadlea, near Clonmel, the 26-year-old Bridget Cleary was beaten and burned to death by her husband, in the presence of her family and friends, for being a fairy changeling. They assumed that the real Bridget had been abducted by fairies. Fairies and witches were associated with misfortune, and in the case of Bridget Cleary, were thought to be responsible for her illness. When Bridget was taken ill a doctor was called in and he diagnosed bronchial catarrh and nervous excitement. A herb doctor was also consulted on the advice of a neighbour, and he claimed that Bridget was a changeling, prescribing a milky drink containing herbs. The drink was forced on to a protesting Bridget while she was repeatedly asked her identity: was she Bridget Boland, wife of Micheal Cleary? She affirmed that she was. On the advice of the neighbour who had recommended the herbalist, she was held over the turf fire and again asked her identity, the idea being that the changeling would leave the house via the chimney. The following evening the procedure was repeated but it had fatal consequences: this time she was covered in lamp oil and Bridget died of her burns. She was buried in a nearby swamp. A court case resulted in 20 years of hard labour for Bridget's husband, six months for her father and two male cousins, and the acquittal of the herbalist and a female cousin.

A belief in a magical world-view did not simply disappear overnight or fade away completely. Rather, ideas, beliefs and philosophies went underground to re-emerge at certain points in time, as they continue to do today in the occult subculture, and also in the various movements that seek to revive a pagan past, such as modern witchcraft. Modern witches do not take on the diabolic stereotype as constructed by the demonologists of the Christian Church, but rather seek to create a pre-Christian pagan alternative, largely modelled on the beliefs and practices of the village wise woman and cunning folk.

Magic and witchcraft was still seen as having the capacity to entice or ensnare, as in this nineteenth-century print.

The witches' Sabbath appears to have an enduring power to fascinate, as in this depiction by Goya painted in 1821–23.

EXPLANATIONS OF THE WITCH HUNTS

The tendency to blame others for misfortune is widespread: the anthropologist Bronislaw Malinowski called it a human universal. Social, political, economic and religious upheaval breed an atmosphere of confusion and uncertainty, a climate of fear in which particular groups or individuals – be they, for example, heretics, witches or Jews – are singled out and labelled the enemy.

THE CHURCH VERSUS WOMEN?

Why were the majority (but not all, as the example of Finland shows) of those accused during the European witch hunts women? Some scholars have suggested that this was because of a patriarchal Christian ideology, which was imposed on ordinary people; that it was a construction that served male supremacy. However, the interesting German case of Anna Ebeler and other cases of conflict between mothers and their lying-in nurses show how witchcraft accusations could involve very deep antagonisms between women.

A simple patriarchal explanation – that men were oppressing and persecuting women – does not address the complexity of the phenomenon of witch hunting. It seems probable that the Christianized ideas of the educated elites of the town were imposed on the country folk of the peripheral areas, and that these went hand in hand with certain patriarchal ideas and values.

THE GODDESS UNDER ATTACK?

Other scholars have gone further and suggested that witch persecutions were part of an organized patriarchal repression of both women and earth-venerating pagan religions, which worshipped a goddess. This hypothesis is based mainly on the evidence of prehistoric cave paintings, pottery remains, carvings and figurines, which suggest the association between women and fertility. However, they do not prove the existence of a belief system founded on the worship of a goddess, and any such interpretation is speculative.

A drawing from the nineteenth century showing a witches' celebration on the first day of May.

WITCH HUNTS IN MODERN TIMES

The persecution of groups of people is not just a phenomenon of the past, and there have been parallel witch hunts throughout history that we can contrast and compare with those of the fiftheenth and sixteenth centuries in Europe. The case of McCarthyism in the United States, in the period 1950–54, demonstrates many of the characteristics similar to those of the early modern witch persecutions.

During the 1950s, Communism was seen to be a threat to America and her allies and there was a widespread fear of government infiltration by the "Reds".

Senator Joe McCarthy, whose motive appears to have been political ambition rather than patriotism, made a number of attacks against what he claimed were "enemies of the people" and accused 205 people working in the State Department of being members of the Communist Party. A Senate Committee was set up to deal with these accusations and McCarthy sought to find proof to back up his claims. To no avail. Out of approximately 81 cases investigated, the Committee found not one of the accused to be a Communist. Undeterred, McCarthy continued his search for Communists in government, using both legal and illegal means, and another Committee was set up to investigate his claims. This Committee also failed to find evidence, yet McCarthyism continued, largely due to the newspapers, which played up his accusations in big headlines, and to a general reluctance to speak out against him for fear of being branded a Communist. Finally, in 1954, a number of Senators took a stand against him and the tide of McCarthyism was turned, but not before a number of people's careers had been damaged by their being unfairly labelled as Communists. McCarthy became dejected and died three years later.

SATANIC RITUALS

Witch hunts to find those who are believed to be enemies of the state can be viscious, but the arguments and the passions involved are reasonably clear cut and well defined. Far more damaging and frightening are the campaigns against those who are accused of satanic rituals. In recent times there have been methodically conducted witch hunts over the suspicion of satanic ritual abuse in America and Britain.

Accusations and prosecutions in both countries led to the convictions of alleged abusers. The evidence was the testimonies of young children who were subjected to suggestive questioning by social workers, therapists and prosecutors. There were accusations of incest and sexual abuse, conducted during organized rituals to worship Satan, made

The interior of the room where Senator McCarthy's committee sat in judgement against members of society who were deemed to be guilty of the crime of Communism.

against the parents of children in Orkney, Rochdale, London and Nottingham in Great Britain, as well as in Edenton, North Carolina, and elsewhere in the United States. Around the same time, parallel accusations were levelled against parents by grown children who claimed that they had been sexually abused in their childhoods but had repressed their memories. These memories may have only been "recovered" and become conscious after a visit to a therapist who had prompted the suggestion, or through the reading of a book on the subject.

HISTORICAL LINKS

These modern day manifestations of witch hunts show how the same social pressures that were evident centuries ago still persist. Belief systems or political ideologies are declared by the establishment to be threats to society. These perceived threats are dealt with in many different ways, but it is possible to make some generalizations. It is also possible to see how the same mistakes are made throughout history, as minorities are persecuted by the state.

The anti-communist committee caused huge unrest in the United States, and was rigorously campaigned and demonstrated against by a wide section of society.

Ungrund
(En Soph)

Ungrund

No. 53.   ad Cap IV

Ungrund

Ungrund

Tom. I. Tab. IV

MODERN MAGIC

Magic today has had a bad press – it is either associated with the work of the Devil, or it is reduced to conjuring tricks and sleight of hand. Magic is seen to be separate from religion, but the way that we view magic in the West has been shaped by Christianity, which has branded it evil. Magic is neither good nor evil in itself and it can be used in a variety of ways depending on who is practising it. During the seventeenth century magic was increasingly seen to be irrational when compared to science. At this time, those who practised the occult arts went underground, and many secret societies – such as the Rosicrucians and Freemasons – were formed. Magical practices today reflect this history.

HOW MAGIC SURVIVED

Since the earliest times, human beings have sought to communicate with, and control, the world around them. Ideas about what we now call magic probably developed naturally from people living together in social groups – through intimate relationships, giving birth to children, mourning the death of a clan or tribe member – and also from the shaman's spiritual link with the animals that were hunted. The idea that there is a subtle, invisible essence that comes from all beings – rocks, stones, plants, fungi and animals as well as human beings – is a basic principle of magical belief. People in different cultures from all around the world have attempted to tap into and control this essence or force.

In many spiritual traditions the human body is seen to be made up of a spirit body (which may be called a soul, an etheric body or an aura) as well as a physical body. The spirit body is often viewed as a life-force. It is thought to be subject to damage, leakage or disease, or even psychic vampirism. It is said that a person's spiritual development can be determined by the condition of their spirit body. A halo – the light that appears around a saint's head – marks advancement. The spiritual aura of the Buddha was said to extend for 320 km (200 miles).

Magicians seek to work directly with the spirit body and use it to link up with

Halos are not confined to Christianity – the spiritual aura of the Buddha surrounded his body as well as his head.

the hidden energies of all manner of beings in the cosmos: from the earth energies of trees, through techniques of visualization to invoke gods and goddesses, to wider planetary influences, of the sun and the moon, for example. Each of the magical tradition works in a different way.

The ways that magicians work today have been influenced by ideas from the past. Modern magical ideas were born in the Renaissance. "Renaissance" means rebirth, and the magicians of the time focused on uniting the individual soul with God in terms of what is now called Neoplatonism. The work most influential to Renaissance magicians was the *Corpus*

Hermeticum, a composite of individual writings by various unknown authors, which was probably of Greek origin and not, as was believed in the Renaissance, the work of an Egyptian priest called Hermes Trismegistus. The works are philosophical and concern magical and astrological ways of making talismans to draw down the powers of the stars, and record the means by which individual souls can find divine knowledge without the aid of a personal god or saviour. Magicians need to try and understand the hidden forces in nature: of external phenomena and within themselves.

Alchemy was highly popular during the fourteenth to the seventeenth centuries, as shown in Shakespeare's Sonnet 33:

> *Full many a glorious*
> *morning have I seen*
> *Flatter the mountain tops*
> *with sovereign eye,*
> *Kissing with golden face*
> *the meadows green,*
> *Gilding pale streams with*
> *heavenly alchemy.*

The halo that surrounds the heads of the Christian saints is a sign of their special holiness.

The sonnet suggests a mystical, alchemical link between the natural elements of mountain, meadows and streams.

Alchemy became the greatest passion of the age, combining the search for the philosopher's stone, which was believed would hold the power to transmute base metals into gold, with an internal (esoteric) spiritual quest. Alchemy was viewed as an art that would lead to transmutation. It was considered an embryonic science – a protochemistry; early alchemists used laboratories for their experiments and study, and made a number of discoveries that contributed to the development of chemistry.

Alchemists conducted experiments with metals and other substances and interpreted their results using astrology, cabbalism and herbalism, frequently employing the language of mystical Christian symbolism.

This was also a time when great store was set by divination. One famous diviner was Nostradamus (1503–66). Born Michel de Notredame, he came from a Jewish family in St Rémy-en-Provence and graduated as a doctor of medicine in Montpellier. He worked with plague victims in Marseilles and Avignon, but he refused to bleed his patients, as was the usual procedure. On a couple of occasions he had to flee the area because the Inquisition thought he was a wizard.

Nostradamus' prophecies were composed with the aid of magical, astrological and cabbalistic books and were published in two parts, in 1555 and 1568. Both Napoleon Bonapart and Adolf Hitler, in their respective centuries, believed that their careers had been foreseen in Nostradamus' predictions, and it is also said that he predicted the French Revolution of 1789.

During the seventeenth century, the rise of scientific rationalism and Protestantism drove magic underground. Scientific rationalism was a mechanistic philosophy that viewed the world as a machine. As Protestantism grew, it attempted to take out of religious practice what it viewed as magical elements – for example the Catholic dependence on the powers of saints'

A contemporary portrait of Nostradamus, whose prophecies are still read avidly today.

A painting from the late fifteenth century of an alchemy master preparing ingredients.

relics. During this period, these two developments in thought meant that people who practised magic did so in secret, and tended to be attracted to underground societies such as the Rosicrucians or the Freemasons.

Left: Conjurors were an accepted part of everyday life between the fourteenth and seventeenth centuries.

Neoplatonism

The philosophy of Neoplatonism originated with Plotinus (c.AD205–270). It was a synthesis of earlier philosophical thought and religious beliefs, combining alchemy and magic to provide not only an image of the universe and the human place within it, but also a method of spiritual salvation. The 'One' as a deity is the source of all goodness and reality. The One is the source from which everything flows, and the gradual dispersion of the original unity results in multiplicity and matter (which is sometimes equated with evil). Human imperfection, which is due to a flaw or the Fall,

stems from the soul's remoteness from the One. The soul is longing to return to completeness, but as the One is beyond description and cannot be reached through rational thinking, it has to be approached through ecstatic contemplative absorption. The soul has many levels: the highest is intellectual thought, and the lowest is the animating principle of the material universe. All humans have all aspects of soul within them and have to choose whether to wake the higher elements or remain immersed in the concerns of the material body.

THE MYTH OF ATLANTIS

Those who continued to work with magic, despite the movement against it, attempted to create meaning by looking for significant connections between things, and this frequently involved the use of myths. A myth is a sacred story that is shared by a group of people who find their most important meanings in it. In Western cultures mythology is often equated with fairy stories, the "unreal" or even falsehood, and contrasted with history, which is associated with the truth. However, myth has played an important part in magic by explaining how the world came to be formed, and by marking out significant relationships with ancestors and other beings. The myth of Atlantis is especially important to Western magicians. It is said to be a sunken continent that occupied most of the area of the Atlantic Ocean, and is the place from which the peoples of Europe arose.

The kings of Atlantis were said to be descended from the sons of Poseidon, the sea god.

THE ORIGINS

The myth of Atlantis has a very import-ant position in Western magic. The name "Atlantis" conjures up visions of a wonderful land of beauty and plenty, a utopian society where peace and justice reigned; a golden country lying in the midst of a wide blue sea. The legend concerns the story of an ancient island

civilization, in conflict with Athens and Egypt, which vanished in a day and a night due to spiritual disaster. It was Plato (c.428–347 BC) who first wrote about the myth in *Timaeus*, telling how a mighty power had once come out of the Atlantic Ocean. The size and position of lost Atlantis was revealed to the Athenian statesman and poet Solon by

an Egyptian priest in about 590 BC. The priest described Atlantis as a kingdom that had been much larger than Libya and Asia Minor put together, which had, some 9,000 years before, been situated beyond the Pillars of Hercules at the western end of the Mediterranean Sea. Its armies had once conquered most of the countries of the Mediterranean:

The idea of the lost land of Atlantis came from Classical Greece, where students of philosophy would discuss utopian societies and ideal states, which were governed by democratic principles or benign dictators.

A seventeenth-century map of the imagined island of Atlantis.

Now in this island of Atlantis there was a great and wonderful empire which had rule over the whole island and several others … This vast power, gathered into one, endeavoured to subdue … the whole of the region … She was pre-eminent in courage and military skill, and was the leader of the Hellenes. And when the rest fell off from her, being compelled to stand alone, after having undergone the very extremity of dangers, she defeated and triumphed over the invaders, and preserved from slavery those who were not yet subjugated, and generously liberated all the rest of us who dwelt within the pillars. But afterwards there occurred violent earthquakes and floods; and in a single day and night of misfortune all your warlike men in a body sank into the earth, and the island of Atlantis in like manner disappeared in the depths of the sea.

Ya-uli, an Atlantean high priest, according to theosophists Besant and Leadbeater.

In *Critias*, Plato describes how, after the Creation, the gods divided up the world:

Athena acquired Greece, and set up the first Athenian state, and the sea-god Poseidon received Atlantis. Poseidon divided the island between his sons to rule, and it was these kings and their descendants who built the city of Atlantis. The kings met every fifth or sixth year to discuss affairs of state after sacrificing a bull during an elaborate ceremony. For a long time the Atlanteans were virtuous but gradually they became corrupt and greedy, and Zeus decided to punish them. The gods were called to a meeting but there ….

Plato's dialogue ends in mid-sentence, so nothing more is known.

THE GOLDEN AGE

The enthusiasm among magicians for the legend of Atlantis indicates a nostalgia for a lost world and a primal state of wholeness before humans lost contact with their spiritual source. The myth forms an ideal vision of a golden age, a time in the past where there was complete social and spiritual harmony: a Garden of Eden before the Fall, when humans were in touch with divinity.

Many modern magicians search for ways to reconnect with this ideal state of existence and, at the same time, work with their internal spiritual selves. Some claim to be in telepathic communication with the erstwhile inhabitants of Atlantis; others have memories of previous incarnations spent on the island. A profusion of books appears each year on Atlantis and a popular theme among Atlantists is that the civilizations of the New and Old Worlds shared a common cultural origin that sprang from it. This would explain common myths, symbols and even language.

Atlantis and the occult

Atlantis is seen to be the home of the initiates of a secret occult tradition, which has been passed on through various sects and secret magical societies, from the Templars, the Rosicrucians, the Freemasons and various occult schools. Some of these schools have claimed to have reconstructed the entire history of Atlantis by means of spirit messages. Edgar Cayce, a well-known American psychic Christian, born in 1877, was disturbed to find out that in trance he had delivered the history of humanity dating back to Atlantis. In a science-fiction like epic, he said that Atlantis had been inhabited by a technological civilization, based on the power of crystals.

An Atlantean pyramid, as imagined in 1923 by Manly P. Hall.

THE TAROT

The methods used to reconnect with the spiritual world are various, but one that is central to many magical practices is the set of cards called the tarot. The origin of cartomancy, or divination by cards, is unknown. The practice was established in Italy, France and Germany by the late fourteenth century and has been attributed to the Knights Templars or the Gypsies, but both are unlikely. Evidence suggests that the idea of playing cards came from China, Korea or India but that the designs of the tarot came from Europe.

The tarot consists of 78 cards, and these are made up of 56 cards of the lesser arcana, and 22 cards of the greater arcana. The lesser arcana is divided into four suits: batons, cups, swords and coins. Each suit has four court cards – King, Queen, Knight and Page – and ten numbered cards. The greater arcana depicts certain symbols and images that are numbered in sequence and range from the Fool (who is unnumbered or zero) to the World (number 21). The images on the cards represent the total energies of the universe, and some magicians say that they concern

Examples of four of the Tarot cards from the Waite-Coleman Tarot deck.

The magician Eliphas Lévi, who first linked the tarot to the esoteric system of the cabbala.

A.E Waite, the co-producer with Pamela Coleman Smith of an extremely popular tarot deck.

initiation into the mysteries. They represent the stages of a life journey and, by solving the riddle that each card presents, they offer an opportunity for spiritual development. The tarot is said to speak in symbols, the language of the unconscious, and, when approached in the right manner, to open doors into the hidden reaches of the soul.

The French occultist Eliphas Lévi (1810–75), whose first work on magic, *Dogme et Rituel de la Haute Magie*, was published in 1855, linked the tarot to the esoteric system of the cabbala and the 22 letters of the Hebrew alphabet. He also connected the four suits of the lesser arcana to the four elements, and to the four letters of the divine name of God. This had a great influence on later occultists. Lévi was also largely responsible for the revival of interest in the nineteenth-century theory of astral light as a fluid force that permeated everything, and which the magician must learn to control.

The Hermetic Order of the Golden Dawn adopted Lévi's system but assigned the cards in a slightly different way; they also linked the 22 cards of the greater arcana with the 22 paths of the cabbala, and added the signs of the zodiac and the planets to combine various systems into one.

TAROT DECKS

The three most important tarot decks of the modern era are those of the Golden Dawn, A. E. Waite and Aleister Crowley. The magician A. E. Waite and the artist Pamela Coleman Smith produced an extremely popular version of the tarot pack in 1910. In 1944, Aleister Crowley (1875–1947), an ex-Golden Dawn member, published *The Book of Thoth*, and directed the artist Lady Freida Harris to illustrate a pack according to this interpretation. All three decks were dependent on a set of tarot papers called Book T, which were issued to members of the inner lodge of the Hermetic Order of the Golden Dawn. These papers suggested that the key to the tarot was found in the cabbala and that the tarot

Tarot cards are used today in many forms of divination. Said to reach the deepest parts of a person's subconscious, they can give personal and spiritual insight.

was an external symbol of the underlying pattern of the cosmos. The book includes lines from the Revelation of Saint John the Divine and suggests that the tarot is the book referred to in this work, and that only those who have been initiated into the secret mysteries can fully understand the tarot. It begins:

> *Hru the Great Angel is Set over the operations of the Secret Wisdom What thou seest write in a Book, and send it unto the Seven Abodes that are in Assiah.*
> *And I saw in the right hand of Him that sat upon the Throne a book sealed with Seven Seals. And I saw a strong Angel proclaiming with a loud voice.*
> *Who is worthy to open the Books and to loose the seals thereof?*

Only an initiate is worthy of loosening the seals and understanding the true mysteries of the tarot.

The cabbala was originally an esoteric aspect of Judaism; today it is interpreted more widely.

The cabbala

The cabbala, originally the inner and mystical aspect of Judaism, provides a framework for many magical systems – such as the tarot, astrology and alchemy – and is thought to represent every force manifested in the universe. Essentially a form of Neoplatonism, Godhead is seen to be brought down to humanity via the spheres (sephiroth) of the Tree of Life. In cabbalistic cosmology, Creation, like the descent of pure light, works downwards from AYIN (God transcendent) to EN SOF (immanent God) through to AYIN SOF OR (limitless light), which becomes manifest in the ten spheres of the cabbala. The relationships of the spheres represent the whole of existence – they are both attributes of God and aspects of human experience – and offer human beings the means of attaining spiritual oneness with the Ultimate.

The Tree of Life is used as a framework for meditation (on the qualities of a particular sphere, for example), or for 'pathworking', an active meditation that engages the imagination, while in a state of trance, on the pathways interlinking the spheres. Cabbalistic

magical training concerns training the mind through visualization – the creation of images using the imagination.

Tarot cards are often used to represent the energies and attributes of a particular path on the Tree of Life. Thus by working on the Tree of Life a magician is said to be able to reach deeper and unknown parts of his or her subconsciousness; this is said to lead to greater self understanding and also spiritual revelation. The Tree of Life represents an inner 'map' of the cosmos and a way of uniting with God.

There are many interpretations of the cabbalistic Tree of Life. This one is from Kircher's Oedipus Aegyptiacus, *1652. More modern ones have distinct pathways linking the spheres to aid meditation.*

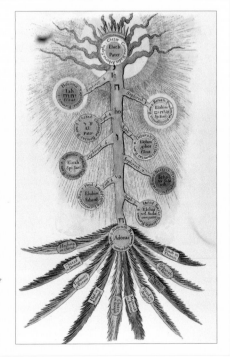

MAGICAL SOCIETIES

The word "occult" conveys the ideas of secrecy and hidden knowledge; a central component of magical organizations in the past was the transmission of esoteric wisdom through initiation rites. During the seventeenth century there was a fascination with secret societies and it was at this time that Rosicrucianism and Freemasonry were established. Rosicrucianism was founded on myths and allegories that were based on the restoration of a divine state through inner experience. The Rosicruicians used alchemy and cabbala to achieve this divine state. In similar fashion, the spiritual aspects of Freemasonry are concerned with making contact with a divine source through the symbolism of the Temple of Solomon. The nineteenth-century Theosophical Society was based on the idea that there was an ancient spiritual science concerned with the mysteries of the interaction between human beings and God. Likewise, the later nineteenth-century Hermetic Order of the Golden Dawn – a synthesis of the practices and traditions of Rosicrucianism, Freemasonry and Theosophy – was also focused on a mystical union with divinity. All these magical societies sought a higher spiritual knowledge or experience as a means of uniting with God.

A Rosicrucian diagram of the spiritual realm in relation to the descent of the reincarnating soul.

THE ROSICRUCIANS

The years 1614 and 1615 saw the publication of two short pamphlets, the *Fama* and the *Confessio*, which became known as the Rosicrucian manifestos. They were utopian myths about bringing humanity back to its divine state before the Fall, and made the stirring announcement of the dawn of a new enlightenment. Their message was framed in an allegory in which the central message was a spiritual opening to divine inner experience. According to this allegory, a Rosicrucian brother had discovered a large brass nail during building alterations. When the nail was removed it revealed a door behind, on which was written the words *"POST CCXX ANOS PATEBO"* ("After 120 years I shall reopen"). When the door was eventually opened,

... there appeared to our sight a Vault of Seven Sides ... although the Sun never shined in that Vault, nevertheless it was enlightened with another Sun ... and was situated in the upper part in the centre of the

ceiling. In the midst ... was a round altar, covered with a plate of brass, and thereon this engraven "I have made this Tomb a compendium of the Universe". Round the brim were the words "Jesus is all things to me". In the middle were four figures, enclosed in circles, whose circumscription was (1) Nowhere a Vacuum (2) The Burden of the Law (3) The Liberty of the Gospel (4) The Untouched Glory of God. Now as we had not yet seen the body of our careful and wise Father, we therefore removed the altar aside; then we lifted up a strong plate of brass and found a fair and worthy body, whole and unconsumed ... In his hand he held the book T, the which next unto our Bible is our greatest treasure.

Behind the walls of the tomb the brethren found books, magical mirrors, bells and even "ever-burning lamps". The first two manifestos were connected with a third publication, *The Chymical*

The Rosicrucian Rosy Cross as depicted by the nineteenth-century Hermetic Order of the Golden Dawn.

Wedding of Christian Rosencreutz, written in 1616 by Johann Valentin Andreae. This concerned another allegory, this time based on the mystic marriage of the soul. By setting forth an alternative to the Jesuit Order, the Rosicrucians promised a prophesied return to a state of paradise through the use of alchemy, cabbala and evangelical piety. Their aim was to promote a programme of research and reform of the sciences.

FREEMASONRY

The origins of Freemasonry are unclear; it has been linked with Rosicrucianism and the Knights Templar, but nothing is known for certain.

The history of Freemasonry is entwined with the Hermetic and cabbalistic traditions, which were studied in England during the second half of the sixteenth century. In 1717 the Grand Lodge was formed, this used a system of symbolism based on the society of stonemasons called the Operative Mason's Craft, together with ideas from the Western mystical tradition. In ancient Greek culture, much effort had been made to capture the gods' characters in stone structures, and this decorative architecture influenced the Roman architect Vitruvius, who wanted to capture the spiritual essence of building to demonstrate that the human being and the building were constructed according to the same plan. The mystical tradition that Vitruvius discovered was handed down through the medieval guilds of stonemasons, and preserved by a small group within the trade.

In the view of Freemasons, the complete human being is made up of a body, a psyche or soul, a spirit and a contact with his divine source. The human psyche contains four levels, which reflect the larger four-level structure described above. In specific terms, Freemasonry represents the psyche with the Temple of Solomon, which it describes as a three-storey temple within which one can be conscious of the presence of divinity.

Freemasonry consists of three basic degrees: Entered Apprentice; Fellow Craft; and Master Mason; as well as "higher" or "side" degrees of the *Rose Croix*. In addition there is the Knight of the Pelican and Eagle and Sovereign, Prince Rose Croix of Heredom, Grand

A nineteenth-century depiction of a Freemasonry initiation.

The ceremonies and symbols of Freemasonry as shown in the frontispiece to a nineteenth-century book on its history.

Elected Knight Kadosh and Knight of Black and White Eagle. There are also many offices within a lodge such as Worshipful Master Deacons and Wardens, which are positions rather than levels of initiation. In Britain, Masonry was responsible for keeping alive the occult tradition from the sixteenth to the nineteenth century. Freemasonry has had an important influence on contemporary magical practices, mainly the Hermetic Order of the Golden Dawn.

THE THEOSOPHICAL SOCIETY

The nineteenth century was an age of independent spiritual teachers in a time of declining established religion, when many people were looking to find a single key to solve the mysteries of the universe. Among these was Emanuel Swedenborg (1688–1772), who developed a theory of correspondences and a view of the universe as a harmonious whole, which was only temporarily disturbed by sin. This was coupled with a belief in the accessibility of the spiritual world together with a trust in the reality of a new political and religious dispensation that would bring together the various orders of science and religion and would combine them with the imagination.

The theory of magnetism propounded by Anton Mesmer (1734–1815) was also popular. This was based on the notion that the human body was surrounded by a magnetic force, which a healer could detect for therapeutic purposes. The movement that became know as spiritualism also attracted many people who believed that the spirits of the dead could be channelled by mediums who had special psychic powers.

HELENA BLAVATSKY

This was the climate of ideas from which the Theosophical Society emerged. It was founded by Helena Petrovna Blavatsky (1831–91) and Henry Steel Olcott (1832–1907) in 1875, and it played a major part in spreading occult ideas at the turn of the nineteenth century. At its inception its objectives were to form a universal brotherhood of humanity without distinction of race, creed, sex, caste or colour; to encourage the study of comparative religion, philosophy and science; and to investigate unexplained laws of nature and the powers latent in humans. These last two objectives were later developed by HPB, as she was popularly known, in *Isis Unveiled*, subtitled "A Master-Key to the Mysteries of Ancient and Modern Science and Theology" (1877), in which she attempted to integrate science and religion. At this stage the theosophical doctrine was still in its formative stages, but was being structured around the idea that there was an ancient, secret spiritual

Anton Mesmer, the Austrian physician who popularized the idea that the human body was surrounded by a magnetic force, a belief that still holds sway in many different natural therapies.

science known to a brotherhood of adepts who would transmit it to select individuals. Blavatsky claimed that science was called "magic" in the far-off days and explored the primary force of nature's mysteries within a universe of cyclic phenomena. These mysteries were in essence the interaction between God and humanity.

The core of Blavatsky's theosophy was that "Man must know himself" and that ordinary religion was just dogma with no scientific foundation. Science, too, was unsatisfactory because it ignored the unseen being. For Blavatsky, the whole was constituted of both the visible and the invisible, the facts of nature being grasped from within the human body as well as without. She was an adamant anti-Darwinian, believing in the spiritual evolution of the psyche rather than the physical evolution of primates. The role of theosophy was to investigate universal religious wisdom by means of science.

Blavatsky claimed that her cosmology was based on her contact with a brotherhood of Himalayan masters whom she

Helena Blavatsky, a co-founder and prominent personality of the Theosophical Society.

Henry Steel Olcott, co-founder of the Theosophical Society.

Annie Besant, a leading Theosophist and a supporter of rights for women, as a young woman, c.1868.

Madame Blavatsky with the emblem of the Theosophical Society above her head. At the centre of the emblem is the six-pointed star of the Seal of Solomon, a sign of the macrocosm, surmonted by a crowned swastica, a symbol of light and life, and surrounded by an ouroboros, a snake biting its own tail and representing cyclicity. The Egyptian ankh to the left symbolizes life, while the square topped by a triangle represents human beings: the triangle signifies the spiritual element, while the square portrays the material dimension.

of women's rights and a socialist, took a maternal charge of Krishnamurti. Eventually turning from Theosophy, Krishnamurti developed his own spiritual teachings on finding truth within and liberation from organized religion. The Theosophical Society has had a major influence on modern Western magic, particularly on Samuel Liddell "MacGregor" Mathers and William Westcott, who were founders of the Hermetic Order of the Golden Dawn. The Society was also responsible for introducing Eastern ideas about reincarnation to Western occultism.

called the "Great White Brotherhood". The masters formed a "cosmic radio" to link humans with the chiefs of the divine hierarchy, which ruled the cosmos.

Blavatsky published *The Secret Doctrine* in 1888 and sought to explain universal creation as a scheme by which the primal unity of an unmanifest divine being filtered down into consciously evolving beings. The spirit was attempting, through a series of rebirths and by moving through the cosmos from planet to planet, to recover from a fall from divine grace. According to Blavatsky's view, a lord of the world originally came from Venus with several helpers who were, in descending order of authority:

Buddha; Mahachshan; Manu (who had an assistant Master Morya or "M"); and Maitreya (who had an assistant Master Koot Hoomi or "KH"). The two assistants Master Morya and Master Koot Hoomi were Blavatsky's masters and probably played a vital role in the founding of the Theosophical Society.

In 1909 a leading Theosophist Charles Leadbeater "discovered" a young Indian boy named Jiddu Krishnamurti who he thought to physically be the avatar – the incarnation of divine consciousness on earth – of Maitreya, and the new Messiah and World Teacher. Annie Besant, a leading free-thinker advocate

Annie Besant with Krishnamurti, the Theosophical Society's chosen World Leader, who later dissociated himself from the organization.

THE GOLDEN DAWN

The creation of the magical society called the Hermetic Order of the Golden Dawn in the late nineteenth century marked an important milestone in the history of Western magic. It was primarily a synthesis of a number of occult traditions, and brought the mystical union with the divine to the forefront of modern magic by combining Hermeticism (which suggested that divine powers are latent within human beings, who may recover them by learning their own true natures) with a study of cabbala (through which humans can achieve union with God by the study of the Tree of life).

The Golden Dawn resembled the Societas Rosicruciana and Freemasonry with its structure of initiations, elaborate ceremonies and use of occult symbolism. Like theosophy it offered leading roles to women, and a number of well-known women played a leading part – such as the actress Florence Farr, the Irish nationalist Maud Gonne, Moina Bergson, sister of the philosopher Henri Bergson, and wife of the founding member Samuel "MacGregor" Mathers, and Annie Horniman, the tea heiress. The society also attracted the eminent Irish poet William Butler Yeats, who had joined the Theosophical Society as an art student in the 1880s.

THE FOUNDING MEMBERS

The Hermetic Order of the Golden Dawn was founded in London in 1888 by three members of the Societas Rosicruciana in Anglia, a Masonic-Rosicrucian body formed by Robert Wentworth Little in 1865 and based on the Rosicrucian legend of Christian Rosencreutz. They were called William Wynn Westcott (1848–1915), a doctor, coroner, Mason and

Left: The Irish nationalist Maud Gonne, a member of the Golden Dawn.

William Butler Yeats, the Irish poet, dramatist and member of the Hermetic Order of the Golden Dawn.

Above: Annie Horniman inherited a large fortune from her father's tea business; she was a theatre manager and founder of the repertory system, as well as a member of the Golden Dawn.

member of the Theosophical Society, William Robert Woodman (1828–91), a doctor, Mason, cabbala enthusiast and Supreme Magus of the Societas Rosicruciana, and Samuel Liddell "MacGregor" Mathers (1854–1918), a Mason who "spent almost half a lifetime in the British Museum in London and the Arsenal library in Paris, delving into magical and alchemical texts". Mathers, a particularly colourful and flamboyant character who assumed the title of Count MacGregor of Glenstrae, was

Dr William Wynn Westcott, co-founder along with Samuel Mathers and William Woodman of the Hermetic Order of the Golden Dawn.

Samuel Liddell "MacGregor" Mathers was mainly responsible for bringing together various magical systems into the Hermetic Order of the Golden Dawn. A lover of ceremony, he is here shown performing the Rites of Isis.

responsible for constructing a coherent magical system from the various elements of Masonic symbolism, cabbala, tarot, astrology, numerology and ritual magic. A fourth founder member, who died soon after the establishment of the Order, was the Rev. A. F. A. Woodford, a country vicar, who had acquired some manuscripts in cypher from the mystic and would-be magician Fred Hockley. He sent them to Westcott to decode and they proved to be a skeletal

description, in English, of five hitherto unknown rituals of a Rosicrucian nature which the writer had witnessed – presumably in Germany, as the manuscript also contained the address of a certain Anna Sprengel of Nuremburg, allegedly a high-grade Rosicrucian. Westcott asked Mathers for his co-operation in working up the bare bones of the system into a coherent whole suitable for "lodge-work", and to this Mathers agreed.

EARLY SPIRITUAL LINKS

In October 1887 Westcott wrote to Fraulein Sprengel asking for occult teaching. This was given in a correspondence course and honorary grades were conferred upon Westcott, Mathers and Woodman. A charter was given for the establishment of a Golden Dawn Temple to work the grades in the cypher manuscript. Temples were set up in London, Weston-super-Mare, Bradford, Edinburgh and Paris. In 1891 the correspondence with Anna Sprengel stopped: a communication from Germany informed Westcott that his correspondent was dead and that no further information would be given to the English students; if they wished to establish a link with the Secret Chiefs of the Order they must do it themselves.

Mathers and Westcott were both friends of Madame Blavatsky and, while she lived, there was a friendly alliance between the Theosophical Society and the Golden Dawn. The roots of the two societies are deeply intertwined and the two organizations saw themselves as an élite, secretly working towards humanity's evolution. In 1892 Blavatsky died; Mathers claimed to have established links with the Secret Chiefs and supplied rituals for a Golden Dawn Second Order: the Red Rose and the Cross of Gold, based on the legend of Christian Rosencreutz. These rituals were adopted and a "Vault of the Adepts" became the controlling force behind the Temples of the Golden Dawn in the Order.

Mathers based his system on Eliphas Lévi's system of magic, which itself drew on Mesmer's theories that the planets influenced human beings

Mesmer's theories of magnetism, as a universal fluid that could be controlled by human will, were extremely popular in the nineteenth century. Here a physician attempts a cure through hypnotism.

through the fluid of animal magnetism. Mesmer claimed to have discovered that animal magnetism, as a universal medium, could be directly controlled by the human will. This became a basis of modern magical theory.

Lévi identified animal magnetism as the "astral light", which, like a magnet, had opposite poles that carried good and evil, and responded to the human will.

He said, "To direct the magnetic forces is then to destroy or create forms; to produce all appearance, or to destroy bodies; it is to exercise the mighty powers of Nature".

ORGANIZED MAGIC

Eclectic in nature, the Golden Dawn used many deity forms including Hebrew, Christian and classical, and

Symbols of the Hermetic Order of the Golden Dawn

Samuel 'MacGregor' Mathers, a co-founder of the Golden Dawn, was fond of saying 'There is no part of me that is not of the Gods'. He paraphrased this from the Book of the Dead. Mathers and other Golden Dawn members used god forms from various cultures as currents or potencies of energies, which could be tapped during ritual. These energies were embodied in the design of wands, banners and badges such as these.

The Order of the Pectoral, with signs of the zodiac. The swastika, as an emblem of light and life, was a spiritual sign before it was adopted by the Nazis.

Pectoral Cross with Hebrew characters showing Judaeo-Christian influences, particularly through Rosicrucianism.

A symbol used in the Hermes Lodge of the Stella Matutina. The triangle represents the number three, symbolizing the highest realm of the spiritual world.

these reflected the spiritual interests of its various members. Mathers declared, in true theosophical fashion, that the order respected the truths of all religions, and he created a flexible system of magic, which could be used in many different ways.

Mathers loved the ornate trappings and highly organized aspects of ceremonial magic, and he ran the Golden Dawn like a military organization. But in 1900 his imperious behaviour eventually caused a rebellion among the other members. Mathers had accused Westcott of forging the foundation documents, and the other members of the Golden Dawn claimed that Mathers had put the authority of the order under question. This infuriated Mathers who decided to curse them all; according to one account, he took a packet of dried peas, rattled them violently in a sieve, and called on the demonic forces of Beelzebub and Seth-Typhon to avenge his opponents.

REBELLIONS AND SCHISMS

Further disagreements splintered the Golden Dawn, and the poet William Butler Yeats took control of the rebel faction for a time. The Christian mystic A. E. Waite took command of the London temple. Born in Brooklyn, New York, Waite was brought up a Roman Catholic, but became interested in spiritualism and theosophy before he joined the Golden Dawn in 1891. He wrote a number of books and is perhaps best known for designing the most widely used modern tarot pack, illustrated by Pamela Coleman Smith.

The Golden Dawn eventually fragmented into four daughter organizations: the Isis-Urania Temple, a Christian mystical organization run by Waite and others; the Stella Matutina run by R. W. Felkin and J. W. Brodie-Innes; the Alpha et Omega run by Brodie-Innes and Mathers; and the pagan A.A. headed by Aleister Crowley.

Aleister Crowley wearing a robe of the Golden Dawn. Note the Rosy Cross on his chest.

A "certificate" of initiation into the Golden Dawn showing that Alan Bennett, a disciple of Aleister Crowley, was initiated by Samuel Mathers.

Below: Samuel Mathers and Mina Mathers, his wife, dressed as priest and priestess.

ALEISTER CROWLEY

Aleister Crowley, a one-time member of the Golden Dawn, is perhaps the most notorious occultist of the twentieth century and is famous for being a "black magician". He is one of the few people whose reputation extends outside the world of magic and witchcraft. Crowley, the self-styled "beast", was a controversial figure and courted publicity of the worst kind, but he was a talented magician and his ideas about magic remain influential today. He developed a system of magical anarchism – his declared creed was: "do what thou wilt shall be the whole of the law" – and his ideas have also shaped the development and organization of modern witchcraft.

"The beast" – Aleister Crowley.

Edward Alexander Crowley was brought up a strict member of the Plymouth Brethren, but he decided to rebel, and as he explains in his autohagiography, at the age of 12 years he "simply went over to Satan's side". Crowley eventually developed his own theology, which was based on personal communication with the Devil against the forces of good, which had "constantly oppressed" him. Thus, Crowley's magical work is a direct rebellion against Christianity

THE BOOK OF LAW

Crowley joined the Golden Dawn in 1898 after leaving Cambridge. In April 1904, Crowley "received" The Book of the Law from an intelligence named Aiwass, mediated through his clair-voyant wife Rose Kelly. From this he developed the religion of Thelema. Thelema (which means "the will" in Greek) was said by Crowley to represent a new aeon, which would release humankind from its obsession with fear and its consciousness of sin. Crowley's brand of magic was based on Lévi's theories, which made the human being the centre of the universe. Lévi's view of magic emphasized finding the "True Will", which is the magician's magical identity – his or her "true self". Drawing on these ideas, Crowley claimed that each individual should be the centre of his or her own universe.

Aleister Crowley's writing on magic is widely regarded by magicians as

brilliant; his excessive, publicity-seeking behaviour, on the other hand, is often deplored (except by his direct followers, the Thelemites) as giving magic a "bad name". In Crowley's scheme of things, the knowledge of the will is the basis of a magician's empowerment, and the evolution of what he termed the Aeon of Horus is the aeon of individualism. Crowley's aim was the emancipation of humankind by the announcement of an "unconditional truth", which was "appropriate for the present evolutionary stage". This truth was to create an interpretation of the cosmos from an egocentric and practical viewpoint.

Thelema was a new cosmology and set of ethics for the Aeon of Horus. This marked a new stage evolving from the previous stage of the worship of the Father, which had followed on from the worship of the Mother. The Aeon of Horus was thus the aeon of the Child, which would, according to Crowley, destroy the Christian formula of the "Dying God" by offering complete moral independence, in this way releasing humankind from fear and the conse-quences of sin. Humanity was to govern itself, and self-sacrifice was viewed as

Aleister Crowley in Golden Dawn robes.

romantic folly, the sacrifice of the strong to the weak was, according to this view, against the principles of evolution.

Do What Thou Wilt

From these ideas Crowley developed the maxim "Do what thou wilt shall be the whole of the law"', meaning that every person had the right to fulfil their own will and in so doing had the forces of the universe behind them. He defined the magician as one who knows the "Science and Art of causing Change to occur in conformity with Will". He believed that magic was the science of understanding the self and its conditions, and was the art of putting that knowledge into practical action.

Thus Crowley's religion of Thelema was based on the idea that the individual was a star within its own galaxy. "In a galaxy each star has its own magnitude, characteristics and direction, and the celestial harmony is best maintained by its attending to its own business."

A self-portrait. Note that the medal around his neck is inscribed 666, denoting the beast from the Book of Revelations in the Christian Bible.

The certificate acknowledging Aleister Crowley as a member of the High Order of the Freemasons of the 33rd Rite in Scotland.

Crowley's version of magic puts the magician as human being in control of his or her will firmly at the centre of magical practices and thus in control of the universe; this creates a sharp break from ideas of theosophical spiritual evolutionism and the Christian notion of union with God as expounded by some members of the Hermetic Order of the Golden Dawn.

LIBERATION PHILOSOPHY

Aleister Crowley was a controversial figure, but there is no doubt that he was extremely influential in the shaping of modern magic. Crowley's major philosophical influence was through a liberation philosophy that focused on recreating a powerful magical self, and his impact stemmed from his connection of themes of human evolution (the Aeon of Horus) with modernism (the development of the self through the will). He is also identified as playing a part in the creation of modern witchcraft as a nature religion, although how much he actually contributed is contested. His poem, *Hymn to Pan*, written in 1929, displays classical themes combined with a focus on nature:

Thrill with the lissome lust of the light,
O man! My man!
Come careering out of the night
Of Pan! Io Pan!
Io Pan! Io Pan! Come over the sea
From Sicily and from Arcady!
Roaming as Bacchus, with fauns and pards
And nymphs and satyrs for thy guards,
On a milk-white ass, come over the sea
To me, to me,
Come with Apollo in bridal dress
(Shepherdess and pythoness)
Come with Artemis, silken shod,
And wash thy white thigh, beautiful God,
In the moon of the woods, on the
marble mount,
The dimpled dawn of the amber fount!
Dip the purple of passionate prayer
In the crimson shrine, the scarlet snare,
The soul that startles in eyes of blue
To watch thy wantoness weeping through
The tangled grove, the gnarl'd bole
Of the living tree that is spirit and soul
And body and brain – come over the sea,
(Io Pan! Io Pan!)
Devil or god, to me, to me,
My man! my man! ...

ORDO TEMPLI ORIENTIS

Crowley was influenced by Eastern schools of thought such as Buddhism and Tantrism, and joined the Ordo Templi Orientis in 1912, becoming its leader in 1922. The Ordo Templi Orientis (OTO) had been founded at the beginning of the twentieth century

Aleister Crowley towards the end of his life.

A card from the tarot deck designed by Crowley and painted by Frieda Harris in 1941.

by Karl Kellner, a German Mason and occultist. It is claimed that it was the product of the German occult revival, which was sparked off by the opening of the Berlin branch of the Theosophical Society in 1884. The OTO was a modern form of Templarism, drawing on the Knights Templars movement, which had been suppressed in the fourteenth century on the grounds of heresy, sodomy and bestiality. Kellner is said to have been initiated into the use of "the sexual Current" by an Arab called Soliman ben Aifa and two Indian Tantrics, Bhima Sen Pratap and Shri Mahatma Agamya Paramahamsa. He was also influenced by a group of French followers of the American occultist P. B. Randolph. The OTO made grand claims that it possessed the key that would open up all Masonic and Hermetic secrets through the teaching of sexual magic. Reuss invited Crowley to rewrite the OTO rituals, and it has been suggested that Crowley saw the OTO as the first great

"The Resurrection of Zoroaster", a drawing by Austin Osman Spare, 1905.

"Blood on the Moon" by Austin Osman Spare, 1955.

A symbolic painting for Crowley's Temple of the A.A., the Order of the Silver Star.

magical order to accept the Law of Thelema, and by doing so to slough off the techniques of ceremonial magic and to revive pagan elements of ecstasy and wonder as the keys to the "Mysteries of Man".

AUSTIN OSMAN SPARE (1886–1956)

Austin Osman Spare was a pupil of Crowley, and he was also the protégé of a Mrs Patterson, who was said to be a hereditary witch descended from a line of witches from Salem, Massachusetts. Spare developed a method of "atavistic resurgence" – the evocation of beings from the primitive depths of the mind, which could make themselves known through visions and art. His magical philosophy was based on the power of the will to influence the subconscious mind, and he believed that it was possible to instruct the subconscious mind through the creation of personal symbols known as sigils. A sigil could be implanted into the unconscious by making the mind blank at the time of a magical act, at sexual orgasm, or through self-hypnosis. Spare's "Cult of the Zos and the Kia" – or Zos Kia Cultus – was informed by his contact with Mrs Patterson and was based on the idea that it was possible to retrace earlier existences. After locating the first personality (Zos) it could be transcended and merged with the void (which he called Kia) through sexual union. Spare's magical ideas have formed an important part of chaos magic practice. Chaos magic is the ultimate expression of liberation philosophy in magical practices.

DION FORTUNE

Considered one of the leading occultists of her time, Dion Fortune was perhaps one of the first occult writers to approach magic and hermetic concepts using the precepts of psychology, in particular of Jung and Freud. Her role was a significant one and the written material she left behind is still used today, valued in particular for its rich source for rituals, and its pagan themes. Dion Fortune also succeeded in bringing about a renewal of interest in British myths and legends, and their importance in the country's historical inheritance. She was also instrumental in emphasising the importance of balance between male and female elements in magic.

A rare photograph of the young Dion Fortune. The picture was taken in 1911, at the beginning of her studies at Warwick Horticultural College.

Dion Fortune was born Violet Mary Firth on 6 December 1890 to a wealthy family in the steel business. She adapted the family motto, "Deo, non Fortuna", to create her magical name. A leading magician of her time, Dion Fortune had been initiated into the Hermetic Order of the Golden Dawn in 1919 but, according to her biographer Alan Richardson, she disliked the idea of pouring the "regenerative spiritual force of the East into the group-soul of the British Empire". Being a staunch British nationalist, Dion Fortune also reacted against the Eastern influence in theosophy and turned instead to a mystical Christianity and what she saw as the indigenous British mythology of King Arthur and the Holy Grail.

Acting on these convictions, in 1923 she formed a Christian Mystic Lodge of the Theosophical Society with the aim of interpreting Christianity in terms of theosophy and vice versa, but she eventually rejected the ideas of the Theosophical Society in 1928 and went on to develop her own magical society.

A pupil of the occultist Theodore Moriarty, who taught that the "Christ Principle" had first been propounded in Atlantis and was manifested through Horus, Mithras, Quetzalcoatl and Buddha, Dion Fortune began to form her own magical contacts. During the winter of 1923–4 she contacted the people she referred to as her secret chiefs, and in 1927 she left the Hermetic Order of the Golden Dawn to found the Fraternity of the Inner Light (still in existence today as the Society of the Inner Light).

Fortune's secret chiefs included a trinity of masters, with Melchisedec of Salem as the source. These three chiefs sent out three distinct "rays" of wisdom, which were defined as the following: the Hermetic, which was concerned with philosophy and ritual; the Orphic or Green Ray, which was devoted to earth mysteries; and the Mystic Ray, concerned with the mysteries of the Son.

From 1926 Dion Fortune published a number of books on magical cosmology,

For Dion Fortune the Knights of the Round Table represented a chivalric era that could be magically tapped into.

The death of King Arthur and his passage to another plane was central to his mystic significance.

cabbala and practical magic, as well as many novels with an occult theme, the most famous being *The Sea Priestess*, first published in 1938.

THE INFLUENCE OF CARL JUNG

Carl Gustav Jung created an individual practice of spiritual rebirth, and he has been called a prophet by spiritual seekers; it has also been claimed that Jungian psychology has helped to legitimize modern paganism, and indeed his psychology has had a major influence on modern magic, primarily through the work of Dion Fortune. Carl Gustav Jung was the founder of analytical psychology. His methods included using the active imagination and amplifying dream and fantasy images; he thought that people from every society were predisposed to form what he called archetypal images – certain symbols that were found cross-culturally in mythology, fairy tales and religious iconography. During the period 1914–18 Jung experienced a psychological breakdown, and for the rest of his life he sought explanations for what had

The ideas of Swiss psychologist Carl Gustav Jung had a profound influence on the magical work of Dion Fortune.

happened to him, trying to understand the images and symbols that had arisen from his unconscious. Jung attempted to liberate the unconscious and developed what has since turned out to be a form of spiritual cult based on trying to understand the mystical process of "inner reality", which will hopefully produce a new secret wisdom. Jung took the idea of the unconscious seriously and developed techniques for encouraging dissociation – freeing the mind from its usual patterns of conscious thought – so that the unconscious could regulate actions.

Much of Carl Jung's theory stemmed from a powerful dream that he once had of a house with two different floors: he took the upper storey to represent his consciousness and the ground floor to symbolize his unconsciousness. From the ground floor was a stairway leading down to a cellar, the cellar led in turn to a cave. This is how he described the dream:

I was in a house I did not know, which had two storeys. It was "my house". I found myself in the upper storey where there was a kind of salon furnished with fine pieces in rococo style ... It occurred to me that I did not know what the lower floor looked like. Descending the stairs, I reached the ground floor. There everything was much older ... The furnishings were medieval; the floors were of red brick. Everywhere it was rather dark ... Beyond it, I discovered a stone stairway that led down into the cellar.

Descending again, I found myself in a beautifully vaulted room, which looked exceedingly ancient ... I knew that the walls dated from Roman times ... I looked more closely at the floor. It was of stone slabs, and in one of these I discovered a ring. When I pulled it, the stone slab lifted, again I saw a stairway of narrow stone steps leading down into the depths ... I descended, and entered a low cave cut into the rock. Thick dust lay on the floor, and in the dust were scattered bones

Much of Dion Fortune's work focused on the magical power of the Goddess as the feminine aspect of a cosmic polarity. Isis, as the sea priestess in one of her novels, was especially important.

and broken pottery, like the remains of a primitve culture. I discovered two human skulls, obviously very old and half disintegrated. Then I awoke.

Interpreting this house as an image of his psyche, Jung saw his consciousness as represented by the salon; the ground floor as his first level of unconsciousness; while the cave represented the world of the primitive human within himself, an area that he thought was scarcely reached by consciousness.

Jung's main theme was of the evolution of consciousness. The first stage of this process was through contacting the "world of memories", which led to a rebirth through the realm of the underworld, the ancestors and the dead. He said that his psychoanalytic techniques were like an archaeological excavation and involved using the active imagination to contact the ancestral past.

The unconscious, for Jung, consisted of all the forgotten material from an individual's own past and the inherited behavioural traces of the "human spirit". Contact with what he called the "collective unconscious" – symbolized by gods – led to access to wisdom and universal human experience. Jung also developed notions of what he called the animus and the anima. The animus was

the masculine aspect of a woman's psyche, while the anima was the corresponding feminine part of a man's psyche. His psychology put much

emphasis on integrating the contra sexual other. In other words, a woman must get in touch with her "masculine" psychic self and a man his "feminine" to achieve psychic harmony.

THE HARMONIOUS UNION

In her magical novels, Dion Fortune utilizes Jung's notions of animus and anima as masculine and feminine forces, whereby a woman develops her masculinity and a man his femininity.

In *The Sea Preistess*, sea priestesses and priests came from the mythical island of Atlantis – which was for Fortune, as for many occultists, the home of divine wisdom – and engaged in selective breeding rites to pass on magical lore. The work focused on the magical power of the Goddess, as the feminine part of a polarity underpinning the cosmos, and, according to the historian Ronald Hutton, drew on three influences: her reading of D. H. Lawrence; her husband Thomas Penry Evans' interest in the god Pan; and the interest shown in

Dion Fortune pictured with her husband on the left, and an unknown friend on the right.

the Great Mother and women's mysteries by Charles Seymour, her magical partner. As Isis, goddess of nature and the fertility of the land, the sea priestess draws her partner, the Lord of the Sun into magical union:

Isis of Nature awaiteth the coming of her Lord the Sun. She calls him. She draws him from the place of the dead, the Kingdom of Amenti, where all things are forgotten. And he comes to her in his boat called Millions of Years, and the earth grows green with the springing grain. For the desire of Osiris answereth unto the call of Isis. And so it will ever be in the hearts of men, for thus the gods have formed them.

At the beginning of World War Two, Dion Fortune became involved in a number of magical operations against Germany. Seeing Britain as being under threat from the forces of evil, she organized a magical meditation group from the Society of the Inner Light to confront the evils of Hitler's Nazi forces. Fortune wrote weekly letters to her students between 1939 and 1942, and every Sunday morning from 12.15 until 12.30 members were asked to meditate on the forces of good overcoming evil.

FORTUNE'S LEGACY

Dion Fortune's work has greatly influenced modern magic, especially the practices, rituals and ceremonies of witchcraft, which is focused on the Goddess. Her ideas and the words she wrote have influenced many different aspects of magic, and she is respected by diverse groups of people.

Dion Fortune's work has also brought a renewed focus on British mythology – especially that of King Arthur – that has revitalized links with historical traditions, and she has also helped to bring about an emphasis on the spiritual harmony of balancing feminine and masculine aspects of the psyche in magical practice.

Inside the Temple of the Grail by W. Hauschild. The Grail represented a source of spiritual wisdom for Dion Fortune.

Dion Fortune and her Society of the Inner Light fought a spiritual Battle of Britain to protect the country from invasion by Hitler's forces.

WITCHCRAFT TODAY

Modern witchcraft, or Wicca as it is also known, is a form of spirituality that seeks harmony with nature. Usually celebrating eight seasonal festivals, witches honour nature – both within their bodies, which are seen as sacred, and the wider environment. Combining a positive view of women and an ecological awareness, this new form of religion seeks a holistic way of experiencing and understanding the world. This modern definition of witchcraft is very different to that of the early modern era, when witches were viewed as evil by the Christian church. This chapter examines the different strands of witchcraft that are practised today, and highlights the various influences and personalities involved in the movement.

TODAY'S WITCHES

Modern witchcraft is a far cry from the witchcraft imagined and created by the Christian Church during the witch hunts of the early modern period in Europe. Rather than being in league with the Devil and practising evil acts, today's witches are seeking a relationship with nature and the changing seasons of the natural world, experienced within themselves as an intuitive understanding. Reclaiming the word "witch" not as an anti-social person who is seen to have magical powers in small-scale communities, but rather as the cunning woman or man of the European village, they attune themselves with the powers of nature. All of nature – the land, mountains, lakes – as well as the past, as seen through ancient cultures, is viewed as sacred.

Modern witches relate to what they see as a time when people were more in contact with nature and the natural environment. Here, at Trethevey in Cornwall, England, offerings have been left near prehistoric rock carvings.

Thus the witchcraft that is becoming increasingly popular today is not the witchcraft practised in small indigenous societies around the world, nor the diabolic type of witchcraft imagined by the Christian church during the European witch hunts. It is a witchcraft that is a form of spirituality: modern witchcraft is a religious practice that venerates nature. It was created in the 1950s using the structure of Western high magic ritual to worship the natural forces inherent in nature personified as various gods and goddesses. This form of witchcraft is not part of an ancient pre-Christian paganism, but instead draws on many sources from the Western magic tradition as well as some of the craft magic of the country cunning folk.

Modern witchcraft is gaining many new members who are disenchanted with mainstream religions; which are increasingly seen by many as being out of touch with direct spiritual experience. People are also attracted to witchcraft because it views women and sexuality as sacred, and this marks an important distinction between this new form of religion and more orthodox faiths, which frequently hold that women are in some ways inferior or less spiritual than men.

Another reason for its appeal is that as ecological awareness increases, modern witchcraft, as part of a wider group of pagan practices, offers a spirituality which is in tune with the natural world – it seeks harmony with nature, rather than its domination or control.

Witchcraft is just one spiritual path within a group of magical practices

A modern witches' altar showing a pentangle, a five-sided star symbolic of the union of the five senses of the human body – sight, hearing, smell, taste and touch – and of the four elements – fire, air, earth and water – and of the spirit.

commonly referred to as paganism. The term "pagan" comes from the Latin *paganus*, meaning "rustic", and was first used to distinguish unfavourably those who did not belong to the dominant urban faith of Christianity. More recently, historians have debated the origins of the word, and it has been suggested that it originally referred to non-military civilians – those not enrolled in the army of God. Another suggestion was that the word *pagani* was used to designate followers of an older religion when the earlier, non-military meaning had ceased to have relevance. However, by the end of the nineteenth century, "pagan" had a clear association with the countryside and the natural world, and this is largely because of its association with the Romantic movement.

Romanticism was one of a range of alternative political visions in the nine-teenth century. Drawing on Renaissance theories of the connections or corres-pondences between the material world and the creative imagination, nature was seen as visible spirit; Romanticism involved a heightened sensitivity to the natural world. The Romantic movement was a reaction against the Enlighten-ment's celebration of reason, progress and notions of a common humanity and universal truth. By contrast, Romanticism valued the individual, the relative and the internal; it explored different levels of consciousness, the supernatural and mythic interpretations of the world. Wild woods, once seen as a threat to the forces of civilization, now offered the opportunity of solitude, contemplation and oneness with nature. The experi-ence of nature became a spiritual act: nature was not only beautiful, but was uplifting and morally healing. This was particularly well expressed in the works of poets such as Wordsworth, Coleridge, Blake, Byron and Keats.

Inspired by the spirit of the Romantic movement and by his knowledge of Western magic and folklore, Gerald Gardner, the founder of the modern witchcraft movement, crafted a new religion based on the creation of a sacred ceremonial circle in which gods,

The land is imbued with history and mythology as here in Cornwall, England, where the Inner Ward of Tintagel Castle, the legendary birth place of King Arthur, may be seen above the wizard Merlin's Cave.

goddesses and the spirits of nature could be invoked. This religion of witchcraft would come to take a prominent place in the spiritual and cultural history of Western Europe, the United States, Australia and other parts of the world.

Modern witchcraft is a new religion – its roots cannot be traced back to an ancient pre-Christian pagan tradition. It draws its inspiration from the past, and although often archaeologically and historically inaccurate in its claims, it nevertheless is in tune with a different, more holistic way of understanding the world, one that would probably have been understood by our ancestors.

The traditional European view of natural springs as sacred places survives today at "clootie wells", where rags are tied to nearby trees as offerings to the spirit of the place.

GERALD GARDNER

The founder of modern witchcraft, Gerald Gardner claimed that he had been initiated into a witch coven in the New Forest, England, in 1939, by a woman named "Old Dorothy". Whether this is true or not remains unclear. However, Gardner was deeply influenced by the work of Margaret Murray who stated that the victims of the early modern witch hunts were practitioners of a surviving paganism which she described as the "Old Religion". Murray's ideas have since been disproved – modern witchcraft is not a form of the ancient paganism practised in pre-Christian times – but her influence on the birth of a new religion created by Gardner is enormous. In 1951, the repeal of the Witchcraft and Vagrancy Acts provided Gardner with the opportunity of promoting and publicizing his witch religion.

Gerald Gardner, thought by many to be the founder of modern witchcraft.

The form that modern witchcraft has taken is largely due to the imagination and creative flair of Gerald Gardner (1884–1964). He united paganism with the figure of the witch; he was what the historian Ronald Hutton calls the originator of a countercultural religion based on a nature goddess and a horned god. Gardner argued that witchcraft was an ancient, pre-Christian, pagan mystery tradition.

THE BEGINNINGS

Gardner had a keen interest in magic and at various times in his life was involved in Freemasonry, spiritualism, Buddhism and other, magical practices. He put many magical ideas and practices in his book *Witchcraft Today*. It was published in 1954, after the repeal of the laws against witchcraft in Britain, and it became the foundation text of modern witchcraft. Gardner was helped by his friend Ross Nichols (then leader of the Ancient Druid Order, and later the founder of the Order of Bards, Ovates and Druids) in the creation of a series of rituals, that were conducted within a purified circle, and the aim of which was to contain and channel the magical powers released from the participants' bodies.

At one time an owner/manager of tea and rubber plantations in Ceylon, North Borneo and Malaya, Gardner later became an inspector in the Malay customs service. He retired to London in 1936 at the age of 52, then moved to the New Forest in 1938. It was there that he joined the Rosicrucian Theatre in Christchurch, and was, so he says, initiated into a surviving coven by a mysterious woman

A modern witchcraft Yule altar with decorations that represent the seasonal festival.

named "Old Dorothy". He worked with this coven until the late 1940s, forming a magical partnership with a woman called "Dafo". In 1947 they created a company to buy a plot of land near a naturist club in St Albans in Hertfordshire, England, and there erected a reconstruction of a sixteenth-century witch's cottage. This cottage, which had cabbalistic symbols painted on the inside, provided the focus for a working coven, which was run by Gerald Gardner and Dafo in the early 1950s.

MARGARET MURRAY

Gardner was greatly influenced by the Egyptologist Margaret Murray. In 1921 she had published a book called *The Witch-Cult in Western Europe* in which she stated that the victims of the early modern witch hunts were practitioners of a surviving pagan religion. Murray claimed that an incarnate deity, in the form of a god, had been worshipped but that this may have been because the god superseded the Mother Goddess; she said that the position of the chief woman was obscure, but that the worship of a female deity had probably been supplanted by that of the male. The witch-craft rites varied with the seasons, but "The greater number of the ceremonies appear to have been practised for the purpose of securing fertility", and a marriage took place, usually once a year.

In her autobiography, Murray describes how ancient religion was her pet subject and that during World War I she researched witchcraft as she was prevented from working in Egypt. She explains how she started:

"I started with the usual idea that witches were all old women suffering from illusions about the Devil and that their persecutors were wickedly prejudiced and perjured. I worked only from contemporary records, and when I suddenly realised that the so-called Devil was simply a disguised man I was startled, almost alarmed, by the way the recorded facts fell into place, and showed that the witches were members of an old, primitive form of religion and the records had been made by members of a new and persecuting form."

A modern representation of a wicker man, a contemporary link with supposed pagan celebrations of the past.

Giving the impression that there was a fairly uniform surviving pagan religion in Western Europe, Murray's work focused on the notion that witchcraft centred on fertility. The horned god represented the generative powers of nature and was personified by a male

A portrait of Margaret Murray, Egyptologist and influential anthropologist.

person during coven rituals. Sabbaths were held four times a year at All Hallows, Candlemas, May Day and Lammas during which there was much feasting, sacrifice of animals and children, processional dances and ritualized sexual intercourse to promote fertility. Homage was paid to the horned god.

Murray even claimed that Joan of Arc and her contemporary, Gilles de Rais, had been members of this ancient pre-Christian religion. In fact Murray had constructed this pre-Christian pagan religion, and simply ignored evidence that did not support her view. She wrote a second book, which was titled *The God of the Witches*, in 1933. In this, she celebrated what she described as the "Old Religion" and linked in folk tales and customs.

GARDNER'S PRACTICAL MAGIC

The historian Ronald Hutton points out four lines of influence on Murray: first, Jules Michelet's *La Sorcière* (1862), which portrayed the pagan witch religion led by women as democratic and nature-loving. (Michelet also claimed

The god Pan is thought to be a manifestation of the ancient horned god in modern witchcraft, largely because of the work of the Egyptologist, Margaret Murray.

that the Renaissance had been caused by the natural wisdom of the witch religion working its way upwards to artists and writers). Second, Charles Godfrey Leland's *Aradia* (1899), which was directly inspired by Michelet and which purported to be the gospel of the Italian branch of Michelet's witch religion. Third, James Frazer's theory of evolution, which suggested that surviving folk customs could be the fossils of old religions. Finally, Murray's association with the Folklore Society. It was Murray's work that gave Gardner the idea of a fertility religion, but how did he put together a practical system for working magic?

Aidan Kelly has made a detailed study of modern witchcraft using his experience of studying the origins of Christianity as a historical problem. He could not discover any "ancient" material in Gerald Gardner's *Book of Shadows* (part of the witch's magical paraphernalia in which ritual details are recorded), and claims that the only magic that Gardner could find out about was high magic, which was inherently Judaeo-Christian and "too complex". Folk magic was too practical for Gardner's purposes:

methods of curing warts, or a knowledge of herbs and charms, do not offer a system or theological structure for working magic, so Gardner had to incorporate elements of high magic. Ronald Hutton says that there are four direct links between ancient paganism and Wicca, or modern witchcraft, and these are: high magic; the knowledge of the use of plants and herbs and spells; folk rites and customs to honour or manipulate the powers of nature; and finally, the literature and art of the ancient world. If Wicca is seen as a form of ritual magic – rather than an age-old paganism – then it has a distinguished and very long pedigree.

CROWLEY'S INFLUENCE

As an initiate of Aleister Crowley's Ordo Templi Orientis (OTO), Gardner was also deeply influenced by Crowley's ideas and, according to one view, hired him to write witchcraft rituals for him. One version of events claims that Crowley was pleased to do this because he saw witchcraft as a "popularized form of his own creed". However, Ronald Hutton claims that there is no evidence for this and points to the fact that Aleister Crowley's writings about witchcraft were brief.

A Secret Wicca ritual that is based on the work of Gardner, with the dramatic addition of lights and theatrical effects.

The historian Gordon Melton claims that Gardner was influenced by high magic as described in Crowley's *Magick* (1929) and *The Book of the Law* (1936). Hutton argues that Gardner was initiated into all the degrees of the OTO and, in addition, that he was held to be Crowley's heir as head of the OTO but that he could not find enough people interested in joining it. Hutton further argues that Gardner had sympathies for both high magic and medieval witchcraft (through a reading of Margaret Murray) and that he "crossed the line" from one to the other, finally devoting himself to witchcraft. From 1947 to 1953 he was writing and devising rituals, which were either copied from existing rituals or were newly created.

VENERATION OF THE GODDESS

Modern witchcraft is a religion that venerates women, the earth, the dark and nature, all of which have been denigrated by Christianity and by Western cultures generally. In *Witchcraft Today*, Gardner links death and rebirth with the myth of the Goddess. When the Goddess journeyed to the nether lands to solve all mysteries she encountered Death:

> The guardians of the portals challenged her. "Strip off thy garments, lay aside thy jewels, for nought may ye bring with you into this our land." So she laid down her garments and her jewels and was bound as are all who enter the realms of Death, the mighty one. Such was her beauty that Death himself knelt and kissed her feet, saying: "Blessed be thy feet that have brought thee in these ways ... " [Death] taught her all the mysteries, and they loved and were one; and he taught her all the magics. For there are three great events in the life of man – love, death and resurrection in the new body – and magic controls them all.

The god of Death falls in love with the Goddess and teaches her that he provides rest and peace, and that if humans love they will be reborn among their loved ones at the same time and in the same place. The myth of the

Goddess often forms part of an initiation ritual into witchcraft.

Gardner wrote another ritual called "Drawing Down the Moon", a term taken from ancient Greece. As Hutton notes, Gardner put his own creative spin on the ancient tradition that saw the malign power of Thessalian witches as so great that the most powerful of them could pluck the moon from the sky and bring it to earth. By contrast Gardner created a ritual whereby the Goddess could be drawn down ino the body of the high priestess in a positive and beneficial way which united human being and deity. When invoked into the body of the high priestess the Goddess was thought to speak through her.

A short time later, Doreen Valiente would make her own contribution to Wicca, both as Gardner's high priestess and by rewriting his rituals to provide some of the most poetic expressions of modern witchcraft. She is particularly well known for revising what is known as "The Charge" – the words spoken by an invoked goddess.

It is no coincidence that modern witchcraft is becoming popular at a time of rapid social change. It often seems to address people's needs in ways that

A sacred altar to the Goddess, piled with offerings of Maiden dolls.

honour both women and nature, both of which have been devalued by a rationalistic, male-dominated society whose main religious traditions reflect this. Only in recent years have matters substantially changed, for example by allowing the ordination of women in the Church of England.

Many established and folk religions throughout the world have viewed women as inferior or less spiritual than men, modern witchcraft offers an alternative space where women and men can relate to each other in a more equal manner.

An illustration from a second-century BC Greek vase showing a female magician "drawing down the moon"; this provided the inspiration for the modern witchcraft ritual.

A modern witchcraft ritual representing the balancing of masculinity and femininity: the priestess inserts the athame, or ritual knife, which is a symbol of masculinity, into a chalice – a symbol of femininity, held by the priest.

THE GODDESS

Women in modern witchcraft are celebrated as the embodiment of the Goddess, and witchcraft is believed by some to have originated in matriarchal times. Others see early agricultural societies in neolithic Europe as matrifocal – focused on women – peaceful and living in harmony with nature until they were invaded by cultures with violent patriarchal religions. There is little to support these views, archaeologically or anthropologically, but the association of women with both nature and peace is a strong one and it shapes contemporary witchcraft practice today.

Diana, a goddess revered and summoned by the followers of magic traditions. In this picture she wears her distinctive moon headdress.

In modern witchcraft, or Wicca, the divine is generally represented by two deities – the Goddess and the God – who take different forms including the Great Mother and the Horned God. Modern witchcraft is unique in that it celebrates women as the embodiment of the Goddess, and this is the essence of the craft; in some cases the Goddess is emphasized almost to the exclusion of a god. Gerald Gardner wrote in *Witchcraft Today* that the witches did not know the origin of their practice, but that he thought it was a cult from a matriarchal time when woman was the chief, and only at a later time did a male god become dominant. By acting the part of the Goddess the priestess is thought to be in communion with her. Later writers on modern witchcraft have suggested that Wicca is, by its very nature, concerned with the development and use of "the gift of the Goddess" – the psychic and intuitive faculties of women. "The gift of the God", which represents the linear, logical, and conscious faculties, is important too, but it is the Goddess who must be re-awakened after too much emphasis has been placed on the God of the monotheistic religions of Judaism, Christianity and Islam.

THE GODDESS'S CHARACTER

The Goddess is called by many names and has many different forms but, as described by the poet Robert Graves, she is usually seen as having three dimensions corresponding with the waxing, full and waning moon; these are her maiden, mother and crone aspects and the trinity is linked with the goddesses Artemis (Diana), Selene and Hecate respectively. As Queen of Heaven, the Goddess represents the moon as the source of feminine attributes connected to intuition, emotion and psychic ability. Her divine feminine force is manifested in a polarity with the masculine principle, often portrayed as the Horned God, her son and consort, who has two aspects related to the waxing and the waning year; these two gods are rivals, and are in constant competition with each other for her favours. The union of Goddess and Horned God is described as a sacred marriage, which transcends all difference.

Persephone is an important goddess in modern witchcraft because she descends into the dark of the underworld before returning to the everyday realm. This is thought to confer great knowledge and often forms part of initiation rituals.

Artemis, seen as one aspect of the triple goddess in modern witchcraft, and symbolic of the waxing moon.

THE GODDESS VERSUS THE GOD

Known as the Great Mother, the Goddess is the creatrix whose limitless fertility brings new life; she is identified with Mother Nature: she creates but she also destroys. It has been claimed by many writers that the worship of the Goddess has been ignored or suppressed by patriarchal religions and that early agricultural societies in neolithic Europe were dominated by goddess-worship; they were focused on women and were peaceful, living in harmony with nature until they were invaded by warlike Indo-Europeans and goddess-worship was supplanted by sky-gods. This idea, according to the historian Ronald Hutton, was taken up by a number of archaeologists who assumed that the concept of a universal goddess was a proven fact; this governed the interpretation of archaeological sites, especially those of neolithic Turkey.

On the strength of these ideas, the archaeologist Marija Gimbutas reissued her original 1974 study entitled *The Gods and Goddesses of Old Europe* in 1982 with the revised title of *The Goddesses and*

Diana (centre), goddess of the full moon and an aspect of the triple goddess in modern witchcraft.

Gods of Old Europe. In the earlier edition she had asserted that the great Goddess was a force of regeneration, responsible for the transformation from death to life; she emerges miraculously out of death, and in her body new life begins. She was

not the earth, but a human female who could transform herself into living aspects of doe, dog, toad, bee, butterfly, tree or pillar. The preface to the revised edition, and later works by Gimbutas, incorporated ideas influenced by her

Drawing down the moon

In his book, *Witchcraft Today,* Gardner describes an example of a witch rite to cause the sun to be reborn and the summer to return. A circle is cast and purified, and the celebrants are also purified. A ceremony called 'drawing down the moon' is then performed in which the high priestess is regarded as the incarnation of the Goddess. This ritual was later formalized by Wiccans so that the high priest draws down the moon on the high priestess, who stands with her back to the altar, with a wand in her right hand and a scourge in her left, held against her breasts in the 'Osiris position'. The priest kneels before the priestess, and after giving her a ritual kiss, he kneels again before her and invokes the Goddess into her with these words:

I invoke thee and call upon thee,
Mighty Mother of us all, bringer of all
fruitfulness; by seed and root, by bud and stem,
by leaf and flower and fruit, by life and love
do I invoke thee to descend upon the body
of this thy servant and priestess.

During this invocation the high priest touches the high priestess with his right forefinger on her right breast, left breast and womb, and then repeats this, starting on her left breast. Still kneeling, with arms outstretched, he says:

Hail Aradia! From the
Amalthean Horn Pour forth thy store of love;
I lowly bend Before thee, I adore thee to the end,
With loving sacrifice thy shrine adorn.
Thy foot is to my lip [he kisses her right foot],
my prayer upborne Upon the rising
incense smoke; then spend Thine ancient love,
O Mighty One, descend To aid me, who
without thee am forlorn.

The high priestess then draws an invoking pentagram of earth in the air with her wand, and says these words:

Of the Mother darksome and divine
Mine the scourge, and mine the kiss;
The five-point star of love and bliss –
Here I charge you, in this sign.

The priest honours the priestess as the incarnation of the Goddess as she stands in the "Osiris position", wand in the right hand and scourge in the left.

The stag god Cernunnos from Celtic mythology; a manifestation of the horned god for modern witches.

This nineteenth-century romantic representation of Pan portrays him as a sensuous half-human, half-goat god in touch with the forces of nature.

personal radical feminist view. It was in these works that she extended Goddess-worship from her area of specialism – the Balkan countries – to all of Europe, the Near East and the Mediterranean region. The early witch trials were the suppression of Goddess-worship, when women were killed for practising the Old Religion of their foremothers.

The Goddess spirituality movement started in the mid to late 1970s as a form of thealogy (*thea* means female divinity); it is a growing form of spirituality – sometimes called "earth mysteries" or "women's mysteries" – that includes witches, pagans, New Agers and druids, as well as some Jewish and Christian feminists. All use female imagery for celebrating the divine and see the Goddess as primary, all-encompassing and immanent rather than as a distant transcendent spirit. A fluid practice that lacks a sacred text, authority is said to lie within the individual. The celebration of the Goddess celebrates a wholeness of self, and a power to define the self is implicit within many rituals.

Mary Daly, a Catholic theologian and feminist who came to abandon the Christian Church, calling it patriarchal, wrote a book in 1973 called *Beyond God the Father*, in which she wrote about changing the perception of "God" as male, and this proved to be an inspiration for many to turn away from what they saw as male-dominated religions. The Goddess is seen as a symbol of the strength and wholeness of women, as Elinor Gadon writes in her book *The Once and Future Goddess*:

In reclaiming the Goddess, in recovering our full human history as men and women, we can learn other patterns of behavior. We can redress the imbalance between the human species and our natural environment, between men and women, exploring the possibility of living in harmony and justice with all things.

Thus the Goddess is an earth-centred metaphor for the earth as a living organism, and also for an alternative, supposedly more egalitarian, social order.

Many other goddesses, as well as a Great Mother Goddess, are venerated. Some, such as Lilith, embody the dark and death as well as more obvious life-giving and nurturing qualities. Lilith, a hybrid bird-woman, was Adam's first wife, but she refused to lie beneath him, and, uttering the magical name of God, flew away to the wilderness where she gave birth to demons. God sent three angels to bring her back to Eden, but she refused to return. Lilith is perhaps the source of ideas about strix, striga, or striges, the owl-like creatures in classical and European folklore, and later the prototypes of the diabolical witch stereotype created and fostered by the established Christian Church.

THE GOD

The partner of the Goddess is the God. He is sometimes called Cernunnos or Herne, but is more frequently referred to merely as the horned god. The historian Ronald Hutton argues that the cultural forces that brought the modern perception of a single goddess also

An owl mask worn to invoke the goddess Lilith. Demonized by the Christian Church, Lilith is seen by many magicians as the first feminist.

delivered a single god as her consort. He points out that before the nineteenth century many gods had a variety of associations and connections, such as Jupiter (ruler), Neptune (sea), Mercury (commerce, education, communication), Vulcan (industry), and Apollo (poetry, the natural world). For the Romantic movement the god Pan, personified as wild nature, overshadowed them all. He became a major theme in the work of Wordsworth, Keats and Shelley, and represented the English countryside. He later featured in the literary works of Robert Louis Stevenson and in Kenneth Grahame's classic children's story *The Wind in the Willows*.

Hutton observes that Pan became the expression of the natural world as sublime, mysterious, and awe-inspiring but also benevolent and comforting; this was in direct contrast to the industrial and urban environment, and represented a return to the lost innocence of a rural paganism. In witchcraft, Pan became characterized as the horned god, not least through Margaret Murray's work *The God of the Witches*, published in 1933, which was formative in shaping modern ideas about a nature god.

A contemporary owl goddess plaque inspired by a dream of Lilith, the fabled first wife of Adam, who rejected him and his God, and fled from Eden.

Baubo, an ancient Greek figure who perched on a well making Demeter laugh when her daughter Persephone was in the Underworld. She represents the sacrality of women's bodies for many witches today.

CELEBRATING NATURE

Referred to as a "nature religion", modern witchcraft honours the Earth and the body rather than a transcendental spirit. The physical body and all of nature are seen as inherently divine and part of a larger whole, commonly seen to consist of interconnecting energies. Many modern witches take the view that their religion is the Old Religion of the village wise woman and cunning man, who practised herbalism and divining as part of their craft. Most now accept that there is no unbroken tradition that connects their current practices with those of the cunning folk, but modern witches talk about a sense of connectedness with nature, which links them spiritually and mythologically, if not historically, to a view of life where everything is connected through various energies and forces. Many are turning to direct action to protect the environment.

A modern witch celebrates a Winter Solstice ritual in a forest.

Witches today seek a relationship with nature, and conduct rituals to create a place where it is possible to be aware of the wider connecting pattern of the universe. This is often visualized as a web, a sacred force that is the very grounding of existence. Sometimes it is envisaged as a "web of wyrd", as outlined by the psychologist Brian Bates in his books *The Way of Wyrd* (1983) and *The Wisdom of Wyrd* (1996). Human beings are seen to be a part of nature, intimately connected via a web of forces and energies.

In *Witchcraft Today*, Gerald Gardner, the founder of modern witchcraft, said that whereas ceremonial magicians used a circle to keep demons at bay, the witches that he knew worked within a magical circle to contain the power generated from their bodies. He outlined four great festivals that the witches celebrated – November eve (Hallowe'en), February eve, May eve and August eve – which corresponded to the ancient Gaelic fire festivals of Samhaim (1 November), Brigid (1 February), Bealteine or Beltene (1 May) and Lugnasadh (1 August). Gardner wrote that the festivals corresponding to midwinter and midsummer were both said to have been founded in honour of female deities, while the two winter ones were those in which the God took precedence (although "he is not superior but merely her equal").

MODERN RITUALS

Today witches create a circle as sacred space "between the worlds" into which the divine, usually personified as the Goddess and God, manifests. The witchcraft circle is always arranged according to the cardinal points of north, south, east and west. Each cardinal direction has certain attributes, which relate to the natural world. Thus the circle is usually ceremonially opened in the east because the east represents light, the first light of dawn and also

All of nature is seen to be part of a pattern of the universe to modern witches; some visualize this as a "web of wyrd", others as a manifestation of the Goddess.

the spring; it is symbolic of air, intellect and rational thought. The magical tool of the east is the athame (a ritual knife or dagger) or the sword. The south represents fire and the energy of the magical will, the summer, sun and heat. It is symbolized by the wand, a slender branch of wood. The west represents water, the emotions, rivers, oceans, streams and autumn; it is symbolized by the cup or chalice. The west flows and merges while the east separates and canalizes. The north represents the earth, mountains, valleys, winter and the body. The pentacle is its symbol: its five points represent the five senses of the human body and all the elements: earth, air, fire, water and spirit. In the centre of the circle stands a large cauldron representing transformation: of the raw into the cooked and, on the spiritual level, of changes of consciousness within the natural rhythms of nature.

Wicca operates a seasonal myth cycle whereby the processes of nature – conception, birth, maturation and death – are portrayed in dynamic interaction with the Goddess and the God as personifications of the forces and powers

Many Wiccan rituals are performed outside. Here two initiates are bound into a coven.

Creative visualizations may be conducted outside, in the midst of nature, for inspiration.

Witchcraft harnesses the power of the mind, using natural objects and visualization techniques.

of nature. Thus the inner self of the individual witch is linked in with the wider mythological cycle.

The Wiccans Janet and Stewart Farrar, in their book *Eight Sabbats for Witches* (1981), work with what have now become the eight standard seasonal rituals for many pagans: Yule or Winter Solstice (22 December), Imbolg (2 February), Spring Equinox (21 March), Bealtaine (30 April), Midsummer or Summer Solstice (22 June), Lughnasadh (31 July), Autumn Equinox (21 September) and Samhain (31 October).

The Farrars have adapted Gardner's ritual year to reflect what they call a solar theme and a natural-fertility theme. The Goddess does not undergo the experiences but presides over them; she is always there but changes her aspect, while the God dies and is reborn. The solar theme, which dominates the solstices and equinoxes, reflects the concept of a sacrificed and resurrected god: he dies and is reborn at the Winter Solstice, and at the Spring Equinox his waxing power impregnates Mother Earth; he reaches his prime at the Summer Solstice, then his waning powers lead through to the Autumn Equinox and his death and

rebirth at the Winter Solstice to complete the cycle. The natural-fertility theme involves the god of the waxing year, represented by the Oak King, and the god of the waning year, personified as the Holly King – both aspects of the horned god, a natural-fertility figure. According to the Farrars, they are light and dark aspects of each other and compete eternally for the favour of the Great Mother. At Yule the Holly King ends his reign and falls to the Oak King, while at Midsummer the Oak King is replaced by the Holly King.

THE ENVIRONMENT

Increasingly modern witches are looking to ritual sites in nature, and ancient stone monuments, to contact the energies of their ancestors, those that practised the "Old Religion". These sites, which often date from the neolithic, are often viewed as places of female mysteries and the land itself is though of as the Goddess incarnate. Believed to be gateways into the otherworld, a "dreamtime" that enables witches to connect with an inner sacred place within, these places are the locations for healing, divination, and the conducting of life rites such as handfastings (weddings). A Wiccan high priestess, Vivianne Crowley has observed that Wicca has changed its focus from the early days. She says that Gerald Gardner's original stress was on witchcraft as a fertility religion but that a more recent portrayal of witchcraft is as an environmental movement. Crowley notes that Gardner made little mention of nature, being more interested in magical powers and the traditional image of the witch as caster of spells, and points out that it was Doreen Valiente, Gardner's high priestess, who recast the concept of fertility into one that included the mind and the soul. Valiente thought that there was a spiritual as well as a material fertility, and that human life was like a desert without it. Valiente talks not so much

Stone circles are especially sacred to modern witches and other pagans as places where the Earth's energies are particularly potent.

Paganism

Nature is central to modern pagan experience, and Selena Fox, Wiccan high priestess and founder of Circle Sanctuary in the United States, describes this side of paganism:

I am Pagan. I am a part of the whole of Nature. The Rocks, the Animals, the Plants, the Elements, and the Stars are my relatives. Other humans are my sisters and brothers, whatever their races, colors, genders, sexual orientations, ages, nationalities, religions, lifestyles. Planet Earth is my home. I am a part of this large family of Nature, not the master of it. I have my own special part to play and I seek to discover and play that part to the best of my ability. I seek to live in harmony with others in the family of Nature, treating others with respect ...

I am Pagan. Nature Spirituality is my religion and my life's foundation. Nature is my spiritual teacher and holy book. I am part of Nature and

Witchcraft, as a part of modern paganism, views all of nature as sacred.

Nature is part of me. My understanding of Nature's inner mysteries grows as I journey on this spiritual path.

about literal fertility but about finding harmony with nature; she calls the star goddess the soul of nature.

According to Vivianne Crowley, Wicca has changed from a secret fertility cult to a more open movement, with nature high on its agenda. This marks a significant transition whereby Wicca moves out of the darkness of witchery to take the moral high ground of environmentalism. To be at one with nature in one's inner self is no longer enough: radical action to preserve nature is now important. While many witches are content to cast spells to help nature, others are becoming involved in direct action. So witchcraft encompasses many different practices but all are focused on nature, both within and without, rather than a transcendental spirit that is separate from the natural world.

To pagans, Nature is a source of divinity and enchantment, thought to be inhabited by spirits or "the little people".

DOREEN VALIENTE

If Gerald Gardner was the founder and "father" of modern witchcraft, then Doreen Valiente surely is his female counterpart. It was she who carried on and expanded his work in formulating and defining this relatively new form of paganism. A modest, unassuming woman, she brought a down-to-earth, yet poetic vision to modern witchcraft practice, as well as a greater emphasis on attaining harmony with nature. At the time of her death, on 1 September 1999, she was held in great esteem as the "mother of Wicca" who had contributed to its growth as a religion, to its poetry and to the beauty of its ceremonies and ritual.

Doreen Valiente, photographed in January 1999.

Doreen Valiente, who was initiated by Gerald Gardner in 1953 and eventually became his high priestess, has had a great influence on modern witchcraft in the form of rewriting, changing and adapting Gardner's rituals. Valiente discovered Gardner's witchcraft in 1952 when she read an article on "Witchcraft in Britain" published in a magazine.

The article quoted Cecil Williamson, the owner of a witchcraft museum on the Isle of Man. He was talking about witchcraft as the "Old Religion" and telling how the witches in the New Forest had raised a "cone of power" to stop Hitler from invading Britain. Doreen Valiente, who had been interested in magic for many years,

wrote to Williamson for information about contacting witches. Williamson passed her letter to Gardner who, after some correspondence, invited her to Dafo's house in Christchurch. There he gave Valiente a copy of his book *High Magic's Aid* to read for information on the witch cult.

Valiente said that her initiation was virtually identical to that described in *High Magic's Aid* except that it included something called "The Charge" (a ritual utterance from an invoked deity) which she recognized as containing passages from Leland's *Aradia* and parts of Aleister Crowley's writings. When she confronted Gardner with the inclusion of this material, he replied that he had had to supplement the fragmentary material from the old coven.

A REVISED CHARGE

Valiente accepted his challenge to revise the wording of The Charge, removing much of the borrowing from Crowley. It begins with a summons to assemble and adore the Great Mother:

A witch consecrates the salt with her athame on an altar which includes flowers to link with nature as well as magical symbolism in the pentagram and the flame of the candle.

*Listen to the words of the Great Mother;
who was of old also called among men,
Artemis, Astarte, Dione, Melusine,
Aphrodite, Cerridwen, Diana,
Arianrhod, Bride, and by
many other names.
At mine Altars the youth of Lacedaemon
in Sparta made due sacrifice.
Whenever ye have need of anything,
once in the month, and better it be
when the moon is full. Then ye shall
assemble in some secret place and
adore the spirit of Me who am
Queen of all Witcheries.
There ye shall assemble, ye who are
fain to learn all sorcery, yet who
have not won its deepest secrets.
To these will I teach things that
are yet unknown ..."*

The priestess representing the goddess identifies herself as the soul of nature:

*I who am the beauty of the green earth;
and the White Moon amongst the Stars;
and the mystery of the Waters; and the
desire of the heart of man, I call unto
thy soul: arise and come unto me.
For I am the Soul of nature who giveth
life to the Universe;
From me all things proceed; and unto
me, all things must return.*

The source of all knowledge lies within:

*And thou who thinkest to seek me,
know that thy seeking and yearning
shall avail thee not unless thou know
the mystery, "That if that which thou
seekest thou findest not within thee,
thou wilt never find it without thee,"
for behold; I have been with thee
from the beginning, and I am that
which is attained at the end of desire.*

Valiente went on to become a formative influence in the development of modern witchcraft, writing a number of books that displayed her own distinct interpretation of the "Old Religion". She recast Gardner's concept of witchcraft as a fertility religion into one that included the mind and the soul, saying that there was a spiritual as well as a material fertility, and that this

A "Path to Female Empowerment", planted by followers of the Goddess, which illustrates the link between nature and the female.

A modern practising witch holding an athame in her right hand and a scourge in her left, in the "Osiris position".

spiritual fertility was found through finding harmony in nature.

In her later work Doreen Valiente came to distance herself from the position taken by Gerald Gardner, critically describing his version of the

craft as rather airy-fairy. She then took instead to working with what she called traditional hereditary witchcraft with Robert Cochrane, who claimed to be a genuine hereditary witch from a long and secret tradition.

A Wiccan initiation.

ALEX SANDERS

At seven years old, Mr Sanders, in an austere and bloody ritual, was initiated into the cult by his grandmother. As a professional, practising witch, and having had first hand experience with the evils of black witchcraft, which brought him an immense fortune but great personal tragedy, Mr Sanders pledged himself thereafter to the furtherance of witchcraft as a benevolent religion. This is how the cover of Alex Sander's book of teachings on Alexandrian Wicca introduces its author. A composite of Gardnerian witchcraft and high magic from the hermetic tradition, Alexandrian witchcraft is often considered to be the "high church" of witchcraft, borrowing as it does from the Judaeo-Christian tradition and having elaborate and highly ritualized ceremonies.

A great showman, Alex Sanders is pictured here with a skull and crossbones.

Gerald Gardner's original formulation of witchcraft was adopted by his followers, who called themselves "Gardnerians", but a later derivative group, whose members came to be known as "Alexandrians", has come to be especially influential in the development of modern witchcraft. Alex Sanders (1926-1988), the self-proclaimed "King of the Witches", was its founder. He attracted many followers and boasted that he had 1,623 initiates in 100 covens, but little is known about his early involvement with witchcraft and it seems highly likely that he derived most of his material from Gardnerian sources. Sanders, who was born Orrell Alexander Carter in Birkenhead, England, was the eldest of six children, and claimed that he was initiated into witchcraft by his grandmother Mary Bibby, a cunning woman, when he was seven years old. Sanders said that he discovered her standing naked in the middle of a circle drawn on the kitchen floor. Ordering him to enter the circle and to take off his clothes, she made him bend over and cut his scrotum with a knife saying, "You are one of us now".

Sanders spent much of his early life drifting from one job to another, drinking and having sexual liaisons with men and women. After pledging himself to the "left-hand path" or "black magic" and making a fortune, he decided to use his powers for beneficent purposes such as healing. He met Maxine Morris in the 1960s and initiated her into the craft. The couple were handfasted (married) and Maxine became his high priestess.

PUBLIC WITCHCRAFT

Sanders courted publicity and a film (*Legend of the Witches*), a biography written in 1969 (*King of the Witches*) and his numerous public appearances in the media brought witchcraft into the public eye, much to the dismay of other witches who shunned the association with such a showman. He upset many prominent

Alex Sanders holds a ritual sword during an Alexandrian ritual. Maxine Sanders sits on his right.

figures, including Patricia Crowther, an initiate of Gardnerian witchcraft. In 1966 Sanders' behaviour prompted Pat Crowther and Ray Bone, another leading spokesperson for witchcraft, to make a public denunciation of Sanders, calling him an impostor because he had not been properly initiated into the Gardnerian witchcraft tradition. This forced Sanders to respond with the story about his initiation by his grandmother. He claimed that hers was the authentic craft, and that Gardner and the Gardnerians were following a later and inferior version.

In fact, Sanders based his version of witchcraft on Gardner's model but incorporated more elements of high magic, being greatly influenced by Eliphas Lévi. Some witches refer to Alexandrian witchcraft as "high church", and Gardnerian witchcraft as "low church". Sanders blurred the boundaries between paganism and Christianity and, according to the historian Ronald Hutton, this marks a distinct difference between the two traditions because Gardner was always concerned to mark a clear separation, preferring to depict himself, like Margaret Murray, as a discoverer of a surviving ancient religious tradition. Alex Sanders and

An initiation ceremony. Here the prospective candidate is blindfolded and challenged by the High Priestess and High Priest.

Maxine Morris, by contrast, portrayed themselves through their life stories as "warriors in a constant battle of good magic against bad". Sanders also placed more emphasis on practical magical techniques such as clairvoyance, astral projection, thought-transference and the use of charms and talismans.

In 1969 a reporter named Stewart Farrar interviewed Sanders for an article in the magazine *Reveille*, and Sanders invited him to attend a witch's initiation. Farrar wrote a two-part feature for the magazine and was sufficiently impressed to become involved himself. He was commissioned to write a book, later

Alex Sanders in ritual regalia.

published as *What Witches Do*, and he started attending Sanders' training classes. In the Sanders' coven he met Janet Owen and they later formed a magical partnership – and their own coven – in 1970. They have published many books on witchcraft.

A film portrayal of a witchcraft ceremony inspired by Alex Sanders' work.

Witchcraft paraphernalia; skull, wand, chalice, cord, candle, crystals and divination cards.

RAYMOND BUCKLAND

It was Raymond Buckland who was largely responsible for taking Gardnerian witchcraft to the United States. An Englishman with Romany blood, Buckland moved to America in 1962 and founded Seax-Wica, a Saxon branch of witchcraft which worships four principle deities: Woden, Thunor, Tiw and Frig or Freya. Buckland had established a relationship with Gerald Gardner when he was living on the Isle of Man and running his witchcraft museum. Impressed with Gardner's museum, Buckland set up a similar one in the United States.

In his introduction to Gardner's book *Witchcraft Today*, Raymond Buckland acknowledged his debt to Gardner, saying that all witches owed Gardner a debt of gratitude for learning his original coven's rituals and adapting them, before breaking from the group and starting his own. Buckland explained that his own life paralleled Gardner's: after being initiated into Gardnerian witchcraft by Gardner's then high priestess Monique Wilson, known as the

Lady Olwen, in Perth, Scotland, he felt it necessary after nearly 12 years to leave this tradition to found his own in the early 1970s. He saw the Saxon tradition of Seax-Wica as a more open branch of Wicca, having no oaths of secrecy.

In Gardnerian witchcraft the high priestess, in partnership with her magical working partner the high priest, is overall leader of her coven. She is seen to be the channel and representative of the Goddess and the coven cannot

Raymond Buckland in his magic regalia.

Raymond Buckland acknowledged his debt to Gardner and adapted many of his rituals.

function without her or a female representative. By contrast, in Seax-Wica men and women are seen to be equally important and a high priest can act alone. Buckland's version of Wicca has no degrees of advancement and therefore differs from other forms of modern witchcraft, which usually have three initiation degrees (in Alexandrian Wicca the second and third may be taken together). The first is often an introduction to the Goddess, and a time for understanding the unconscious: a man must find aspects of himself in the Goddess, while a woman must absorb qualities that she has projected elsewhere. The second initiation concerns the descent to the underworld, to face fears and find the self. The third initiation concerns the bringing together of all aspects of the person to discover the wisdom within.

SEAX-WICCA

Buckland's system allows for self-initiation by the performance of a rite of self-dedication, after which the initiate may start their own coven. The self-initiate stands with both arms lifted facing an altar and says:

> Woden and Freya, hear me now!
> I am here a simple pagan
> holding thee in honor.
> Far have I journeyed and long
> have I searched,
> Seeking that which I desire above all things.
> I am of the trees and of the fields.
> I am of the woods and of the springs;
> The streams and the hills.
> I am of thee; and thee of me ...

However, it is preferred that the initiate is introduced and trained in the customary manner, and there are three categories of relative involvement in Seax-Wica. The first is the Theows: those who do not belong to the Saxon craft, but attend the rituals by invitation. This introduction may lead to a request for further involvement and training leading to initiation, when the neophyte is termed a Ceorl. After a period of time – anything from a month to a year depending on the person's spiritual

A Wiccan Samhain (Hallowe'en) ceremony with the high priestess crowning the high priest.

development – the neophyte is initiated and becomes a Gesith, after which there is no further degree of advancement. Buckland claims that this counters any tendency for one person to become too powerful, and helps to stop any egoism developing. Recognizing that it was not

possible for everyone to go through the course of training, Buckland tried to make the craft more accessible to earnest seekers. He started many covens and established the Seax-Wica Seminary correspondence school in Virginia in the early 1970s, later moving to San Diego. He has written many books about witchcraft but has subsequently turned his attention to writing about Gypsies. He notes that the Romany word for "witch" is "shuvihani" (the masculine form is "shuvihano") meaning "wise one", the implication being that the witch is knowledgable in all aspects of the occult. A shuvihani has experience of magical beliefs and practices; she is not considered evil in any way. Many shuvihanis undertake a vision quest similar to the Native American Indians to gain previously unknown knowledge.

Thus Buckland has, as a "poshrat", or half-blood Romany, sought to understand and practise both witchcraft and gypsy magic. Like Alex Sanders he adapted Gardnerian witchcraft to his own ideas and experience. In this sense Wicca has proved to be a flexible set of techniques open to much interpretation.

Wiccan high priest and priestess of the Gardnerian tradition, the foundation for Buckland's own interpretation of witchcraft.

HEREDITARY WITCHCRAFT

While most witches now accept that their religion is a modern recreation of paganism that links back to a past spiritually rather than historically, others reject this and assert that their practices have been handed down through family tradition. Many of the beliefs and practices of hereditary witches can be traced back to the work of Charles Godfrey Leland, and his research on the supposedly secret religion of witches who worshipped the goddess Diana and the god Lucifer.

It is now fairly well estblished that modern witchcraft was formulated in the early 1950s. A significant minority, however, claim that they do belong to an unbroken inherited tradition, that comes to them through their own family rather than any social inheritance. Scholarship on this subject has so far failed to provide any proof to support these claims. Most hereditary witches draw on the work of Margaret Murray and her view that the Old Religion was a fragmented form of pagan religion, which had managed to survive centuries of Christian persecution. Others claim that their traditions stem directly from the Italian witchcraft explored in the writings of Charles Godfrey Leland, especially his book *Aradia: Gospel of the Witches*, published in 1899.

THE COCHRANE COVEN

Robert Cochrane claimed that he was a hereditary witch who was initiated at the age of five, his practice passing through his family. A former blacksmith, he named his coven the Clan of the Tubal Cain after a smith in Hebrew legend. Doreen Valiente was initiated into Gardnerian Wicca in 1953. In a book called *Witchcraft: A Tradition Renewed* (1990) she collaborated with another initiate from Cochrane's coven, Evan John Jones, to put forward the basic ways of working according to this tradition.

An ideal coven structure consisted of 13 members: six men and six women, with the Lady – who directed proceedings, dedicated the circle, led celebrants in, dedicated the cakes and wine, and closed the ritual – as the thirteenth.

Each of the correspondences had an officer associated with it: the north was attended by the "Dark One", the Hag; the south by the Mother aspect of the Goddess; the east by a young man who symbolized light; the west by a male guardian of the gates of the underworld. The rest of the coven was made up of initiates and apprentices, who served an apprenticeship of a year and a day. A "Man in Black" maintained contact between covens; and a "Summoner", while keeping contact with the Man in Black, acted as a record-keeper and also organized such things as transport to ritual sites. Cochrane's coven followed a Gardnerian pattern of rites – celebrating

Lucifer, or the Devil, is another representation of the horned god or Pan, the goat-footed god of nature, life and vitality.

Tradition is an important part of modern magic and much folklore and many beliefs are passed on through museums, such as this witchcraft museum in Cornwall.

the Great Sabbats of Candlemas, May Eve, Lammas, and Hallowe'en, and also the Lesser Sabbats of the equinoxes and solstices – but there were also important differences. They assigned air to the north (earth in Gardnerian Wicca), earth to the south (fire in the Gardnerian tradition) and fire to the east (air in Gardnerian Wicca), while the west was associated with water as in the Gardnerian tradition. Ronald Hutton noted that there was more emphasis upon the God as Lord of Death than in Gardner's tradition, and that the Man in Black or "Magister" functioned as high priest in the role of divine sacrificial king; in this he was supported by the Maid or Lady. The Magister also conducted a rite before the ceremonial consumption of cakes and wine, dipping his knife into a cup of wine in which the moon was reflected by the use of a mirror. Doreen Valiente noted that Cochrane's rituals were more spontaneous and shamanistic, more earthy than those of Gardner, and that this was partly because the coven did not use a Book of Shadows in which to record rituals, leading to more creativity.

A hereditary coven will often work its rituals and celebrations outside.

Charles Leland

Raven Grimassi used the works of Charles Godfrey Leland, particularly *Aradia* (the Italianized name of Herodias, who was portrayed as a villain in the New Testament for her part in the death of John the Baptist) to trace the alleged origins of his craft. Leland wrote that the Italian witch came from a family in which her calling or art had been practised for many generations. In 1886 he had met a woman called Maddelena who claimed to be a witch. She had apparently inherited a collection of family charms and invocations that could heal, break curses and invoke certain spirits. Leland used these and employed her as a research assistant to find out more about the secret religion of the witches. In particular he sought to find the gospel of its body of beliefs, and eventually Maddelena managed to provide him with such a manuscript obtained from oral sources. What Leland considered to be an ancient pagan religion was thus recorded.

A portrait of Charles Godfrey Leland.

The frontispiece of Leland's seminal and highly influential work, Aradia.

Ronald Hutton concluded that Cochrane used a Wiccan framework to develop his own ideas and practices, and called it hereditary witchcraft.

Cochrane's hereditary legacy lives on in a coven named the Regency, which was formed on Hallowe'en in 1966 by two former members of Cochrane's coven. They combined his ideas with those of Ruth Wynn Owen, who also claimed to be a hereditary witch coming from a family with psychic skills whose rituals were similar to Wicca in their veneration of a god and goddess. The hereditary craft spread to America through the work of Joseph Wilson, who developed the "1734 tradition", a special numerological value based on Robert Graves' *The White Goddess* (1948).

RAVEN GRIMASSI

Also claiming to be a hereditary witch in the "Strega Tradition" of old Italy, Raven Grimassi was taught by his mother about the Old Religion. He says that the old faith is based on the belief that spirits inhabit both physical objects and all of nature, and that he learnt that it was possible to call up the fairy folk. This was done by pouring milk, honey and wine into a bowl, putting it under a myrtle bush and then swinging a reed tied to a string in a clockwise circle while whistling. A rustling of the leaves signified that the fairies had come.

DIANA

The old faith focused on deities personified as the great Goddess, represented by Diana, and the horned god, represented by Lucifer. The myth of Diana tells that she was the first to be created and in her were all things. She divided herself into darkness and light: her brother and son Dianus was her other half and was the light, while she was the dark. When Diana saw the beauty of the light she yearned for it and swallowed it up in delight. This desire was the dawn. However, Dianus fled from her and would not yield to her wishes. Diana lamented to the Fathers of the Beginning, to the Mothers and the Spirits, and they told her that to rise she must fall and that therefore she had to become

The goddess Diana is closely associated with the moon in hereditary witchcraft. She is seen here in part of a series of reliefs depicting the planetary symbols and signs of the zodiac.

Diana is always depicted as a beautiful goddess with an essentially feminine aspect.

mortal. So Diana descended to earth with Dianus, where she taught magic and sorcery; thus witches and magicians came to be. Her brother Dianus had a cat, which slept on his bed. One day Diana took the form of a cat like her brother's; she lay with her brother and in the darkness assumed her own form. This is how Diana became the mother of Aradia. Dianus was angry, but Diana sang a spell to keep him silent. She hummed a song like the buzzing of bees and the spinning of a wheel. Like a spinning wheel spinning life, she spun the lives of men. All things are said to be spun from the wheel of Diana, while Dianus turned the wheel.

Grimassi says that the Gardnerian tradition took on elements of Italian witchcraft from the works of Charles Leland: part of the Charge of the Goddess contains elements of Leland's material, and other borrowings are full-moon gatherings, worship of a goddess, ritual celebrations involving cakes and wine and worshipping naked.

Wiccan ritual celebrations may have been inspired by traditions that were handed down by hereditary witchcraft, according to some.

Some hereditary witches say that Gardnerian witches borrowed elements – such as worshipping naked – from their tradition.

FEMINIST WITCHCRAFT

Feminist witchcraft is a later variant of modern witchcraft. It is now primarily associated with the work of Starhawk, an influential figure in feminist witchcraft, and has a strong political dimension. Feminist witches often work with what they term ecstasy, rather than the feminine/masculine polarity, which is central to Gardnerian Wicca. Magical work for social change – to end patriarchal oppression – is also a predominant part of their rituals.

Jules Michelet, the French historian who studied the records of the witch hunters.

In the 1970s the women's liberation movement produced a general critique of world religions, which, it was said, denied women's experience. Two differing branches of feminist spirituality emerged: those keen to reform orthodox religions and those who looked to pre-Christian goddesses such as those celebrated in modern witchcraft. Ideas of the witch as a freedom fighter against patriarchy were used by American radical feminists. According to Rachel Hasted, writing in the magazine *Trouble and Strife* (1985), the original WITCH (Women Inspired To Commit Herstory) group accepted ready-made "facts" about the witch-craze in Europe and claimed that nine million witches had been burned as revolutionary fighters against patriarchy and class oppression. They drew on the work of Jules Michelet, Joslyn Gage and Margaret Murray. Each of these writers had contributed to the idea that there was an underground movement of women's spirituality, originating from matriarchal times, which had been suppressed.

The French historian Jules Michelet's *La Sorcière* (1862) had interpreted witch hunters' records as a massive peasant rebellion and rejection of Christianity in which pagan priestesses led a doomed peasants' revolt against the oppression of a Christian ruling class. Matilda Joslyn Gage, a radical leader of the US suffrage movement, had argued in *Woman, Church and State* (1893) that witchcraft and the occult were a form of knowledge that was based on the worship of a female deity which had been outlawed by a jealous patriarchy. Margaret Murray's *The Witch-Cult in Western Europe* (1921) had claimed that European witchcraft was an ancient pre-Christian fertility religion, which had survived among the peasantry.

Feminist witchcraft's mythical origins lie in a golden woman-centred age before patriarchal religions came to dominate both women and nature. Judaeo-Christian traditions were seen to have deepened the split, finally establishing a duality between spirit and matter. Women became identified with matter, nature, the body, sexuality, evil and the Devil, and had to be controlled, while the male God was uncontaminated by birth, menstruation and decay and was removed to the realm of the spirit. Feminist witchcraft, in common with Wicca, has a holistic vision of the world: the Goddess is seen to link people with nature; she is seen to be within every human being and her worship involves celebrating life: she is associated with renewal and the regeneration of life.

The origins of Goddess-worship are traced to ancient, peaceful, egalitarian cultures where the change of seasons and lunar and solar cycles were experienced as mystic bonds linking humanity with nature. Much of this feminist reinterpretation of witchcraft is based on the work of the archaeologist Marija Gimbutas, who attributed a single religious system of Goddess-worship to both palaeolithic hunter-gatherers and neolithic farmers and horticulturalists. Gimbutas claimed that when food-gathering gave way to food-producing, leading to a settled way of life, there was no corresponding change in the religious symbolism – the Goddess ruled throughout. According to Gimbutas, this peaceable old European culture was overrun by violent patriarchal invasions between 4300 and 2800BC. The anthropologist Ruby Rohrlich disagrees with this view and

The old stereotype of the witch shown in this illustration has recently been recast by feminists.

points to the earliest civilizations in Sumer, Egypt, India and China, and also the societies of the Incas and the Aztecs, claiming that they gradually transformed themselves from peaceable, women-centred enclaves into warring, stratified cultures. She argues that the changes were made from within rather than by patriarchal invaders from without. Nevertheless, the idea that there was a peaceable, Goddess-focused, pre-patriarchal society is very common among feminist witches.

ZSUZSANNA BUDAPEST (1940–)

In 1971, "women's mysteries" were created in Malibu, USA. According to Zsuzsanna Budapest, a group of women sat around a weatherbeaten old café table eating eggs and potatoes, drinking coffee, talking and fantasizing and laughing, and knowing that they were doing something revolutionary that was going to influence the world. Budapest, who claims that she comes from a long line of witches, and that she is the "last branch of an 800-year-old family tree", says that her mother, Masika, was the result of a virgin birth, and was taught all the arts of witchcraft by a very well-known witch from Transylvania.

The American feminist Susan B. Anthony.

Spiritual Suffrage

The Susan B. Anthony Coven No.1 was started by Zsuzsanna Budapest on the winter solstice in 1971 in Hollywood. It was named after the suffragist Susan B. Anthony, a leading campaigner for women's suffrage and president of the National American Woman's Suffrage Association. When Anthony was asked what she would do in the afterlife, she reputedly answered 'When I die, I shall go neither to heaven nor hell, but stay right here and finish the women's revolution', a comment that inspired Budapest to acknowledge Anthony as an ancestress, whose work should be honoured and continued.

Budapest was part of a Malibu core group of eight women who created what has been termed the "Dianic tradition" of feminist witchcraft by celebrating rituals together and contributing their experiences to *The Holy Book of Women's Mysteries* (1989). Dianic tradition witches are usually either celibate or lesbian.

This form of witchcraft is based on Wicca and shares its structure: the coven is composed of up to 13; sabbaths are held on the same festivals; the ritual structure is based on a circle and four quarters. Other similarities are the emphasis on feasting and sexuality; witches are supposed to enter the circle "in perfect love and perfect trust"; the naked body is seen to represent truth; and the abiding moral maxim is "Do as thou wilt and harm none". The main differences focus on the central role of politics and an emphasis on democratic working (whereas Gardner's system was based on a hierarchical, initiatory system of three degrees); and the primacy of the Goddess, sometimes to the total exclusion of the God.

Feminist politics have been central to the practice from the start and Budapest speaks of the difficulties of combining religion with politics in the early days. For Budapest, spirituality concerns the struggle to liberate the religious woman inside by the creation of a faith system that will serve women. She has written that in the true beginning, before the Judaeo-Christian Genesis, "the Goddess was revealed to her people as the Soul of the Wild. Called Holy Mother, she was known to be a Virgin who lived in wild places and acted through mysterious powers. Known also as Artemis, She was worshipped in the moonlight, and young nymphs and maidens were called to serve in Her rituals. The Holy Mother, Virgin, Artemis was also called by the name Dia Anna, 'Nurturer Who Does Not Bear Young'."

Women and the earth are seen as especially sacred in feminist and Goddess spirituality. This is a ritual at the Goddess Festival in Glastonbury, England, honouring the powers of nature.

Starhawk leading a spiral dance in America: she is the central figure holding a drum. The spiral dance gathers everyone and engenders a feeling of collectivity and connectedness.

STARHAWK (1951–)

Starhawk (Miriam Simos), the woman who has had the most formative effect on feminist witchcraft, attended her first ritual with the Susan B. Anthony Coven, according to Budapest. Starhawk's background is Jewish and she still sees herself as Jewish but she sought an alternative spirituality because "in Judaism there were no images of powerful women". She also had powerful spiritual experiences, which did not fit Judaism because they "seemed to take place in nature or in the context of sexuality", and in traditional Jewish circles at this time these were not discussed.

THE FAERY TRADITION

In 1975 Starhawk began to study with Victor Anderson and was initiated into the Faery (Feri) tradition as taught by him. Victor Anderson and Gwydion Pendderwen founded the Faery tradition of witchcraft, and it is likely that Anderson was influenced by Margaret Murray's work on fairies. Anderson was allegedly initiated into the craft by witches who called themselves faeries, and he worked in covens with people from southern America and practised a "devotional science", harmonizing with nature, performing magic and engaging in ecstatic dancing. Anderson was also

initiated into the Harpy coven in Oregon in 1932. This was eclectic, mixing Huna from Hawaii with varieties of folk magic more common in the rest of the United States. There was an emphasis on practical magic and little concern with worship, theology, ethics or ritual.

According to the Faery tradition, there is a Mother-Father God called the

"Drychton" (after the Anglo-Saxon word for "lord" or "ruler") who is the male-female power, being both the God and the Goddess. In the beginning, according to the mythology, the light from the stars bounced off the curved mirror of space in the directions of left and right and produced the other deities: the gods on one side and the goddesses on the other. Above all, the Faery tradition is an ecstatic one – rather than one that is based on fertility, as in Gardner's original formulation of Wicca – and the aim is to become one with the gods. The sexes are seen to be equal and there is no high priestess in overall charge. Later, Alexandrian witchcraft material was incorporated into the tradition.

In her first work, *The Spiral Dance: A rebirth of the ancient religion of the Great Goddess* (1979), Starhawk located the origins of Goddess-religion in peaceful neolithic Europe, which suffered attack from patriarchal Indo-European warrior tribes. Starhawk's view of the history of the "Goddess peoples", which is heavily influenced by the now discredited theories of Margaret Murray, is based on their escape from persecution from waves of invasion by warrior gods, who drove the Goddess peoples out of the

Another performance of the sacred spiral dance, this time in Glastonbury, England. The dance begins with all the participants holding hands and beginning a winding snake-like movement around the room, during which a complex pattern allows everyone to have contact with each other at some point.

fertile lowlands into the hills and high mountains, where they became known as the sidhe, pixies, fair folk or faeries.

Murray had claimed, in *The Witch-Cult in Western Europe* (1921), that witch beliefs were associated with an early European dwarf race, which at one time inhabited Europe and survived in stories of fairies and elves, and that every seven years they made a human sacrifice to their god. According to Murray, fairies gradually became identified with witches. Both fairies and witches were said to cast and break spells, heal, divine for lost objects and the future, "traffick" with the Devil, change shape, fly, levitate and steal unbaptized children.

Starhawk builds up a picture of the faeries based on the ideas of Victor Anderson and Margaret Murray. According to her version, the faeries preserved the pre-Christian, pre-patriarchal Old Religion: they bred cattle in the stony hills and lived in turf-covered round huts. Clan mothers, called Queens of Elphame, led covens, together with a priest, the sacred king, who embodied the dying God who died a mock death at the end of his term of office. They celebrated the eight festivals of the wheel of the year with "wild processions on horseback, singing, chanting, and the lighting of ritual fires". Starhawk writes that the sacred king, or high priest, held office for nine years, after which he underwent a ritual death, abdicated and joined the council of elders.

POLITICS

There is a political thread running through all of Starhawk's writing. She contrasts a peaceful vision of society where all are honoured and live in empathy with the natural world, with a culture based on the dominance of some people over others and the destruction of the environment. In *Dreaming the Dark* (1982) she says that the "burning times", when women were persecuted as witches in Europe, were linked to a stealing of common land, natural resources and knowledge by a culture based on what she calls a "consciousness of estrangement". She contrasts this with the "consciousness of immanence",

The Goddess is worshipped in many guises. Here a "black Madonna" is venerated at the Goddess conference in Glastonbury.

which she claims is found in women, sexuality and magic. In her next book *Truth or Dare* (1990), she focused on ancient Sumerian Mesopotamia, and wrote about a spiritual battle of power between the priestesses of the temple and the king. Initially, she says, these roles were elected and based on an equal relationship, ritually maintained, but eventually the king usurped power: refusing to relinquish his kingship to an elected successor, he passed it on to his sons instead. This changed the relationship with the priestesses of the temple, and relations with women in general, by establishing an oppressive patriarchy with its consciousness of estrangement. In her novels *The Fifth Sacred Thing* (1993), which is set in the

year 2040, and *Walking to Mercury* (1997), which is a fictionalized autobiography, Starhawk finally developed the "fantasy of a living future", which is briefly outlined at the end of *Truth or Dare*. Starhawk's works offer a vision of the future by using the imagination, which is the basis of magic, to envision a different reality.

Moving away from Dianic witchcraft, Starhawk includes men in her version of witchcraft. However, men have to learn how to be non-oppressive and how to discover, or rediscover, the parts of themselves that have been repressed by patriarchy. Starhawk's vision of witchcraft combines political activism and therapeutic techniques within a spiritual system loosely based on Wicca.

WESTERN MAGIC TODAY

Western magical practices, including modern witchcraft, offer a kaleidoscope of paths or techniques for attaining alternate forms of consciousness. All of these attempt to go beyond ordinary, everyday awareness to achieve a heightened state which some, such as high magicians who practise "Western mysteries", describe as contact with a deity or angels. Others, such as chaos magicians, strive to achieve an altered state of consciousness by deconditioning the self to obtain inner knowledge. Many, but not all, of those who have an interest in Western magic see the world in a spiritual way, and so the link that magic has had with religion in the past is still in evidence.

TODAY'S MAGICIANS

B y using a variety of different techniques, magicians learn to see themselves as part of a magical whole – a wider pattern underlying all of life, including the seen and the unseen. There are many different paths – from the various forms of modern witchcraft, where people of either sex work alone or with others, to New Age, which has a very wide variety of different expressions and beliefs. What these different branches of Western magic share is that most followers and practitioners seek communication with what is often termed the "otherworld", a realm of spirit beings, defined or personalized in many ways. A trained magician can move in and out of contact with the otherworld with facility, in much the same way as shamans have done in times past, and still do today.

Modern Western magic often forms an alternative religious or spiritual practice today, and much of the symbolism remains the same.

Who are the people who practise magic today in Western cultures? To call them magicians is likely to conjure up an image of Tolkien's Gandalf striding into the unknown, staff in hand, long robes and hair flowing in the wind. This romantic image has currency among those who practise magic, helping to add glamour and bring mystery into many magical traditions. Alternatively, magicians may be seen as Satanists, evildoers, part of a malevolent cosmic force working against God and the forces of good. Neither of these images are how most modern magicians see themselves, and most would strongly assert that they use magical powers for healing and positive purposes rather than for negative or destructive ends. There are many magical practices and paths to choose from today. A glance at the noticeboard in a local occult or New Age bookstore will reveal advertisements for courses, groups, healing, astrological consultation and much more; as will any of a number of specialist magazines. It is possible to join a witchcraft coven, train as a high or ceremonial magician in an occult school, become a druid, engage in a whole variety of New Age activities, practise Western forms of shamanism, perform magical rituals within the Northern or Nordic tradition, or become a chaos magician. These magical groups and traditions offer a kaleidoscope of ways of engaging in magic.

A magical world-view is a different way of seeing the world; it is holistic – often viewed as an interconnected web of forces and energies, which may be communicated and worked with, or controlled and directed. Each magical tradition will have a slightly different

White-robed druids celebrating Spring Equinox at Tower Hill, London, by sowing seed and making blessings for new life.

emphasis and way of working. For example, witches may prefer to work outside in nature, while high magicians may work in a specially consecrated temple dedicated to Egyptian deities, and a modern Western shamanic practitioner may go on spirit journeys conducted within a drumming circle. Many modern magical practices have adopted the eight seasonal festivals of the year developed by Gerald Gardner and his druid friend Ross Nichols. These festivals are seen to be the points where the magician links in with the wider forces of the cosmos. This is based on the understanding that the human being, as magician, witch, druid or shaman, is part of a wider pattern of life. This pattern of life includes the unseen as well as the seen.

Some magical practices offer training and a series of graduated initiations as part of a process for opening up awareness of magical forces and energies. By using various different techniques, such as meditation, guided path-workings or visionary journeys, the initiate is encouraged to value and focus on realities that are not always apparent in the everyday, ordinary world. This may mean learning to experience and

feel using intuition as well as using the critical faculties of the mind; it also involves learning to see significant connections between what would previously have been seen as separate events. It concerns coming to value the

Not all magical practices are viewed as spiritual traditions. This Baphomet statue is celebrated by chaos magicians who see magic primarily as a technique for changing consciousness.

Modern witchcraft can be practised in many different ways. People work alone or together and are free to formulate their own rituals.

connections of the whole as part of a spiritual journey that leads into another reality. This reality is often called the "otherworld" and it may be described in terms of spirits, deities and a whole range of other beings that are believed to inhabit this other dimension. Communication with the otherworld is possible through the active imagination, when the mind is in a state of light trance. The otherworld is said to co-exist with the ordinary world, and a trained magician can move in and out of these different forms of awareness with ease.

An important part of many magical practices is being able to see the seen and the unseen. Here, a crystal ball is being used to access the deeper parts of consciousness to gain what is seen to be spiritual truth.

WESTERN MYSTERIES

Modern magic's central ethos is working with the idea of spiritual evolution – the bringing down of higher angelic or elemental forces into the magician. This bringing down is a process that is thought to enable the soul to evolve; an idea which has been at the centre of much religious thought. Practitioners of Western Mysteries often work with esoteric versions of Christianity to seek unity with God. They may also use Egyptian myths, such as that of Isis and Osiris, to access what they see as deep levels of inner knowledge and wisdom in the name of spiritual and divine truth, or the legends and myths of other cultures, such as the British Arthurian legends.

Angels play an important role in Western magical traditions.

High or ceremonial magic, or "Western Mysteries", is a form of European magic distinguished by modern magicians from eastern magical systems. For those magicians who practise the Western Mysteries, all life forms – animals, plants, rocks – are evolving, but human beings are often seen as the supreme carriers of divinity, and they consequently have a responsibility to other life forms.

Magical rituals are frequently based on mythological themes and cycles concerning life and death, such as those of Isis and Osiris, and the descent into the underworld as undergone by Persephone. Each myth is seen to reveal a deeper inner truth. Western Mysteries are a magical form of Neoplatonism whereby the individual soul of the magician seeks reunion with the divine One. This frequently encompasses versions of esoteric Christianity which seek unity with divinity after the Fall, and concerns the mastery of the lower self and baser nature in the spiritual pursuit of the Ultimate Being. This is seen in terms of a union of the magician's soul with the One. It is said that the primordial teachings came from Egypt and were derived from the lost island of Atlantis.

The Western Mysteries are usually taught in occult schools and have initiation schemes whereby the apprentice may progress to a number of different levels or degrees, each of which

Each angel is seen as a being of pure consciousness in profound union with God.

has an appropriate outward insignia – for example, a distinctively coloured robe or girdle. Western Mystery magical work is usually focused on working with Cabbalistic path workings or meditation on certain spheres of the tree of life. Group rituals are conducted in a lodge or a temple dedicated to a deity.

ANGELS

Most Western Mystery schools work with the idea of spiritual evolution and the bringing down of higher angelic forces into the magician to aid the soul's progress. This developed from the Hermetic tradition, which attempted to rise above the deceptions of sense by attunement to the divine mind through the contemplation of the universe. The practice is concerned with raising a fallen human nature in a wider movement of spiritual evolution. According to the high magician David Goddard, from the One, which is beyond understanding or comprehension, comes an overflowing of eternal love that expresses itself in a multitude of beings. The One is a creator and through this overflowing of love comes creation. The One becomes many – the seven great spirits of the Elohim, seven princes, archangels or "lords of flame": the Elohim form a prism through which the One is refracted and through which the One acts. Each angel is a being of pure consciousness and is in profound union with the One, beyond time or space, channelling the divine light without distortion. An angel is a focus of power, wisdom, beauty and love, and they have a teaching function. For David Goddard, Michael helps in matters of achievement and ambition; Gabriel is concerned with psychic development; Samael is invoked for courage or perseverance; Raphael is a specialist in healing and communication; Sachiel helps in financial matters; Asariel rules in mediumship and trancework; Haniel is associated with the devas of nature; Cassiel supervises the energies of the planet; and Uriel transmits the Magical Force. Thus angels can be invoked in times of trouble or consternation to give practical and spiritual insight.

Some modern magicians use Egyptian myths as part of their magical practices.

Angels are called on to help in a whole range of human concerns and dilemmas.

THE ARTHURIAN LEGEND

The mythology of King Arthur and his Knights of the Round Table is important to magicians following the Western Mysteries because, like most other mythologies, they provide a moral and spiritual model on which to base magical practice.

Arthur is a Celtic hero, the son of King Uther Pendragon and the Lady Igraine, and his birth was made possible by the magical workings of Merlin the magician. The earliest written historical record of Arthur is in the *Historia Brittonum* (compiled in the early ninth century) which says that "the warrior Arthur" fought with the kings of the Britons against the Saxons, whom he conquered in 12 battles conducted in the sixth century. Arthur's entry into legend was effected by Geoffrey of Monmouth, who mixed these historical fragments with local traditions and Celtic myth. Consequently, Arthur and Merlin are hybrids, blending historical people with mythological characters.

THE ROMANCE OF ARTHUR

According to legend, Arthur was a fifth-century Christianized British warrior who made a stand against the barbarian Anglo-Saxon invaders from Denmark and Germany when Roman rule collapsed in AD400. Writing in the twelfth century, Geoffrey of Monmouth portrayed Arthur's reign as the climax of the history of the kings of Britain. Drawing on Welsh monastic writing, Breton folklore, poems and legends, he created the realm of Arthur as a piece of literary fiction. Arthur came to preside over a court with complex codes of etiquette and expression: jousts and combats were conducted under strict

Bedivere returns the sword Excalibur to the lady of the lake, as Arthur dies in the foreground.

moral and ethical rules of behaviour. The language of courtly love was based on the theme of unattainable passion – the beloved was seen to embody the image of the divine and was married to another. Underpinning the whole was a deeper dimension of the spiritual quest: the court was the point of departure for adventures into the otherworld.

The Round Table was set up by Merlin and had places for 150 knights, who were all equal in rank and loyal to King Arthur, who was first among equals. The knights embarked on quests, venturing deep into primeval forests, and these were metaphors for the soul's journey through uncharted

The central magical figure of the Arthurian legends is Merlin. Here, he comes under the enchantment of the Lady Nimue, the female magic figure who inherited his wisdom and who acts as a benign counterbalance to Arthur's sister, the malevolent female sorceress, Morgan le Fey.

worlds. The quest is an archetypal image of a spiritual search for the soul: Jason's quest for the golden fleece and Dante's wanderings in the dark forest to find an earthly paradise are but two examples. The goal of the quest could be a person, such as a maiden in distress, or a divine object such as the Holy Grail.

THE QUEST FOR THE GRAIL

The Grail is a complex symbol with many meanings. Allegedly the cup from the Last Supper used to collect the blood of Christ, it was said to have been brought from Palestine to Britain via Spain and North Africa by Joseph of Arimathea. It is associated with Glastonbury in Somerset, sometimes called the sacred Isle of Avalon, where Joseph of Arimathea founded the first Christian community. The Grail is seen to be a sacred vessel that contains the potentiality of all wisdom, intuition and knowledge; it is also thought to be the source of creativity and inspiration; it is a magical chalice of transformation, a cauldron of rebirth. It is thought to be able to effect a form of spiritual alchemy, bringing about a higher form of consciousness; it is held that it can bring healing; it is also symbolic of the female power of the womb, and of the Goddess. The myth of King Arthur offers magicians a range of heroic patterns or archetypes with which to identify in a personal quest for a higher form of consciousness whereby the ordinary, everyday consciousness is dissolved, purification ensues, and the individual soul is reunited with the One.

AN ETHICAL MODEL

The Arthurian legend and the figures within it are important components of the Western Mysteries for many magicians. This is because the Western Mysteries are a form of Neoplatonism – a philosophical view of the world that gives a view of the universe and explains the human position within it. Above all, it outlines how human beings can achieve salvation by restoring their original divine nature in union with God. Arthurian mythology offers a moral and ethical model for this purpose.

The Grail was allegedly the cup used by Jesus and his disciples at the Last Supper, and then later to collect the blood of Christ during his crucifixion. Once thought of as a mark of spiritual purity, the Grail today represents the potentiality of all wisdom, intuition and creativity for many magicians.

Symbolic of magical transformation, the Grail represents a form of spiritual alchemy to bring about a higher form of consciousness. This twelfth-century depiction shows the cup standing at the centre of the round table, another very potent symbol within the Arthurian legend.

DRUIDRY

The druids are thought to have been Celtic spiritual leaders, but exactly who they were and what they did remains unknown. What information is available comes from Roman sources but pagan Celtic beliefs were intensely localized and few generalizations can be made. It is clear that the druids have been imagined in various ways in different periods, from the Renaissance to the Romantic movement, and more recently in the 1970s as part of the general expansion of spiritualities in Western cultures. Once only associated with men in white robes, celebrating the solstice at Stonehenge, today druidry is interpreted more widely as a spirituality in touch with nature.

Stonehenge is particularly associated with the druids, as this nineteenth-century aquatint shows.

The esoteric origins of modern druidism are located in the Western Mystery mythological tradition. Philip Carr-Gomm, the current chief of the Order of Bards, Ovates and Druids, says that the magicians of Atlantis discovered the secrets of nature and worked in tune with her powers. However, some used their powers for selfish ends and there developed a struggle between good, or white, magic and bad, or black, magic. The battle lines were drawn between those who saw in nature the great divine Mother of men and used her gifts for human welfare, and those who saw nature as a Satanic temptress with cruel power. As catastrophe struck Atlantis, the dark lords were engulfed while the white sages, having greater gifts of foreknowledge, journeyed both east and west. In the west they landed on the shore of America, and in the east, on the shores of Ireland and the western coasts of Britain, and so druidry spread.

Human sacrifices were said to have been put in wicker-work images and burnt by the Celts, supposedly to promote the fertility of the land.

DRUID FESTIVALS

Today, modern druids celebrate the same eight festivals as witches. In druidism these are called: Samhuinn (31 October–2 November), Winter Solstice or Alban Arthuan (Light of Arthur), Imbolc or Oimelc (2 February), Spring Equinox, Beltane (1 May), Summer Solstice or Alban Heruin (21 or 22 June), Lughnasadh (1 August) and Autumnal Equinox or Alban Elued (21 September). Of these festivals, Samhuinn is the time when "the veil between this world and the World of the Ancestors is drawn aside" and druids prepare to make contact with the spirits of the departed as living spirits of loved ones who hold the "root wisdom of the tribe" as a source of guidance. There is much variety in druid rituals and they differ from group to group. Sometimes members adapt or completely rewrite rituals for their own use. According to Philip Shallcrass, the British Druid Order rituals are based on the story of Lleu Llaw Gyffes in the *Mabinogion*, a collection of supposedly Welsh Celtic myths. According to Ronald Hutton, however, they were popular international tales with their origins in Egypt, India or China, which had spread across Asia and Europe and were mixed with Irish and British myths. They were put in their final form by a courtly entertainer by the late eleventh century, when they were probably not more than a century or two old.

DRUID BELIEF SYSTEMS

Shallcrass points out that there is no central druid theology but that two generalizations about druid beliefs can be made: the first is that there is a belief in a power or energy resident in the earth or in nature, which is often represented as a mother, but it is left to individuals to decide how they wish to look upon this entity; the second is that there is some kind of unified force underlying the manifest world, but again that force is defined by each individual.

Emma Restall-Orr, head of the Druid network, and one time joint head of the British Druid Order, says that druidism includes a whole spectrum of beliefs but that a love of the earth is what holds druids together. Restall-Orr describes druidism as an animistic faith, not a "call of the gods". Communing with nature means learning to grow, to trust and to hear the response of the earth. Nature as deity is drawn down into the ritual circle and this is experienced as joy and love. The internalization of love, joy and inspiration is called "Awen" in modern druidism, and it is the role of bards – as poets and musicians – to encourage the flow of Awen. Ovates, or vates, have a different function: they listen to the voices of the otherworld using various forms of divination such as tree lore and

Modern druids celebrate dawn within the circle at Stonehenge at the Summer Solstice or Alban Heruin. A vigil is held through the night and as dawn breaks a ceremony marks the sun's rising. A further ritual is held at noon.

runes. Ovates are facilitators, healers, "changers of situations", and their role is to interpret signs and ask questions. Tree lore is associated with a symbolic language called Ogham (pronounced o'um), which links a tree with a letter of the alphabet, and runes are a series of symbols often inscribed on wood or stone. They are associated with the Norse god Odin, who hung upside down on the cosmic tree Yggdrasil, and through his suffering came to understand the cosmic meaning of the universe, which he then revealed to humans through the runes. Modern druidism is a quest for a spirituality that connects the individual with the natural world through artistic expression and inspiration.

THE DRUID'S HISTORY

Modern druidism developed from the late eighteenth-century Romantic movement, but this was not the first time that the druids had been "discovered". Stuart Piggott shows that from the Renaissance onwards those steeped in the philosophy and scholarship of the Greek and Roman thinkers had sought to rediscover the beliefs and practices of the druids. In the eighteenth century, when "fashion shifted from classical to

romantic, the druids were quietly waiting to take on a new life in the contemporary modes of Western thought and emotion". The druid story has an evidential basis in archaeology and what can be deduced of ancient Celtic religion from texts and iconography. In searching for the origins of the druids, Piggott has outlined three types of source material. The first is archaeological evidence from graves, ceremonial sites or representations in Celtic or Romano-Celtic art; the second is the writings of Greeks and Romans on the Celts; and the third is the development of ideas about the druids that originated in the antiquarian speculations of the seventeenth and eighteenth centuries, and were used by scholars as well as imaginative writers and artists. Piggott concludes that the combined evidence from all available sources leaves modern knowledge of pagan Celtic religion in a "state of the most rudimentary vagueness".

The Reverend William Stukeley (1687–1765) revived a cult of the druids. Stukeley had visited Stonehenge and believed that druidry was the native religion of the British Isles. He laid out a druidical temple in his garden, complete

Emma Restall-Orr, former joint chief of the British Druid Order.

with apple trees and mistletoe. His numerous publications on the Celtic past led to an interest in discovering and recreating a Celtic past.

Ronald Hutton notes that a number of writers between 1760 and 1840 "set out to 'reconstruct' the principles of a noble and natural religion worthy to be associated with prehistoric philosopher-priests". Of note is Edward Williams (1747–1826) who assumed the name Iolo Morgannwg and "revived" the medieval Order of Bards to teach a "prehistoric system of mystical belief". He added ritual, ceremonies, regalia and hierarchy to texts. The first ritual, the "Gorsedd" (the assembly of new Bards), was held on Primrose Hill in London in 1792. Hutton observes that the notion of a home-grown system of very old wisdom akin to those of the East is very important to many people in the British Isles. This has, he argues, resulted in the belief in the importance of national characters, racial identity and folk-memories as a product of the Romantic movement of the late eighteenth century. The Celts have come to represent the

Sacred mistletoe

Mistletoe is often called the 'druids' plant'. Godhead is seen to be located in the oak, and the white berries of the mistletoe are thought by some druids to resemble drops of semen. At the druid Winter Solstice ceremony (Alban Arthuan) the mistletoe is ritualistically taken from the oak tree and laid upon an altar. Mistletoe is seen to bring fertility to the earth through its representation of the semen of the oak god given to the earth goddess, thus fertility is renewed.

A nineteenth-century romantic portrayal of a druid priestess with sacred mistletoe.

emotional, mystical, creative and "feminine", while the Anglo-Saxons have been defined as the embodiment of progress, industry, utilitarianism, science and masculinity.

HISTORICAL EVIDENCE

According to Hutton, the Graeco-Roman writers agreed that the Celtic intellectual elite was divided into bards, druids and vates (only the latter two were religious officials). The druids were more prestigious and were more concerned with philosophy and theology, but according to Julius Caesar they were also teachers, healers and judges. The vates specialized in divination and sacrifice. Hutton points out that the druids were male and that the formal religion of the Celtic peoples was mediated through men, although bards, physicians and women were all depicted as skilled in magic and capable of communing with deities in Irish literature. As far as religious beliefs are concerned, the Graeco-Roman writers tended to agree that the Celts had some sort of theology but it was not recorded

This painting depicts the druids of Anglesey, North Wales, being massacred by the Romans by order of the governor Suetonius Paulinus.
It is conveying a specific nationalistic message and was painted during a Celtic revival by the Scots, Irish and Welsh against
English imperialism, and also against the rationalism of the Enlightenment.

An arch-druid at the Avebury stone circle in England during the Summer Solstice celebrations.
The growing informality of the druid order is shown in the different types of clothing worn.

in any detail. Most of the early Irish and some of the early Welsh tales described a divine otherworld – a version of the mortal world – where people enjoyed eternal life. This otherworld could be entered via certain doors concealed in mounds, islands, hills, lakes or the sea, and some humans could visit and return.

THE MODERN INHERITANCE

A great deal is unknown about the religious beliefs of the ancient druids, but modern druids interpret druidism in terms of worshipping the natural forces of the environment through the creative arts. Gone are the days when druidry was represented by men in white robes. Now it attracts a variety of people interested in a Celtic heritage and wanting to relate to nature.

Druids celebrate the Winter Solstice at Stonehenge. Much controversy and publicity has surrounded the solstice celebrations at Stonehenge. For a number of years rituals were strictly controlled or banned altogether, but at the Summer Solstice in 2000 all restrictions were lifted and many people were able to enjoy being in the midst of the stones as the sun rose over the eastern horizon.

THE NEW AGE

The New Age movement originated in 1971 when it emerged in America as a self-conscious form of spirituality. The New Age was originally world-denying in its search for a new order based on spiritual enlightenment. The Earth was seen to be entering a new cycle of evolution marked by a new human consciousness, which would give birth to a new civilization – the "Age of Aquarius" – which would overcome the present corrupt culture by cataclysm and disaster. The idea of a New Age was an amalgamation of various predictions: those of Nostradamus; the American psychic Edgar Cayce; the Theosophical Society; and the Lucis Trust, Rudolf Steiner's anthroposophy. These prophecies were founded in the spiritual traditions of the Maya, Aztecs and Hopi people, and also the Judaeo-Christian belief in the second coming of Christ. When the anticipated apocalypse did not arrive there was a "turn inward" and nature became a source of revelation rather than something that obscured real spirit.

New Age philosophy involves connecting with nature and all its beauty.

The term "New Age" has become a diffuse term applied to anything from New Age travellers to a particular type of book or music. The New Age is primarily a movement which aims to bring about social change by many and diverse means. By its very nature, according to the sociologist of religion Michael York, it is a term of convergence, one that is more than the sum of its parts, or at least is not to be equated with any one of its parts. According to Marilyn Ferguson there is an "Aquarian conspiracy" – without a political doctrine or a manifesto – which aims to bring about a new form of human consciousness. The Aquarian conspiracy, as advocated by Ferguson, is a new world-view, which has arisen as a response to a crisis. In this vision of a different reality, nature's powers are seen as transformative and a powerful ally, not as a force to be subdued. Ferguson sees human beings as stewards of inner and outer resources, and fundamentally embedded in nature. An expansion of consciousness is required to effect a reunion with all living things, she says: "Just as science demonstrates a web of relationship underlying everything in the universe a glittering network of events, so the mystical experience of

A holistic perspective – whereby everything in the cosmos is seen to be interrelated – is an underlying theme of the New Age.

The Edgar Cayce Foundation, Virginia, USA.

A New Age group invoke the Earth Spirit at the Merry Maidens stone circle, Cornwall, England.

James Lovelock, formulater of the Gaia principle.

wholeness encompasses all separation".

More recently, the popularization of New Age ideas has been given an immeasurable boost by the publication of James Redfield's *The Celestine Prophecy* in 1994. Combining a new view of science with a conspiracy adventure drama conducted in the rainforests of Peru, Redfield introduces nine "insights" that teach the perennial wisdom that all religions are concerned with humanity creating a relationship with a higher source of divinity. This is a means of stopping the abuse of power and of finding a positive vision of a way to save this planet.

NEW AGE AND GAIA

For New Agers, the earth is entering a new cycle of evolution marked by a new human consciousness. David Spangler, a leading proponent, describes the New Age as a time of abundance and spiritual enlightenment guided by advanced beings, "perhaps angels or spiritual masters or perhaps emissaries from an extraterrestrial civilization whose spacecraft were the UFOs, [who] would help to create a new civilization". This new cycle of consciousness concerns the invisible and inner dimensions of all life and is, according to William Bloom, a prominent spokesperson and writer on

the subject, made up of different dynamics that constitute four major fields: ecology, new paradigm science, new psychology and spiritual dynamics.

The ecology field draws on the work of the British scientist James Lovelock who, in 1969, proposed the revolutionary principle known as the Gaia hypothesis – that life shapes and controls the environment rather than the other way around. Every individual life form, from

microbe to human, is involved by its own life processes. Earth's atmosphere is actively maintained and regulated by life on the surface for all the species of living beings. Lovelock's work has helped promote a new scientific understanding of life at all levels, from organisms to social systems and ecosystems. It involves a distinct shift in perception from the mechanistic world-view to an encompassing ecological view.

The New Age is eclectic in its beliefs and practices. Here, a tourist performs the Chinese art of Tai Chi, at the Temple of the Condor, Machu Picchu, Peru. Machu Picchu is said to be the lost city of the Inca, once full of thousands of people as well as various religious shrines and temples.

A ceremony involving group dancing at the Findhorn Centre.

The New Age physicist Fritjof Capra has probably done more than most to popularize New Age science thanks to his critique of mechanistic science, *The Turning Point* (1983), and by his exploration of the parallels between modern physics and eastern religions in *The Tao of Physics* (1976). He calls this change an ecological paradigm. Capra points out that in twentieth-century science a holistic perspective – involving a change in focus from the parts of mechanistic philosophy to the whole, where knowledge is seen as a network of relationships with no firm foundation – has become known as "systems thinking". Systems thinking was pioneered in the early twentieth century by biologists who emphasized the view of living organisms as integrated wholes. It is concerned with context, connections and relationships, and how the essential properties of an organism, or a living system, are properties

Eileen Caddy, of the Findhorn centre.

The meditation room at Findhorn.

of the whole. Living systems are viewed as part of an interactive web or network.

FINDHORN

A New Age community in northern Scotland, Findhorn is run according to messages and guidance received from God through Eileen Caddy, one of its founders. It has become a horticultural mecca for communication with nature spirits, devic presences, fairies and other such beings. Eileen Caddy, her husband Peter, and Dorothy MacLean moved to Findhorn in 1962 and established a community of over a hundred members as a centre of light for the Aquarian age. MacLean communicated with devas, which she felt were part of the myriad forms of thought of the divine potential with a vibrant energy that is the very essence of life.

These ideas are influenced by Theosophy, and have been influential in bringing New Age thinking in line with a Christian interpretation of the divine, largely through a focus on the light and communication with angels. The artist and writer Monica Sjöö has launched an attack on such a view, calling the New Age movment patriarchal and fascistic. She claims that New Age embraces reactionary, anti-life views, which are not in tune with the power of women, symbolized as the Goddess. She argues that by creating a God who is all light and transcendent, the rest of creation is demonized. Consequently, the New Age is concerned with a transformation of nature, both internally as healing and a form of development of a higher consciousness, and externally as a relationship with the wider environment. The interconnectedness between all beings, within a network symbolized as Gaia, is very important, and its spiritual aspect is expressed through harmony and light, often within a Christian interpretation.

Healing is an important aspect of the New Age, and complementary or alternative therapies, such as shiatsu, acupressure, reflexology, reiki and various visualization techniques are very much part of the whole picture.

New Agers see all life as connected. Here, on a Californian beach, musicians prepare to play music for whales in a ceremony to link humanity with the animals.

The Findhorn Foundation, like other New Age groups, communicates with nature spirits, devas, fairies and beings from the otherworld. This painting of a Fairy Tree shows the enchanting world of Faerie.

WESTERN SHAMANISM

The central precept of shamanism in the West is regeneration and a revitalization of earth-based "ways of knowing". Inspired by the idea that shamanism is humanity's most ancient and authentic form of spirituality, many modern Western shamanic practitioners turn to what they see as a primordial means of healing and creating connections to nature. Practices include drumming and journeying, as techniques for self-realization and making contact with an otherworldly realm of spirits. Some emphasize the importance of traditions – such as those practised by the Native American Indians – others place more importance on finding new ways of engaging with the living world.

Many modern Western shamanic practitioners attend drumming classes. Drumming helps to induce a trance state for journeying.

The 1970s saw the emergence of contemporary shamanism, sometimes called neo-shamanism, as a new form of spirituality emanating from the USA. It has been claimed that Mircea Eliade's book *Shamanism: Archaic Techniques of Ecstasy* (1964) was the prototype for the Western shamanism movement, but it took Carlos Castaneda's *The Teachings of Don Juan: A Yaqui Way of Knowledge* (1968), which sold hundreds of thousands of copies, to bring the living experience of an indigenous shamanism to Western culture. This work and nine other books by Castaneda on the same subject are now widely regarded as hoaxes, presenting fiction as fact, but they did popularize shamanism and lead to a fascination with the alternate realities of the shaman.

Shamanism is seen as primordial and authentic by those in the West who are jaded by world religions, particularly Christianity. Native American shamanism, with its circular notion of power and knowledge, symbolized by the medicine wheel, taught about the balance and relationship of all things, and this form of shamanism became particularly fashionable. An alternative to a focus on a particular culture is core shamanism, developed by Michael Harner in his influential book *The Way of the Shaman* (1980). Harner peels off cultural traditions, leaving an essential core, which reveals techniques for changing consciousness during journeying to find power animals, restoring power and

In earlier centuries, as well as today, shamans have been portrayed in ways that reflect Europeans' fascination with the exotic, and rarely in ways that reflect the shaman's own culture. It is an appalling fact that most shamanic societies have been wiped out by European colonialism and imperialism.

healing: the essence is in the technique rather than the specific culture. Harner created the Foundation for Shamanic Studies, which has promoted core shamanism techniques through the widespread use of workshops, and now has a number of accredited teachers.

SHAMANISM IN HISTORY

Traditionally a shaman is a ritual specialist who communicates between different worlds – the ordinary world and the spirit domain – on behalf of his or her people. In the Western, usually urban, context, shamanism may stand for a regeneration and revitalization of ancient Earth-based "ways of knowing" for those who see themselves as dispossessed or alienated from nature as a spiritual source. Westerners can be fascinated with the exotic world of shamanism, but they can also fear it as something that takes them beyond the known.

The West's fascination with shamanism is not new. The historian Gloria Flaherty notes that the curiosity of intellectuals was raised in the fifth century BC when Herodotus reported the death-defying feats of the Scythian soothsaying poets Aristeas and Abaris. She notes that classical scholars throughout the ages have studied Herodotus and have also pointed out numerous other "shamanic" practices of antiquity.

The general view of shamanism as an ageless human activity connected with nature has accounted for its rise in popularity in the West. This is the aspect that has led many people to search for a spiritual path in shamanism. According to some Western shamanic practitioners, it is the oldest way in which humanity has sought connection with spirit; it is seen to be an authentic spiritual experience far removed from the dominant religious institutions in the West, which are thought to have lost touch with the experience of spirituality.

THE MEDICINE WHEEL

Modern Western shamanism ofers a series of techniques for self-help and self-realization; it is believed to lead to personal empowerment but also teaches that the individual is part of a broader framework that connects with the rest of the cosmos. The Native American medicine wheel teachings offer a framework for understanding what is, for Westerners, a very different way of seeing the world. The medicine wheel has many meanings and manifestations,

During the eighteenth and nineteenth centuries, Western Europeans saw shamans as primitives who worshipped evil spirits.

They have seen in shamanism the origins of theatre, fairy tales and Greek mythology. Flaherty points out that in the eighteenth century there was a good supply of information about shamanism from all over the world, and that by this time certain notions of shamanism had become assimilated into the intellectual mainstream.

Most eighteenth-century observations of shamanism were written from the point of view of interested yet disbelieving western Europeans. Shamanism was viewed in a variety of ways. For some Christian missionaries it was related to native peoples' belief in evil spirits and worship of heathen idols: these "primitives" were thought to have no sense of the true god. For others it concerned a scholarly pursuit of truth into unknown "otherness" and shamanism was subjected to empirical tests and rational analyses. Some attempted to record the activities of vanishing peoples; for others, shamanism epitomized an ageless human activity; while for others there was a fascination with discovering what were seen as the hidden secrets of nature.

A modern shamanistic drum showing symbols of the seasons and the zodiac. The drum is an instrument that the shaman can "ride" to take him or her into the spirit otherworld; the symbols relate the shaman to the cosmos.

Native American "dream catchers" have become part of popular Western shamanism and the New Age. Adopted from Native American Indian traditions, they are believed to hold on to good dreams and dispel the bad ones.

ranging from structuring ceremonies and a means for the expression of dreams and visions, to methods for healing. The path of personal transformation on the medicine wheel is said to take the knower and the known through a spiral of experiences that link the individual, and his or her own course from birth to death, with the seasons and the wider whole.

The teachings of Sun Bear, who is of Chippewa descent, are based on his vision of the medicine wheel and incorporate elements from various Native American cultures. The wheel revolves around a Creator Stone, which is the centre of all life and radiates energy to the rest of the wheel. Seven stones surrounding the Creator form the centre circle, the foundation of all life. They are, in sunwise direction: Earth Mother, Father Sun, Grandmother Moon, Turtle clan, Frog clan, Thunderbird clan and Butterfly clan. Four stones mark the outer circle, and these are the Spirit Keepers: Waboose in the north, Wabun in the east, Shawnodese in the south and

Mudjekeewis in the west. From the Spirit Keeper stones radiate qualities – such as cleansing, renewal, purity, clarity and wisdom – that are necessary to gain the sacred space of the Creator in the centre of the circle. Between the four Spirit Keeper stones are the 12 moon stones of the outer circle.

Issues of cultural appropriation or, in other words, the stealing of an oppressed people's spiritual heritage by the descendents of Western colonialism, are slowly infiltrating popular books and journals aimed at those interested in practising shamanism in the West. There is a move to search for Western "indigenous" versions, and a whole range of shamanisms – from Celtic to Wiccan – are being "rediscovered". Weekend workshops and drumming circles, where participants can journey in trance to find their spirit guides, are becoming more and more popular.

Healing is often a central component of much of this work, and shamanic

Soul journeying is an important part of modern Western shamanic practice.

practitioners journey to retrieve lost soul parts – for themselves and for others – on a regular basis. The essence of shamanic healing concerns the spiritual removal of aspects of a person that should not be

there, and returning those spiritual parts that should. This is often done with the aid of spirit beings sometimes called power animals, or totems.

However, shamanic practitioners are not the same thing as shamans: a shamanic training does not make a shaman. For Gordon MacLellan, who is a contemporary Western shaman working in environmental education, being a shaman is a practical job of mediating between the human world and the world of spirits. Seeing the role of the shaman in modern Britain as one of communicator and "patterner" with nature, he says that a modern shaman has to find new ways of engaging humans with the living world. Shamans work with communities and draw their inspiration from the Otherworld, which is an abode of spirits where we "meet the talking foxes and watch the shapes of the stone people unfold from the rocks on a hillside ... This is the shaman's world. The shaman moves through an Otherworld that may

The medicine wheel links the individual into a wider sacred whole. Here a man is meditating at a medicine wheel at Sedona, Arizona, USA.

Shamanic tools

Smudge sticks and smudge fans are used to cleanse the body, mind and surroundings before a spirit journey is commenced, or simply as a way to clear the mind and purify the body. A smudge stick is lit and the fragrant smoke that comes from it is directed to the appropriate place by the fan. Smudge sticks are often made from white sage, but also from other sweet smelling herbs that have particular significance or cleansing qualities. Rattles are sometimes used instead of a drum to help a shaman go into a trance; they can also be used during a healing to call spirits, diagnose illness and open a person to the spirits.

A smudge fan made from feathers.

A rattle made from dried seed pods.

White sage smudge sticks for cleansing.

correspond exactly with the territory she calls home but here is midnight and a world frosted with energy like ice on every leaf, where the mist at dawn is a swirling, pouring cloud of spirals spilling out of damp hollows". The Otherworld is not other at all, it is also this world.

Not tapping directly into an extant tradition, and gaining inspiration from a number of sources, Gordon MacLellan claims that some of the most exciting ceremonies have grown with grass roots environmental action: "Whole rituals take shape through the need of people to draw upon their own energy, to recognize their strength and to acknowledge the land and their feelings for it that can bring them to battle on its behalf." MacLellan feels that these rituals represent a growth that breaks traditions, bridges class, belief and age distinction, and suggests that these eco-warriors are the latest practitioners of a particular magic of the modern age, and the inheritors of shamanic traditions.

Gordon MacLellan, a modern Western shaman.

Western shamanism today is often concerned with healing, and here Jo Crow, a Western shaman, drums herself into a trance during a ceremony.

THE NORTHERN TRADITION

Heathens, or practitioners of the Northern tradition of magic, attempt to recapture an ancient Indo-European way of life through the mythology of Odin and other Scandanavian gods and goddesses. Northern cosmology is focused on the world tree Yggdrasil, the connecting point of nine worlds, at the bottom of which sit the three sister Norns who weave a web of fate called the "wyrd". This is a very specialized tradition and one which, unlike the Western Mysteries, does not take strands of belief from other traditions. The spiritual path that practitioners of the Northern tradition follow looks to the Icelandic Sagas for inspiration in matters concerning human dilemmas and conflicts.

Odin the Norse god with his two crows Huginn (Thought) and Muninn (Memory).

While many modern pagans claim Celtic origins for their practice, some are drawn to the traditions and history of Germanic, Scandinavian or Anglo-Saxon peoples, the spiritual beliefs that are said to be indigenous to northern Europe.

Comprising Germanic, Baltic, Norse and Celtic strands, these beliefs relate to areas of Germany, the Baltic countries of northern Poland and western Russia, Iceland, Scandinavia, Austria, the Czech Republic, Switzerland, northern France, Ireland and Britain, and are collectively described as the "Northern tradition". Often preferring to call themselves heathens, practitioners of the Northern tradition attempt to recapture and reconstruct what they see as the ancient Nordic tribal religion, mainly through the lore and the sagas as outlined in twelfth- and thirteenth-century literature, especially that of the Icelander Snorri Sturluson (1179–1241). Seeing their beliefs as part of an ancient Indo-European way of life, practitioners of Northern magic create a different spiritual path to those who follow the Western Mystery tradition, with its focus on Egyptian and Judaeo-Christian mythology.

While most practitioners of the Northern tradition see their magical practices as part of a rich variety of spiritual paths and welcome all interested seekers, it is unfortunate that in the past this form of magical organization has

The goddess Freyja, mistress of magic and witchcraft. She is said to own a falcon skin that enables her to fly to the underworld. She is depicted here flying with swans.

attracted a minority who have neo-Nazi sympathies. A tendency to nationalism by some in the Northern tradition in Britain has led to tensions with other pagan or magical groups, but now the general consensus among most heathens is that they will not hold with any form of racism or nationalism.

TROTH TO THE GODS

The main Northern tradition is known as "Odinism" or "¡satr·", meaning "loyalty or troth to the gods", or "allegiance to the deities". The principle god is called Odin in Scandinavian, Wotan in German and Woden in Anglo-Saxon. Odin is associated with inspiration, writing, combat and the dead. He has one eye, wears a wide-brimmed hat and often a blue cloak, and carries a magical spear. Two ravens, Huginn (Thought) and Muninn (Memory) sit on his shoulders, birds of battle and also symbols of flights to find wisdom.

Although the goddesses are equal with the gods in Northern mythology, little is known about them. For example, there is not much information on Odin's partner, the goddess Frigg, who is Queen of the Heavens. There were 12 gods and 13 goddesses in the Norse pantheon, and these included the fertility god Freyr and his sister Freyja, who is associated with war and rides to battle in a chariot drawn by two cats. Freyja is mistress of magic and witch-craft, and owns a falcon skin, which enables her to take falcon form on journeys to the underworld. The god Thor is the son of Odin and the Earth, is second in importance to Odin and represents order, law and stability. Loki, the son of two giants and the foster-brother of Odin, is a trickster figure who embodies all that is dark, unpredictable, and ambiguous. Loki is necessary as a catalyst to create change, without which no movement could take place.

Northern cosmology is centred on the world tree Yggdrasil, which is the connecting point of nine worlds; each world is populated by one race or type of being, such as giants, dwarves, elves, deities and humans. In Norse myth-ology, the Norns are three sisters who sit

A twelfth-century Viking tapestry depicting Odin on the left carrying an axe, with a representation of the cosmic tree Yggdrasil, from which he hung. In the centre is the god Thor carrying a hammer, and on the right is the fertility god Freyr holding an ear of corn.

at the base of Yggdrasil and spin a web of fate called "wyrd". The past and future are not seen as separate, and the future is seen to be in the present; time is not viewed as a linear progression and wyrd can be changed to some degree. The amount of influence that it is possible to exert on wyrd has been likened to sailing by the psychologist Brian Bates, who is the author of two popular books on the subject. According to him, a skilled magical practitioner is like a sailor who has the ability to trim the sails in order to change or adjust direction but cannot alter the overall course of the

The Norse tradition was depicted in heroic, Romantic terms by a variety of artists, as in this nineteenth-century painting by Hans Gabriel Jentzsch showing a Winter Solstice festival honouring the onset of winter.

current. According to Ronald Hutton, there is not enough information to make comparisons between the cults of the Celts, Romans, Greeks and Eastern peoples and those of the Germanic and Norse peoples, but wyrd, the idea of an overwhelming web of destiny that shapes the whole world, appears to be a significant northern characteristic.

Since 1973, Ásatrú has been one of the officially recognized religions of Iceland, and while it has not reached that status in other countries it is growing in popularity. Northern tradition groups in Britain are the Odinic Rite, Odinshof, Hammarens Ordens Sällskap and the Rune Gild. In America the Ásatrú Alliance, the Ásatrú Folk Assembly, the Odinist Fellowship, the Ring of Troth and the Rune Gild are prominent. Some heathens celebrate the eight pagan seasonal festivals and lunar cycles but others dismiss these as of

A modern heathen celebration of May Day in Navan, Northern Ireland.

recent origin and observe what they see as more authentic Northern European rites of Winternights, Yule and Sigrblot. Winternights is the celebration of the onset of winter, harvest festival and an honouring of the dead; Yule is the observance of the longest night and New Year, a time of oaths and fateful encounters with otherworldly visitors such as the dead and divinities. Sigrblot is a victory celebration of the beginning of summer – of vitality over winter gloom or a celebration of coming victories in trading or raiding.

The runes are used as a divination system in the Northern tradition. Divination was important to the Germanic

peoples, and according to the Roman writer Tacitus, they paid much attention to the "casting of lots":

Their method of casting lots is a simple one: they cut a branch from a fruit-bearing tree and divide it into small pieces, which they mark with certain distinctive signs and scatter at random onto a white cloth. Then the priest of the community, if the lots are consulted publicly, or the father of the family, if it is done privately, after invoking the gods with eyes raised to heaven, picks up three pieces, one at a time, and interprets them according to the signs previously marked upon them.

A modern heathen celebration of midsummer or Sigrblot, the victory of summer over winter. People join hands around a decked pole to celebrate the return of the sun.

A ninth-century casket with runic inscriptions.

Rune stones in Gørlev church, Zealand, Denmark, from the tenth or eleventh century.

The true nature of the runes is said to have been revealed to Odin as he hung upon the world tree Yggdrasil for nine days and nine nights. Odin's account is recorded in the Håvamål:

> *I know that I hung on the*
> *windswept tree*
> *For nine days and nine nights,*
> *Wounded by a spear,*
> *And given to Odin,*
> *Myself to myself,*
> *On that tree*
> *Which no man knows*
> *From what roots it grows,*
> *They gave me no bread*
> *Nor drinking horn.*
> *I looked down,*
> *I picked up the runes,*
> *Screaming, I took them.*
> *Then I fell back.*

Heathens, like practitioners of magic in other traditions, seek to live in contact with the "spirit of place", seeing their gods as unique entities and as part of the all-embracing web of wyrd.

Stone runes.

Table of Runes:

Today, modern magicians of the Northern tradition use the runes as a system of sacred knowledge and expression of eternal universal laws; like the Tarot, they represent the deeper mysteries in symbolic form. The Elder Futhark is an alphabet of 24 runes or staves, and there are many variations of this basic pattern: some have more characters, like the Anglo-Saxon variant with 29, and others have less, like the Scandinavian version that has 16.

LETTER	SIGN	NAME	MEANING
F	ᚠ	Feoh	Cattle
U	ᚢ	Ur	Auroch
TH	ᚦ	Thorn	Thorn
A	ᚫ	Ansur	A mouth
R	ᚱ	Rad	A cartwheel
K	ᚲ	Ken	A torch
G	ᚷ	Geofu	A gift
W	ᚹ	Wynn	Happiness
H	ᚺ	Hagall	Hail
N	ᚾ	Nied	Need
I	ᛁ	Is	Ice
J	ᛃ	Jara	Harvest
Y	ᛇ	Eoh	A yew tree
P	ᛈ	Peorth	A dice cup
Z	ᛉ	Elhaz	An elk
S	ᛋ	Sigel	The sun
T	ᛏ	Tyr	The god Tyr
B	ᛒ	Beorc	A birch tree
E	ᛖ	Ehwaz	A horse
M	ᛗ	Mann	A human
L	ᛚ	Lagu	Water, sea
NG	ᛜ	Ing	The god Ing
D	ᛞ	Daeg	Day (light)
O	ᛟ	Othel	A possession

SATANISM

For Satanists, Satan or the Devil is symbolic of a hidden force in nature responsible for the workings of earthly affairs and representing the spirit of inspiration and human progress. Revolting against organized religion – which is only suitable for "the herd" – Satanists allegedly seek to harness what have been called dark forces to liberate the will in the advancement of evolution. Claims that Satanists conduct rituals to abuse children are reminiscent of early modern witchcraft accusations, and are vigorously denied. Satanism concerns the self-affirmation and freedom of the individual.

A pact supposedly signed by demons in looking-glass Latin, and used in evidence at the witchcraft trial of Urbain Grandier in 1634. The reversed signatures of Satanas, Beelzebub, Lucifer, Leviathan and Astararoth may be seen.

The Christian division of the world into light and dark or good and evil, the battlelines drawn between the God of good against demonic forces of evil headed by the Devil or Satan, has been a positive invitation to some to join the dark side. Anton Szandor La Vey, the founder of the Church of Satan, has taken this position one step further by formulating a religion based on worshipping the dark forces. La Vey was a great showman and played to his audience by dressing up as the Devil but, in his view, the Devil was not a deity that represented the opposite of God but a hidden force in nature responsible for the workings of earthly affairs. The Devil represented the spirit of progress and inspiraton for the advancement of human beings, as well as the spirit of revolt that leads to freedom from organized religions like Christianity, which are only suitable for the "herd".

On Spring Equinox or Walpurgisnacht, 30 April 1966, Anton La Vey shaved his head and declared the beginning of the Age of Satan. This marked the start of a number of Church of Satan workshops, seminars, and rituals that were open to the public and conducted at his home, the "Black House". This was the first church of its type, but it was not the first group that had met to honour Satan. In England in the eighteenth century, Sir Francis Dashwood had formed the Hellfire Club, and Rabelais' fictional utopia, the "Abbey of Thelema", had inspired Aleister Crowley to found his version in

Sicily in 1920, with the motto "Fait ce que voudras" ("Do what thou wilt").

ANTON LA VEY

La Vey was born in Chicago on 11 April 1930, and was allegedly taught legends of vampires and witches by his Gypsy grandmother, who passed on to him the folklore of her native Transylvania. Dropping out of school because it was boring, La Vey joined the Clyde Beatty Circus as a cage boy, watering and feeding lions and tigers. He became an assistant trainer and also played the organ. Later he joined a carnival and it

Sir Francis Dashwood (1708–81), pictured seated, formed a Satanist group called the Hell-Fire Club in the eighteenth century.

Francois Rabelais' (1494–1553) fictional utopia the "Abbey of Thelema" inspired the notorious magician Aleister Crowley to found his own version in the early twentieth century.

was stopped and Church of Satan activities were carried out in Satanic grottos in several countries. La Vey's stated goal was the creation of a police state in which the weak were weeded out and an achievement-oriented leadership was permitted to pursue the mysteries of black magic.

The Satanic Bible is a book that outlines the theory and ritual practice of Satanic magic. Magic is separated into lesser, everyday magic, such as that used for psychological manipulation and tricks to get people to do what the Satanist wants, and greater or ceremonial magic. Satanic rituals, according to La Vey, do not involve the sacrifice of animals or babies; they do not involve a negative reversal of Christian ritual – as in the

Below: Anton Szandor La Vey, the founder of the modern Church of Satan, has followed in the satanic tradition of Dashwood and Crowley in liberating the individual will from the fetters of organized religion. He is shown here on the left with "Satania" lying on an altar and "Hellas" and his wife "Elysia" (on the right) looking on.

Above: Satan is seen as an arch-rebel and individualist by modern Satanists and in Blake's portrayal of him rousing the rebel angels.

was here that he learnt hypnosis and studied the occult as assistant to a magician. During a period when he worked as a photographer for the San Francisco Police Department he saw the worst side of humanity, and came to detest the sanctimonious attitude of people who saw in human violence the work of God's will. He left the Police Department to play the organ in night-clubs and theatres.

In the 1950s La Vey started gaining a reputation for black magic in San Francisco and formed a group called the Order of Trapezoid, which later evolved into the governing body of the Church of Satan. It espoused a down-to-earth philosophy with an emphasis on the "carnal, lustful, natural instincts of man" without guilt or sin. Its methods sought to harness the dark forces to change situations according to will. His publicity stunts included baptizing his own three year-old daughter Zeena in 1967, dedicating her to the Devil. The following year he played the part of the Devil in the film *Rosemary's Baby*. In 1972 the public work at the Black House

The Nine Satanic Principles

1 Satan represents indulgence, instead of abstinence!

2 Satan represents vital existence, instead of spiritual pipe dreams!

3 Satan represents undefiled wisdom, instead of hypocritical self-deceit!

4 Satan represents kindness to those who deserve it, instead of love wasted on ingrates!

5 Satan represents vengeance, instead of turning the other cheek!

6 Satan represents responsibility to the responsible, instead of concern for psychic vampires!

7 Satan represents man as just another animal, sometimes better, more often worse than those that walk on all-fours, who, because of his divine spiritual and intellectual development, has become the most vicious animal of all!

8 Satan represents all of the so-called sins, as they all lead to physical, mental, or emotional gratification!

9 Satan has been the best friend the Church has ever had, as he has kept it in business all these years!

Anton La Vey, the great showman.

popular stereotype of a black mass conducted by a defrocked priest worshipping a naked woman on an altar – but allegedly concern celebration and purges from sin. A Satanic wedding, for example, consecrates the joys of the flesh with a lust rite. La Vey outlines nine Satanic principles (see box above).

The Satanic Church attracted an international following and at its peak it was said to have about 25,000 members (although this claim was probably greatly exaggerated). It also included celebrities among its number; the best-known was the actress Jayne Mansfield, who was killed in a car accident that was allegedly foreseen by La Vey.

THE TEMPLE OF SET

By the mid-1980s another Satanic organization, called the Temple of Set and also based in San Francisco, had attracted several hundred members. It was founded by Michael A. Aquino (a lieutenant-colonel of the US Army Reserve), Lilith Sinclair and Betty Ford (not the First Lady of that name) and is a society based on the worship of the Egyptian god Set or Seth, who is viewed as the forerunner of Satan. The Temple

of Set is an initiatory society that is interested in people of high intelligence and the advancement of genetic evolution. Aquino prophesied an apocalypse in which only the members of the Temple of Set, as the elect, would survive. There are many who are attracted to Satanic activities – the frisson of being

Jayne Mansfield, the hollywood actress, was a member of La Vey's Satanic Church.

a part of an organization that is seen by Christians as the very essence of evil is compelling to some.

SATANIC RITUAL ABUSE

In the late 1980s a moral panic about Satanism that took the form of ritual abuse led to scores of children being taken into care in Britain. The panic started in 1988 in the USA, when allegations of Satanic ritual abuse were made by social workers, and these ideas were passed on to their British counterparts at an international conference. Satanic abuse was seen to involve extreme acts of human sacrifice, cannibalism and the sexual abuse of children in orgiastic rituals, the purpose of which was an act of Devil-worship or witchcraft.

These allegations, which are strikingly similar to those levelled at witches during the early modern witch hunts, were fuelled by evangelical Christian groups.

The work of Aleister Crowley has been an inspiration to many Satanists. This seal was designed by him and depicts an inverted pentagram, or five-pointed star, a symbol now used by Satanists.

Satanism and witchcraft bring up people's deepest fears. Here a woman is portrayed as the Devil, and combines femaleness and evil in a manner common to the early modern stereotype of the witch.

"Satanic" activities, from the use of masks and costumes to the invocation of supernatural powers.

In 1994 the British government ordered a report to investigate the abuse. Eighty-four cases of alleged ritual abuse were investigated. Three did show evidence of ritual used to entrap the children by claims of mystical powers, or to prevent them from telling, but none were considered Satanic. In other words, the motivation for the abuse was sexual rather than Satanic. The report was critical of the interviewing techniques of the social services, saying that interviewers had employed leading questions, and used repeated questions, the report said that the children had told the adults what they thought they wanted to hear. This last aspect is reminiscent of the early modern European witch trials in which confessions were extracted to conform to the judge's views of diabolic witchcraft.

Satanism, like witchcraft, tends to bring up peoples' deepest fears. Undoubtedly there are individuals who perform immoral acts – but this does not justify the tendency that society has of branding a whole system of belief on the basis of conjecture and unproven rumour, a lesson that should have been learned from the times of the European witch hunts.

These groups offer counselling to people trying to sever their links with the occult. They claim that an interest in the occult starts people off on the slippery slope towards Satanism, and that people are recruited via New Age fairs and international Satanic organizations. At the time of the allegations, newspaper stories of survivors of Satanic abuse and confessions of former Satanists – who told about young girls being used as "brood mares" by being made pregnant and then forced to have abortions at five months so that the foetus could be used as a sacrifice – added to the panic.

In Britain, the social services and the charity the National Society for the Prevention of Cruelty to Children organized a survey of social workers, and the results reported a wide range of

Charles Manson as he appeared in court in California accused of Satanic murder

CHAOS MAGIC

Unlike most other magical practices chaos magic is not a spiritual path. Using the maxim "Nothing is true, everything is permitted", chaos magicians emphasize pragmatic techniques and observable results in the world as it is directly experienced as a form of sorcery. The aim is to achieve alternative states of consciousness or "gnosis". Chaos magic has acquired a certain notoriety for being sinister, even Satanic. This is because it rejects spiritual elements in its practices. Above all, it offers an opportunity to explore non-ordinary reality without the hindrance of accepted beliefs, and in the process, its practitioners claim, inspiration, knowledge, power and heightened perception are gained.

The Great Cthulhu, lord of dreams, telepathy and madness, is an entity with octopoid head and wings and is based on the work of the science fiction writer Howard Phillips Lovecraft.

Chaos magic was created in the late 1970s with the emergence of punk rock and the theoretical explorations in science that came to be called chaos theory. Influenced by both Aleister Crowley and Austin Osman Spare, chaos magic is above all a practical approach to practising magic. Chaos magicans claim

that all the methods of working magic are the same, despite differing symbols and belief systems. Chaos magic is thus a means to an end, rather than an end in itself. It claims to eschew the dogma of other approaches in its emphasis on avoiding the use of any one magical "system", advocating experimentation

Austin Osman Spare, artist and occultist, and source of inspiration to chaos magicians.

Chaos magic came into being at the same time as punk rock, a movement that was epitomized by the band The Sex Pistols.

with many practices. According to chaos magician Phil Hine, chaos magic is concerned with deconditioning from "the mesh of beliefs, attitudes and fictions about self, society and the world". Through the idea of the "paradigm" (which in chaos magic means the individual taking up a personal, magical role model), the magician can switch into and out of many magical techniques using the maxim. "If it works, use it", while leaving his or her beliefs behind. Chaos is not a religion – its focus is not on what may be termed "spirituality" – it is more specifically the utilization of magical techniques for the attainment of alternate states of consciousness or "gnosis". "Spiritual truth" has no meaning; whatever feels right is important. It glorifies fantasy and is a conscious and deliberate dislocation from any historical and spiritual tradition.

BASIC PRINCIPLES

The basic principles of chaos magic are expressed by the maxim "Nothing is true, everything is permitted". They may be summed up as: an avoidance of any form of dogmatism; a focus on personal experience; technical excellence in development of skills and abilities in the performance of a magical act; deconditioning the self by modifying and discarding beliefs and "ego-fictions"; and an eclectic and diverse approach, choosing from themes as wide apart as science fiction or tantrism, or adopting the beliefs of a spiritual system, if they are thought to serve a useful function. The overall aim is to achieve gnosis as a form of inner knowledge.

Eight forms of magic are represented on the "chaosphere". Octarine is pure or raw magic, representing the development of theories and philosophies. Black magic is death magic and concerns the ritual rehearsal of death. Blue magic is concerned with the control of other people and the creation of wealth. Red magic is associated with war. Yellow magic is involved with the ego or self-image. Green magic is about love. Orange magic concerns thought and living by the wits. Purple or silver is associated with sex magic.

The chaos magician Phil Hine holding a chaosphere-headed staff.

Peter Carroll, in his book *Liber Kaos* (1992), sees magic as a consequence of the structure of the universe, and he visualizes it as five serpents – of space, time, mass, energy and aether – each biting their tails and giving birth to themselves out of their own mouths. Carroll's view of the universe indicates that it is random, as is the individual's relationship with it: he offers no permanent model. His early writings appeared in the magazine *The New Equinox*, and it was here that the magical order the Illuminates of Thanateros (IOT) was first advertised. The IOT was formed in 1978 by Peter Carroll and Ray Sherwin to provide inspiration for chaos magicians. It was not a teaching order with initiated hierarchies but rather an organization where people could come together to practise and publish practical magic. This was not as easy as it sounds, some people expected teaching and leaders, but no rules or instructions were ever given, only suggestions on how to reach "that which could not be taught".

A chaos magic altar demonstrating its eclectic nature: Baphomet sits in the centre surrounded by a skull mala, a glass thunderbolt, a green baboon fetish, a lizard fetish, a crystal with a demon inside, a metal thunderbolt, and a three-dimensional chaosphere in the bottom right hand corner.

THE THANATEROS RITUAL

Phil Hine, writing in *Condensed Chaos* (1995), describes magic as "a doorway through which we step into mystery, wildness and immanence", and ritual is one way of achieving this. For chaos magicians there is no one shared reality when ritual workings are conducted, but rituals are seen to create opportunities for experiencing a magical state of consciousness. Before any magical work is undertaken a "banishing ritual" is performed. This is a preparation and centring exercise, which allows the magician to focus on the task ahead rather than on more mundane thoughts, and it also is supposed to clear the ritual space from unwanted atmospheres. Banishing rituals typically have three parts. The first section focuses awareness on the magician and is aimed at clearing the mind of unwanted thoughts by the visualization of white light being drawn through the body. The second creates a symbolic universe with the magician at the centre. The following is a suggestion by Phil Hine, and may be done by focusing on the eight rays of magic of the chaosphere and declaring:

The chaos Thanateros ritual is a process that simulates an encounter with sex and death – in the death of self in the act of sex, and the birth of self in an encounter with death. This is a nineteenth-century painting of Thanatos (Greek god of death) depicting aspects of sex and death.

> These are my weapons
> Expressions of my will
> I grasp them lightly
> I stand poised, at the centre
> The Universe dances for my pleasure.

The third section involves an identification of the chosen source of inspiration.

The Thanateros ritual is an example of a "celebration of Chaoist principles" according to Peter Carroll, and it concerns the invocation of the power of chaos. The magician tricks his or her consciousness into an ecstatic magical state by what is called the "neither-neither" effect. By meditating on the death of self in the act of sex, and the birth of self in an encounter with death, the ritual simulates encounters with both sex and death, and then with both of these experiences simultaneously, which is said to force conception beyond its normal limits. After a statement of intent and litanies, Eros and Thanatos are invoked:

> *Invocation to Eros:*
> *So come Eros, we invoke thee*
> *You who created us*
> *In the chaotic conjunction*
> *Of genetic roulette*
> *Come create us anew*
> *And kill us again!*
> *Our lovers approach*
> *Our breathing quickens*
> *As they come closer*
> *Our breathing quickens*
> *As we are clasped together*
> *Our breathing quickens*
> *At the thrill of touch*
> *Our breathing quickens*
> *We begin to gasp*
> *We are ready to surrender*
> *Three, Two, One,*
> *(Cry of Climax)!*

> *Invocation to Thanatos*
> *So come Thanatos, we invoke thee*
> *We accept your bargain*
> *Come kill us again*
> *And create us anew*
> *Our nemesis approaches*
> *Grinning skull and upraised scythe*

> *Our breathing quickens*
> *Closer it comes and closer*
> *Our breathing quickens*
> *Death stares us in the face*
> *Our breathing quickens*
> *Upraised terrible scythe*
> *We begin to gasp*
> *When it falls we shall die*
> *Three, Two, One,*
> *(Cry of Death Terror)!*

The ritual finishes with ecstatic laughter as an expression of the neither-neither; the energy being raised is either used for itself or to cast a spell.

THE CTHULHU MYTHOS

Another way of working with chaos magic is with what is known as the Cthulhu Mythos. Cthulhu, high priest of the "Great Old Ones", created by science fiction writer Howard Phillips Lovecraft (1890–1937), is a zoomorphic entity with an octopoid head and wings. Contact with him is said to unite the chthonic roots of primeval consciousness to the stellar magicks of the future. Phil Hines writes, in *The Pseudonomicon*, that the Old Ones, who are alien to human civilization and rationality, have a close relationship with wild places – particularly stone circles and "strange manifestations" – and have been cast forth from the earth and forgotten by civilized humanity and its materialistic vision. They are ever-present, "lurking at the frontiers of order, in places where the wild power of nature can be felt". They are chaotic, as Nature is chaotic, and they retain their primal power since they cannot be explained.

The Old Ones manifest into the everyday world through gateways in wild, lonely places entangled with local myth and folklore; associated with "strange lights, subterranean noises, stone circles, ancient ruins, strange angles, tunnels, wells and the gates of dreaming, trance and madness". A core feature of the Cthulhu Mythos is said to be transformation into a new mode of being. After initiation by fear and near madness that shatters the old conception of self, and by dreaming and astral visions, the magician reaches a form of consciousness that is more tenuous and chaotic than ordinary reality.

A statue of Baphomet, who is popular with chaos magicians, displaying hermaphroditic qualities.

Masks are an important part of magical work: they ease the identification with otherworldly beings and the loss of a sense of the self. This is a spirit of Chaos mask.

Tantric Altar

Chaos magic takes an eclectic approach to magic, and may utilize other magicial traditions. Altars are ideal for demonstrating this, as the symbolism and connections can be so diverse. Here, on this Chaos Tantric altar, is a selection of items that takes in several different traditions. It includes a yoni lingam (top right), a small statue of Kali, goddess of death and destruction (top left), a thunderbolt (bottom right), and a Tibetan phurba, or ritual dagger (bottom left), used for 'nailing demons'. The altar contains eight bowls of water for the eight directions and is surrounded by a skull mala.

A Chaos Tantric altar.

APPRENTICED TO MAGIC

In days gone by, a magician might take an apprentice, a young novice as yet lacking in magical skills and knowledge but having the desire and potential to become a great magic-worker. Similarly, wise women passed on their knowledge to the next generation, teaching which herbs were safe and which were poisonous, and how to use "magic" to treat all manner of ills – or else to protect and empower. In this way, knowledge of the occult was passed on, often in secret, and over time a great body of magical knowledge has built up. Today, the written word has largely replaced this oral tradition, and we can rediscover some of this ancient knowledge through books, although of course many teachers of magic still exist. The first part of this section is designed to initiate the reader into the ways of magic. Take time to absorb and digest the information contained in this section – it will stand you in good stead when you come to put your knowledge into practice.

INTRODUCTION

Essentially, magic is the art of making things happen by drawing on the powers of the natural world. But even if we are not yet able to influence events, most of us retain a sense of the magical, despite living in an urban, technological society and, for the most part, out of touch with the natural world and its powers.

"Magic" is often the word we instinctively use to describe a stunning sunset, a leafy forest glade, or a wintry landscape transformed by a carpet of snow. It may also be how we refer to an idyllic time, such as a love affair or dream holiday, or to one of life's very special moments, such as the birth of a child or an outstanding achievement. All of these experiences, however diverse, have something in common: they touch us at our deepest core, enchanting, surprising and delighting us.

We may also use the term "magic" to express our sense of wonder and awe at creation and our place in it: the feeling that for this moment at least, all is right with the world. Magic is what can happen when we step outside our everyday reality to connect with something precious and much bigger than our "little selves".

THE OTHERWORLD

Regardless of time or place, magic is based on the understanding that behind the ordinary, everyday world, there exists another dimension, or "otherworld", a spiritual domain that is said to co-exist with the mundane. A realm of deities, spirits and other discarnate beings, it is also a place of knowledge and sacred power, and whenever we experience a "magic" moment, we are tapping into this dimension, albeit accidentally. In this context we can say that the word "magic" describes the inner nature of the beings that make up the universe – the spiritual part of all things that is cosmic and eternal.

The practice of magic involves making contact with this otherworld through special rituals and ceremonies, and because this world is invisible to the naked eye magic is often referred to as "the occult" (literally "concealed" or "hidden" in Latin). Magic then is primarily concerned with a spiritual experience of hidden worlds; this lies at its heart and informs magical practice.

REDEFINING OUR VALUES

In modern western society, with its emphasis on reason, logic and scientific enquiry, a living relationship with the otherworld has largely been lost. Although we are materially wealthy, many people feel dissatisfied with their lives; there is the feeling that something is missing

Rituals are enhanced by the use of special items kept for magical purposes, such as a chalice.

Using the four Elements in your magic is one of the most obvious magical links to the natural world.

One of the most challenging and rewarding ways to practise magic is to use your mind to access other worlds and dimensions.

but we are not quite sure what. This condition has engendered a search for meaning and a spirituality that makes sense, and it is in this context that interest in magic is steadily growing.

Magic suggests that there is more to our world than can be seen with the naked eye, and that a rational and objective approach is not always the best way. In fact, to establish a relationship with the otherworld, it is necessary to put logic and reason aside, and to engage with the irrational, emotional and intuitive, or the forces of "unreason". Connecting with the world of magic means rediscovering the languages of dreams and visions, imagination and fantasy, myth and story, image and symbol and to be prepared to enter the unknown.

ABOUT THIS SECTION

The aim of this section is to give the reader enough information and practical techniques to enable them to establish their own unique relationship with the otherworld and learn how to use its powers for self-mastery. While there are many schools of magic, each with its own path and set of disciplines, this book does not adhere to any one particular way, but draws on material from a diversity of magical traditions, including shamanism, wicca and "high magic". An important central theme in the book is that to become a magic-worker involves responsibility – towards yourself and others – and teaches that magic powers should always be used for the greatest good of all.

The book is divided into two parts: the first part covers the basics of magical "theory" and tells you all you need to know before you begin practising magic. The first section of the book starts with important background information on some of the key principles of magic and includes a cultural overview of magical practice throughout the world. This is followed by detailed information on the magic-workers' toolkit, which includes herbs and spices, incenses, crystals and natural objects. It goes on to explain the significance of cosmic powers, such as the sun and moon and the four elements, before concluding with a discussion of how timing can affect your magic. The second section of the book is practical and includes detailed instructions on how to work with specific spells and rituals and create and nurture sacred space. Information on divination, including tarot and astrology, is also given, while a special section shows how to develop intuitive powers.

Hopefully, as you turn the pages that follow, you will discover how to step outside your everyday self and enter into a magical world full of self-discovery and adventure.

A magic circle, whether it is made of candles, a cord, or is one that you conjure up in your mind, will protect you from negative energies.

Learning how to choose your tools and ingredients is a key part of gaining magical expertise.

The natural world is full of its own special magic, and this book will help you access it, and become part of it.

MAGIC AND THE SACRED TRADITION

Since the earliest times, magic has been practised in many different guises throughout the world, despite opposition from orthodox religion and mainstream society at various points along the way. Magic is an ancient art, and far from being something "bad" or "evil", it has played an important part in the psycho-spiritual development of the human race. To many, this may sound preposterous, yet if we look at cultures other than our own we can see evidence of "magical" thinking and how this informs the way people live. For instance, Native American Indians regard the Earth as a living spirit whose voice can be heard in the roaring, sighing or whistling of the wind. Consequently, they believe in treating the land with respect and living in harmony with nature's laws.

In this chapter we shall look at the link between magic and sacred tradition and how magical thinking is embodied in the myths and rituals

that have played a central part in shaping human society. We shall look at the differences and similarities between different practitioners of magic – witches, magicians, sorcerers and shamans – and give a brief overview of some of the main schools of magic in existence today. Sacred places, various gods and goddesses, angels, fairies and spirit beings also play a special role in magic, but underlying almost all magical thinking is the idea that the universe is a living and interconnected entity whose energies we can work with once we know how.

THE ORIGINS OF MAGIC

Throughout the world, human beings have developed a multitude of beliefs and practices to explain and give meaning to the cosmos. Almost without exception, early cultures evolved with a world view wherein magic and spirituality were inextricably bound, and in some parts of the world this is still true today. In fact, the word "magic" comes from the Greek *mageia*, which derives from *magoi*, an ancient Persian caste of priests who studied astrology and divination. Even before written records were kept, however, cave paintings dating back some 30,000 years indicate that our earliest ancestors practised what we would now call magic in the form of shamanism.

A medicine man of the Moquis people of North America performing a snake dance.

SHAMANISM

Claimed as the oldest spiritual practice, shamanism is still embraced by many small-scale societies around the world – from Siberia to the Amazonian region to Africa – albeit under increasingly difficult conditions. A shaman takes on the role of mediator between the everyday world and the spiritual dimension. By entering into a trance, he or she "journeys" to the otherworld in an attempt to resolve some difficulty or dilemma in the human domain. Shamanic cosmologies are frequently formed from three regions: a middle world corresponding to our everyday reality on earth; an upper world relating to the sky and celestial realms; and a lower or underworld, which reaches deep down into the earth. These three regions are connected by a central axis, and are often represented by a tree.

Most of the world's sacred traditions have been influenced in one way or another by shamanism. For instance, magic was very important in the Chinese royal-ancestral religion of the Shang and early Chou (16th–8th centuries BC), where the wu was a shaman or sorcerer who sacrificed to and invoked the spirits, and also cured physical and spiritual complaints or maladies by means of medicinal plants and spells.

The beliefs of the Ancient Egyptians were expressed in complex creation myths involving the of deeds all-powerful gods and goddesses, and were administered to the people by priests, and later magicians.

ANCIENT EGYPTIAN BELIEFS

The dual development of magic and religious custom and belief became more sophisticated in ancient Egypt. Egyptian magic dates back to a time when the region's pre-dynastic, prehistoric inhabitants believed that the earth, the underworld, the air and the sky were populated by countless supernatural beings, some of whom affirmed life and were friendly while others caused death and destruction. Complex rites and rituals were devised to honour or appease these beings – the vast pantheon of Egyptian gods and goddesses – and temples were constructed in their honour. Priests became the guardians of a secret knowledge revealed by the deities to help humanity, and their books of spells and other magical formulae were safeguarded in temple and palace libraries. In popular tales, they were credited with the power to bring wax animals to life, or roll back the waters of a lake. The priests' role was eventually taken over by magicians (*hekau*), who carried metal or ivory wands as symbols of their authority and ability to summon and control powerful spirits.

Mainly concerned with healing and self-preservation, ancient Egyptian magic permeated every aspect of daily life. Rituals were conducted for all kinds of purposes – to protect the king, to safeguard a woman and her baby during childbirth, or even to help the dead in the afterlife. Egyptians of all classes wore protective amulets inscribed with magical symbols and the names of gods or pharaohs.

Destructive magic was also practised in ancient Egypt. It was believed, for instance, that foreign enemies and Egyptian traitors could be weakened or destroyed by inscribing their names on clay pots and figurines, then smashing, burning or burying these. Enemies of the divine order could be similarly cursed. For example, to counter the influences of Apophis, the chaos serpent, his image would be drawn on papyrus or modelled in wax and then spat on, trampled, stabbed or burnt in temple ceremonies; any remaining pieces were dissolved in buckets of urine.

A Hindu Brahmin, wearing an iron collar, raises funds for a hospital.

MAGIC AND RITUAL IN INDIA

In India magical thought was inseparable from the sacred tradition. According to legend, the ancient sacred texts known as the Vedas (meaning "what is known" in Sanskrit) were revealed more than 4,000 years ago to 52 great rishis, or seers, during meditation. The Vedas praise and appease forces of nature and "higher beings", which are depicted as deities. A rich source of magical ideas, they reveal the unity of creation as a mysterious interconnectedness and co-dependence. Each bio-organism, element or species has a purpose within a larger scheme and is sacred, and reality is built up from various networks of affinities or connections, which can be evoked and controlled by human beings.

MAGICAL RITES IN THE INDIAN VEDAS

The ancient Indian Vedas are divided into smaller books, of which the Atharva-Veda contains a rich collection of spells and magical rites. These are arranged according to those concerned with positive welfare and the pacification of

A Brahmin shows his religious devotion by suspending himself over a fire.

evil influences, and those directed against hostile powers or individuals. The priestly Brahmin caste, or class, performed the rituals, which were to do with restoring equilibrium rather than controlling nature. Their purpose was to keep the life processes of the universe moving and to maintain good relations with the powers of the unseen. They were held on special occasions, such as festivals, and for specific purposes, such as curing disease or exorcizing spirits.

A ritual might include divination and the manipulation of spirits or deities. Sacred sounds, such as a ceremonially uttered word or mantra, were often used in spells and rituals as a way of making contact with the hidden world. Many mantras were believed to hold so much power in awakening the spirit world that they could only be performed under the guidance of a guru. Extensive preparation – such as astrological readings, long recitations and a knowledge of how to regulate breathing – was also necessary before it was considered safe to use them.

MONOTHEISM AND MYSTICISM

Unlike the plural religions of ancient Egypt and India, Judaism and Christianity are monotheistic, holding a belief in one creator God who is separate from humankind. Both traditions officially condemn magic, describing it as evil and seeing it as a way of manipulating supernatural power for human ends. Islam also believes in one God, Allah, who is separate from humans: he has no likeness and is transcendent. He is believed to preside over two worlds: the visible al-Shahada, which is accessible to humans, and the unseen al-Ghaib, which is unknowable, mysterious and only revealed through divine revelation, such as miracles. However, both the Judaeo-Christian tradition and Islam have inspired unorthodox mystical traditions that teach that it is possible to be reunited with or to know God.

A 17th-century Indian painting depicts a mystical conversation between Sufi sheikhs.

THE CABBALA
In the Judaeo-Christian tradition, a form of mysticism was developed that sought to reunite human beings with God. Known as the Cabbala (also spelt Kabbalah and Qabalah), this secret

A pilgrim meets a messenger of necromancy, standing in a circle of Cabbalistic signs.

doctrine concerns the unexplained "mysteries" in Genesis and is passed on to initiates only. It contains a series of meditations on the 22 letters of the Hebrew alphabet and the four-letter name of God (Yod-Heh-Vav-Heh) and is a collection of the writings of various anonymous learned authors, the most important being the Sepher Yetzirah (Book of Creation), probably produced in Babylonia around 2,000 years ago, and the Sepher Zohar (Book of Splendour) written in 13th-century Spain.

Cabbalists believe that God created the universe in stages, with not one world but four. The "highest" of these is

a world of pure light and closest to God, while the lowest is the everyday world we humans inhabit. In each world, creation moves through a series of ten emanations, known as "sephiroth" and symbolized by the Tree of Life, through which the infinite relates with the finite. By meditating on the sephiroth, a person is said to be able to link up with the greater plan of the universe and so become closer to God. Because the Cabbala challenges interpretations based on the scriptures and encourages a direct and unmediated relationship with God, it is regarded as heretical by orthodox Jews and Christians.

Renaissance Christian Cabbalists

During the Renaissance, some Christians interpreted the writings of the Cabbala as a means to bring higher angelic forces down to the ordinary world. Three magicians of this time were particularly influential. A priest and physician, Marsilio Ficino (1433–99), developed a system of 'natural magic' that was concerned with drawing down the powers of the cosmos. His theory of magic was based on the guiding of spirit from the stars using the natural sympathies running through nature.

Giovanni Pico Della Mirandola (1463–94) was influenced by Ficino's natural magic but, in an attempt to increase its power, incorporated the mysteries of the Cabbala to tap the higher powers of angels and archangels.

Giordano Bruno (1548–1600) sought to return magic to what he saw as its purer pagan origin in Egypt. Bruno also used the Cabbala, but in contrast to Pico, who wanted to work only with angelic forces, he used it in attempts to unlock demonic forces.

People of the Masai gather underneath a tree at sunset. African traditions are closely linked to the land and its spirits.

SUFISM

In Islam there has always been a strong emphasis on the difference between human beings and God, yet Sufism developed as a form of mystical training that aimed to overcome this distinction. Sufism (so called after the suf, or woollen garments, worn by its first practitioners) introduced an inner spirituality into Islam, proposing that the self and God could merge through the purification of consciousness. The idea of attaining union with God is seen by some as blasphemous and is rejected by more orthodox Muslims.

AFRICAN TRADITIONS

Although African cultures are very diverse, they are similar in the way they connect human beings (both living and deceased) and the natural world with a strong magical power. This power is viewed as a kind of vital force that flows through the universe and permeates all aspects of life. Some societies see it as originating from a creator spirit, and in many places the notion of a named supreme god is well established. The Janjero of Ethiopia, for instance, believe in a supreme being called Hao, while the Nupe of Nigeria say that their deity, Soko, is in the sky.

There is often a hierarchy of spirits in African tradition: from the nature spirits of rivers, rocks, trees and animals, through ancestor spirits, to divinities who derive their power from the creator spirit.

In the Lugbara cult, which is centred on the spirits of the dead, the living are seen to belong to the "outside" world while the dead belong "in the earth". If the dead are neglected, they punish their descendants by inflicting misfortune and sickness on them, and so need to be appeased by the living. Magical power is seen to come either directly from the creator spirit, or through the spirits of the ancestors, or as part of the invisible force of nature in the universe.

Voodoo

Essentially a fusion of African spirit beliefs with Roman Catholic Christianity, voodoo is today a peasant religion practised by 90 per cent of Haitians. The Christian God (known as Bondeye in Haitian Creole) presides over a variety of voodoo rituals, ranging from the lighting of candles to animal sacrifice, and sends down his loa (angels or spirits) in response. Voodoo ceremonies may involve ancestor worship, spirit possession, dance, song and drumming. When the loa takes possession, a new devotee has to be baptized and take holy communion.

MAGIC IN MYTH

A myth may be described as a way of explaining humanity's attempts to understand the universe and its place in it; it is a sacred legend or story, shared by a group of people and expressing their most important meanings. In Western cultures, mythology is often equated with fairy stories, the "unreal" or even falsehood, in contrast with history, which is associated with truth. However, myth has played an important part in magic by explaining how the world came to be formed, and by marking out significant relationships with ancestors and other beings. Many myths are celebrated and re-enacted through ritual and ceremony, and are used by magical traditions, both ancient and modern.

The mythology of Atlantis is based almost entirely on the imaginations of writers and artists.

MYTH AND CULTURE

It is impossible to separate myth from its cultural context. In ancient Egypt, for instance, all life was said to originate from the waters of the Nile, while Norse cosmology tells us that life was created through the union of fire and ice, with Ymir, the frost-giant, being one of the first creatures. Magic played a central part in early Graeco-Roman culture, too, and was a common theme in literary works, such as Homer's *Iliad* and *Odyssey*. The *Odyssey* in particular was recognized primarily as a book of magical deeds, and Homeric verses were used later as magical formulae.

In early societies myths were often linked to religious ceremony and ritual. For instance, the Greeks practised a form of rites called "Mysteries" (the most famous being the "Eleusinian Mysteries"), which were known only to initiates. After a preparatory purifying stage that led a neophyte to a state of readiness, sacred objects were shown to him. It is likely that the myth of Demeter and Persephone was performed as a form of initiation into the process of life and death. Similarly, the myth of Isis and Osiris played an important role in the religious ceremonials of ancient Egypt, with the death of Osiris and the lamentations of Isis (his half-sister and wife) being re-enacted each year.

THE ROLE OF MYTH

As well as playing an important role in the enactment of ritual and ceremony, myths also provide a moral and spiritual framework on which magical practice can be based. For instance, modern magicians who follow the Western

Mystery Tradition (a form of magical practice based on initiation into secret knowledge) embrace the mythology of King Arthur, while the myth of Atlantis also has a very important position in Western magic.

THE ARTHURIAN LEGENDS

Arthur is a Celtic hero, whose birth was made possible by the magical workings of Merlin, the magician. A blend of history has combined with oral traditions and myth, making Arthur and Merlin hybrids – historical people with mythological characteristics.

According to legend, Camelot was Arthur's famous court where he established a knightly order, made up of the greatest and most chivalrous warriors in Europe. Arthur and his knights became known as the Knights of the Round Table, named after a huge round table that was set up by Merlin, with places for 150 knights, all equal in rank and loyal to Arthur. In the Arthurian legends the knights embark on quests, venturing deep into primeval forests, which are metaphors for the soul's journey through uncharted worlds. The

Sir Galahad personified the chivalric ideal, and being noble in thought, courageous in action and pure in spirit was destined to achieve the Grail.

quest is an archetypal motif of a spiritual search for the soul. Its goal may be an individual, such as a maiden in distress, or a divine object such as the Holy Grail. The Grail itself is a complex symbol with many meanings. Allegedly the cup from the Last Supper used to collect the blood of Christ, it is a sacred vessel that symbolizes the potentiality of all wisdom, intuition and knowledge. It is also thought to be the source of creativity and inspiration, a magical chalice of transformation, a cauldron of rebirth.

The King Arthur stories offer magicians a range of heroic patterns or archetypes with which to identify in a personal quest for a higher form of consciousness whereby the individual soul is reunited with the cosmic source of all things, or the One.

THE ATLANTIS MYTH

According to legend, the "lost continent" of Atlantis occupied most of the area of today's Atlantic Ocean. Destroyed by natural disaster, the civilization was highly sophisticated, a pinnacle of truth and beauty. The Greek philosopher Plato (c.428–347BC) refers to it in his writings as a wonderful empire, pre-eminent in courage and military skill, that was destroyed by earthquakes and floods. He wrote: "and in a single day and night of misfortune all your warlike men in a body sank into the earth, and the island of Atlantis in like manner disappeared in the depths of the sea."

The myth of Atlantis forms an ideal vision of a golden age: a Garden of Eden before the Fall, when humans were in touch with divinity, and peace and harmony reigned. Many magicians share a great interest in the legend, some claiming to be in telepathic communication with the erstwhile inhabitants of Atlantis, and others having past-life memories of previous incarnations spent on the island. Today, the legend's power may be attributed to nostalgia for living in harmony with nature and the longing of the soul for perfection. Many people see magic as a path to reconnect with this ideal state of existence, while at the same time working on their inner, spiritual selves.

Demeter and Persephone

In Greek mythology, Persephone is the beautiful daughter of Demeter, the goddess of corn and the harvest, and Zeus, the mighty king of the Olympians. While picking meadow flowers, the young maiden was abducted by Hades, the ruler of the Underworld, who made her his queen. Consumed by grief and sorrow, Demeter searched for her daughter. The land became barren as crops withered and died and it became perpetual winter.

Zeus intervened, sending Hermes, the messenger god, to bring Persephone back. Persephone had eaten the food of the dead (in the form of pomegranate seeds), however, and so was not able to return to the upper world forever. Instead, she was restored to Demeter for two-thirds of the year only. Her arrival each year is marked by the rebirth of spring, but when she has to return to Hades for one-third of the year, the earth once again becomes barren.

The grief of Demeter is so intense and unremitting that it blights the world with perpetual winter.

MAGIC-WORKERS

Nearly all societies have some concept of witchcraft in which individuals are thought to possess a form of extraordinary power. A belief in witchcraft is part of a magical world view that sees inherent in the universe powers and forces that may be directed by certain people. These "magic-workers" have been called by many different names, most commonly witches, magicians, sorcerers, shamans or witch doctors. Having all manner of special abilities, they are thought to be able to change their shape, fly and sometimes trick and deceive. Often regarded as frightening, they have been the subject of folklore in numerous countries and used as scapegoats for unexplained or unexpected elements of everyday life.

A Zulu witch doctor depicted in an engraving from the early 1900s.

WITCHES

The word "witch" comes from the Old English wican, meaning "to cast a spell", but the meaning of witch and witchcraft changes from society to society and there is no neat and precise definition with which everyone agrees. In general, however, witches are usually female, associated with darkness and night-time, and with the reversal of normal human lives. Roman literature is full of references to a creature called a strix (a word of Greek origin meaning "to screech"), which flew about at night,

uttering piercing screams and feeding on the flesh and blood of human beings. The Yoruba of Nigeria believe that witches are generally women who fly about at night and meet in secret places. In European folklore, a witch is frequently depicted as an ugly old hag, or else a beautiful enchantress, who uses her powers to allure and seduce. Witches are also commonly believed to have special spirit animals or familiars that perform services for them; typical examples include black cats, newts and snakes. They also have knowledge of plants and herbs, and they concoct their spells using a giant pot, or cauldron.

Theories about how witches get their power vary. In some parts of the world it is thought that power derives from an association with carnivorous predators; gained through acquired knowledge or

skills; or inherited, as in the African society of the Azande. At the time of the witch hunts in Europe (16th–17th centuries), the Christian church was convinced that a witch's power was the reward for making a pact with the Devil.

WISE WOMEN, CUNNING MEN

Alongside the idea of "bad" witches there co-exists the idea of magic-workers who use their powers for the good of the community. In the European tradition these are often referred to as "cunning folk", also known as wizards, wise folk, wise women or white witches. Once found in every village, these magical practitioners were commonly consulted for identifying witches (of the bad kind), fortune-telling, finding lost or stolen goods and naming the thief, as well as for providing remedies for a wide range of

This photograph, c.1915, entitled Medicine Man, shows a North American Indian shaman.

The crime of practising magic

Over the centuries, thousands of men, women and children have been tortured, tried and condemned to death for the 'crime' of practising witchcraft. In Europe, witch-hunting was at its peak from 1580 to 1650, a period when the growing strength of the Christian church coincided with the emergence of the modern nation state and new attitudes to science. Zealous Puritan ministers condemned magic, and witch-finders were appointed on behalf of

church and state to seek out and try those individuals who were suspected of sorcery. The focus of the witch-hunting process was on finding so-called 'Devil's marks' on the accused. In the United Kingdom, witchcraft remained illegal until 1951, when the British Witchcraft Act was repealed. Until then people could be tried and imprisoned; the last such case involved a spirit medium, Helen Duncan, who was sent to jail during World War II.

illnesses. In fact, many illnesses and misfortunes were attributed to the workings of spirits, so that a sick or unlucky person or animal was considered to be "bewitched". It was the job of the cunning worker to lift spells and to provide antidotes to, and protection against, witchcraft.

SHAMANS

Common in early traditions, and still practised by some societies in Siberia, the Amazonian region and Africa, shamanism is a tradition whereby an individual works magic for the benefit of the social group. Shamans use their power to communicate with the spirit world to protect the group from magical aggression and natural calamities. They also heal sick people, communicate with the spirits of the dead, find lost objects and predict the future. They can do this by entering a trance during which the soul leaves the body and changes, or shape-shifts, into spirit forms, such as various animals. This altered state enables shamans to battle with spirits or forces, or to gain valuable information.

MAGICAL MEDICINE

The link between magic and medicine exists in many cultures and healers are often referred to as medicine men or women. A medicine may be used for more than healing the body, however. In many traditional African societies, for instance, magical "medicines" may be used to bring or prevent rain, to delay sunset, as an aid in hunting, for success in love affairs or to find stolen property, as well as for treating illnesses.

The medicine man, or diviner, may also use spiritual power in amulets or charms to protect individuals. The magic may also involve rites using medicines

The link between magic and medicine has always been strong, and the image of the witch with her cauldron steaming on an open fire is a part of this.

Sorcery

A sharp distinction between witchcraft and sorcery is impossible to maintain. However, the latter is usually associated with maleficent magic, evil spells and injury, which some claim is purposely intended.

made from trees and plants, with the magician telling the medicines what he wants them to do. In most Bantu languages the term used to refer to a medicine man, magician, herbalist or shaman is nganga. The nganga goes into the forest to collect herbs, roots, bark, and plants for the medicine. Some nganga families have a tradition of healing that goes back many generations; the living members receive guidance from their ancestors, who speak to them in dreams, instructing them about which herbs to use and where to find them.

MAGIC IN THE MODERN WORLD

Today, Western magical practices, including modern witchcraft, offer a kaleidoscope of paths or techniques for attaining alternative forms of consciousness. Many of these, such as Western shamanism, have their roots in ancient practices, while others, such as Wicca, have been developed in more recent times for use in the modern Western world. All see the world in a spiritual way, perpetuating the link between magic and sacred tradition. There is no one right way to practise magic and many modern magic workers use a synthesis of techniques drawn from different traditions.

Ancient woodlands hold much power and mystery for many magical traditions.

WICCA

A far cry from either the type of witchcraft practised in small traditional societies around the world, or the diabolic type that was once so feared by the Christian church, Wicca is a modern form of witchcraft that venerates nature. Created in the 1950s by Gerald Gardner, it uses the structure of Western high magic ritual to worship the powerful forces inherent in nature and personified as various gods and goddesses. It has also reclaimed the word "witch" as meaning the resident "wise woman" or "cunning man" of the old European village.

Wiccans are usually members of a coven, or group, led by a high priestess and high priest. As independent bodies, covens follow their own path, although all have a series of rituals and prayers that are written down in what is sometimes called a Book of Shadows. Essentially, Wicca is a spiritual movement, based on witchcraft, but dealing with modern themes and issues. Many Wiccans, for instance, are ardent environmentalists and campaign in many ways to protect the planet's resources.

By returning to nature and ancient practices, Wicca offers a spiritual path for those searching for meaning in today's materialistic, fast-paced modern world. Wiccans are prevented from using negative magic through their adherence to the Wiccan Rede, or rule: "As thou harm none, do what thou wilt". Their rites and celebrations are centred around their oneness with life and the earth, and the passing of the seasons, and use many ancient magic symbols.

PAGANISM

Like Wicca, modern paganism is a religion that honours women, the earth, the dark and nature, all of which have been denigrated in Western society.

Gerald Gardner

An English witch, Gerald Gardner (1884–1964) is regarded as the founder of modern-day Wicca. He argued that witchcraft was an ancient, pre-Christian pagan mystery tradition and, after the repeal of the witchcraft laws in 1951, published *Witchcraft Today* (1954), which described witchcraft as practised in his coven. He also rewrote many rituals and charms for his coven's *Book of Shadows*, which he also published.

A pagan ceremony using the ancient magical symbols of the circle and the pentagram.

Summer solstice celebrations at Stonehenge take inspiration from ancient Celtic and druid traditions.

Pagans worship the Great Mother and the Horned, or Solar, God as supreme deities, above lesser gods and goddesses, and their year is defined by a cycle of sacred celebrations. They employ the seasons and tides of the earth, moon and sun to strengthen their spells, and work with the energy of the full moon. Some pagan witches function as individuals, performing their rituals alone. Others are members of a family or tradition, while many are initiated into covens and share meetings and festivals with a group throughout the sacred year.

CEREMONIAL MAGIC

The central ethos of ceremonial magic is based on the idea of spiritual evolution – the bringing down of higher angelic or elemental forces into the magician – which process is thought to enable the evolution of the soul. Ceremonial, or ritual, magicians usually follow one of the aspects of the Western Mystery Tradition, which goes back to the time of ancient Egypt. There are several schools. Many magicians follow the Cabbala, of which there are at least three branches – the Jewish, the Christian and the

mystical or magical Cabbala. Others work with the Arthurian legends and the Holy Grail, or the Celtic, Greek, Roman or Egyptian traditions. Each school provides a framework of symbols, mythological stories of the deities, magical practices and a great body of inherited wisdom. As we forge our way into the 21st century, many magicians are involved with research, in a quest to develop new magical techniques.

DRUIDISM

The esoteric origins of modern druidism are located in the Western Mystery Tradition, with links to Atlantis. As catastrophe struck Atlantis, those magicians who had used their powers for selfish ends were engulfed, but those who had used magic to help humanity escaped the destruction due to their greater gifts of foreknowledge. These magicians journeyed eastward and westward, landing on the shores of Ireland and western Britain and the east coast of America respectively, taking their knowledge with them. Modern Druidism encompasses a wide spectrum of beliefs and practices, but a common

love of the earth is central and fundamental. Communing with nature means learning to grow, to trust and to hear the response of the earth – nature as deity is drawn down into the ritual circle and is experienced as joy and love.

WESTERN SHAMANISM

The 1970s saw the emergence of contemporary shamanism, also called neo-shamanism or Western shamanism, as a new form of spirituality emanating from the USA. The central precept of Western shamanism is regeneration and a revitalization of earth-based "ways of knowing". Inspired by the notion that shamanism is humanity's most ancient and authentic form of spirituality, many modern shamanic practitioners turn to what they see as a primordial means of healing and creating connections to nature. Practices include techniques for self-realization and making contact with an otherworldly realm of spirits. Some practitioners emphasize the importance of traditions, such as those practised by Native American Indians, while others place more importance on finding new ways of engaging with the living world.

THE WEB OF LIFE

A web holds all kinds of mystical significance, and is often used as a magical metaphor.

Natural magic honours the earth and the physical body rather than a transcendental spirit. The idea that the physical body and all of nature are inherently divine and part of a larger whole is based on the underlying principle that everything in the universe is connected to everything else and that each part has an influence on the whole. In Anglo-Saxon times this magical interconnectedness was known as "the Wyrd", which translates as destiny, power and also prophetic knowledge. It may be visualized as a giant web in which everything links up with everything else along fine pathways or channels of energy. This view is backed up by modern physics, which essentially recognizes that we are living in an energy universe. Magic workers draw on the powers of nature to learn how to tap into this web in order to influence events – and this is what natural magic is all about.

CONNECTING WITH SPIRIT

Spirit is the essence of creation, the unifying force that is present throughout the universe, the energy possessed by all things. Spirit not only connects us with each other, but also with animals, plants, rocks, water, air, the stars and the space between the stars. It is the skein of being beyond the physical, the otherworld that can be accessed for communication, healing and understanding. Using the symbol of the web, spirit is the first thread from which all other emanations are produced, creating webs within webs, or worlds within worlds, as we interact with our families, friends, workmates, wider social groups and physical environment.

The fundamental link in the web is energy. All of us are aware of energy on an instinctive level. For instance, we may sense the atmosphere or energy vibration in a room after an argument and describe it as thick or heavy. On a more subtle level, there is the instinctive feeling when we are liked or disliked by someone. Energy suffuses all things, but the energy of each part of creation vibrates at its own particular frequency. The extent to which we can be affected by these energetic communications depends upon how receptive we are. Learning about natural magic involves developing sensitivity so that we can

Sacred for thousands of years for the Aborigines of Australia, Uluru is just one part of that culture's conceptualization of the dreamtime.

attune to vibrations in other parts of creation, be they a rock, a blade of grass, a faraway star or another human being.

THE DREAMTIME

Aboriginal Australians conceptualize the "web of life" in a unique way. In their view, Australia is covered by a web of "Dreamings". The Dreamtime relates to a state of reality beyond the everyday, an otherworld in which ancestral creators travelled across the land, shaping it as they went. During the Dreamtime an all-encompassing law bound people and the natural world together as one organic whole, and it is through Dreaming affiliations and ritual associations that people remain connected to one another and to the land.

THE HUMAN ENERGY FIELD

Our first point of contact with the physical world is through the body and its five senses – touch, taste, sight, hearing and smell – and many traditions have seen the body as a microcosm of the macrocosm (the universe). During medieval and Renaissance times it was quite common to link the body's organs with cosmology: the astrological sign of Cancer (ruled by the moon) was associated with the upper chest, the sign of Leo (ruled by the sun) with the heart and solar plexus, and so on. These ideas are more sophisticated in the East, where it is understood that it is spirit, or energy, that suffuses us with life and that it flows through the body along invisible channels known as meridians, or nadis.

The subtle bodies

The aura (energy field) around the human body is said to comprise seven different layers, each layer vibrating at a higher frequency than the preceding one.

1 Etheric body: closest to the physical body
2 Emotional body: seat of the emotions
3 Mental body: mental activity, thoughts, ideas and day-to-day concerns
4 Astral body: 'out of body' experiences; dream travel; journeying
5 Causal body: seat of willpower and gateway to higher consciousness
6 Celestial soul body: spiritual essence, the 'higher self'
7 Illuminated spiritual body: cosmic unity, the One or the Divine

SUBTLE BODIES AND CHAKRAS

Oriental sensitives have documented the existence of seven subtle bodies (layers of the body's electromagnetic energy field, or aura) and seven energy centres known as "chakras" (from the Sanskrit word for "wheel") to which they are linked. A chakra is like an entry/exit point or gateway for each energy body, with each chakra roughly corresponding to its equivalent in the subtle body. As vortices of energy chakras connect us with the energies of the universe, and in this context the idea of an organ of the

The chakra system

The chakras (energy centres) of the human body are connected with different colours, organs and levels of experience that encompass all aspects of life – from the mundane to the sacred.

Chakra	Colour	Governs	Concerned with
1st chakra: base of spine	red	skeletal structure, lower body	physical survival; ambition; security
2nd chakra: just below the navel	orange	bladder, circulation	sexuality; creativity; feelings, emotions; pleasure
3rd chakra: just below ribcage	yellow	adrenal glands, stomach	identity; self-confidence; personal power; desires and wishes
4th chakra: centre of the chest	green	immune system, lungs	relationships, compassion; personal development
5th chakra: at the throat	blue/turquoise	lymphatic, immune and neurological systems	self-expression; communication; trust
6th chakra: "third eye" at the centre of the brow	indigo	pituitary gland, central nervous system	understanding; perception; intuition; spiritual knowing; psychic abilities
7th chakra: crown, at the top of the head	violet, also magenta	pineal gland, ancient mammalian gland	openness; connection to higher energies and spiritual realms; self-realization

body being "linked" to a particular constellation of stars may not seem so far-fetched. Each one vibrates at a particular frequency and is connected with different organs, colours and qualities.

Developing psychic ability and fine-tuning sensitivity to subtle energies is especially connected with the 6th chakra, or "third eye", situated between the brows.

ANIMISM

Magic involves an animistic world view. "Anima" means "the soul", the innermost part or essence of a being and its animating principle. Animism is the belief that the world is profoundly alive and that all of nature – the trees and rocks, animals, insects and fish, and even the weather, as well as human beings, has vital essence. Everything that exists has consciousness. The consciousness of spirits can merge into human consciousness, and the soul of a living human is believed to become spirit when they die, becoming either an ancestor spirit or part of an elemental spirit.

Chakras are wheels of energy in the body that are reflected in the world outside by nature's spirals.

SACRED PLACES

I n natural magic, the earth is regarded as a sacred manifestation of spirit and, like everything else in the universe, it too is made up of invisible energies. Over time, the places where these energies were most powerfully felt became sacred sites, where people gathered to perform rituals and sacrifice offerings in order to give thanks, seek protection from harmful influences, and gain the favour of spiritual powers. In ancient times, rites of earth worship would have been associated with the times of year when the spirits were most active and their help most needed. Modern witches and pagans work with the seasons and the energies of the earth to forge a link with nature and all her powers.

The power and majesty of the pyramids has endured for thousands of years.

SACRED SITES

Many sacred sites around the world have special significance to particular communities: Stonehenge for Druids; Mount Olympus for the ancient Greeks; the San Francisco Mountains for the Native American Zuni tribe; the Black Hills of South Dakota for the plains tribes; the Great Pyramids for the ancient Egyptians; and Uluru (formerly known as Ayers Rock) for the aboriginal tribes of Australia. These sites are usually associated with the ancestors, gods or spirits of a given culture and are important to the community's collective psyche. Acting as gateways to the otherworld, such energy hotspots play an important role in natural magic.

Geomancy

The particular branch of natural magic that involves reading and relating to the subtle energies of the earth is known as geomancy. It is a core part of the relationship that all magical traditions have had with the environment and is intimately woven into the cultural fabric of indigenous people everywhere, be they Celt or Saami, !Kung or Inuit, Aboriginal Australian or Native American. Feng Shui, the Chinese code of geomancy that stems from the imperial culture of China, has become popular in the West and is widely studied.

STANDING STONES

The oldest megaliths in the world are at Carnac in Brittany, France, where thousands of large stones are arranged to form avenues, chambers and mounds. Stone circles, the best-known of which is Stonehenge in England, began to be constructed from around 3000 BC. These mighty structures required huge resources of materials and manpower, and their survival demonstrates that those who built them certainly intended them to be permanent structures.

Megaliths may have had astronomical as well as spiritual significance, and it is likely that priests attended them and used them for measuring time, foretelling eclipses and predicting the movement of the stars. A prehistoric burial chamber surrounded by a circle of 12 great stones in Newgrange, Ireland, is an excellent example. At the winter solstice, the rising sun shines directly into the passage to the chamber, while the circle stones, which are carved with magical symbols recording the movements of the sun, moon and planets, are aligned with sunrises and sunsets at the solstices and equinoxes. At a number of sites in North America large, wheel-like circles orientated to the points of the compass have been outlined in stone. Traditionally, people come to them to pray and leave offerings.

Early Christian churches and abbeys in Europe were often built on the site of, or close to, megaliths and stone circles, presumably in recognition of the sacred energies that were present there.

HOLY SPRINGS

Water is one of life's essentials, and when it flows underground it carries strong earth energy, which can be detected by dowsing. The point where water forces its way out from the depths of the earth is a powerful focus for energy, and natural springs are often associated with natural magic. Most of us have at some time tossed a coin into a well or pool while making a wish, and in many places local folklore claims that drinking or bathing in the water of a particular spring or well can help promote fertility or cure disease. Every year, thousands of people make their way to Lourdes, France, where the holy water is said to have cured many illnesses. The holy "chalice well" at Glastonbury, England, has also become a focus for pilgrimage.

THE POWER OF TREES

Large trees are also powerful energy centres, and their sheer size reminds us of the enduring presence of nature and can help to put our human life span into perspective. A great mature tree, with roots locked deep in the earth and

It is believed that megalithic monuments such as these standing stones may have had astronomical as well as spiritual significance. They were usually erected at natural power spots – places where earth energy is particularly strong – and were lined up to connect with the yearly movements of the sun and stars.

branches reaching up into the sky, can also help us to appreciate and celebrate the "connectedness" of creation.

The image of the Tree of Knowledge occurs in the mythologies of many cultures, such as Yggdrasil, the Norse world tree, and the holy trees that grow on the Japanese Mountain of Heaven. In ancient times, sacred groves were sites of worship and divination, while pagan aspects of tree magic lie behind the modern custom of bringing evergreens indoors at Christmas.

In hot and arid lands, where trees indicate the vital presence of water and therefore life, they were often honoured as fertility symbols and associated and involved with fertility rites.

A PERSONAL SACRED PLACE

Many people find their own personal sacred space, somewhere that inspires a feeling of being part of creation, a place to meditate on the complexity of nature, feel its vitality and reflect on their own part in the immensity of the universe. There is no set formula for finding or nurturing a personal sacred place; each magician or witch has his or her own personal awareness of the land and therefore of the places where they feel particularly attuned to it. Some people are instinctively drawn to a traditional energy hotspot, while others seek a place that is uniquely special to them, such as a beautiful meadow or an ancient fallen tree in a glade. Although it seems more obvious to choose somewhere far from human habitation to connect with the earth's energies, the neglected hearts of cities and towns are just as important and have their own potency. Urban areas can offer healing and a new current of life-giving energy if they are located, cleared out, honoured and acknowledged.

GODS AND GODDESSES

A belief in gods and goddesses often originates from the pagan religions of ancient times, which acknowledge both a male and a female aspect of deity. In many traditions, these are thought of as the Sky Father and the Earth Mother, personifications of the forces and powers of nature – the essential energies of male and female that combine to create life and are present in all aspects of creation. In classical paganism, these two energies were further divided into whole pantheons of gods and goddesses, each with their own powers and specialities. It is possible to work magic with an eclectic mix of deities taken from many pantheons, or to work within one tradition.

Lilith is a complex figure from Judaic mythology who embodies many of the characteristics and contradictions of the Dark Goddess.

ARCHETYPAL PATTERNS

While gods and goddesses occur in various guises in mythology and sacred tradition, they very often share essential characteristics, which gives them an archetypal or primordial quality that transcends time and place. They can be seen as archetypal patterns, a way of expressing the enduring themes of human existence. In the ancient Greek pantheon, for instance, Aphrodite is recognized as the goddess of love, and Hermes is the patron of messages, healing and teaching, yet to the Romans, they are Venus and Mercury respectively. The Anglo-Saxon sky-god Tiw (from whose name we derive Tuesday) can be identified with Tyr in Scandinavia, Tiwaz in northern Europe, Ziu in Germany and Dyaus in ancient India, as well as with the Greek Zeus and the Roman Jove.

SUN AND MOON DEITIES

In many traditions, the sun is a male god of light, and the moon a goddess with three faces. Encountered in several ancient religions, these deities form the foundation upon which much natural magic is based; they can also be thought of in terms of lunar and solar principles, or feminine and masculine energies.

The lunar principle is associated with the earth, fertility, the dark, gestation, growth and decay. Her powers include intuitive, non-linear thinking. Artemis (Greek), Diana (Roman), Isis (Egyptian) and Ceridwen (Celtic) are all names of different aspects of the moon goddess. The solar principle is associated with the heavens, with creativity, light, clarity and truth. His powers are reason and logical, linear thinking, embodying the principle of rational consciousness. Names for the sun god include Apollo (Greek), Re (Egyptian), Odin (Norse), Wotan (Teutonic) and Tawa (Native American).

THE GODDESS AND THE GOD

In modern witchcraft, the divine is usually represented by two deities – the Goddess and the God – who take different names and forms. The Goddess is usually seen as having three dimensions, which correspond with the waxing, full and waning moon. These are her Maiden, Mother and Crone aspects, a trinity that is linked with the goddesses Diana (or Artemis), Demeter and Hecate respectively. When the Goddess is known as the Great Mother, she is the creatrix whose limitless fertility brings new life. Also identified with Mother

Diana is the Roman manifestation of the maiden, one of the three aspects of the moon Goddess, and is associated with hunting, wild nature and the protection of women.

Nature, she can be destructive as part of her regenerative cycle of birth, growth, death and rebirth.

As Queen of Heaven, the Goddess represents the moon as the source of feminine attributes connected to intuition, emotion and psychic ability. Her divine feminine force is manifested in a polarity with the masculine principle, often portrayed as the Horned God, who has two aspects related to the waxing and the waning year. As both her consort and son, these two gods are rivals and in constant competition with each other for her favours. The union of the Goddess and the Horned God is described as a sacred marriage that transcends all difference.

Also known as Cerunnos, Herne, Pan or the Green Man, the Horned God is not to be confused with the Christian Devil, which is a demonization of pagan god forms. Horns were a common attribute of gods in ancient cultures, and those of the Horned God are a symbol of male authority and sexual potency.

THE DARK GODDESS

In addition to the Great Mother, modern witchcraft venerates many other goddesses. Some of these embody the dark and death as well as more obvious life-giving and nurturing qualities. Typical is Lilith, a hybrid bird-woman who according to legend was Adam's first wife but refused to lie beneath him. Uttering the magical name of God, Lilith flew away to the wilderness where she gave birth to demons. God sent three angels to bring her back to Eden, but she refused to return.

The figure of Lilith is perhaps the source of ideas about strix, or striges, owl-like creatures of classical and European myth, and later the prototype of the diabolical witch stereotype fostered by the Christian church.

ACCESSING DIFFERENT TRADITIONS

Perhaps the most accessible of all the pantheons are those of the classical world. This is because the Greeks and Romans had a written tradition, so their mythologies have been handed down to us largely intact. However, the Celtic

The gift of the goddess

By its very nature, magic depends on the development and use of our psychic and intuitive faculties – the 'gift of the Goddess'. Although the 'gift of the God', which represents the linear, logical and conscious faculties, is also important, the Goddess in particular needs to be reawakened. It has been claimed that the early agricultural societies in Neolithic Europe, which lived in peace with nature and focused on women, were dominated by goddess-worship until they were invaded by warlike Indo-Europeans, whose sky gods supplanted the Goddess. Subsequently, she has been sidelined by the emphasis placed on the God of the monotheistic religions of Judaism, Christianity and Islam.

gods and goddesses are also very popular, even though they come from an oral tradition. The King Arthur legends, the Mabinogion (a Welsh mythological epic) and many modern fantasy cycles inform the Celtic tradition. The pantheon of ancient Egypt is also widely used in magic. These deities took both human and animal form, like Bastet the Cat Goddess. The gods and goddesses of the Northern Tradition (Scandinavian, Germanic and Anglo-Saxon) are easily accessed, too, while most indigenous peoples also have a rich pantheon.

The Horned God has many manifestations. In Greek mythology his name is Pan, but in all traditions he is associated with male authority and sexual potency.

ANGELS, FAIRIES AND OTHER GUIDES

Ideas about magic are often associated with spirit forms that are believed to inhabit the otherworld. These spiritual entities act as intermediaries between the ordinary everyday world and the enchanted realm, appearing in various guises, but commonly as angels, fairies or guides. Tales of fairies have often become mingled with tales of witches and sorcery, while angels are generally seen as high and pure spiritual energies that act as messengers, protectors and guides to humans. The concept of a guiding spirit appears in many traditions; the guide may be an angel, an ancestral spirit or that of any deceased person, a mythological being or even an animal.

Angelic beings emanate a powerful radiance. They can be called upon for healing and protection.

ANGELS

The concept of angels is familiar in the Judaeo-Christian tradition. Some, such as Gabriel, are mentioned in the Bible, and there are famous stories of individuals claiming to have been saved by angels. Angels predate the biblical period, however, and references to such beings have been found in the earlier cultures of Sumer, Babylon and Ur (modern Iraq). Angelic invocations form the basis of many ancient occult practices and individual angels are traditionally associated with various entities, such as

The attributes of angels

When calling on the power of the angels, use this guide to help you direct your plea to the right being.

Angel	Planet	Influences	Day	Colour	Symbol	Incense
Michael	Sun	Guardian and protector; encourages success with issues involving the maintenance of stamina or physical health	Sunday	Orange/red	Six-pointed star	Olibanum, frankincense
Gabriel	Moon	Protector of women and children; summon for fertility, healing and psychic abilities	Monday	Pale blue	Nine-pointed star	Myrrh, jasmine
Zamael	Mars	Protector and guardian guide to men; summon to protect against violence, to dispel negative opposition and for justice	Tuesday	Red	Five-pointed star	Tobacco, dragon's blood
Raphael	Mercury	Summon to protect during times of change and upheaval; travel; mental stress	Wednesday	Yellow	Eight-pointed star	Galbanum, storax
Sachiel	Jupiter	Summon for justice or to protect finances	Thursday	Purple	Square	Cedar
Anael	Venus	Summon for love, when conflict involves relatives or friends, where emotional harmony is lacking	Friday	Green	Seven-pointed star	Rose, sandalwood
Cassiel	Saturn	Summon for protection of property, land or possessions; to clear obstacles	Saturday	Indigo or black	Straight line	Myrrh

the seven ancient planets, specific days of the week, certain colours, incenses, symbols and powers. When an angelic power is called upon in making magic, it will leave behind a lingering protective energy and some of its special character.

FAIRIES

There are many types of fairies, including pixies, elves, lubberkins, goblins, hobgoblins, banshees, sidhes and leprechauns. Ranging in height from the size of a human being down to minute proportions, their appearance varies from extreme beauty to grotesque ugliness. The land of fairies, Faerie, is an enchanted world of captivating beauty, humour, mischief, laughter and love; it is also a world of darkness, ugliness, superficiality, terror and tragedy. It is an otherworld, a place of magical power that can reveal itself to certain people. Many fairies were believed to live inside hollow hills or barrows of the dead, which were thought to be entrances to the otherworld.

In Celtic folklore the fairy king and lord of the underworld is Gwyn ap Nudd, a wild huntsman who rides a demon horse in waste places at night accompanied by a pack of red-eared white hunting dogs. Numerous folk

myths are associated with similar chases, usually referred to as "The Wild Hunt", with many different leaders, including the Scandinavian Odin, or Anglo-Saxon Wotan, and England's Herne the Hunter. The goddess Diana, later identified in Shakespeare's play *A Midsummer Night's Dream* as Titania, queen of the fairies, is also sometimes associated with this spectral rout.

GUIDES

Mythological figures and ancestral spirits are also believed to inhabit the otherworld, and can be called upon to guide and assist you when working magic. Which figures you choose to work with will be up to you and will depend to some extent on the culture or tradition within which you are working. For

instance, if you work with the Arthurian legends, King Arthur would represent the master of mysteries, while the knight Gawain would be the defender of all that is right. The Lady of the Lake would be the guardian of the ancient mysteries and secrets, and holder of the Holy Grail; a pagan priestess, this dreamer and all-knowing visionary is mistress of wisdom. As the Arch Mage, Merlin would be the master of magic, ready to teach all who are willing to learn. If you follow Western shamanism your guide figures may appear as animal or totem spirits.

The spirit of a deceased loved one will sometimes appear to guide and direct you through the otherworld, while some people make contact with the powerful spirits of great teachers or magicians who lived long ago.

Meeting your guardian angel

Everyone has a personal Holy Guardian Angel. You can try to visualize your own angel in the following way.

1 Light a candle and burn some incense. Sit with your eyes closed and imagine a long ladder reaching up to the sky.

2 Ask to see your angel, and as you do so, imagine one coming down the ladder.

3 Imagine your angel in as much detail as you can. Feel its angelic power flowing all around you. Thank the angel for its visit; it will fade away when it has blessed you.

The land of Faerie is a place of enchantment and a popular subject in myth and legend. Rings of dew on morning grass are known as "fairy rings", a tell-tale sign that the fairies were dancing while humans lay sleeping.

INNER AND OUTER WORLDS

Many people who have become disillusioned with the dogma and rules of organized religion have sought a more individual and less regulated direction. Attracted by the very personal approach to spirituality, many have turned to the old arts of magic. Although these are very old, they are quite simple, and can be mastered by anyone who has a little patience and application. To practise natural magic it is not necessary to belong to any particular group or to follow any particular path. It is about finding a spiritual source or way of working magic that has meaning for you. The best maxim is, "If it works, use it", but always followed by the adage, "So long as it feels right for you and harms none".

The expression "pearls of wisdom" is based on the understanding that wisdom is hidden deep inside us, just like pearls in an oyster shell.

PATHWAYS TO NATURAL MAGIC

You can choose to work magic within a particular tradition, or adopt a more eclectic approach, adapting myths and symbols that resonate with you at a particular time. Similarly, it does not matter if you see these otherworldly beings, the gods and goddesses, angels, fairies and guides as actual spirit entities or as archetypal forces, as symbolic representations of cosmic powers and energies. All witches and Wiccans are pagan in that they are individuals who venerate nature, but not all pagans are witches or Wiccans. It is possible to be a pagan Druid, a pagan follower of the Norse deities, or a pagan worshipper of the gods of ancient Egypt, Greece, Rome or of many ancient deities of other lands around the globe. If you dislike the idea of labels of any kind, it is also possible to practise natural magic without identifying yourself as a pagan at all – it really is up to the individual.

TUNING IN TO THE INNER WORLD

It is easy to assume that the otherworld is somehow "out there" and divorced or separate from us. Paradoxically, however, it is both within and without, for it is only by tuning in to our inner world, the deepest centre of who we are, that we are able to make a connection with the world of spirit, the etheric vibrations of the cosmos that are all around us. This connection thrives not on logic and reason, but on a felt sense, often referred to as our "sixth sense", or intuition. Intuition is our inner knowing; the word is derived from two Latin words that mean "to look" and "in", and it is through this "looking in" that we are able to know things that are "out there" directly, without having to reason or think about them. This is why the disciplines of meditation and creative visualization have always played a key role in the practice of magic. Both of

Meditation is a way of stilling our senses so that we are able to connect with our inner knowing, or intuition – one of the most powerful magical tools we have.

these skills help to put us in touch with our inner world and increase our powers of concentration. It is concentration, or focus of intent, that helps to keep the desire of a spell or ritual in mind, and it is this that makes magic happen.

MEDITATION

In both the East and the West, meditation is practised as part of many ancient religions and cultures. This art of utter relaxation enables the practitioner to "drop" into that quiet, inner space deep inside. Essentially, it is a way of stilling the conscious mind; it involves letting go of everyday concerns and allowing the deeper, more subtle senses to awake and inform your conscious awareness. You can use meditation to put you in touch with your inner sense of power and creativity, and then with the gods and goddesses, angels and elemental beings – the partners of witches and magicians in their rituals. Unless you can withdraw from the everyday world for a few minutes each day, these archetypal forces will be unable to connect or resonate with you in any meaningful way.

There are literally hundreds of different ways to meditate, so you need to find one that works for you. Most meditation involves sitting quietly and focusing attention on an object, such as a candle flame, or on your breathing. It is also possible to meditate while lying down (provided you don't fall asleep) or even while walking or moving about, as long as you bring conscious awareness to every movement you make. Early morning meditation is generally better than late night sessions, but any time is good as long as it works for you, and you will not be disturbed. Your results will only become reliable if you persist with regular practice, so try to set aside at least 15 minutes each day, six days a week, for a couple of months.

VISUALIZATION

To practise natural magic, it is essential to develop your skills in imagining, or visualizing, alongside those of meditation. As children, most of us are able to imagine quite well, but as we get

The swirling smoke of incense, flickering candle flames and subtle scents are all used in natural magic as aids to meditation and to open up our senses to the otherworld.

older we tend to lose this ability. Fortunately, as with meditation, practice makes perfect.

There are various exercises you can try to improve your ability to visualize. A good way to start it is to close your eyes and imagine a series of simple objects in your mind's eye. For instance, these could include a ball, an apple, a tree, a flower, or even an animal. It doesn't matter what you pick, the aim is to try and see it in as much detail as possible.

A more complicated exercise is to close your eyes and see yourself travelling a particular route, choose one you are familiar with. See it in as much detail as possible, noticing any colours, signs, or other landmarks. When your attention wanders, come back and start again. Finally, another very useful visualization exercise is the Sphere of Protection described below. Practised regularly, it can help strengthen your aura while improving your ability to meditate.

The sphere of protection

Try combining the following visualization technique with your meditation practice to develop the two skills at the same time. Sit comfortably and close your eyes. Now imagine or mentally create a ball of white fire about arm's length in front of you. See it spinning and glowing strongly. See the ball begin to expand so that it surrounds you, below your feet and above your head, enclosing you in a sphere of brilliant light like a luminous bubble. Continue to imagine yourself seated within this rainbow-hued globe, and notice how it feels. To come out of the visualization, gradually let the image fade away and take a few deep breaths.

MAGICAL TOOLS

When practising natural magic there are a great many tools at the disposal of the witch or magician. Many of these are special objects that hold particular symbolism and magical power, and they are usually associated with the natural world in some way. These objects can be real or imagined, and are a personal expression of the magic worker. As you go

along, you will build up your own collection of tools that have meaning for you. It is important to keep them safe and use them solely for magical purposes – in this way they will build up subtle vibrations of power that are uniquely attuned to you.

This chapter covers a wide range of equipment that can help you in your magical practices – from altars, shrines and robes to crystals and gemstones, and even mundane items such as pens, paper and furniture. It includes information on herbs and spices, trees, fruit and flowers, incenses and oils as well as preparing candles for magic. The symbolism of light and colour, as well as the traditional witch's tools (like the cauldron, broomstick and pentacle), is also discussed, together with information on charms and talismans and animal totems. The chapter finishes with the power of ancient symbols, such as the spiral, cross and circle, all of which are used in magic.

ALTARS AND SHRINES

We're all familiar with altars, and the term probably conjures up some richly decorated object that may be seen in a temple or a church, but of course they don't have to be like that. The earliest kinds of altars were open to the sky, with the smoke of burnt offerings rising towards the gods, and it was only later that they were enclosed in temples erected to honour specific deities. Like the hearth at the centre of the home, the altar was the focal point of sacred activity, where ritual took place. Altars have always played an important role in magic: they serve primarily to focus attention, turning it away from the mundane towards the sacred and the magical.

A simple altar in which the yellow flowers, candle and burning incense represent the Air element.

WHERE TO PLACE AN ALTAR

If you are going to create a permanent altar in your home the first thing you need to consider is where to place it. In the Judaeo-Christian tradition, altars are positioned in the east of a building, the direction of the Holy Land (from Europe) and the rising sun. Similarly, whenever Muslims pray they face the Ka'aba in Mecca, Islam's holiest shrine, believed to be the site of God's first house on earth. You might want to follow the Wiccan tradition, however, and place your altar in the north, the compass direction associated with the Earth.

The altar should be in proportion with the space it is in, so do not create a huge one in a small room, or make it obstructive in any way. Don't clutter your altar with too many items, and keep it clear of dust and debris.

ALTAR SYMBOLISM

What you place on your altar depends entirely on you. You can choose symbols to represent the four elements of earth, water, fire and air using a stone for earth in the north, a bowl of water to represent water in the west, a lighted candle for fire in the south, and either some scented flowers, a feather, joss sticks or incense

If you dedicate a permanent space in your home as an altar you can change the items on it to reflect your prayers and wishes. This healing altar enlists the cleansing energy.

for air in the east. Represent the fifth element, ether or spirit, at the centre of the altar; a clear quartz crystal is a good choice. Square altars are said to represent the sky, while circular altars symbolize the earth. Most people have a selection of favourite objects that can be dedicated for use in magical work, such as statues or simple objects of beauty that have a special significance for them. For rituals or specific purposes, other elemental objects can also be added to your altar. These may include a centre lamp, salt for cleansing and purification, and some incense grains burned on charcoal.

A cup of wine or fruit juice and a platter of bread may also be positioned on the altar, to be drunk and eaten as part of the sacred meal during ritual.

TYPES OF ALTAR

Big, brightly coloured altars are good for large places, and have a greater impact on the subconscious and therefore a greater power. Bright colours also have specific purposes, such as helping to improve creative powers. But small, low-impact altars have their own power and purpose, and a little personal altar, using something like a small table or a flat stone, can be easily placed in your home or garden. An altar does not have to be permanent: you can create small, temporary altars that serve a specific purpose or simply reflect how you are feeling at the time.

Whatever you use, and wherever you place the altar, look after it, keep it clean and give it your attention for a few minutes each day. This will help to focus your awareness and strengthen your spiritual connections.

CREATING A SHRINE

An altar is set out specifically for each piece of work, but a more permanent display is usually called a shrine. A shrine can be created in a small corner or on a tabletop; it may be indoors or outside (or both). The point is to create something that has meaning for you and helps you connect to the power of natural magic and focus your meditations. The objects you choose to display should be very personal, evoking a special response in

Altars are best kept simple, with just a few well-chosen objects that have personal meaning.

you. Typical items that are often selected include a statue of a god or goddess, or a picture of an angel or other sacred symbol. Shrines displaying seasonal symbols, such as flowers, fruit or foliage, are useful to celebrate the festivals of the year; or if you are working with the phases of the moon, you can select different symbols to represent the moon in all her phases. These can be changed as time passes.

An outdoor shrine is sometimes referred to as a grotto. This is generally bigger than a shrine and should contain growing flowers and herbs, larger rocks, pieces of sea-washed wood and other pleasing items that help you connect to the natural world. Many people also like to include a goddess statue to symbolize Mother Nature and all her bounty.

OFFERINGS

An altar or shrine is also a place to leave offerings. Offerings play an important part in magical rituals. When you make an offering you are exchanging energy, as well as giving thanks. It helps to reinforce your connection with the universe; the conscious intent, coupled with the physical action, makes this a powerful ritual. Typical offerings may include tobacco, a sacred herb for Native American Indians and widely used in their ceremonies and rituals, and salt, regarded as sacred by the Celts. You can also leave a small coin to represent material wealth, or natural items like a shell, a pebble, a single flower that you've gathered on a country walk. It doesn't really matter what you offer as long as it has meaning for you and your intent is clear.

An outdoor shrine can be something you maintain in your own garden, or a way of honouring nature on the spur of the moment as you walk through the countryside.

ROBES AND OTHER EQUIPMENT

Since antiquity, those who have worked magic have worn ceremonial robes and used special equipment, and these still form an important part of a magic-worker's tool-kit today. The idea behind them is that such objects will facilitate the psychological transition from everyday life to being a worker of magic. Many of the tools also have a practical purpose and will be needed in rituals and spells. It is important that you set aside your magical clothes and equipment and only use them when making magic. Thus they will absorb the subtle energetic vibrations of your magical work and over time will become imbued with magical power. Keeping your clothing and equipment in a safe and private place, as well as keeping them clean, is also important.

A straight-backed chair, a small table and a box for your materials are important for magic work.

CEREMONIAL ROBES

A special robe or other ceremonial costume is important to the working of magic. Although many people do just change into clean clothes for rituals, actually wearing a robe specifically dedicated to magic can really help put you in the right mood.

Traditional costumes are simple T-shaped garments, reaching to the ankles and with long sleeves, similar to a kaftan or kimono design. The important thing is that the robe should be loose-fitting so as not to restrict the flow of energy through your body. Ideally costumes are made from natural fibres, such as cotton, silk, linen or wool, as a reminder of your connection to nature.

Some organized groups have a specific colour or design, but for working on your own or with friends, a simple garment in any design will be fine. Some people like to embroider or decorate their robes; some have long sleeves, which may be wide or close-fitting (although the latter are safer when dealing with lit candles and fire); others are sleeveless or short-sleeved: really it is up to you to choose something that you feel comfortable in, but which you also feel is appropriate. Treat your magic-making clothes with

Sleeveless robes work well as magical garments as they leave the arms free.

respect, keep them clean and crease-free, and hang or fold them carefully when you put them away.

MAKING A ROBE

The most basic robe can be a tube of material, with armholes but no sleeves, and a simple neckline that is big enough to put on over your head. All that is needed is a piece of material that reaches from your neck to your heels, and is wide enough to make two matching pieces for the front and back. Obviously the actual design will depend on how much skill you have at dressmaking, and how much time and effort you spend on decoration. The choice of colour will be important: let your intuition guide you when picking the fabric. If you need design ideas, historical costumes or stage-costume books can be a good source.

TEMPLE OR SANCTUARY FURNITURE

As most people do not have the space for a full-time temple or sanctuary area in their homes, your temple furniture may have to serve a dual role. In this case, make sure you clean it before and after using it for magical work. If you do decide to invest in special furniture, it should always be chosen for its practicality. Don't be tempted to pay a lot of money for fancy items that may look good but won't work well in practice, or which are too large to be stored easily.

You will need a table for an altar, a comfortable and supportive chair (ideally one that has arms and is straight-backed) for meditations and inner work, and some kind of cupboard, chest or box in which to keep your equipment when it is not in use. Magical equipment should definitely be kept separate from other household items as this will help to increase its magical significance, and a special box or chest to keep it in is the one item that you should consider buying if you don't already have anything suitable. If you decide to set out a shrine to celebrate the changing seasons or moons, you will need a small area for a few flowers, symbols, statues or pictures to reflect the patterns of your own land and surroundings.

The materials that are needed for spells should be kept together and used only for magical purposes.

Filling a magic casket

Start to build up a store or 'casket' of general magical ingredients and equipment. Your casket can be a cupboard, chest or special box, or a collection of several different sized boxes, perhaps kept inside a cupboard. You can often find something interesting in a second-hand or antique shop, or perhaps you, or someone you know, can make something specially. If you buy something that has been used, make sure you cleanse it thoroughly first to rid it of any unwanted emanations from its previous owners. Ideally your casket should be made of wood or other natural material rather than anything man-made.

The casket will need to contain the following basic elements:

- natural sea salt (for cleansing and purifying)
- a length of white cord for casting circles
- a selection of incenses and essential oils
- candles in various colours
- special crystals, stones and gems of your choice
- a selection of dried herbs
- feathers
- gold and silver pens (to represent the sun and the moon respectively)
- silk and cotton fabrics in a choice of colours
- a variety of coloured threads
- good-quality natural paper (for writing spells)
- a goblet and platter
- a spell bag (a drawstring pouch for keeping spells in)

SYMBOLIC TOOLS

Several tools traditionally associated with magic-workers may seem archaic or stereotypical, but do have a number of functions and have not been bettered. They include the cauldron, wand, broomstick and pentacle, as well as the sword, athame or dagger. Also known as magical weapons, each of these instruments has a number of practical purposes and is richly imbued with symbolic meaning. Understanding this symbolism is essential if you are to work with these tools confidently and effectively, and successfully follow the well-trodden path of ancient magical practice.

THE CAULDRON
The meeting place of all four elements, cauldrons are used in nearly all traditions of natural magic. The iron pot itself represents the earth, the fluid it contains stands for water, the burning wood or peat below for fire, and the rising steam and aromas are air. In medieval times, most cooking was done in an iron pot hanging over an open fire at the centre of the home. The hearth had to be regularly tended and stoked up with fuel by the woman of the house and her cauldron was usually the focus of household life, providing physical nourishment and inner wisdom. Some women were sensitive to the strange patterns that might be seen in the swirling water, and some could see the future, or events

happening far away, in the drifting spirals of smoke. Today, many witches do not have an open fire in their homes, so will light a candle in a cauldron to represent the hearth fire of old. If it is not possible to find a suitable cauldron, you can use a chalice or goblet to symbolize it.

THE BROOMSTICK
Another vital piece of household equipment in days gone by was the besom, or traditional broomstick. It was made up of materials that were easy to come by, and many lands have their own simple versions. In Europe many besoms were made with birch twigs for the bristles, a handle of hazel, and a binding of willow withies. Each of these plants has magical associations: birch being

The besom, made of birch twigs, is still used as a magical tool by modern witches.

linked to birth and beginnings, hazel to wisdom or far seeing, and willow to the healing power of the old Crone Goddess.

The whole implement was used domestically for sweeping the floor, and magically for clearing out any invisible disturbances from a place used as a magical circle. In the days when houses had earth floors, a circle would literally be swept into the dust, and this ring would form the limits of magical work. Modern witches sometimes still sweep the area they are about to use for magic, and may place the besom on the edge of the ritual circle to symbolize a doorway through which their companions may enter the sacred ring.

THE WAND
Traditionally associated with wizards, wands are still much used by modern magic-workers. The simplest kind is a straight stick from which the bark may have been cut in a spiral or other pattern. Carved or painted, the wand basically is a symbol of the magician's power and authority to command the forces of

If you have a small cauldron, a candle placed inside can represent Fire.

Once you have made a wand you can adapt it to fit your spell-making.

Making a wand

While witches mostly use simple wands – such as a plain hazel stick, perhaps carved with a spiral – you might also want to make a more elaborate wand.

you will need:
*a willow stick, cut about 1 m (3 ft) long, 1.5 cm (23 in) thick
coarse sandpaper
fine sandpaper
PVA (white) glue
ribbons in the seven colours of the rainbow
a quartz crystal
copper wire*

1 Strip the bark away from the stick and sand it down with coarse sandpaper. Sand again with fine sandpaper until the wand is completely smooth.

2 Glue strips of ribbon to the wand in order of the rainbow: red, orange, yellow, green, blue, indigo, violet.

3 Attach the quartz crystal to the top of the wand, using copper wire.

You can adapt your wand for different purposes by attaching small symbolic items to it, such as rose quartz for love, seashells for fertility, fresh mint for prosperity or holly and oak leaves for protection.

The traditional tools of the Wiccan practitioner are the chalice (representing the cauldron), the athame (or knife), the wand and the pentacle.

A pentacle is a five-pointed star. It can be painted on a surface or made from twigs.

magic. Sometimes it is used to mark a magical circle, either by physically scratching a line or describing a circle in the air, to create the "place that is between the worlds of time and space" where all natural magic is performed.

THE PENTACLE

The five-pointed star known as the pentacle has been closely associated with different kinds of magic and religious symbolism for thousands of years. It has been found painted on the walls of the temples of ancient religions, carved on the stones of Christian churches by the masons who built them, and used as a pattern for many stained-glass windows in cathedrals.

The five points of the pentacle are sometimes seen as symbolizing the head, hands and feet of the witch, and it is sometimes also enclosed in a circle, representing wholeness and oneness with the universe. Sometimes witches wear this symbol as a pendant or on a ring, traditionally in silver, the metal of the moon and the pagans' Goddess.

THE SWORD

Based on the idea that metal is a good conductor of energy, many witches use a sword to draw the magic circle. The use of a sword probably derives from ritual magic and freemasonry. In his Book of Shadows, Gerald Gardner, founder of the modern Wicca movement, refers to an athame, or black-handled knife, as "the true witches' weapon". It is used for drawing pentacles and may also be used for drawing the circle if you do not have a sword. A wand may be used in place of the sword or dagger if you prefer.

Magic symbols

The tools described here differ from those of a ceremonial magician, whose four magical instruments are the pentacle, chalice, sword and wand, chosen to represent the four elements of earth, water, air and fire respectively. These tools also correspond to the four suits of the Minor Arcana in a traditional Tarot deck.

DARKNESS, LIGHT AND COLOUR

According to the wisdom of ancient China, everything in the universe is made up of two opposite but complementary forces. Known as "yin" and "yang", these polarities are seen to represent certain energetic qualities that exist in all things to a greater or lesser extent. Yin is the female or negative polarity, and represents the forces of darkness, while yang is the positive or masculine polarity, and represents the forces of light. Neither yin nor yang is superior to the other and each contains the seeds of its opposite. The universe exists in a state of energetic tension between these two forces, each ready to transform into the other, just as day follows night. Magic is also based on this principle: the forces of darkness are as important as light and understanding these two polarities forms the basis of magical thinking. Colour, which is an important part of the magic-worker's tool kit, is essentially composed of more or less light.

Understanding and implementing the opposite, and complementary, forces of light and darkness will add power and depth to magic work.

THE DARK AND THE LIGHT

In Western culture, we tend to split the world into "good" and "evil", embracing all that is "good" while rejecting all that we see as "evil". In its turn, "evil" is associated with darkness, which has long been feared, for both rational and irrational reasons. Although darkness is negative – it is an absence of light – magic teaches us that it is an essential and profound part of life. The dark is associated with gestation, rest and renewal. Night-time is when we dream and drift into otherworlds that are as valid as the ordinary everyday world we consider reality. In magical thinking, the darkness represents Earth and the moon. It is the unconscious, psychic power, intuition, imagination, emotion, and irrationality; it is soft, yielding and feminine. The light on the other hand is associated with the sun and the Heavenly Sky. It is conscious awareness and represents reason and logic, ambition and the desire to forge ahead in the world. Like an arrow shooting forth, its qualities are focused, disciplined, hard, unyielding and masculine. A magic worker needs this power to have the intent to direct or focus energy.

Nature's cycles of light

At sunrise, the sun low on the horizon is red. As it climbs into the sky, the widening angle with our point on the earth's surface allows more orange and then yellow light to reach the ground. Experiments have shown that red light increases blood pressure, pulse rate and breathing rate, and that these functions increase even more in orange light and reach their peak in yellow light. Our physiological response to light has evolved so that the rising sun stimulates us into activity and alertness.

Other experiments have shown a decrease in blood pressure, pulse rate and breathing rate when people are exposed to green light. As daylight fades the green light is subdued, and changes to the blue of evening, when relaxation increases further and is at its fullest in complete darkness. Night, or no-light, is the natural time of rest and reflection.

Colours, when used in magic making, can have great energetic powers.

Colour chart

As each colour has its own distinct properties and effects, we can also use the vibrations of colour for particular purposes when making magic. Essentially this means we are working with the subtle interplay between the powers of light and darkness, with intense colours such as deep reds, purples and indigo blues having more darkness as well as different qualities from sunny yellows, sharp greens and bright oranges. Different colours are chosen according to the type of magic that is being worked.

Colour	Energy correspondence	Chakra correspondence	Useful for
Red	Stimulating, energizing	1st, or base	Low energy, sexual problems, blood disorders, lack of confidence
Orange	Cheering, enlivening	2nd	Depression, mental disorders, asthma, rheumatism
Yellow	Inspiring, helping mental clarity and detachment	3rd, or solar plexus	Detoxifying, hormonal problems (menopause, menstrual difficulties)
Green	Fresh, vibrant, harmonious	4th, or heart	Antisceptic, balancing, tonic; good for shock and fatigue; soothes headaches
Blue	Soothing, calming, promoting truth and inner reflection	5th, or throat	Insomnia, nervous disorders, throat problems, general healing
Indigo	Transforming, purifying	6th, or third eye	Painkiller, sinus problems, migraine, eczema, inflammation, chest complaints
Violet/ Purple	Regal, dignifying	7th, or crown	Love of self, self-respect, psychological disorders and scalp problems
Magenta	Letting go	7th, or crown	Emotional hurts and upsets, accepting life's problems
Black	Absorbing, secretive; night-time; the occult		Power and control; self-discipline
White	Reflecting, purity, innocence; day-time		Tonic; replaces all colours
Gold	Divine power, purity; the Sun		Depression and low energy; digestive disturbances
Silver	Cosmic intelligence; the Moon		Hormonal and emotional balance, calms the nerves

THE ENERGY OF COLOURS

Colour has always been associated with certain types of energy that are useful in magic. In the Middle Ages, colour was one of the correspondences used in magic along with planets, elements, spirits and angelic beings, metals, herbs, shapes and numbers. However, it was the German philosopher, dramatist, artist and scientist, Goethe (1749–1832) who combined scientific observations with metaphysical concepts, describing colour as an interplay of the polarities of light and dark. He saw colour as an expression of spirituality and a way of expressing the inner nature of humanity. His thinking influenced later theorists, such as Rudolf Steiner, who was influential in forming colour theories in the 20th century.

We know instinctively that colours affect us in different ways. We speak of feeling blue, being green with envy, red with anger, or in the pink when we are feeling especially happy. Each band of energy in the colour spectrum vibrates at a particular frequency that not only influences our mood, but also corresponds to the body's organs and energy systems. What is more, it is not necessary to be able to see to have a sense of these resonances of colour. Many blind people have developed their sensitivity to the subtle vibrations of different colours, so that they are able to identify colours without ever being able to see them.

CANDLES

Traditionally, candles have always played a significant part in magic and sacred ceremony and no altar is complete without them. They embody the positive symbolism of light as spiritual illumination, and a fragile candle flame is a powerful emblem of the individual soul, especially in times of darkness and difficulty. Other lights, such as oil lamps and lanterns, can have a similar reassuring significance, and a perpetual flame on an altar stands for the constant presence of the divine.

CANDLE RITUALS

The lighting of candles is a simple ceremonial act that initiates and hallows ritual. It acts as an announcement of your intention to work magic, perhaps to revere your chosen spirit beings or gods, or to summon their presence to your work. It is common practice in many sacred traditions to light a candle and leave it to burn out before the shrine of a saint or deity as an act of devotion, symbolizing both prayer and sacrifice. Candles are also used to mark rites of passage, from baptism to funerals. Placed around a coffin, their light is believed to protect the dead from harm during the vulnerable time of transition from this world to the next.

The Christian feast of Candlemas (the lighting of candles) at the beginning of February was grafted on to the pagan fire festival of Imbolc, when all the candles that were to be used in the year ahead were blessed. Candlemas is a time of purification and a good time to clean or re-dedicate your magical tools and equipment. In pagan tradition, the candle flame represents the element of

Lit candles represent the Fire element, but their colours and shapes can also be used symbolically.

Snuffing a candle flame, rather than blowing it out, gives greater power to the ritual or spell.

Colours for candles

When using candles in your spells or rituals, make sure their colour reflects the magic you are working.

White: enlightenment, healing, peace, purity; can be a substitute for another colour
Yellow: communication, concentration, movement
Orange: attraction, strength, luck.
Gold: confidence, health, prosperity; honours solar deities
Pink: love, harmony, family, affection
Red: sexuality, courage, passion
Violet or purple: spirituality, inner harmony, wisdom
Indigo: cleansing, meditation
Blue: wisdom, inspiration, truth, healing; honours lunar deities
Green: love, nature, renewal, abundance
Brown: home, wealth, stability, family elders
Silver: secrets, psychic power, lunar magic
Black: conclusions; banishes guilt, regret and negativity

fire, associated with life, creative energy and passion. Blowing candles out is said to have the effect of blowing away your intent or desire, so it is best to let the candle burn down completely. If this is not possible, then you can pinch out the flame instead. For the same reason, incense sticks should be waved rather than blown before the altar.

CANDLE

Casting spells using candles is one form of basic magic that is quite easy to do. A spell is a set of words (sung, chanted, spoken or written) that asks for a specific kind of change to come about. Lighting a candle to signify you are beginning the spell, and then snuffing it out at the end, gives your spell definition and focus.

Another simple form of candle magic involves writing the name of something you wish for on a piece of paper and then burning the paper in the candle flame, so that the wish is carried away in the smoke. In another candle charm, a symbol of the wish is engraved in the wax. As the candle burns down, you may find that the melted wax dripping down its side forms an image to indicate how your wish might come true.

Once you have made up your mind exactly what you intend to achieve, you will need to set out a place to work and find a suitable candle and holder. If the candle is central to the spell, it is generally best to use a new one. You may also want to mentally conjure up your desired wish, or a symbol associated with it, and hold this in your imagination as you work your magic. For instance, if your wish is for a new job, then you might want to visualize your desired working environment and the kind of colleagues you would like to work with.

Burning a spell or blessing in the flame of a candle is one way to complete your magic work.

PREPARING A CANDLE

A candle is often used as the focus for magic, but it needs to be properly prepared. For ritual use, candles can be empowered by "dressing" or anointing them with oil, to clean them of any unwanted energies and to personalize them to your needs. If you prefer, you may use a cotton bud to put the oil on to the candle rather than your fingers, particularly if you have sensitive skin.

1 Choose a new candle and an essential oil that corresponds with the spell. Take a few drops of the oil and "anoint" the candle with it. If the ritual is intended to send energy out, you should wipe the oil along the candle from the middle to the ends. If you are performing a spell that aims to achieve or attract something, wipe the oil from the ends of the candle to the middle.

2 As you concentrate on your aim, wind a length of narrow coloured ribbon around the candle to bind your intention to it. Choose a colour that corresponds with your magic.

You can now use the candle in a ritual to accomplish your will.

PSYCHIC ATMOSPHERES

You can use a lighted candle to see if the psychic atmosphere of an area is clear. Put the candle in a holder and stand it on a table or other surface away from draughts. Light it and notice how it burns. In a well-balanced room, the flame should burn gently with a small golden-yellow flame, flickering only now and then, perhaps in the natural movement of air in the room. If the candle flame splutters, burns blue, behaves erratically, jumps rapidly or sparks, or does anything else unusual and unexpected, it indicates a charged psychic atmosphere that would benefit from a space clearing.

Candles in sacred tradition

In the Catholic church, a prescribed number of candles must be lit before each mass, the number varying according to the solemnity of the service. However, the Christian use of altar candles was adopted from much older traditions. For instance, the ancient Egyptians used candles when practising dream incubation as a way of seeking answers; the questioner would sit in a cave staring at a candle flame until he saw a deity in it, then when he fell asleep, the deity that had been seen would provide an answer.

INCENSE AND AROMATICS

Like candles, incense and aromatics have a long tradition of use in both magic and sacred ceremony. In ancient temples, incense was burned to purify the atmosphere, focus the mind and calm the senses as well as to symbolically carry the prayers and requests of the worshippers to the gods and goddesses above. As it spirals up to the heavens, the fragrant smoke forges a link between earth and the heavenly realms, becoming a flight-path for prayers, spells and incantations to deities and angelic beings. Furthermore, each fragrance has its own unique properties, which can be used in magic to stimulate, relax, rebalance, transform or purify energetic states, as well as to influence possible outcomes. A working knowledge of aromatics is essential in the practice of natural magic.

Fragrant smoke gives atmosphere to magical ritual, and provides a link between worlds.

HOW FRAGRANCE WORKS

Our sense of smell is registered in the part of the brain that is connected with memory, emotion and instinctive activities. Fragrance plays a very important part in controlling our feelings and responses: foul or acrid fumes repel us, whereas sweet or fragrant aromas tend to draw us closer to their source. This response is the basis for the choice of the different incenses and oils used in magic: just as they attract or repel us,

some scents can be used to attract positive vibrations, and others to drive away negative influences. Similarly, some scents have a refreshing or energizing action, while others promote calm and relaxation; some aromas invoke sexual desire, while others quell it; some are head-clearing and encourage clarity of thought, while others promote dreams and intuition, creativity and inspiration. It is a matter of knowing which scents do what and learning how to use them.

INCENSE AND ESSENTIAL OILS

Deriving from the Latin *incendere*, meaning to kindle, incense is the term for the fragrant aroma that is produced when certain plant material is burned or vaporized. It is also the term for the actual material – typically resins and barks, herbs and spices, and essential oils. Essential oils are contained to a

Incense in ancient Egypt

The ancient Egyptians regarded fragrant resins as the life-breath of the tree that provided them, and placed them in graves to assist the souls survival in the next world. Rites and prayers accompanied the creation of incense-burning mixtures and the recipes were recorded in 'magic books'. One of the most precious mixtures was kyphi, meaning 'welcome to the gods', which was used as an aid to sleep and dreaming as well as for treating all manner of complaints. Frankincense and myrrh were two key ingredients of kyphi, while other substances, such as cinnamon, spikenard, sandalwood, coriander, raisins and wine, were added to make fragrant incense pellets.

Resins, such as frankincense and myrrh, produce impressive clouds of fragrant smoke.

greater or lesser extent in all parts of a plant and are believed to represent its "quintessence" or life-blood. These oils have always been imbued with magical, transforming properties. The ancient Chinese, for instance, believed that by extracting a plant's oils they were liberating its soul, and alchemists strove to find the elixir of life in these "magical" essences. It is the essential oil present in all parts of a plant that gives it its distinctive aroma.

USING AROMATICS

You can use incense and essential oils in different ways – as ready-made sticks or cones, loose as resins or incense pellets, or by vaporizing one or two drops of an essential oil in a burner. You can also make up recipes to suit your particular needs, or take them from books. If you have the chance to try out single-scented incenses one at a time you will soon learn those that you like and those you don't, and which evoke the kinds of powers you require. You may find that the scents you like tend to fall into the same fragrance group or family. Fragrance families are a way of classifying scents according to their aroma as follows: floral, herbaceous, woody, spicy, earthy, resinous and citrus. Floral scents are sweet and flowery, and

A starter kit of magical scents and aromas would include resins and gums, as well as the more familiar incense cones and sticks.

include rose and jasmine; herbaceous are the fresh "green" herbal scents such as rosemary or eucalyptus; fresh, uplifting citrus scents include bergamot and grapefruit. Woody, earthy and resinous scents are taken from bark, roots and resins, and include sandalwood, cypress and frankincense. Spicy fragrances include cinnamon and coriander.

This is an ancient craft, but with a little experience you can create a selection of scents that will conjure up just the right mood and atmosphere for any ritual or celebration. Having a mixture of loose resins and barks, dried herbs and spices, and a range of good-quality essential oils is a good place to start.

BURNING LOOSE INCENSE

You will need a suitable fireproof container for burning loose incense. A censer is a vessel designed for burning loose incenses and resins: a church thurible is ideal, although incense stoves made of clay and other materials are also available. You will also need the special charcoal blocks that are sold by occult supply houses. Light the charcoal with a match and leave it for a few moments. When the charcoal is hot, sprinkle on a very small amount of the incense mixture. A mere pinch will be enough to discover whether you like the smell and how much smoke it is giving off.

White sage has magical and cleansing properties.

An incense kit

When building up a collection of oils and incenses, try to include as many different types of fragrance as possible.

Loose resins: frankincense, myrrh, copal, dammar, mastic

Wood barks: agarwood (also known as 'aloes'), sandalwood, cypress, cedar, pine

Herbs and spices: star anise, cinnamon, cloves, sage, sweetgrass, rosemary, basil

Earthy: patchouli, vetiver

Florals: rose, lavender, jasmine, ylang ylang, geranium, tuberose

Citrus: orange, lemon, bergamot, grapefruit

Solar incense recipe

This multi-purpose loose incense will suit any healing ritual, or you can use it to celebrate a solstice or equinox. To make it, you will need a pestle and mortar.

1 Crush about 5ml/1tsp frankincense resin. Add a little crushed cinnamon quill, some marigold petals and a few drops of honey and orange oil.

2 Mix well until the texture is like breadcrumbs. Leave to blend for a few hours. Burn on hot charcoal.

HERBS AND SPICES

The use of herbs and spices in natural magic is centuries old. In the past, magic and medicine were inextricably bound, and in some parts of the world this is still the case today; for instance, in the Fipa language (spoken in Tanzania and Malawi) separate words for either concept do not exist. It is not difficult to see why. Plants are the basis on which all other life depends, providing us with life-giving oxygen as well as materials for other essentials such as fuel, food, clothing and shelter, together with healing medicines and mind-altering drugs. Knowledge of plant lore is the foundation on which shamans, medicine men and wise women have based their magic, using herbs and spices in healing potions to treat "dis-ease" and in spells and amulets to ward off "the evil eye", or negative influences.

An illustrated herbal can help you identify which plants are safe to use and which are poisonous.

PLANT MEDICINE

In Western society our idea of a "medicine" is comparatively limited compared to many other areas of the world. In some cultures, medicines are not just substances that possess healing powers, but can also make people fall in love, appease the spirits, gain prosperity or do anything else that is sacred, unusual and imbued with magical power. In this context medicine means using the inherent potency of a plant to maintain, restore, attract or repel energies from a person, place or thing. This is because every plant has special attributes, some of which are helpful and have positive effects, while others may be dangerous.

In days gone by, knowledge of plant lore was passed on from generation to generation, particularly through the female lineage. Today, much of this received wisdom has been lost, so we need to re-educate ourselves in order to learn about herbs. Ideally, you can do this by finding a teacher who can show you how to recognize each plant, where it grows, how to cultivate and harvest it and how to prepare it in the most effective way. Many places now have herb societies that run training courses and there are also some very good correspondence courses available. Alternatively, a family member or friend may be able to pass on information, while a good, well-illustrated reference book can help you begin to learn how to identify what you are dealing with.

Once you know all about a plant and its properties, you will need to learn how to prepare it properly for use in herbal remedies and your magic work.

Collections of dried herbs should be kept in airtight containers and thrown away if they lose their scent.

Using Herbs and Spices

There are a number of ways to use herbs and spices to give a spell its potency: they may be ingested in food, or drunk in teas, infusions or decoctions, and even used in bathing or steam inhalations. Knowing which part of a plant to use – leaves, fruits, roots or seeds – is as vital as knowing exactly which plant you are dealing with, especially if you are going to eat or drink it. As a general rule of thumb, any herb that is commonly used in cooking will be safe to use for any other purpose, although you need to learn its special properties before attempting to use it in magic.

Decoctions

Spices are usually derived from a plant's bark, fruit, seeds or root rather than its leaves and flowers, and these tougher plant pieces need to be simmered or "decocted" in boiling water in order to extract their essences and magical properties. Use approximately 5–20g (¹/₄–1oz) dried spice to 750ml (1¹/₄ pints/3 cups) cold water, reduced to about 475ml (16fl oz/2 cups) after simmering. If you are using fresh herbs or spices, double up the quantity.

Talismans

Herbs are used as talismans in magic: St John's wort (*Hypericum*), for example, can be hung over windows and doors on Midsummer's Day to cleanse and protect the house, while cloves of garlic are a traditional protector against psychic disturbances or harmful presences. In folkloric traditions, strings of garlic are hung around windows, doors or even people, for protection.

Offerings

Another use for some kinds of herbs, such as tobacco, is as an offering. Tobacco is seen as a sacred herb by the Native American Indians, and is left as a gift on altars, or burned in a flame as an offering. Salt is used in rituals in the same way, and also as a means of cleansing or grounding. White sage is also used as an offering by the Native American Indians; the smoke it produces is thought to be especially pure.

Native American sacred herbs

For thousands of years, the indigenous people of North America have maintained a very close relationship with the plant kingdom. They use many herbs for healing, protection and blessings, but their four most sacred herbs for purification and protection are sweetgrass, sage, cedar and tobacco.

Sweetgrass: this is traditionally used for self-blessing, for keeping evil spirits away from the home and to purify tools and equipment, because its sweet smell calls up the good spirits. It is plaited into a braid, then the end is lit and the smoke wafted over magical tools or around the room.

Sage: a powerful cleanser and purifier, and Native American Indians have been known to sit on sage leaves in sweat lodges, thus physically being submerged in its purifying abilities. The leaves can also be used for smudging (burning and waving it where the purifying smoke is needed), either loose or in smudge sticks. The most effective types are white or mountain sage.

Cedar: an evergreen tree also known as the Tree of Life. It is a very powerful psychic and spiritual cleanser. Smudging with cedar is advised when conditions are particularly difficult or obstructive, as its powers deal with the more problematic energies.

Tobacco: used for offerings to the Great Spirit and to the elemental and natural powers of creation. Tobacco is also cast into the sweat lodge fire as an offering to the fire spirits, and is sometimes given to elders and medicine men as a mark of respect.

Steep a handful of fresh sacred herbs in hot water to release their aroma and cleanse the atmosphere.

TREES, FLOWERS AND FRUIT

E ven if urban living makes us feel removed from the natural world, a walk through a leafy forest glade, a summer display of garden flowers, shells and driftwood from a beachcombing trip, or a bowl of autumn fruits, all remind us of our connection with the Earth and can help us appreciate nature's bounty. As powerful emblems of nature, trees, fruit and flowers have their own attributes and symbolism. This symbolism has always played an important role in natural magic: the unique properties of each species are harnessed to create spells and charms and used in ritual and ceremony for a wide variety of magical purposes.

Flowers have symbolic meanings and play an important part in natural magic. A single blossom makes a stunning altar display.

THE BEAUTY OF TREES

Possessing a unique natural beauty, trees have a timeless quality. With roots reaching deep down into the earth below and branches rising into the sky above, they are a perfect symbol of our connection with both the underworld and the heavenly realm. Trees were used in the development of one of the first alphabets: the Celtic Ogham alphabet, consisting of horizontal and diagonal strokes, which were inscribed on pieces of wood. Wood rituals have been used for love charms all over the world. By walking through a forest and noticing how each tree is different, you can find something that speaks to your heart and soul and so can be used in creating natural magic. Remember that if you are taking a twig from a tree you must ask permission of the tree's spirit, and give something back in return. Also, bear in mind that wild flowers are protected by law, and must not be picked.

Groves of trees were sacred to the Druids and played an important part in their magic and ritual. Just by standing next to a huge and ancient tree you can feel its power for yourself.

TREES IN MYTHOLOGY

The symbolism of trees is to be found in sacred and mythological traditions all over the world. Through the symbolism of the Tree of Life in the Cabbala tradition, for instance, the universe is seen as encompassing different levels of reality at the same time. Northern European cosmology is focused on a world tree, Yggdrasil, the connecting point of nine worlds, each of which is populated by one race or type of being,

Making a floral essence

Infuse your chosen tree or flower blooms by placing them in cold water and leaving to stand for several hours in sunlight. Strain off the water and add a preservative, such as brandy, vodka or vinegar. Use up to seven flowerheads to 300ml/ $^1/_2$ pint/1 $^1/_4$ cups of water and 150ml/$^1/_4$ pint/$^2/_3$ cup

preservative. The essence will keep for several months in a dark glass bottle, and you can use this when you want to call on a particular tree or flower for a spell. Many trees and their fruits are poisonous, so always check on a plant's properties before using its medicine.

such as giants, dwarves, elves, deities and humans. In Norse mythology, three sisters known as the Norns sit at the base of Yggdrasil weaving a web of fate called the Wyrd, where past and future are not separate but co-exist, world upon world, with actions in one influencing events in the other.

FLOWER SYMBOLISM

With a long history as lovers' gifts, a "language" of flowers has evolved wherein we understand a flower in terms of its symbolism. They are a universal symbol of youth and gentleness, and an appreciation of their beauty has helped civilizations to flourish artistically since ancient times. The brief life of a flower encapsulates the cycle of birth, life and return to the earth to nurture the next generation. A single bloom is an expression of natural but fleeting perfection; gazing into one, you can find a peace and serenity that you can take into yourself.

FRUIT AND REBIRTH

A universal symbol of nature's abundance and generosity, fruit represents the harvest, when we reap what has been sown. Each fruit also contains the seeds for the next generation. In this way fruits symbolize completion and endings as well as new beginnings, reminding us of nature's cycle of growth, decay and rebirth.

MAGICAL ESSENCES

It is possible to capture the vibrational pattern of a tree or flower in a magical essence. Such an essence may be used for healing negative emotional and psychological states as well as fostering the development of certain "soul" qualities. Several plant essence systems have been developed by sensitives who have attuned themselves to a plant's auric field (subtle energy field, or aura) and then noticed how this influenced their mood. The most well-known of these systems include the British Bach flowers, the Australian Bush flowers and the Californian flower essences, which are widely available. Alternatively, you can make your own essence.

Magical trees and fruit

- **Apple:** particularly associated with peace and the giving and receiving of love; 'poisoned' apples represent seduction, wickedness and false knowledge.
- **Oak:** sacred in many traditions, including Druid, Judaeo-Christian and Norse; it is particularly associated with protection and endurance. Fruit: acorns.
- **Hazel:** tree of knowledge and wisdom. Hazel rods are traditionally used for dowsing, while hazel twigs woven into 'wishing caps' were said to grant the wearer's desires.

Hazelnuts have long been revered as the food of the gods.

- **Silver birch:** the 'Lady of the Woods', a tree of enchantment, especially associated with feminine intuition and wisdom. The twigs were traditionally used to make brooms, with an ash or hazel handle. Fruit: catkins.
- **Willow:** represents forgiveness and acceptance; sitting in a willow grove was said to produce inspiration and visions.
- **Holly:** protection against evil spirits and lightning; used in dream magic.

Fruit is one of Mother Earth's gifts and a symbol of her abundance and generosity. Peaches are particularly associated with love magic.

FAIRIES AND DRYADS

If you pay close attention to a tree or plant's physical make-up you may start to notice various qualities or characteristics. Some of these may be visible, observed from the plant's physical structure – its shape, how it moves or how it sounds in the wind – while others may be experienced as a subtle resonance or aura emanating from it. In natural magic, this is attributed to the plant's guardian spirit, usually referred to as a dryad, wood-nymph or fairy. These elementals protect the plant and may also give us counsel when we approach the tree or flower with an open heart and honest intent.

CRYSTALS AND STONES

Treasures from the earth, crystals and stones are not only objects of great beauty, but are also storehouses of powerful energies that are of great value in natural magic. Created in the darkness of the earth, sparkling crystals are potent symbols of spiritual illumination, purity and durability. The word "crystal" is derived from the Greek *krustallos*, meaning ice, and to the ancient Greeks, all quartz crystals were believed to be fragments that had fallen from the perfect crystal of truth that resided on Mount Olympus, home to the gods. Gemstones have a long magical tradition, too. For instance, wearing emeralds was said to give protection against poison and negative spirits, while rubies helped those gifted with psychic powers to see into the future.

Choose stones that you feel drawn to when you are building up your own collection.

MAGICAL PROPERTIES

As part of the earth's structure, crystals and gemstones are coherent, organized forms of matter. The properties of quartz crystals in particular are derived from their special orderliness and the stability of their atomic structure, which is not upset by outside forces such as heat or pressure, giving them unusual strength. Both crystals and gemstones are able to store, magnify and transform energy, emitting energy waves at natural frequencies that are in harmony with our own biological make-up.

Each type of crystal and stone has a particular vibration, derived in part from its colour but also from its atomic structure, which exerts a specific influence on our subtle energy system at the level of mind, body and soul. This is what gives crystals and stones their magical properties and their long association with ritual and healing.

CHOOSING STONES

It is very likely that you will be attracted to different stones at different times, depending on your need. The best way of choosing a stone is to let your intuition guide you rather than thinking too much about what it means. Often the stone you are first drawn to is the one for you, and it is better to check its magical correspondences afterwards, although some spells will call for specific stones. You can put your stones on your altar or shrine to lend power to your invocations, or else you can programme them for specific results.

The way crystals absorb and reflect light gives them a unique visual appeal.

Every crystal is unique in shape and size as well as magical potency, and using them will inspire your senses as well as engage your powers.

The colour properties of crystals and gemstones

The colour transmitted by crystals and gemstones is a particularly focused, powerful vibration. Remember that translucent crystals have a more pronounced effect than opaque stones. Use your intuition as well as the guide below to help choose the right stone.

Colour	Useful for	Crystals and gemstones
Red	Warming and energizing	Garnet, ruby, jasper, quartz
Orange	Shock and trauma	Carnelian, orange calcite, topaz
Yellow	Energizes solar plexus, reduces tension and anxiety, promotes confidence	Citrine, yellow fluorite, tiger's eye, amber
Light blue	Communication skills, immunity boosters	Turquoise, aquamarine, blue lace agate, celestite
Dark blue	Inner peace, calming the mind, developing intuition	Lapis lazuli, sodalite, sapphire, kyanite
Violet	Meditation, integration of the self	Amethyst, fluorite, sugilite
White and clear	Clarity, purification and order	Clear quartz, calcite and selenite energize, while moonstone and milky quartz are soothing
Black	Energy imbalances, focus awareness inwards, speed release of unwanted energies	Obsidian, smoky quartz, black tourmaline and haematite
Pink	Releasing emotional tension	Rose quartz, rhodonite and kunzite

Cleansing crystals or stones with incense smoke is especially suitable for magical purposes.

CLEANING STONES

Because crystals and gemstones hold energy, it is important that they are always thoroughly cleansed. Do this whenever you bring a new stone into your home, and keep your stone collection free of psychic dirt at all times. You may be able to detect negative vibrations in a stone by a feeling of heaviness or unpleasantness when you handle it, or you may suddenly feel an impulse to give your stone collection a thorough clean. Stones should always be specially cleansed before using them in a particular piece of magic.

To clean hard stones, place them in a bowl of salt water and leave overnight. Throw away the salt or salt water afterwards. A gentler method is to use pure spring water, or simply to leave the stone in direct sunlight. All hard or soft stones can also be cleansed using the smoke from incense cones or burning resin and smudge sticks.

Programming stones

It is possible to direct your conscious intent into a stone to help you achieve a result. This is called programming, and it is very simple.

- Take a clean stone of your choice and sit with it quietly.
- As you hold the stone, visualize your desire and see it entering the stone. As you do this, 'speak it' into the stone.
- If you are working with any gods or angels, you could ask for their assistance to empower the stone, offering it up to their guidance. For instance, if you are working on a sleep problem, you may ask Hypnos, god of sleep and dreams, to empower your stone.
- Spend some time each day with your stone, or wear it throughout the day. Remember to clean it once you have finished using it for a particular issue.

MUSIC AND SOUND

Sound is a form of vibration that is at the root of our existence. It is one of our first experiences of life – the heartbeat is the first sound we hear in the darkness of the womb – and different sounds evoke different responses. For instance, we feel most at ease with naturally occurring sounds, such as waves breaking on a beach, a running stream, birdsong, or rustling leaves. Conversely, discordant noises and high levels of background noise, such as from traffic, or music we don't want to listen to, undermine the sensitivity of our hearing. The vibrations of sound – whether from musical instruments or the human voice – can be used in natural magic to summon spirits, dispel negativity and to cleanse, purify and heal.

Bells and chimes can be used to gently vibrate the energies in a room, and calm discordancy.

VIBRATIONAL FIELDS

Albert Einstein asserted that what appears to be solid matter is actually a dance of atoms in space, and when we look closely at our physical nature, this is indeed the case. All matter vibrates, emitting waves of energy, and within a certain range of frequencies we respond to these vibrations as sound. We pick up on these sound waves not only through our ears, but also through our vibrational energy field. The subtle bodies, the chakras, and the physical body all vibrate at particular frequencies. When these vibrations are out of balance, we are literally "out of tune", but certain sounds will help us to realign. When our energies are aligned we are empowered and are more easily able to manifest magical results.

USING THE VOICE

One of the easiest and most effective ways of using the voice magically is with mantras and chants. These sacred sounds have been used in ritual for thousands of years to create a harmonious inner and outer environment. In India, for instance, the sound of "Om" is said to contain the vibrations of the universe; it is the primordial sound from which all others arise. Tibetan overtone chanting is also very powerful, particularly when done with a large group of people. Teachers of this technique usually run regular workshops and courses, so look out for some in your area. One of the beauties of mantras and chants is that everyone can do them, regardless of their singing ability. However, if you have a natural talent for singing it is a good idea to develop your skills – you will have plenty of chance to use them in connection with magic at festivals, rituals and on ceremonial occasions.

DRUMMING

A well-known symbol of shamanism, the drum is also used in many sacred traditions. The beat of a drum carries primal memories of the heartbeat in the womb, and the Earth herself, reaching deep into the atavistic recesses of the human soul. The sound of drumming is

Singing bowls can produce a variety of sound vibrations that can have a powerful healing effect.

Rhythmic sounds, especially in the form of drumming, are used in shamanic ritual to summon the assistance of the spirit world.

said to wake up the spirits and is a good way of opening a ceremony or ritual, naming those whom you wish to call upon. It is also a good complement to any singing or chanting. A rattle can also be used for healing purposes, to call in allies to help with a problem, or like the rattlesnake, to warn intrusive energies that they should step back and withdraw.

You can buy a rattle or you can make your own. A very simple version is to put a handful of dried peas in a jar or tin, but you may be able to find a workshop where you can make one from hide mounted on a wooden handle and filled with dried beans or pebbles.

SOUNDS AND THE ELEMENTS

Each element can be invoked by using particular types of instruments. Percussion instruments such as drums and rattles will strengthen Earth energy, while wind instruments, as one might expect, are connected to the element of Air. The Aeolian harp, which is actually "played" by the wind, has long been associated with magic. Stringed instruments, bells and crystal singing bowls are linked with water, while the brilliant sound of brass instruments invokes Fire. If you have no instrument, even hand clapping will generate sound vibrations and raise energy. As a general rule, fast or loud sounds increase energy, whereas quiet, slow, rhythmic sounds induce peace and tranquillity.

helpful for entering a spirit body, journeying to the otherworld or accessing cosmic energy. The optimum drumbeat is around 200 beats per minute (bpm), so practise until this is your natural rhythm. The sound of rhythmic drumming helps to raise the Earth element. If it is played loudly and with authority, it also helps to dispel any unwanted negative energies.

The most desirable drum is one made by hand, using natural materials, because a well-made drum is a powerful tool,

holding not only the energy of the materials used in its manufacture, but also some of the energy of its maker. Although it is possible to buy hand-made drums, a great deal of satisfaction can be gained from making one yourself.

RATTLES

Together with the drum, a rattle has many associations with shamanism and is used in magic and sacred ceremony all over the world. The sound of the rattle is

In the absence of any musical instrument, clapping the hands will raise Earth energy.

Mantra to Lord Shiva

The Om Namah Shivaya (pronounced 'Omnarmar Shiv-eye-yah') mantra to the Hindu deity Lord Shiva is a powerful way to clear negative vibrations, remove obstacles and to give you inner strength.

Light a candle and sit behind it. You may like to have a statue of Lord Shiva in front of you. Begin

chanting the Om Namah Shivaya mantra rhythmically, and continue for at least ten minutes. If you have a mala (a string of 108 beads used in the Hindu tradition), you can perform the chant the traditional 108 times, moving one bead along with each repetition, or adapt a Christian rosary to help you keep count.

ANIMAL TOTEMS

To people who live close to the land and the natural world, animals have always had a great significance. All over the world, certain animals are thought to embody particular traits and strengths that are relevant to the history and geography of the particular culture. Because there is such a diversity of creatures and cultures, a number of animals have come to represent the same characteristics. For example, the tribes of the northwest Pacific coast of America revered the orca (killer whale) as a holder of great strength and wisdom, whereas to the plains tribes of North America, who had never seen a whale, that quality was fulfilled by the mighty bison. Animals can be adopted as a totem or emblem on an individual or group level and used in magic as allies or helpers, sharing their qualities to empower us and make our magic more successful.

A totem animal could be any kind of creature, and each brings its own special characteristics.

MOON ANIMALS

Certain animals have long and deep links with the moon and for this reason are often favoured as totems by natural magic workers. They include the wolf, hare, frog, cat, cow and owl, although any animal linked to water – such as various types of fish, for instance – will be pertinent to the moon to some degree. Moon totem animals can be carried as charms or talismans, which should ideally be made of silver, the metal of the moon. Dreams about any of the moon totem animals could well signify that an important change is imminent, or may signify a time of increased fertility (such as ovulation), a birth, the death of an old person, or a time for learning and growth.

DISCOVERING YOUR TOTEM ANIMAL

If you feel drawn to the idea of enlisting the help of a totem animal you might want to follow the shamanic tradition and make a journey in your mind to find your own personal power animal. As with any kind of creative visualization, or mind travel, its intensity and power depends on how much mental energy you devote to the process. The more detail you add, and the better your concentration, the more real the experience will be.

Once you have found and made contact with your power animal you will be able to summon her or him whenever you need their guidance. Don't try and force an image into your mind, let your animal totem find you, whether it is a mighty eagle or a humble hedgehog it will have its own virtues and qualities.

When working with your totem animal, spend a few moments tuning in to its particular medicine. Bears have a strong connection to the earth.

The lesson of the wolf totem is about loyalty, trust and devotion.

The horse represents nobility of spirit, freedom and also endurance.

You can perform the following simple meditation to discover which animal is your totem at any particular time.

A MEDITATION FOR A TOTEM ANIMAL
Sit somewhere quietly where you won't be disturbed. Burn a little copal resin or incense such as sandalwood or frankincense. Attune yourself to the rhythm of your breathing, and as you do so, start to visualize yourself in a secret garden. This garden is your own special place and no harm can ever come to you while you are here.

As you sit in the garden, feel the warmth of the sun on your skin and a soft breeze through your hair. You can hear the sound of a fountain in the background. Now see yourself walk over to the fountain and a beautiful pool of water. Look down into the water and see your face mirrored back to you.

Keep looking at your reflection and as you do so, notice the image change from human to animal form. What animal is looking back at you? See it in as much detail as you can.

This is your totem animal. Carry its image with you as you step away from the pool and out of your garden, back into the room where you are sitting.

Animal symbolism

To get you started, the following list represents a few of the more common totem animals and some of their counterparts from different cultures. If you want to find out more, invest in a good book on the symbolism of animals.

Bear: lives fully in the summer, retreating in the winter to hibernate and renew earth-connection. Represents the receptive female energy, having the ability to go within to seek answers. A similar totem is the badger.

Bison: evokes the strength and wisdom of the elders, who are providers for and protectors of the people. Similar totems include the bull, the reindeer and the orca.

Coyote: related to the wolf, the coyote exhibits the trust, innocence and playfulness of the child that is present in all of us. It is also the trickster, and, through mischief, can expose pretensions and foolishness in others.

Dolphin: represents understanding and awareness, and is possessed of a gentle, loving energy. Similar totems are the manatee and the deer.

Eagle: associated with the ability to fly high and free, without fear and with the gift of far-sightedness. The eagle symbolizes the restless male energy and the quality of seeking and striving for higher goals. Similar totems include the buzzard and the condor.

Horse: runs like the wind and is capable of covering distance with endurance. The horse symbolizes swiftness, freedom and faithfulness. A similar totem is the elk.

Lion: the king of the jungle and a powerful hunter is associated with the powers of the sun. Proud, regal and dignified the lion establishes his authority and has few enemies. His consort, the lioness, a protective mother, nurturer and fierce hunter, is associated with the moon. Similar totems are the panther, tiger and other big cats.

Owl: hunts by night and is able to see in the dark, flying on swift silent wings. Symbolically it represents the ability to see that which is indistinct, to pierce the veil of reality and understand hidden truths.

Wolf: fiercely loyal and true, yet maintains its freedom and independence. The wolf is particularly associated with the psychic aspects of lunar lore. A similar totem is the hound or dog. Seek wolf medicine when in need of protection and support.

Cats in myth and magic

The cat has long been known as a 'familiar' to magical practitioners, especially those who work with lunar magic – the cat is a symbol of the moon and represents her mystery. During the time of the witch hunts the black cat was relegated to the realms of sorcery. In mythology, the cat is associated with the Greek goddess Artemis, known in Roman mythology as Diana. In ancient Egypt, where harming a cat in any way was punishable by death, it was a sacred animal. The Egyptian cat goddess, Bastet, daughter of the sun god Re, was believed to have the power to ripen crops. Shosti, the Hindu goddess of childbirth, is depicted riding a cat, and Freya, the Norse goddess of love and fertility, rides in a cat-drawn carriage. Seek cat medicine when you want to improve your psychic abilities, or during psychic protection ceremonies.

CHARMS AND TALISMANS

In natural magic, certain objects act as mystical "telephone numbers", summoning a specific power, be it god, angel, elemental force or a kind of luck. These mystical objects differ for witches and for ceremonial magicians. Witches tend to use natural objects as charms or amulets. Ceremonial magicians, however, make talismans specifically for their workings. Traditionally made using astrological principles and with particular thought for the purpose in mind, talismans are a means of drawing down the power of the planets into a scroll, or an object, which can then be used as a powerful magical tool.

Holey stones were used in witchcraft as a means of protection for animals.

CHARMS, AMULETS AND TALISMANS

A charm should be something from the natural world that you respond to, a simple stone you found that you felt compelled to keep for example, and can really be anything at all. An amulet is more likely to be a precious piece of jewellery that you can wear while you are working. A talisman is usually made for a specific magical purpose.

MAGICAL CHARMS

Charms are always a natural substance, perhaps a plant that has a strange shape, such as four-leaved clovers, said to bring luck, or pebbles in the shape of an eye, which are thought to be protective.

Stones with natural holes in them are a classic example of magical charms. Known as holy or holey stones, these perforated flints or fossils were traditionally used to protect animals. The stones were collected from a beach or riverbank, and hung on red wool or ribbon over the doors of barns or stables to stop elves milking the cows, or to prevent the horses being stolen by night-hags during the hours of darkness. It was thought that the hole in the stone would trap any bad spirits. After seven years, the stones were thrown into running water so that any harm trapped in them could be washed away, then new stones were found and hung up.

Some fossils were thought to have magical powers: belemnites were believed to be "elf shot", arrows fired by spirits to make cattle sick; and ammonites were snakes turned to stone by the magic of wizards. Such charms were carried for protection, to bring health or luck.

Other charms include plant materials, such as herbs: for example, mint is a charm for money if carried in the purse, and sage is for wisdom. Oak is believed to protect from lightning when it is put into a red charm bag and worn every day.

AMULETS

Similar to a charm, an amulet has a single purpose and may be worn or carried all the time. Amulets can take all shapes and will have particular relevance for the person who carries one. They are often made in the shape of a hand, like the Arabic Hand of Fatima, which is said to ward off harm.

TALISMANS

A talisman is used to focus magical powers on a particular short-term aim, such as healing sickness or for success in finding a new job or house. Ideally they

Talismans are still written in ancient alphabets, or use magical symbols that summon the help of angels or gods and goddesses.

should be made for the person whose life is intended to change. In the past they may have been made of precious metal set with jewels, written in magical ink on parchment, carved into wood or else inscribed on to clay. Today, the easiest way to make them is on coloured paper.

The art of making talismans is extremely old. Some have been found on sites in ancient Mesopotamia (modern day Iraq) that seem to predate writing, and it is possible that our various alphabets originated in the symbols used to request magical help.

Using the Zodiac Signs and Planets

To make a talisman you need to understand the basic powers of the zodiac signs and their correspondences: each sign is associated not only with a particular planet, but also with a number, a colour, jewel, incense and symbol. It is also connected to a day of the week and time of the year.

Creating a Talisman

Refer to the chart in the Magical Correspondences section of this book and decide on the powers that most fit with what you are trying to achieve, then work out which colours of paper, ink and silk you need, and which symbols to use for the inscription.

You will need

coloured paper
coloured inks
the correct planetary metal or a symbol of it
connecting link to another, such as a photograph, if the talisman is for someone else
coloured silk

1 Write the magical inscriptions on the paper with coloured ink, focusing as you do so on the person or situation for which the talisman is intended.

2 If it is for yourself, add a drop of your blood or saliva, or if it is for someone else, include the connecting link to that person.

3 Fold the paper and wrap it up in the coloured silk. Keep it in a safe place, until you are ready to consecrate it.

A charm or talisman should be taken great care of, and stored in a special bag or pouch.

Consecrating the talisman

You will need some holy oil; this is usually almond or olive oil with added appropriate herbs, resins, or essential oils associated with the planets concerned. You will also need an altar on which to place a bowl of water, a lit candle, incense, a stone, wine and some bread. The words you use and whom you invoke will depend on what powers you wish to invest it with: for courage, for instance, you would invoke the energies of the planet Mars, and use these words:

I call upon Zamael, Angel of the planet Mars, to lend assistance with this talisman. Please imbue it with your power, so that it may give courage to (say the person's name for whom the talisman is intended) when this is needed.

1 Work out an invocation to reflect your purpose and directed at the powers you have chosen to make your request to.

2 To cleanse the talisman, first sprinkle it with water and place it on your altar. Then energize

it with fire by circling with the lit candle. Now wave the talisman through the incense smoke. This will blow life into it, so that it is fully effective.

3 Dip your index finger into the holy oil and imagine a pool of light which transfers to the talisman. Say the words you have decided on firmly and clearly.

4 Wait for a surge of energy or the incense smoke to swirl or until you perceive light around the new talisman. Place it under the stone to ground its power. Drink a cup of wine and eat the bread to complete the ceremony.

5 When you have completed the ceremony, put your equipment away, disrobe and come back to earth. Leave the talisman on the altar for one month, then give it to the person for whom it was made, or use it for the purpose you intended it.

ABSTRACT SYMBOLS

Symbols predate writing as a means of conveying ideas, and in ancient times were carved, painted, stitched or worked in metal for magical purposes, to ward off evil or to invoke gods and spirit beings. They were also worked into talismans for luck, health and inspiration. Some signs, identified as archetypes, appear to be universally understood. A symbol gains its significance from the emotional and spiritual weight it carries. It has its own energetic vibration and can influence the spirit world as well as resonate at a deep soul level with the human psyche. Among these powerful signs, or sigils, are the spiral and the circle in their various forms, which – together with other abstract symbols – have always played a central role in magic.

The natural world is full of circles, and its connotations and symbolism are numerous.

SPIRALS

Formed by tracing a point that is moving simultaneously out and around, the spiral is an evocative image, symbolic of a life path, the lessons and learning that come to us throughout life. The circular motion relates to the cyclic nature of existence, and the outward motion to the spiritual and emotional growth of a person as they progress through life, apparently repeating experiences, but each time moving to a new level.

Spirals can be combined to make double or even triple forms. Double spirals symbolize the duality of life and the natural world, seen in pairs of complementary opposites, such as light and dark, male and female, young and old, or mind and body. In Celtic lore, the triple spiral is linked with the moon and relates to the three stages of life: maiden, mother and crone. This symbol displays the cycles that are present within cycles, showing that the whole is made up of different periods of growth and development but that each stage is directly linked to the others. The spiral may also represent the pathway that a shaman may take to reach another realm.

CIRCLES

A line without end, a circle represents the continuous cycle of birth, death and rebirth as shown in the moon's journey through the sky and the seasonal cycles connected to the sun. For one cycle to begin another must end, but they do not really begin and end, merely transmute.

The circle symbolizes the cycles that are present in all of creation, the relentless progress of life in all its forms. Many traditional circular dwellings reflected this idea, symbolizing living within the whole. Circles that incorporate another solid circle speak of the totality of creation, showing that all things are connected and that creation encompasses the individual.

THE CROSS

Best known today as the emblem of the Christian church, the cross is an ancient symbol. In pre-Columbian America it was a fertility symbol related to the four rain-bearing winds. In some native American traditions, the four points of the cross represent the four directions and the four elements, with the centre point representing the source from which all life arises. The ankh, a cross with its topmost arm in a loop, was an ancient Egyptian symbol of immortality.

THE MAGIC CIRCLE

It is customary when making magic to create a circle as sacred space "between the worlds" into which divine or angelic beings are summoned. The witchcraft circle is always arranged according to the

The spiral is an inspiring symbol of the soul's journey through life.

The cross has many meanings, including our "crucifixion" while bound to the physical world.

There are many different ways of creating a magic circle. This one has been created using a ring of candles, whose light symbolizes protection and spiritual illumination.

The medicine wheel

Many shamanic practices are based on the teachings of the Native American Indian medicine wheel, which offer a framework for understanding the way these people see the world. The medicine wheel has many meanings and manifestations, ranging from structuring ceremonies and a means for the expression of dreams and visions, to methods for healing. The path of personal transformation on the medicine wheel is said to take the 'knower' and the 'known' through a spiral of experiences that link the individual, and his or her own course from birth to death, with the seasons and the wider whole.

Also known as the sacred hoop, the medicine wheel is a circle bisected by two lines (forming a cross), which symbolize the blue road of spirit (east to west) and the red road of life (south to north). The four sections of the circle represent the seasons of the year. As with the magic, or stone, circle, each point is associated with a direction of the compass, and with particular attributes that can be related to times and situations in your own life. The east is the place of inspiration and the inception of a new ideas. The south is related to consolidation, while the west is the place where the fruits of an endeavour can be harvested. The north is the place to recuperate and reflect.

cardinal points of north, south, east and west. Each cardinal direction has certain attributes that relate to the natural world, thus the circle is usually opened in the east, because this represents the first light of dawn. In the centre of the circle stands the cauldron, representing transformation of the "raw" into the "cooked", or on a spiritual level, of changes of consciousness within the natural rhythms of nature.

Whether you are working indoors or outside, you should visualize the magic circle as a place of stillness beyond normal time and space. It may be outlined with a wand or staff, created with cord or stones, or visualized.

THE PYRAMID

A geometric structure with five points, a pyramid synthesizes the symbolism of the square with the triangle, and the numbers three, four and five. The square at its base has four points and represents the Earth plane and the material world – structure, order and stability. The number four not only reminds us of the four elements, the four seasons, and the four directions, but also the four stages of life – childhood, adolescence, adulthood and old age – and even the four stages of the alchemical process – origins (or creation), division, opposites, and union of opposites. The four upward-pointing triangles of the pyramid's sides echo the

symbolism of four, while bringing in that of three. Three is the trinity of man, woman and child, of body, mind and spirit. There are also many examples in mythology of the gods appearing in triad groupings, or having three aspects – such as the mother, maiden and crone aspects of the triple goddess.

At the apex of the pyramid, the four triangles meet to form a fifth point, suggesting the fifth element: ether or spirit. As the pyramid reaches up to the sky, this point represents the strivings of the human soul towards perfection, the attempt to reach up to the heavens to unite with the One.

The power generated by the pyramid shape was recognized by the ancient Egyptians.

COSMIC FORCES

The mystery of the sun and moon, the stars and planets has always fascinated human beings. Over thousands of years, a rich heritage of myth and magic has grown up around these cosmic forces. Stories of solar gods and lunar goddesses exist in nearly every culture, perhaps in an attempt to understand and explain some of our most fundamental questions about life on Earth. From the earliest times people noticed that these faraway lights in the sky exerted a tremendous influence upon many aspects of our daily life, including our health and well-being (in body, mind and soul), as well as patterns in the weather, the tides of the oceans and the changing seasons.

This chapter presents an overview of these cosmic forces – the sun and moon and the constellations of the stars and planets in the zodiac. It shows how the sun is linked with health and vitality and how the mysterious moon affects our moods, intuition and psychic senses. It looks at the cardinal points of the compass and the symbolic power and meaning of these "Four Great Powers". It also includes a breakdown of the symbolism of the elemental energies of Fire, Water, Earth and Air, and looks at ether, or spirit, the intangible "fifth element" that plays such an important part in natural magic.

THE SUN

Throughout the ancient world the sun, the centre of our solar system and the source of light and heat, was worshipped for its life-giving energy and healing powers. Today, magicians and witches take the light of the sun into account when they are working magic, and as you become more aware of it, you will notice how it affects your life, your dreams and your magic. The sun is often seen as a representative of the individual in his or her world, the light radiating is the way he or she is seen by friends and family. If someone is ill, it is as if the light of their personal sun is dimmed and so spells that encourage the light to shine are sung.

Ancient societies worshipped the sun as the source of life and prosperity.

BRINGER OF LIFE

The power of the sun is concerned with life. It is the motor that drives this world and any change to the energy we receive on the surface of the earth is like a change in gear that speeds up or slows down all life processes. It is not a matter of choice: life has evolved to take advantage of the energy of the sun and so is automatically connected to its cycles – the seasons of the year and the shifting rhythm of day and night, light and dark.

Before the invention of electric lighting and the rise of our modern "indoor" culture, we would have been very aware of these cycles. In the past, people spent a great deal more time working outside and ate a diet largely based on seasonal produce. Now we can eat sun-ripened fruits in the middle of winter and are active far beyond the hours of natural daylight. To a large extent our natural connection with the sun's energies and the balance between light and dark has been lost, which in turn affects our health and well-being.

Studies have shown that spending a great deal of time in artificial fluorescent lighting increases fatigue, hyperactivity, and irritability, while the reduction of sunlight on a cloudy day, or more profoundly, in the long months of winter, has a significant effect upon our mood. For some people, the lack of sunlight can be seriously debilitating. Seasonal Affective Disorder (or SAD syndrome) causes mood swings, low energy levels and depression that begins as the days grow shorter and only gradually improves with the onset of spring. The sun is an energizing, active, dynamic force whose light is necessary for health, and makes us feel brighter, happier and well.

SUN MAGIC

Observing the path of the sun through the year, and celebrating the seasons, is one way of working with the sun's energies. This is described in more detail in The Wheel of the Year, but two of the most important festivals of the sun are at the summer and winter solstices, when the power of the sun reaches its peak and nadir respectively. You can also work with these cycles on a daily basis: the first rays of sunlight appear at dawn, gaining in strength to peak at midday, and then fading and disappearing at sunset each evening. Tailoring your activities to suit this natural pattern can help you make the most of the sun's power: this would mean being active and outgoing through the morning and early afternoon, and then gradually reducing your activities and energetic output as evening approaches.

Eating a diet consisting largely of seasonal produce is another way to attune yourself to the sun's energies. Freshly grown, locally harvested food is ideal, as the energies contained in the

The sun not only has cosmic powers, its effect can be felt in a very real way in many aspects of our life, from the food we eat to the way we structure our waking hours.

Sun legends

Within northern European mythology, the Sun God is born at the dead of winter soon after the solstice. He grows with each passing day, and receives his sword and arrows from his Mother, the ever-virgin Earth Goddess. Later, as the year turns, he becomes her lover. At midsummer he is at his height and yet, to feed the people, as the corn king, he has to be cut down at harvest. The Earth Goddess receives him and takes him into her house, symbolized by the corn dolly, made from the last sheaf of standing corn. Autumn brings the bonfires of Halloween, Summer's End. One tradition holds that on this ghostly eve, all the dead return to join the revels, and unborn children meet their parents in spirit. As the king of winter, the Sun God at his lowest ebb rules with his queen, the Lady of the Night, and at midwinter he is born again, the star child, the Child of Promise, the bringer of hope in darkness.

These legends form part of the ritual pattern of many modern covens of witches, with the high priest and priestess acting out the story of the God and Goddess. The Druids follow this cycle, and many other pagans also work their way through the cycles of stories of the old gods.

You don't have to sit in the sun to feel its regenerative powers. Try a meditation that calls on them in order to transform your negative energies.

If you have a sick friend, encourage them to spend a few moments feeling the sun's healing rays.

food will most closely match your own energy patterns, rather than foodstuffs that have been grown in another place hundreds or even thousands of miles away. You can also use "sunny" colours such as gold, oranges, yellows and reds in your clothing and surroundings as well as in your magic when you wish to connect with solar energies. Sun metals and gemstones include gold, diamonds and amber, the sun's incense is golden frankincense resin and its number is six.

THE SUN'S HEALING POWER

To use the sun directly as a healing force requires little in the way of equipment or preparation. If you are feeling low or tired, then simply sitting quietly in a sunny spot and relaxing for twenty minutes can work wonders. If this is not possible, then use your magical powers of imagination instead.

1 Sit quietly and visualize yourself surrounded by golden light beams.

2 Now imagine the beams entering your body at the crown of your head. Feel the warmth of the golden light circulating through your entire system. See the light reach into all parts of you, driving out any darkness and releasing stuck energy.

3 Finally, imagine the light leaving your body through your feet, travelling down deep into the earth where any negative energies will be transformed.

THE MOON

The moon is intimately linked with fertility and a woman's reproductive cycle. The full moon is a particularly potent time for women.

Mysterious, magical and ever changing, the moon shines her silver beams upon the shadows of the night. Many ancient civilizations venerated her because they observed how she influenced the germination and growth of crops, the tidal flows of the oceans, and weather patterns as well as a woman's "moontime" cycle. She also affects our moods, our sleep and dream patterns and our mental health. But perhaps more than any other celestial body, it is the moon that is most intimately linked with magic weaving and the occult. She is associated with intuition and psychic sensitivity, and her changing rhythms offer the magic-worker great scope for understanding life's mysteries.

LUNAR POWER

The moon is strongly associated with the imagination and psychic, intuitive powers. She is also particularly associated with women and the production of children: many ancient civilizations performed fertility rituals and celebrated the moon at annual festivals dedicated to the goddess, to seek her help and favour with conception. The time of ovulation, when a woman is at her most fertile, is most likely to occur during a full moon. During menstruation, women's powers of perception are heightened, and in many traditional societies it is customary for a woman to remove herself from the rest of the community at this time. In societies that revered the goddess, this was never intended as a punishment, but a chance for a woman to nurture and protect herself and to reconnect with her inner wisdom. Often all the women in a community would menstruate at the same time, so it was also a time of fellowship and bonding.

Developing an awareness of the moon and her phases helps to increase trust in the more subtle aspects of the psyche, including perception, intuition and psychic awareness.

Moon lore

There are many folklore sayings and warnings about the moon, from many cultures around the world, reflecting her mystery and power. These are some of the ones that have survived down the years.

- Do not leave your washing out at night – if the moonlight shines upon it, it shines upon clothes for a funeral.
- If you touch a silver coin when you see the moon, it will bring you good luck.
- Move house on a new moon.
- It is considered unlucky to marry during the month of May or during any of the waning/ dark quarters. Conversely, it is considered lucky to marry in June and during any waxing or full moon phase, but do not let the light of the moon fall on your marriage bed, or you will be courting bad luck.
- A baby that is born at the time of a full moon is a child of fortune.
- It is lucky to hold a newborn child up to the light of a new moon, and give thanks as well as offer up prayers for a long life.

Dedicate a Moon altar with white or clear stones, sandalwood incense, and riverside flowers.

LUNAR MAGIC

The moon has four phases: waxing, full, waning and dark. Understanding these phases and what they represent is an essential part of natural magic. These are discussed in greater detail in The Cycles of the Moon, in the following chapter, but essentially the waxing phase is when the moon's energy is growing and so is a good time to initiate new projects. Full moon is a time of great fertility and powerful magic, while during the waning phase the moon's power is decreasing, so it is a good time for completion and letting go. The dark moon (or no moon) is a time for rest and retreat. The colours to use when working with moon energies are silver, white and dark blue, and the gemstones are pearls and moonstones. The scent of jasmine is associated with the moon and her number is nine.

THE MOON AND DREAMS

Once you start to observe the phases of the moon and her movements in the sky, you may begin to notice the rhythms in your own life. There are natural peaks and troughs of energy, feelings and inspiration or creativity, and to some extent these may be reflected in the way you dream. Many people have difficulty remembering their dreams, or even fail to remember any at all, but it usually helps if you make an deliberate decision to write them down each morning. At first the dreams may drift away, but if you tell your subconscious to

Although the moon appears as a beacon in the night sky, it is actually a large reflective surface mirroring the light of the sun.

recall your dreams, just before you go to sleep, you will find memories start to remain. To enhance your connection to the inner world of dreams, try placing an aquamarine or other moontime crystal, such as a moonstone or piece of clear or smoky quartz, under your pillow as you sleep. Or to develop sensitivity to the dreaming aspect of the moon, you could try meditating with the moon and/or High Priestess Tarot cards. As you hold the card in front of you, softly gaze on the image, letting its wisdom speak to you.

Moon legends and deities

Known by many names and in different guises, the moon has been depicted in many ancient legends as both the giver and the taker of life. Because of her ever-changing yet regenerative cycle, she was seen as immortal and as the place to which souls departed at death. She could bring gentle rains to water the fields, but because she could also raise storms and ruin crops she was considered unpredictable and potentially destructive. Goddesses chosen to represent her were therefore double-sided as well, endowed with both destructive and creative powers. In Aztec mythology, the moon was named

Xochiquetzal, companion to the sun and protector of lovers. She was also linked to the family, and to childbirth. The Mayan moon deity was Ixchel, who was feared as the bringer of floods and storms. She wore a skirt decorated with bones, and her crown was a serpent. Despite this she was also considered a protector of women in childbirth. The life-giving qualities of the moon are universally linked to the spider, and in the mythology of many native tribes of North America, the spider is the weaver of the web of creation, producing the physical world, and then supporting and nurturing life on earth.

THE ZODIAC'S INFLUENCE

In magic, all astral or psychic energies are intimately connected with the influences of the zodiac. The zodiac is a series of starry constellations, each of which is rich in symbolic associations that can be used in magic to make predictions or influence the outcome of an event. While the earth makes its annual orbit of the sun, from earth we perceive this movement as if the sun is travelling along an imaginary line across the sky, called the ecliptic. The zodiac is the name given by astrologers to the band of constellations that appear along the ecliptic through the year. During each 30-day period of the year, or thereabouts, the sun appears to rise against the background of one of these groups of stars, and that constellation is said to be the sun sign of anyone born in that period.

Astrologers take into account the position of the moon, as well as the sun and all the other planets, when constructing a horoscope.

THE SIGNS OF THE ZODIAC

In Western astrology there are 12 signs of the zodiac. Each sign has a planetary ruler and is governed by one of the four elements. The moon travels through these constellations approximately every 27–28 days, whereas the sun takes a year. The dates shown for each sign refer to the approximate time when the sun is in that sign, although this can change by a day or two depending on the year. If your birthday falls near the beginning or end of a sign, it is on what is known as "the cusp", and it is worth checking to find

out your correct birth sign. To find out when the moon is travelling through a particular constellation, you need to refer to a book of planetary tables known as an "ephemeris". This is available in specialized astrology bookshops or over the internet.

THE HOROSCOPE

To construct your natal horoscope, an astrologer needs to know not only the time and date of your birth, but the exact geographical location in longitude and latitude. From these data a unique chart

can be constructed that will not only establish your "star sign" (which merely shows the position of the sun at birth), but also the position of the moon, the "ascendant", or rising, sign and all the other planets, and the complex relationships between them. For instance, some planets may appear next to one another, while others may be diametrically opposite, some planets may be moving forwards, while others have an apparent backwards or "retrograde" motion. All of these things are very important when reading a horoscope and can explain why popular astrology of the type found in newspapers and magazines is usually far from accurate as it only looks at one particular aspect of the horoscope – the position of the sun.

LEARNING ABOUT ASTROLOGY

Each sign of the zodiac has certain qualities and influences, as do each of the planets, and it is the individual configuration at a person's birth that shows their potential, highlighting their strengths and also areas of difficulty or challenge. An astrologer will be able to interpret a horoscope in great detail and show hidden potential, possible illness and positive or difficult times in a person's life.

The starry night sky has fascinated humankind since the dawn of time. Before the invention of the compass, people looked to the stars to help them navigate.

A guide to the signs of the zodiac

Remember that when consulting a horoscope, it is not only the position of the sun in the zodiac that is important, but the moon and all the other planets too. Here is a little information about each of the zodiac signs, each of which is governed by one of the four elements: earth and water are feminine and fire and air are masculine.

Star Sign	Emblem	Ruling Planet	Element	Quality
Aries (21 March – 19 April)	The Ram	Mars	Fire	Cardinal
Taurus (20 April – 20 May)	The Bull	Venus	Earth	Fixed
Gemini (21 May – 21 June)	The Twins	Mercury	Air	Mutable
Cancer (22 June – 22 July)	The Crab	Moon	Water	Cardinal
Leo (23 July – 22 August)	The Lion	Sun	Fire	Fixed
Virgo (23 August – 22 September)	The Virgin	Mercury	Earth	Mutable
Libra (23 September – 23 October)	The Scales	Venus	Air	Cardinal
Scorpio (24 October – 21 November)	The Scorpion	Pluto/Mars	Water	Fixed
Sagittarius (22 November – 21 December)	The Archer	Jupiter	Fire	Mutable
Capricorn (22 December – 19 January)	The Goat	Saturn	Earth	Cardinal
Aquarius (20 January – 18 February)	The water bearer	Uranus/Saturn	Air	Fixed
Pisces (19 February – 20 March)	The Fishes	Neptune/Jupiter	Water	Mutable

In astrology, the planet Saturn is concerned with teaching us life's lessons. Many say its position in the horoscope is connected with karma and past lives.

Horoscopes can also be constructed for many other purposes apart from the birth chart. For instance, it is possible to draw up a horoscope for a new business venture or a relationship, based on when and where the thing first started, in just the same way as the birth of a child. Studying such horoscopes, as well as the birth charts of individuals, can be useful for many kinds of magical work.

SUN AND MOON SIGNS

In astrology, the position of the sun is said to represent your inner or life essence, whereas the moon indicates how you respond emotionally and intuitively and is a barometer of your feeling world. So an Aries moon, for instance, can indicate someone with a quick temper who "sees red", whereas a Cancer moon would be more placid and easy-going.

THE FOUR GREAT POWERS

The four cardinal points of the compass – north, south, east and west – are honoured in many ancient traditions, and over time a litany of knowledge attributing specific qualities to each direction has been built up. Together, the four points symbolize balance and wholeness, the horizontal west-east axis representing the formative, receptive force or the feminine principle, the vertical north-south axis representing the active or conceptual force, which is masculine. Various cultures have referred to these four points as the Four Great Powers and have associated them with gods, angels and spirit beings. Understanding these great powers and their particular symbolism is fundamental to practising natural magic.

The medicine wheel of Native American Indians is a cross within a circle, representing the cycles within nature.

THE MEDICINE WHEEL

There are many different approaches to understanding the four directions, but the Native American medicine wheel is particularly rich in symbolism and magical ideas. Unlike the typical modern European approach to life, which is based on linear thinking, to the Native American life is thought of in terms of circles and cycles, symbolized by the medicine wheel. It is a physical thing, typically made of stones or rocks, with four directions – east, south, west and north. Understanding the four directions can help us to realize our connection with the earth's cycles and with all of life.

THE EAST

At the beginning of each day, the sun rises in the east. The power of the east is light: it is the arising of dawn whose light dispels darkness; it is the arrival of spring after the dormancy of winter. The east is the place of enlightenment or awakening, symbolism that is understood in Christian churches and Buddhist temples where the altar is positioned in the east. The east is the triumph of rebirth over death, and is new beginnings, fresh ideas and inspiration.

The colour of the east is yellow, the colour of the rising sun and of illumination. Its element is Air and its totem animal is the eagle. The eagle is prized for its clear vision, linking to the quality of perception or seeing, which is associated with the east. The eagle also flies higher than any other bird and is therefore closest to the sun, the source of light and sustainer of life. Eagle feathers are highly prized in the Native American tradition and often used in headdresses, to connect them to the eagle's powers of vision and closeness to the Great Spirit.

A magic circle is usually opened in the east. It is the direction to work with when seeking enlightenment or illumination, when beginning a new project, when looking for original ideas and inspiration, or when starting a new phase in life.

THE SOUTH

It is customary to move around a magic circle clockwise from east to south, symbolizing the movement of the sun from dawn to high noon, or from spring to summer. The power of the south is exploration, investigation and experience; it is the curiosity of the growing child who wants to find out about things. The south is a place of blossoming and unfolding as purposes become clear. It is also connected with trust and intuition.

The east's colour is yellow, and its power is light. Its association with enlightenment means that it is used in Christian and Buddhist places of worship to position the altar.

The Wheel of the Four Winds

Each of the four compass directions relates to a time of day, to a particular element and to an angel. Use this Wheel of the Four Winds to help you place your offerings or materials in the right place within a magic circle, or on an altar.

East

Direction of the infant, of beings and creatures of Air. Its time is dawn, its season is spring, and its angel is Raphael. Its animal totem is the eagle and its colour is yellow.

South

Direction of the child, of beings and creatures of Fire. Its time is midday, its season is summer, its angel is Michael. Its animal totem is the mouse and its colour is red.

West

Direction of the adult, of beings and creatures of Water. Its time is sunset, its season is autumn and its angel is Gabriel. Its animal totem is the grizzly bear. Its colours are black, dark blue and purple.

North

Direction of the elder, of beings and creatures of the Earth. Its time is midnight, its season is winter and its angel is Uriel. Its totem animal is the buffalo and its colour is white.

THE WEST

Journeying around the wheel, the west represents the time of day when the sun sets, and the annual movement from summer to autumn. The power of the west is consolidation and strength; it is where the fruits of an endeavour can be harvested. It is also the time to look within, a time for self-examination and reflection, allowing transformation of experience into knowledge, or matter into spirit.

The totem animal of the west is the grizzly bear, the strongest and fiercest of all the bears. The grizzly eats well in autumn, strengthening its body in preparation for the sleep of winter. It also makes careful consideration before taking action, hence its association with the qualities of introspection. The element of the west is Water, and its colours are black, dark blue and purple.

West is the direction to use when you need to take stock and evaluate a situation; it is a time for self-evaluation as you prepare for new action.

THE NORTH

Final resting point on the wheel, north is the place of rest and renewal. It is the power of winter, a time when nothing appears to be growing but inwardly the earth is gathering her energies for the new life to come. The north is the power of night, the time when the body lies sleeping but the spirit is active, dreaming and learning. North stands for focus and clarity, the white snow of purity; it is wisdom and knowing.

The element of the north is Earth, and its colour is white, the sum of all other colours and the essence of perfection. Its totem animal is the buffalo, an animal that gives totally of itself to sustain life. Sometimes the north is represented as the White Buffalo, a rare animal with sacred significance, associated with the legendary White Buffalo Woman who is said to have brought the Sacred Pipe to the Native American people.

North is the path that is used to gain strength of will and clarity in one's intentions. It is also a place of refuge, the place where you are able to retreat to find rest and rejuvenation.

The element of the south is Fire and its colour is red, the colour of our lifeblood and vital energy. Its totem animal is the mouse, which may seem an unlikely creature to represent such a powerful force, but a mouse is very sensitive to any vibrations in its environment. The wisdom of the mouse tells us not to confuse power with size and ferocity, and to learn how to develop a finely attuned "felt-sense" by trusting in our feelings and emotions.

South is the direction to work with for growth and development. It is a place to consolidate ideas, to build on what was started in the direction of east. South is the place of gathering experiences and learning from them.

THE ELEMENT OF AIR

The universe is made up of the four elements of Fire, Water, Earth and Air. Life is a balance between these forces, both as energies in the outer world and within every human being. When weaving spells and making magic, witches work with these elemental energies, each of which has particular characteristics and symbolic correspondences. The element of Air symbolically corresponds to a spring dawn: a light breeze whispers through the trees, the sky is blue and the day is just beginning. The lightness and clarity of the invisible air element governs the realm of the mind and all structured mental activity. The air element has the following magical associations or correspondences.

Air presides over the mountain tops of the world, and also over clear and cloudy skies.

THE BREATH OF LIFE

Air is the element of life and breath; to breathe is to be alive, and when we take our last breath, our life expires. The speediest and most ethereal of the elements, Air rules the east, the direction of sunrise, and its season is spring. Because it is associated with the new day and with the freshness of the new year, Air symbolizes new beginnings, enterprise, infancy and the generative energy of the seed. It is creative, focused and aware. In the form of wind, air may

be a gentle, cooling breeze or it may have the destructive force of a hurricane. Its energy is directed outwards. Because Air is the element of the wind, it governs all movement and is associated with travel, freedom and new discoveries. It is also the element of thought and ideas – the fresh moving force of the open mind, of intellect and the imagination.

In daily life the areas governed by Air include workplaces, meeting rooms, schools and libraries, as well as places concerned with travel, such as railway stations, airports and bus terminals. In terms of professions, Air is connected with the law, mathematics and science.

Air presides over the eastern quarter of a room or building, while in the natural world, Air's places are mountain tops, windy plains and clear or cloudy skies.

GODS OF THE AIR

Deities associated with the Air include Shu, Thoth, Hermes and Mercury. Shu was the Egyptian god of the Air who, with his consort Tefnut (the goddess of moisture), created the earth and sky. The Egyptian moon god Thoth was the scribe of Osiris, the god who ruled the underworld and judged the dead. As god of wisdom, Thoth was endowed with secret knowledge. It was said that his book of magic contained spells that

Air is manifest everywhere, from fiercely raging storms to the gentle stirring of grass in the wind.

Air correspondences

Direction: east
Season: spring
Time: dawn
Moon phase: new
Planets: Mercury, Uranus
Gender: masculine
Colours: light blue, yellow
Senses: hearing and smell
Magical tools: wand, athame (sword)
Musical instruments: wind instruments
Creatures: birds, winged insects

Natural symbols: feathers, fragrant flowers
Celtic sacred trees: alder, birch
Trees: elder, eucalyptus
Herbs: comfrey, lavender, mint
Incense: sandalwood, lemon
Minerals: mercury, aventurine, topaz
Zodiac sign: Gemini, Libra, Aquarius
Archangel: Raphael
Alchemical symbol: upright triangle with a horizontal line

Altars dedicated to the Air element can include the colours violet and yellow, and objects such as feathers and fans. Smoke and smell are also associated with air, in particular the scent of sandalwood and of lavender.

would give the user power over all the gods, and that together his books contained all the wisdom of the world. He eventually became associated with the Greek god Hermes, messenger of the Olympian gods, who could travel as fast as thought.

In many ways, Hermes is the personification of Air. He was versatile and changeable, eloquent and inventive. His lively mind, quick wits and slippery character made him the patron of thieves and merchants as well as travellers. Hermes' Roman equivalent was Mercury, whose cult spread widely among the Celtic and Germanic peoples of the Roman Empire. The Norse people identified him with their most powerful god Wotan or Odin, the god of speech, breath, wind, storm and magic. Mercury gave us the word "mercurial" to describe a volatile, lively, quicksilver character, all of which qualities are associated with Air.

THE AIR PERSONALITY

When Air features strongly in a person's horoscope, they will have a tendency towards being rational and analytical, preferring logic and carefully thought out ideas over irrational impulses. Air types enjoy mental stimulation in their relationships, and their idea of a good evening would include a lively exchange of ideas. However, the key to working with any of the elements is balance. Too much or too little of a particular element creates problems and challenges that need to be overcome. When Air is out of balance it can become critical and judgemental. It has a tendency to nit-pick and over-analyse until it almost literally blows a thing apart. This tendency can be particularly destructive when a creative idea or project is in its infancy, when maybe a little tender, loving care is what is needed. Too much Air (talking, discussion) and there is a danger that things can become "airy fairy" and plans will never materialize. In many ways Air is a tricky element to work with as its mercurial nature is not to be pinned down.

Exploring the air element

The best way to understand the qualities of an element is to explore it for yourself. Try going outside and notice how it feels to be out in the fresh air. What difference does it make if it's windy or if the air is still? Do all winds feel the same or are some easier to be in than others?

You could also try sitting indoors and working with your breath. In India, the concept of prana, or the sacred breath, plays an essential role in learning mastery over the mind. Adepts have discovered that when the rhythm and length of

the breath are controlled, specific changes in consciousness occur. Attuning yourself to your own breathing patterns and learning how to change them will lend greater power to your magic. A simple way to start is to sit with your eyes closed and breathe in to a count of six, hold for a count of three, and then breathe out. Hold again for a count of three and repeat. Vary the counts to suit your breathing, as it is important to do what works for you without causing strain or shortness of breath.

THE ELEMENT OF FIRE

Associated with the sun, Fire is the spark of life. It governs the realm of passion and intensity and is the element that ignites our desires. It is the intuitive flash of understanding, the leap of imagination that creates exciting new possibilities. Fire is both creative and destructive: it can cleanse and purify, but it also consumes. It is the only one of the four elements that cannot exist without feeding on something else. It makes our homes warm, and welcoming, and cooks our food, but it is dangerous and can get out of control. It has the power to transform everything it touches.

Fire is a creative force, and has been used for industry ever since it was discovered.

CREATOR AND DESTROYER
Fire rules the south, the direction of the sun's fiercest heat in the northern hemisphere, and is related to motivation, creativity and passion. Its energy is fast, forceful and positive and its power can be frightening. It symbolizes the inner child, the spirit within and the creative spark. Because it is the element of the passions, it gives courage and strength to fight for quality of life. Those in whom it is dominant are passionate and intense. Fire consumes obstacles to faith, and banishes negativity. Fire governs the sense of sight; it also inspires the need to offer and accept the power of touch. It is the element of physical challenge, sensation and sexual energy.

Areas governed by Fire are kitchens, fireplaces and boiler rooms, gyms and athletics fields and creative spaces such as studios and playrooms. Professions in the arts and entertainment industry are all linked with Fire. Fire presides over the southern quarter of a room or building. In the natural world its places are deserts, hot springs and volcanoes.

GODS AND GODDESSES OF FIRE
Some of the deities associated with Fire are Re, Sekhmet, Apollo and Lugh. The ancient Egyptians worshipped Re as their pre-eminent solar deity. As a creator god, he brought order out of chaos and from his tears were formed the first human beings. Reborn each morning, he journeyed daily across the sky in his solar boat, entering the underworld each night to do battle with the cosmic serpent, Apep. "Son of Re" was one of the titles bestowed on the pharaoh. Re's daughter was the sun goddess Sekhmet, "the Powerful One", usually portrayed with the head of a lioness. She was the terrifying aspect of Hathor, the goddess of joy and maternal love. Re sent Sekhmet as his "Eye", the terrible burning power of the sun, to punish the wickedness of humankind, but at the last

The cleansing force of Fire makes it a powerful symbol of change and transformation, in many levels of magical thought and philosophy.

moment saved his creation from total destruction by diverting Sekhmet's frenzied rage.

In Greek mythology, Apollo, who represented light, truth and clarity, guided the sun across the sky. He was the god of medicine and music and the patron of the nine Muses, the mythical embodiments of the creative imagination. The Celtic sky god Lugh was a deity of the sun and the weather, and his spear was sometimes seen as a fork of lightning. As the god of skills and arts, he could be honoured by an offering of a creative work. The pagan festival of Lughnasash, celebrated at the beginning of the harvest, is held in his name.

IRON AS A FIRE METAL

One of the Fire metals, iron is found on earth in its pure form only in meteorites. It is present in our blood, and is essential for physical energy and clear thinking. Wearing it as a talisman is said to increase physical strength. In some cultures an iron talisman is worn as protection against evil or negative energy: for this reason Sikhs wear an iron or steel bangle called a kara on their right wrist.

EXPLORING THE FIRE ELEMENT

One of the best ways of getting to know the Fire element is to sit in front of an open fire. Notice how it warms and energizes you, its variations in colour and how shapes alter and shift in the flames. Hear the sound that it makes as it burns. If you don't have access to an open

Fire is vital for humanity's survival, and when under control is a nurturing symbol of the home.

fireplace, then an outdoor garden bonfire would be fine. If neither of these options is practical, then try a candle flame meditation. Light a red or orange candle and sit in front of it. Soft-focus your gaze on the flame for a few minutes, as if searching for its centre. Feel yourself a part of its vibrant, dancing energies. Then close your eyes and form a mental picture of the candle flame in your mind's eye. As you breathe in and out, imagine you are inhaling and exhaling the qualities of Fire through every pore of your body. Let yourself merge with its essence. Remember when working with

fire to make sure that it is always properly contained: never leave a burning candle unattended.

THE FIRE PERSONALITY

Fire types are warm and extrovert, with a strong sense of fun and playfulness. Often charming and charismatic, passionate and intense, they like to live life to the full. They are usually very intuitive and tend to base decisions on their "gut instincts" rather than on careful consideration and deliberation. They are often attracted to creative pursuits or leadership roles where they have a chance to shine. In relationships they enjoy risk-taking and adventure and can feel trapped or bored by too much domestic routine.

When Fire is out of balance it becomes destructive, too much Fire can cause "burn-out" at work, and needs boundaries, and control: setting limits and saying "no" rather than taking on too many projects, for instance. Fire enjoys drama and the limelight, but too much of this and it becomes selfish, feeling that others only exist to fan the flames of adoration. Too little Fire, however, can be linked with a lack of vitality and low energy, which can lead to hopelessness, depression and lack of motivation.

Fire correspondences

Direction: south

Season: summer

Time: midday

Moon phase: first quarter

Planets: Mars, Pluto

Gender: masculine

Colours: red, orange

Sense: sight

Magical tools: wand, candles, lanterns, all solar icons

Musical instruments: stringed instruments: guitar, harp

Creatures: dragon, snake, lion, ram, phoenix

Natural symbols: flame, lava

Celtic sacred trees: oak, holly, blackthorn

Herbs: basil, bay, garlic, hyssop, juniper, rosemary, tobacco

Incense: frankincense, cinnamon, basil

Minerals: brass, gold, iron, fire opal, garnet, hematite, red jasper sardonyx, flint

Zodiac signs: Aries, Leo, Sagittarius

Archangel: Michael

Alchemical symbol: upright triangle

THE ELEMENT OF WATER

In the realm of the subconscious, dreams and emotions ebb and flow, exerting their subtle influences on our conscious thoughts. The element of Water is connected with our feeling world and it is the power that shapes all our relationships. Water is the element of love and the emotions because it is as fluid as our feelings. It rules friendship and marriage. It also relates to the subconscious mind, constantly shifting and active beneath the surface, and affecting our moods and emotional responses. It influences sleep and dreaming, as we sink down into the swirling depths of the subconscious to discover our deepest desires.

THE EBB AND FLOW

The moon tugs at the oceans of the world to create the tides, which follow her ever-changing cycle. She exerts the same pull on the fluids in our bodies, affecting our emotions, moods and a woman's menstrual cycles. Thus the ebb and flow of water is mirrored in the cycles of our own lives.

The energy of Water is feminine and receptive. It rules the west, the direction of the setting sun, and its season is autumn. Water is an element of purification and healing; this can take the form of healing counsel leading to emotional release, sweeping away stale feelings and inducing us to face the truth about ourselves. Water is cleansing and essential to life, and our own lives begin in water. The element is thus symbolized by the womb and is related to fertility.

Areas of the home ruled by Water are the bathroom and the kitchen sink. Because it presides over friendship and relationships, it also governs the living room, the arena of social interaction. In its cleansing and healing role, Water is also the element of medical rooms and hospitals. Those in caring professions,

The still waters of a lake remind us of Water's hidden and mysterious depths.

psychotherapy and those with a strong aesthetic sense are connected with Water. In the natural world its places are seas, lakes, rivers, marshes, pools, wells and rain-drenched lands.

GODS AND GODDESSES OF WATER

Deities associated with Water include Tiamat, Venus, Neptune and Epona. In Mesopotamian mythology Tiamat represents chaos and the raw energy of the salt ocean, she was the primeval mother whose salt waters mingled with the fresh water of Apsu to initiate the creation of the gods.

Neptune, the Roman god of the sea, was revered by seafarers whom he generally protected, but they feared his temper: his mood could change in an instant, giving rise to perilous ocean storms. Venus, the Greek equivalent of Aphrodite, archetype of love and beauty, was said to have been created from the foam of the sea, and to have been carried on a seashell to Cyprus. As she stepped from the sea, the drops of water that fell from her body turned into pearls at her feet. The goddess had the power to calm the sea and ensure safe voyages, just as she could bring balance and harmony to

To appreciate the power of the Water element, spend some time in nature next to running water.

human instincts and emotions. Epona was a Celtic horse goddess worshipped during the period of the Roman Empire. She was portrayed carrying fruit or corn to show her connection with fertility and the earth's abundance. She was also a goddess of Water and healing, and the presiding deity of healing springs.

EXPLORING THE WATER ELEMENT

The best places to connect with Water are in nature: spend some time by the sea or at natural pools, streams, rivers or lakes. If it is safe for swimming, then that would be ideal. Being out in the rain is another good way of experiencing the Water element. Notice how it feels as you get wet: is it a pleasant feeling or are you unable to let yourself go into it because you are afraid to get wet?

A convenient way of connecting with Water in our own homes is, of course, in the bathroom: take a long soak in the bathtub, or enjoy a refreshing wake-up shower. Don't think only of the purpose of getting clean, but immerse yourself fully in the water and notice how you feel before and after the experience. As you soak in the bath, close your eyes and visualize yourself as a fish: as you breathe in, imagine the element of Water suffusing your body; let yourself melt into the water and become one with it.

Water correspondences

Direction: west
Season: autumn
Time: dusk
Moon phase: full
Planets: moon, Neptune, Venus
Gender: feminine
Colours: black, dark blue, purple
Sense: taste
Magical tools: chalice, cauldron, mirror
Musical instruments: stringed instruments, gongs, bells
Creatures: cat, frog, turtle, dolphin, whale, otter, seal, fish

Natural symbols: shells, water, river plants, watercress
Celtic sacred trees: willow, alder, yew
Plants: camomile, hops, lemon balm, seaweeds, yarrow, belladonna, lotus
Incense: jasmine, rose, vanilla
Minerals: silver, copper, amethyst, aquamarine, turquoise, tourmaline, opal, jade, pearl, sapphire
Zodiac signs: Cancer, Scorpio, Pisces
Archangel: Gabriel
Alchemical symbol: downward pointing triangle

THE WATER PERSONALITY

People dominated by Water are emotional, sensitive and spiritual. They often have a well-developed "sixth sense" and incline towards mediumistic tendencies. Water types are the poets and dreamers, approaching life from a felt sense, rather than from thought (Air), spontaneity (Fire) or practicality (Earth). In relationships they are romantic, nurturing and empathic but can be prone to imagine insults where none exist.

Lack of Water creates problems in forming relationships. The person keeps an emotional distance and finds intimacy and close contact difficult, possibly because they find it hard to access and share their own feelings. A lack of empathy and poor psychic and intuitive skills are also indicated.

Too much Water, on the other hand, leads to being awash in a sea of emotion; flooded by feelings that can't be contained, it becomes difficult to function and operate in the everyday world. This can also happen when the conscious mind is overloaded by psychic material, so it is particularly important to be well grounded or earthed when dealing with this element.

Water is essential to life and its powers are healing, rejuvenating and refreshing.

The humours

At one time, it was accepted as fact that everything in the universe – both animate and inanimate – was made up of a combination of the four elements. Formulated by the Greek philosopher Empedocles in the 5th century BC, this theory of the 'humours' classified individuals into one of four character types. People of the earth, were said to be 'melancholic', fiery people were 'choleric', watery people were 'phlegmatic' and airy people were 'sanguine'. Until the 19th century, doctors, philosophers and other professionals employed these words as technical medical terms, and would treat illness by trying to balance the humours, but they are now widely used to describe character types.

THE ELEMENT OF EARTH

Densest of all the elements and the one most closely linked to our physical world, the Earth element governs stability, security and material concerns – whether these relate to the physical body and health, money or property, business affairs or anything that is connected with our material well-being, such as food, clothing and shelter. Stability, loyalty and reliability are the qualities of the Earth element, keeping us grounded and secure in loving families and comfortable homes.

Like rocks or soil, the Earth element is connected with matter and is the densest of all the elements.

THE ROOT OF OUR BEING

Earth is the element of all physical and material things and its energy is grounding. This feminine element is the realm of the Mother Goddess, and her body is where we sink our roots as we reach out toward new experiences. Whether it is represented by hard rock or

Gardening is one of the best ways to get to know the Earth element.

fertile moist soil, Earth stands for stability and growth. It is the solid foundation over which all the other elements move.

Earth's energy is receptive, teaching patience, endurance, self-sufficiency and reliability. It helps us to recognize and accept the limitations and potential of our characters. Earth shows us how to take responsibility for our lives and our destiny. Its symbol is the wise elder.

Earth's season is winter and its direction is north, where in the winter darkness the shifting, moving waters are frozen into ice. In the natural environment, Earth's place is a cave, the primal symbol of shelter. The cave's womb-like magic makes it a symbol of birth and rebirth, where oracles speak and enlightenment is achieved. Forests, valleys and fields are other places of the Earth element. In the home, Earth governs areas of physical needs (the dining room and toilet) and practical tasks (the workshop, greenhouse and garden). It is the element of buildings and their construction, and presides over financial institutions. Professions that are

connected with the Earth include catering, gardening, farming, business, and anything that involves making things or working with the hands.

GODS AND GODDESSES OF EARTH

Some of the deities associated with earth are Gaia, Pan and the Horned God. Gaia is the ancient Greek Earth goddess whose name has been given in modern times to the life force of the earth. The daughter of Chaos, she gave birth to Uranus, the sky, and Pontus, the sea. Her union with Uranus produced the Titans, including Cronos (lord of Time), father of Zeus. Gaia, pre-eminent prophetess, was the first deity of the great oracle at Delphi. Even the other immortals were subject to her law. The Greeks worshipped Gaia as the giver of dreams and the nourisher of plants and children.

In Greek mythology, Pan was a shepherd; his name may derive from a word meaning "pasture". Easy-going, lazy, sensual and unpredictable, he represents the spirit of untamed nature. He was usually said to be the son of Hermes, and was portrayed with the hind legs and horns of a goat (one of the first animals to become domesticated). Pan was a very ancient god of wild things, and his importance increased until he came to be worshipped as the Great God and father of all living things.

Grounding meditation

Being grounded is very important in any piece of magical work. If you are not grounded your power will be considerably less. Try this grounding meditation before or after a spell. Sit in a quite spot and imagine yourself in a leafy forest glade; feel the earth supporting you. As you breathe in, imagine yourself drawing the

energies of the earth up through the soles of your feet, like roots coming up into a tree. Feel the element of earth run through your whole body. As you breathe out, imagine the energy returning through your feet and 'roots' back down into the earth. Repeat this cycle several times until you feel strong and grounded.

The pagan Horned God, who is related to the Celtic fertility deity Cerunnos, represents sexuality and vitality. He is the consort of the Triple Goddess. Like Pan, he is represented as half-man, half-animal. As lord of the woods he is the hunter, but he is also identified with the sacrificed and hunted animal.

EXPLORING THE EARTH ELEMENT

Spending time outside connecting with nature is the best way to get to know the Earth element. Any outside activities, but especially walking and gardening, are very good ways of coming into contact with Earth, particularly the latter as it involves getting your hands dirty. An awareness of the seasons and the weather is essential when you are gardening, while physical contact with plants and soil is very "grounding". Even if you don't have access to a garden or an allotment, keeping plants in the house or tending a window box will help you connect with Mother Earth.

THE EARTH PERSONALITY

People in whom the Earth element is dominant are home-loving, dependable

Earth correspondences

Direction: north
Season: winter
Time: midnight
Moon phase: dark
Planets: Earth, Saturn
Gender: feminine
Colours: natural 'earthy' colours: browns, ochres, burnt orange, olive green, black; white
Sense: touch
Magical tools: pentacle
Musical instruments: percussion
Creatures: ox, dog, wolf, goat, stag

Natural symbols: fossils, stones, grains and seeds, salt, earth
Celtic sacred trees: ash, hawthorn, pine
Herbs: pennyroyal, lovage, sage, mugwort
Incense: vetivert, patchouli, myrrh
Minerals: lead, emerald, aventurine, pyrites, coal, onyx
Zodiac signs: Taurus, Virgo, Capricorn
Archangel: Uriel
Alchemical symbol: downward pointing triangle with horizontal line (reverse of Air)

and loyal, and happiest when surrounded by their family. Physical touch and affection are important to them and they enjoy the pleasures of the senses – food, material comforts and a healthy sexuality. Too much Earth element is stodgy, plodding and dull. Overly concerned with security and material possessions, negative Earth is unable to take risks, to branch out and try something new, for fear of the unknown. It becomes easy to get stuck in a routine, staying in a job or

relationship where we no longer really want to be because it seems the easiest and safest option and to do otherwise presents too much of a risk to our material comfort.

Too little Earth can be associated with someone who is unable to focus properly or concentrate for very long. Lacking determination and perseverance, they may dream up ever more wonderful schemes (especially if strong on Fire or Air), but never bring them to fruition.

The physical formations of the landscape remind us of the Earth element, where change takes place very slowly and over a long period of time.

THE FIFTH ELEMENT

Usually we think of there being only four elements, but in many systems of thought there is also a fifth element – ether or spirit. Because of its nature, this is the hardest element to define. Spirit is intangible, ineffable and mysterious. It is the divine soul, the magical "x" factor that in the end cannot be explained, categorized or defined, although mystics and artists through the ages have attempted to express the divine language of the soul.

ETHER OR SPIRIT

The word for spirit in the Sanskrit language is *akasha*, from which we get the "akashic records", a sort of mystical "log book" that occultists claim contains knowledge of everything that has ever happened in the material plane, existing as an energetic "imprint" in the astral world. In Latin, the word is *aether*, derived from the Greek *aithein*, which means "to kindle". In the Middle Ages ether was referred to as the quintessence (*quint* meaning five or fifth), and it was the alchemists' goal to find this fifth essence, which they believed contained the secret of everlasting life. Early European occultists regarded ether as the substance that made up the heavens, which filled the void in space.

Spirit does not have a place or location in any occult system: it is perceived to be everywhere and also nowhere, for as soon as we say "it is here" we have lost it. Unlike the other four elements, it is not possible to tie up the fifth in a neat package and attribute to it qualities that we can work with. Spirit perhaps is not so much an element as a force, it is the centre of the web that unites and animates all other emanations.

THE POWER OF SPIRIT

The qualities of the spirit are often best expressed through media other than words: musicians, poets, artists, saints and sages have used the power of sound, visual image, metaphor, prayer and feeling to try to convey what can only be

The fifth element is the spirit of the universe, which can be evoked by the starry night sky.

described as the "religious" experience, an experience of something so sacred that we are transported beyond the narrow confines of how we normally define ourselves into something much bigger. The fifth element is concerned with the timeless and the universal, with the cosmic and the mysterious. It is the

Dream-like images, such as these mountain tops above cloud height, are a way of reminding us of the connection with spirit, which is the most difficult element of all to define.

source of all, the One that permeates the cosmos. Some traditions call this God, others refer to it as Great Spirit, while in the East it is sometimes known as the Tao, or the Way. Spirit is the empty space between the stars, the blank canvas of the mind that is untroubled by thoughts and emotions. In the Buddhist tradition, experience of spirit has been likened to the moment that a dewdrop disappears into the ocean of infinite being.

MAGICAL CORRESPONDENCES

Spirit is the path or channel along which magic travels from the otherworld to this. Although there are no standard magical tools used to represent spirit, it is sometimes associated with any item that connects or unifies disparate things. For this reason spirit may be represented by magical cords, cloaks or medicine bags.

In the chakra system spirit is associated with the crown, or 7th chakra, while in the Tarot deck it is represented by The World, the last card of the Major Arcana.

Swirling clouds of fragrant smoke can transport our thoughts from the everyday world to the invisible world of spirit.

Connecting with the otherworld

Incenses have traditionally been used to help us connect with the otherworld and the realm of spirit, transforming the mundane into the sacred.

You will need
10 ml (2 tsp) frankincense resin
10 ml (2 tsp) mastic resin
5 ml (1 tsp) dammar
5 ml (1 tsp) sandarac
pestle and mortar
charcoal

1 Light the charcoal and place on a heatproof surface. Crush the frankincense and mastic resins into small pieces and mix together, along with the dammar and sandarac .

2 Sprinkle a little of the incense over the hot charcoal. Sit back and relax, allowing yourself to drift away.

Spirit's colours are white and/or black, as these essentially contain or reflect all other vibrations of light and dark.

CONNECTING WITH SPIRIT

For ceremonial magicians, the goal of magic is essentially to connect and become one with spirit, and magic is a path that is used to achieve this end. However, we all connect with spirit in our own way and it reveals itself to us only when we are ready.

The traditional magical symbol of spirit is the six-pointed star, also known as the Star of David or Solomon's Seal. It is one of the oldest symbols of the divine source from which all life is created (sometimes referred to as the One, the All, or God), and when broken down it contains all the other alchemical symbols for the four elements.

Working with the six-pointed star can be one way of helping you to connect. You could do this by drawing the symbol, wearing it, studying it each night before you go to sleep, or using it as an aid to meditation. When you meditate, imagine the symbol residing in your heart. Ask it to teach you its secrets and be open for any learning that follows; you will need to trust your "inner voice" rather than your rational mind for this.

Another magical symbol that recalls the fifth element is the pentagram. The five points of the pentagram represent Air, Fire, Earth, and Water, with spirit at the apex. Its symbolism reminds us that all four elements emanate from spirit in the astral world, and in a sense, that spirit is the cosmic "glue" that binds everything together.

The Star of David is an ancient symbol that represents the divine source of all life.

CYCLES AND SEASONS

All life on earth is governed by cycles. These vary in length; for instance, there is the 24-hour cycle of day and night, the moon's cycles last roughly 28 days, while the sun waxes and wanes through a whole year. Each cycle has its use in magic, and every time and season has benefits and strengths that can be used to gain insight, develop skills and assist the magic-worker to grow in wisdom. Being in touch with these natural cycles, rather than struggling against the tides of the world, makes our way through life smoother and our magic more effective. For no matter how good or powerful our magic, if our timing, or synchronicity, is wrong then all our efforts will be in vain and what we are capable of manifesting will be much diluted from our original purpose or intent.

This chapter considers the timing of magic, looking in particular at the cycles of the moon and the journey of the sun through the "wheel of the year". It gives information on the major festivals and celebrations in the magic-worker's calendar and also looks at the distinct qualities of each of the four seasons, the lessons we can learn from them, and how best to use them in natural magic.

NATURE'S TIMING

Just as day follows night, and spring follows winter, everything in nature happens in a certain chronology. This chronology is very important when working with natural magic because everything has a point or place of greatest power. The lunar and solar cycles influence energy patterns over short and long periods of time – through the days, months and seasons of the year. They are also present within human beings. By harmonizing with the cycles of the moon and sun your magic will be in harmony with the natural forces of the cosmos, rather than going against them.

Monday, or "moonday", is the day of the week that is dedicated to the Moon.

TELLING THE TIME

Before the advent of clocks and calendars, people measured time, or the passing of the year, by the patterns of movement in the starry night sky. Because the stars appear to move on cyclic paths, time can be marked as they return to an earlier position.

It is thought that the first henge monuments, technically ring-ditches and embankments, were fixed observatories. By standing in the ditch, the astronomers would have had a flat circular horizon against which the moon or stars could be observed. Posts could be driven into the top of the bank so that patterns of movement could be gradually traced.

ALIGNING WITH NATURE

Our modern lifestyle is pushing us further and further away from the natural rhythms of nature and we are losing contact with her cycles and seasons. Furthermore, as the delicate balance in the earth's biosphere is disturbed through man-made "greenhouse gases", the ozone layer is being damaged and the earth is getting hotter. This is disturbing the harmony of nature and causing changes in climate and weather patterns that could have a catastrophic effect if nothing is done to reverse the trend. Consequently many modern-day witches and magicians are using their magic to try to realign energies in the environment.

The wisdom of Saturn

Ancient astrologers knew Saturn as Rex Mundi, Lord of the World. He was also known as Cronos to the ancient Greeks, and Geb, god of earth, to the Egyptians. These gods governed time, one of life's limitations and restrictions. Saturn is the leveller or teacher. He teaches that we are subject to the cycles and rhythms of nature as we move from one stage of life to the next.

It is thought that megalithic monuments, such as Stonehenge, were used to help monitor the passage of time by observing the movements of the sun, moon and stars in the sky throughout the year.

Days of the week

Each day of the week is dedicated to a particular kind of magic and is governed by one of the "inner" planets.

Day	Planetary influence	Magical use	Colour	Incense	Number	Metal
Sunday	Sun	Use the power of the sun for personal healing or for a new impulse to assist your life.	Gold/yellow	Cedar Frankincense	6	Gold
Monday	Moon	Use the silvery light of the moon to strengthen psychic or dreaming powers, enhance meditation, and for inner work.	White/silver	Jasmine Water lily	9	Silver
Tuesday	Mars	Use the energy of Mars to end conflicts, for lack of motivation and for self-assertion. Also for anything that needs to be kick-started or needs physical work.	Red	Tobacco	5	Iron
Wednesday	Mercury	Use the energy of Mercury for communication: writing letters, talking, connecting with friends.	Orange	Mastic	8	Mercury
Thursday	Jupiter	King of Gods, Jupiter rules business, material growth, justice and legal matters. Energy of expansion and good fortune.	Royal blue	Cedar	4	Tin Brass
Friday	Venus	Goddess of love, Venus rules all kinds of partnerships, harmony and beauty. Use her energy to beautify yourself and improve your life. She is not a goddess to ask for help if you are wishing someone else to fall in love with you – you can use her powers only for yourself and to influence someone else would be a misuse of magic. If you want love, be loveable.	Green	Rose Patchouli	7	Copper
Saturday	Saturn	End of the week, ruled by Saturn, father of the gods. Use Saturn for anything to do with old age, with setting up or breaking down boundaries or limitations. His magic works slowly but it can be gentle and extremely powerful; patience is needed.	Black	Myrrh	3	Lead Pewter

MAGICAL HOURS

Several hours of each day are dedicated to each planet's power. These are not ordinary clock hours but represent one-twelfth of the time between local sunrise and sunset, and sunset and sunrise. This means that in summer the day hours are more than 60 minutes long and the night hours less. The first hour of each day from sunrise is dedicated to the planet whose day it is, and the following hours are ruled by the planets in the following sequence: Moon, Saturn, Jupiter, Mars, Sun, Venus, Mercury; returning to Moon, Saturn, Jupiter and so on for the night-time hours. From this you can calculate Moon or Mercury hours in any day, should you wish to work on a talisman at that time. The Moon hour on the Moon day is the strongest available lunar force, especially if it falls during the sign of Cancer (governed by the Moon). To bring in the greatest energies to a talisman, you would ideally also look at the actual planetary positions within the signs of the zodiac, and take into account your own birth sign, and the various aspects between your chosen planets.

BIORHYTHMS

The forces of the sun and the moon are also present within human beings. The male solar energy is focused on action in the world outside, while the female lunar energy is inwardly focused. According to the theory of biorhythms, we all have an internal solar cycle and lunar cycle that affect us physically, emotionally and intellectually. These cycles produce a pattern of "highs and lows", so that some days we have lots of energy and feel able to do anything, while at other times we are more introspective.

CYCLES OF THE MOON

Because the moon has such a strong daily influence upon the rhythms of ebb and flow in our lives, its phases are closely observed when working with magic. Teach yourself to understand how the positions of the earth and the sun cause the moon to wax and wane, and change her rising and setting place and time throughout her cycles – which are actually 18 or 19 years long – before the earth, moon and sun return to their starting places. Find out how she affects your moods and the tides. The different phases of the moon are conducive to different kinds of magic work.

The phases of the moon are a way of recording the passage of time as she moves through her cycle.

WORKING WITH THE MOON'S CYCLE

Moon times are shown in many diaries or in *Old Moore's Almanac* (*The Old Farmer's Almanac*, in US). If you wish to utilize the powers of the moon more precisely when casting spells, refer to the lunar calendar or an ephemeris; it will take you deeper into working with the four faces of the moon. The best time of the year to remove an obstacle, for instance, is in autumn or early winter, whenever the moon is in Capricorn, or during a waning moon. If you wish for love, the best time would be when the moon is in Taurus or Libra, and during her waxing moon face.

THE BLUE MOON

Very occasionally, two full moons can occur in the same calendar month. Known as a "blue moon", this occurred only 40 times during the 20th century – on average once every two or three years and usually during a month that has 31 days. The event signifies a special time: a doubling of the moon's powers during the month that she appears. Considered unlucky by some, the blue moon is seen by many as a magical moon, when long-term objectives can be set. So a blue moon can be used to sow seeds for your future, giving them time to germinate and grow until the next blue moon rises. But you should be careful if you intend to weave magic during a blue moon. Be very clear about what you ask for, because this moon will be potent, doubling your wish and intent.

MOON-DREAMING

Many of the mental arts of magic are similar to inducing dreams to happen when you are awake, so the clearer the

Observing the moon's cycles can help attune us to the ebb and flow of natural energies, which it is easy to lose touch with in the modern world.

The four phases of the moon

The moon has four phases – waxing, full, waning and dark – each of which is associated with one of the four winds. Witches observe the phases of the moon and time their magic in accordance with her cycles, tapping into the specific powers associated with each phase.

The first phase: waxing (new) moon
Wind: East
Timing: beginning of a new cycle; development and growth; new opportunities.
Lesson: to invoke – knowing.
Magic for: health and personal issues; put plans into action for the month ahead.

The second phase: bright (full) moon
Wind: South
Timing: the moon is full and ripe; a very fertile time, but care is needed as the energies are very powerful.
Lesson: to expand – manifesting.
Magic for: increase and expansion in your day-to-day affairs; a good time for personal power and magnetism.

The third phase: waning (old) moon
Wind: West
Timing: the moon's power is decreasing; release and letting go.
Lesson: to let go – courage.
Magic for: letting go of the past; a powerful healing time. It is also the time for insights and increasing psychic power.

The fourth phase: dark (no) moon
Wind: North
Timing: the moon disappears; time for retreat and withdrawal; recharging energies before the new cycle begins.
Lesson: to learn – to keep silence.
Magic for: gaining wisdom, understanding and insight. This time is best spent in contemplation, meditation and preparation, or seeking guidance; destructive magic is often practised at this time.

communication between your inner and outer mind at night, the brighter will be the visions seen when you scry (divine by crystal-gazing) or meditate. Because the moon's phases affect dreaming cycles in most people, this can be used to enhance the power of magic. You can work a spell to bring about finding a new job, for example, and then dream of finding yourself in the sort of place where you would like to work, or even meeting a friend who tells you about the kind of position you are seeking. Then, in real life, you find the dream being played out before you. That is how effective magic shows itself.

THE TRIPLE GODDESS
The goddess of the moon is also known as the Triple Goddess. The Triple Goddess represents the maiden, the mother and the crone and is also known

as the Great Mother or by her Latin name, Magna Dei.

The Maiden is associated with the new moon. She is everyone's daughter, playmate and inspirer. To the ancient Greeks she was Artemis, the huntress with her silver bow, protector of animals and children, the spotless maiden.

The Mother is associated with the full moon. She guides our lives, teaches us the skill of living, heals us. In Classical Greek mythology she was Aphrodite, the goddess of love and beauty, born of the foam of the sea.

The Matriarch or Crone is associated with the waning and dark moon. She gives wisdom, magical knowledge and the power to see into the future. The ancient Greeks worshipped her as Hecate, the dark goddess of the underworld, who teaches magic and ancient wisdom when the sky is dark.

Moon magic

The three phases of the moon are related to the Triple Goddess: new or maiden moon; full or mother moon; and waning or crone moon. Using moon magic often involves the use of three candles, which may be white or silver, or perhaps the colours associated with each of the three moon goddesses – white for the Maiden, red for the Mother and black or dark blue for the Matriarch.

ESBATS
Lunar festivals are called "esbats" and are held on the first night of the full moon. They are times of celebration and power, when requests and dedications are made and a feast is shared to honour the Mother aspect of the moon goddess and her great abundance and fertility.

THE WHEEL OF THE YEAR

In natural magic, the seasons and cycles of nature show that life is a never-ending journey of birth, growth, death and rebirth. This journey is represented by the wheel of the year, which is divided into eight festivals or sabbats. Four of the sabbats are solar festivals (solstices and equinoxes) while the other four are Celtic in origin. Celebrating the sabbats is a chance to sharpen our awareness of the changing season, and to fall into harmony with the rhythms of nature. Any one of the festivals can be treated as a time for endings and beginnings as we move from one cycle to the next.

The colours of autumn are a reminder that the wheel of the year is turning and that the sun's powers are fading.

THE EIGHT SABBATS

The sun and the moon represent the polarities of light and dark, or yang and yin. When one is at the height of its power, the other is at its nadir and vice versa, and so the universe is held in a state of dynamic tension. The solstices and equinoxes are key moments in the solar cycle, while the other sabbats, or festivals, are more linked with agriculture and humans' relationship to the natural world.

WINTER SOLSTICE (YULE)

The midwinter solstice, or Yule, is the shortest day of the year, when the sun is at its lowest point. Night overshadows day and the moon's power is at its height. It is a time of great feasting and celebration as the sun is once again reborn, a light offering hope for the future. From this point, the sun will begin its ascent through the skies, the hours of darkness will decrease and new life will return to earth. Traditional Yule customs include putting up a holly wreath to symbolize the wheel of the year and giving gifts. Yule is a good time to relax and celebrate.

IMBOLC (CANDLEMAS)

The Celtic word *imbolc* means "ewe's milk" and this festival heralds the beginnings of new life. It is the start of the lambing season, when the first green shoots appear, and the sun's strength is slowly increasing as the days grow longer. To celebrate the return of the light, a traditional custom is to light candles (hence "candlemas"). This is a good time for spring-cleaning the temple, and throwing out any lingering mental, physical and emotional baggage.

SPRING EQUINOX

Day and night are equal, but from this point the moon's power is waning and

The power of the sun is weakest during the winter, when the weather is cold and the hours of daylight are at their shortest.

The year's main festivals

Different regions of the world have different seasonal and directional patterns, but the sabbats can be celebrated anywhere following the seasons, rather than the specific dates given here.

Winter solstice: (Yule) December 21 or 22
Imbolc: (Candlemas) February 2
Spring equinox: March 21 or 22
Beltane: April 30 or May 1
Summer solstice: June 21 or 22
Lammas: August 1
Autumn equinox: September 23 or 24
Samhain: (Halloween) October 31 through November 11

the sun is getting stronger as the hours of daylight increase. Fertility returns to the land as the life force gathers strength and the sap rises. At this time it is customary to plant the first seeds. Now is a good time to symbolically plant the new seeds for your life, to make plans and lay the foundations for the future.

BELTANE

The name for this festival of light and life comes from a Celtic word meaning "bright fire". It heralds the first day of summer and was traditionally marked by the lighting of bonfires to symbolize the strength of the rising sun.

May Day festivals and fairs, maypole dancing and other fertility rites are some of the customs associated with this sabbat. This is a good time to take part in creative projects, to socialize and have fun. Beltane is also associated with fertility magic.

SUMMER SOLSTICE

The sun's power is at its strongest at midsummer and it is the time when crops and fruits ripen. The longest day is celebrated at summer solstice, an occasion marked by the stones of many of Northern Europe's ancient megalithic monuments. At this time the mystical marriage between earth and heaven is celebrated as the God and Goddess make love. This is a time of perfection, but we also know that on its heels is the ascendancy of the dark. Healing herbs were harvested at midsummer, and it is a good time to be dynamic and active. Use magic to help with material matters, such as jobs, houses or money, or for fulfilling sexual relationships.

LAMMAS

Traditionally Lammas (or "loaf mass" in the Saxon language) was a time when the first grain was baked into bread. This festival celebrates the giving of thanks to nature for all her bounty, a time to reap what has been sown. Lammas is a good time for reflection, to go within and "count your blessings", to be grateful for what you have, and to understand why there may be a lack in certain areas of your life and how you might address this.

Celebrating the sabbats

The word 'sabbat' comes from the Hebrew word, *shabbath*, which means to rest. In natural magic, the sabbats are holidays that mark important turning points of the sun's journey through the wheel of the year. They fall roughly every six weeks and are normally celebrated with feasting and rituals, using the energies of the changing seasons for peace, prosperity, health and good luck. The celebrations usually last from sunset until sunset the next day.

AUTUMN EQUINOX

Once again, day and night are of equal length, but now the sun's power is diminishing, giving way to the power of the moon. According to ancient Greek legend, this is when Demeter, goddess of the harvest, mourns the loss of her daughter Persephone, as a result of which the earth becomes barren. It is customary at this time to gather orchard fruits and the later harvest, celebrating nature's goodness yet being aware of the cold, dark months ahead. This is a good time to prune your life of non-essential activities; gather your energies and turn your attention inwards. It is also a good time to develop magical powers.

SAMHAIN (HALLOWEEN)

Also known as the Witch's New Year, Samhain marks the end of summer proper and the start of winter. It is a time when the veil between past, present and future is thin and it is possible to see beyond into the otherworld.

In Christian times, Samhain became the Feast of All Saints, a day when the dead heroes of the Christian church were commemorated. Traditionally, Samhain is associated with divination, being a good time to seek guidance for the coming season. It is also a good time to look back over the past and see how it has shaped the present; see what is holding you back and let go.

Spring is a time of renewal as daylight hours increase and the sun's life-giving energy grows stronger.

SPRING AND SUMMER

The four seasons of the year are nature's moods, each with its own unique characteristics. Following the seasons is at the backbone of modern magic, whether Wiccan, Druid or pagan, and there are many different ways of working with the gifts of the seasons. These include seasonal altars, ritual and celebration and many different kinds of magic, all of which are linked with other magical correspondences such as colours, incenses, the elements and so forth.

FRESH BEGINNINGS

After the long, dark days of winter, the first green shoots of life reappear in spring, a sign that life goes on. It is a time of birth and growth, of hope and optimism for the future.

The element of spring is Air, its direction is east and it is heralded in nature by bursts of fresh, vibrant colour: lively yellows, verdant greens and shots of bright blue, purple, pink and white adorn gardens, parklands, woods and hedgerows. Some of nature's sweetest perfumes scent the air – the delicate yet intoxicating scents of narcissus, bluebell, jonquil and hyacinth for instance. When using incense and incense oils at this time, all the citrus scents are fresh and uplifting; bergamot in particular is good for calming the feelings of insecurity that can accompany new ventures, and grapefruit is helpful for procrastination. Fresh green herbal scents, such as coriander, basil, sweetgrass, rosemary and thyme, are also stimulating and can help shake off any sluggishness left over from winter.

A SPRING ALTAR

Set your altar in the easterly quarter of a room, and, if possible, arrange it under a window so that it is bathed in the

The yellow and violet flowers of spring can inspire us to begin new ventures in life.

morning sunshine. Invoke the element of Air to inspire you with confidence and hope for a new beginning. To symbolize new growth and natural energy you could add a vase of spring flowers or a planter containing spring bulbs. For a spirit of hope and new beginnings, burn a little elemi resin. Its spicy, lemony scent combines well with lemongrass or other citrus scents.

A summer altar for creativity can be as over the top as you wish, with vibrant pinks, purples and blues.

RITUAL FOR A NEW START

The best time to begin this springtime ritual is at new moon, or failing that when the spring moon is still in its first quarter. You will need a piece of yellow paper cut into a triangle, and a large circular piece of violet or sky-blue paper or cloth. You will also need a bell, an appropriate incense, and a few spring flowers. As you meditate before your altar, focus on your hopes and wishes for the future, allowing whatever thoughts or images come to mind to be there. Next write these down on the yellow triangle (this symbolizes the Air element). Put the triangle face down on the paper or cloth circle and place a bell on top. Each morning during the waxing moon, and as near to sunrise as possible, come to the altar, burn a little incense and ring the bell three times. As you do this, you can either ask your chosen deities or angels to help you, or else visualize your hopes and wishes being realized and achieved.

SUMMER'S ABUNDANCE

As the sun's power increases, the season ripens and almost imperceptibly spring becomes summer, the time of nature's bounty and abundance. Summer is the season of relaxed and easy living, a gift to be enjoyed. It is a time to recharge and enjoy the sweetness of life. The element of summer is Fire, its direction is south

The yellow triangle and violet circle on this spring altar both symbolize the Air element, which will help to inspire confidence and hope for new beginnings.

and everywhere in nature a riot of colour and fragrance assaults the senses. These aromas include wallflowers, roses, sweet peas, honeysuckle, lavender, jasmine, carnations, clove, pinks and sweet Williams, while in the evening, night-scented stocks and nicotiana (tobacco plant) add their heady perfume. The colours of summer are hot pinks, crimson reds, royal purples, rich yellows and golden oranges, tempered by cool whites and creams and pale blue, pink and lilac.

A SUMMER ALTAR

Position your altar in the south and invoke the element of Fire for creativity, fertility, expansion and growth. Remember that creativity is not the same as having artistic ability: rather the spirit of creation flows through every one of us, and may be described as the quintessential energy that we put into everything that we do. Use orange, red or deep pink candles and fabric, and images associated with solar power. Make the altar a place to try out your dreams and bring your own creations to beautify it.

SUMMER RITUALS

Bonfire celebrations are a traditional way to celebrate summer. In Cornwall, England, a ritual is enacted whereby a bunch of nine good herbs and nine useless weeds is tossed into a fire by a young woman representing the goddess

of the land. The idea is that the good plants will be increased by the fire and the weeds destroyed. Other summer rituals often re-enact the story of the Goddess and the God, who having mated at the spring equinox, marry at Beltane, so that their Child of Promise may be born at midwinter. Some Beltane rites reflect this idea of the sacred wedding, or allow couples to renew their vows, often by jumping over a bonfire, or casting bunches of sacred herbs into the fire as a kind of sacrifice.

Work with the magic of the full moon during summer to encourage fertility, passion and abundance. In ancient times, women would rise before dawn on the day of the full moon and go to the fields. There they would wash in the morning dew, asking the moon to bless them with children. If you want to have a baby, then you could also include a figure of the Goddess on your altar to ally yourself with her fertile power.

APHRODISIACS

Certain fragrances are associated with love and romantic longing and even said to stimulate sexual desire. Best known of these are the distinct scents of summer flowers, especially rose, jasmine, ylang ylang and neroli (orange blossom). Sandalwood and patchouli are also renowned aphrodisiacs. Use any of these to stimulate love and fertility magic.

Focus incense

If you are having trouble deciding on or setting your goals for the year ahead, this incense mix should help you to focus and clarify your thoughts.

2 parts dried rosemary
1 part dried thyme
1 part lemongrass
few drops rosemary essential oil
pestle and mortar

Pound all the dry ingredients together using a pestle and mortar, then add the rosemary oil, mixing it in well. Burn a few pinches of the mix on your altar, on a charcoal block.

AUTUMN AND WINTER

Early morning mists and cooler days signal the advent of autumn. There are many ceremonies and rituals built around autumn's harvest, a time to give thanks for summer's bounty as resources are garnered and stored for the long winter months ahead. The long, dark days of winter are rich in magical tradition and mystery, having a unique quality and flavour associated with the moon and darkness, as well as feasting and celebration for the rebirth of the sun god at the winter solstice.

Some of the negative associations of autumn are decay and barrenness.

HARVEST AND DECAY

After the glorious crescendo of summer, everything in nature begins to contract. Russets, golds, amber, dark reds and nut-browns are the paint-box of autumn as leaves change colour and fall, blown about by the season's blustery winds. Autumn is a rich tapestry of colour and the earthy scents of decay, a time to reap nature's bounty at the harvest as the old withers and dies. It is a season of endings and completion, a turning point on the wheel of the year between the free and easy living of summer and the restrictions of winter. The element of autumn is Water and its direction is west. Any earthy, or woody fragrances will represent the mood of autumn; suitable incense and oils include myrrh, cedar, patchouli, pine, or rosewood.

AN AUTUMN ALTAR

Position your altar in the west and use rich autumnal colours for candles and fabric. You might like to use nuts, fruit or berries as an offering to the deities, angels or other powers that you are working with. As well as the abundance of the harvest, autumn is also associated with death, loss and mourning and so is a good time of year to reflect on the past and to come to terms with any unfinished business.

Water, autumn's element, is linked with emotional healing and letting go, so make sure this is symbolized on the altar too. To heal emotional hurts and disappointments, incenses such as frankincense, myrrh, sandalwood and agarwood are all helpful. Burn them during the time of the waning moon.

HARVEST RITUALS

Traditionally, magic was worked to keep the weather dry and calm so that the harvest could be gathered in. At this time, the God, as Spirit of the Corn, becomes Lord of the Underworld, a place of magic and eternal youth. The last sheaf of standing corn was sometimes cut in a ritual way to keep his spirit of fertility alive until the spring sowing. Today, ears of wheat are still saved and woven into corn dollies or "kern kings", then decked with red ribbons, the colour of blood and vitality, to be set over the hearth until spring.

An autumn altar of abundance and thanksgiving could include harvest fruits as an offering to the deities. Position it in the west and use rich autumnal colours.

The saving of the seed for next year's crop thus symbolizes the hope for the future that is kept alive during dark and seemingly barren periods of life.

USING MUSHROOMS

In addition to being a source of food and medicine, mushrooms can also inspire visions of the past and the future. A great number of mushrooms and other fungi are edible, but require expert guidance to be gathered safely; they vary from the expensive truffles, traditionally hunted by dogs or pigs, to the common horse mushrooms and puffballs that are found in many places. Some of the poisonous toadstools, however, are considered to have special properties. One of these is the fly agaric, the red and white mushroom typically shown in fairytale books. Shamans in Lapland would traditionally feed these mushrooms to their reindeer, then drink a potion made from the reindeer's urine. Having got rid of the dangerous toxic effects via the reindeer's metabolism, the potent potion causes visions of flight. It is thought that this might be the origin of the flying reindeer associated with Santa Claus.

Frost and snow outside signify the indoor months of winter, the season of introspection.

THE POWER OF WINTER

As the harvest draws to a close, the weather changes and winter takes over, bringing with it cold days and long nights. Crisp icy weather and clear open skies reflect winter's radiance, while the stark silhouettes of trees stripped bare remind us that nature is ultimately uncompromising: what is born will one day die and return to the earth. Winter is the indoor season. It is time to close the shutters and spend more time alone or with those closest to us, away from the busyness of the world. It is the season for introspection and reflection in preparation for the rebirth of spring: this means nourishing ourselves in mind, body and soul and the focus is on wholesome food, plenty of sleep, brisk walks and generally taking care of ourselves. The direction of winter is north and its element is Earth. Its moon is the dark or no-moon phase. Warming, comforting, or spicy scents such as orange, cinnamon, cloves and nutmeg are all appropriate for winter rituals.

A WINTER ALTAR

A minimalist style for your winter altar will reflect the stark simplicity of nature. Ice white, silver and black are all winter colours, while adding a touch of crimson or dark blue links with the moon's symbolism. Position your altar in the north and choose maybe one or two beautiful objects to represent the Earth element: a fallen branch, a piece of driftwood, or twisted willow branches. Appropriate incenses include vanilla, benzoin resin, sandalwood, frankincense and dammar (cat's eye resin). Spend time each day at your altar, meditating and journeying deep within yourself.

YULETIDE MYTHS AND RITUALS

In some traditions, the winter solstice (on or around 21st December) is known by its Saxon name of Yule. Yuletide is a time of feasting, when the Yule log, made of the root of a great oak tree, or the Ashen Faggot (a bundle of sticks from an ash tree) burns in the hearth for the 12 nights of the festival. It should be as big as possible and is lit from a piece of the previous year's log. As many homes

A stark, minimalist winter altar could be as simple as a stone pot and sandalwood incense.

no longer have an open fire, today's Yule log is usually symbolized by a log-shaped chocolate cake.

For pagans, Yule is the time of the birth of the Star Child, Modron, also known as Mabon, the sacred Son of the Mother. He is the Child of Promise, whose coming brings hope to the wintry world. Like the birth of a real child, his coming is eagerly awaited within the ritual, and gifts of magical significance are offered to the young boy who takes his part in the Mystery Play of Mabon. The ritual tells of the magic child's birth and as he ages one year for one day, by Twelfth Night he is old enough to earn his magical instruments and symbols, which are shown to the whole company. This time of year can also be a time of initiation for other young people into the tradition of the clan. It is customary to exchange gifts at Yuletide.

MAGIC IN ACTION

Having become apprenticed to magic, by now you are doubtless keen to try putting what you have learned into action, and to start testing your powers as a magic-worker. So prepare to cast reason and logic aside as you shape-shift into the world of magic. This is where the boundary between this world and others begins to dissolve and the impossible becomes possible. It is where dreams can become reality, for magic becomes a tangible force that touches on many different areas of your life.

 Although the otherworld is a place of magic and mystery, it nevertheless operates according to its own internal rules or logic. These rules are known as metaphysical laws and magic workers need to recognize and respect them. One of the most important of these principles is the law of karma – whatever you sow, so shall you reap. Misuse of magical power is not recommended, for whatever you give out returns to you threefold. So before creating magic always make sure it will harm none and is done for the highest good of all.

INTRODUCTION

Make a special time and place for your rituals.

As your understanding of magic grows and you prepare to practise it yourself, you may feel increasingly drawn to a particular magical technique. Many different practices and ceremonies are described in this section of the book, offering templates for rituals and suggesting spells for specific purposes, together with tables of magical symbols and correspondences for you to use in your own spellweaving and ritual. This survey is designed to help you find ways to bring magical power into your life, using the suggestions on the following pages as starting points for the development of your own magical practice.

Using Spells and Ritual

The rituals and spells described here draw on numerous forms of natural magic, but all share a reverence for the long traditions that underlie them and for the integrity of the natural world. In embarking on your magical journey you are becoming part of these ancient traditions, and it is important to approach them with care and respect.

Though magic can suffuse your daily life, it should not be compromised by the everyday. By setting aside a special time and place that you can devote to magical ceremony you will give your spells the full force of your own attention and belief. Your ritual space should be a place in which you feel comfortable and safe: an outdoor altar, in a garden or a beautiful landscape, could help to inspire you with a feeling of oneness with nature, or you could create a space with an equally special atmosphere indoors. Wherever you intend to weave your spells, take time to inhabit the space and make it feel peaceful and blessed so that it empowers your magic. Give the same time and attention to all your magical tools, equipment and props, lavishing care and thought on choosing them and taking care of them, so that you come to know them as friends, supporting you in your practice.

Developing your Abilities

You may be seeking a closer connection with the timeless energies of the Earth, or have a desire to tap into its rhythms and cycles. You may be searching for the power to improve or transform your life, or to deepen your relationships with other people, or you may want to provide protection for those dear to you. You may be hoping for good health, a happy home, or a garden full of flourishing plants. Whatever your need for magic, you will intuitively find the right way to allow it empower you for the good of all. And in time, your magical skills may lead you to a greater recognition of your psychic powers, allowing you to practise the more advanced arts of mental prowess, such as divination, astral travel and lucid dreaming.

Sharing rituals and ceremonies with a magical partner can be a source of strength and inspiration.

Cleansing, by smoke or by water, at the beginning of a ritual or ceremony helps to give it particular resonance and meaning.

Incense has been used for centuries to help create a magical atmosphere.

PLANNING AND PREPARATION

Before you undertake any piece of magic, there are certain set procedures that must be followed, more or less, all the time. For magic to be successful adequate preparation is essential, and putting in the effort during the initial stages will set the scene for the magic itself. It is worth making the time to track down all the correct ingredients and also to prepare yourself and your workspace so that you are in the right frame of mind for making magic. Contraindications to making magic would be when you feel tired or drained, or when your mind is busy and won't switch off.

This chapter will give you a good grounding in all the practical information you need to start working magic, beginning with ethics and responsibilities. It goes on to explain how to consecrate yourself, your space and your equipment through bathing and cleansing rituals that include smudging and the use of herbs and oils. It also describes techniques for

raising energy, invoking spirits, angels and other beings, and for aligning yourself with higher powers. It finishes with instructions for opening and closing a magic circle – the sacred space in which magic happens – and how to make offerings and give thanks to your magical allies for their support.

THE POWER OF MAGIC

When you work with magic you are working with powerful forces for change, and it is important to realize this before you begin to send wishes and weave spells. The energy you put into magic increases as it is released and what you give out returns to you threefold. So be careful with what you wish for, as you might have to live with the consequences for a long time. It is important not to be fearful of magic, however, but instead learn how to be humble and ask for the right things in the right way. When you ask with sincerity, and from the heart, you ask from the right place, and this is the way to exercise the true power that you hold within you.

ETHICS AND RESPONSIBILITIES

The witches' law states that "if you harm none, do what you will." At first, this may appear like a licence to do whatsoever you like, and magic-workers are often criticized for having no moral code. However, it actually means that as long as you cause no harm to any person, animal or thing, you may follow your True Will. True Will is not a personal choice or desire, but the purpose of your existence here on earth. The reason you are alive is to discover your True Will, or purpose, and work towards realizing it. Furthermore, it is a universal law that whatever we give out is reflected back, hence the biblical saying, "as you sow, so shall you reap".

Reaping the consequences of our actions – good or bad – is inevitable, if not in this life, then in another incarnation. Consequently, it is always a good idea to align yourself with the divine will of the universe before starting to perform a magical act. You may think of the divine will as the God or Goddess, your Higher Self, the ultimate source, or the One – whichever description best works for you.

The energy and concentration you devote to your magic making will return to you threefold.

MAKING THE PLEDGE

Before starting to weave magical spells or rituals, it is important that you pledge yourself and your actions to the light. This is a way of reminding yourself of your intentions and should be done simply and from the heart.

1 Place your hands upon your heart and ask that you be filled with the light of love. Imagine the golden light and feelings of love filling your heart and then your whole being.

2 Open your arms and raise them above your head, palms facing up towards the heavens, and say the pledge. Then bring your arms down to your sides.

When making the Spellweaver's Pledge imagine golden light filling your whole being.

Raising your arms, as you say the pledge, links you with the heavens.

The Spellweaver's Pledge

I call upon the divine will of the universe to send a blessing upon my heart, so that I may be filled with the light of love and truth in all that I do. I pledge that from this day I will do my best to harm none with my thoughts, words or deeds. I pledge that any magic I perform will be for the highest good of all. So mote it be!

Hedgewitches

Of course, it is not necessary to work with others or to belong to any recognized group in order to practise magic. A magical practitioner who works alone and according to his or her own individual style and belief is sometimes known as a hedgewitch. In days of old, the hedgewitch, or country witch, or wise woman, would have been called upon regularly by members of the community. They would have performed such things as house blessings and clearings, to help with the protection of vulnerable people, property and personal possessions, and also to act as an oracle for discovering the reasons behind particular problems or hindrances.

Hedgewitches, who live in harmony with nature, use their knowledge of herbs, flowers, roots and leaves to make up concoctions for such purposes as healing, protection or fertility. The country witches of today seldom write anything down, relying – as did their predecessors – on memory and inspiration for their workings, which are usually conducted in a sacred place. Their knowledge is passed on in the old way, by apprenticeship, whereby a newcomer is gradually taught magical rituals, healing spells, chants and movements, or else may be self-taught. A hedgewitch is so named because she is able to keep one foot in the material world and the other in the world of spirit, and the "hedge" represents the veil between the worlds.

Covens and Lodges

Many practitioners of magic like to work with others, either within a coven or group of witches, or in a magical lodge. Traditionally, these organizations have been kept secret, but one way of discovering other like-minded people is to look for announcements in popular occult magazines, which may list societies or training schools. Alternatively, seek out publications written by specialists in the area of magic that most interests you. It has never been easy to find a way into the Mysteries, but these basic steps are open to all.

Having found a suitable coven or lodge, the next step will be to undergo a ceremony of admission, or initiation. The word "initiation" means beginning, so this is a first step, rather than the conclusion of a magician's work. No one should accept initiation into a group unless they are certain that it is right for them, and that the group is trustworthy. If there are any doubts in your mind about a group, it is far better to wait than to rush into a situation.

Commitment and Secrecy

Although society is far more tolerant now than it was in the past, it is still best to keep some things secret and go about your magical work in privacy and silence, both of which will add to its power. Effective magicians never speak of some things, including who is working magic, when and where any magic or ritual is being done (unless it is some sort of public festival) and any magical names and mottos used. These are only ever known to the magicians and the gods. While you can read books on most techniques or activities, it is the practical experience of magic that makes it work, and that is a particular secret that cannot be shared.

Go about your magical work in quiet privacy: it is not a sideshow or something to do in public, but a personal commitment that you should take seriously.

TIME AND PLACE

An offering on an outside altar can be as simple as a few flowers on a tree branch.

Before you rush into any piece of magical work you need to consider timing and location. Timing is important because everything has a point of greatest power and therefore a right time and purpose. By utilizing the season, the correct phase of the moon, the four winds, the right planets, herbs, minerals and affirmations, you can increase the efficacy of your magic. Similarly, every place has a certain energy field, or spirit of place, that will be naturally better suited to some types of magic than others.

TIMING

To plan the best time for your magic you need to use your knowledge of the phases of the moon, the time of day and the season. Current positions of the planets and the kind of "energetic pattern" they are creating are also worth noting. You can consult an ephemeris, a table showing the movements of the planets, for this kind of astronomical information.

Consider whether the purpose of your magic is to attract or create something, or to reflect or dissolve something. The waxing phases of the sun or moon are for the former, while their waning phases are associated with the latter. The moon's cycles last roughly 28 days, while the solar cycle takes 365 days, or a calendar year; the sun is waxing, or growing in strength, from the winter to the summer solstice, and waning thereafter. To find out about the phases of the moon you can consult a diary or almanac.

PATIENCE

Modern society is fast-paced and based on instant gratification. We are not accustomed to having to wait for things and even the length of time it takes to cook our food is getting shorter and shorter. Yet magic does not work in this way. It takes time for things to manifest on the material plane, and we must resist the temptation to think it is not working if, once we have set magic in motion, we don't see an immediate result.

One of the golden rules for every magic worker is patience. Just as it takes time for a sown seed to germinate and develop into a healthy plant, so it is with magic – and the bigger the plant you are trying to grow, the longer it may take to come to fruition. So once you have set your magic in motion, leave it alone. Do not keep repeating the spell or ritual without need as this shows a lack of faith in its original power. Another thing to remember is that magic can move in mysterious ways, so try not to be cynical or disappointed if the results are not exactly what you had planned or envisioned; they will be exactly what your inner self called for to meet your true needs at this particular time.

INSIDE OR OUTSIDE

You have two choices about where to perform your magic – indoors or outdoors. Traditionally, spells are cast outside. Some covens meet out of doors, in woods or high hills, in all weathers. These outdoor witches use whatever is around them for their symbols: water in a seashell from rain or a spring, a small

One of the most important elements of your magic work is patience. If you are naturally impatient then you will need to work on your ability to wait.

Woodland clearings, or the tops of hills, are traditionally places where magic is made, but anywhere outside will do, so long as it is quiet and secluded and you can be sure you will not be interrupted.

bonfire, a tree branch for a wand and their hand for a sword. If you want to work outside it is helpful to find a natural beauty spot that is peaceful and secluded, where you won't be disturbed. Such a place could be part of a garden, near a particular rock or tree, or in meadowland. It will be somewhere that inspires a feeling of being part of creation and where you feel safe. You may also want to set up a natural altar in your chosen spot, using "found" objects that you come across, such as stones, feathers, nuts, flowers, leaves, pine cones etc.

If you do not have access to an appropriate place outside, you can use a room in your home. If you have the space, it should be a room or section of a room that is primarily dedicated to making magic. If this is not possible, you will need to create a magical space each time you work, but in any case, it is important to keep the atmosphere clean and balanced. This can be done by cleaning it regularly with salt and burning purifying herbs.

Visualizing sacred space

Sometimes it is not possible to travel physically to a special place for magic work. However, everyone has the ability to create an inner sacred space that can become a sanctuary or temple, a retreat from the everyday world where magic can happen.

Your inner sacred space can be any kind of place in which your spirit feels happy and at home – a woodland clearing, a cave, a deserted beach, even a corner of your own garden. Concentrate on creating the place and remembering it in detail. You will need a candle and some incense.

1 Take five deep breaths to centre yourself and focus your mind on what you are about to do. Voice your intent out loud. Light a candle and burn some incense, holding your intention in your mind. Contemplate the candle flame for a while, imagining it lighting up the recesses inside you, so that you may find a way to the place you seek more easily.

2 When you feel ready, sit in a comfortable position and focus on your breathing. With closed eyes, take deep, slow, relaxing breaths from your diaphragm. Now picture an opening, a natural doorway such as a hole in the ground or the mouth of a cave. This will lead you to the sacred space you seek.

3 When you pass through the doorway, and enter your sacred space, pay attention to details that will make the place seem more real. Notice what you are standing on: is it grass or stone, sand or pebbles? Pause to smell the fragrance of a flower, reach out and touch trees or rocks, hear the sound of birdsong and the sighing of the wind, sit by a freshwater spring and drink its water.

4 When you feel it is time to leave your sacred space, give thanks and promise to return. Retrace your steps through the entrance and come back to your physical body.

Natural objects or representations of them are good for working magic outside.

PREPARATION RITUALS

Taking the time to prepare yourself before you start working magic is an important part of the magic itself. If you work spells or rituals when you are feeling tired or when your mind is busy with other things, then you can't expect to achieve good results. In fact, because magic involves connecting with powerful energies, it is not recommended that you attempt to perform magic at all when you are like this. Wait instead until you have more vital energy and are able to switch off your thoughts and become like an empty vessel. Magical energies will then be able to flow through you without you becoming drained or too attached to the result of your work.

Add some essential oils to your bath and bathe by candlelight as preparation for magic work.

PREPARING YOURSELF

There is a saying that "cleanliness is next to godliness", and it is an esoteric belief that harmful negative energies will fasten on to any dirt on the body of an

After your bath you might like to anoint yourself with rose water or an oil blend containing rose geranium essential oil before performing a ritual.

individual engaged in magic work. Traditionally, initiates fasted, refrained from sexual activity, bathed and anointed themselves with oils and herbs to prepare themselves for magic. While it is not necessary to go to such extreme lengths, some level of deliberate preparation will give your magic work more significance. Eating a light, plainly cooked meal rather than one that is rich in spices and sauces is preferable before you begin, for example. When we have sex our energies mingle with those of the other person, so make sure that any sexual contact is especially loving and nourishing as it can affect our magic – for better or worse, depending on the qualities of the relationship.

Bathing is highly recommended; an invigorating shower or a long soak in the bath are both appropriate. Water not only cleanses the physical body but also washes away psychic dirt from the subtle bodies. We pick up this psychic dirt all the time – from negative energies in the atmosphere created by our negative thoughts, anxieties, stresses and petty jealousies as well as from vibrations in the environment. If you do not wish to bathe, simply washing your hands and face is helpful.

While you are bathing, imagine that you are cleansing away all impurities from your body, mind and soul, and as the water drains away visualize all those impurities draining away from you. Using essential oils or herbs in the bath is

Cleansing herbal bath mix

The ingredients for this mix are associated with purification and cleansing. Use fresh herbs if possible.

You will need
7 basil leaves
3 bay leaves
3 sprigs oregano
1 sprig tarragon
small square of muslin (cheesecloth)
10 ml/2 tsp organic oats
pinch rock or sea salt
thread
Pile the herbs in the muslin, then add the oats and the salt. Tie the corners of the muslin with thread. Hang the sachet from the bath tap so that the running water is infused with the essence of the mixture.

Golden light breathing exercise

The more concentrated and positive effort you fill your magic with, the more potent it will be, so to be successful as a worker of magic you need to know how to raise or increase energy. Energetic breathing will help you build up your concentrated energy. This technique is cleansing and empowering; it increases energy in the body and gives you more resources to work with.

1 Stand with your feet hip-width apart and feel them make contact with the ground. Rest your hands on your stomach and take a few deep breaths into the stomach area.

2 Place your hands just below your sternum. Begin to breathe, not too deeply, but slowly and with concentration.

3 Breathe in through your nose and visualize drawing golden light into yourself. Hold the breath for a short time (do not strain) and imagine your heart opening. Breathe out through your mouth, letting the golden light circulate around your body.

4 Continue breathing in this way until you feel energized and wide awake. Then rest your hands on your heart for a few moments, letting the breath gradually return to normal.

Spend some time preparing yourself mentally, with a period of meditation, to achieve the right frame of mind before you begin your magic work.

also helpful: lavender, geranium or rose are good choices, or look for any others that are particularly purifying.

Next, choose what you are going to wear. A robe is ideal, otherwise select loose-fitting garments that do not constrict the flow of energy through your body. Don't worry about looking fashionable – comfort is much more important when making magic. In fact, many witches like to work "sky clad", or naked, as they feel much freer and closer to nature like this, but this is up to you.

MENTAL AND PSYCHIC PREPARATION

When undertaking any magic work it is important to be in the right frame of mind, so mental and psychic preparation is recommended. After you have bathed, a period of meditation immediately preceding the start of a ritual will help to achieve calm composure. Meditation can be accompanied by some quiet, spiritually inspiring music and the burning of a suitable incense. A light fragrance such as geranium or a head-clearing scent such as rosemary is best, leaving the heavier aromas for the ritual.

PREPARING THE TEMPLE

Whether or not you have an actual "temple" room in your home, you will need to create a sacred space for working magic. Again, this needs to be properly prepared. The first step is to create a "clean slate", as any psychic impurities or negative energies present when magic is performed can intrude and interfere, contaminating the result and perhaps changing it completely. As a modern analogy, we might think of such impure energy as a kind of occult computer virus, with a purifying and cleansing routine acting like an anti-virus program.

Every culture has its own favoured purifying and cleansing methods, many of which date back thousands of years. In Old Testament times, for instance, brooms made of hyssop were used to clean out temples and other sacred buildings. Today, many occultists like to use the Rose Cross ritual. This involves lighting an appropriate incense and carrying it around the room while wafting the smoke in a pattern from corner to corner in a cross shape, then making the shape of a circle in the middle of the cross. This shape represents a cross with a rose in its centre, which is the symbol of the Rosicrucian Brotherhood, a secret occult order that dates back to the fifteenth century.

A feather can be used in smudging, fanning the fragrant smoke around your body to cleanse your aura of any negative energies.

Smudge sticks are densely packed and can burn slowly for a long time.

SMUDGING

One of the most popular purifying and cleansing techniques, smudging is a shamanic practice that has enjoyed widespread revival in recent years. Its shamanic origin means it lends itself to just about any magical path without causing contention. It is very simple but extremely effective, and because it needs a little input from the practitioner, it encourages magical thought and activity while the basic tools for the ceremony – a smudge stick and a smudge fan – are being put together.

A smudge stick is a densely packed bundle of herbs, which usually includes sage – a plant that smoulders when lit, producing clouds of fragrant smoke. The fan should be made of feathers, or else a single feather can be used. The purpose of the fan is to waft the smoke all over the area being cleansed – over the walls, floor and ceiling and around the doors, windows and any other openings into the room, such as the fireplace or air vents. The nature of the herbs, the intention of the person who gathers and ties them together, and the action of the fan will drive away any negative thought-forms lingering in an area.

MAKING A SMUDGE STICK

It is very rewarding to grow and dry your own herbs, thus ensuring that their magical qualities are tended during all stages of growth, and that you honour the spirits of the herbs when cutting them. The three herbs suggested here are all for purification. The best variety of sage to use is American white, or mountain, sage (*Salvia apiana*). All the herbs must be thoroughly dried.

You will need
dried sage stalks
dried lavender flower stalks
dried thyme stalks
natural twine

Gather all the dried herb stalks together and arrange them in an intertwined bundle. Tie the stalks together at the end, and then wind both ends of twine upwards around the bundle until it is bound together. Light one end, extinguish the flame and let the smoke rise to fill the area. As you fan the smoke, strengthen the action by visualizing the herbs' cleansing qualities.

BLESSING YOUR EQUIPMENT

In the same way that you prepare yourself before performing magic, all equipment and materials that you intend to use should also be cleansed and consecrated beforehand. Once blessed, the items can be stored, ready for use. The blessing described here is for a cord, but you can adapt it for any other item. You can also perform this ceremony on an altar if you prefer.

you will need
compass
incense
candle
bowl of spring water
bowl of sea salt
cord

1 In a cleared space outside or on the floor, mark out a circle with the four points of the compass. Put the incense in the east quarter, the candle in the south, the bowl of water in the west and the bowl of salt in the north.

2 Begin with the east quarter. Light the incense and say the first line of the blessing. Pass the cord through the smoke rising up from the incense, while imagining a clear, cool breeze passing through the cord.

If you do not have a smudge stick or dried herbs, then you can use incense sticks for your cleansing and purification rituals.

3 Turn to the south quarter and say the second line of the blessing, passing the cord through the candle flame as you do so.

4 Turn to the west quarter and say the third line of the blessing, while sprinkling the cord with water.

5 Turn to the north quarter and say the fourth line of the blessing, sprinkling the cord with salt. Finish by saying the final lines of the blessing.

THE BLESSING
I cleanse, bless and consecrate this cord with the powers of Air.
I cleanse, bless and consecrate this cord with the powers of Fire.
I cleanse, bless and consecrate this cord with the powers of Water.
I cleanse, bless and consecrate this cord with the powers of Earth.
Finish with
May this cord now be cleansed and purified for the highest good of all.
And so mote it be!

Thought-forms

In occult terms, an atmosphere can contain 'thought-forms'. These subtle vibrational patterns are produced by the workings of the mind and are picked up at a subliminal level, rather like how a radio set receives broadcast messages. A received thought-form reflects the nature of the original broadcast: happy, sad,

gloomy, cheerful, and so on. Thought-forms that are deliberately created by a magician can be extremely valuable and they form a major part of magic. But unconsciously produced thought-forms tend to be negative and can get in the way of making successful magic, which is why purification rituals are so important.

CASTING A MAGIC CIRCLE

Whether you work inside or outdoors, it is traditional to create a magic circle before starting a ritual, spell or other piece of magic. The circle will help you concentrate on your work and will banish any unwanted thoughts or influences. With practice, you will come to know it is there, protective and empowering, each time you begin your ritual. You need to visualize the area within the circle as a place of stillness beyond normal time and space. It is a place where physical, social and spatial boundaries are redrawn, and represents the wholeness of the human, the natural and the divine. It is where the internal and external are connected and where all is incorporated into one – matter and spirit reunited. You may outline the circle using a wand or staff, and as you turn to draw the line in the air you may see it burning with golden fire.

The working place is a circle of light, whether visualized, or made with physical elements.

MAKING YOUR CIRCLE MAGICAL

A legacy from ceremonial or high magic, the circle traditionally recognizes the four points of the compass. North is the place of Earth; west is the place of Water; south has the heat of Fire; and east possesses the breath of Air.

It is customary to open the circle in the east, which through its association with Air symbolizes intellect and rational thought. Its magical tool is the athame (dagger) or sword, although a feather may also be used. The next point on the circle is Fire in the south, the energy of the magical will that desires to create. Its magical tool is the wand, which can be a slender branch of wood; hazel is especially appropriate as it has the capacity to bend, although a candle may also be used to represent this point. The south is the quarter of the circle for energizing, for setting in motion a course of action. Through its association with Water, the west is associated with emotions and feelings. While the east separates and divides, the west flows and merges; beginnings are initiated in the east, while letting go is the theme of the west. The west's symbol is the cup or

Making a magic circle

You can make a magic circle in many different ways. It can be visualized in your mind's eye, drawn in the air with a wand, a dagger or just your hand, or created physically – with stones, candles, or other symbolic objects. One popular way is to use a length of white, silver or gold cord, laid out on the ground. This will need opening and closing down before and after the spell.

You will need
2.7 m/9 ft length, 5 mm/¹/₄ in thick white cord
salt water

The Light Invocation
By the powers of Heaven and Earth, I cast this circle in the name of love, wisdom and truth, for the highest good.

1 Place the cord in a circle with an opening in the east. Step through the opening with whatever items you are going to use for your spell or ritual. Place them in the centre of the circle. Close the circle behind you and seal it with a sprinkling of salt water.

2 Go clockwise around the circle, sprinkling salt water on the cord as you go. Visualize yourself surrounded in golden light and say the light invocation. The circle is now ready to work within. When you have finished your spell, close the circle as detailed on the opposite page.

chalice, or else a bowl of water. The north corresponds to darkness and winter, the polar opposite of the south's fiery heat. It is the quarter for containment and inner reflection and is represented by the pentacle or sometimes salt.

CASTING THE CIRCLE

There are many different ways of casting a magic circle. It may be drawn in the air with an athame or with your hand, visualized as a ring of fire, or you may prefer to create an actual, visible circle, such as a cord circle – if you are new to magic, you may find this easier to work with. If you are working outside, you could make one out of rocks, pebbles, pine cones, pieces of wood, or even flowers: choose objects that seem to "speak" to you in some way and are in harmony with your magic.

One of the most versatile circles is a basic cord circle, which can be used indoors or outside. Remember that a magic circle is always opened in the east and should be cast in a deosil (clockwise) direction. It should always be closed before any magic work takes place, and you should not step out of it until you have finished. When you are finished, you must ritually take the circle apart or dissolve it.

CLOSING THE CIRCLE

At the end of your magic it is important to take the circle apart. This is to keep the magical energy pure and contained, marking the boundary between magical and everyday activity. Doing so also acknowledges that endings are part of

life's cycles. Work "widdershins" (anticlockwise) until you end up where you began. For instance, if you started working a spell or ritual in the south, you would close the circle by beginning in the east and moving round through north and west until you reach the south. Gather up your tools from each quarter as you go round and as you do, say the following words:

I give thanks to all who have helped me
and leave my magic with you.
And so mote it be.

Nature's circles

If you are creating a circle from natural objects, use 12 items. Ask permission to use each object in your magic before taking it. Purify each item with a pinch of salt and say:
I bless this stone/rock/flower or whatever with love,
light, wisdom and truth.
Then sprinkle salt on the object, asking for a dedication to the light. Welcome it to the circle and explain what you are going to do.

One way of making a magic circle is using candles or tealights.

Some magicians and witches visualize a circle to create a place between the worlds, and trace it with their finger at the beginning of a ritual or spell.

INVOCATIONS AND OFFERINGS

Once you have created your magic circle, it is customary to invoke the spirit beings that you wish to call upon to assist you in your magic. Their subtle yet powerful presence will help to connect you with the otherworld and make your magic more effective. At the same time, every magic worker knows that magic is a give-and-take relationship, so will always give thanks to these unseen helpers as well as to the spirit or energies of the place and the equipment that has been used. In this way, you ensure that your magic is aligned to the highest good of all.

A sacred herb in the Native American Indian tradition, tobacco is often used as an offering.

GUARDIANS OF THE WATCHTOWERS

In casting a magic circle, great importance is attached to astral beings called the Guardians of the Watchtowers. The "watchtowers" are the four quarters of north, south, east and west. The purpose of the powerful guardians is to protect those who invoke their aid and ensure the security of the circle. They will be with you while you work and should be thanked at the end.

The guardians may be seen as angels, totem animals, gods and goddesses, holy living creatures, elementals or any other kind of otherworld beings – every tradition has its own set, but it's up to you what you choose to work with. Cabbalists, for instance, often invoke the four archangels: Raphael (Healer of God) in the east; Michael (Like unto God) in the south; Gabriel (Strength of God) in the west; and Uriel (Light of God) in the north. Some practitioners may prefer to work with the Arthurian legends: King Arthur, master of the mysteries, in the east; Gawain, defender of all that is good, in the south; the Lady of the Lake, guardian of the secrets, in the west; and Merlin, the archmage with the power of vision, in the north.

INVOKING THE GUARDIANS

There is no single right way to invoke your heavenly powers, what matters is the spirit with which you do it, so be creative. Just remember that you cannot command or order these powers to be with you, but only ask or invite them from a humble heart. The following invocation calls upon the Guardians of the Watchtowers (the four directions), but if you are working with a different

Angels and Arthurian heroes are both called upon in magical working as guardians and helpers. Here Sir Galahad achieves the Grail, a potent magical symbol, watched by other knights of the Round Table, and three archangels.

An offering of salt is made on a very simple and impromptu altar.

Leaving an offering outside

When you are taking something from the natural world, show your gratitude by leaving something behind. If you are taking something from the land, always ask its spirit for permission first. Remember it is illegal to pick wild flowers or disturb protected species.

1 To make an offering, hold your gift in your hand and present it up to the sky.

2 Present your offering to the earth to show appreciation to the Great Mother.

3 Hold it out to each of the four directions – north, south, east and west – keeping in mind the connection between all things.

4 As you leave the offering in your chosen place, voice your thanks and intention. Speaking the following words aloud will help to focus your attention and energy:
I offer this in gratitude for the gifts given, in honour of creation and my part in it.

set of guardians, then you may insert their name after "I call".

1 Stand inside your magic circle, close your eyes and take a couple of breaths to centre yourself.

2 Face north, raise your hand and say:
I call the Guardians of the North to protect this place from earthly wrath.

3 Turn to face the east and say:
I call the Guardians of the East to calm the airs and bring me peace.

4 Turn to the south and say:
I call the Guardians of the South to protect me from the fire's red mouth.

5 Finally, turn to the west and say:
I call the Guardians of the West to lay the stormy seas to rest.

6 When you have completed the circle and are again facing north, say the following words. As you do so, imagine the circle you have cast is spreading

through the universe like ripples in a pool, bringing tranquillity and peace to its centre, which is you and your circle.
*Let blessings be upon this place
And let my Circle clear this space
Of spirits wicked, cruel or fell,
So that in peace I may dwell.*

GIVING THANKS
It is always advisable to give thanks to your unseen helpers. One way to do this is by making an offering to the spirits. This must be natural or biodegradable. Not only will this acknowledge them as important, it will also encourage a

cooperative relationship, for when you make an offering you exchange energy as well as giving thanks. You may also make an offering if you need special help, or in gratitude when your magic bears fruit.

You can make offerings on your altar or shrine, in your magic circle, or outside. In the North American Indian tradition, tobacco is often used, while the Celtic tradition favours salt. The offering can be anything that has special meaning to you and is in harmony with your magic – flowers, stones or coins, or something made especially for the purpose, such as a loaf of bread you baked, or a cake.

Elementals

Archetypal spirit beings associated with each of the four elements are sometimes known as 'elementals'. Believed to inhabit the realm of Faerie, they are sylphs, salamanders, undines and gnomes. Sylphs are the fairies of Air in the east, and their name is taken from the Greek *silphe*, meaning 'butterfly'. Salamanders rule Fire in the

south, and their name is from the Greek *salambe*, meaning 'fireplace'. Undines are the ruling spirits of Water in the west, and their name is derived from the Latin *unda*, meaning 'wave'. Finally, gnomes are the creatures of Earth in the north; their name comes from the Greek *gnoma*, meaning 'knowledge'.

RITUAL THROUGH LIFE

A ritual is a way of making contact and communicating with the otherworld, thereby bringing transformation – or magic – to the individual and to the wider cosmos. Traditionally, it is a way of honouring transitional states as we move from one stage of life to another, and it provides an opportunity to step outside routine ways of thinking and behaving in order to connect with the unseen forces of the cosmos that shape our lives. Major life events, such as birth, marriage and death, are usually acknowledged by some kind of ritual ceremony, while seasonal festivals are also acknowledged by ritual acts. It is also possible to transform everyday events into something special through ritual.

This chapter looks at the power and purpose of ritual, differentiating between rites, ritual and ceremony and the role they have to play in magic.

It includes a variety of rituals that can be performed to assist with many different aspects of life. These include the banishing ritual of the pentagram, a traditional magical ritual to clear psychic energies, as well as rituals for inner calm and healing. It looks at how we can use rituals for blessing ourselves and our homes and how to make rituals a part of our daily lives. It concludes with information on rites of passage and how magic is being used to create meaningful rituals for the modern world.

THE POWER OF RITUAL

Since ancient times, rituals have played an important part in magical and sacred ceremonies. Rituals are patterned acts, performed to bring about specific objectives. For our earliest ancestors, they were often accompanied by sacrifice and were an attempt to placate, if not to control, forces that were potentially life-threatening, such as wild animals or extreme climatic conditions for instance. In magic, rituals are a way of connecting with the otherworld to give thanks, make offerings, ask for guidance or make requests. The tools that are used in ritual, the elements and the powers that are invoked, all have particular meaning and significance and must be used with care.

Lighting a candle focuses the mind, and acts as a signal to all present that the ritual is beginning.

THE PATTERN OF RITUAL

A ritual is a patterned activity. This means that it follows a recognizable structure and sequence of steps, time after time. What is important is that you engage with it in mind, body and soul and do not just "go through the motions". The latter would make it an empty gesture devoid of meaning and therefore it would lack any real power to make magic happen.

To begin with, it is essential that a clear and precise objective is outlined and that everyone who is involved is fully aware of this purpose, which is often stated at the start of the work. Most magical rituals follow four basic stages: purifying mind, body and soul; getting dressed or robing; preparing the place; and creating the circle. Whether the ritual is for divination or a celebration, to consecrate a talisman or work for healing, its

purpose is then said aloud so that all those taking part are clear about why they are there, and agree to its purpose.

WORKING THE RITUAL

Once you have made the necessary preparations, opened the sacred space and stated your purpose, you can proceed to magically do whatever you have decided upon. This could be creating a talisman, weaving a spell, sitting in meditation, enacting a traditional myth, or celebrating a special time of year. Towards the end of the ritual it is usual to have a sacred sharing, or communion, with the deities, angels

Preparation for a ritual often begins with cleansing or purification. This can be symbolic, such as passing round a bowl of warm water, scented with essential oil, and floating flowers.

Outdoors or indoors?

Old-fashioned village witches often performed their rites and rituals alone or else with a close group of family and friends, and as far as possible they would work outdoors. Modern-day magic workers tend to hold their rites, rituals and ceremonies indoors for the sake of convenience.

and otherworldly beings who have been called upon to help your magic, as well as with any other people who are enacting the ritual with you. Something to eat, which may be bread and salt, biscuits, fruit or any other sacred food, placed on a platter, is blessed, often in the name of the Earth Mother who provided it, and eaten. Then wine, water, milk or any other drink in the chalice is blessed in the name of the Sky Father, or by the power of the Sun God, before being drunk. The chalice is taken with both hands to show complete involvement.

After the communion there is often a pause to meditate on what has been begun by the ritual, or if you are with others, to discuss business or any other matters. Then it is customary to say "thank you" and release the higher powers that you summoned to your ritual and to unwind the circle widdershins (anticlockwise), the opposite direction to the one used at the beginning. You may feel a shift of energy and gentle return to ordinary awareness at this point. When you are clearing up, you might find it useful to discuss the ceremony, although if you are working for an ongoing

Food is often a part of a ritual, and preparing it – such as dividing up bread or pouring out glasses of wine – can become part of the ceremony.

If you are passing round a chalice, hold and take it with both hands to show involvement.

purpose it is best not to talk about it so that the magic has time to develop in the silence of secrecy. If it was a festival, then that has been completed and may be shared.

RITES, RITUALS AND CEREMONIES

There is sometimes confusion over the difference between rites, rituals and ceremonies. The words "rite" and "ritual" are often interchangeable, but rites tend to have shorter and simpler workings, and are often performed by someone working alone. Much less emphasis is placed on the preparation and the closing of a rite, with the concentration instead on the central stages. They come in many shapes and forms, which vary depending on their source or tradition and on their purpose. Simple rituals veer more towards a rite, while those that are more elaborate and complex could more accurately be described as a ceremony.

A ceremony usually involves several people, and has a more complicated pattern and more elaborate equipment. Ceremonies may be held in public or in front of an audience. They are used by many traditions worldwide to mark special times – to celebrate birth and naming, to join two people in marriage, or to lay the dead to rest. Some ceremonies are performed by a priest before a congregation, while others allow the wider participation of the faithful, in processions, public offerings, hymn singing or ritual dance.

STICK WITH IT

It can take time before you can perform rituals and ceremonies with ease and confidence and at first you may feel embarrassed and rather self-conscious, particularly if there are others present. However, most people feel like this when they start doing something new and out of the ordinary, so persevere. It is worth putting up with a few uncomfortable feelings in the beginning, as these will begin to subside once you start to reap the rewards of natural magic.

A BANISHING RITUAL

A highly respected ritual that has been used by a number of the main magical disciplines for hundreds of years is the Lesser Banishing Ritual of the Pentagram. It is called "lesser" only to distinguish it from its counterpart, the Greater Ritual of the Pentagram, which is used for magical invocation rather than for banishing or clearing. The Banishing Ritual involves invoking angelic powers for the purpose of purification and is often used to space clear a place of unwanted energies or create higher vibrations for magic.

CABBALISTIC INFLUENCES

Because the banishing ritual is Cabbalistic in origin, much of its wording is in Hebrew (including some words from the Lord's Prayer) and it calls upon the archangels of the Judaeo-Christian tradition. The ritual is divided into three sections: the Cabbalistic cross; the drawing of the pentagrams; and the invocation of the angels. To close the ritual, the first section – the Cabbalistic cross – is repeated.

THE HIGHER SELF

The main reason for performing the Cabbalistic cross as part of the Banishing Ritual is to enable the magic-worker to get in touch with his or her "higher self". This higher self is visualized as white light that is present above the head, and is drawn down by the ritual. The higher self is able to bridge the gap between the everyday world and the higher astral planes, the source of infinite knowledge and wisdom.

PERFORMING THE RITUAL

Before you begin, prepare yourself by bathing, drinking spring water and sitting quietly in meditation for a while. You should be dressed in clean, comfortable clothes. Make sure you will not be disturbed at any time. Unplug or switch off phones, close the curtains if you are overlooked. When you are ready to begin, place yourself in the middle of the space you are working in. Work through the following steps slowly with reverence and respect.

1 Visualize a sphere of pure, clear light, about the size of a football, a little way above your head. Reach up to it with the fingers of your right hand and visualize that you are drawing a shaft of

The first movement of the ritual is to reach up to an imagined sphere of light above your head.

The traditional gesture of the god Osiris completes the cabbalistic cross part of the ritual.

light down to you by touching your forehead. Say:
Ahte (pronounced "Ach-tay" and meaning "Thou art").

2 Touch your fingers to the centre of your chest, visualizing the shaft of light travelling down to infinity through the floor, as you say:
Malkuth (pronounced "Mal-koot" and meaning "the Kingdom").

3 Touch your right shoulder, saying:
Ve-Geburah (pronounced "vay-Geboorah", meaning "the Power").

4 Touch your left shoulder, saying:
Ve-Gedulah (pronounced "vay-Gedoolah", meaning "and the Glory"). As you do this, visualize a shaft of light emanating from infinity to your right, crossing your body as you perform the action and plunging away into infinity again on your left.

5 Now cross your wrists at the centre of your chest with the right wrist outermost in the "Osiris risen" position. As you do this, say:
Le Olahm (pronounced "lay-Ola-chiem" and meaning "Forever").
Now bow your head and say:
Amen ("So be it").

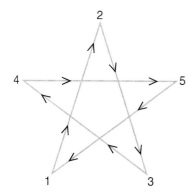

This diagram shows the order you should trace the pentagram. Begin at point number one.

DRAWING THE PENTAGRAMS

The next part of the ritual consists of drawing four pentagrams, one in each direction of the compass, starting with the east. The particular pentagram used here is called the "earth banishing pentagram". Each pentagram should stretch from about shoulder to knee height and is best drawn with the arm at full stretch if possible. As each one is completed, it should be "fixed" with a stabbing gesture of the fingers into the centre, accompanied by a Hebrew word.

1 Face the east to draw the first pentagram. When it is complete, fix it while saying the names of the letters that spell the name of God – Yahveh in Hebrew, or Jehovah in English: *Yod-He-Vau-He.*

2 Turn to face the south and draw the next pentagram. Fix it by saying: *Adonai* ("Lord").

3 Then draw the western pentagram, fixing it with the name by which God identified himself to Moses, pronounced Eeh-heh-yeh: *Eheieh* ("I am that I am").

4 Finally, draw the northern pentagram. The word to fix this with is pronounced "Ah-geh-lah". It is made up of the initial letters of the phrase Aith Gedol Leolam Adonai: *Agla (*"Thou art mighty forever Lord").

As you invoke the archangel Gabriel, turn your palms to face you.

THE INVOCATION OF THE ARCHANGELS

The third part of the ritual involves the invocation of the archangels.

1 Raise the palms of your hands to face forward and say:
Before me, Raphael (pronounce the angel's name "Raff-eye-ell").

2 Turn your palms to face behind you, saying:
Behind me, Gabriel (pronounced "Gab-rey-ell").

3 Lower your right hand, palm upwards, and say:
On my right hand, Michael (pronounced "Mick-eye-ell").

4 Lower your left hand the same way and say:

On my left hand Uriel (pronounced "Ur-eye-ell").

5 Finish by saying the following words. Raise your hands above your head and put them together as you utter the last line:
For about me flame the pentagrams. Above me shines the six-rayed star!

The Cabbalistic Cross

It should be noted that the hand makes the cross from right to left, not from left to right as in the Roman Catholic crossing gesture.

EVERYDAY RITUALS

R ituals help strengthen our connection with the universe. Just as vibrations spread across a spider's web or ripples radiate across water, a simple ritual can have far-reaching effects on you and those with whom you relate. By performing rituals based around your daily activities you can consciously strengthen the connection between your everyday self and your higher self, and life itself becomes a ritual.

HABITUAL ACTIONS

In everyday life habitual actions such as cleaning our teeth or making a cup of tea are sometimes referred to as rituals, yet we do not generally associate them with magic. What differentiates habit from magical ritual is the consciousness we bring to the action. Performing an act with awareness has the effect of increasing the efficacy of that act. This is because the intent carries to other levels of our being: for instance, if you take a shower with the intent of cleansing your spirit as well as your body, the overall cleansing effect is greater. It will empower you and make you stronger. It

Ritual food can be chosen so that it embraces the essence of the four elements.

will also "charge" your energy body with spiritual vibrations so that you will radiate a certain aura wherever you go and life becomes a magical experience.

FOOD AND DRINK

Preparing and eating food are powerfully symbolic activities and mealtimes provide a very good opportunity to incorporate ritual with day-to-day practicality. When you are preparing food, do it with love and appreciation of what has been supplied by Mother Earth to give you nourishment. Choose your ingredients carefully – ideally you should always use organic, locally grown and seasonal foods, and those that you have grown yourself are even more special.

Even the most ordinary activity can have ritual significance. Taking the time to buy and arrange some special flowers, for example, gives your home love as well as decoration.

Tea ceremony

Throughout the world, there are many customs associated with the brewing and serving of tea. The most notable of these comes from Japan, where the classic tea ceremony is a complex ritual that elevates drinking tea into a spiritual experience. The tea ceremony has many rules and set procedures and is presided over by a master of ceremonies. It is a good example of how a daily activity can be transformed into a magical experience.

Making food for rituals

Although for rituals many people just use commercial bread, broken into pieces, and any kind of wine, mead, cider or fruit juice as a drink, you may wish to try the old ways where special biscuits or scones and your own home-brewed wines or beer are made for rituals. Any type of food, or recipe will do, it is the act of making it that adds power to your ritual. As you become more experienced, you can adapt traditional recipes by adding favourite or appropriate ingredients. Although not everyone has the time to make wines for rituals, it is a pleasing skill to master. Country wines can be made with fruits, vegetables, herbs, berries and dried fruits. It is very important that you sterilize all the equipment before use.

Baking bread yourself for a specific magical purpose gives the ritual greater power.

Eating foods that are as close to their natural state as possible is not only beneficial for your body, but is also helpful from a spiritual point of view. Remember we are what we eat, and the plants and animals are all gifts of Mother Earth, so by sharing her bounty at mealtimes, we are also taking in some of the eternal blessings of creation.

In magical ritual, it is customary to bless our food or drink before taking it into our body. You can do this by holding your hands over the meal, closing your eyes and inwardly saying thank you to Mother Earth for her goodness. Make time to eat away from your normal activities, even if this is a quick snack. Take time to experience the different tastes, colours and textures of your meal. Don't work, read, watch TV or talk excessively to others while you are eating as this only takes energy away from eating. When you eat with awareness, even ordinary meals can become a ritual that nourishes body and soul.

FOOD FOR FESTIVALS

All over the world, special dishes are served at festival times throughout the year. These can range from a simple kind of special bread eaten occasionally to elaborate feasts with many courses to celebrate a major event such as a wedding or seasonal festival, like Yule.

But you may not want to wait for big occasions, and could make one meal a month (at new moon for example) an opportunity to share some simple dishes with others on your path, to discuss the arts of magic, and celebrate the passing seasons. It can be a time when you decorate your shrine with new flowers and symbols, and use that as the centrepiece of your gathering.

Home-brewed wine and mead are free from chemicals and full of goodness, and have the added value of having been made yourself, so adding to their magical purpose.

RITUAL THROUGH THE DAY

Just as everyday acts can be transformed into ritual, it is also possible to use rituals throughout the day to help strengthen your connection to your magical powers. Morning and evening are two especially potent times of day for ritual activity. Morning is the beginning of a new day and rituals performed at this time will set up a pattern of energy that you can take with you throughout the day. Evening is about endings and winding down; rituals performed at this time will help you come back home to yourself.

MORNING RITUALS

Greeting the morning puts you in touch with the rhythms of nature and is a great way to start a new day. You can work out your own simple ritual involving a few stretches or breathing exercises to wake up the body, perhaps followed by a moment of quiet or meditation to collect yourself for the day. Taking a shower is also energizing and refreshing and changes your energy from sleep to awake; use fragrances such as rosemary, all the citrus scents, peppermint or eucalyptus in your shower products.

As you touch your forehead to begin, say clearly and firmly, "I am Spirit!"

START-THE-DAY RITUAL

The following ritual summons a fresh charge of personal psychic energy to strengthen your being and encourage you to appreciate the joy of a new day.

1 Light your chosen incense or vaporize your essential oil. Stand facing a window, towards the east (during warm weather this ritual can also be performed outside facing the morning sun). Take some slow, deep breaths.

2 When you feel calm, make the sign of the pentagram on your body. Touch your forehead with the fingertips of your right hand, and say:
I am Spirit!
Then touch your left hip and say:
I am Earth!
Touch your right shoulder and say:
I am Water!
Touch your left shoulder and say
I am Air!
Touch your right hip and say:
I am Fire!
Finally, touch your forehead again to complete the figure of the pentagram and say:
Thus I seal my affirmation.

3 Inhale the fragrance of incense or oil for a few moments before beginning the new day.

It's good to make time for a period of quiet contemplation or meditation, accompanied by purifying incense, to prepare you for the day.

Wake-up herbs

For protection and purification:
frankincense, juniper
For success: cinnamon, carnation, cloves
For a clear mind: rosemary, basil,
peppermint
To dispel sluggishness: grapefruit,
lemon, lime, bergamot.

EVENING RITUALS

Just as you began with energizing and
empowering rituals to greet the day,
evening time is about winding down and
relaxing and giving thanks for the day
that has passed. It is a time of transition
between wakefulness and sleep, and it is
important that you allow yourself to slow
down before going to bed. A simple
night-time ritual is to make an offering
on your altar last thing at night using
incense and candles to give thanks and
let go of the day that has passed. Useful
herbs, incense or oils for encouraging
peaceful sleep include lavender,
marjoram, hops, camomile, rose and
passion flower.

END-THE-DAY RITUAL

To end the day, you can use this specially
modified version of a much more
elaborate ritual known as the Middle
Pillar Exercise, which has its origins in

*Placing an amethyst under your pillow will help
you achieve a deep and untroubled sleep.*

*After you have finished your bedtime ritual, relax with a cup of dreaming herb tea and allow the
tensions of the day to disperse.*

the teachings of the Cabbala. To add to
its effectiveness and enhance your ability
to sleep, place an amethyst or clear
quartz crystal under your pillow before
you settle down to sleep.

1 Before you begin, calm and centre
yourself. Stand facing west – the
direction of the setting sun – and for a
few moments focus on the sun setting
on the horizon, whether it is actually
still daylight or already dark.

2 Imagine a beam of brilliant white light
shining down on you from an infinite
height. As it touches your head and
enters your body, it transforms your
entire body into light-filled glass, like a
clear bottle of human shape.

3 As the light courses down through your
body, see it changing hue, moving
through all the colours of the rainbow.
As these colours flow down, imagine
any dark areas of your body being
cleansed by the rainbow light, pushing
the blackness downwards and out
through the soles of your feet.

4 As the rainbow-coloured light flows out
of your body through your feet,
imagine that it is forming a pool or
puddle of black mire, and that this pool
is then draining away into nothingness,
leaving you clean and filled with
brilliant opalescent, rainbow hues.

Dreaming tea

Mix the following herbs to make yourself a
goodnight tea. It can help you to recall your
dreams and have a restful night's sleep. (It is
not advisable to drink this tea if you are
pregnant.)

1 heaped tsp dried jasmine flowers
1 heaped tsp dried camomile flowers
2 sprigs fresh marjoram
a large cup or mug of freshly boiled spring water
honey (optional)

Place all the herbs in a jug and pour over the
boiled water. Infuse for 5 minutes, strain into a
cup and sweeten with honey if desired. Sip this
tea about half an hour before you go to sleep.

A RITUAL FOR INNER CALM

When you are flooded with emotion, desires and restless thoughts it will be difficult to focus on making magic, as all you will be able to think about will be yourself. A magic-worker needs to be able to switch off from their personal concerns in order to connect with the higher self and the cosmos. This means being calm and still inside with your energies contained and focused. Methods to achieve this state form an essential part of Eastern sacred traditions, most notably Zen Buddhism, from which this ritual has been adapted.

Meditation is an ideal practice to help you move towards a clear-minded state.

ZEN PHILOSOPHY

The word Zen is derived from the Chinese *ch'an*, which in turn originates from the Sanskrit *dhyana*, meaning "meditation". A philosophy of Chinese origin that was adopted by the Japanese in the 12th century, Zen has its own unique identity within the wider practice of Buddhism. Its essential concept is that perfection (nirvana) can only be achieved when all is reduced (or expanded) to nothing. Zen rituals therefore tend toward simplicity, quiet, stillness and deep inner reflection to create an atmosphere of intense and almost tangible peace.

RITUAL FOR INNER CALM

This ritual is ideal when you are feeling stressed and anxious and are unable to settle yourself by your usual methods. To perform it, you will need as much silence and stillness as your surroundings permit. Ideally your space should be as empty and clutter-free as possible, as this will help to induce calm and composure. Remember to turn off your phones.

If possible, use a gong to mark the beginning and end of the ritual; otherwise find something else that will produce a similar clear, simple sound. You will also need a low table or altar covered with a plain black cloth and a few sticks of sandalwood incense in a suitable container. Set up the altar so that you can sit or kneel before it facing east.

THE RITUAL

Light the sandalwood incense. Kneel on a cushion or sit on a straight-backed chair before the altar. If you prefer, you may sit cross-legged in a half- or full-lotus position. When you are comfortable, perform the fourfold breath to still your thoughts. To do this, breathe in to an unhurried count of four, hold your breath for a count of four, breathe out for a count of four and hold your breath again

A simple sound is used to mark the beginning and ending of a Zen ritual.

The sound of Om

'Om' is spoken after taking as deep a breath as possible. It begins with the sound 'ahh', moving into 'oh' and ending with 'mm' for as long as the out-breath lasts. All of these three sounds should merge into one. The sound of Om is said to symbolize all the sounds in the universe.

Zen koans

Koans are exercises in paradox, used in Zen teaching, and are designed to baffle the mind until it is defeated and reduced to nothingness. They take the form of questions that defy reason; perhaps the most famous is 'What is the sound of one hand clapping?' When everything is reduced to its ultimate state of non-being, then the perfection of union with the higher spiritual forces of the cosmos becomes possible.

for a count of four. Take the next breath and repeat the sequence. Continue to practise the fourfold breath for a few minutes until you feel a state of great calm begins to unfold.

When you feel sufficiently calm and at ease with your surroundings, gently sound the gong once. As the sound fades, begin to chant the single word "Om" as slowly as possible. Keep your head bowed towards the altar. Repeat the chant 10–12 times, taking care throughout to avoid any feeling of "hurrying things along".

Once you have reached the end of the chanting, take two or three more fourfold breaths, then slowly bow towards the east, with your hands held at your chest in an attitude of prayer. In this position, repeat a single long "Om". Your mind should now be clear enough to concentrate your thoughts. Close your eyes and visualize a circular ripple of light in the centre of your abdomen, slowly spreading out horizontally, like the ripples from a stone tossed into a pool filmed in slow motion. As this circle of light reaches the horizon, it continues out into the universe and to infinity. Continue to observe this visualization for several minutes. As you do so, make your mental image as sharp as you can, ideally you are aiming for a reality equivalent to having your eyes open, but this takes a little practice.

To end the ritual, stand up, place your hands in the prayer position at your chest as before and bow deeply from the waist. Sound the gong one more time to close the meditation.

The Zen philosophy epitomizes simplicity, and ritual in the Zen style will therefore also be very simple and unadorned.

Incenses for inner calm

In the East, several incenses are particularly valued for their affinity with meditation, but two of the most noteworthy are sandalwood and agarwood (or 'aloes'). Hindu temples were often made from sandalwood, while yogis (masters of yoga) use a yellow sandalwood paste to mark the 'third eye' chakra. This paste is cooling and helps calm restless thoughts. Burning sandalwood incense has the same

effect. Little known in the West, agarwood has been valued in Middle and Far Eastern countries for thousands of years. Its indescribable fragrance has been compared to a blend of sandalwood and ambergris and is reputedly one of the finest (and most costly) fragrances in the world. Agarwood is used in Japanese incense and is said to open up the heart to compassion while calming the mind.

A HEALING RITUAL

In many traditional societies, it is the medicine man or woman who performs healing rituals for the sick – whether this is a person, situation or even an environment. The healing ritual described here is based on traditional shamanic practices in its use of herbs, drums and chants to summon the assistance of the spirit world for the purpose of healing or rebalancing energies.

THE ROLE OF THE SHAMAN

The word "shaman" comes from the Tungusic dialect of the Ural-Altaic tribes of Siberia. Shamans were the priest-doctors of the tribes, responsible for officiating at ceremonies and rituals, tending the sick and caring for all aspects of the spiritual wellbeing of the people. The term is now used more broadly to describe individuals who commune with the natural and supernatural world for the good of their community using traditional shamanic practices, such as drumming, journeying and dreaming.

A SHAMANIC HEALING RITUAL

The shamanic ritual outlined here calls upon the powers of the drum, of sacred herbs, and of the Inyan (the stone people of the Native American Indians) to summon dream spirits for healing, cleansing and purification. Have a representation (such as a picture) of the person, situation or place that you are doing this healing ritual for and place it on your altar or shrine. This ritual is best done in a fairly large open space so that you are able to move around, or if possible outside.

As you hold the stone to your heart, visualize the person you are working on.

You will need
loose dried sage
heatproof bowl or shell
black or dark feather
large stone chosen for its individuality
tobacco
drum

1 Place the sage in the bowl and light it. Use the feather to fan the smoke around yourself and over the large stone. This is known as "smudging".

2 Take a pinch of tobacco and stand in the centre of your space facing north. Say the following words, then place the pinch of tobacco at the centre.
Great Spirit I honour you and humbly seek your presence within this grandfather rock.

3 Pick up the large stone and, holding it to your heart, ask it to help you clear any negative energies from the person, situation or place you are working on. Set the stone down on top of the tobacco saying the words:
Mitake oyasin ("For we are all related").

Sit for a moment in front of the burning sage, and breathe in its cleansing smoke.

The shaman's drum

The drum is one of the shaman's most powerful tools. Its primal sound touches the deepest recesses of mind, body and soul, connecting us with the heartbeat of Mother Nature and life itself. Before using a drum for a ceremony, it is customary to make an offering to the spirit of the drum. The spirit is made up of the essence of the animal that gave its hide, the tree that gave its wood and the maker who gave his or her skill and intent. The offering is given to honour the separate units that came together to make the whole. To make an offering, sprinkle a little tobacco over the drum before you begin to use it, saying thank you.

Drums play an important part in shamanic rituals. The sound of the drum is said to call healing spirits, while driving away sickness.

4 Take another pinch of tobacco and, still facing north, hold out your hand in that direction. With feeling and respect call out "Buffalo" and place the tobacco on the floor to the north.

5 Repeat the gestures for the east, south and west, calling out "Eagle", "Mouse" and "Bear" respectively.

6 Turn to the north again and say the following words, then stand the smudge bowl on the stone so that the smoke coils up through the room. *Guardians of the four winds, I, your brother/sister, do call your presence here.*

7 Take up the drum and, beginning at the edge of your space, walk deosil (clockwise) in a spiral until you reach the centre, drumming the atmosphere towards the stone. Drum over the stone into the herbs, visualizing any negative energies coiling away in the smoke. Thank the Great Spirit, grandfather rock, and the four totem animals for their help.

8 Repeat the words "Mitake oyasin" and then remove the smudge bowl from the stone. Take the stone outside to rest on the earth so that any remaining energy can be safely discharged into the ground.

RITUALS FOR BLESSING

One of the most essential arts in the witch's or magician's set of skills, is the ability to perform blessings. As well as blessing yourself, sometimes you may also need to bless places. You may sometimes have felt, when entering a place, that the atmosphere did not feel right or, when moving somewhere new, that it still had psychic disturbance caused by the previous occupants. Performing a blessing can change this and put the atmosphere right.

When you are performing a ritual to change an atmosphere it is important to use a new candle.

BLESSING YOURSELF WITH COLOUR

Before dealing with a difficult situation or if you need healing, or want to work a particularly powerful piece of magic, you might find the following ritual very helpful. It will help you to feel balanced, protected and able to deal with problems. Work through it slowly, really seeing or sensing the colours and their different energies. You can also use it to bless another.

1 Sit comfortably upright and close your eyes. Imagine that you are standing on a dark, black, curved surface. It is so intensely black that you could almost imagine it is the night sky, spangled with brilliant stars. Moving up your body from your feet, watch the colour changing to a dark, peaty brown, fading gradually as you move up your legs to a russet brown.

2 At the top of your legs, the colour is crimson red. Above that is a band of orange across your stomach, fading into a yellow band in the region of your solar plexus. Above the yellow, the colour changes to a rich leaf-green over the heart region. At the top of your chest and throat, the colour changes through turquoise to a bright blue at your Adam's apple. From the bright blue, the colour changes to deep violet on the level of your "third eye", in the centre of your forehead, and finally there is a change to brilliant diamond white at the top of your head.

3 Allow these colours to become vivid and definite and try to discover a gradation of tone, from very dark at your feet to a brilliant white light above the top of your head.

4 See the vivid and shining white as a great ball above your head and then imagine drawing this force downwards through each colour band. It comes from beyond you, for it is the healing power of the creative force, or perhaps one of the healing angels.

5 As the light flows down through you, have a sense of it opening up like a rose unfolding. The chakra at the crown of your head is the link with your higher self through which you may work magic.

When blessing yourself with colour you need to be sitting comfortably before you begin the meditation.

Blessed colours

The colours that you visualize during the blessing have the following significance.

At the forehead the intense violet-purple represents your psychic faculty. As the brilliance flows downwards through your body, the blue rose of communication and speech flowers at the throat. Below that there is a green flower at the heart centre, from which the power of love and compassion flows to others. Next is the main healing centre of the solar plexus, through which the magical life force of the universe may be directed, in rays of golden sunlight, to those in need.

Across your abdomen is the orange-coloured flower that helps you cope with the mundane aspects of healing the sick, and will assist indigestion. Below that is the crimson blossom filled with the brilliance of white light that enlivens your most basic urges of sex and true unity. This can be used to heal and balance your own life, but you shouldn't use this healing power with others until you have fully mastered control of this centre of energy. Below that is a darker region of stability and strength. It is the strong base on which the blossoms of sacred light grow. This is a mysterious firmament, often envisioned as sprinkled with stars.

Traditional tools for changing an atmosphere: words recited from a book of power, the sound of a bell, and the cleansing power of a candle flame.

CHANGING THE ATMOSPHERE

When someone moves into a new home a common problem is that they feel disturbed by the atmosphere left by the previous occupants. You can deal with this matter fairly easily, if you are just changing the atmosphere to suit the new tenant, not trying to shift a ghost or a haunting – that is a job for the highly experienced.

You will need
twig of rowan wood
piece of red ribbon or thread
new white candle
candle holder

1 Bless yourself with colour as described in Blessing yourself.

2 Tie the piece of red ribbon or thread around the rowan twig, and then carry it around the whole dwelling clockwise in every room and space, from top to bottom, mentally sweeping out old energies. Sweep these out of the front door as if they were dust.

3 Go outside, light the new white candle and carry it in. Carry the candle around all the rooms and spaces, clockwise, visualizing bright, new light entering.

4 When all feels well, stand in the centre of your home and stand quietly for a few moments. Before you snuff out your candle, you can recite this Navajo blessing:

This home will be a blessed home.
It will become the house of dawn.
Dawn light will live in beauty in it.
It will be a home of white corn,
It will be a home of soft goods,
It will be a home of crystal water,
It will be a home dusted with pollen,
It will be a home of life-long happiness,
It will be a home with beauty above it,
It will be a home of beauty all around.

Psychic upsets

Many psychic upsets are the result of people playing with the occult when they don't know what they are doing, such as using a Ouija board or attempting to set up a séance without knowing how. These actions can open a crack between the ordinary self and the inner one, and if people have fears or phobias, or repressed memories, these will be the first through the gap. These methods for contacting magical powers are not recommended for the novice, and should be left to trained witches and magicians.

A large number of candles placed in the corner of a room will dispel stagnant energies.

RITES OF PASSAGE: BEGINNINGS

L ife is a journey with many milestones along the way. Different cultures around the world have many different ways of acknowledging these phases with ritual and celebration. Also known as "rites of passage", these rituals are designed to acknowledge the transition from one stage of life to another, and usually involve not only the individual but also their family and sometimes the wider community. For instance, most traditions have a way of naming a baby, others have rites at puberty or first menses, while marriage is almost universally acknowledged as one of life's major stepping stones. These rites of passage are usually embedded in the established religion of the society, although many customs also have their roots in magic.

A ring is an excellent symbol of commitment, as it is the unbroken circle without beginning or end.

WEDDING RITUALS

Although a traditional church "white wedding" is still the favoured option for many people, others are looking for ways to unite in marriage that do not involve the church. There are other marriage ceremonies, which although they may not be recognized by the state, suit many couples, particularly as they can decide for themselves the words and format of the ritual rather than following a fixed set of procedures. Weddings over the broomstick have taken place in many parts of the world, in which the couple step over a besom to indicate they are entering a new phase of a shared life. Pagans have a ceremony called "hand fasting" where the bride and groom have their hands bound together with a ribbon and there is an exchange of rings.

Although a priestess and priest officiate at pagan ceremonies, the format of the actual ceremony is always directed by the couple, allowing them to promise to love, support and remain with each other for a traditional "year and a day", or

The pagan ceremony of hand fasting involves tying the couple's hands together with a ribbon to signify their commitment to each other.

for a lifetime or forever. They usually have a pair of wedding rings blessed by the priestess and priest, and exchange these as a sign of long-term commitment. There is often a ceremonial sharing of bread and wine, and often the bride and groom break the wine glass to show that no one else can break their union. Many pagans like to conduct these marriage rites out of doors, in a sacred circle, ringed by lighted candles, flowers and ribbons. Their guests are instructed as to what may happen, as they may be from many faiths, perhaps being asked to light a candle of their own, to offer gifts or to speak personal blessings and wishes for the future of the couple. There is a wedding feast with a special cake, usually followed by a party.

NAMING CEREMONIES

Many parents today in more modern, secular societies, are not comfortable with having their baby baptized or christened into the Christian faith and are looking for other options. In former times one of the tasks of the village midwife was to bless a baby at its birth, before the priest of the orthodox religion named it. Today, pagan priestesses trained in these arts are much in demand. Within the blossoming pagan religions, new ceremonies are being constructed which can be offered to adherents, so that their children can be named and blessed in the power of the old gods and goddesses.

Affirm the life you are living now and keep mementos and reminders of the days that are passing. The stages of childhood in particular should be marked and recorded with reverence and joy.

COMING-OF-AGE RITUALS

In the Jewish religion, a boy's coming of age is marked with the "bar mitzvah" ceremony, symbolizing the end of childhood and an initiation into adulthood at puberty. For the most part, however, coming of age is not officially recognized within modern society and many people are once again looking to the pagan tradition for meaningful rites that honour the young person's passage. By officially recognizing their status in society, a young person is given a more

clearly defined role and a sense of belonging that is often lacking among modern teenagers whose "difficult" behaviour can be connected with a struggle for identity.

Rituals are being set up so that young people can be seen to have passed into adulthood, and they are given the symbols of the responsibilities they are taking on. These rituals are different in character from those of earlier traditions, which might have involved a hunting ritual for boys, or a time apart for girls, but in content they can still be part teaching session and part celebration.

In a magical community, at the chosen age in years, or moment in life, a ritual is organized where the young person is presented with their own magical tools, their Tarot pack or symbol of the clan or community. They will be told of their responsibilities, which may increase if they are initiated into the Mysteries of their family, and they are shown the kind of assistance and support that is available to them within the community.

In most magical and witchcraft groups young people do not receive full initiation until they are adults. Some groups take 18 as the age of adulthood, others wait until the age of 21.

Traditions of marriage

The wedding ring: having no beginning or end, the ring symbolizes the unbroken circle of lives and the couple's commitment to each other for eternity.

The bouquet of flowers: this is a vestige of the sacrifice, which in days gone by would have been an animal or bird, offered on the altar and then becoming part of the wedding feast. Flowers symbolize beauty and perfection, with particular blooms having different meanings. Brides cast their bouquet over their shoulder to pass on the expectation to be the next to be wed.

The stag and hen night: the Stag is reminiscent of the Horned God and a symbol of male sexual potency and authority, while the Hen, with her power to lay eggs and create new life, symbolizes the fruitful mother aspect of the goddess. The traditional stag and hen parties, or bridal shower, may have evolved from the competitive games that were once held. Often, the bride had to be 'stolen' from her family and taken into the groom's community, and the groom would swoop into the bride's territory on a horse and carry her off to a new life, chased by her family and his friends.

RITES OF PASSAGE: ENDINGS

While most of us welcome beginnings and the start of something new, we tend to find endings more difficult. This is partly because of the way we are taught to see life, as something that progresses from start to finish. In magical thinking, however, an ending is not something final but is merely another stage in the infinite cycle of birth, growth, decay and rebirth. It is yet another transition from one stage to another as we journey through the wheel of life. It is important to acknowledge endings as this helps us to move on to the next stage of the soul's journey.

In magical thinking, an ending is not seen as final, but as another stage in an infinite cycle which is reflected in the cycles of nature.

DIVORCE RITUALS

In the past, people struggled to make a marriage or partnership last, trying to hide their differences or finding ways of respecting them and continuing to live together for a variety of practical reasons. Today, people are more ready to separate if they have grown apart and there is less social stigma to being divorced, but as yet, mainstream society does not have any official rituals, other than legal ones, that acknowledge this transition.

For this reason, rituals of division have been created by modern pagans, which try to signify an ending that is peaceful and not acrimonious. In a ceremony, the couple acknowledge that they cannot reconcile their differences, have fallen out of love, and desire to part. Then the wedding rings are taken off, and possibly thrown into running water, or given to a goldsmith who can melt them down,

undoing the magic of joining. A ribbon that has been tied around the couple is cut and they are set free, perhaps by burning a paper on which their original bonds or promises were written. A cake may be cut in half in the presence of those assembled, or some other symbolic representation of the parting performed, to help at this difficult time.

FUNERALS

In orthodox places of worship, a funeral is usually a rather sombre and gloomy affair. While the death of a friend, family member or colleague is very sad for those that are left behind, pagan funerals try to focus on celebrating the dead person's life. Many pagans choose a woodland burial in a biodegradable coffin and to have a living tree planted over their grave, rather than a cold headstone, as a memorial. Others are cremated so that

their ashes may be ritually scattered at some sacred or beloved spot by their friends. Some funeral centres will allow for a magical circle to be cast about the coffin and floral tributes can be offered in the shapes of stars, moons or circles. Ritual prayers or poetry may be read at the service. Symbolic acts of casting off mortal life for an eternal spiritual one can be shared by family and friends, and anecdotes of the deceased's life, including photographs of them at different life stages, are often included.

OTHER ENDINGS

As we go through life, we will encounter many endings. Some of these, like death and divorce, are fairly major, but "smaller" endings, like leaving home, changing a job, or moving to a new area, all signify the ending of one phase of life and the start of something new. These endings are often acknowledged by the people we are leaving behind with cards

Severing the ties

When relationships are no longer able to sustain themselves, a ritual severing of the ties that bound the couple together helps to set them free and to heal any bitterness or uncertainty. In earlier times, the partners' names were written on a log which was then split; each partner would burn the half log bearing the partner's name on their own fire to release any lingering bonds.

As in any kind of ending ritual, splitting a log with the couple's names written on it was a way of letting go and moving on from a painful situation, and marking its passage.

For those who are left behind, a remembrance shrine can bring comfort, and a feeling of continued closeness to someone who has died.

and gifts, but we can also acknowledge them for ourselves. We can light a candle on our shrine or altar and say goodbye to the old life, acknowledging and giving thanks for all it has given us, before we embark on our new journey.

REBIRTH

Many occultists believe that after death the immortal soul is drawn towards a great light. People who have had a near-death experience often describe passing through a dark tunnel towards a place of brightness, and perhaps encountering a divine or heavenly being or spirit guide who leads them to a glorious garden. But when it is not their time to die, they return to complete their life on earth, usually as changed people. Occultists

believe that when we die, after a period of rest the soul once again prepares for rebirth into the temporal plane.

Those who have evolved through many thousands of lives and, according to the Buddhist belief, have been able to step off the wheel of incarnations, may still choose to return to earth, to teach others, or to act as a beacon, guiding lost

souls towards their heavenly or divine heritage. Some people seem to return quickly to a new life; it depends on the purpose of each particular incarnation, and time as we understand it in the physical world has no meaning in the realm of spirit. Others return after long intervals of earthly time.

IMMORTAL LIFE

In magical thinking, a burial or scattering of ashes is essentially returning the person's physical remains to the Great Mother, which is part of all life. Through the food we eat and the air we breathe, our lives are created with the substance of earth, which is also part of the cosmos. Along with the earth, moon and stars, the sun and planets, we are part of this vast creation, ever changing but immortal.

Remembrance shrine

When someone has died, the ones who are left to grieve may find comfort in marking a particular place in the house where they can go to remember and celebrate a life that has moved on. A remembrance shrine can be made using

photographs, a lit candle, some burning incense, some fresh flowers or a keepsake that reminds you of that person. Make the shrine an affirmation of the person's life rather than a continual mourning for a loss.

SPELLWEAVING

Magic doesn't just happen all by itself: spells are woven, crafted, worked and cast in order to bring about a desired result. This means making spells is an active process that requires effort, energy and commitment on the part of the spellweaver.

Essentially, a spell is a magic recipe containing many different ingredients and needs careful thought and planning. Before you start, you need to be clear why you want to cast a particular spell and to make sure your intent is in line with your highest purpose. You also need to assemble all your ingredients – and this may take several hours or even days as you search for exactly what the spell requires. And even once the spell is cast, you will need to back up your magic on the physical plane by taking whatever action is necessary to set things in motion.

This chapter contains 27 spells to bring magic into all areas of your life. The spells begin with meeting angels and guides, and then you can start to work magic for healing and protection, self-empowerment, luck and prosperity, love and romance, friends and relationships and more. It will show you how to work with a variety of magical ingredients including talismans, charms, spell bags and an assortment of stones, plants, herbs, trees and oils. You will also learn to record your efforts by creating your own spell book or Book of Shadows.

THE SPELLWEAVER'S ART

The art of weaving, or casting, spells is what attracts many people to magic. Spells are magical formulae that are designed to change or adapt reality to the magic-worker's will. They are serious matters, so be sure that your motives are pure and that your object is both achievable and desirable. You should never use magic to interfere with the free will of another, and whatever you give out in magic is returned threefold, so always make sure you are working for the highest good of all concerned. Spells are usually cast once the magic circle has been created and the otherworldly beings have been summoned. Always have your spells planned out in advance and make sure you have all the equipment gathered together before you step into your magic circle.

Spells are usually worked in a circle that is large enough to hold you and your equipment.

SIX STEPS TO SUCCESS

Natural magic requires six basic components for success, so before you embark on a spell, check that each one is in place. The first requirement is desire and need. This may sound obvious, but if you don't truly desire what you are working for then your energy won't really be behind it and your thought-forms won't take shape in the astral plane.

The second requirement is emotional involvement. This fuels your desire and need, and further strengthens the links between the astral and the physical planes: once your thought-forms are strong enough on the astral level, they cannot help but manifest themselves on the physical.

Thirdly, you need to have enough knowledge and to have set realistic targets. Knowledge is power. It includes knowing which tools to use and when and how to use them. For instance, in a spell to attract love, some herbs will be more suitable than others, and certain times will be more favourable than others. Having realistic expectations means knowing which magical goals are naturally within your reach, and which are not. No spell can make you superhuman and achieve the impossible.

How many spells?

If you are new to working spells it is likely that the first one you perform will use up a lot of psychic energy, so try not to wear yourself out. In the beginning it is probably best to confine yourself to one or two spells in a session, although as you become more practised you may do three or four.

A magic circle can be made out of individual items as well as an unbroken cord. If you are doing this kind of circle, use numbers and symbolism to add power to your spell.

The fourth component is belief. This can be difficult in the beginning, but having enough confidence and belief in the outcome of your spells is crucial. Lack of belief and negative thoughts about it will undermine what you are doing. The popular tag on the end of spells, "so mote it be" ("so may it be"), is an affirmation of belief and has been used for centuries to assert a spell's reality in the here and now.

In the spirit of the old occult saying that declares "power shared is power lost", the fifth requirement is the ability to keep silent. This helps to protect the energy you have put into your spells from outside influences, some of which may be negative. Lastly, you need to be willing to take whatever practical steps are necessary to back up your magic in the everyday world. For instance, it is no good doing a spell for prosperity and then sitting around waiting for money to shower down on you from above. You will have to create and work your spell by taking appropriate action, being confident that your magic will guide you in the right direction.

The Book of Shadows

The traditional name for a witch or magician's spell book is a 'Book of Shadows'. Its title may allude to the shadows cast by the flickering candlelight that the practitioner worked by as they wrote up their magical diary, in the days before electricity. On another level, it may also refer to the fact that the book, like the magic itself, should be kept hidden and out of sight in the 'shadows'. According to legend, these books were once written in secret alphabets in case they fell into the wrong hands. The first time such a book was ever made public was when Gerald Gardner, founder of the Wicca movement, published his own early in the 20th century.

Making your own collection of precious and symbolic items will help you to be more creative with your spells. Invest time in your equipment to imprint them with emotional energy.

KEEPING A SPELL BOOK

Get into the habit of recording your spells and other magic work in a personal magical diary, or spell book, usually known as a Book of Shadows.

Originating in the late Middle Ages, when literacy became more widespread, the practice of keeping a log has become a standard tool in modern magic. It is traditional to write up the diary by hand and to record in detail your spells and magic work, including the words that you used and any equipment, as well as the outcome. Many people also like to include transcriptions of dreams and astral travel, insights gained during meditation and other discoveries on their personal journey in their spell book. Over time, it will prove an invaluable record of your findings, failures and successes. Today, there are an infinite variety of beautiful notebooks available in the shops, made with handmade paper, coloured paper, tissue leaves and so on. Look for something that appeals to you, or spend some time making your own record book, and enjoy transforming it into a magical treasure trove.

BE CREATIVE

Once you have grasped the fundamentals of how magic works and the different attributes of the various magical tools and helpers – be they herbs, oils, gemstones, colours or deities – you can begin to create your own spells. The possibilities here are endless; it is a question of experimenting and trying out different combinations until you find something that is effective. In many ways your own formulae will be more potent, as you will have invested time, thought and emotional energy to give them an energetic imprint that is uniquely yours.

Golden rules for spellweaving

- Work from the heart and do what you do with gentleness and responsibility.
- Seek no revenge and send no ill will - for whatever you send will return to you.
- Do not manipulate the free will of another, or attempt to control events to suit yourself.
- Keep yourself, your working space and equipment clean and free of psychic dirt.
- To insure against negative influence always include the words 'for the highest good of all' in a spell.
- At the end of every spell affirm your belief in its power by saying 'And so mote it be!'.

Undoing a spell

If you wish to undo a spell, write it down on a piece of paper. Light a white candle and some frankincense then burn the written spell in the candle flame and say:
This spell is undone. So mote it be.

SPIRIT AND ANGEL SPELLS

There are many different ways of connecting with angels and celestial beings, but weaving spells is an excellent method. You can use these spells whenever you are seeking guidance, clarity or inspiration from on high, during times of vulnerability or for blessings. Always remember to thank the Beings of Light; whether you sense their presence or not, they will be there.

The six-pointed star used in the Spell for Connection is a powerful mystical symbol.

A SPELL FOR CONNECTION

Sitting within the six-pointed star will help to develop your connection with celestial beings. Bless your equipment before you begin.

You will need
rhythmic spiritual drumming music
lotus oil
natural sea salt
6 violet candles
6 amethysts
gold candle

1 With spiritual drumming playing in the background, face east and anoint your head, hands and feet with lotus oil.

2 Draw a six-pointed star, made of two overlapping equal-sized triangles, in salt around you. The star should be big enough for you to sit in the centre.

3 Sit or stand in the centre of the star and place a violet candle on each of the six points, beginning at the south. Light the candles in turn, saying the following. As you light the first, say:
O Angel Gabriel, lift my spirit to Levanah, to draw down her magic into my heart.

Light the candle to your right and say:
O Angel Raphael, lift my spirit to touch Kokab that I may draw down his wisdom and truth.

Turn to the next candle, light it and say:
O Angel Zamael, lift my spirit to touch Madim that I may draw down courage and strength.

Light the next candle, and say:
O Angel Cassiel, lift my spirit to touch Shabbathai that I may draw down understanding and patience.

Light the next candle, and say:
O Angel Sachiel, lift my spirit to touch Tzedek that I may draw down righteousness.

Turn to the last candle, light it and say:
O Angel Anael, lift my spirit to touch Nogah that I may draw down love and beauty.

4 Then place an amethyst next to each candle, in the same order as above. Put the gold candle in front of you, inside the star, light it and say:
Mighty Michael, Angel of the Sun, lift my spirit to touch Shemesh that I may be drawn closer and closer to the light of the Divine. This I ask of you, that I may grow ever closer to the truth. Adonai, Lord of Light, Adonai, Adonai.

5 Now close your eyes and sit with your hands in your lap, palms up. Stay here for up to 20 minutes and feel the essence of spiritual light filling your body, mind and soul.

6 To close your spell, pick up the amethysts and blow out the candles, starting with the last one you lit and ending with the first. Close your cord circle, saying:
May divine will be done.

The colour violet, and the amethyst, are both connected to the crown chakra, the chakra of spirituality.

The angel blessing can be spoken on its own, if you feel it is needed, without candles and incense.

An angel altar should be left for 24 hours, and then dismantled.

ANGEL BLESSING

This spell can be performed as a way to bless and consecrate yourself.

You will need
2.7 m (9 ft) white cord
white candle
frankincense
charcoal burner

1 Open your cord circle and place the candle, frankincense and burner in the centre. Turn to the south and set light to the candle and the charcoal. Sprinkle some frankincense on to the hot charcoal saying:
Lord of Light, this offering I make.

2 Next, say the Angelic Invocation. While you say the first line, touch your head, as you say the second line touch your stomach, as you say the third line touch your left shoulder, and say the remainder of the invocation as you touch your right shoulder:
Uriel above me
Michael beneath me
Raphael to my left
Gabriel to my right
By the power of these Great Angels
Surround me with light.

3 Visualize an angel in each of the four directions. Bow your head and say "thank you" to each one. Ask them for what you feel you need; humility, an open heart, strength etc.

4 When you have finished thank each angel again and let him depart. Blow out the candle and close your circle.

AN ANGEL ALTAR

You can use this altar for someone you know is in need of angelic protection or healing, but never perform spells for another without their permission.

Cast a circle of salt on your altar, then place a white candle, some frankincense and a photograph of the subject within it. Light the candle and the frankincense and say the Angelic Invocation while touching the head and relevant parts of the person's body in the photograph and saying their name rather than your own. Leave the altar as it is for 24 hours, then remove the circle of salt, gathering it up so that it can be sprinkled on the earth outside, or over a pot of earth. For serious situations, leave for 48 hours, repeating the invocation after 24 hours.

A spell seeking guidance

Spells can be used as oracles when you need an answer to an important question. This simple version uses a 'magical book', which could be any book containing spiritual teachings. It is best done during a waning moon.

You will need
blue candle
your thickest magical book
sheet of paper
black ink

1 Light the candle and place it beside the magical book. Concentrating on your question, write it down on a new sheet of paper in black ink. Fold the paper into a narrow bookmark shape. Say:
In this book I seek; in this book I peek.
Reveal a clue, now heed me.

2 Slide the paper into the book at random, then read the words next to the paper. This should help answer your question if it was clear. Pinch out the candle.

SPELLS FOR PSYCHIC HELP

Psychic powers can be developed by learning to trust our instinctive, intuitive responses rather than rationalizing and analysing everything that we do. Traditionally, women are said to be more in touch with this aspect of themselves than men, but this is not a hard and fast rule. Regardless of our gender it means cultivating a relationship with the "feminine" or "yin" aspect of the life force, and one way of doing this is by drawing on the powers of the moon when casting spells and working magic.

Round white stones are used to represent the full moon, or increase your connection with her.

DRAWING DOWN THE MOON

Draw on the powers of the moon to refresh and rejuvenate you for the month ahead and help you get in touch with your sensitivity and powers of intuition. The best time for this spell is 2 days before the full moon.

You will need
13 circular stones of any size
salt
aromatherapy burner
jasmine essential oil
9 white or cream candles

1 Beginning in the south, make a circle of 12 of your chosen stones in a clockwise direction. Place the 13th in the centre.

2 Sprinkle the stones with salt. Light the aromatherapy burner and put in 3 drops of jasmine oil.

3 Place 8 candles around the circle and one by the centre stone. Then light the candles as you say these words: *Magna Dei, Light of the Night, I light these candles to guide your moonrays here. I ask you to come and bless this circle.*

4 Stand facing south, with your arms outstretched above your head and your feet quite wide apart. Reach towards the sky and say this lunar invocation: *Hail to thee, Sophia, holy spirit of the wise moon. I call upon you to enter and fill me with your light. Protect me and guide me on the moonway. Teach me your wisdom and truth as I seek your clarity and guidance.*

5 Draw down the powers of the moon. Allow yourself to be refreshed and refilled with the feminine virtues of wisdom, beauty and grace. Let the moon bless your feelings and perceptions until you feel energized and content. Lower your arms.

6 Finish by saying "thank you". Blow out your candles and close the circle.

The spell is particularly of benefit to a woman, as the moon cycles reflect her own.

Psychic Dreams

You can encourage psychic dreams with an aquamarine crystal. Store your dream crystal in a little pouch made of shiny pale blue or silver material, decorated with moon charms and sequins. Before you use the aquamarine you need to clear your dreamtime by first using jet in your pouch under your pillow, until any nightmares you may have been suffering from are gone. Then dedicate or bless your aquamarine, place it in the pouch, and put the pouch under your pillow for perceptive dreams.

You can dedicate or bless your dream crystal every month, at the full moon, for extra potency.

Opening the Inner Gates

The gate of inner vision is situated at the 6th, or brow, chakra, also known as the "third eye", which is located just above the eyebrows. Seeing with this "inner" eye is associated with clairvoyance. Best time: Monday, waxing moon.

You will need
2.7 m (9 ft) white cord
flower
red candle
small bowl of water
stone
sandalwood incense
picture of an open door or gate, or the Moon Tarot card

1 Open your cord circle and place the flower in the east, the candle in the south, the bowl of water in the west and the stone in the north. Light the incense in the centre of the circle.

2 Sit in the centre of the circle with the picture or Tarot card on your lap. Close your eyes, centre yourself and focus on the intention; be sure that your wish to work with inner vision is for the highest good of all.

3 Stand up and make an opening gesture to each of the four quarters in turn, saying the appropriate sentence as you pick up each object. Light the candle as you speak the following words about candle fire:
Open my mind like a growing flower, may my vision now empower.
Open my mind to the candle fire, may my vision now inspire.
Open my mind to the water's flow, that on vision journeys I may go.
Open my mind to this stone so cold, that visions I shall safely hold.

4 Pick up the picture or card and hold it out in front of your heart. Circle or turn around four times, saying:
Open gates that I may roam,
Safely bring my knowledge home.

5 Sit down and close your eyes again. Relax and sit in meditation for a while, letting any pictures or images come and go freely.

6 When you are ready, open your eyes and put out the incense. Close the circle widdershins and dispose of your equipment appropriately.

Psychic protection

As you become more sensitive to spiritual energies, you need to make sure that you are protected. Feeling excessively tired and drained is often a sign that you are picking up too much psychic dirt. Best time: Saturday, waxing moon. Carry this spell with you for the next few days.

You will need
12 tealights
indigo blue candle
myrrh incense
carnelian stone
vervain Bach flower essence
15 cm (6in) square of indigo cloth
red thread

1 Arrange the tealights in a circle, then open it deosil, lighting the first tealight in the east. Sit in the centre of the circle, facing west, and light the indigo candle and the incense.

2 Close your eyes and visualize yourself in a golden globe of pale blue light with orange flames around the surface.

3 Take the carnelian stone and bring it to rest on your hara, the body's life energy centre about 5cm (2in) below the navel. Hold the stone here and repeat this invocation three times:
Bright angels of the astral plane, please come and bless this stone and fill it with your power, love and protection.
After the third repetition, say:
Thank you (to the angels). And so mote it be!

4 Add two drops of vervain essence to the stone and wrap it up in the cloth. Tie the parcel with the thread. Extinguish the candle and incense then close the circle widdershins, pinching out each tealight, starting in the east. Dispose of the candles with respect and do not reuse.

The carnelian is connected to the hara, the personal power centre or Shaman's Cave.

Carnelian

This deep red or orange stone has the ability to protect you from negativity. It links to your own inner power and strength during times of psychic stress.

SPELLS FOR HEALING

There has always been a strong link between magic and medicine, and any distinction between the two is often very blurred. In many cultures, spells and incantations have been used for a variety of healing purposes. Traditionally, knowledge of healing spells was the province of the village wise woman, the shaman or the medicine-man. However, it is accepted that recovery from illness has much to do with state of mind, and with a little knowledge of the art and craft of magic, it is possible for you to practise healing magic for yourself or those who are close to you.

A SPELL FOR HEALING

This is a spell to bring healing. Ask permission if you are doing it for another. Before you perform this spell, find a suitable tree – ash, birch, juniper and cedar trees are all good. You may prefer to cast your circle outside next to the tree, and work within nature. The best day for working this spell is a Sunday.

You will need
2.7 m (9 ft) white cord
gold candle
gold pen
15 cm (6 in) square of natural paper
knife
lime
gold thread
15 cm (6 in) square of orange cloth

Binding the spell with gold thread (the colour of the sun), before burying it under your chosen tree, helps to invoke the sun's healing powers.

1 Open the circle and honour the four directions. Light the candle and say these words:
Angel Och, healing spirit of the sun,
I light this flame to honour your presence
And ask you to hear this prayer.

2 Write the name of the person to be healed on the paper, visualizing health and wellbeing surrounding them.

3 Cut the lime in two lengthways. Fold the paper three times and place it between the two halves. Bind it together with gold thread and say:
Powers of lime
Health is mine/thine
Cleanse the body, cleanse the mind
Spirit pure, fill my (or say another person's name) being
With health, with health, with health.

4 Place the bound lime in the orange cloth and bind it with gold thread. Close the circle in the usual way.

5 Now take the spell and bury it near the base of the tree. Ask the spirit of the tree to help you (or another person) to return to good health. Thank the tree, and depart.

The colours of gold and orange, used repeatedly in this spell, are colours of the sun, which is renowned for its healing powers.

A SPELL TO HEAL THE EARTH

Modern magic workers like to use their skills to help heal the damage that we are causing to our planet. Choose a place where the Earth's resources are being used or abused, such as a polluted river or a quarry. This is a spell of atonement.

You will need
moss agate crystal
white rose

1 Holding the moss agate crystal in your right hand and the rose in your left, repeat the following prayer of atonement. As you say the last line, lay down your moss agate.
Spirits of this place, I come in peace but with a heavy heart. I wish to say how sorry I am for what my brothers and sisters are doing to you in their ignorance. I come to make an offering to show you that I am sorry for taking from you without respect. I ask your forgiveness. I ask you to help humanity to see how precious all life is.
I make this offering to you.

2 Transfer the rose to your right hand. Hold it to your heart, say the following:
Creator, guide us all in the ways of peace, love, wisdom and truth. I call you here to (say the name of the place) to bring the Divine to this area, to bless it with your healing love. May (say the name of the place) now be sacred again.

3 Lay down the white rose on the earth. Visualize the whole area filling with white light, embracing it with illumination. End the spell with the Native American saying:
"Mitake Oyasin" (we are all related).

The white rose stands for purity and innocence, and is an appropriate gift for the Earth.

Frankincense is the incense associated with the sun. It is not difficult to see why when you see the rich ambers, yellows and golden colours of the loose resin.

A spell for good health

Each planet has its own magic symbol, which can be used to harness its powers. The sigil of the sun is used in this spell for health; it can also be used for success and prosperity. Sunday is the best day to perform this spell.

You will need
2.7 m (9 ft) white cord
gold candle
frankincense and burner
gold pen
15 cm (6 in) square of natural paper
a lock of your hair

1 Open the circle, taking with you all the ingredients for the spell. Light the candle, and begin to burn the frankincense, and say these words:
Angel Och, healing spirit of the sun,
I light this flame to honour your presence
And ask you to hear this prayer.

2 Take the piece of paper, and write the name of the person whom the spell is for, visualizing health and wellbeing surrounding them as you do so.

3 On the other side of the paper draw the sigil of the sun, and write the words 'Angel Och'. Hold the piece of paper to your heart, with the name facing inwards, and visualize golden-orange light filling your heart, and then the whole of your body. Repeat:
I am healthy and well.

4 Take the lock of hair and lay it on the spell, on the side of the sigil of the sun. Fold the piece of paper six times so that it forms a small packet. Keep it in a very safe place, or preferably, carry it with you, close to your heart.

The sigil of the sun is often used for healing.

SPELLS TO EMPOWER

T he path of magic is the road towards self-empowerment. Instead of being a victim of circumstance, magic encourages us to use our free will to make creative choices for ourselves, in line with our soul's highest purpose. A universal law is that "like attracts like", so whatever we give out returns to us. Lack of self-confidence and negative self-beliefs stand in the way of us getting what we want for ourselves, but we can use spellweaving to help remove these obstacles and increase our personal power and magnetism.

Before you undertake the Aura of Confidence spell, you should perform the Golden Light Breathing Exercise, to energize yourself.

A SPELL TO REMOVE AN OBSTACLE

If you feel that you are stuck and unable to move on for some reason, and can identify the cause, try this spell to remove the obstruction in your life. For this you will need to create a gift to Mother Earth, it should be something you have made yourself, like a cake or painting, or it can be a loving action such as clearing a stream, picking up litter, or planting a tree. This spell needs to be performed outside.

You will need
a gift for Mother Earth
a fossil or a blessed stone
natural sea salt

1 Take your gift and fossil to the place you have chosen to perform your spell. Beginning with the east, with the salt draw a deosil circle around yourself, large enough to sit in, repeating the opening circle invocation.

2 Place yourself comfortably on the ground, facing north. Say the following invocation three times with as much feeling as possible.
Mother Earth, I bring you a gift of (state what) because I have come to you today to ask you to help me. I wish to remove (state your obstacle).
I ask you with all my heart if you will talk with the Angel Cassiel on my behalf, and that together you help me to lift the condition. Please help me to understand why it is there, so that I may move forward, safe in the knowledge that I am
part of a loving universe. Teach me, Mother Earth, to be wise and to trust in the beauty of all life. Show me the way to remove this obstacle so that I may grow in understanding and wisdom. (Take your fossil).
I ask that this fossil, when it is buried in your being, may take away my burden and help me to endure, because it is within you and you are with me.

3 Add "thank you" at the end of the third time. Bury your fossil. Send the energies home by saying "So mote it be", while visualizing the completion of your task.

4 Leave the earth your gift, or tell her your pledge has been done, or will be done on a certain day. It is important to give, or you may not receive.

5 Starting with the west, break your circle of salt widdershins and brush it away into the surrounding area, until you are back at west again. Walk away, leaving your troubles behind you. Do not look back.

If you have a weakness for chocolate cake, make this your gift to Mother Earth.

AURA OF CONFIDENCE

Tap into the sun's powers to radiate self-confidence. If you are not confident, then it is unlikely that your magic will be very successful. Make sure you practise Golden Light Breathing (see Preparation Rituals) before you work this spell to energize you. The best time for this spell is Sunday during a waxing moon.

You will need

2.7 m (9 ft) white cord
gold candle
gold pen
15 cm (6 in) square of natural paper
larch Bach flower essence
envelope
gold ribbon
goblet of golden drink
round, golden biscuit
tin box

1 Open a circle in the east. Sit in the centre, facing south, light the candle and say:
O Michael, Angel of the Sun, I call upon your presence and ask you to shine your golden light upon my life. Strengthen my aura with your positive rays.

2 Close your eyes and visualize yourself surrounded by an egg-shaped space. This is your aura. Breathing gently, watch as the Angel of the Sun beams

Think carefully before you write down the things you would like to achieve.

As you drink the golden drink, and eat the biscuit, visualize the sun's warming powers.

his golden light rays towards you. With each inbreath, feel the light warming and energizing your whole being.

3 As you breathe out, see the egg-shaped space filling up with golden light and becoming bigger and brighter as your aura expands outwards. Repeat to yourself six times these words: *I can.*

4 Open your eyes and write down six things that you would like to achieve in the next six months. Choose things that seem out of reach at the moment, but not so far away that you feel they

are impossible. Drip six drops of larch essence on the paper, fold it up and put it into the envelope. Tie the gold ribbon around the envelope.

5 Eat the biscuit and drink the drink; both represent the power of the sun. Snuff the candle, thank the angel Michael and close the circle.

6 Put the spell into the tin box. Bury the box under a hazel tree and leave it for six months, undisturbed. When this time has passed, you may unearth the spell to check your progress.

Amulet for strengthening willpower

Making magic is about focusing your will to achieve a result. The more focused and determined you are, the better the likely outcome. Keep this amulet in your pocket and carry it with you; whenever you feel weak-willed, holding on to it will remind you of your resolve. The best time to perform this spell is on a Tuesday, during a waxing moon.

You will need

wand
red candle
haematite stone
centaury Bach flower essence
12.5 cm (5 in) square of red cloth
gold thread

1 Cast a magic circle with your wand and visualize it as a ring of fire. Put your spell ingredients in the centre and light the candle.

2 Begin in the east; hold the stone in your left hand and pass it over the candle flame, saying the first line of the following words. Then turn to the south, west and north in turn saying the second, third and fourth lines respectively and passing the stone over the candle each time.
I call the Sylphs, the helpers of Air.
I call the Salamanders, the helpers of Fire.
I call the Undines, the helpers of Water.
I call the Gnomes, the helpers of Earth.

3 Then continue with the rest of the incantation:

O elemental beings, please bless this stone so that it may remind me that I have the mental power to achieve my goal (or say whatever particular goal you are trying to achieve), sticking to what I feel is right for me. For I know that I am as firm and as steadfast as a rock.

4 Place the stone on the red cloth, together with a few drops of centaury essence. Bind the stone in the cloth with the golden thread.

5 Say 'thank you' to your elemental helpers and let them depart. Blow out the candle and use your wand to close the circle.

GOOD FORTUNE SPELLS

In everyday language, a lucky life is said to be a "charmed life", and good luck charms and talismans have always played an important role in natural magic. They have been worn or carried as protection against the "evil eye" since ancient times. They have also been given to those embarking on any of life's "journeys" – whether a literal journey or a metaphorical one like a wedding, the start of a new job or the birth of a child.

A SPELL FOR GOOD LUCK

Work with the magic of the oak tree when making a good luck spell. You will need a spell bag or pouch, which you should make yourself, and a suitable oak tree. The best time for this spell is on a Thursday, during a full moon.

You will need
small amethyst
turquoise stone
oak leaves
cinquefoil essential oil
sprig of rosemary
spell bag

Turquoise brings blessings, and amethyst offers protection, so these two stones make an ideal combination for a good luck spell.

If you make the spell bag yourself it will have far greater potency than if you buy it. It can be used again and again, and don't forget, the effort, time and energy you invest will be returned threefold.

1 Greet the spirit of your tree and tell it your intentions. Place the amethyst at its base as an offering. Walking deosil round the tree, repeat the following four times:
   O Sachiel, Angel of Jupiter, I ask you to hear my call.
   Light my path, guide my actions, words and thoughts and those of all I am yet to meet, that by the power of your might, all will be fortunate to my sight.
   Good fortune growing, growing.

2 Anoint the turquoise stone and the oak leaves with the cinquefoil oil, while visualizing yourself surrounded by the arms of the mighty oak tree.

3 Place the turquoise, the oak leaves and the sprig of rosemary in your spell bag. Hold the spell bag up to the oak tree and say the following words:
   Heart of Oak, you are my heart and with honour I shall carry you by my side.
   Thank you.

4 Carry this spell with you for good fortune, and store it carefully when not in use. You could also do this spell as a special gift for a friend, and then give them the spell. But ask first.

A SPELL TO IMPROVE BUSINESS

Repeat this spell regularly to keep your business affairs flowing smoothly. Giving a gift to the energies that are helping you with your business pleases them and encourages them to work positively on your behalf. Rice and wheat are symbols of new life, and they encourage fertile opportunities. Do this spell every month for a while. It is best performed on the first day of a new moon.

You will need

3, 7 or 9 fresh basil leaves
bowl of spring water
spoon
citrine stone
dried ears of wheat
rice grains
mint leaves

1 Bless your equipment and ingredients. Soak the basil leaves in the bowl of water for one hour, stirring occasionally in a deosil (clockwise) direction.

2 Beginning to the right of the entrance at your place of work, walk deosil round the building or work area,

Potency is added to magic if you use special tools for the task. This beautiful silver spoon is used for stirring the water in the spell to improve business.

sprinkling the aromatic water as you go and repeating the following invocation until you are finished:
Business expand, business grow
secure and successful –
my dealings flow.

3 Bless the citrine stone, wheat, rice and mint leaves again, then place the stone where you keep your money or transactions. Offer the corn and the rice to the energies that are helping you with your business affairs by sprinkling them in discreet places around your office or workplace.

4 Carry the mint leaves with you in your money pocket or purse. Replace them with fresh ones each time you re-work the spell.

Spell for safe travel

For this spell you need to find a stone that is different in some way from other stones in your area. Ask its permission to be used in a spell for safe passage. Use it for yourself or another. The best time to do this spell is a Wednesday.

You will need

2.7 m (9 ft) white cord
yellow candle, blessed
lavender essential oil or incense
aromatherapy burner (if using oil)
an unusual stone from your area
yellow and violet or blue paints
artist's paintbrush

1 Open your cord circle in the east and honour the four directions (see The Four Great Powers in chapter 3). Place the candle and oil burner (if using) in the centre and light them, adding a few drops of lavender oil to the burner. Alternatively, light the incense.

2 Sit in the centre of the circle facing east and paint your stone bright yellow. When it is dry, paint a triangle in violet or blue, with a line near its base as shown. This is the alchemical symbol for Air.

3 Hold the stone up to the east and repeat the following invocation eight times, making sure that you say 'thank you' to the angel Raphael after the eighth time.
O Raphael, Angel of the East, fill this stone with
your blessing and protection. I pray to you for a
safe journey for me (or say someone else's name).
Guard me (or say someone else's name) and guide
me (or another name) on the path this journey
takes, until I (or another name) can return.

4 Close your spell and circle in the usual way. Carry your stone with you on your travels, returning it to Mother Earth when the journey is ended and you are safely home.

This is the alchemical symbol for Air that you need to paint on the stone for the travel spell.

SPELLS FOR THE HOME

Our homes and possessions are like an extension of ourselves. In magical terms they are connected to us along fine energy pathways and we can use magic to make things happen in our physical surroundings. Traditionally, many home spells are concerned with blessing and protection, although we can also work spells to help us find things that are lost and to buy and sell property successfully.

Sweep your house with a birch broom to cleanse the physical and spiritual environment.

A HOUSE BLESSING SPELL

If you have recently moved into a new home or there have been upheavals in your domestic life, perform this blessing to consecrate the space. The best time is on a Sunday morning during a waxing moon. You should be alone.

You will need
natural sea salt
small bowl
rose geranium essential oil
white candle
aromatherapy burner
a few grains of organic rice
15 cm (6 in) square of golden fabric

1 Bless and consecrate yourself using the Angelic Invocation. Place the salt in the bowl. Starting in the top right-hand corner of your home and working deosil through the building, sprinkle a pinch of salt in the four corners of every room, door and window. As you sprinkle, say:
I cleanse and purify this room of all unnecessary or negative vibrations.

2 Take the rose geranium oil and light the white candle. Again working clockwise around the building, place the candle in the centre of each room. Anoint all doors and windows with a little of the oil as you say:

I call upon the Angels of Light and Love to bless this home and all who enter here. May love, happiness and harmony prevail.

3 Place the candle in the centre of your main living room. Light the aromatherapy burner and add six drops of rose geranium oil to it. Sit quietly, visualizing your home filled with the qualities that you desire.

4 Let the candle burn down almost completely, then anoint it with rose geranium oil and sprinkle with rice as thanks to the helpful energies. Snuff the candle, wrap it in the gold fabric and place the spell beneath your front door mat or as close to your door as possible, saying:
This I place so that all who enter here will be blessed.

5 Leave the parcel undisturbed until the next time you perform a cleansing or blessing ceremony, when it can be replaced by a new parcel.

Grains of rice are a precious gift from the Earth and are often used in magical spells and rituals as a symbol of giving thanks.

Horseshoes, hung with the open ends upwards on front doors, provide protection and strength.

A spell for finding

This spell uses your powers of visualization in which you imagine a lost object being drawn back to you. It is best performed on a Wednesday, the day of the week associated with Mercury, the god of thieves. You will need to find a hazel tree to cut yourself a wand. Ask permission of the spirit of the tree first and leave a lock of your hair as a gift. Perform this spell during a waxing moon, on a Wednesday.

You will need
20 cm (8 in) wand of hazel
honeysuckle essential oil, diluted in carrier oil
yellow cloth

1 Find a quiet place where you won't be disturbed and draw a deosil circle around yourself with the hazel wand, saying these words:
By the powers of heaven and earth I cast this sacred circle in the name of love, light, wisdom and truth.

2 Perform the Golden Light Breathing exercise (see Preparation Rituals in chapter 5), then anoint your temples, forehead and hands with honeysuckle oil. Sit or stand in the north, facing south, close your eyes and visualize yourself on a high mountain peak made of magnetic crystals. You can see for miles in any direction.

3 Now see yourself opening your hands, palms are facing upwards. Say this invocation:
Swift and sure, my (name the object) return to me.

4 Imagine that your property is being drawn back to you, by the strength of the magnetic mountain. Draw it back with as much willpower and concentrated thought as you can. Note any pictures that come into your mind and from which direction your property returns to you in the visualization.

5 To add to the spells effectiveness, write what you have lost on a piece of paper and pin it up where you will see it.

6 Say 'thank you' to the energies that have helped you. Close your spell then move your wand widdershins from the end to the beginning of the original circle, saying:
This spell is done.

7 Wrap the wand in the cloth and store it in a safe space with the rest of your magical equipment. If the lost object is in someone else's possession, he or she should feel compelled to return it. If nothing happens, try the spell again a week later, or accept that it is irretrievable.

The hazel wand in a spell for finding gives magical protection during the ceremony.

Burning frankincense in a spell for selling will cleanse your home and purify it of old vibrations.

A SPELL FOR SELLING

When you need to sell your house, or any other object, work a spell to attract the right buyer. Burning frankincense will cleanse your home and purify it of old vibrations, making it ready for the next keeper. The best time for this spell is on a Wednesday during a waxing moon.

You will need
an altar
a vase of yellow flowers
frankincense and burner
item for sale, or a picture or symbol of it
yellow ribbon

1 Hold the item being sold, its picture, or a symbol of it in your right hand. Stand in front of your altar and turn to face west, the direction for letting go. Turn slowly, from west to east, moving deosil as you say:

I let go of this (name the object), so that something new can come in its place.

2 Place the vase of flowers on the altar and burn the frankincense. Tell the spirit of the item you are selling that it is time to part company and that a new keeper is coming to take over.

3 Tie up the item or its symbol with yellow ribbon and put it on your altar in the east. Call on the east wind, saying:
Hail to thee East Wind. This (name the object) sells, this (name the object) sells. Please guide the next keeper here speedily so that I am free for something new.

4 Say thank you to the East Wind, saying:
For the highest good of all concerned, so mote it be!

Flowers to help a sale

To enhance the magic of a spell for selling, change the vase of flowers on the altar each day of the week for one week. Repeat the spell if the item hasn't sold, and repeat weekly until it goes.
Saturday: evergreens, cypress
Sunday: orange flowers
Monday: white flowers, river plants
Tuesday: red flowers
Wednesday: yellow flowers
Thursday: violet or purple flowers
Friday: pink flowers, roses

SPELLS FOR FRIENDSHIP

Attracting love and friendship are among the most popular reasons for spells, but remember that when you make magic you cannot use your powers to influence the free will of another. You may ask for someone to share your love with, but do not name them: whoever answers will be right for your needs. If you are having trouble manifesting results in this area, you may need to look at what is blocking you – this may be negative self-beliefs or else others may be gossiping behind your back.

Warm pink and gold are both colours associated with love and healing.

A LOVE SPELL

Try this spell for your perfect love match. Before you start, take a long bath or shower, then spray your whole body with rose water. Work this spell on a Friday, during a waxing moon.

You will need
bottle of rose water
2.7 m (9 ft) white cord
4 green candles
charcoal and heatproof burner
pink candle
rose petals
rose essential oil
cinnamon stick
gold pen
glass bowl of spring water

1 Open your cord circle and step inside with your equipment. Light a green candle in each direction. Invoke the four winds in turn, repeating the following words four times, each time substituting the next direction:
Hail to thee East/South/West/North Wind. I call for love and make this offering of light to you.

2 Place some charcoal in the heatproof burner in the centre of the circle and light it. Light the pink candle next to it. Do the Golden Light Breathing exercise until you feel full of energy.

3 You are calling for new beginnings, so face east. Put seven rose petals to one side, then rub a little rose oil into the rest. Crush the cinnamon stick and place it on the burning charcoal with the scented rose petals.

4 Focus your heart upon feeling love. Write the word "love" in gold ink on the seven reserved petals. Float them gently in the bowl of water.

5 Sit in the circle and breathe in the scent of rose and cinnamon. Take time to centre yourself and build up charged energy. Open your hands, open your heart and repeat your request seven times, with genuine feeling:
O Anael, Angel of Venus, I call upon you to fill me with love, that I may feel a joyous heart. I ask that I may share this love with another who will come to me of his/her free will and together we shall know the beauty of a loving union. I ask this for the highest good of all.

6 At the end of the seventh request say "thank you". Blow out the candles, and close the cord circle widdershins. Pour the water and petals respectfully on the earth.

Cinnamon brings success, and is also an aphrodisiac. Breathe in its warm, sensual smell as you work.

A SPELL TO STOP GOSSIP

Gossip produces negative thought-forms that can become attached to our energy field and create problems for us. You will need to find a suitable holly tree to bury your spell under – you might want to perform your spell next to it, too. Do this on a Tuesday, during a waning moon.

You will need

2.7 m (9 ft) white cord
red candle
red pen
very small square of natural paper
snapdragon (antirrhinum) flower
thorn
red ribbon

1 Open your cord circle. Light the red candle, face south and sit down.

2 Using the red pen, write the name of the person or organization that is gossiping about you on the paper square. If you do not know the source of the gossip-mongering write "whoever is".

3 Carefully take one of the larger flower heads from the snapdragon and gently open it up. Roll the piece of paper into a tiny scroll and place it inside the flower, repeating the following words five times:
Speak only goodness, think only kind. Look to your own faults and not to mine.

4 Keep the scroll of paper in place by sealing the flower head with the thorn, and as you do this say:
Flower seal, flower heal
lips that speak not from the heart.

5 Take your spell to a holly tree. Tell the spirit of the tree your intention to bury it there and ask it to protect your good name.

6 Bury the snapdragon flower head under the holly tree. Say thank you by tying a small red ribbon to a branch.

7 As you walk away, know that you are leaving the malicious gossip behind you. Do not look back.

The colour red is associated with bringing change in difficult circumstances, and with courage, while snapdragons are used to redirect negative energies into a more creative outlet.

A spell to make friends

Perform this spell in a horseshoe shape within your magical cord circle. The colour green and the apple are both sacred to Venus, and sweet peas are the traditional flower of friendship. Work this spell on a Friday, with a waxing moon.

You will need

2.7 m (9 ft) white cord
7 green candles
aromatherapy burner
sweet pea essential oil, diluted in sesame oil
5 seeds from a sweet organic apple
gold pen
natural paper
heatproof container

1 Open the cord circle in the east. Place the green candles in a horseshoe shape, with the open end facing north and you facing south in front of it.

2 Place the aromatherapy burner in the centre of the horseshoe shape and add seven drops of sweet pea oil. Lay the apple seeds in the centre too. Light the first candle to your left and say:
Nogah, Nogah, light of love,
I honour and illuminate your beauty and call upon you to help me today.

3 Using the lit candle, light the next one. Light all the candles this way, then light the burner.

4 Using the gold pen, draw the sigil of Venus on the paper. Beneath this write your wish:
By the powers of the four directions, above me and below me, within me and without,
I call for favour with Anael, Angel of Venus,
I call for friends of the same heart, that joy and celebration shall prevail.

5 Burn your spell in the flame of the last candle to be lit, dropping it into the heatproof container. Visualize the smoke carrying your wish to the sky. Blow out the candles widdershins and close your circle in the usual way. As you extinguish the last candle say: *And so mote it be!*

6 Take the apple seeds to a prepared site or pot and dedicate them as follows:
Nogah, these apple seeds I plant to honour you and please you. And as they grow, so is my life blessed with joy of friendships new.

The seal of Venus.

SPELLS FOR PARTNERSHIPS

Many marriage customs have their root in magical thinking. In some cultures, for instance, grains of rice (symbols of fertility) are thrown as confetti, while a horseshoe is traditionally associated with luck, and the wedding ring is a symbol of the eternal bond of lives. Spells for a long and happy partnership are some of the most popular of all. These not only include spells for luck and fertility but also for removing conflict and reminding a partner of your love.

A SPELL TO REMOVE CONFLICT

This spell will help remove conflict in a relationship. It will work best if both people in the relationship do it together. If only one of you wishes to do it, write down what you wish to let go of, and work to heal your own difficulties. The best time for this spell is Tuesday during a waning moon.

You will need

5.5 m (18 ft) white cord
a small round table or stool
5 red candles
charcoal and burner
coriander seeds
red pen
2 pieces of natural paper
heatproof container

1 Open your cord circle. Place the round table or stool in the centre and on it position the red candles, also in a circle, and light them, remembering which candle is the last to be lit.

2 Light the charcoal in the burner. When it is hot, face west and sprinkle on the coriander seeds, saying the following dedication:
O Zamael, Angel of Mars, we call upon you to help us today/tonight and dedicate this offering to you.

3 Breathe in the aroma of the burning seeds. Both of you should then use the red pen to write down the emotion to be let go – jealousy, anger, etc.

4 Swap papers and, without looking at what the other has written, add your negative feelings on the other side of their paper. Then walk widdershins around the table five times, visualizing the way you express your emotion.

5 When you have circled the table for the fifth time, each of you should burn your own piece of paper in the flame of the last candle that was lit, dropping the paper into the heatproof container.

Red is the colour of Mars. Call on the energies of this planet when working with conflict situations.

Burn coriander seeds to invoke Zamael, angel of Mars. Coriander is sacred to this angel.

A joint wish

Write your names together on natural paper, stating a positive wish you both want. Place it between the two halves of an organic apple, seal the join with green candle wax and bury the apple near to your home in a prepared spot. If the apple pips (seeds) grow, tend them carefully because they represent new growth in your relationship that needs looking after.

A SPELL FOR JOINING

For a romance that is blossoming, work with the energies of spring to create this love token, which is inspired by the Maypole, an ancient fertility symbol. During the spring May Day festival (Beltane), people traditionally danced around the pole, interweaving coloured ribbons as they did so, symbolizing the joining of the male and female. Give the love token to your partner to represent the weaving together of your lives. Work this spell on a Sunday at full moon.

You will need
wand
straight wooden stick
two green ribbons
two yellow ribbons
thread or wool (yarn)
beads, pendants or stones for decoration

1 Find a comfortable place to work, then cast a circle around you. Assemble your materials in the centre. Sit facing south.

Green is the colour of new growth and fertility, while yellow symbolizes health and happiness.

2 Invoke the winds of the four directions in turn, repeating the following words and each time substituting the next direction:
Hail to thee South/West/North/East Wind. I call upon your assistance in the making of this charm for (say the person's name). Please lend it your power and give it your blessings and protection for the highest good of all concerned.

3 Secure the lengths of ribbons around the top of the stick using the thread or wool. Hold the stick firmly in place and lay out the ribbons in the four directions, green in the north and south, yellow in the west and east.

4 Weave the ribbons around the stick, crossing alternate adjacent pairs in a continuous pattern, until you reach the base. Wind the north and south ribbons deosil and the east and west ones widdershins around the wood, weaving the north ribbon over the east one, and the south ribbon over the west one.

5 Secure the ends with thread or more ribbon. Tie beads, pendants or stones on to them as decoration, or leave the ribbon ends free if you prefer.

6 When you have finished, thank the Four Winds for helping you, and close the circle in the usual way.

Love's protection

In many cultures giving a cloak or scarf to a loved one signifies the offer of protection, and that the giver will always be there for the other. You can make a love charm to symbolize the cloak by using a smaller piece of fabric decorated with symbols of your love. Think carefully about the colours, patterns and fabric you wish to use. The best time to make and present this love charm is in the autumn, during a waxing moon.

You will need
square of fabric
soft pencil
needle and thread
small pieces of fabric
beads and charms
paintbrush and fabric paints or needle and embroidery thread (floss)

1 Use your hand to create a magic circle around your workspace. See it as a ring of fire and know that it protects you as you make your spell.

2 Draw out the pattern of your design on the cloth in pencil. Sew on the pieces of fabric you have chosen. You can also tie on beads and other charms if you feel they are needed, or have a particular significance.

3 Using either fabric paints or embroidery thread, fill in the pattern. Close your circle when your spell is complete.

4 Give the charm to your partner as a token of your love; remind them that you will always be there when they need you.

SPELLS FOR SEPARATION AND ENDINGS

When relationships are no longer able to sustain themselves, many couples decide that it is best to part. This is usually the last step in a painful process that involves a lot of soul-searching and talking together. Magic can help you to achieve an ending that is peaceful and not acrimonious, that recognizes your differences without seeing one another as wrong. Ending spells may also be performed after the death of a partner to help you let go so that you are free to move on.

As you work on the talking stick, concentrate on the issues you want to resolve.

EFFECTIVE COMMUNICATION

Separation is a difficult and complex process, particularly if children are involved. Clear communication can help each partner let go of unspoken resentments and painful feelings, so that each can move forwards as peacefully as possible. Using a "talking stick" is a Native American technique designed to facilitate open and honest dialogue to help people move on and progress a difficult situation. The charm can be used for any problem and is particularly good for moving forward in a relationship, even if it is towards an ending rather than a reconciliation.

MAKING A TALKING STICK

Traditionally, a talking stick was made from wood, but it can be made of any material – this one is made from paper. Decide how you are going to symbolize the relationship problem you are having, as you will inscribe this on your stick. The best time to work this charm is during a waning moon, on a Tuesday.

You will need
pencil
sheet of natural paper
coloured paints or pencils
paintbrush
coloured ribbon or string

1 Use your hand to cast a magic circle around your work area. Visualize it as a ring of bright fire.

2 Draw your inscription on paper. Spend time designing and choosing the words or symbols, remembering that they stand for the problem that you and your partner are going to discuss.

3 Using coloured paints or pencils, add colour to the design; think about talking and listening to your partner concerning this particular issue as you work, and about letting go of the problem so that you can both live without its shadow hanging over your relationship.

4 Roll the paper up into a scroll and tie it in place with the ribbon or string. The symbols, along with your intentions are now bound up into the roll of the charm.

5 Close your circle. You are now ready to use your charm. Begin by presenting it to the person you love and suggest how it may be used.

When you and your partner have finished using the talking stick it should be burned.

Before you begin using the talking stick, make sure you both agree on the rules.

HOW TO USE THE TALKING STICK
One person holds the stick and talks while the other person, without interrupting, listens intently and respectfully in silence. When the speaker is finished he or she places the stick on the ground for the other person to pick up. When you both feel you have finished, throw the talking stick on to a fire, or burn it in a heatproof container. Watch the flames devour it, symbolizing the ending and letting go of an issue. This talking ceremony will need to be repeated many times during a separation process, which is a series of endings, letting go a little more each time.

A spell for helping to cut the ties

This spell can help you to say goodbye at the end of a relationship, and let go of your partner. It can be performed at the end of any relationship to ease the transition from one life stage to another. The best time to perform this spell is on a Saturday during a waning moon.

You will need
purple altar cloth
aromatherapy burner
cypress essential oil
30cm (12in) black ribbon
white candle
black candle
photograph of yourself
photograph of your partner
clean pair of scissors

1 Clean and prepare your altar space and put the cloth on top. Place the oil burner in the middle of the altar towards the back. Light the burner and add three drops of cypress oil.

2 Tie one end of the black ribbon around the white candle and the other around the black candle. Position the candles on the altar so that the ribbon forms a 'tightrope'.

3 Place the two photographs side by side in the middle of the altar, beneath the ribbon; the photograph of you should be on the side of the white candle, your partner's photo should be on the side of the black one.

4 Light the white candle and say:
White candle, please hear my plea and represent me.
Help me to part from (say your partner's name) in a spirit of love and friendship.

5 Light the black candle and say:
Black candle, please hear my plea and represent (say your partner's name).
Help (say your partner's name) to part from me in a spirit of love and friendship.

6 Hold the scissors over the taut ribbon and prepare to cut the ribbon as you say these words, actually cutting it as you finish the second line:
Scissors shiny, scissors sharp
Make me and (say your partner's name) move apart
Neither harmed nor alarmed
May we now go our separate ways,
Scissors clean, scissors new
Make a clean break.

7 Put the white candle on top of your photograph, and the black one on top of your partner's picture. Let the candles burn for three minutes as you visualize you and your partner happily walking away from each other.

8 Move the photographs a little further apart and repeat the visualization. Repeat once more. Close the spell by saying 'thank you' to the spirits and blow out the oil burner. Repeat the spell for up to seven days.

A spell for emotional healing

Try this spell to help you through the grieving process at the end of a relationship. The best time for this is a Sunday, during a waning moon.

You will need
16 tealight candles
pink candle
rose essential oil and aromatherapy burner
pansy

1 Arrange the tealights in a circle and open it in the west by lighting the first tealight, followed by the rest of the tealights.

2 Sit in the centre of the circle, facing south, and light the pink candle and the oil burner. Add a couple of drops of rose oil to the burner. Close your eyes and breathe in the soft fragrance of the rose essential oil. As you do so, imagine yourself surrounded by a pink light. This soft pink light permeates your whole being and fills the sacred circle where you sit.

3 Bring the pansy to your heart chakra. Hold it there and, speaking softly, tell it your troubles and how you are feeling. When you are finished, slowly get up and close the magic circle in the usual way, giving thanks to the spirits for listening. Take the pansy outside and bury it in an appropriate spot.

Imagine yourself surrounded by pink.

SACRED SPACE

The idea that we can connect with higher powers through the many different spaces we inhabit is an ancient one. The Romans, for instance, believed that each home has its resident *genius loci* – the individual deity of the place – and each household had a special altar, where at certain times the family would gather to give thanks for their security. The same idea occurs in traditional Chinese and Indian thought, and similar spiritual belief systems have existed all over the world throughout the ages. Today, a growing awareness of the importance of sacred space is rekindling this ancient need to sanctify our environment – whether at home, at work or in nature – and many magical and mystical practices are being put into action.

This chapter begins with hints and tips for how we can encourage good vibrations in our homes using herbs and stones as well as creating altars for

household gods. It includes a hedgewitch salt cleansing ritual and a shamanic rattle ceremony to be used for clearing negative energies. Information is given on how to create different atmospheres, how to make a place feel special and how to change the function of a room by banishing the old spirits and welcoming the new ones. A special technique is given to clear negative energies in the workplace, as well as ideas on creating personal altars and placing altars around the home. Finally, a section on outdoor magic describes ways of honouring nature and receiving nourishment from it.

GOOD VIBRATIONS

A home where we feel secure is one of the most basic human needs, but what exactly gives us that feeling of security is something most of us would find hard to define. It has nothing to do with material wealth and luxury – some of the most palatial buildings can feel cold and uncomfortable. In magical thinking, this is because all locations have a spirit of place, or "genius loci" as the Romans called it. When this spirit is properly acknowledged and cared for, it can have a positive effect on the place and all those who occupy it. We can use many techniques based on natural magic to help generate positive vibrations in our everyday environments.

A bead curtain hung in a doorway adds a sense of mystery and magic to the place of transition.

DOORWAYS

In magical terms, the doorway is very important. It is not only the means by which we enter and leave a particular space, but it also symbolizes the transition between entering and leaving different psychic realities. A doorway, therefore, is an ideal setting to affirm the atmosphere you wish to create inside your home or a particular room. Bead curtains add a sense of mystery and magic, while fairy lights strung around the doorway create a sense of light and warmth, and invite the fairies into your space. Flowers and herbs encourage connections with the natural world and convey a sense of ease and relaxation, while garlands of foliage, such as rosemary, ivy or laurel, on a door symbolize protection. Many people like to hang images or charms over the door to attract specific qualities: angels invite blessings, protective deities offer strength and coins invite prosperous

Furnishings in the home

Today we choose our carpets because we like their colour or pattern, but the traditional designs from the Far East, Turkey and North Africa were woven to attract good fortune and domestic tranquillity. Similarly we hang pictures on our walls because we like to look at them, but originally the murals of ancient civilizations served a spiritual purpose in placating and invoking local deities. All these devices were originally intended to drive away bad vibrations and attract good or harmonious ones in their place.

In the Japanese sacred tradition, candlelight and flowers represent the innocence of the heart.

exchanges. You can also place spells for protection or good luck under the front doormat, so that you step on them each time you go in or out of the home.

HOUSEHOLD GODS

Many cultures have a tradition of honouring the household gods or ancestral deities. In ancient Greece, for instance, Hermes and Hestia were the twin protectors of the home. A statue of Hermes, the god of transition and exchange, stood by the front door, while one of the goddess Hestia presided over the hearth, representing stability and permanence. When a new baby was born, it was the tradition for Hestia's blessing to be sought by ritually carrying the child around the hearth. In the Chinese tradition, the spirits of the ancestors are venerated at the family altar or shrine, so that they will confer their blessings on the family.

ALTARS

The idea of having an altar at home may take a little getting used to, but in many parts of the East it is common practice. In the Japanese Shinto tradition, for instance, the *kamidana* is a small altar enshrining protective deities, where offerings of food, water and flowers are regularly placed. The tokonoma, an alcove in the north wall where scrolls are hung and flower arrangements or beautiful artefacts are displayed, also serves as a spiritual focus.

A domestic altar embodies the sanctity of home and family, and its presence helps to create a positive environment. It is a constant reminder of the search for spiritual fulfilment, anchored in the context of daily life. It can be a focus for prayer, a shrine to honour those you love, a place where you choose to meditate, or somewhere to spend a few minutes in quiet contemplation. An altar does not have to conform to any particular size, shape or colour but is your own unique creation.

DARK CRYSTALS AND STONES

Any dark crystal can be programmed to draw in negative vibrations from its local environment. Placing dark stones in a

Protective herbs and spices

Many herbs and spices can be used to help banish negative spirits or energies and protect the home. These are some of the most common:

Angelica: an all-round protective plant.

Asafoetida: removes all negativity, but smells acrid, so is used only in severe cases.

Cactus: all spiny plants and tree branches offer protection. Prickly plants or stems in the home or workplace will deflect negativity from the surrounding area.

Fumitory: to expel negative thought-forms.

Garlic: a powerful psychic protector. Its strong smell and taste deters unwanted energies. Cloves of peeled garlic can be strung over door frames,

or placed in strategic positions and replaced once a week with fresh cloves. In folklore garlic was used to keep vampires at bay.

Rowan: all parts of the rowan tree have magical protective properties. String the leaves and berries into a garland and place them around whatever you wish to gain protection for but keep the garland out of reach of small children or babies.

Salt: central to many magical practices, salt is one of the sacred items for all magical practitioners. It is a crystal and its cleansing powers mean that it is held in great respect.

Yarrow: a powerful psychic protector.

problem area can help to cleanse it before it is filled with symbols and objects of warmth and light. Flint, a dark stone commonly found throughout most of the world, is a powerful protector against negative psychic energies.

SHARP OBJECTS

To give protection against negative influences, you can place needles, pins, thorns, prickles or any other sharp objects in a jar, then fill it with a mixture of protective herbs. The jar should then be sealed and left in the area that seems

to be causing problems. It can also be placed under the bed for protection at night. Another traditional means of protection against psychic opposition is to put rusty iron nails around a property, facing away from the walls.

A HORSESHOE

Iron is the metal of Mars – the Roman god of power, strength and courage. An iron horseshoe can be displayed with its "horns" facing to the left, in the shape of a crescent moon, to reflect the properties of Mars, and also of the moon goddess.

In the English folklore tradition it is believed that a jar of needles, pins and thorns, together with protective herbs, gives protection against negative influences or psychic opposition.

SPACE CLEARING

Shaking the rattle as you say the words imbues them with the power of the rattlesnake.

A ny kind of good, positive atmosphere is welcome and wholesome, but we sometimes need to cure a negative, unwholesome one. Negative energies in the environment will have an adverse effect on the people who live or work there: common symptoms include feeling tired or drained of energy, poor concentration, loss of interest in present circumstances and being stuck in a rut. Space clearing is a way of clearing negative energies – it is like a psychic spring-cleaning. We can also perform space clearing ceremonies on ourselves to free ourselves from negative thought-forms and psychic energies.

SPACE CLEARING IN FOLKLORE
Many ancient space clearing ceremonies have persisted as part of the folklore tradition. "Beating the bounds" is an old custom whose original purpose was the spiritual protection of the community. The village boundary line was beaten with birch wands to ensure the safekeeping of the village by establishing a magical barrier around it that no evil spirit could cross. Similarly birch broomsticks were not only used domestically for sweeping the floor, but magically for clearing out unwanted psychic energies and for creating a magic circle. In the days of earth floors, a circle could literally be swept into the floor, this ring forming a visible barrier to the inner realm and a protection against any outside influences that might disrupt the work within. Sometimes today witches still sweep the area they use for magic.

Space clearing can also be about clearing negative energies from the body. For instance, the Northern European folk tradition of "wassailing" (the giving of a New Year salutation for health and wellbeing with a cup of spiced ale) was thought to clear away any evil spirits residing within a person's body. The term "wassail" comes from the Anglo-Saxon *waes hael* meaning "be whole" or "be well".

A HEDGEWITCH SPACE CLEARING
This ritual can be performed once a week to keep your home or workplace clear and clean. Sweep up any old salt and take it outside your property boundary before repeating the ritual.

Begin at the doorway and move deosil (clockwise) around the room. Take a pinch of natural sea or rock salt and sprinkle it in the first corner, saying:
Clean and clear this corner (or window, fireplace etc) be, from all that is not good for me.
Repeat these words as you sprinkle more salt in all four corners, then around the doorframes and fireplace before moving on to the next room you wish to cleanse.

Performing the fourfold breath will calm and centre you before a space clearing ritual.

Changing ourselves

Because 'like attracts like', there is no point in space clearing the environment if we do not also change our own state of mind, banishing negative thoughts so that unwelcome vibrations are no longer received. Most psychic negativity is produced by our own mental and emotional states. Rituals that produce changes inside ourselves - changes of consciousness - need to be approached with care and sensitivity and work best when they are short and simple.

Rattles, such as this North Amerian Indian one, are made from seed pods.

SPACE CLEARING YOURSELF

To perform this self cleansing you will need a selection of white candles, including one large one, together with tealights and a rattle. Rattles conjure the ominous sounds of the rattlesnake as it warns of its presence by shaking its tail. When used in ceremony, a rattle can either summon the energy of the snake to protect, or can warn intrusive energies that they should step back and withdraw.

1 Distribute the candles about the floor of the room and light them, using as many or as few as you feel is appropriate but reserving the large one.

2 Sit on a cushion in the centre of the room. Light the large white candle and place it directly in front of you.

3 Spend some time performing the fourfold breath: breathe in for a count of four, hold for four, breathe out for four, and hold for four before taking the next breath. Then pick up your rattle in your right hand and repeat the following words, shaking the rattle at the end of each line except when you say "It is true":
Pay attention (shake rattle)
Snake is here (shake rattle)
It is true
Snake is coming (shake rattle)
So beware adversary – snake is ready to strike (shake rattle loudly).

4 Then repeat the following chant:

Life is love; love is life; let there be an end to strife.
Let the good replace all bad; let love release all spirits sad.
Let my will reveal the power, starting at this present hour,
To enhance the energy, so that I possess the key,
To allow all ills to go, and to let the goodness flow
Into this place where I now kneel, let love begin all things to heal.

5 Repeat the chant several times. Visualize all negativity departing from you at great speed as you chase it away and reclaim what is rightfully yours.

Making a space clearing rattle

If you don't have a ceremonial rattle, you can make one. You will need an aluminium drinks can, some paper, a handful of rice, glue, scissors and some sage for burning.

1 Wash and dry the empty can, making sure the ring pull has been completely removed.

2 Place the can on the paper and draw round the circular base to form a circle the same size. Cut out the circle. Pour the rice into the can through the ring-pull hole and place the paper

circle over the top of the can to cover the hole. Glue in place.

3 Cut out another piece of paper big enough to wrap around the sides of the can. Glue it around the can, decorate it if you wish.

4 When the rattle is complete, dedicate it to Sosho (the snake) by passing it through the smoke of burning sage. Call for the powers of the rattlesnake to enter your rattle and to help you in your magic.

As with all magical equipment, if you make it yourself it has greater power.

CHANGING ATMOSPHERES

Natural magic can be used to change and create atmospheres for a variety of different purposes. For instance, sometimes you may want to change the function of a room in your home, in which case you will not only need to think about how to decorate and rearrange the room, but you will also need to think about its energetic personality. If the change in use is particularly radical, like the change from a work space to a bedroom, you will need to banish the old spirits of place before the new ones can be welcomed in.

If a former bedroom, which has acquired a relaxed atmosphere over the years, is changed into a sitting room, psychically sensitive people may feel drowsy when they spend time in the room. If the planning department of a company moves out of an office and the accounts department moves in, employers may notice the accounting staff spending time in discussion. The atmospheres in these spaces are not particularly negative – they are misplaced echoes of former thought-forms, each with a residual power of subliminal persuasion, that need to be overwritten by a more appropriate one.

This atmosphere is being changed from the masculine atmosphere of an office – symbolized by a pen – to the gentler atmosphere of a girl's bedroom – symbolized by the little pink bag.

TO CHANGE AN ATMOSPHERE

Transmuting one positive atmosphere into another can be done with a ritual in which you begin by focusing on the old atmosphere, then swing your focus to the new, whatever it may be. This could also be described as stamping a new psychic impression upon a place. Here, the aim is to change what was a home office into a bedroom for a young girl.

You will need
4 small tumbled rose quartz crystals
altar
white candle
2–3 candles in a colour that reflects the new usage of the space
a token of the original use of the space (in this case a pen)
black cloth large enough to cover or contain the token
rose geranium essential oil and burner
a token of the new atmosphere (in this case a pink bag)

1 Set up an altar in the middle of the room using colours that suit the new atmosphere you wish to create. Put the white candle in the centre of the altar with the three coloured candles arranged in a triangle around it.

As you clap your hands, visualize the sounds driving away the old atmosphere of work, business and stressful activity.

Using colour to change atmospheres

Use this list to help you choose the most appropriate colours to represent the new function of the room and enhance the atmosphere you are seeking to create.

Red: best used in active areas, such as a living room or dining room, or to add a touch of energy to a more neutral backdrop

Orange: use in creative areas and for a supportive ambience

Yellow: best used in work places, its happy, sunny colour also works well in the kitchen

Green: use in areas of relaxation and harmony, such as a living room or bedroom

Blue: ideal for areas of peace and relaxation, such as a living room, bedroom or bathroom

Violet: as a combination of blue and pink it is ideal for areas where both liveliness and rest are required, such as a dining room

Pink: for inspiration and happiness, this could be used in a bedroom, living room or office

Purple: good for areas requiring stillness, depth and meaning, such as a bedroom, or any restful, contemplative 'inner' space

Silver: symbolizes magic and dreams; can bring a touch of feminine (yin) energy into a more masculine (yang) space

Gold: symbolizes happiness and abundance; can bring masculine (yang) energy into an overly feminine (yin) space

Brown: for an atmosphere that requires stability and reliable energy; ideal when changing a mentally orientated space to a more practical one

An element of red will bring energy and dynamism to a room.

2 Put everything you are going to use in the ritual on the altar for a few moments, then take the rose quartz crystals and put one in each corner of the room.

3 Take the object you have chosen to represent the old atmosphere, and place it in the western quarter of the room. Take the object that is representing the new atmosphere of the room and place it in the eastern quarter. Light all the candles.

4 Start the ritual at the east side of the altar, facing west. Take a few deep, calming breaths and say the following:
Go! Depart! Begone ye hence!
Avaunt I say, this is my will!
Be ended, finished, changed, transposed,
Leave no disturbing echoes still!

5 Clap your hands loudly, then take the cloth over to the object in the west and cover it. Return to the altar, but this time stand at the west side facing east, in the opposite direction to the earlier part of the ritual. Say the following:
Now welcome be, now welcome stay,
Now welcome is for evermore!
Be started, newborn, fresh, unfurled,
And bring thy presence to the fore!

6 Go to the object in the east that represents the new atmosphere and bring it reverentially to the altar to place it there. Sit beside the altar and leave the item there for several minutes while you meditate on it. As you do so, absorb the new atmosphere that is emerging in the room and reflect it back at the object.

7 When you feel this is complete and the atmosphere has been altered, close the ritual by extinguishing the candles. Dismantle the altar and remove the object that represented the old atmosphere from the room. Leave the object that represents the new atmosphere in a prominent position on a windowsill or shelf.

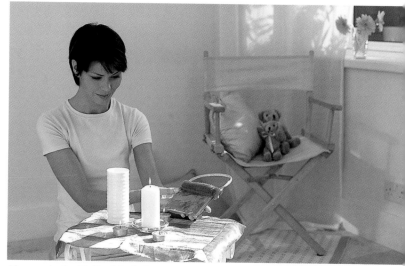

After removing the old object, bring in the new one, and place it in a central position in the room as a focal point for the new energies.

CREATING A SPECIAL FEEL

When we expect visitors and spend time preparing for their stay, our aim is to make our home feel especially welcoming. If we are holding a dinner party, we take great care both to prepare good food and to provide a pleasant atmosphere. It is important to us to provide for our guests' physical comfort, and we are also concerned about doing the equivalent on a psychic level. There are also times when a special atmosphere is called for – when entertaining friends, celebrating the season or marking some other important event, such as a wedding or naming ceremony.

The solar hexagram is a six-rayed star with a representation of the sun in the centre.

There are two key words that relate to making a place feel special, both materially and magically, and these are "pride" and "respect". Without one, we will not feel the other. When both these elements are brought into play, our place – whatever and wherever it may be – will begin to fill with that special atmosphere of sparkle and excitement.

FOR A SPECIAL FEEL

Every now and again, we want to make a place feel especially welcoming. This ceremony uses frankincense, rose water and orange candles to create a "golden" atmosphere. Frankincense is one of the most precious incense ingredients, while rose water is delicately purifying and leaves a lingering subtle fragrance.

Orange candles symbolize the life-giving, creative power of the sun. As you perform it, you should notice your space begin to change and fill with that special atmosphere of sparkle and excitement.

You will need
altar and orange altar cloth
2 orange or gold candles
frankincense and charcoal burner
  or essential oil and burner
wand
additional orange candles for dark areas
rose water in small bowl

1 Position the altar so that you will face east when standing before it. Arrange the cloth and the two candles in holders upon it, together with the incense or essential oil burner and the wand.

2 Place the additional candles around the room in the shadowy areas that light does not normally illuminate, and where the candle glow will enhance the richness of the room's appearance. The aim is to achieve a depth of perspective in the room, so arrange the candles in a non-linear way, and avoid having them at a similar distance from the altar.

3 Light the candles, then stand in front of the altar and bow your head. Take several deep and calming breaths.

4 Use the wand to "draw" a solar hexagram in the air in front of you, above the altar. The hexagram, a six-pointed star (identical to the "Star of

The many candles that are randomly arranged in this ritual will brighten every corner.

As you perform this spell, focus your mind and concentrate on what you are doing, and visualize a sphere of happiness being created.

Elemental imbalances

Sometimes the atmosphere of a place is spoilt by an elemental imbalance, that is to say, where there is either too much or not enough of one of the four elements. These elemental imbalances can be corrected by introducing any of these quick fixes:

Air: music, wind chimes, images of air creatures such as birds, lavender fragrance;
Fire: candlelight, gold or orange materials, fire creatures such as the phoenix, lion or dragonfly, frankincense or copal fragrance;
Water: an indoor fountain, water garden, fish-tank or bowl of water, images of water creatures or plants, jasmine fragrance;
Earth: plants, herbs, crystals, images of earth-dwellers such as prairie dogs or badgers, cypress fragrance;
Elemental lightbulbs: Another way to change the atmosphere is by replacing a plain lightbulb with one you have painted with particular designs, using glass paint. To introduce more Air use a patterned lightbulb painted with violet circles on a yellow background; to add more fire to a room use a lightbulb painted with red flames on a green background; to add Water use a lightbulb painted with blue bands on an orange background; and to introduce Earth use a lightbulb painted with citrine and russet-brown diamonds.

Painted lightbulbs add instant elemental influences to a room.

David"), is associated with the zodiac, the planets and the sun.

5 At the centre of the hexagram, "draw" the symbol of the sun: a small circle with a dot in the middle. As you do this, visualize the outline appearing as a line of brilliant golden light. Then, in a commanding voice, say:
Let none undo the spell I cast,
For it is well and three times good;
This place is special now at last,
Be it now full understood!

6 Now pick up the bowl of rose water and, as you walk clockwise around the edge of the room, dip your fingers in the water and then brush your hand over the walls and floor areas. As you do so, say, "Blessed be this boundary". Where there are areas of the room that might be damaged by the rose water, pass your hand over the walls a little distance away. It is helpful to visualize the blessing water creating a sphere of happiness and peace, as you mark out the boundary of the room.

7 To close the ritual, extinguish all the candles, starting with the furthest away from the altar and ending with the nearest. Then give thanks and go outside to discard any remaining rose water into the earth.

MAGIC IN THE WORKPLACE

Unless you have a private office or work from home, it may be difficult to imagine using magic in the workplace. However, there are a number of ways of using magical tools and equipment to protect against negative energies at work. It is a good idea to do this, as we are exposed to many vibrations that can adversely affect us. Common problems include allergies, poor concentration, high stress levels and feeling tired all the time. Such problems have been linked to excessive exposure to artificial light, electromagnetic radiation (the energy waves emitted by electronic equipment such as computers, mobile phones and photocopiers), and "sick-building syndrome". The latter is a term used to describe a cluster of health problems associated with inhabiting certain kinds of buildings.

THE POWER OF THE MIND

It is a good idea to perform regular space clearing rituals at work to transform negative energies. Although it can be awkward to conduct any kind of overt ceremony or ritual, there are ways around this. At its purest and most powerful level, magic needs no special equipment or physical actions, not even speech: the entire ritual, including all scents, colours and tools, can be imagined through creative visualization. An occult master can use his or her mind and willpower to achieve astonishing results using this

As offices are usually crowded and busy places, space clearing at work often needs to be a private, mental exercise.

technique, but fortunately even a shadow of this ability is good enough for your needs.

PREPARATION

Try to choose a time when you are unlikely to be disturbed. Even though your outward actions will not raise any eyebrows among your colleagues, you will be better able to concentrate if you are alone. Beforehand, you will need to obtain a small notepad suitable to make into a scrapbook. You will also need to collect a number of appropriate images to represent your working environment. These could be taken from magazines and catalogues. Your tools for this ritual will be nothing more complicated than scissors, glue and paper.

Cut out the pictures you have collected and use them to assemble a collage, or compound image, of your workplace, by arranging and sticking them together. Remember that it does not need to be a realistic impression of the place, nor does it need to be artistic or to scale, or to have perfect perspective. You are simply aiming for a symbolic general impression of your working environment, not an accurate representation.

Create a scrapbook of images that represent your working environment, and use this as a focus for your thoughts.

Crystals

As natural parts of the earths structure, the energies of crystals are radiated at natural frequencies. You can use these to help balance the emissions of modern appliances by placing them around equipment such as computers and printers or televisions. To remain effective, the crystals will need to be cleansed once a month.

SYMPATHETIC MAGIC

Everyone is familiar with the voodoo practice of sticking pins into a doll that represents someone you don't like. This is based on the principle of sympathetic magic: the idea is that the doll and the target become inextricably linked, so that whatever happens to one will transfer itself to the other by association. Though this practice is a form of destructive magic and is not recommended, the principle of sympathetic magic can be used in a positive way – in this instance, to clear negative energies at work.

So just as the doll is only a rough image of a real person, your workplace collage need only be an approximation of the actual place. You can make a single collage or as many versions as you like, until you find an image that you resonate well with. Once you are satisfied, sit quietly with the image and visualize it being filled with golden light. See the light filling up the picture until everything is surrounded by a golden glow – pay particular attention to areas of heavy or particularly negative energy,

such as photocopiers, computers and other machines. Say these words quietly to yourself:

Darkness be gone! May this space be filled with golden light. And so mote it be!
Repeat the visualization regularly for maximum effect; each time you practise it your powers of visualization will become more powerful and effective.

GUARDING AGAINST NEGATIVITY

There are other steps you can take to repel negativity and to promote good vibrations at work. Keeping the area clean and free from clutter is one of the most basic – negativity attaches to dirt. If you are having trouble with another worker, a cactus plant positioned between you will offer protection.

If when you are at work you feel a sudden vulnerability, use your mind to project an image of a guardian figure standing next to you. This could be your guardian angel or guide, a totem animal or someone you know with whom you feel safe and happy. Remember the guardian will never take the offensive against the person or situation that is causing you to feel vulnerable, but will offer a mantle of protection around you, strengthening your auric field so that negative energies cannot get to you.

PROTECTION STRATEGIES

There are also other ways to keep your workplace psychically protected:

◇ Display plants and flowers that have protective qualities, such as fern and geranium. Put them in waiting rooms

If you need protection from a difficult colleague, position some cacti on your desk between you.

and reception areas to reduce invasive effects from the energy of visitors.

◇ Place smoky quartz crystals in the four corners of the room to help absorb stray energies. Make sure you clean them once a month.

◇ Position clear quartz crystals near computers and electronic equipment to help to absorb and transform electromagnetic radiation.

◇ Include plenty of green plants in the building to provide oxygen, and let their vibrations help to connect you with the natural world.

Altars at work

In many parts of the East, you are just as likely to find an altar or shrine in a shop or office as at home. You can make an unobtrusive 'altar' at work by creating a small display of personal objects on your desk or workstation. These could include a photograph, a natural object, such as a stone or crystal, a piece of fruit, and some fresh flowers or a plant.

If you need protection, make a display of suitable plants and keep it on your desk.

Smoky quartz crystals, placed in the corners of a room, will absorb stray energies.

PERSONAL ALTARS

Creating a personal altar is a way of inviting magic into your home. The sacred space it occupies is available to you all the time; it is a meeting point where the divine reaches down to touch the everyday world and where you can concentrate your intentions and desires for spiritual growth. There is a two-way flow between the individual and the world of spirit, and the altar is its channel. It can be both a setting for a journey into a spiritual dimension and a place to gain deeper understanding of your own character and place in the universe.

A personal altar is probably best used for prayer or meditation rather than spell-making, ritual or ceremony, when special altars are usually set up for that particular purpose. As it is used, it becomes energized and its influence widens, flowing out through and around you, to bless your home and everyone in it. A personal altar can be a physical expression of your deepest attachments and longings: by giving them form you bring them into your daily life and empower yourself to achieve what you desire. There is no set way of creating your own personal altar – the form it takes is up to you. What is important is that it has meaning for you.

NATURAL OBJECTS
In natural magic, a personal altar would usually contain symbolic representations of the natural world. Placing natural objects on an altar helps to reinforce its connection with earth energies and underlines our commitment to preserving the natural world. It is also a reminder of our own connection with the web of life. When looking for objects for your altar, you may prefer to take only things that have fallen ("found" objects), rather than by cutting flowers or trees, for instance. Remember to always give thanks for what you have taken by leaving an offering or by a simple action, such as clearing away litter.

Stones represent the Earth element. Their presence on an altar can help stabilize stress-filled places.

SACRED IMAGES
Deities from any religion may have a personal symbolism for you that you would like to represent on your altar. For instance, a statue of the Buddha in meditation could help you to focus on your own meditation, while the Goddess could be represented by a fertility figure or a statue or painting of one of her many aspects. By invoking the Goddess and seeking her ancient wisdom you will find an aspect of her in yourself. Bringing her into the heart of your home in this way upholds a tradition that has been practised throughout history. Similarly, if you call on a guardian angel for spiritual support, you can place a picture or figurine of an angel on your altar to focus your prayer.

ABSTRACT SYMBOLS
Symbols predate writing as a means of conveying ideas. Ancient symbols were carved, painted, stitched and worked in metal for magical purposes, to ward off evil or to invoke gods. A symbol gains its significance from the emotional and spiritual weight that it carries. Some of the most compelling symbols are the simplest, such as the circle that

Feathers represent birds, who are honoured as a link between earth and heaven.

Natural symbolism

The natural world is full of symbolism, whether in trees and plants, rocks and shells, or feathers, flowers and pieces of wood.

Feathers: represent the Air element and also symbolize the connection between the earth and the heavens.

Stones: bring grounding, Earth energy to the altar. A stone also brings some of the character of the place where it came from.

Fossils: even more than stones, a fossil is a striking reminder of the antiquity of the earth and carries the resonance of millions of years of history.

Seashells: a reminder of the ocean and the element of Water. Seashells are associated with the unconscious and feminine energy. They also have traditional links with regeneration, baptism and prosperity.

Fruits, nuts and grains: are a reminder of the abundance of nature and the changing seasons of the year.

Flowers, herbs and trees: plants are great healers, with particular species being linked with different properties. For instance, ash is associated with purification and cleansing, roses with love and beauty, and basil is said to protect from pain.

Driftwood: a piece of driftwood, carried by the oceans, conveys the blessings of the Goddess.

---

represents the wheel of life, death and rebirth. The spiral too stands for the cycle of existence, but its outward motion also symbolizes growth and energy. The pentacle, or five-pointed star, is an ancient symbol of harmony and mystic power. Placing ancient graphic symbols such as these on your altar will bring their energy and associations into your life. By painting or carving them yourself, you will enhance your connection with them further.

PRACTICAL CONSIDERATIONS

A personal altar is essentially a work of intuition and imagination. Any flat surface can become an altar when it is hallowed by intent. The surface could be a shelf, a windowsill, the top of a chest or even the top of a refrigerator. Some people like to know that their personal altar is completely private to them. If you feel this way, you could arrange a beautiful shrine inside a cupboard or box. A small wooden box makes a lovely

Elemental altars

Another way of creating a personal altar is through a symbolic representation of the elements. For instance, if you are working on creative issues, then you would focus especially on the Fire element, for relationship issues on Water, on Earth for stability and material prosperity, while Air represents freedom, change and new ideas.

Fire: symbolized by the colours orange or red and by yellow or gold flowers

Air: symbolized by incense, scented candles, a fan or feathers and silver-coloured cloth or ornaments

Water: symbolized by the colours blue and green, and by water, wine or any liquid

Earth: symbolized by stone or terracotta objects and earthy colours such as russet, brown and deep orange

---

altar because you can arrange all your sacred things on the flat lid and it is also portable. Having a portable altar is a good idea if you are often travelling away from home and wish to carry the essence of home with you.

Statues of female or male figures can be used to represent the archetype you wish to honour.

A portable altar will remind you of home.

ALTARS IN THE HOME

Most people have one room that feels special, where the sense of positive energy is most complete. It could be the living room, the kitchen, or a welcoming entrance hall. Traditionally the hearth is regarded as the centre of the home and it is really a prototype altar. Deciding where to position your altar will influence its style as well as how you use it. For instance, your altar can be for you alone, or to share with others. A family altar can work for cohesiveness, like the traditional ancestral altars of the East, while a couple could share in the creation of an altar to promote a deeper commitment to one another. In each case certain locations in the home are more suitable than others.

This simple bedside altar to Gaia, the goddess of dreams, includes lilies to invoke calm.

POSITIONING THE ALTAR

All the different activities that we pursue create distinct types of energy in each room. This is why it can be very difficult to go to sleep in a room that has been full of lively conversation, for instance, or to concentrate on a piece of analytical work in the kitchen. Similarly, every altar will be influenced by the energy of its surroundings. You can use this power to create a life-enhancing altar in any room by drawing on the intrinsic energy of the space, and there is no reason why you shouldn't have several small altars around the house, wherever you feel they are appropriate.

To help you position your altar, you could look into Feng Shui, the ancient Chinese art of placement. There are many good reference books available on the subject, but essentially the different rooms in a building as well as the different corners in a room correspond to

A bedroom altar could include the scent of lavender to help promote peaceful sleep.

An office altar dedicated to Thoth, the scribe and guardian of knowledge to the Egyptian gods, encourages inspiration.

A child's altar

Children have a wonderful ability to invest all kinds of objects with magic. A handful of toffee wrappers can become jewel-coloured windows, and fragments of translucent sea-worn glass are as valuable as any precious gemstone. Young children naturally make collections of their favourite things. Creating a special place for them – or an altar – will encourage the child to build a magical relationship with their spirit, which grows and develops as they journey through life.

particular areas of life. For instance, south-west-facing rooms are linked with love and relationships, while those that are north-facing suit business affairs. Alternatively, you could use a pendulum to dowse for the most suitable spot (see Divination), or follow your gut feeling and be guided simply by your intuition.

THE BEDROOM

Most of us want our bedroom to be a sanctuary where we can be wholly ourselves. It is where we take our secrets and prayers, joy and grief. A bedroom altar acts as a focus for these, and for daily rituals to help you greet the day and prepare for night.

For peaceful rest, place sleep crystals on your altar: amethysts, a piece of jade or obsidian. Burning a little lavender incense or essential oil will also help you sleep. Honour the earth deity and goddess of dreams, Gaia, with barley grains or laurel, or include an image of Nephthys, who sheltered the sleeping pharaohs beneath her protective wings.

At bedtime, set a bowl of water scented with jasmine oil near your bed and place your sleep stones or crystals in it. To help your wishes come true, write what you wish to come to you in your sleep on willow leaves.

THE STUDY OR OFFICE

An altar in the workplace will generate positive energy to help you concentrate. Wisdom and inspiration are personified by Thoth, the scribe of the Egyptian gods, who wrote down the wisdom of the universe. Yellow candles assist communication and learning. Helpful crystals include emerald to give insight, azurite for clarity, and haematite to aid reasoning and memory. There are also many fragrances that are useful for mental work. Eucalyptus, peppermint and camphor can clear muddled thinking and are an antidote to daydreaming, while rosemary and basil have head-clearing properties, aid concentration and sharpen the intellect.

THE HALLWAY

An altar or shrine in the doorway or near the entrance to the house is traditional in many parts of the world. The Roman god Janus is a traditional protective deity, while a guardian totem animal such as a dog, lion or tiger is also appropriate. Sacred objects at the entrance to your home help to sanctify the whole of it and you and your visitors will carry blessings with you as you leave.

To create the welcoming smell of home, warm and spicy fragrances such as cinnamon, cassia, star anise and clove work well in the winter season, while summer blooms such as stocks, lilac, sweet pea or cabbage rose can permeate the whole house with their fragrance and particular characteristic.

THE KITCHEN

At the hub of the house, the kitchen is a potent place. The magical process of preparing and cooking food transforms the energy of the earth into a form that we are able to take in. An altar for hospitality could be dedicated to Hestia, the goddess of the hearth, or to Demeter, goddess of abundance and unconditional love. Leave offerings of rice, grains, fruit or honey for the nature spirits and light the altar candles each time you prepare a meal. A shrine behind the sink would engage your attention as you work there. You could hang herbs and flowers, chilli and garlic around the window like a garland, or decorate it with evergreens.

THE LIVING ROOM

To promote harmony between your family and friends, set up an altar to the four elements in the living room. This could combine salt for Earth, a red candle for Fire, sea shells for Water and feathers for Air. You could also put photographs of loved ones on the altar.

Create a prayer bowl, placing a clear quartz cluster in a bowl filled with spring water, with floating green candles for harmony. Invite members of the family to write down their prayers and tuck them under the bowl.

A kitchen altar could include offerings of food in honour of Demeter, the grain goddess.

A prayer bowl in the living room can be a family focus for wishes and requests.

OUTDOOR ALTARS

Magic is about relating to the natural world and finding our place in it. Visiting nature is a good way to find peace, tranquillity and inspiration and most people have a particular place that they visit when they need time alone, to meditate or just to relax. Such a place could be anywhere – part of a garden, a spot near a favourite tree, a rock on a hillside, or a cool, leafy forest – it doesn't really matter as long as it is special to you. Like the traditional holy sites, these places have a natural power, but they also take on the energy of those who visit them: they become magical or sacred space.

A flat rock makes a good outdoor altar, especially when it is in a spectacular setting.

NATURAL ALTARS

You can set up an altar in your sacred outdoor space. This may be a temporary or more permanent feature depending on the location. A flat rock or a tree stump can work well, or a sacred circle can be made with stones, twigs or cones, although nothing should be done that disturbs the natural harmony of the place. An outdoor altar can be adorned with anything that has a special significance for you, such as crystals, feathers, flowers or sticks. It can show appreciation for the moment and it has the advantage that others might see it and add their energy. Remember to leave an offering on your altar when you visit.

TREE ALTARS

Trees make very beautiful natural altars, pleasing to the eye and very calming when attention is focused upon them. Being firmly rooted, a tree has a deep

Salt is part of the crystal kingdom and is the blessed representation of the earth. Use salt to purify, consecrate and protect.

Ritual sites in nature

Increasingly, those involved in magic today are looking to ritual sites in nature and ancient stone monuments to contact the energies of their ancestors, those who practised the 'Old Religion'. These sites, which often date from the Neolithic era, are often viewed as places of female mysteries and the land itself is thought of as the Goddess incarnate. Believed to be gateways into the otherworld, a 'dreamtime' that enables magic workers to connect with a sacred place within themselves, these places are the locations for healing, divination and the conducting of life rites, such as hand fastings (pagan weddings).

connection with Mother Earth, and that energy can be tapped into when you talk to it, leave offerings and pray or meditate there. You can tie things in the branches for decoration, or place tiny items in the trunk. A flat rock placed at the base of the trunk can serve as an altar stone. Be aware of which trees attract you, because they all have their own attributes and symbolism. For example, oak is the keeper of wisdom and possesses great strength; willow represents love and regeneration, being very ready to grow a new tree from a cut branch; the tall and graceful beech symbolizes aspirations to higher ideals; yew, associated with ancient burial sites, represents transformation and inner wisdom.

ROCK ALTARS

Rocks are the bones of the Mother, supporting her and therefore us. Because they take millions of years to form, they hold ancient Earth wisdom and knowledge, power and strength. They can help you to connect with these primordial energies and you can call upon this strength when you pray or meditate at a rock altar. Feel the strength of its timeless wisdom helping, supporting and connecting you.

THE GARDEN SANCTUARY

Whatever the size of your garden, you can create an outdoor sanctuary to connect with the magical powers of nature. If space permits, this can be achieved through planting trees or shrubs to form an enclosed area. This can contain seating, such as a wooden bench or chair, as well as a shrine or grotto. A water feature is also recommended; this could be a fish pool, or some kind of running water in a stream or fountain. It does not need to be very big, but the energy of water is refreshing and cleansing for the subtle bodies. A statue of the Goddess and/or a nature deity such as Pan can be part of your garden altar. If your garden area is small, consider creating a miniature garden with Japanese bonsai trees, or arrangements of pebbles, or making a nature table to reflect the changing seasons of the year.

Trees have enormous symbolic and magical powers, and are also vital for the sustenance of life on our planet. Offer them respect and reverence in your magical work.

Making a cairn

The beauty of making something to use as an altar is that your energy is blended with the materials in a focused way. A cairn looks like a haphazard pile of stones but, to make it stable, care must be taken in selecting stones that fit together well. Take time to gather the stones.

1 Begin by selecting a few large, flat, roughly circular rocks to act as the base of the cairn. Start to build up a tapering dome by laying smaller flat rocks in an overlapping pattern.

2 As you work, keep the intent of honouring creation, and that will help focus your energy. Work slowly and methodically so that the stones are evenly balanced.

3 When the cairn is complete, decorate it with objects found close by.

Making a cairn takes time and care, and so gives the end result greater significance.

MAGIC IN DAILY LIFE

Caught up in busy schedules and coping with the demands of everyday life, it is easy to forget to take care of your own needs and to become dissociated from the core of who you are. But at the centre of everything that is going on in your life, ultimately there is only one person – you. If you don't take care of yourself then everything else in your life will suffer. Practising natural magic puts you firmly at the centre of life's wheel and encourages you to look for practical ways to nourish yourself in body, mind and soul and to reconnect with the magic of daily life.

The focus of this chapter is finding ways to use magic for everyday concerns. It begins by recognizing that care of your inner self forms the basis from which the rest of your life will grow and blossom, before turning to specific areas of life such as your goals and ambitions, the quality of your relationships and your health and wellbeing. It also offers suggestions for

how to increase wealth and prosperity by focusing on abundance, and how to deal with change with the minimum of stress. It concludes with a special section on lunar gardening, which shows you how to work with the cycles of the moon for strong and healthy plants. By bringing magic to bear on all aspects of your life, you will be enriched on many levels.

THE INNER YOU

I t is what you are within, rather than what you do, that is important so far as the life of your soul is concerned. The meaning and purpose of your life, and your connection with the greater whole, are to be found deep within you. There are many ways of nourishing your connection with your inner self, but before you begin you should take care of your physical, mental and emotional needs. Natural magic is based on balance and harmony between all aspects of creation, and you need to reflect this before you can succeed.

Regular meditation is a very good method of staying in touch with your inner self.

BODY CARE

Physically, you are influenced by your lifestyle and what you choose to eat and drink. You may like to consider changing things in your daily life that do not serve you – or are actually harmful to you – such as too many late nights, poor eating habits, or addictive patterns such as alcohol or drug consumption. On a physical level, it is helpful to be disciplined about transcending your "bad" habits, as a weak or sick physical body will significantly affect your emotional, mental and spiritual health.

Taking the Bach flower crab apple essence can help you to detox, while walnut and chestnut bud can help reduce addictive cravings.

MENTAL AND EMOTIONAL WELLBEING

Albert Einstein once said; "A clever mind is one that is trained to forget the trivial." On a mental level, being unable to switch off our thoughts is associated with many common stress-related problems such as tension headaches, anxiety and insomnia. White chestnut flower essence can be helpful, and it is

also advisable to consider physical exercise, or to begin practising a spiritual discipline such as yoga or tai chi, all of which will help reduce stress levels.

On an emotional level, you need to consider "relationship" – how you relate to others and from what emotional

Take time out, find a private space, and don't let yourself be distracted by other people. Cultivating self-awareness will give you the confidence to take a break when you need one.

A woman's moontime

The female menstrual cycle mirrors the cycle of the moon in duration, and both the hormonal changes in the body and the phases of the moon have a profound efffect on the emotions. The time of ovulation, when a woman is at her most fertile, is likely to occur during a full moon. During their menstruation, women are sensitive and highly perceptive; it is particularly important at this time of the month for women to look after themselves. Book a date with yourself and use your 'moontime' to let go of the past and to allow the flow to cleanse and take away any problems or difficulties in preparation for the new cycle ahead.

this is carving a sculpture, writing a letter, making a meal, or simply interacting with others. In this sense, creativity is not restricted to "artistic" pursuits, and everything you do can be approached with the spirit of creativity, giving spiritual value to all aspects of your daily life. Being mindful of this is one of the best ways of staying in contact with your inner self as you go about your daily affairs.

Mindfulness is another name for meditation, and meditation is one of the best ways of connecting with your creativity and inner self. Its benefits have been well documented: it allows you to relate to who you truly are without falling into the common traps of everyday life. It also helps you to think clearly and sharpens your intuitive, spontaneous responses. Spending regular time in meditation each day is a good discipline to foster; it is like washing your inner senses and will give you the eyes to see the magic that is all around us, ever-present all of the time.

Playing music is just one of the ways to express the creativity you hold within you.

AN ALTAR FOR INSPIRATION

The creative process is about inspiration, hard work, discipline, exercising judgement and discernment and the courage to make mistakes and learn from them. Making an altar to inspiration will encourage you to go beyond your limits, so that your open mind will attract fresh ideas like a magnet, faster than they can be expressed. It is in this state of intuitive awareness – a form of meditation – that creativity flows and life itself becomes a magical experience.

There are really no rules for making an inspirational altar. You might like to make it very vibrant, dressing it with a variety of colours so that its flamboyance

perspective you see things. When you look closely at your emotional responses to life, you may realize that they are out-dated, linked to wounds from the past that have yet to heal. There are several Bach flower remedies that can help with emotional healing, including using honeysuckle for someone who dwells on the past, holly for jealousy, anger and destructive feelings and impatiens for irritability and excessive reactions. Understanding and sorting out your feelings will help to alleviate heated arguments, high stress levels and heavy atmospheres.

LIVING LIFE CREATIVELY

The spirit of creation flows through every one of us. We may describe it as divine inspiration, chi, life force or quintessence, but it is the energy that we put into everything that we do – whether

will give you the confidence to express yourself in your daily life. Or you may choose a theme or colour scheme and work with that. The objects you choose to put on the altar can reflect the creative opportunities you want to explore, such as brushes and paints for artistic endeavour, or pens and paper if you are searching for the courage to express yourself. Use this special place to try out your dreams, and bring your own creations to beautify your altar.

HARMONIZING WITH NATURE'S CYCLES

To a greater or lesser extent, most of us are disconnected from the natural rhythms of nature, the journey of the sun and moon through day and night, the months and the seasons of the year. Effectively this cuts us off from our own nature, our innate, inner wisdom that is central to who we are. Spending time in nature and observing the seasons through ritual and celebration, as well as changing our diet and lifestyle to adapt to nature's patterns, can help us to reconnect with nature's cycles and our central core.

Imbolc: the light of inspiration

At the beginning of February, the festival of the return of light, or Imbolc, honours the Celtic triple goddess Brigid, a fire deity, and celebrates her union with the god of light. It is a time of inspiration and creativity, when rituals are performed to bless new love, fertility and the

planning of new projects. Imbolc is predominantly a female festival and Brigid blesses women's self-expression and creativity. By tradition, if a white cloth is left outside overnight at Imbolc, the goddess will bless it with inspiration.

GOAL-SETTING

Wherever our real ambitions lie, striving for achievement is necessary if our lives are to be fruitful and valuable. If we aim for nothing, we may end up achieving just that. And if we don't set our own priorities, someone else will. So setting out the things we want to achieve over the next week, month, year or five years, is a valuable exercise in establishing what our goals are. We can then use magic to help us in our journey towards them.

If your goal is physical fitness, picture yourself running along a beach or climbing a hill.

ESTABLISHING GOALS

Achieving something that we want to do is a great boost to confidence and self-esteem, helping us to raise our sights to even higher goals. Aspirations need not be set in stone: they need re-evaluating as we learn from experiences and as our outlook and priorities change. Re-evaluating current goals is therefore the first step. Very often we find ourselves pursuing ambitions that no longer satisfy us and, in some cases, maybe never did.

For instance, our work may leave too little time for relationships, family life or creativity, or perhaps we realize we are doing the wrong job altogether – a career path chosen perhaps to satisfy our parents – in which case it might be time to change track and consider retraining for something that we would really like to do. To help establish your goals you can divide your life up into different categories and look at each one in turn:

Asking yourself what you want from life and then thinking about the practical steps you can take to achieve it is part of goal-setting.

Setting goals

- Visualize your long-term goals and set short-term targets - weekly or monthly - to help you get there.
- Set specific daily goals to keep you motivated.
- Goals should stretch you, but not defeat you before you begin. If you make them too easy, they won't motivate you. Make each goal a challenging and positive one.
- Limit the number of your stated goals and make sure they don't clash or contradict each other.
- Write a list of your goals and read it at the start of every day.
- Re-examine your list from time to time; if your goals have changed or seem unrealistic, you can change them.
- Give yourself small rewards for each of your achievements.

A wishing box

One way of working towards your goals is to create a wishing or dream box. Write down your wishes and then keep them in a special wooden box on your altar. Surround the box with oak leaves to sanctify and protect your dreams. The sacred oak will aid your rituals with its strength and bring the promise of success. If you are unable to find oak leaves, you can sprinkle a few drops of the Bach flower oak essence on the wishes.

Keep some frankincense in your wishing box. This most ancient incense has been burnt on the altars of many cultures to summon the aid of the divine. Its uplifting scent banishes negative thoughts and promotes success. Burn a little each day as you visualize the goal you are working towards manifesting.

relationships, work, home, health, creativity, leisure and money. Some of these categories may overlap and you may notice that some areas are more important to you than others. Take as much time as you need, until you have found goals that have meaning for you and are going to help you create the life you want for yourself.

The Power of Now
Magic only recognizes the here-and-now: the past has gone, the future is not yet, and the point of power is in the present moment. So when working with goal-setting, always use the present tense for your targets. For instance, instead of saying "I want", begin with "I now have /am". Similarly, visualize the result you desire as if it is already happening. For instance, if your goal is to get a new job, you can visualize yourself opening the letter of appointment telling you it is yours. Or if your goal is a return to health and fitness, visualize yourself striding up a hill or running across a beach. Hold on to your vision for as long as you can, so that it sinks into your unconscious mind, forming a new pattern into which you can grow. Even when you seem to be making no progress, your spirit will still move in the direction you have chosen.

Ritual for Worldly Success
For material achievements such as making money and success at work, include Earth element as well as Fire on your altar. Earth is the element of stability and prosperity, and supports us in taking responsibility for our own destiny. Fire is the element related to ambition and creative projects and helps burn away any resistance there might be to achieving our goals.

1 To represent the Earth, use the colours of the land, such as olive green and russet, and place two green candles, and one darker one, on the altar, together with some salt or a stone.

2 Place a bowl of the Fire incense, frankincense, on the altar; it is best to use pieces of frankincense resin.

3 Now write your goals (remembering to use the present tense) on a piece of paper. Fold the piece of paper up and put it into the bowl of resin.

4 Close your eyes and visualize the realization of your ambitions, seeing the successful outcome rather than the process of getting there. When you have fixed the images in your mind, take the piece of paper and burn it in the candle flame, dropping it into a fireproof bowl.

5 To finish, pinch out the candles and take a few moments to gather your thoughts. Remember that you need to remain open to whatever happens and that you always seek the highest good of all concerned.

Burning the paper symbolizes letting go and trusting the universe to bring you a result.

When working for worldly success, Earth colours such as greens or russets and symbolic representations of Earth, such as salt or a stone, will help your magic along.

MAGIC AS MEDICINE

Originally, medicine and magic were not two separate disciplines but one. Medicine has largely moved away from magic, but there are many ways of using magic therapeutically, whether with herbs and plant medicines, with the assistance of cosmic powers and divine beings, or by using the vibrations of colour, sound or crystals. You can use magic as medicine to treat yourself or another (with their permission of course), to restore harmony in body, mind and soul. It is about listening to your body and working in harmony with its innate self-healing powers to restore wholeness.

A quartz crystal will help you to transmit your healing power as you voice your prayer.

A HEALING CEREMONY

Healing ceremonies play an important part in magic and medicine. Traditionally they are conducted by the shaman or medicine man, who uses a combination of ritual, spells and charms to drive out the bad spirits causing the illness from the sufferer. This ceremony enlists the healing energy of Water.

Set up an altar for healing in the west and stand facing towards the west to make your offerings or to say prayers. Make the altar a vision of pure watery beauty, fresh with the colour blue and decorated with flowers such as jasmine, lilies, lotus, iris or poppies, or with water-smoothed pebbles or seashells. These beautiful natural items will speak of the vibrancy of the world outside that waits to be enjoyed.

Choose sandalwood incense, which is associated with purification and healing, or camphor or eucalyptus for their cool, cleansing scents.

A healing ceremony will be most effective during the time of a waning moon – particularly in the four days following full moon. This is the time when things can be cast away or released,

The goddess of compassion

Chinese worshippers flock to the shrines of Kuanyin to seek her favour because they believe she can cure almost every sickness and alleviate every distress. Her name means 'One who sees and hears the cries of the whole world' and her image stands on many family altars in the East. She is usually shown carrying a vial containing the dew of compassion, and she cures the seriously ill by sprinkling a few drops on their heads.

On your healing altar, place a bowl of water, a quartz crystal, the colour blue, and some beautiful white flowers, such as lilies, to echo the vibrancy of the outside world.

including grief and anger. To perform a healing ceremony on behalf of someone who is ill, light two blue candles on the altar and present a bowl of clear spring water as an offering.

Ask for the healing help of Archangel Gabriel or Ceridwen, the white goddess of the Celts, or try appealing to the compassion of Kuanyin, the Buddhist goddess of mercy. Using a silver pen, write down the name of the person and their ailment on white paper or a petal from the lily, and then float it in the water. Visualize the ailment being lifted out of the sufferer and give thanks for their recovery. Place a clear quartz crystal in the water, and hold a second crystal in your hands while voicing your prayer, so that the healing power is transmitted.

MAGICAL HERBALISM

Every culture has had its own tradition of plant medicine, sometimes widely known and sometimes kept as secret wisdom by certain members of the society. Today many people in the western world are turning to more natural, plant-based medicines, but to understand this vast subject fully and use plant material safely takes many years of study and commitment. It is not recommended that you try to treat serious conditions yourself, but there are some traditional herbal remedies that you can use to treat everyday complaints. Generally, the herbs are best made into a tea or decoction and then drunk. If you are unsure about the safety of any herb, seek professional advice before using it.

Moon medicine

The phases of the moon are associated with important healing energies. The new moon is for health, vitality and regeneration; the full moon for fertility and empowerment; and the waning phase is the time when unwanted symptoms and ailments may be banished. The following moon medicine combines the power of crystals with the appropriate moon phase, depending on what is being treated.

To make the moon medicine you will need to make sure the moon is in the correct phase of her cycle and perform it either outside on a calm night, or inside by the light of the moon. Choose an appropriate stone that has been cleansed. Traditionally, all white, clear or watery bright stones are associated with the waxing and full moon ('bright moontime'); examples include moonstone, pearl, aquamarine and clear quartz. Black, dark or cloudy stones are used at the time of the waning moon ('dark moontime'); examples include jet, smoky quartz, obsidian and black tourmaline.

You will need
9 white tealights
matches
glass bowl
appropriate moon stone
spring water

1 Place the glass bowl on the floor in front of you, then position the nine tealights in a circle around it. Light the tealights, starting with the one in the south, saying while you do so:
Hail to thee Levanah, Queen of Heaven.

The nine tealights correspond with the moon's magical number of nine.

I call for your blessings and ask that your moonrays fill this essence with healing.

2 Put your moon stone in the bowl and pour in the spring water until the stone is completely covered. Leave it in place for at least three hours. Do not leave the tealights burning unattended and replace any that burn out.

3 After three hours, blow out the tealights, remove the stone, pour the infusion into a glass and sip slowly while visualizing yourself being touched by the moon's gentle rays.

Traditional ways with herbs and spices

The use of herbs and spices for healing, spiritual cleansing and magic has a long history. Many remedies are tried and tested, and almost every plant is useful in some way.

Feverfew leaves: eaten in honey sandwiches these are a traditional cure for migraine. This daisy-flowered herb with its peppery scent is fairly common, growing wild in some places.
Lemon balm: this is said to make the heart merry and the soul joyful. Bees love this plant

and bee-keepers traditionally rub their hives with it to keep their bees contented and settled.
Garlic: this offers protection from negative influences, including everyday infections such as the common cold, as well as bad spirits like vampires and ghosts.
Dandelions: these have a detoxifying and cleansing action. At one time, dandelions were a rustic oracle for telling the time: the flowers were said to open at five in the morning and close at eight in the evening.

Camomile: this brings down a fever, soothes the stomach, and is cooling and calming; it is also a tonic for blonde hair.
Ginger: this is warming and energizing; it is said to be a prescription for a happy love life in your later years.
Rosemary: said to be an aid to memory and concentration; it is also used as a conditioning tonic for dark hair.
Cloves: this warming spice is a traditional remedy for toothache in its oil form.

CHAKRA BALANCING

When our chakra system is balanced we enjoy good health. However, the chakras can be thrown out of balance by many things, including poor diet, lack of sleep and exercise, stress and modern medicines. Negative environmental influences such as electrical energy fields, geopathic stress and pollution also upset the chakra system. There are many ways to balance the chakras. For instance, you could work with colour therapy and gemstones, placing the appropriate coloured stone on each of the chakra points. Or you could use the healing properties of sound by intoning the mantra (healing sound) relevant to each energy centre, beginning from the base and ascending to the crown, and going down again. The box below on chakra properties tells you what colours and sounds to use for each chakra.

To diagnose which chakras are out of balance, you can use a pendulum to dowse them; you can also use dowsing after the treatment in order to check that the imbalance has been corrected.

The healing power of colour

Choose colours according to your healing need or preference.

Colour	Healing uses
Red	low energy, sexual problems, blood disorders, lack of self-confidence
Orange	depression, mental disorders, asthma, rheumatism
Yellow	detoxifying, hormonal problems
Green	antiseptic, balancing, tonic; soothes headaches
Blue	insomnia, nervous disorders, throat problems, general healing
Indigo	painkiller, sinus problems, migraine, eczema, inflammations
Violet/purple	psychological disorders; fosters self-love and self-respect
Magenta	emotional hurts and upsets, accepting life's problems
Black	for when you need to hide (such as when grieving)
White	tonic, replaces all colours
Gold	depression and low energy; digestive disturbances
Silver	hormonal and emotional balance, calms the nerves

Bottles of dual-coloured liquid can be used to diagnose colour imbalances. The bottles you are drawn to will tell you what colours you need more or less of in your life.

Chakra properties

Each chakra governs distinct organs and functions, and corresponds to a colour and sound.

1st chakra; colour: red; mantra: "lam":
Governs the gonads or ovaries, skeleton, large intestine and lower body; physical survival, energy distribution, practicality

2nd chakra; colour: orange; mantra: "vam":
Governs the bladder, circulation, sexuality; feelings, emotions, creativity and pleasure

3rd chakra; colour: yellow; mantra: "ram":
Governs the adrenal glands, spleen, pancreas, stomach; identity, self-confidence, personal power

4th chakra; colour: green; mantra: "yam":
Governs the thymus gland, immune system, lungs; relationships, personal development, self-acceptance, compassion

5th chakra; colour: blue; mantra: "ham":
Governs the thyroid, lymphatic, immune and neurological systems; self-expression, communication, trust

6th chakra; colour: indigo; mantra: "om":
Governs the pituitary gland, central nervous system; understanding, perception, intuition, spiritual 'knowing', psychic abilities

7th chakra; colour: violet; mantra: silence:
Governs the pineal gland; openness, connection to higher energies, self-realization

Crystal healing

Gemstones and crystals are attributed with specific healing powers. You can use them to transform poor health (whether physical, mental or emotional) into wellbeing by placing them on the chakras. You can also programme stones to deal with specific complaints, and then place it on the relevant part of the body to draw out the sickness. It is important to use only cleansed stones in healing and to clean them again afterwards.

Amber: relieves depression

Amethyst: protects the immune system; calms fear; aids sleep

Aventurine: soothes the emotions

Bloodstone: blood detoxifier; strengthens physical body

Carnelian: increases physical energy

Chrysocolla: assists in the relief of grief, worry and pain

Clear quartz: a powerful talisman for healing, known in many cultures as the 'all-healer'. guards against loss of vitality and strength; draws out pain, raises self-esteem, balances emotions, increases insight

Garnet: relieves depression, boosts sexuality and fertility

Haematite: helpful for blood disorders, anaemia; eases the effects of jet lag

Jet: dispels irrational fears; protects from illness and infection

Malachite: releases trauma, relieves depression, protects against negativity

Rose quartz: comforts and heals the emotions; strengthens the heart

Tourmaline: good for psychic protection; relieves stress

Crystals whose colour corresponds to a chakra will enhance its natural qualities, whatever the situation. For a simple chakra balancing, place a stone on the relevant chakra for a few minutes.

COLOUR HEALING

There are many different ways of harnessing the vibration of colour for health and wellbeing. You can wear it, use it in your surroundings, make colour infusions, eat coloured food or even bathe in coloured light.

A colour infusion draws on the energizing, health-giving powers of the sun. To make one, use coloured stones, fabric or any other colourfast item and soak the "colour" in a bowl of mineral water. Leave the bowl in sunlight for several hours, then pour the water into a glass and drink the infusion. Always make sure the coloured item you are using is clean before you soak it.

Coloured foods can also be used for healing. Red, orange and yellow foods are hot and stimulating. Yellow foods can help with weight loss and red foods restore energy. Green balances and detoxifies and is a tonic for the system. Blue, indigo and purple are soothing; blue curbs activity so is useful when you are trying to gain weight.

Another way of healing with colour involves shining coloured light on to the body to relieve physical, mental and emotional problems. You can try it yourself on everyday ailments. Place a coloured gel over a spotlight, making sure it is not touching the hot bulb. Turn off any other lights, and bathe in the coloured light, taking in the healing vibrations of your chosen colour. The main colour choice is often followed by its complementary opposite. For instance, if you are being treated with green, this may be followed by magenta to ensure a healthy balance in the body.

FLOWER ESSENCES

The subtle vibrations of flowers and trees are contained in flower essences. These are very useful for treating negative mental and emotional states and helping to rebalance the body's subtle energy system.

These properties of flowers were first discovered in the early twentieth century by Dr Edward Bach, who found himself drawn to certain flowers when suffering from particular emotions. The essences are made from flowers that are gathered when the dew is on them, floated in water and placed in the sun to allow the water to absorb the subtle vibrations. There are 38 Bach remedies, each one representing a negative emotion, plus rescue remedy, a mixture of five essences that is used for treating shock.

COLOUR AND CRYSTALS

Just as everyday acts can be transformed into ritual, it is also possible to use rituals throughout the day to help strengthen your connection to your magical powers. Morning and evening are two especially potent times of day for ritual activity. Morning is the beginning of a new day and rituals performed at this time will set up a pattern of energy that you can take with you throughout the day. Evening is about endings and winding down; rituals performed at this time will help you come back home to yourself.

As in many traditional systems of healing there is a close correlation between the colour of gemstones and their healing properties. Once the key concepts for each colour are recognized, it is easy to identify how a crystal or gemstone will bring the qualities of its planet to interact with our personal energy. For example, red is the colour of Mars, so red stones are used to enhance Martian qualities like courage, strength and protection. Green is the colour of Venus, and green stones help with relationships and creativity.

The colour of a crystal affects us in two ways – through our eyes and by its placement on the body. Crystals are coherent, organized forms of matter and the colour they transmit is a focused, powerful vibration. Crystals that are transparent, letting light right through them, will generally have a more pronounced and focused effect than opaque stones, where the light frequencies are both absorbed and radiated outwards in a more diffuse manner.

WARM COLOURED STONES

Red stones will be energizing and stimulating. Rich, bright reds, such as garnet, ruby and zircon, can be quite dramatic in their effects. The opaque or tawny reds of jasper and iron quartz create a more grounded, practical energy.

Orange stones are excellent for use in situations of shock and trauma. They will energize the repair mechanisms within the body. Carnelian and orange

Selecting the right crystal for a magical ritual can be made by an intuitive process. Simply hold in your mind the purpose for which you need a stone or crystal, and then let your gaze wander over a group of stones until your eye picks one out.

calcite will soothe and restore, while topaz and rutilated quartz help to strengthen and reintegrate dissipated energies.

Yellow stones support the sense of self, energizing the solar plexus and so reducing tension and anxiety. Citrine, yellow fluorite, tiger's eye and amber create clarity, awareness and confidence.

The endless range of coloured minerals and crystals make them an ideal way to introduce colour into a magical ritual or healing session.

COOL COLOURED STONES

Green stones balance the heart, calm the emotions and stimulate personal potential for growth. Green aventurine and green tourmaline are good emotional stabilizers. Emerald and moss agate encourage harmony with our surroundings. Malachite, dioptase and peridot help to release emotional pain.

Light blue stones support communication skills and work well to strengthen immune systems. Turquoise and aquamarine encourage flexibility and support the subtle energy systems of the body. Blue lace agate and celestite release tensions and lift heavy moods.

Dark blue stones such as lapis lazuli, sodalite, sapphire and kyanite quieten the normal thought processes and encourage intuition. They can also help to release long-held stresses, encouraging deep peace.

Violet stones, such as amethyst, fluorite and sugilite, make excellent objects for meditation and contemplation. They encourage the integration of all aspects of the self.

Green and turquoise stones help to calm the emotions and enhance subtle psychic skills. Green stones are used to stimulate personal growth.

Peace and quiet can be quickly experienced just by holding or gazing at a blue stone. Use your intuition to choose the right stones, and then simply hold them in your hands.

CRYSTALS OF OTHER COLOURS

White and clear stones generally amplify the life-sustaining energies of the body. They bring clarity, purification, orderliness and harmony. Clear quartz, calcite and selenite energize, while moonstone, milky quartz and other translucent white or cloudy stones have a soothing, gently cleansing effect.

Black stones – obsidian, smoky quartz, black tourmaline and haematite – can help to release deep energy imbalances. They focus awareness inwards, calming the body and mind by speeding the release of unwanted energies.

Pink stones are useful for releasing emotional tension and helping to improve self-confidence and acceptance. Rose quartz, rhodocrosite, rhodonite and kunzite remove the stresses that prevent us from being at ease in the world and can be helpful to counter aggressive situations.

HEALING STONES

Any crystal, if you are drawn to it, will have a healing effect. If you want one to help you with a specific problem, look at a collection of different stones and work with those you are attracted to. The colour correspondences of the crystals can indicate the root of the difficulty or may give you some clues to other steps you can take to enhance your health and wellbeing.

HARMONIOUS RELATIONSHIPS

The people in our lives can be one of the greatest sources of happiness, yet they can also present us with some of our biggest challenges. Every relationship will have its ups and downs and you should consider the effect your moods and emotions have on those around you as well as vice versa. Relationships require a level of self-discipline and a commitment to work things through if they are to be nourishing and supporting. There are many ways of using your magic skills to foster an atmosphere of love and understanding and to honour your closest relationships.

To help communication between members of your family, use blue stones on the altar.

A FAMILY ALTAR
Making a family altar is a good way of celebrating and deepening the bonds between you. It is best positioned somewhere that is at the heart of family life, such as in the living room or kitchen. An old piece of furniture that has been handed down to you through the generations could be the perfect site for an altar dedicated to your family. It will carry the blessings of those it served in the past. You could place the altar in the west where the Water element governs relationships. If you wish to observe Feng Shui principles, the area of your home or room that corresponds to the family is positioned in the west, and to love and relationships, in the south-west.

You might invite all the members of the family to help you make the altar, each bringing an object that symbolizes an aspect of themselves. Photographs of your loved ones will act as a focus for your prayers and thoughts about your

Zodiac candle colours

Each sign of the zodiac can be symbolized by a coloured candle as follows:

Aries: dark red
Taurus: green
Gemini: yellow
Cancer: silver
Leo: gold or orange
Virgo: yellow
Libra: sky-blue or rose
Scorpio: burgundy or red
Sagittarius: purple or black
Capricorn: black
Aquarius: rainbow
Pisces: sea-green or indigo

Place pictures and gifts from children on the altar, to honour their contribution to the family.

family. To honour your relationship with your partner, choose a happy and harmonious picture of the two of you together. Other items could include gifts to you from your children, especially presents or drawings made by them, which bring with them fond memories and the resonance of the love that motivated the gift. But remember to include objects that represent family members as they are now – acknowledging your children as complex teenagers, not just as enchanting toddlers, for example – so that the altar grows with the family and remains relevant. If pets are part of your family, you can also include reminders of them on the altar.

RELATIONSHIP DIFFICULTIES

When you or other family members are going through a difficult time, try to stay open and talk about what is happening. Because of their link with the throat chakra, all blue crystals aid communication. You can put the stones on the altar, or else use them as a charm and carry them with you. Blue lace agate helps you express feelings, turquoise fosters partnership, light blue angel stone heals anger and lapis lazuli aids in the release of emotional wounds. Rose quartz is the stone of love.

If someone close to you is having problems in their relationship with others, perhaps with friends or at work, surround a picture of them with rose

---

The symbolism of flowers

In folklore, flowers are believed to speak the language of the heart. Using flowers and herbs is another way of working with whatever qualities are being expressed or are needed in a relationship.

Apple blossom: love, friendship
Clover: fidelity
Coltsfoot: peace and tranquillity
Cyclamen: love and truth
Gardenia: peace and healing

Hyacinth: love and protection
Jasmine: friendship
Lavender: peace and happiness
Lily of the valley: peace, harmony and love
Narcissus: harmony
Passion flower: peace and friendship
Rose: love
Sweet pea: friendship and courage
Vervain: inner strength and peace
Violet: contentment

---

quartz crystals for harmony. While you do this, think about the person close to you and imagine them at ease with themselves and others.

GIVING BLESSINGS

When someone leaves home or begins a new life journey, write a protective blessing and tuck the folded paper into the frame of their picture on your altar. When loved ones are away, you can light candles that represent their sun sign to send them your love and support. You can also burn candles to bolster confidence and self-esteem or to celebrate significant dates such as birthdays and anniversaries.

HONOURING THE ANCESTORS

In cultures with an established tradition of family altars, the ancestors are the most honoured family members.

Photographs and mementos of your forebears keep those you loved as a positive influence in your life, and provide a sense of continuity for your children, helping them to see themselves as links in a chain of existence.

In Spanish-speaking countries – particularly Mexico – the Day of the Dead is when the dead are entertained as respected members of the family. One of the most important religious occasions of the year, families have picnics in the cemeteries and build altars covered with flowers and food to welcome their dead relatives home for the night, burning candles and copal incense to help them find their way. Veneration of the ancestors is also an important tradition in the East. To prevent their spirits from becoming restless or vengeful, rituals are conducted that ensure proper respect and provide the family with a means of consulting the wise elders; the family includes past and future generations, as well as the present.

Copal

One of the most important and valuable incense burning substances used by the Mayans, Incas and Aztecs of Central and South America was copal, the gift of the jaguars. According to the Mayan's holy book, copal resin was extracted from the Tree of Life and given to humanity as a gift. There are three types of copal resin: black, golden and white.

If someone in the family needs special love and care, surround their picture with rose quartz.

COPING WITH CHANGE

O ur lives follow cycles that are continually changing, evolving and shifting from moment to moment, and nothing in the physical realm remains the same forever. In modern society, we have come to fear or abhor most endings, seeing them as associated with failure or as the loss of something we value or want to keep. However, natural magic teaches us that change is good, and when we are able to let go of things that do not really serve us, or of an experience that has run its course, our lives can open up in very positive ways.

A ritual purification of your new home, using sun-charged water and rosemary, will cleanse the psychic space to make it yours.

ENDINGS

To attract a new beginning, we must first close the door on that which is ending. This could be a work contract, a relationship, a house move or perhaps grown-up children leaving home; whatever the situation it is important to create an ending that honours the change, while remaining positive about it. The simplest way to honour an ending is to voice the fact, and give thanks for what you have experienced as you indicate your intention to let it go and move on to a new beginning. The ceremony can be as simple or as elaborate as you wish. For instance, you could light a candle on your altar and say a prayer, or give some other offering as a thanksgiving for what is ending. Water is the element associated with letting go, so you could also include this on your altar.

MOVING HOUSE

If you are moving house, cleaning and clearing out is something that you will do naturally in the process of moving on. After the physical clearing and cleansing has been finished, an ideal way to acknowledge the act spiritually is to sweep the house symbolically with a bundle of birch twigs or a birch broom, imagining each area being purified as you do so. In ancient times, brushwood from the birch tree was used to sweep out the spirits of the old year, preparing the way for the beginning of the new one. Let the house know of your intentions in performing this act and thank it for having been your home. You can also use the birch broom to sweep the new house you are moving into, as a

A traditional witch's broom made from birch twigs can be used symbolically to sweep away the old to make way for the new.

first step to claiming it as your new home. Here, it will have the effect of sweeping away the atmosphere created by the previous occupants, making space for your own spiritual energy.

To prepare your new home for the beginning of your life there, you can bless it by walking around all the rooms and sprinkling them as you go with drops of water that you have charged with the energy of the sun. Use a sprig of rosemary to sprinkle the water, as it is a protective herb that favours new beginning. This will add vitality and vigour to your new environment.

A TALISMAN FOR CHANGE

Endings and beginnings may be accompanied by feelings of insecurity, fear, and sadness, and you can use this talisman to help you come to terms with your feelings. Make it during a waxing moon if you are more concerned with beginnings, during a waning moon for endings and letting go.

You will need
2 silver or white candles
silver pen
23cm (9in) square of natural paper
moonstone

1 Light the candles, saying these words as you do so:
Hail to you Levanah, I light these candles in your honour and ask for your help with the endings/beginnings (whichever you are working on) in my life at this time.

2 Draw the symbol for Alpha (beginnings) or Omega (endings) in the middle of the paper, depending on whether you are working with endings or beginnings. If you want to work with both, then draw both symbols.

3 Fold the four corners of the paper into the centre to make a diamond shape, then fold in the same way twice more.

4 Pinch out the candles, place the moonstone on your talisman and leave it in moonlight for several hours. Afterwards, put it in a safe place or carry it with you.

Symbols of new beginnings

Add a wish to a bowl of pumpkin seeds.

A white lily holds a rolled-up wish paper.

There are many ways in which you can call for a new beginning, once you have recognized and acknowledged an ending in your life.

- A pair of lodestones placed together in a central area of a room will call for the attraction of a lover.

- If you see shooting stars and comets together in the sky, wishing upon them calls the Sky Father's protection and blessing for any wishes you make.

- The cowrie shell is sacred to the Goddess and empowers wishes for love, friendship and family. Decorate a small pouch with cowrie shells and drop your written wish inside.

- A bowl of seeds (such as sesame, sunflower or pumpkin) with a wish tucked into them, placed on an altar or on the kitchen windowsill, will encourage the growth of whatever you have called for.

- A birch broom propped up beside a doorway will encourage the old to depart and the new to arrive, and will also provide protection for your home.

- When you are seeking new work or prosperity opportunities, turn silver coins in your pocket on the first night of a new moon to invite growth in your finances.

- Write a wish on a piece of paper, fold or roll it and place the paper within the cone of a white lily flower; this bloom is sacred to Ostara, the goddess of birth and new life.

- Written symbols, such as Beth from the Druidic tree alphabet, or the Greek letter Alpha, will encourage new beginnings. Write them in places of significance, such as over a written wish, or trace them in the air in a space where new beginnings are being called for. You could also include them on a talisman.

A talisman to the moon can help you cope with change.

ABUNDANCE AND PROSPERITY

Prosperity is not only a matter of material possessions, physical or otherwise – feelings of satisfaction with our lot often bear little relation to what we actually possess. Abundance is about tuning in to the blessings of life, shifting emphasis away from personal limitation and all that we lack, and opening ourselves to new and prosperous possibilities. It has long been acknowledged that if you have a clear idea of what you want you are far more likely to achieve it. Magic recognizes that thought is a form of energy, and positive thinking contributes energetically to the fulfilment of your desire: ideas are the first step to abundance.

An altar of abundance, dedicated to Lakshmi, should reflect Earth colours and scents.

PERSONAL BELIEF SYSTEMS

When you want to focus on creating abundance a good place to start is to examine your belief systems. For instance, many people believe that material wealth is at odds with spirituality, and that being poor is somehow virtuous. Another widely held view is that you have to work hard in order to have wealth, or that only money that is "hard won" is deserved. Similarly, many wealthy people are unable to enjoy their riches as deep down they harbour a sense of guilt, alternatively some people are actually afraid to have more money for fear that they won't be liked or won't fit in any more with their social group, or even that they will become a target for people's jealousy.

Most of us have many barriers that stop us from receiving the abundance that we deserve – whether on the material plane (money), on the emotional (love) or on the spiritual (godliness). The first step in bringing more abundance into your life is to feel that you are worth it and deserve it: a person living in abundance has much more to offer than someone who is living in lack or "poverty consciousness".

One way of increasing your feeling of self-worth is to practise "affirmations", sayings that you use to help redirect your thoughts from negative to positive. The words you use for attracting abundance can be whatever you feel fits the situation, but here are two suggested affirmations:

I (say your name) am now open to receive (say what it is you are wishing for),
or *I (say your name) give thanks for the ever-increasing blessings in my life, now, today and always.*

One of the best ways to find abundance is to have gratitude for everything you have, as well as anything else you may receive.

An Altar to Abundance

Dedicating an altar to abundance is a powerful symbol of your intent to welcome more of life's goodness and to give thanks for the gifts you have already received. As Earth is the element associated with the material plane, use warm earth colours such as russet, deep yellow, rich browns and olive greens. Add spicy scents to your altar to attract prosperity, scents such as patchouli, star anise, clove and cinnamon are ideal – or make up some prosperity incense mix.

Make an offering of some silver coins, and as you do so, think of all the things that already enrich your life and represent them on the altar to create a positive reminder of what you have already been given and to express your gratitude. If you focus your attention on what you have, and keep giving thanks for it, you will find greater abundance being drawn into your life, based on the "like attracts like" principle.

Hindu Gods of Abundance

If you are seeking to manifest greater wealth, call on the Hindu goddess Lakshmi and/or the god Ganesha.

In the Hindu tradition, Lakshmi is the personification of abundance, wealth and harmony. She is portrayed as a beautiful woman seated on a sacred lotus throne; with two of her four hands she offers blessings of love and joy, while gold coins

Chai Shen, the god of wealth

For generations, Chinese families have set up an altar outside their homes on the eve of the Lunar New Year, in the hope of receiving the blessings of Chai Shen, the god of wealth, for the coming year. Each year, the god arrives from a different direction and this must be carefully calculated to make sure the altar is correctly positioned, otherwise it would welcome the god of evil instead.

All the family members say prayers and make offerings that symbolize abundance and good fortune, including sweets, fruit and wine. Everyone writes their wishes for the year on red paper, which is burned with offerings of incense. The previous year's portrait of Chai Shen is burned, and firecrackers are set off. After the ceremony, the god's portrait is carried inside to watch over the household for the year to come.

fall from the other two into the ocean of life. She is a symbol of everything that is fortunate and it is the nature of good fortune that it is distributed randomly. Deepavali, the third day of Diwali (the Festival of Lights), is dedicated to her worship; lamps are lit inside every home to welcome her and fireworks are exploded in her honour.

Ganesha, the elephant-headed god and lord of obstacles, helps to clear the path of anything that stands in the way of us receiving Lakshmi's blessings, so his presence can also help to bring abundance into your home.

A Prosperity Box

To help you focus on what you want to bring into your life, choose a suitable container to be your "prosperity box". Using black ink, make a list of what you

wish for. Be specific with what you are asking for – for instance, if you would like more money, state how much you need. Then write another list using energy-enhancing orange ink: this list should contain all the things you are prepared to do to help you achieve your desires. Remember: you have to take practical steps to help magic happen.

Fold the pieces of paper and place both lists in the box, together with a handful of prosperity incense, a few silver coins and a small piece of jade. Keep the box on your altar. When you receive a gift, place it on the altar for a while and give thanks to sustain the flow of abundant energy.

Prosperity incense

1 part cassia bark or cinnamon
1 part grated nutmeg
1 part finely grated orange rind
1 part star anise
few drops orange essential oil
2 parts frankincense grains

Pound the first four ingredients using a pestle and mortar, sprinkle on the oil and mix in the frankincense resin. Burn small amounts of the mixture on a charcoal block placed in a heatproof bowl.

A mixture of frankincense and rich spices can help in your prosperity magic.

Prosperity boxes can be filled with wishes for others, and offerings to a wish-granting power.

LUNAR GARDENING

Because the moon has such a strong influence over crop yields, for hundreds of years farmers, agriculturists and gardeners have all observed the moon's phases when planting, tending and harvesting crops. The phases of the moon, and also the zodiac sign that it is passing through, seem to affect the way plants grow, so timing gardening activities according to the moon helps make them more effective. The principles of lunar gardening take a while to adjust to, but after a while, you will find that your flowers bloom brighter, crops grow more succulent and flavoursome, and trees have stronger roots. In fact your whole garden will benefit from this ancient way of gardening and be filled with healthy plants that are a joy to behold.

Watery or fleshy plants, like courgettes and cucumbers, should be planted during a full moon.

GARDENING BY THE MOON

If, to begin with, you find it a little too complicated to check the zodiac signs for your gardening tasks, you can simply follow the moon's phases of waxing and waning. The moon is increasing in influence between the new and full phases (brightmoon) and decreasing in influence during the waning and dark phases (darkmoon).

NEW MOON

Seeds of plants that flower above the ground should be sown at the new moon. This is also the time for farmers to sow cereals such as barley and sweetcorn (maize), and for leafy and fruiting crops such as asparagus, broccoli and Brussels sprouts, squash and tomatoes to be planted. This is also the time for fertilizing and feeding anything that you wish to flourish.

FULL MOON

Because full moon has the strongest influence over the Water element this is the best time to plant watery or fleshy crops like marrows (zucchini) and cucumbers. This is also a good time for harvesting the leaves, stems, or seeds of herbs for drying, especially when the moon is transiting a Fire sign. It is important to pick your herbs on a dry day, so that they dry quickly, without rotting. The best time to harvest is just before midday. String the stems together

and hang them upside down in an airy, cool but dry atmosphere, until ready for use. The full moon is also an excellent time for baking bread. The influence of the full moon proves the yeast better and encourages the dough to rise.

Traditionally, mushrooms are picked at full moon, the best time being just after dawn, when the dew is still on the grass. Take them home and have them for breakfast. Remember that some fungi are poisonous, so be very careful that you

pick only edible mushrooms and do not eat anything you are unsure about.

WANING MOON

The waning moon is the time in the moon's cycle for root vegetables, peas and beans, and garlic. Anything undertaken during this time will benefit

Tend leafy plants and feed the garden well during the new moon. This is also the best time for sowing many types of seeds.

underground development or retard growth. This is therefore an excellent time to mow the lawn, as its new growth will be slowed, or to plough and turn the soil. Gather and harvest crops during the waning moon, especially in late summer, the traditional harvest time. This is an excellent time to prune trees, roses and shrubs, and to water the garden. Making jams and pickles should also be done during a waning moon, for best results.

Crops that are suited to planting during the waning moon are endive (chicory), carrots, garlic, onions, potatoes, radishes, beetroot (beets) and strawberries. All flowering bulbs, biennials and perennials should be planted during this time, especially when the moon is in a Water sign. Saplings also benefit from being planted during the waning moon, when it is in Cancer, Scorpio, Pisces or Virgo.

DARKMOON

The fourth quarter, or darkmoon, is the best time for garden maintenance: for weeding, cultivation and the removal of pests. Start a compost heap during the darkmoon time, or harvest and dry herbs and everlasting flowers, especially if the moon is in a Fire sign. A watermoon is the best time to water fields and gardens.

Elemental gardening table

When gardening according to the moon's sign of the zodiac, your timing needs to be a little more accurate than is the case with the moon's phases. The moon takes only about a couple of days to pass through each sign, so to coordinate both factors will take careful planning. For details on the moon's phases and when it is passing through a particular star sign, you will need to refer to a lunar almanac or an ephemeris. Then check the chart below to discover which zodiacal sign is most appropriate for each activity.

AIR
Gemini (barren and dry): weeding, clearing, pest control
Libra (moist): plant fruit trees, fleshy vegetables, root vegetables
Aquarius (barren and dry): garden maintenance, weeding and pest control

FIRE
Aries (barren and dry): weeding, clearing, garden maintenance
Leo (barren and dry): bonfires, ground clearance, weeding
Sagittarius (barren and dry): plant onions, garden maintenance

WATER
Cancer (very fruitful and moist): best sign for planting, sowing and cultivating
Scorpio (very fruitful and moist): very good sign for planting, sowing and general cultivation, especially vine fruits; start a compost heap
Pisces (very fruitful and moist): excellent for planting, especially root crops

EARTH
Taurus (fertile and moist): plant root crops and leafy vegetables
Virgo (barren and moist): cultivation, weeding and pest control
Capricorn (productive and dry): good for root vegetables

Carrots and other root vegetables develop best during the time of a waning moon.

LUNAR PLANTS

Particular plants and trees come under the influence of the moon. These have been used in ceremonies and rituals to the moon goddess, and were also depicted in traditional art and sculpture. Flowers of the moon include all aquatic plants like waterlilies, seaweed and lotus, as well as jasmine and poppy. All flowers that are white or that blossom at night, such as jasmine or night-scented stock, are also moon flowers.

Trees of the moon include sandalwood and camphor, both of which were used in the ancient world in ceremonies to attract the attentions of the moon goddess, as well as the willow, aspen, eucalyptus, pear, plum and lemon. The willow is also known as the moon's wishing tree, and calling for favour by tying white, silver or light blue ribbons to her branches on lunar festival days can help to empower a wish.

Foretelling the weather

Because the moon influences weather patterns, it is possible to predict changes in the weather according to where the moon is in her cycle, or her appearance.

- a new moon always brings a change in the weather, and if the horns of the moon are sharp it indicates the onset of windy weather
- a crescent moon cupped and on its back means rain
- if you can see a star close to the moon, expect to have 'wild weather'
- a bright full moon heralds good weather and a mottled full moon will bring rain
- storms and other dramatic weather patterns are more likely just after a full moon

ARTS OF DIVINATION

The word divination shares the same Latin root as divine, meaning sacred, godly or pertaining to the heavenly realm. Divination is a sacred art; it is the means by which we can discover the unknown (or what is hidden) by means of intuition, inspiration or magic. In ancient times, it was very much a part of both religious and secular life. In Old Testament times, for instance, the priest would cast stones or lots when important decisions had to be made, while in the Ancient and Classical world, oracles were regularly consulted to assess the best time for an undertaking or to predict the outcome of a course of action. In all cases it was believed that God or the gods were speaking through the divining tool.

Divination embraces a number of arts that use symbols or patterns to help you focus your clairvoyance or psychic vision on matters that may be

occurring at a distance, back and forth in time, or simply at a deep level within yourself.

There are a variety of different methods by which the doors to your own psychic abilities are opened in a way that permits intuition to work. This chapter includes some of the most widely popular systems of divination in use, including numerology, astrology, the Tarot, the I Ching and runes. Dowsing, a relatively straightforward art, is also included, along with scrying, which is perhaps one of the trickiest to master.

DIVINATION

Above the entrance at the celebrated Delphic Oracle in ancient Greece was carved the inscription, "Know Thyself". Indeed, increasing self-awareness can be said to be the ultimate purpose of divination. Rather than being a method to predict a future that is already certain, it is a way of seeking guidance from the gods or our "higher self" about possibilities. If we accept that we are the creators of our own destiny, it follows that the more information we have at our disposal, the more we are able to make choices that are in line with our highest purpose or destiny.

The I Ching can give you greater insight into your situation and help you make wise decisions.

HIGH AND LOW MAGIC

At its most elevated level, divination is a sacred art designed to exalt the consciousness of the individual seeking guidance (the inquirer) and to increase self-acceptance. At the other end of the spectrum, divination is also associated with "fortune-telling" and prediction.

This can place the inquirer in a passive position, a victim in the hands of fate. Practitioners of natural magic are more inclined to use divination for its original sacred intent. This puts the onus of responsibility firmly in the hands of the inquirer and means that the divinatory arts are approached with the same care and respect as any other aspect of natural magic. When interpreted correctly, a reading will direct the inquirer's attention to the forces shaping his or her path in life – and present choices or suggest a course of action.

SYNCHRONICITY

The practice of divination stems from a desire to know in advance what is going to happen. Through the ages many

Divination can be done for yourself and for others. If you undertake to perform any kind of reading for someone else, be careful about how you give them difficult or challenging information.

Uses for divination

Divination can be used to:

- analyse problems
- clarify a decision-making process
- help you to understand yourself and others better
- reveal aspects of a situation that are out of conscious awareness
- stimulate intuition
- open up your mind
- assist healing
- predict future patterns or trends

Ethics – the dos and don'ts of divining

Traditionally the divinatory arts were taught by oral and practical exposition, where the student would naturally assimilate the level of responsibility needed to stand as mediator between the inquirer and the spiritual realm. Whenever you undertake to perform any reading for another person, you should treat them with respect and compassion: do not give them more information than they can handle, and do not frighten them if you see difficult or challenging aspects in their reading. The following guidelines may also be helpful:

1 Do not use divination for guidance obsessively: this can be counter productive and indicates giving away your power and responsibility.

2 Always obtain the permission of another person before doing a reading for them.

3 Do not use divination for entertainment or in inappropriate circumstances.

4 Respect your spiritual allies; seek their advice seriously and remember to give thanks.

5 Don't divine when you are low in energy or feeling upset; wait until you feel balanced and centred.

6 Remember that divination is a means of spiritual clarification, not sorcery.

7 Dedicate your art to the highest good of all.

8 Encourage the inquirer to see the reading as a pattern of possibilities based on their current situation; remind them that they have choice.

different methods have been used to foretell the future, from signs and portents in the sky to the patterns made by tea leaves or the innards of slaughtered beasts. Sticks, coins, coloured stones, pictures and dreams have all been used to predict events, often with an uncanny accuracy. No one really knows how divination works, but the theory of "synchronicity" may come close to giving us a plausible explanation.

It was the twentieth-century psychologist, Carl Jung, who used the term synchronicity to account for "meaningful coincidences". In rational thinking, mysterious or amazing coincidences are ascribed to chance, but during the course of his work Jung noticed a pattern of coincidences in seemingly unrelated events that caused him to challenge the predominant scientific view of cause and effect. He ascribed this to a deeper level of the mind, which he referred to as "the collective unconscious". Archetypes and symbols operate at this level.

According to magical thinking, nothing happens at random; everything is connected and has meaning, as events in one area of the web of life correspond to patterns in other areas. This means that in theory, almost anything can be used for divination; it is all a question of being able to read the signs or patterns. A divinatory reading can reveal a minute part of the greater pattern; during that moment, it is as though a veil is twitched aside and we glimpse the otherworld.

Palmistry has been used as a divination tool for centuries and can take years of study and practice to perfect.

PREPARATION

Before divining, it is important to create a calm environment with soft lighting. Too much background noise or bright lights can disturb your concentration. Privacy is also vitally important because quite personal and intimate subjects may be discussed while doing any kind of reading. Eye contact and a friendly smile always helps the other person to feel at ease. Before you start, the inquirer

should focus on the subject or issue that they are seeking guidance with. If you are using any tools – such as Tarot cards or the Rune stones – let the inquirer handle these as they focus on their issue. Some people will take only a short time to get their issues clear in their minds, while others will take longer to focus. The inquirer should then pass the cards, stones or whatever is being used back to you so that you can begin.

NUMEROLOGY

Aside from their practical use in counting, numbers also have a symbolic value. Numerology is the art of understanding life by studying the symbolic value of numbers and the relationships between them. Since time immemorial, cultures and religions all over the world have either devised their own system of numerology or borrowed from and expanded on existing ones. All of them have been used to explain and gain a deeper understanding of ourselves in relation to the cosmos, and numerology has always played a part in magic and divination.

The numbers of our birth date help us discover and express our core personal qualities.

LIFE CYCLES

The numbers 1 to 9 form the basic building blocks of numerology. Aside from zero, all other numbers can be reduced to arrive at one of these single digits. For example, 39 reduces to 3; this is arrived at by adding 3+9=12; 12 is then reduced to 1+2=3. Numerology is based on the principle of reduction, which mirrors the process of life. For instance, our time in the womb from conception to birth is nine months, which consists of three terms, while traditionally our lives are said to be made up of three cycles of three nine-year periods. The first cycle (ages 0–27) is concerned with the birth and growth of the individual; the second cycle (ages 28–54) is about how we engage with the world; while the final cycle (ages 55–81) is about engaging with the spirit. Similarly the numbers 1 to 9 form three nests of three with their symbolic meanings fitting within this bigger framework.

NUMEROLOGY AND YOU

Numbers affect every area of our lives and almost any set of numbers can be broken down and have meanings assigned to them. Many numbers are uniquely ours, from our telephone or house number to the number on official documents such as passports, driving licences and bank accounts. Many people also have a number that they consider "lucky". In numerology, however, the most significant numbers are those that relate to your date of birth (the life path number) and to the letters of your name (personality number).

THE LIFE PATH NUMBER

Everyone has a life path number that represents their potential. It is derived from the sum of the digits of their birth date. For example, a birthday of 9 November 1968 (9/11/1968) has a life path number of 8, reached in the following way: 9 + 1+1 + 1+9+6+8 = 35, then 3 + 5 = 8. Your life path number is a guide to what you need to do in life.

THE COSMIC AND PERSONAL YEAR

Like astrology, numerology can also provide a clue for the best timing of

The personal year number helps us all to work in harmony with unfolding events.

events. Every year, the calendar changes and different possibilities are available to us. The cosmic year number is calculated by adding up the digits of the current year. For example, the year 2004 was a 6 year, which showed that there was potential for universal peace and harmony (the vibration of 6) that year. While the number of the cosmic year symbolizes the potential that exists around you, there is also a personal year number that relates more directly to you. To calculate this, you use your birth date, substituting the current year for the year of your birth.

NUMBERS AND THEIR MEANINGS

Traditionally, the symbolic meanings of numbers are ascribed as follows:

0 The lens; the all-seeing eye that encompasses everything but cannot act; reflective; withdrawal from life to take stock before embarking on the next adventure.
1 Initiative and independence; the leader; goal-setting and ambition; Great Father; the sun.
2 Nurturing and relationship; balance; carer, mediator; Great Mother; moon.
3 Creativity; self-expression; the birth of ideas; aspiration; Cosmic Child.

4 Structure and order; stability; material structures; self-discipline and consolidation.
5 Breaking free from limits imposed by structures leading to growth and change; restlessness; adventurous; exploring new possibilities; self-discovery.
6 Emotional harmony and sensitivity; perfection and ideals of family life; love of heart and home.
7 Spiritual transformation; meditation, mysticism; spiritual learning and development; life and spirit combine.
8 Strategist and organizer, regulating relationship between spirit and matter; moves between spheres of heaven and earth; connects with cycles of life. Karmic number.
9 Wisdom gained through experience; the great teacher; completion and ending before a new cycle begins.
11 Speaking with inspiration; channelling the spirit; visionary; the prophet or seer.
22 Building the dream; the master builder; systematic approach combined with gentleness and sensitivity.
33 Unconditional giving; devotion to great causes; saint or martyr; the tireless helper.

Personal year numbers

Your personal year number is calculated by adding the day and month of your birth with the current year.

1 Fresh beginnings, both in your personal and professional life
2 Finding peace; revising and strengthening what you have started
3 Self-expression; personal as well as professional development
4 Discipline and consolidation; application, hard work and self-discipline
5 Exploring new possibilities; change
6 Self-esteem; love and romance
7 Soul-searching; self-awareness and personal spiritual growth
8 Go with the flow; try to connect more with inner self and others
9 Resolution; assess the past and note and enjoy your achievements

The personality number

Although many people will have the same life path number, the unique path that their life will take will be influenced by their personal attributes. A clue to these can be gained from the personality number. This number represents your identity; by recognizing and using its inherited qualities, you are better able to express yourself. In numerology, every letter of the alphabet has a numerical equivalent. The personality number is obtained by finding out the numerical value of every letter in your full name and reducing it to a single digit. For example, the name Ann Helen Myers consists of the numbers 1+5+5 + 8+5+3+5+5 + 4+7+5+9+1 = 63 which reduces to 9. Name changes and nicknames will reflect the personality number most representative of you at the time.

Numerical equivalents of the alphabet

1	2	3	4	5	6	7	8	9
A	B	C	D	E	F	G	H	I
J	K	L	M	N	O	P	Q	R
S	T	U	V	W	X	Y	Z	

The letters of our names can give us clues to our inherited patterns.

ASTROLOGY

Before the modern scientific age, it was widely believed that the movements of the celestial bodies regulated life on earth. The cycles of day and night, the waxing and waning of the moon and the movement of the planets across the starry night sky follow regular and predictable patterns. Our ancestors related these patterns to natural phenomena, including not only the weather and seasons, but also different kinds of destiny. Astrology is the study of these cosmic patterns pin-pointed in the continuum of time and space and represented symbolically on an astrological "chart" or horoscope.

The universe is constantly evolving and new planets are still being discovered today.

ORIGINS OF ASTROLOGY

Astrology is one of the most ancient of all the magical arts. It seems to have evolved in Mesopotamia, where it was practised by priests who concerned themselves with the prediction of major events, from whether or not the harvest would be good to the destinies of kings and princes. Later it became the province of mathematicians, and the Greeks and Chaldeans used their knowledge of the heavens to delineate

The zodiac signs

In modern-day Western astrology, there are 12 signs of the zodiac, each related to a constellation.

Aries: The leader; 'me first'; loner, pioneer, go-getter; enjoys action, adventure; quick to anger; ruled by Mars

Taurus: The builder; practical, patient, steadfast; enjoys material comfort and wellbeing; ruled by Venus

Gemini: The talker; quick-witted, restless, easily bored; enjoys travel, new ideas; constantly on the look-out for new experiences; ruled by Mercury

Cancer: The nurturer; empathic, sensitive to needs of others; imaginative; enjoys home and family; ruled by the Moon

Leo: The actor; plays centre-stage, dramatic, generous, warm, affectionate; enjoys good living, romance, and 'to play'; ruled by the Sun

Virgo: The perfectionist; precise, meticulous, pays attention to detail; enjoys work in the service of others; sincere, dependable; ruled by Mercury

Libra: The adjuster; seeks to bridge or reconcile opposites, to balance; relationships important and need for peace and harmony; enjoys aesthetics and beautiful things; ruled by Venus

Scorpio: The transformer; death and rebirth, endings and beginnings; going to the depths, emotional intensity; enjoys the occult, the mysteries of life; ruled by Pluto and Mars

Sagittarius: The traveller; journeys to expand horizons; free spirit, adventurous, buoyant and exuberant; enjoys humour, having fun, new experiences; ruled by Jupiter

Capricorn: The climber; works hard to achieve ambitious and lofty goals; patient, cautious, responsible, committed; enjoys the status of success, black humour; ruled by Saturn

Aquarius: The reformer; intellectual revolutionary, seeks social justice, a 'brotherhood of man'; freedom of thought, originality and emotional independence; enjoys gadgets, machines, electronic media; ruled by Uranus and Saturn

Pisces: The dreamer; impressionable, imaginative, sensitive and artistic; psychic development, meditation, spiritual transformation; refines and idealizes; enjoys the arts, but also has a tendency towards escapism; ruled by Neptune and Jupiter certain characteristics associated with each pattern that could be applied to life on earth.

USES OF ASTROLOGY

A horoscope involves plotting the position of the celestial bodies at a given moment in time. It is possible to draw one up for almost any life situation: we can use it to help us determine the best time or place for an event, such as a wedding or business venture, or we could also examine the potential of a relationship by comparing two charts and looking at the symbolic interaction between them. However, the most useful place to start with astrology is with your own birth chart.

The birth chart can be used as a tool for self-awareness: personality types and psychological traits as well as information on the building blocks of life – such as career, health and relationships – are all covered in the birth chart. It can also be used to predict future life-trends, although be aware that these are "trends" and not absolute certainties. Drawing up a birth chart involves complex numerical calculations and unless you want to spend the time learning how to do this, it is a good investment to get your chart drawn up by a professional astrologer. Once you have your chart, it is yours for life. The next step is learning how to make sense of it.

UNDERSTANDING ASTROLOGY

Your horoscope will be drawn as a circle divided into twelve sections, each section representing a sign of the zodiac

(Aries, Taurus, Gemini and so on); the word zodiac itself comes from the Greek meaning "a circle of animals". Each of the celestial bodies (referred to as "planets" for convenience) will appear in a sign of the zodiac. Most probably you already know your "Sun sign" (often referred to as your "star sign") but in addition you will find that you will also have a zodiac sign for the Moon, Venus, Mars and all the other planets. The basic layer of the birth chart shows the disposition of the planets and how they are influenced by the nature or character of the signs in which they fall. The next layer is to look at the relationships or "aspects" made by these planets to one another; some of these aspects will be easy and harmonious, while others will be stressful and present challenges. On top of this, the chart is further divided into twelve "houses". These represent areas of life – such as work, relationships, creativity and health for instance – that show us where the energies of each planet are expressed.

Astrology is the study of the patterns made by the planets and how these can influence life on Earth.

The symbolism of the planets

The word planet is derived from the ancient Greek 'wanderer'. In ancient times, the planets were regarded as mysterious wanderers of the night sky and linked with the gods and goddesses of classical mythology. Each of these divinities is contained within the horoscope, and can be seen to represent different energies or aspects of the psyche. How these are expressed will vary according to which of the 12 zodiac signs the planet falls in, and whether this is a Fire, Water, Earth or Air sign.

Planet	Symbol	Function
Sun	☉	Wholeness; integration of the self; inner purpose; vitality; conscious authority; the heroic impulse to 'be'
Moon	☽	Emotional response; imagination; receptivity; rhythm and mood; memories
Mercury	☿	Thought and communication; mental faculties; intelligence
Venus	♀	Love, beauty, art; relationships (friends and lovers); harmony; money and resources
Mars	♂	Action; self-assertion; desire, ambition, competition; physical energy; ego
Jupiter	♃	Expansion, freedom, opportunity; search for meaning; luck, learning, philosophy
Saturn	♄	Limitation, structure, perseverance, responsibility; life's lessons; karma
Uranus	♅	Originality and inventiveness; eccentricity; urge to reform; radicalism; change, the unexpected, intuition
Neptune	♆	Idealism and inspiration; spiritual values, transcendence; clairvoyance, the subconscious
Pluto	♇	Transformation; death, rebirth and regeneration; intensity, power

The Houses

Just as there are 12 signs, there are also 12 astrological houses that closely reflect the meanings of the signs. The houses are "areas of life", compartments of experience that indicate where the energies of each planet are expressed. If the planets show us "what" then the houses indicate "where".

The first house is concerned with childhood and the development of personality. It governs physical appearance and is the way we present ourselves to the world. The second house represents possessions and values; it is the domain of accumulated wealth, income and everything to do with material comfort. It is connected with a person's capabilities and resourcefulness. The ability to communicate is contained within the third house. This house also governs neighbours, relatives and the immediate environment. Home is the domain of the fourth house; this includes our homeland, as well as the actual building in which we live. The fifth house is about pleasure and creativity, and includes love affairs, our sex life and children, as well as creations of an artistic sort. Our health and wellbeing falls into the sixth house, which also includes our work and how we fulfil our role in society. Close relationships and

Aspects

Reading a birth chart is extremely complex. Not only does the astrologer take into account the position of the planets in the signs and houses and where they fall in the circle, they will also look at the 'aspects' or relationships between the planets. Like relationships, some aspects are easier to handle than others. The challenging aspects are often what motivates psychological growth. The main astrological aspects are as follows:

The conjunction (0°): planets are in close proximity to one another. The conjunction is like a marriage, with each planet strongly influencing the other; it is usually a harmonious aspect, depending on the planets and houses involved.

The opposition (180°): planets are placed on opposite sides of the circle, suggesting tension and confrontation. The opposition is a challenging aspect and means that we will struggle to integrate these opposing forces.

The trine (120°): planets are in a harmonious relationship forming one (or more) sides of a triangle, enabling easy synthesis. If all three points of the trine (or triangle) are completed, it is known as a 'grand trine'.

The square (90°): planets are in tension with one another, forming one (or more) sides of a square. The square produces restless striving in order to get to grips with the planetary energies involved; being at right angles to one another, the planets involved may also go off at a tangent, causing blocks.

The sextile (60°): planets are in harmony; sextiles produce motivated activity, a working relationship between the planets and the angles involved.

partnerships (both marriage and business) fall into the seventh house, while the eighth house is the house of transformation and covers endings, death and rebirth. Inheritances, wills and life's challenges and upheavals are found in this house. Travel, higher education and spiritual voyaging are ninth house matters, while the tenth is concerned with public position, our reputation and status in the world. Friends and social groups are contained in the 11th house, while the 12th house is the area of spirituality and transcendence.

The first of the 12 astrological houses is concerned with childhood.

Our love affairs and our sex life are governed by the fifth house, which is also about pleasure and creativity.

Work comes under the governance of the sixth house, which also includes our role in society.

The moon through the signs

Unlike the Sun, the moon travels through all the signs of the zodiac in a month, spending two or three days or so in each sign. Because the moon is so important in magic and ritual, it is especially useful to understand how it functions through the different signs.

Moon in ...	Key word	Magic for ...
Aries	energy	starting new projects, leadership, goal-setting
Taurus	dependability	love, money and material things
Gemini	communication	talking, writing; travel (short journeys)
Cancer	nurturing	home and family, emotional support; issues to do with motherhood
Leo	courage	creativity and fertility; daring to take risks
Virgo	self-improvement	work (on self or in the world); health; attention to detail
Libra	balance	emotional harmony, giving and receiving; artistic and spiritual work; legal matters
Scorpio	transformation	making real changes in your life; sexuality and desire
Sagittarius	exploration	travel (long journeys); pursuit of spiritual values
Capricorn	achievement	getting organized; pushing forwards with career, ambitions; status in the world
Aquarius	revolution	freedom and originality; any work that involves creative expression, problem-solving
Pisces	compassion	healing; working with dreams, psychic abilities, clairvoyance and telepathy; trusting intuitive powers

THE ASCENDANT AND DESCENDANT

The houses of your horoscope begin with the ascendant. This is the precise degree of the sign on the eastern horizon at the time and place when you were born. Also known as the rising sign, the ascendant is very influential; it is like the outer mask or persona that we present to the world and is largely how we create a first impression with others. So, for instance, someone with Leo rising but with a moon in Pisces may seem bold and brash, but their moon sign indicates sensitivity and that they are liable to be easily hurt. Opposite the rising sign is the descendant; this marks the cusp of the seventh house (the house of relationships) and describes the "other", the natural partner. The ascendant and the descendant form a polarity, so that neither can be understood without the other. The ascendant-descendant axis divides the circle into upper and lower halves, the upper part symbolizing the "world out there" and the lower part our subjective, inner experience.

THE MIDHEAVEN AND THE IC

The uppermost point of the chart is known as the "midheaven"; this point symbolizes the height of worldly success and public position, and with most house

The 11th house governs our friends and our social groups.

systems is on the cusp of the 10th house. It describes our aspirations and the type of career we are likely to develop.

At the other end of this axis is the IC, or *imum coeli* (Latin for "bottom of the sky"), on the cusp of the 4th house. It describes the least exposed parts of ourselves and is a link to our personal and ancestral past. The IC and the midheaven form an axis of innermost and outermost life experiences, which further divides the circle into eastern and western hemispheres. The eastern hemisphere is concerned with the self, while the western hemisphere is linked with the impact of others.

THE TAROT

The origins of the Tarot are shrouded in mystery. Some say it dates back to ancient Egypt, while others see strong links with Hebrew mysticism. However, we do know that in fifteenth-century Italy the wealthy Visconti family commissioned an artist to paint a set of 78 unnamed and unnumbered cards that depicted religious allegories, social conditions and ideas of the time, to celebrate a family marriage. These cards formed the deck for an Italian gambling game called "Tarocchi", and by the late eighteenth century we find them being used as a divinatory tool. Since then, hundreds of different Tarot decks have been produced but the core meanings of the cards remains largely unchanged.

Pick a Tarot card each day and meditate on the image, or think about what you feel it shows.

WHAT IS THE TAROT?

Essentially the Tarot is a deck of 78 cards, which divide into two clear parts: the 22 cards of the Major Arcana and the 56 cards of the Minor Arcana. The Minor Arcana is further sub-divided into four suits, each of which is related to one of the four elements: Wands (Fire), Swords (Air), Cups (Water) and Pentacles (Earth). The Minor Arcana closely parallels a normal pack of 52 playing cards with its suits of clubs (wands), spades (swords), hearts (cups) and diamonds (pentacles). It is therefore possible to transpose the meanings of the Tarot cards on to a deck of playing cards and to use these for readings.

The word "Arcana" is related to arcane, which means mysterious or secret, and the Tarot has also been known as a "Book of Secrets". The Major Arcana deals with archetypal themes and reflects the major turning points in our lives: our commitments, triumphs and tragedies, our greatest challenges and most powerful impulses. The cards of the Minor Arcana deal with more day-to-day aspects of life, such as work, relationships, our ideas and our ambitions. Taken together, they constitute a guidebook to the incidents and issues that we have to handle in our lives, from the past, in the present and looking to the future.

DECODING THE TAROT

Most modern Tarot decks have a picture on every card, and the best way to learn the meanings is to shuffle a new pack thoroughly and take one card each day. Place it somewhere you can see it and think about what it seems to show, or meditate on the image. Write down your conclusions in a book kept for the purpose, and next day go on to another card, until you have examined all 78. You may simply focus on the name or number of the card, or try to decide what the picture shows at first, but gradually meanings will start to emerge.

Many books on interpreting the Tarot system are available and they take a wide variety of approaches – from light-hearted fun to a deep magical or psychological orientation. It is best not to rely too heavily on the meanings given in books, however, but to use your own intuitive understanding.

Understanding the cards

This numerical guide can be used as a quick reference to the Minor Arcana definitions, by cross-referencing the generic numerical meaning for any card with the general background to a particular suit. Take the Nine of Cups, for example. The suit of Cups is concerned with emotional issues, whilst a general definition for any of the number nine cards concerns fulfilment. By combining these two pieces of information, you can work out a general definition for the Nine of Cups to signify emotional contentment.

King:	Competition, realization
Queen:	Fulfilment, deep satisfaction, skill, maturity
Knight:	Focus, single-mindedness
Page:	Information
Ten:	Culmination and change
Nine:	Integration, contentment
Eight:	Organization, evaluation, experience, commitments
Seven:	Imagination, options, variety of choice
Six:	Poise, contentment, relaxation, victory
Five:	Adjustment, challenge, possible conflict
Four:	Manifestation, creation of a plan
Three:	Clarification, plans made public
Two:	Affirmation, some sort of choice, commitment
Ace:	Potential, new beginnings; the 'raw' energy of the suit

THE MINOR ARCANA

The 56 cards of the Minor Arcana are divided into four suits. The suit of Wands is concerned with energy and ambition, our goals and desires; it is also connected with sexuality. The suit of Swords is concerned with the mental realm of thoughts and ideas; it is also the area where conflicts are likely to surface. Emotions are connected to the suit of Cups dealing with love relationships, artistic endeavours and contentment. Lastly, the suit of Pentacles is concerned with everyday material matters, such as money and property.

The Major Arcana

The cards of the Major Arcana represent the powerful cosmic forces at work in our lives and are always the most important cards in a reading. These cards represent archetypal forces and have traditional astrological correspondences.

Number	Card	Correspondence	Traditional meaning
0	The Fool	Uranus	Fresh beginnings; spontaneity; taking risks and stepping into the unknown; change
I	The Magician	Mercury	Manifesting results in the material world; communicating; bringing different elements of life together
II	The High Priestess	Moon	Trust your intuition; don't take things at face value but look behind the scenes; patience
III	The Empress	Venus	Fertility or pregnancy; domestic bliss; abundance and the good things of life; enjoyment of sensuality. The 'mother' principle
IV	The Emperor	Aries	Power and authority. Established structures and organizations; banks, schools, offices, companies. The 'father' principle
V	The Hierophant	Taurus	Traditional ways of doing things; seeking advice from figures in the establishment or a higher authority (a teacher or spirit guide)
VI	The Lovers	Gemini	Intensity and choices in relationships; instant chemistry and attraction between two people; the feeling that something is 'meant to be'
VII	The Chariot	Cancer	Moving forwards on the path through life towards success; staying focused on goals
VIII	Strength	Leo	Recognizing and using your inner strength; having self-confidence
IX	The Hermit	Virgo	Look before you leap; take time out to be alone; cultivating wisdom and self-awareness; the guide
X	The Wheel of Fortune	Jupiter	Luck, expansion and growth; fate taking a hand in your life and possibly redirecting the path you are on
XI	Justice	Libra	See what is out of balance and make necessary adjustments; reaping what is fair and just
XII	The Hanged Man	Neptune	Sacrifice and letting go; reversal of fortune, a time to sit back and wait until circumstances improve
XIII	Death	Scorpio	Changes and endings (not usually a physical death), followed by regeneration and rebirth
XIV	Temperance	Sagittarius	Testing the waters before diving in; compromise and cooperation, allowing feelings to flow. Treading a middle way and not jumping in where angels fear to tread
XV	The Devil	Capricorn	Trapped by fears, compulsions and addictions; being overly attached to security; can also be rediscovery of passions and sexual energy
XVI	The Tower	Mars	Disruptive changes that are sudden and unexpected; life will never be the same again; a radical upheaval
XVII	The Star	Aquarius	Realizing dreams and visions, a wish comes true; renewal of hope and faith
XVIII	The Moon	Pisces	Dreams and illusions, everything may not be as it appears at face value; the power of the subconscious
XIX	The Sun	Sun	Extremely positive card denoting growth, life and an increase of potential in all or many areas of life; vitality, joy and happiness
XX	Judgement	Pluto	Decisions are pressing and need to be made; coming to terms with the past. Moving forwards with a more positive attitude; the lifting of karmic restrictions
XXI	The World	Saturn	The most auspicious card in the deck. You have come a long way and can now enjoy great success in all areas of life; completion of a cycle

USING THE TAROT

One of the main differences between using the Tarot compared to other divinatory tools, such as astrology or numerology, is that it is a pictorial system. The visual images give this system an impact that is real and immediate. It is even possible for some people without any knowledge about the Tarot to give accurate readings simply by looking at the images, having an instinctive response and then conveying what is seen, felt and understood.

We can use the Tarot for many purposes: to ask for advice about a best course of action, to gain insight into life's spiritual "lessons", as a tool for meditation and self-discovery, and also to develop our psychic ability and interpret what we see for others.

TAROT FOR YOURSELF

It is possible to do readings for yourself. One way of doing this is to begin each day with a simple question such as "What kind of day is in store?" Shuffle the pack, then pick a card. At the end of the day you may be able to understand how the card related to the day's events; it will also help you come to terms with a card's meaning, as experience is the best form of learning there is.

A quick three-card reading is also useful. Shuffle the pack and pick three cards, laying them out from left to right. The first represents yourself and your current situation; the second and third cards represent the situations and people you are about to encounter, respectively.

READING FOR OTHERS

When giving a Tarot reading, almost as much thought needs to be put into the preparations as into the actual reading itself. It is important to create a calm environment, preferably with soft lighting and no disturbing background noise. Privacy is also very important because quite personal and adult subjects may be discussed while doing a reading for another (the inquirer). Eye contact and a caring smile can help the inquirer to feel at ease when you are reading their cards, and remember it is not part of your remit to make scary predictions or give negative feedback. Always focus on the positive messages of the cards.

Ask the inquirer to concentrate on the subject or issue of their reading, as they shuffle the cards. Some people will take only a short time to get their issues clear, while others will take longer to focus. When the inquirer feels they have shuffled for long enough, they should pass the deck back to you. Now you are ready to lay out a spread. There are many different types of spread you can choose from, with two of the most popular being the "Celtic Cross" pattern, or one based on astrology. There are many good books on the Tarot, which will give information on different spreads for you to try.

Lay out the cards, face up, in the correct sequence. Notice any patterns or clusters of cards (for instance two or more

Before you begin to work with your Tarot cards, take some time to get to know them.

Care of your cards

Many people like to keep their Tarot cards wrapped in silk or in a special pouch or box. Do not loan out or let others handle your cards (except when giving a reading), as they will absorb your psychic impressions and become special to you.

of the same number, or a predominance of a particular suit), as this will give you a clue to the overall theme of the reading. You should also pay particular attention to any Major Arcana cards.

When you have interpreted all that you can from the cards, draw the reading to a conclusion and gather them together.

A TAROT SPELL FOR INSIGHT

The Tarot is a powerful divination system. Use this spell to empower a new pack of cards, or before doing a particularly important reading.

1 Take your cards and a square of silk, either red or bright blue, and a large surface with a clean flat cloth on it. Place a tall yellow or gold-coloured candle in a gold-coloured holder and light it.

2 Place the cards face down on the cloth and, with both hands, mix them up very thoroughly, saying the following:
Cards of wisdom, cards of grace, cards with magic on their face,
Open in me the holy power, to answer truly at any hour.
Open in me the skill of sight, to speak the truth by day and night.
Let the knowledge in me rise,
Let all I speak be good and wise.
Help me, Lord of the Tarot,
Help me.

Keep your Tarot cards in a safe place, and don't let anyone else use them.

3 Clap your hands over the cards three times, then select three cards and turn them over. These will show how well your spell has worked by their meanings. Snuff out the candle.

4 Collect up all the Tarot cards, wrap them in the silk square, place them in their box and put it in a safe place to retain their power.

The Celtic Cross formation is one of the best Tarot spreads to use.

Tarot meditation

One of the best ways of getting to know the Tarot is through meditation. To do this, sit quietly and comfortably with your eyes closed and take a few deep breaths to calm and centre yourself, allowing your thoughts to settle. Keeping your eyes closed, reach out and pick a card, feeling its energy in your hands. Open your eyes and allow your gaze to softly focus on the image, absorbing all its details, colours and characters.

Now close your eyes again and start to re-form the image in your mind's eye. Let it become bigger and bigger, until it becomes like a doorway. See yourself walking through it and into a living world peopled with the characters and symbols of the card. Notice your thoughts and feelings, and let yourself interact with the figures you find there. When you have finished, say goodbye and step back through the doorway. See the scene you have visited shrinking until it is once more the size of a card. Take a deep breath and open your eyes. Record your findings in your Book of Shadows.

THE I CHING

Paradoxically, the only certainty in life is change. In all change, however, there are certain patterns, and it is this predictability that the shamans of ancient China referred to when they were called upon to give advice and divinations on forthcoming events. Originally, an answer to a question was divined from the patterns on animal hides or tortoise shells; later this developed into the I Ching, or the Book of Changes. As the I Ching developed, it became more than an oracular device; the ancient sages saw that it could be used as a blueprint for understanding the way the whole universe works in all its complexity.

You may be able to obtain some old Chinese coins to use for divining, but any coins will do.

WHAT IS THE I CHING?

At its root, the I Ching is made up of eight trigrams, said to represent the eight fundamental forces of nature. At some point they were arranged into an octagonal form known as the Bagua, showing opposing pairs or forces, and were given specific names taken from nature. As its name suggests, a trigram is an arrangement of three lines, with a solid line used to represent yang energies, and a broken line to depict yin. In Chinese thought, yin and yang are the

Throw combinations

3 heads	= 9	_ _ changes to _ _
2 heads, 1 tail	= 8	_ _
1 head, 2 tails	= 7	___
3 tails	= 6	_x_ changes to ___

two opposing principles that underlie all of creation, the complementary opposites that are apparent in everything. When combined with one another, the trigrams make up the 64 hexagrams of the I Ching.

CONSULTING THE ORACLE

A physical way of constructing a hexagram is needed and the most common is to throw or cast three coins. It is a good idea to dedicate your coins to the I Ching and only use them for this purpose. The "heads" side of a coin is considered yang, and is given a value of three, while the "tails" side is thought of as yin and has a value of two. When the coins are thrown, a total of six, seven, eight or nine is obtained, giving lines that are either yin (even numbers) or yang (odd numbers).

Begin by preparing yourself and letting go of everyday thoughts and concerns. Light some incense and burn a candle to help put you in the right frame of mind. When you are ready, hold your question in your mind's eye and then drop the

coins on to a hard surface, making a note of the pattern to give you a number. Repeat this process a further five times until you have six totals. The hexagram is then constructed upwards, following the path of organic growth, so that the first total makes up the bottom line.

CHANGING LINES

A line totalling six (old yin) or nine (old yang) changes to its young opposite. The changing lines give deeper insights into a reading, being used to produce a second hexagram. The initial hexagram relates to present conditions, while the second hexagram relates to the future outcome of a situation, or can help to clarify the original question.

The eight forces of I Ching

Ch'ien/Heaven: the creative
Chen/Thunder: the arousing
K'un/Earth: the receptive
Sun/Wind: the gentle and penetrating
Li/Fire: the clinging
Ken/Mountain: the stillness
K'an/Water: the abysmal
Tui/Lake: the joyful

When you are consulting the I Ching, light a candle to help focus your mind.

The 64 hexagrams

1 Ch'ien:	The Creative	Masculine, dynamic, inspiring
2 K'un:	The Receptive	Feminine, yielding, receptive
3 Chun:	Difficult Beginnings	Immaturity, new growth, sprouting; perseverance
4 Meng:	Youthful Folly	Inexperience, guidance, enthusiasm, tuition
5 Hsu:	Waiting	Correctness, patience, perseverance, nourishment
6 Sung:	Conflict	Opposition, disengagement, communication
7 Shih:	The Army	Unity, harmony, acting in concert, strength, division
8 Pi:	Holding Together	Union, bonding, cooperation
9 Hsiao ch'u:	The Taming Power of the Small	Patience, yielding, strength; gentle action
10 Lu:	Conduct	Caution, courtesy, simplicity, innocence
11 T'ai:	Peace	Balance, harmony, new growth, prosperity
12 Pi:	Standstill	Lack of progress, barriers, stagnation
13 T'ung Jen:	Fellowship with Others	Cohesion, bonding, strength in numbers, co-operation
14 Ta Yu:	Possessing Plenty	Feminine, yielding, receptive, gentle, providing, bountiful
15 Ch'ien:	Modesty	Quietly progressing, steadfast, deepening, developing
16 Yu:	Enthusiasm	Energy, opportunity, support
17 Sui:	Following	Acceptance, following, joy
18 Ku:	Work on Corruption	Disruption, decay, disorder, spoiled, repairing
19 Lin:	Approach	Advance, waxing power, strength, benevolence
20 Kuan:	Contemplation	Meditation, understanding, perceiving, example
21 Shih Ho:	Biting Through	Clarity, decisiveness, obstacle, unity
22 Pi:	Grace	Adornment, beauty, simplicity
23 Po:	Splitting Apart	Strong, enduring, patient, non-action
24 Fu:	Return	Change, turning point, improvement
25 Wu Wang:	Innocence	Purity, innocence, sincerity, intuition
26 Ta Ch'u:	The Taming Power of the Great	Keeping still, tension, practice, staying firm
27 I:	Corners of the Mouth	Nourishment, discipline, meditation, fulfilment
28 Ta Kuo:	Preponderance of the Great	Pressure, regeneration, growth, cautious progress
29 K'an:	The Abysmal	Depths, despair, danger, alertness
30 Li:	The Clinging	Dependence, passion, brilliance, creativity
31 Hsien:	Influence	Harmony, mutual benefit, coming together, courtship
32 Heng:	Duration	Persistence, progress, endurance, stamina
33 Tun:	Retreat	Withdrawal, conserving strength, stillness, order
34 Ta Chuang:	The Power of the Great	Self-possession, strength, heaven, patience
35 Chin:	Progress	Advancement, dawning, rising
36 Ming I:	Darkening of the Light	Oppression, damping, sunset, inner light
37 Chia Jen:	The Family	Harmony, togetherness, loyalty, health, balance, structure
38 K'uei:	Opposition	Misunderstanding, contrary resistance, adversity
39 Chien:	Obstruction	Obstacles, barriers, blockage, stuck
40 Hsieh:	Deliverance	Relief, release, growth, progression
41 Sun:	Decrease	Discipline, simplicity, limited, drawing in, restriction
42 I:	Increase	Improvement, gain, progress
43 Kuai:	Breakthrough	Resoluteness, determination, resistance
44 Kou:	Coming to Meet	Caution, awareness, temptation, tolerance
45 Ts'ui:	Gathering Together	Peace, harmony, cooperation, prosperity, leadership
46 Sheng:	Pushing Upwards	Direction, ascending, growth
47 K'un:	Oppression	Exhaustion, stretched, adversity, endurance
48 Ching:	The Well	Spiritual nourishment, counsel, guidance, wisdom
49 Ko:	Revolution	Change, advance, devotion
50 Ting:	The Cauldron	Growth, sacrifice, nourishment
51 Chen:	The Arousing	Shock, movement, stimulation
52 Ken:	Keeping Still	Stillness, observing, quietness, clarity, readiness
53 Chien:	Development	Gradual progress, patience, steady growth
54 Kuei Mei:	The Marrying Maiden	Impulsiveness, disturbance, desire, proper conduct, discipline
55 Feng:	Abundance	Fullness, power, wise actions, plenty
56 Lu:	The Wanderer	Moving, restless, temporary, transient
57 Sun:	The Gentle	Gentle, penetrating, wind, persistence
58 Tui:	The Joyous	Inner strength, fulfilment, harmony, joy
59 Huan:	Dispersion	Division, dissolution, rigidity, stubbornness
60 Chieh:	Limitation	Restraint, moderation, guidelines
61 Chung Fu:	Inner Truth	Prejudice, understanding, acceptance
62 Hsiao Kuo:	Preponderance of the Small	Non-action, caution, patience
63 Chi Chi:	After Completion	Order, balance, awareness, culmination
64 Wei Chi:	Before Completion	Caution, regeneration, potential, clarity

THE RUNES

A system of sacred writing from northern Europe, runes are said to
have appeared to the Norse god Odin, during a shamanic
initiation rite. The runes then became his gift of knowledge to
humanity and as such they are empowered with ancient wisdom. The
word "rune" comes from the Middle English *runa*, meaning "a
whisper" or "a secret", and traditionally knowledge of the runes was
granted only to a runemaster, who guarded it closely. A runemaster
performed a similar role in Norse communities to the shaman, or
medicine man or woman.

*Runes can be written on small round pebbles, or
on specially cut rounds of wood.*

RUNE LAW

Runemasters underwent many initiatory
experiences to discover the secrets of
rune lore. They knew how to use them
for divination, but also for magical and
healing work. Runes can still be used as
guides for meditation, as protective
talismans, and in spells and charms.

THE RUNIC ALPHABET

The angular script of the runes points to
the fact that they were not intended for
writing but for carving. Many stone
memorials bear runic inscriptions and it
is likely that the earliest alphabets were
inscribed on to pieces of wood, stone or
bark. There are many different varieties

of runic writing, but the most widely
used runic alphabet is the Early
Germanic or Elder Futhark. The word
"futhark" refers to the first six runic
letters f, u, th, a, r and k, just as our word
"alphabet" refers to the first two letters
of the Greek alphabet, Alpha (or a) and
Beta (or b). The Elder Futhark has 24
letters and some scholars believe it was
probably in existence as early as the 2nd
century BC. Traditionally, it is divided
into three "families", or aetts, of eight
runes each, which were named for the
Norse gods Freyr, Hagal and Tyr.

In the ancient runic alphabet, each
inscription (also known as a glyph)
possessed a signifying sound and a
meaningful name. Over time, they have
also become associated with particular
trees, colours, herbs and gemstones.

*A rune bag is essential for storing your runes, and it is also important that you keep them cleansed
and that no one else uses them, as they are imbued with your unique energy.*

Care of your runes

The following guidelines will help you take
care of your runes:

- cleanse them regularly with spring water,
  salt or by smudging
- to empower your runes, leave them
  outside for 24 hours to let the sun and
  moonlight energize them
- keep them in a special bag or box, and do
  not lend them to anyone

A guide to the runes

There are 24 rune symbols, each of which stands for a different letter of the Early Germanic, or Elder Futhark, alphabet. Each of these inscriptions has a divinatory meaning, as well as tree, colour, herb and gemstone associations.

Sign	Name	Meaning	Divinatory meaning	Tree	Colour	Herb/plant	Gemstone
F	Feoh	Cattle	Spiritual richness	Elder	Light red	Nettle	Moss agate
ᚾ	Ur	Auroch (recently extinct cattle)	Strength in time of change	Birch	Dark green	Sphagnum moss	Carbuncle
ᛈ	Thorn	Thorn	Contemplation before action	Thorn/oak	Bright red	Houseleek	Sapphire
ᚨ	Ansur	A mouth	Messages and new opportunities	Ash	Dark blue	Fly agaric	Emerald
ᚱ	Rad	A cartwheel	The wheel of life, a journey or quest	Oak	Bright red	Mugwort	Chrysoprase
ᚲ	Ken	A torch	Enlightenment and inspiration	Pine	Light red	Cowslip	Bloodstone
ᚷ	Geofu	A gift	A spiritual gift, love and partnership	Ash/elm	Deep blue	Heartsease	Opal
ᚹ	Wynn	Happiness	Success and achievement; balance	Ash	Yellow	Flax	Diamond
ᚻ	Hagall	Hail	Strength to face a challenge	Ash/yew	Light blue	Lily-of-the-valley	Onyx
ᚾ	Nied	Need	Everything is as it should be; your needs are met	Beech	Black	Bistort	Lapis lazuli
ᛁ	Is	Ice	Standstill, preparation before moving on	Alder	Black	Henbane	Cat's eye
ᛃ	Jara	Harvest	Harvest, reward for past effort	Oak	Light blue	Rosemary	Cornelian
ᛇ	Eoh	A yew tree	Transformation; letting go, endings ready for beginnings	Yew	Dark blue	Mandrake	Topaz
ᛈ	Peorth	A dice cup	Choice, taking charge	Beech	Black	Aconite	Aquamarine
ᛉ	Elhaz	An elk	Protection within	Yew	Gold	Angelica	Amethyst
ᛋ	Sigel	The sun	Good fortune	Juniper	White/silver	Mistletoe	Ruby
ᛏ	Tyr	The god Tyr	Initiation	Oak	Bright red	Sage	Coral
ᛒ	Beorc	A birch tree	New beginnings	Birch	Dark green	Lady's mantle	Moonstone
ᛖ	Ehwaz	A horse	Progress	Oak/ash	White	Ragwort	Iceland spar
ᛗ	Mann	A human	Destiny	Holly	Deep red	Madder	Garnet
ᛚ	Lagu	Water, sea	Attunement to creation	Willow	Deep green	Leek	Pearl
◊	Ing	The god Ing	The inner spark	Apple	Yellow	Self-heal	Amber
ᛞ	Daeg	Day	The light	Spruce	Light blue	Clary	Diamond
ᛟ	Othel	A possession	Focus and freedom	Hawthorn	Deep yellow	Clover	Ruby

CONSULTING THE RUNES

The runes can be used in a variety of ways. A single rune may be picked to give you guidance for the day ahead or to help clarify a problem or issue. The message of a single rune can help bring you back down to earth when you are losing touch with reality, or reassure you about a course of action you have already decided upon, confirming what you already know. You can also draw a rune to honour significant events, such as birthdays, anniversaries, a wedding, or getting a new job, or to celebrate the changing seasons and festivals throughout the year. The most common issues or questions on which people seek guidance, whether from the runes, Tarot, I Ching or any other divinatory method, tend to fall into categories such as love and relationships, work, home and family, health, and general life guidance.

When using the runes for clarification or guidance, avoid asking "closed" questions that demand a "yes/no" answer. Instead, turn the question into an "issue" statement: for instance, the question "should I change my job" becomes "the issue is my job". The runes will never tell you what to do, but what they can do is comment on a situation, giving you a new perspective.

Keeping your issue in mind, focus your thoughts on it while holding your runes. This will send a vibration of your

The three-rune spread

A line of runes is referred to as a 'spread', and a three-rune spread is helpful for giving an overall picture of an issue by placing it in its context. It is like a signpost at a crossroads showing where you are, where you have been, and where you can potentially go if you learn the lessons you need to learn. Focus on the situation and pick out three

runes from your bag. Lay them one by one in a row, and read them in turn as follows:

1 The past: this provides background to the situation and shows events that led up to it.

2 The present: the issue as experienced now.

3 The future: the most likely developments given 1 and 2.

thought-forms into the runes, and then you will unconsciously be attracted to pick out the rune that resonates with you. You can pick a rune directly from the bag or box, or else lay them all face down in front of you and then pick the one you are most drawn to. You may notice your body becomes warmer as you are drawn to the right rune; you will just need to trust that whichever one you pick is right for you for this moment.

ADVANCED DIVINATION

As well as providing insight into everyday situations, the runes can also be used to give deeper insight to help you

on your spiritual path. The following spread is based on the World Tree and is designed to act as a guide to the next stage of your spiritual journey. Similar to the Tree of Life, the World Tree is one of the very oldest and most universal symbols in the world. Known as Yggdrasil in the Norse tradition, its roots are said to connect to the underworld, home nature spirits and elementals, while its upper branches ascend to the sky and the realm of angels, advanced souls and supernatural entities.

Beginning at the base of the tree and working upwards and from left to right, lay the runes out in the correct positions,

Rather than picking the runes one by one from the bag, you might prefer to spread them all out in front of you and then pick the one you are most drawn to.

For guidance for the day ahead, simply pick one rune from the bag.

The layout of the World Tree spread of runes.

Working with a partner to read runes will help you to work out their meaning.

asking the following questions of the runes as you pick each one:

1 *What do I need to learn?*
2 *What will challenge me?*
3 *What is my guiding rune?*
4 *What power will help me?*
5 *What comes to warn me?*
6 *What do I need to let go of?*
7 *What will be the outcome of learning this lesson?*

INTERPRETING THE RUNES

The meaning of a particular rune may change depending on whether it is picked upright or upside down (reversed). This is largely a question of individual preference, and there are many books available with more detailed meanings for each of the runes, including upright and reversed meanings. However, as with any other method of divination, to become adept at interpretation you need to train your intuition. This is the connection to your higher self, the part of your being that knows everything, including your purpose in life and how it can best be achieved. Meditation is one of the best ways for training intuition.

At the beginning of each day, pick out a rune and sit with it quietly in meditation for ten minutes or so. As you go through the day, reflect on its symbol and notice any particular themes or patterns to your day; at the end of the day, you can check the rune's official meaning and see if it relates to your experience. When checking the rune's official meaning, pay attention to any particular passages or words that seem to jump out at you, as these will be the ones that have the most relevance for you at this time. When we look up a meaning, a lot of what is said doesn't seem to apply, but then suddenly we will come across something that strikes a chord and that seems to speak to us directly. This is when divination is at its most powerful.

Creating your own rune set

If you want to get to know the runes, a good way of doing this is by making your own set. The two materials from which runes are commonly made are wood and stone, although other materials such as crystals, glass beads or clay can also be used. If you are using stones, you will need to collect 24 of a similar size. Some of the best stones for rune making can be found on beaches and in streambeds; remember to leave behind an offering in thanks for what you are taking.

For stones: using a fine paintbrush and an acrylic paint in your chosen colour (preferably a neutral, earthtoned shade), paint the runic inscriptions on each stone. When the paint is dry, apply a coat of varnish over the stones to protect the paint. For wood: you will need a long branch. Ask permission from the tree before you cut it. Use a handsaw to cut the branch into 24 slices. Burn the inscriptions into the runes with a soldering iron. Rub over with beeswax to protect the wood.

Making your own runes makes them personal.

DOWSING

Everyone has the ability to dowse and it is a skill that every witch and magician should hone and perfect. Dowsing is essentially the art of asking a "yes/no" question and using the movement of a dowsing device – usually a pendulum or rod – to divine the answer. It is a simple process that connects the rational, intellectual part of ourselves with the intuitive, wise part. It is like a doorway between the mind and spirit, using the body as a threshold. The more respect we bring to our dowsing, the more reliable and effective it will be.

When holding a pendulum, keep your fingers pointed downwards, to allow it to swing freely.

HOW DOWSING WORKS

A genuine need to know is a key factor for dowsing to work well. You ask a clear and unambiguous question in your mind, to which the answer can only be "yes" or "no". The second important step is then being able to let go of the question and any emotional attachment to the answer one way or the other, and waiting with a "detached curiosity", or an open mind, for the answer to come back from your inner self.

The most familiar tools that are used in dowsing are the pendulum and L-rods, although other devices such as Y-rods and "bobbers" are also used. The movement of the dowsing tool occurs involuntarily, in the same way as a yawn or a laugh, without your needing to make it happen. But before dowsing can start, you need to establish your personal basic dowsing responses.

PENDULUM RESPONSES

Before you begin, you need to establish the pendulum motions that will mean "yes" and "no" for you, as these vary from person to person.

1 Sit in a relaxed, upright position and hold your pendulum in a central position just above the height of your knees. Start swinging it in a to-and-fro motion towards and away from you. This is the "neutral" position and indicates that you are ready to start.

2 Now move your hand over your dominant-side knee (right for right-handers, left for left-handers). State clearly to yourself the following words: *Please show me my "yes" response.*

3 Notice what the pendulum does; it may swing in a clockwise or anti-clockwise direction, or from side to side, or even diagonally. Whatever it does, this is your signal for "yes".

4 Take the pendulum back to the neutral position and move your hand to the other knee. Repeat the procedure as in step 2, this time asking for your "no" response. It should be something clearly different to "yes" and will be your signal for "no".

5 Repeat the exercise several times to become confident and familiar with your responses. After a short period of time, your chosen responses will become automatic and spontaneous and you will be able to dowse with confidence.

DOWSING AND HEALTH

There are an infinite number of possible situations in which you can use dowsing, but using it as a tool for information and

Crystal pendulums are widely available and are also very beautiful objects to work with.

Choosing a pendulum

Almost anything that swings freely can be used as a pendulum, but ideally it should be symmetrical and attached to its cord centrally so that it can swing in any direction. Natural materials such as wood, stone, metal or crystal can all work well, but find one that feels right when you pick it up and swing it, or make your own from whatever you feel is appropriate.

With practice, you can learn to detect problems in specific parts of someone's body.

guidance around your health is one of its most valuable uses and also one of the best ways to build up experience and confidence. You can experiment with lists of herbs, vitamins, massage oils, Bach flower remedies or forms of treatment with which you have become familiar, so that you can dowse along the list, picking out things to try in a particular case.

You can also dowse for someone else, but you should always get their permission first. Unless you are very experienced and able to hold them in mind as you dowse, it is a good idea to obtain something from them, such as a

You can use a pendulum for sensing the energies around a person's aura to judge their health.

lock of hair or a ring, to help "link" you to them while you investigate. If they are present, you can ask questions while swinging the pendulum over their hands, or you might feel more confident if they

supply the sample and allow you to work on their problem by yourself. Always be sure that you are dealing with an ailment you can handle, and if either of you are in any doubt, seek medical advice.

Typical dowsing responses

This is the kind of pattern of responses that you might establish:
Anti-clockwise for 'no'
Towards and away for 'neutral'
Clockwise for 'yes'
Diagonal to the left for 'no'
Diagonal to the right for 'yes'

Dowsing the life-force in food

As well as its nutritional properties, our food carries the 'life-force', or vital essence. This is most intensely present when the food is at its freshest and diminishes over time. Food that has high life-force tastes better and gives us more nourishment; we may find that we need to eat less of it. You can dowse over your food to assess its vitality, using a scale of 0–10, with 0 being

absence of life-force, and 10 being the optimum. As you dowse over the food, ask questions such as "is the vitality of this (say what it is) higher than 5? Higher than 8? Does it have a vitality of 10?" and so on to assess the score. You will find that freshly picked fruit and vegetables have the highest score, while packaged foods and ready-meals will be at the lower end of the scale.

DIVINING THE LAND

In magical thinking, etheric energy (known as "chi" in Chinese thought) flows through every energy system, including that of the earth. We can use dowsing to detect energy patterns in nature and to observe the different effects they have on us. We can also use dowsing to repattern chi paths and to bring healing to traumatized environmental energies.

Although you can use your pendulum for dowsing in relation to earth energies, it is often more useful to use another of the basic dowsing tools, the L-rod. So called because of its shape, the L-rod can be constructed from any material, including an ordinary wire coat hanger, cut and bent into shape. You will need a pair of rods, one for each hand. Mostly used for searching for things while the dowser moves around, they can also be used for "yes/no" questions in a sitting or standing position.

L-ROD RESPONSES

To establish your "yes" and "no" responses, stand in a comfortable upright posture, spine straight and shoulders relaxed, and hold the shortest "handle" part of the rods. The rods should be pointing straight out and away from you, parallel with each other. This is the neutral or search position.

Keeping the rods the same distance apart, move them over to the dominant

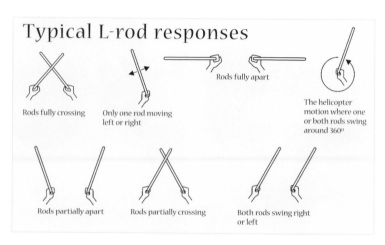

Typical L-rod responses

Rods fully crossing

Only one rod moving left or right

Rods fully apart

The helicopter motion where one or both rods swing around 360°

Rods partially apart

Rods partially crossing

Both rods swing right or left

side of your body and ask to be shown your "yes" response. Return to neutral and repeat on your non-dominant side to be shown "no".

DRAGON ENERGIES

In traditional Chinese thought, the chi paths of the earth's subtle body are known as dragons. Dragons inhabit every landscape. Typically described as having the body of a serpent, the scales of a fish, wings of a bat and claws of a bird, they symbolize the energy that is present in all animals and throughout nature. Sinuous and mercurial by nature, their energies fluctuate and change with sunrise and sunset, with the waxing and

waning of the moon, with the passing of the sun through the seasons and with the deep, quiet cycles of planetary time. The West recognizes its own dragons or energy lines, referred to as ley lines, which form more or less rectilinear grids across the earth. Where ley lines cross are points of power. In addition, there are energy paths for each of the elements of Earth, Air, Fire and Water.

SEARCHING FOR DRAGONS

Centre and calm yourself. Position yourself so that you are standing comfortably, feet flat on the ground, with your rods in their neutral position. Then say the following:

To establish your own responses, first hold the rods straight out and away from you, parallel with each other; this is neutral.

Saying in your mind, "please show me my response for yes", move the rods over to the dominant side of your body and note the signal.

Go back to neutral, then to the opposite side of your body, asking for the "no" response. Observe the signal. Test the responses several times.

I wish to dowse for earth energies; is this timely and appropriate?
If the response is "yes", ask:
Please show me any energy paths of significance to my health.

Walk forwards at a slow, steady pace. When you reach the first path, your rods may start to split apart as though meeting something solid like a wall. Once they are completely apart you have arrived at an energy line. Conversely, you may find that the rods cross – this is an equally valid "here it is" sign. You can continue to dowse to find out more about the dragon, such as how big or small it is (some lines are very narrow while others are several metres wide). You can also ask if the line is predominantly yin or yang, and find out how strong it is, using a scale of 0–10. The effect of being in a predominantly yin chi path slows us down, rather like a glass of wine or heavy meal. Predominantly yang chi, on the other hand, acts like coffee, stimulating and speeding us up. These effects increase with the intensity of the etheric field, and are more extreme the more strongly the etheric field is polarized to yin or yang.

HEALING TRAUMATIZED ENERGIES
Traumatic changes to the surface of the landscape, such as quarrying or excavation or new construction projects, can create stress and trauma in an otherwise healthy energy field. If the chi has been traumatized it is likely that one or more blocked, stagnant or overly stimulated chi paths runs through the space. Let your dowsing guide you to where to work.

Place your hands where your L-rods indicate, visualize yourself channelling healing energy from the divine source, and ask that the etheric field receive whatever healing energy that it needs in order to regain health and balance.

At the end of each session, visualize yourself filled with golden light and give thanks for the healing that has occurred.

Dowse intermittently to see if the process is complete. It may take several sessions over a period of days, weeks, or even months, the earth's cycles of time are slower than those of a person.

Repatterning energies

If you find a chi path that is detrimental to your health, you can ask the spirit of place that the energy be repatterned. Remember that the energy itself is neither good nor bad, and that something that may be harmful to us, can be helpful to other species. Repatterning may take hours or days, but once you have begun the process you don't need to stay. You can return to the place every few hours and check with your dowsing to find out when it is complete. You can use a pendulum to do this exercise.

1 Hold your pendulum and begin by checking with the spirit of place if it is timely and appropriate to communicate with it. If the answer is 'Yes', continue by saying:
I wish to spend time in this space and need the energy here to be supportive to my health. Are you willing to repattern the energy here to be supportive of my health?
If the spirit of place is not willing, then you might want to ask it to suggest an alternative place where you can work.

2 If the spirit is both willing and able, make a special request almost like a prayer. You may also visualize golden light filling the entire space as you make your request:
I request that the energy in this space be repatterned at this time to be supportive of human health at every level, and that it may remain so for as long as may be the divine will.

3 Once your dowsing indicates that the repatterning has occurred, give thanks to the spirit of place by leaving an offering.

L-rods are probably the most popular and widely used tools for water dowsing.

THE SPIRIT OF A HOME

In one study, people were asked to list their most stressful life experiences in order. The results of this showed that the most stressful event of all was to move to a new home. This tells us a great deal about our relationship with the place where we live and which we identify as home.

DOWSING YOUR HOME

The practice of dowsing will help to deepen your awareness of the nature and character of your home, and orient you to high and low energy spots and the flow of chi through it. It also gives you a means of dialogue with the spirit of place. Begin by greeting the spirit of place. You can use either your pendulum or L-rods for the opening dialogue of "Yes" and "No" questions and answers, and your L-rods for identifying and tracking the energy paths through your home.

Clear and centre yourself, and visualize yourself in a column of golden light. Introduce yourself first. State the nature of your relationship with the place, such as if you own or rent or are visiting, and your intentions in regard to the place, whether it is only a home or also your work place, how you intend to develop and so forth.

"I am (name) and this is my home. I live here with my family and wish this to be a safe and nurturing place to live. I wish to communicate with the spirit of place here. Is this timely and appropriate?" If the answer is "Yes" then go on. "Is this a safe and healthy place for me to live? Is there anything that I need to know about the energy here? Is any healing required in this space? Are there any chi-paths of health significance that run through this space? Are there any power-centres here?"

Gather as much information as you can, dowsing with "Yes/No" questions. Once you have an overall feel for the energy field, dowse your home room by room with your pendulum or L-rods to find out the peace or otherwise of the energies present, whether any healing is needed, and what the overall polarity and field intensity is using your ten-point scale.

One way to deepen our relationship with the spirit of place is to create a simple altar in our home.

CHI-PATHS IN YOUR HOME

Get to know the energetic anatomy of your space as intimately as you can. If there are any chi-paths present, find them with your L-rods and track them through the room, then on through the house and outside – you will want to track these all the way from where they enter your property to where they leave. Find out their polarity and intensity, their state of peace or trauma, and how they affect the human health aura.

Notice the health of any plants that you find on the chi path, and whether it runs under beds or chairs or through places where animals sleep. It is best not to spend prolonged periods sitting or standing directly in chi-paths, particularly if they are of a strong yin nature.

Placing plants in certain positions can sometimes help to balance energy paths.

The most important place to have healthy, sweet and gentle energy is in our bedroom, especially for children. Do you sleep well? Do you wake feeling refreshed after a night's sleep?

Rooms that work well in a house tend to have a good match of their energy to their function. Rooms where the energy field is incongruous to the use of space feel awkward and difficult.

Energy Fields to Activities

Different energy fields are appropriate for different human activities. During sleep for example, it is most appropriate to be in a serene, very gentle and moderate energy field, without any strong or highly polarized chi.

Ideally our bed is placed where only the tiny capillary lines of chi feed a constant and gentle energy to us. The bed and bedroom generally should be kept in a state of energetic clarity and cleanliness. Healing any etheric traumas and clearing the space of disturbed memory is important before you start using a room as your bedroom. You may also want to clear and balance the energy after an argument or any period of illness, or if your dreams seem troubled and tense.

Dowsing in the Bedroom

If you routinely sleep heavily and wake unrefreshed you should dowse carefully to ensure that there is not an excess of yin chi running through your bed. If you do find energetic problems in your bedroom, apply the healing techniques that seem appropriate.

Ask for the help and co-operation of the spirit of place to ease and repattern the energy flow and create a safe and nurturing space for you at every level. Our sleeping position is the most important environmental factor for our sustained health.

High Energy Areas

You may find one or more power spots in your home of varying magnitude. These are ideal areas for any creative activity, whether cooking, writing, painting, doing healing work or other spiritual practices. It is best to limit your time in intense power-centres and it is very important to keep them clean and clear, because they hold and amplify thoughts and emotions. They are very useful, and should not be neglected.

Cleaning and clearing a space can be as simple as asking the spirit of place to heal and balance all the energies there, or you may need to use one or more tools such as bells, candles, incense and so on to raise enough focused intention to restore health.

Your dowsing will guide you as to whether peace and balance are present, and if not what you need to do to restore it. Begin a practice of dialogue with the spirit of your home and of monitoring the energies present.

Pay attention to your imagination and your intuitive feelings as well as your dowsing. Observe the energy changes that follow the daily, monthly and yearly cycles. You will find this increased awareness both revealing and richly rewarding.

Becoming intimate with the spirit and energy of your home will greatly deepen your relationship with the space. Be sure to keep high-use areas energetically clear and well balanced.

Scrying

From the earliest times, people have seen supernatural images in shiny surfaces such as a pool of dark water, a black stone, a concave mirror or a crystal ball set against black velvet. In Tibet, seers sometimes gaze at a wetted thumbnail. The process is called "scrying", which means "perceiving", and it is an art that many magicians aim to master as a way of answering questions about the future. To be able to scry you need to be able to switch off from the distractions of everyday life and enter an altered state of consciousness. It uses the same kind of inner vision as dreams, so you may find that by improving dream recall, scrying gets easier, or conversely if you learn how to scry you will remember your dreams.

An ordinary picture frame can be turned into a scrying vessel by placing a piece of black paper behind the glass.

FINDING YOUR RELAXED STATE

To improve your success at scrying, it is necessary to be able to enter a deeply relaxed state, so performing this preparatory exercise might help.

Find a time and place where you won't be disturbed for at least half an hour. You will need an upright chair and a notebook and pen for keeping a record – you may wish to use your Book of Shadows or else create another magical diary which you keep for recording your work with dreams and/or visions.

1 Sit with your feet flat on the floor or on a thick book so that your knees are at a right angle, and find a comfortable relaxed position. Close your eyes.

2 Breathe out fully and then, counting at your own speed, breathe in for a count of four. Hold your breath for a count of four, breathe out for a count of four, then hold your breath out for another count of four.

3 Repeat this entire breathing cycle at least 10 times. If you lose count, it will be necessary to start again from the beginning. You may find this pattern difficult, in which case you can try a slower 10–5–10–5. You can count quickly or slowly or, if you can feel your pulse while sitting in a relaxed position, count that.

4 Focus all your mental attention on breathing slowly and rhythmically, and relaxing physically. Gradually, you will find that this helps you to become calm and focused.

5 Bring your attention to the scrying glass, and gently open your eyes. You are in your relaxed state and ready to begin scrying.

Scrying within a magic circle of candles will protect you from harmful or negative visions.

Steps to scrying

You can learn to develop your ability to 'see' by following these steps.

1 Allow yourself to sink into a relaxed state. Open your eyes to regard the glass, crystal, sphere or other 'speculum'.

2 Look within the glass, ignoring any reflections or points of light on its surface. Sink within it, forming the question in your mind. In a while, you will find that the glass seems to cloud over, or become dim. Through the mist, a dark patch may appear.

3 You might find yourself sinking into this dark patch, then pictures, signs, numbers, words or other symbols may appear before you. This will probably not happen in the first experiments you perform but will come with practice.

4 Continue for a number of regular sessions and you will gradually master this ancient and very valuable skill.

LEARNING TO SCRY

Scrying is not a skill that you can learn automatically. Like riding a bicycle or swimming, there is a knack to it and it takes time, practice and concentration. A common mistake in beginners is that they try too hard, which only creates tension. Rather relax, and you will see words, images, still pictures or actions flitting through your mind's eye, rather like watching a film. The trick is not trying to hold on to what you see, but to let it go.

After a while, you will find that the film slows down and the images or non-visual concepts remain visible long enough for you to study them. Like remembering dreams, you may need to tell yourself what is happening in order to fix it in your longer-term memory, but it does get easier with practice. You may find that it helps to cast a circle around yourself and the table with the scrying vessel (known as the "speculum") on it, or that to light a candle and some sweet incense will bring on a more psychically open state of mind. Really it is a matter for patient experimentation to see what works best.

TRUST WHAT YOU SEE

In order for scrying to work, there must be no distracting reflections on the surface of the object, so the ambient light where you are working should be soft and diffuse. If a vision is to emerge, the mind and body need to be stilled and calmed by a period of quiet contemplation, with the eyes closed so that residual images fade from the retina.

Once you feel you have reached the right state of mind you are ready to begin to gaze into your scrying object. Gazing into the speculum induces a trance-like state and allows ideas to emerge from the unconscious mind, as they do in dreams. The first impression may be of a mist, which eventually darkens and resolves into colours, shapes, symbols or complete images. Like the images seen in dreams, these are likely to relate to deep-seated issues and offer information that the conscious mind does not have access to. They may seem inexplicable at first, but become relevant later.

Making your own scrying vessel

Real crystal balls are difficult and expensive to obtain, so before you decide whether to get one you can make your own scrying vessel. Use black enamel spray paint to coat the outside of a balloon-shaped wine glass. You may need several coats. Alternatively try scrying in a clear glass bowl of water. You can also make a simple mirror by painting the glass of a picture frame, or as follows, using a sheet of black paper.

1 You will need a picture frame, a piece of black paper and a pair of scissors. Take the frame apart and cut out a piece of black paper to fit. Place the paper in the frame behind the glass and put the frame back together again.

2 Once the frame is properly secured, polish the glass thoroughly with a soft cloth. Your scrying glass is now ready to use.

Crystal balls are closely associated with magical arts, especially the ability to see into the future.

Interpreting visions

Although visions in a scrying vessel can only be interpreted by the individual who sees them, like the symbols perceived in dreams they sometimes seem to represent archetypes that have universal significance. Some visions are simply a mist of colour.

White: good fortune
Yellow: obstacles to come
Orange: troubled emotions, anger

Red: danger
Blue: business success
Green: health and happiness
Grey/dark: misfortune
Rising clouds: affirmative
Sinking clouds: negative
Far-off visions: the distant past or future
Foreground visions: the present or near future

DEVELOPING THE SUPER SENSES

From ancient times, every worker of magic has made use of psychic abilities of one kind or another. Some of these are immediately available, inherited perhaps as a gift from the gods, from ancestors, or from past lives; others may be less accessible, but can be developed just like any other skill. Most magical training is aimed at working with these "super senses", but it will require commitment, dedication and hard work.

The ability to enter an altered state at will is probably the most important key to developing psychic abilities. Meditation and creative visualization are two of the most powerful tools in this respect and this chapter begins with a variety of techniques designed to develop these skills. This is followed by information on psychic training using games and experiments to develop telepathy and intuition, as well as how to sense auras and chakras. Astral travel and dreamworlds – including information on dream control and lucid dreaming – are also included, as well as how to journey to the otherworld and inner planes. Through psychic powers it is possible to meet spirit guides, teachers and angelic beings, while exploring past lives can provide many valuable insights into your current situation here on the Earth plane.

MEDITATION

Psychic ability may be seen as the gift of the Goddess, the great Earth Mother. A heightened sensitivity to the unseen relies on a strong intuitive sense that we can develop through cultivating a strong relationship with the Goddess or "feminine" aspect of ourselves. For men and women alike, this means learning to trust our body sensations and having a "felt sense" that is accurate and reliable. To be able to do this we need to be as relaxed and free in body, mind and spirit as possible. Meditation is one of the best ways of achieving this; it helps to ground and centre us in the root of our being and opens up the doorway to the otherworld.

THE POWER OF MEDITATION

Many ancient religions and many cultures in both East and West have practised the art of meditation, and today we have a huge variety of techniques at our disposal – some active, some passive. What is important is to find a method that works for you and to practise it regularly; over time, you will be able to "switch off" from everyday concerns and enter an altered state more readily, while along the way you will be developing an increased sensitivity, heightened perception and intuitive awareness.

Essentially, meditation is the quality of awareness that we bring to an act. It is about raising our levels of consciousness so that we are aware of our activity and of

Burning white sage before you begin to meditate clears the head and promotes insight.

any thoughts and emotions that we are experiencing in the moment as we do it. In which case, any act can become a meditation; if you enjoy walking for instance, you can make this activity your meditation. Instead of hurriedly rushing to be somewhere, slow down and take the time to feel your feet connect with the earth as you take each step. If you enjoy dancing or jogging, you can also make this your meditation, allowing yourself to relax ever more deeply into your body's natural rhythm and movement.

Active meditations such as these are particularly helpful when you are feeling stressed and find it difficult to sit still

Meditation is the best gateway to inner wisdom, opening you up to previously unknown dimensions.

Going in

Meditation is a way of 'going in' to meet yourself. As everyday concerns begin to fade and your conscious mind quietens, the deeper more subtle senses begin to awake and inform your conscious awareness. Unless you can withdraw from the everyday world for a few minutes each day, there is no way that these inner forces can develop.

The three "S's" for meditation

Follow this checklist of the 'three Ss' – Stillness, Silence and Sensitivity – to help make meditation easier.

Stillness. If you sit relaxed and completely still, this helps you to drift into the poised state of awareness where inner material can begin to flow. As soon as you start to wriggle about, or become aware that you are not comfortable, you will break the stream of concentration.

Silence. Don't be tempted to use background music to blot out noises in the environment. It is far better to find a quiet time of day and learn to create inner silence. This matters because as well as seeing images many people also hear sounds, and any music will make this much harder. The more you focus inward and allow any images or feelings to surface, the less you will be distracted.

Sensitivity. You need to listen, watch and perceive whatever images, sounds, symbols or other sensations start to occur in your mind. These will be vague and fleeting to begin with, but the more physically and mentally still you become, and the quieter the background noises are, the sharper your own awareness will be.

and relax; they help to "burn off" your outer layers of energy and bring you back into contact with your inner self.

Letting Go

Meditation teaches us to relax and let go of everyday concerns as we move into deeper levels of our being. It is from these deeper places in ourselves that we are able to experience our connection with the universe; the more deeply we can let go, the more powerful our experience of the hidden realm and cosmic oneness. Many meditation techniques are based on passive "non-doing" states. Bringing awareness to the breath is a good way of bringing attention into the here and now, using each out

breath to relax a little more deeply. Many meditation practices involve working with the breath in a sitting or lying down position, as the mind and body can most easily unwind in these positions.

Active and Passive Meditation

Active meditations can include dance, walking, jogging or any day-to-day activity, providing it is performed with conscious awareness. With a modern sedentary lifestyle, there are many advantages of using active meditation methods. They help to burn off excess energy, which if it is not used, has a tendency to produce an imbalance in the mental body, making it much harder to quieten the mind. They also help to move energy through the body's subtle energy system. Passive meditations usually involve sitting or lying down in a comfortable position and letting go of tensions held in the mind or body through focusing on the breath.

Embracing Darkness

From a seed that sprouts in the soil to a child growing in the womb, all life begins in the dark. The darkness is a place of mystery and tremendous power; it is the realm of the Goddess and is associated with the "feminine" creative force. In modern society, we have become afraid of darkness and have created many sources of light to help us escape from it; but being able to embrace darkness is a necessary part of life. It is also essential if we are to develop as a worker of magic and to feel comfortable entering the otherworld, itself a place of mystery.

A Darkness Meditation

This guided meditation is a good way of connecting with the beneficial power of darkness; it may be a little tricky to master at first, but with practice it does get easier. It is best done in the evening.

1 Sit in a relaxed, upright position in a darkened room. The darker it is, the better, with no chinks of light coming in through the curtains or under the door. Breathe gently and, keeping your eyes open, stare into the blackness. Feeling at ease, imagine the darkness

Using the flame of a candle to help your mind to focus is a good meditation technique.

that is all around you entering your open eyes. It should give you a deep, soothing feeling.

2 At this point, you may like to close your eyes and imagine yourself disappearing into the darkness, just as a shooting star disappears in the rich dark of the night sky. Feel yourself being absorbed, so that just for this moment in time, you don't have to be or do anything. Allow yourself to fully experience the deep relaxation of letting go.

3 Come out of the meditation slowly, lighting a candle to allow your eyes to get used to the light, before you turn on electric light or allow daylight in.

4 As you go about your usual activities following the meditation, imagine that you are carrying a patch of this darkness within you; silent, deep and relaxed. If you do the darkness meditation before bed, try and carry this patch of dark silence with you into sleep.

THE MIND'S EYE

Meditating with lapis lazuli helps promote a lively silence, and aids thought processes.

Perhaps the most powerful tool of any witch or magician is their mind. It is estimated that we use only a tiny percentage of our mental powers, leaving vast reservoirs untapped. Learning to train and use the mind is one of the most basic yet far-reaching skills of any magic worker. The ability to exert control over our thoughts and to direct the focus of our attention is a necessary prerequisite for successful magic; it is also how we can develop the extraordinary powers of the mind to travel in space and time. One of the best ways of doing this is through the faculty of imagination. This is because the imagination deals in pictures, not words, and can influence the unconscious mind on a much deeper level.

THE IMAGINATION

The words imagination and magic share the same root. To imagine is to allow our thoughts to wander freely and conjure up pictures or concepts that are not actually present but seen in the mind's eye as though they are – and the more vivid our imagination, the more real these things seem. Imagination can be seen as the ability of the mind to be creative or resourceful. William Wordsworth, the eighteenth-century English poet, described it as "another name for absolute power and clearest insight".

A vivid imagination, directed by magical training, is the most effective tool we have for changing the world from within, yet for most of us it is something that has lain dormant since childhood. Creative visualization is a way of accessing and training the imagination and beginning to harness its power.

Using creative visualization

Creative visualization can be used in many areas of life, including personal relationships and health and business situations, as well as to improve memory, overcome problems and counter negative thinking. It is also one of the most powerful tools for developing psychic abilities.

A grounding visualization is helpful whenever you feel unconnected to reality, or to the natural world. Sit in front of a green candle on a wooden table to represent the earth.

CREATIVE VISUALIZATION

Essentially, creative visualization uses the power of the mind to consciously create pictures at will. For instance, if you are sick, you could use creative visualization to imagine or see yourself healthy and well; this is much more effective than simply using positive thinking, although accompanying a visualization with a positive thought or affirmation increases its power. Techniques similar to creative visualization have been used for centuries in some parts of the world to heal or prevent disease, although it can be used for any aspect of life.

For instance, creative visualization is a good technique to use for grounding and protection. When developing your mental powers it is particularly important to take care of yourself. Being grounded (or "earthed") is essential; a lack of grounding makes you unable to channel higher energies successfully. You can become overwhelmed by extra-sensory perceptions and get swept away. Similarly it is also a good idea to learn how to protect yourself so that you don't become drained or tired, or else vulnerable to negative energies.

Holding a grounding stone can reduce feelings of confusion and anxiety.

GROUNDING VISUALIZATION

Practise the following grounding visualization before undertaking any work on the mental plane. It will help to connect you with the natural world and to focus, stabilize and renew your positive energies. To do it, you will need a green candle and a dark stone, such as black onyx or smoky quartz.

1 Light the candle and sit on the floor in front of it, or else sit on a chair with your feet on the ground. This is to connect you with the earth. Take the stone in both hands.

2 Breathing slowly and deeply, visualize the roots of a tree gradually growing down into the earth. Think of the strength of numerous small roots, locking themselves into the fertile soil, anchoring the tree firmly and working silently down towards the earth's core. See yourself connecting with the earth.

3 Concentrate on your out-breaths and with each one, feel the energy flowing downward through your body into the ground. You can also see it as a stream of light, passing through you and "earthing" through the soles of your feet. Become aware of the constant, sustaining strength that lies beneath you, supporting you.

4 Now on each in-breath, feel the earth's strength flowing back into you. Picture it as a green energy flowing up through the roots of the tree into the trunk and branches that is your body. Visualize its power flowing into you until you feel calm and centred. When you feel you have come to the end of the visualization, release the stone.

Stones for grounding

Black onyx: protection against negative energy, good for emotional stability; encourages connection to material goals and their achievement

Black tourmaline: grounding and protective, absorbs negativity.

Haematite: banishes fuzziness and aids concentration, memory and self-discipline; self-healing

Jet: grounding, earth power; wards off nightmares and avoids ill-health

Obsidian: very powerful grounding stone; dissolves anger and fear; snowflake obsidian has a softer effect, restores balance and clarity

Smoky quartz: lightly grounding and balancing, counteracts hyperactivity; fosters self-acceptance and awareness of divine protection

PSYCHIC TRAINING

You may already have found that your magical interests have led to your getting "hunches" about doing, or not doing, certain things, or that hints and clues are found in dreams, or that you actually perceive future events clearly in meditations or during divination sessions. Gradually, these psychic impressions will become clearer and easier to interpret, especially if you are able to devote some time to learning which skills you already have, and which need to be rehearsed. There are many simple techniques that you can practise to train your psychic abilities, but it is important that you work at a level and pace that feels comfortable for you; too much progress too quickly could make you feel overwhelmed by your ability to pick up impressions from the otherworld.

The human mind can be trained to realize its full psychic potential.

PSYCHIC GAMES

Some of the most valuable training techniques are psychic "games" which you can experiment and have fun with. It is worth trying some experiments in extra-sensory perception (ESP), psychokinesis (PK, affecting material objects by "mind power"), and expanding psychic awareness. You and your magical companions, or perhaps a slightly wider group of your friends and family, for example, can get together to try out skills such as telepathy (conveying information from one mind to another), precognition or clairvoyance (guessing which card, for example, will be turned up next), or retrocognition (listing the order of an already shuffled pack of cards).

If you have a pack of ordinary playing cards, you can begin some simple tests. Get someone to spread out the playing cards face down on a table and shuffle them very thoroughly, and then give you the whole deck, face down. You then take this pack and, picking the cards up one at a time, still face down, try to guess, imagine or see what colour each one is. Place each card in turn, still face down, on one of two heaps, representing black and red. If you get stuck with some cards, make another heap and go back to them at the end. When you have reached the end of the pack, turn over the heaps and see what has happened. You might

be surprised how many you get right first go! Let a companion have a turn and see if they do better or worse.

ZENER CARDS

To test a psychic's powers of telepathy, a popular research tool used by parapsychologists is a pack of "zener cards". Designed in the 1920s by JB

Rhine, a Harvard biologist, each pack consists of 25 cards depicting five different symbols: a circle, a cross, a square, a five-pointed star and three wavy lines. Each symbol appears on five cards, and is boldly printed against a

Use packs of cards to work on your psychic skills. Innate powers of telepathy, precognition and retrocognition can all be improved on with practice and training.

white or plain-coloured background. In a typical experiment, the cards are shuffled and turned over one by one by a "sender", who then concentrates on the image for a minute or so while the "percipient" (the person who is trying to pick up the image telepathically) tries to identify each card by drawing or saying whichever image comes into his or her head. Sometimes the sender and the percipient are in separate buildings, and the test is repeated several times, with the deck shuffled each time, to reduce the possibility of a chance good result. If you come across zener cards you might like to try some experiments yourself; alternatively it would be relatively simple to make your own deck.

PSYCHIC TAROT

Another experiment, which may be more interesting to magicians, uses Tarot cards. There are layers of interpretation attached to every Tarot card, which may be contradictory, depending on which of the 500 or so Tarot decks you are using. In other words, your view of the cards may be linked to the symbolism of the card, or to your own or a more traditional interpretation.

Place a pack face down across the floor or a large table and stir them about. The experimenter then picks up a card and, without seeing the picture, tries to name it, or describe the feelings, symbols or meaning of the card to a partner. Then both of you look at the card and see if any of it fits. Often, because the

It is important to discuss your results together, as the images you receive telepathically might not always be identical to what was being transmitted.

experimenter gets immediate feedback, by seeing the card after they have guessed, they will get better, more accurate impressions. This "game" has the added advantage of helping you to form telepathic links with your partner, as well as possibly discovering deeper levels of meaning to the Tarot. You could also try this with runes.

TAKING YOUR SKILLS UP A LEVEL

Later on, you may be able to send each other messages at a distance. For instance, you could agree with a friend that at a certain time you will "send" them a thought form which they should try and "tune in" to. To begin with, think of something relatively straightforward, such as a colour, shape or number, or you could try a feeling, such as calm, upset, happy and so on. With practice, you might be able to make the information more complex. For instance, you could try sending a number and a suit of playing or Tarot cards that would include a message, derived from the interpretation of that card or cards.

Find out what sorts of information you can pass from mind to mind and use your imagination to invent experiments to try. Each will help awaken, strengthen and control your psychic faculties.

PICTURE POSTCARDS

Start making a collection of picture postcards that contain clear images or graphic designs that you can use for telepathic experiments. The sender picks a card and tries to convey the illustration to the receiver in another room, who will attempt to draw or describe what they see.

When you are receiving telepathically, you need to be able to enter a relaxed and meditative state, allowing your mind to empty, so that the message can be clearly seen on the "blank screen" of your mind. Although it is not easy to draw exactly the same picture, receptive people should get some aspect of the design, or indicate the feeling of the sender's mind. For example, if the card showed yachts sailing on a calm sea, with birds flying above, the receiver might draw triangles and say it felt windy, or sunny, or that there was a feeling of swaying, etc. Sometimes the emotion of a picture of lovers, or the scent of a flower, or the speed of racing cars can be sent more easily than the actual shapes, colours or minor details of the design. Another technique is to allow the receiver to try to recognize the target card from a selection of the cards. Record your results and see how you improve.

Psychic experiments

Parapsychologists, working in laboratories with carefully selected subjects and using well-tested methods under strictly controlled conditions, have found that new subjects often score higher than those who have tried, and become bored with, card guessing, or attempts at bending metal. It has also been found that a relaxed frame of mind is a help to 'remote viewing' (astral travel to the magician).

SENSING AURAS

An aura is an emanation of the subtle, non-physical energies that infuse and surround every living thing in creation. In magical thinking, this includes rocks and stones, as well as trees, plants, animals and human beings. An aura is like an invisible extension of the physical form and through psychic development it is possible to be able to see or to sense it. This ability can be used to "read" what is going on for a person on a mental, emotional and spiritual level, and for the purposes of healing and rebalancing energies.

Before you use a pendulum to discover a person's aura, make sure you have established your yes and no responses.

THE THREE LAYERS OF AN AURA

Auras are a form of radiant energy that we can learn to detect. Many psychics see them as a halo of energy that has three distinct layers. These layers extend for about 30 cm (1 ft) from the human body, although the greater a person's spiritual vitality, the bigger their auric field. The inner etheric is easily visible to ordinary eyesight in a dimly lit room as a smoky band outlining the figure, and is seen best against naked flesh. Beyond that is a wider band of the astral health region, seen as faint-coloured filaments, such as you sometimes see around power lines on misty days. Outside that is an even fainter layer, the very fine threads of the emotional aura, which connects to all the people, places and objects with which you have any link.

MEASURING AN AURA

One of the easiest ways of discovering the extent of a person's aura is with a pendulum. Start about 10 m (30 ft) away from them and walk towards them, stopping every pace and testing by asking the question "Does the aura reach here?" and waiting for the "yes/no" response. It is also possible to use your hands to sense an aura. Approach the person very slowly with your hands stretched out, and notice any changes to your body sensations. Your hands may become warm or tingle, or you may "feel" their energy field as a springy "ball" that you can push up against. You will have to trust your intuition.

SEEING AURAS

It is also useful to be able to see auras, and this is a skill that can be learned with patience. Ideally, you should have your subject standing in front of a plain, pale surface and ask them to sway slightly from side to side while you stand about 5 m (15 ft) away, looking at the body's

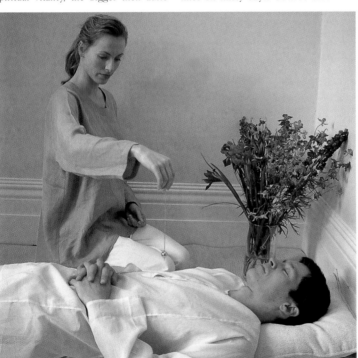

A pendulum is a useful tool to help you sense the condition of a person's aura. You can ask specific questions, as with other kinds of dowsing.

outline. After a while, you will see a light colour that moves as they do. With practice over a number of sessions, you will start to be aware of layers of lighter or deeper tone surrounding them. This is usually a series of bands, starting close to their body with the etheric, which is a dense, pale, smoke-coloured layer a few centimetres wide. Beyond that, stretching some distance, are a number of bands of what you will come to see as varied shades, going all around their outline, and in front of them too. You can try half-closing your eyes so that you are seeing through your eyelashes – some people find this helps. The aura is constructed of rays of light, to get an idea of what it looks like, try squinting at a candle flame. You may well see a kind of radiating rainbow of light around the centre. This is what an aura looks like, and it is a matter of time and practice before you can identify the bands, and eventually the separate colours. Some of these are beyond normal vision and may be hard to name or identify.

INTERPRETING AURAS

There are numerous books on interpreting the colours of auras, as to state of health, mood and so on, but remember that you are also looking through your own aura so the colours are a combination and may seem murky. You can see your own aura by standing naked

in front of a mirror in a dimly lit room, and gazing softly at your reflection. The colours of the outer aura will be changing all the time, varying with emotion, hunger and temper, as well as our general state of health, and concentration on other people, which will brighten the filaments of auric material by which we are linked. Each individual's aura is different, and interpreting an aura's health is dependent upon the individual and the intuition of the viewer.

It may well be that it is along these delicate threads that the shared thoughts of telepathy flow; when you are psychometrizing an object (sensing its history), the impressions you receive are obtained from the same source.

SENSING CHAKRAS

Within everyone's aura are the chakras, a series of seven energy centres that run right through us. The base, or 1st, chakra

is red and centred in the sexual region. It rules raw emotion. Next, is an orange sphere in the belly (the 2nd chakra), dealing with absorption and elimination, both physically and psychically. Above that at the solar plexus is a golden yellow chakra (3rd), our Sun and self centre. In the chest is the emerald green heart chakra (4th), for love and harmony. At the throat is a brilliant blue flower of living light (5th chakra), our power of communication and speech. At the forehead is a violet purple chakra (6th), linking to our intelligence and wisdom. At the top of the head is a brilliant white chakra of light (7th), which connects us to the Creative Spirit, through which spiritual feelings flow in and out.

You can use a pendulum on a partner to detect the vitality of each of their chakras; you can also tune in using your hands, in a similar way, to detecting the auric field.

Meditating on a candle flame can help to open your inner vision and make it easier for you to see auras.

ASTRAL TRAVEL

The starry, or astral, plane is thought to be another layer of reality that is separate from the everyday world that we inhabit during our waking lives. Many people believe the astral plane is the realm of dreams, while the astral body, which includes your aura, is thought to be able to leave the physical body and visit other locations. Those who walk the paths of witchcraft and magic teach themselves consciously to enter the astral planes and bring back information or power. Although some dreams may be thought of as astral travel – particularly those that involve flying – being able to travel at will rather than by accident is a skill that can be learned through meditation and visualization. This is also known as astral projection.

It is possible to teach your mind to travel to other worlds, leaving your body behind.

LEAVING THE BODY

Meditation is a doorway to the inner landscapes and guided meditation, creative visualization and pathworking all teach the astral traveller how to shift from the outer, mundane level of awareness to the inner, and return safely with a full awareness of what has been observed. This does take practice, however, and you are unlikely to be able to travel if you do not have a regular meditation practice. Before attempting to travel, you need to get comfortable with moving in and out of your body.

As you enter meditation, visualize yourself splitting into two: in your mind's eye, see the physical you that is sitting in meditation, and your astral or auric body as a shadow or outline, separating from your physical body, but connected to it with an "umbilical cord" of white light. You may start to feel floaty or light-headed (this is why it is important to be well-grounded before attempting this sort of work); you may even find yourself being able to look down on or at your physical body and having what is known as an "out of body" experience.

LEARNING FROM A TEACHER

Out-of-body techniques are probably best learnt from someone who has a lot of experience of this work. Mastering the techniques can take years of practice and you have to have the passion to really want to do it. Some people don't like the feeling of loss of control that goes with out-of-body travel, so it is important to work within your own limits of what feels comfortable and safe for you.

Meditation is the doorway to astral travel. Burning incense will help you to achieve the mental state necessary for your journey.

Concentrating on the flame of a candle will help to focus your mind during meditation.

Flying witches

It is quite possible that the stereotype of a witch flying across the night sky on her broomstick actually came about as a result of reports of mind travel and out-of-body experiences. These in turn are linked with traditional shamanic practices such as shape-shifting and journeying between the worlds.

THE COLLECTIVE UNCONSCIOUS

Influenced by Jungian depth psychology, some esotericists believe that the astral realms are not outside of us but lie deep within the collective unconscious, the primordial part of the mind that is universal and where archetypal themes and symbols reside. The astral plane, it is argued, is the realm of feelings and emotions and its forms reflect the beliefs of every human being who has ever lived. Hence it is a land of demons and angels, dragons and unicorns, and all the saints and sinners, heavens and hells, and gods and devils of myth and legend.

MAKING AN ASTRAL JOURNEY

Like many of the other aspects of magic, you will need a quiet time and place. If you are intent on going into the astral levels you will also need a companion for basic guidance to share your visions with and help clarify their meaning.

1 Clear a physical and mental space, set up a basic circle and sphere of light around yourself and, having chosen a simple aim, say:
I wish to travel to the astral realms in order to discover....

2 Sit with your companion nearby. Your friend could speak a narrative leading you to the kind of place in which you imagine what you seek would exist. You have to find the landscape, which really already exists on the astral plane. Look on it as another continent or a different dimension of space. Acknowledge that it is real, and that, unlike some images you make, you can't change what you see.

The inspiration for inner journeys can be provided by a magical companion, who can lead the traveller onwards, and then bring them safely back.

3 Once you have seen the surroundings, which may be sufficient for one day, come back to normal awareness, report to your friend, and close your circle.

4 A second attempt will require a different exercise. Here you need to create your protective circle, but instead of setting off into the other dimension, begin to construct an image of your own body, perhaps

Bilocation

The ability to be in two places at the same time is known as 'bilocation'. Essentially a double of you (the astral body) can go out into the world and allow you to see what is going on while you remain going about your daily affairs. To do this, you enter a state of deep meditation and envision a filmy image of yourself leaving your body behind. Bilocation is a very advanced technique and usually takes many years of practice before it can be mastered.

dressed in the costume of the astral realm, standing before you, but facing away. In other words, see your own back in front of you. Work on this until you are really able to see it.

5 Once you have built your own figure, you need to transfer your awareness to it, by a kind of mental leap. This immediately puts many people back to themselves, but with gentle effort you can succeed. You then need to transfer to your "astral self" and insert that self into the inner surroundings so that you can meet your hero or Goddess. For this you may need help from your companion, who will describe the setting when you have indicated that you are in your astral body. What you will experience there is completely real but it has a different look or feel to "real life". With practice over a number of short sessions, most people find that they can do this if they don't force it. A few short sessions of half an hour are far better than a prolonged attempt lasting hours.

DREAMWORLDS

To dream is to move beyond the bounds of everyday reality and to enter the dreamworlds. This is a place where anything can happen – a magical world of limitless possibilities, where the dreamer can fly, shape-shift, walk through solid objects or swim in the sun. And, especially while the dream is going on, it is every bit as real as the common reality that we all share in our day-to-day existence. Magical thinking recognizes the validity of these other worlds and even suggests that our everyday world could be the "dreamscape" of some other dimension of reality. Being able to work with dreams is an invaluable skill for workers of magic: it develops intuition, heightens sensitivity to otherworldly experiences, and increases self-awareness and personal power.

THE DREAMING TRADITION

Whether or not we can remember our dreams, dreaming is something that we all do every night. Through the ages, workers of magic have always valued dreams and taken them seriously. Dreams have been regarded as messages from the gods and used as oracles to predict the future. They have also been attributed with the power to solve problems, heal sickness and bring spiritual revelation, and shamans and

priests, wise women and sages have all acted as dream interpreters.

In magic, a dream is often seen as a way for the spirit self to communicate with the physical body, relaying information in allegorical frames that relate to the dreamer's life and experiences. This has an analogy with modern depth psychology, where dreams are widely believed to contain messages from the unconscious mind; in this context, dreams can be used to work out

Dreamscapes have an otherworldly quality to them, with a special, magical atmosphere.

personal problems as well as a tool for emotional and spiritual growth.

PREPARE TO DREAM

Throughout the ancient world, "dream incubation" was widely practised at holy sites and shrines, many of them dedicated to the gods and goddesses of sleep and dreaming. This was an

Herbs, incense and oils for dreaming

Certain plants are conducive to relaxation, dreams and visions. You can use them fresh or dried, burn them as incense, or vaporize them as essential oils. You could also try making a dream pillow, using a mix of some of your favourite ones.

- Frankincense
- Sandalwood
- Agarwood (aloes)
- Dream herb (zacatechichi)
- Nutmeg
- Valerian
- Hops
- Passion flower

We can nurture the dreaming process through using herbs and oils that prepare body and mind for a restful night's sleep.

intensely ritualistic procedure designed to encourage an especially informative dream from the gods on a variety of issues – from everyday matters to omens and portents for the future. When you want to "incubate" a dream, it is important to put yourself in the right frame of mind before you go to sleep. This means using the evening as a time to relax and let the cares of the day float away as you reconnect with your inner self. Taking a leisurely bath with oils and/or herbs, burning incense, and practising meditation before going to sleep are all helpful.

DREAM RECALL

By their very nature, dreams are elusive and have an annoying habit of slipping away from the wakening mind very easily. Keeping a dream diary is one of the best ways to help with dream recall. Dedicate a special book or folder as your dream journal – you could use your Book of Shadows if you wish – and get into the habit of recording your dreams. Dreams can offer valuable insights into life situations, and keeping a record not only gives you material to work with, but

Record your dreams in a dream diary. You will need to write them down as soon as you wake up, even if that is in the middle of the night.

sends a message to your subconscious mind that you are interested and wish to remember your dreams. Keep the book and a pen by your bed so that you can write the dreams down the moment you

wake up, even if this is in the middle of the night. Don't worry about it making sense, and even if you can only remember a fragment, this can be enough to work with.

Dream catchers

The 'dream catcher' charm is a traditional Native American Indian device for capturing good, wise dreams and for letting the bad ones pass through it and into the night. It has a single thread that is wound in a spiral from the outside to the centre, symbolizing the journey from the waking world to

the world of dreams. The native Americans believe that their dreaming selves pass through the heart of the dream catcher and return with knowledge of the dreams of their true selves.

Making a dream catcher

Dream catchers are available ready-made but it is also possible to make your own. A dream catcher is a very personal thing and making one gives you plenty of scope to design it in a way that says something about you.

You will need

a thin bendy stick about 60 cm (2 ft) long
twine, such as fishing line, or strong cotton thread
coloured ribbon
knife
beads
feathers

1 Curl the stick into a circle and fasten it with twine wrapped around. Some people like to cover the whole of the wood in ribbon before they start, but it is up to you. Cut off any sharp ends of wood at the join and wrap some ribbon around it.

2 Tie one end of a length of twine on to any point on the circle and thread it across $\frac{1}{4}$ of the

circle. Tie it onto the circle and cut off the long end.

3 Come back towards your starting point and tie another cross-twine across the circle. Repeat this four times until you have four lengths going around the circle.

4 From the centre of each of these tie one twine to each of the other three. This gives you a sort of 'cat's cradle' effect. Experiment until you have a pleasing criss-cross of lines resembling a spider's web. An alternative way to do this is to use a single length of twine, but this might take some practice before you succeed.

5 Add a bead in the centre of the web to represent the spider.

6 Finish by decorating the dream catcher with some ribbons hanging from the bottom of the circle. Add some feathers and beads to these downward-hanging ribbons.

INTERPRETING DREAMS

There are many dream dictionaries and interpretative guides to dreams, yet ultimately the best expert on your dreams is you. One way of unlocking the meaning of a dream is to decode its symbolism. Traditionally, certain symbols (such as an animal, a building, fire and so on) are associated with certain meanings, but it is probably best to ask yourself what a particular symbol means for you: dreaming of water, for instance, may mean quite different things to two different people. Another way to start to understand your dreams is to ask yourself how you feel when you first wake up: are you happy or sad, angry or fearful? Notice if this feeling is connected with your dream. You could also ask questions of whoever or whatever is in the dream and let that "part" speak to you.

REPLAYING DREAMS

It is very useful to be able to replay your dream again later when you are relaxed and awake as you may gain fresh insights. You can also interact with dream characters and landscapes to try to find out more information; for instance, you could ask the characters and even the places involved: "Who are you? Why are you here? What are you telling me? Why am I here?" Go with the first answer that comes to mind but don't accept "No". A character may run away, or try to frighten you, but don't be intimidated, follow them – they will lead you to an answer.

Learning to lucid dream

The most important key to learning how to generate lucid dreams is your level of motivation. The second is being adept at recalling your dreams, which comes through practice. However, the following techniques may also be used to encourage lucidity.

pre-sleep suggestion: as you drift into sleep, repeat a request or statement in your mind about becoming lucid in your dreams.

periodic questioning: develop a 'critical-reflective attitude' to your state of consciousness while awake, asking yourself 'could I be dreaming now?' through the day.

rehearse dreaming: sit down and pretend that you are dreaming. Use your imagination to create a dream.

if this were a dream: several times a day, stop and ask yourself 'if this experience were a dream, what would it mean?'

meditation: practice your ability to meditate; people who regularly practise meditation seem to have more lucid dreams.

dream groups: it is possible to join up with other people who are interested in exploring their dreams. People with a regular forum in which to discuss their dreams tend to become regular lucid dreamers.

CHANGING DREAMS

Because all worlds are dreamscapes, the ability to change or direct a dream means that we can decide how we would like events to turn out, rather than letting things "just happen" to us by chance. Usually, the dreams that we want to change are ones that cause fear, pain or anger, and by taking control over them in the dreamworld, we are affirming our strength here, in this physical world.

When changing a dream, don't try to force things to happen, just let your intuition flow and allow your creativity to

One way of becoming more at home in your dreamworld is to replay your dreams when you are awake.

Consider every aspect of your dream, noticing figures, landscapes and any symbols.

If you dream of falling, and wake up before impact, revisit the dream and control its ending.

Your dreams are about you

Usually the main characters and events in a dream represent various aspects of yourself. For example, disturbing dreams – perhaps involving death or violence of some kind – are not necessarily portents that some harm is about to befall the characters involved. Rather, the injured parties represent aspects of yourself that are

being harmed, perhaps by not being allowed their full expression in the waking world, and that harm has a detrimental influence on the whole. By questioning the characters in the dream you can determine what aspects of your personality are trying to communicate with you, such as the child-self or the male/female-self.

Many people believe that when you dream, essentially you are dreaming about one person – and that is you.

come to the fore. Remember, anything can happen in a dream, so don't restrict yourself to the logical constraints of everyday life.

CHANGING WHAT OCCURS

To change a dream, you will need to replay it, looking out for where you want to make the changes. For instance, say you have a dream in which you feel powerless, perhaps chasing someone who eludes you. A way of changing that type of dream is actually to catch the person you are pursuing. They may continue to escape when you re-enter the dream, but be persistent and persevere until you reach your goal.

CHANGING YOUR RESPONSE

In a similar way to changing the events, changing your response is another method of taking control. Fear dreams are often recurrent, and many feature being chased or stalked by a menacing presence. This can cause a great deal of anxiety and the dreamer may wake up short of breath and with a pounding

heart. A way of taking control in this situation would be to transmute the reaction; instead of being tense and afraid in the dream, be light-hearted and happy. This will help dispel anxiety.

EXTENDING A DREAM

Most of us have experienced dreams that end prematurely when we wake, usually with a fearful start. A good way of changing this type of dream is to allow it to continue and see where it goes. Simply recall the dream and, at the point where you woke up, carry it on using your creative intuition. A typical situation in this type of dream is that the dreamer is falling, which can signify a leap into the unknown. The dream usually ends abruptly just before impact with the ground – but who knows what

might happen if the dream were allowed to continue? Perhaps the ground might open up to allow safe passage, or maybe it would be soft and resilient. One way to find out is to give your creative intuition free rein and take that leap.

LUCID DREAMING

The term "lucid dreaming" is used to describe the state of being aware that you are dreaming whilst you are in the dream state. Lucid dreams seem to introduce us to that part of ourselves that creates our dreams. Consequently, learning how to recognize and generate such dreams has enormous magical potential – once we can direct our dreams at will, we are in touch with powerful forces for changing our lives in accordance with our wishes.

JOURNEYING TO OTHER WORLDS

We all have the ability to journey to different worlds, and indeed do so when we dream. As we know from dreams, these otherworlds are places of limitless possibilities, where information is relayed in a format the traveller can relate to. Unlike dreams, however, the journey to another world is undertaken with conscious intent and with a specific goal in mind. You may like to light a candle and cast a magic circle around you before you begin.

When you are preparing for a journey you need to focus your attention before you begin.

PLANNING A JOURNEY

When journeying to another realm, it is important to be open to whatever may happen and to anything you might meet. Trust your intuition, because what first comes to you is the right thing, whatever it may be. Just go with the flow and don't try to force anything. Remember that you have control over what you can accomplish in this otherworld that you travel to and don't be inhibited by fear. Be creative in circumventing problems and challenges that may arise.

As with physical travel in this world, if you prepare yourself properly before a journey, things will go more smoothly and it will be a more fruitful experience.

PREPARING FOR A JOURNEY

This simple ritual helps to prepare you for any kind of journey by centring you and focusing your attention on the journey you are about to undertake.

1 Gather your tools together (these may include musical equipment and an appropriate piece of music, incenses, oils or candles) and create a

Before you begin your journey make sure you are comfortable and relaxed, and that you will not be disturbed.

comfortable place where you feel relaxed and safe from disturbance. Light a candle for inner illumination and contemplate it quietly for a while.

2 Smudge yourself, the tools and your surroundings. Make an offering to whichever spirits, gods or goddesses or angelic beings you are working with and voice your intent:
I call on (say the name) to assist me in this journey to (state reason of journey) and I make this offering in honour of you and in gratitude for your aid.

3 When you are ready, sit or lie comfortably and breathe deeply to get relaxed. Start the music if you are using it, and take some deep, regular breaths as your journey begins.

JOURNEY TO THE HALL OF THE GODS

Here is an inner journey to a place that is peaceful, powerful and magical, and where it is easy to sink into an altered state of awareness to commune with the gods. Make sure you will not be disturbed for about half an hour and get into a meditative frame of mind. If possible, record the narrative on tape, pausing after every sentence to allow the images to build up, or get a friend to read it to you, or go through it a number of times until you can recall the various stages. Allow the images to become as real as possible. You are creating the pictures partly from memory or imagination, and partly because they are real in another realm or dimension.

1 Sit upright, close your eyes and concentrate on your breathing. Allow it to slow down and become deeper.

2 Begin to build up a picture of an elaborate doorway; see the frame and the details of the closed door. What is it made of? What does it feel like? Does it open? This is the door from your world to the realm of the gods. There may be a guardian who is there to ask who you are and why you wish to go through, or ask for a password or token. You will have to find the answers.

You might like to perform your dream journeys within a magic circle, so that you benefit from the protective energy field that no hostile or negative forces can penetrate.

3 After a few moments, as you continue to relax and make the experience deeper, you will find that the door can be opened. At first a great light seems to be shining through the doorway, and you stand on the threshold while your inner vision adjusts.

4 The light dims so that you can look into the place beyond, and what you see is a glorious hall, built of golden stone. Upon the walls are paintings or hangings picked out in bright colours. You step forward on to a paved floor covered in mosaics.

5 Everything you see is on a grand scale. The ceiling is high above but that too is painted and gilded, and everything is beautiful. To one side of the room there is a platform reached by several

steps covered with marvellous brocade, and on the dais is a throne, carved and covered in gold. Upon it you start to make out a figure that is awe-inspiring but also approachable.

6 You move towards the steps and try to make out the face of the figure seated above you. This is the deity you have come to meet. Take as long as you need with them, and when you have had your audience, give thanks, even if the advice is not immediately clear, and act with respect.

7 Allow the image of the great hall to fade, so that you see again the door and threshold. The light dims and gently you return to your own place. Come back to normal awareness slowly, allowing yourself to recall every detail.

SHAMANIC JOURNEYING

The ability to journey to otherworlds is a traditional shamanic practice. It is a very powerful way to gain insights into problems, to look for healing, to seek allies or just to relax. When you journey, you enter a different world. It is essentially one that you create and guide yourself through, although your conscious self relinquishes control to your spirit. Before starting a journey, make sure you are in a place where you feel safe and won't be disturbed.

THE DRUM

Traditionally, a drum is used in shamanic journeying and it is good to have someone drum for you, as a regular rhythm of around 200 beats per minute helps you achieve the focus needed for the opening of a gateway. It is good to build up the rhythm gradually to allow the traveller to become acclimatized.

At first it is best to journey for a set time of around five minutes. At the end of this period the drummer can initiate the return with a call-back signal – say, four one-second beats followed by some very rapid drumming. With experience, the drummer will be able to use their intuition to tell when the journey is complete. Making a drum tape for journeying can also be very useful, as you can record several sessions of various lengths and incorporate your own call-back signal.

JOURNEY TO MEET A POWER ANIMAL

A power animal is your own personal spirit ally which takes the form of an animal. Meeting a power animal is a useful journey to start with because the animal can accompany you on future adventures and give you guidance, wisdom and protection. How to do this is described in the section on Animal Totems. This is not a deep journey but it does expand your awareness, taking you to the edge of your sacred space, where it borders the realms of other spirits. The

Entrances to the upperworld

The way into the upperworld could be:
- A gap in the sky which can be reached by flying or leaping
- A cave mouth high up a cliff that you need to scale
- A tall tree to climb
- A mountain that pierces a cloud
- A flight of stairs
- A ladder

animal you find could be anything, and it may not be what you were expecting, but once you have found each other you should spend some time together on subsequent journeys. Be aware of the love it has for you. Remember, the greater the detail the more real it will seem. If it feels appropriate, transform yourself into the same animal and run, fly or swim. Above all, have some fun.

When you have returned from your journey, go over it in your mind or, better still, write it down to help fix the details. This will aid you in future travels and make it easier to contact the animal.

JOURNEYING TO OTHERWORLDS

Deeper journeys to otherworlds require going beyond your sacred space. The otherworlds that shamans journey to are many and varied and can encompass any number of features, because each is a construct of the shaman who enters it. Essentially though, otherworlds are confined to two realms and when you journey from your sacred space you can travel downwards to the underworld or upwards to the upperworld.

The drum plays a very important part in Shamanic rituals. If you are working alone it is a good idea to make a drumming tape for your journeys.

Entrances to the underworld

The way into the underworld could be through any of the following openings:

- A cave or crevice in the side of a rockface
- A recess or a knothole in a tree
- An animal's burrow in a bank
- A wormhole
- A well
- A doorway or gate
- A waterfall or stream

THE UNDERWORLD

Most shamanic journeys involve going to the underworld, which is not comparable with the hell of Christianity and other faiths, but represents the inner recesses of the traveller; you could also think of it as the deepest recesses of the unconscious mind. It is not a sinister place but a place of challenge and adventure. A shaman enters it to seek solutions and understanding. The challenges you might encounter are all manifestations of your own fears and problems. By confronting them and finding solutions in the underworld you are facing them within yourself and allowing your spirit to communicate the solutions to your conscious self. Because you are journeying deep within yourself, you are seeking an entrance that will lead downwards and in. Remember, to gain entry you can transform yourself to any size and shape required.

THE UPPERWORLD

Associated with the higher self or the soul, the upperworld is the place to go to for inspiration and communion with

When you are journeying for another person, spend some time tuning in to your partner's mind.

other spirits. Whereas the underworld is about confronting your inner fears, the upperworld is more concerned with seeking assistance from others, by meeting other spirits on an equal basis and sharing knowledge with them.

This realm is very light and tranquil, with a feeling of limitless space that stretches away forever. Because it is related to the higher self, it is reached by going upwards. As with a journey to the underworld, it is good to have some structure to follow to help maintain your focus. Because going upwards relates to the soul, a good focus to have is to connect with your higher self. This part of your being is calm and all-knowing. It is dissociated from the emotions that have such a strong influence on the physical, and can therefore give counsel with a dispassionate objectivity that will cut to the heart of a problem.

JOURNEYING FOR OTHERS

Sometimes a shaman may be required to journey to the upperworld or underworld on behalf of another, for purposes of healing or to seek the answer to a question. The principle is always the same: go with a specific aim in mind and be open to what befalls you on the way to your goal. The meaning of the tests and solutions might not be immediately apparent, but when you describe your experiences to your partner, they may understand the symbolism in ways that you did not.

Journeying on behalf of another person is mutually beneficial, and can form a close bond between the people involved. When you are doing this, take some time to develop a level of empathy with your partner by sitting quietly for ten minutes, holding hands and feeling each other's energy.

INNER GUIDES

The occult arts have always recognized the reality of the unseen forces that may help and heal, instruct and guide. Magicians and witches do not usually call up the spirits of the dead, accepting, on the whole, that the immortal human spirit needs to rest and assess its past life before being brought back into incarnation. Although there are discarnate sources of knowledge that may be contacted through magical applications of some of the spiritualists' methods, magicians and witches generally prefer to use their own ways to receive information from hidden masters or inner guides.

MEETING INNER TEACHERS

Magicians and witches may have the ability to talk to teachers of wisdom from the past, or their own ancestors, or the people who founded their magical tradition. This can be done by creating an inner journey to the place in which these wise beings would dwell, and going there to hear what they have to say. Throughout, the modern magic worker is in control and able to terminate the experience if necessary.

INNER PLANE ADEPTI

Some schools of magic have named inner teachers who are known as the Inner Plane Adepti or Hidden Masters of Wisdom. These great instructors may once have been famous living people or they may be angels who have never lived on earth.

A well-established magical lodge will have one or more of these teachers, who are invited to witness the workings of the magical order and give guidance or instruction as necessary. If a group is fully aware of its Inner Plane Adept, they may see him or her during group meditations, or else one member of the group may have the skill to perceive this inner teacher and convey their words or philosophy to the other members. It requires a lot of faith and trust to enter a mind-to-mind contact with some unseen

The one-eyed god Odin, leader of the Wild Hunt, had a central role in Nordic mythology.

being, but those who are experienced in this method gain a great deal of genuine and original teaching material.

MYTHOLOGICAL HEROES

Legends and myths have given inspiration for guides and teachers to many traditions, in particular the Arthurian legends and Norse sagas. The Norse god Odin, leader of the Wild Hunt and giver of knowledge, is a complex figure who traded one of his eyes to drink in the underworld well of the wise god Mimir, and is therefore seen as a source of wisdom himself.

ANGELIC BEINGS

Among the other unseen beings who are often called on to help in magical work are the angels and archangels. They have many functions: as healers, teachers, protectors and illuminators of humanity.

Angels, whose name means "messenger" in Greek, are thought of as the active hands of the God or Goddess,

Egyptian temple pictures sometimes show deities and other celestial beings, as having wings. Here it is Isis who is shown as possessing angelic qualities.

Angels appear in many different spiritual traditions, acting as intermediaries and guides between this world and the next.

you see them as huge, delicate cloud formations like wings or feathers blown by the wind, and tipped with sunlight. They are always beautiful, and if you find yourself in their presence, it can be very moving and inspiring.

MEETING YOUR HIGHER SELF

Your higher self resides in the upperworld, or starry realm. It is the wisest and purest part of yourself that wants only what is best for your highest spiritual purpose – which is not necessarily the same as what your "lower" or everyday self desires.

To meet your higher self, you will need to journey to the upperworld (see Journeying to Other Worlds earlier in this chapter). Once there, pause and take a moment to observe your surroundings. Your higher self, or soul self, might be right there or you might have to go in search of it. When you meet your higher self, greet it with love. Pose any questions you may have and receive the answers gratefully. They might not be what your mortal self wants to hear but they will be honest. When it is time to return, thank your higher self for the meeting and slowly come back. Make a record of the events in a journal, because the meaning may not be immediately apparent and you may wish to read through the account again at a later date.

the source of all, or the One. They have no free will and travel between Earth and Heaven, bringing news or offering assistance. Working with angels is very popular because they appear to be benevolent beings of light, and are found

in many religious philosophies. Pictures from ancient Egyptian temples show winged goddesses who seem to have many of the qualities of angels, and Christians, Muslims, Jews and many other faiths have accounts of angels in their religious texts.

Many different kinds of angels are particularly important to followers of the Hebrew mystical system of the Cabbala. The central glyph of this philosophy is the Tree of Life, which has ten spheres of creation. These are commonly linked to the powers of the planets, but each sphere also has an angel who rules over its working in the Earth plane.

MEETING ANGELS

Angels may be called upon by lighting a candle, relaxing and asking them to appear, or they might offer help unasked, if you genuinely need their assistance. They don't always look like we imagine them to be, as they can be vast in size, and as subtle as auric light. Sometimes

The planets and archangels

The Earth and seven 'personal' planets are each associated with an angel, who rules over its working in the Earth plane.

Earth: Sandalphon
Moon: Gabriel
Mercury: Raphael
Venus: Anael
Sun: Michael
Mars: Zamael
Jupiter: Sachiel
Saturn: Cassiel

A word of warning

It is wisest not to attempt trances or try to contact discarnate spirits unless you have a reputable teacher, or expert help is at hand. Some people who have taken part in séances, played at 'raising ghosts' or light-heartedly dabbled with Ouija boards have scared themselves. A few have opened doors to psychic perceptions that they did not know how to close, or have attracted the attention of entities they could not control. If you are aspiring to master the skills of magic, always work in the power of light, act sensibly and treat all beings - be they angels, gods, ghosts or elementals - with respect.

EXPLORING PAST LIVES

atural magic honours the cycles of nature and its eternal round of birth, growth, death and rebirth. In human terms this is mirrored by a belief in reincarnation, which holds that each soul lives through many lifetimes, gradually gaining skills and strengthening its power to evolve. An aspect of this divine spark is within everyone – it is immortal and does not die when our bodies do. We recognize this eternal factor within us and probably think of it as our "inner self". Just as plants grow, blossom, fruit and die, so the human being grows, learns, reproduces, dies and is born again.

Trees "die" in winter and are "reborn" in spring, symbolizing the soul's eternal round.

THE SOUL

Throughout our time on the Earth plane, our soul gains new experiences and becomes more complete. When we die, it rests in a state that might be thought of as "heaven". Here it is not "judged" or made to account for "sins" but assesses its own progress and sees dispassionately how it has done in life. If a certain part of its development has been overlooked, it will reincarnate in another physical form to learn the lessons it needs to learn. The soul continues to reincarnate until its lessons on Earth are complete, when it transcends the birth, death, rebirth cycle by becoming one with the cosmic unity or the One.

KARMA

The theory of karma is central to the idea of past lives. Karma is a Sanskrit term to denote the concept of action and reaction, similar to the idea in Western thought of reaping what you sow. This means that every action has a consequence, and even if we may appear to "get away with it" this time around, our actions can return to haunt us in a future incarnation. Some people think that the qualities we are born with are the results of either "good" or "bad" karma, or that misfortune could be the results of karmic debts being paid off. Others believe that it is possible to choose to come to Earth in imperfect bodies in order to learn hard lessons quickly, and so evolve spiritually. It is impossible to agree on a precise doctrine,

Once the cycle of rebirth is over, and the soul has learned all it needs to know, it transcends birth and death to become one with the cosmic unity.

Discovering past lives

One way of discovering past lives is through hypnotic regression. This is not something that you can do by yourself and should only be undertaken with expert guidance. However, an effective way of finding out about past lives by yourself is to develop an inner journey to the Hall of Records where you can locate your own personal Book of Lives and look in that to see who you have been. It also avoids the emotional impact of re-living the past, which can be associated with regression techniques.

1 Sit in meditation and visualize yourself entering an old building and climbing a staircase to a great library. This is the Hall of Records and in it there are a great number of books of all ages, sizes and types. Explore the place fully using all your senses.

2 Librarians are available who can help you find your own records; you just need to ask for their help. The volume of your lives will have your current name on it and it can be taken to a quiet corner to study.

3 Continue to relax and allow whatever symbol

of this personal record that arises to do so, rather than making it have a particular form. It could be a book, a stone tablet, or even a computer screen – there is no right form.

4 When you are focused, look at your personal record and you are sure to find something of interest. It could be a family tree, written words in familiar or ancient languages, pictures, or an image that is more like a window, through which you can pass to explore your own past.

5 Take your time and enter into the experience as deeply as possible, while making a mental note of everything that you find. You may experience life from the outside, merely witnessing domestic events as an onlooker, or you may find yourself viewing some past incarnation. What you get, and how deeply you are affected, will depend on how much you can go with the process.

6 Write up your experience in your Book of Shadows or other journal. You could also add drawings and anything else you gain from research later on.

Use the smoke from a snuffed candle to draw you into the meditation, and light it again afterwards to ground yourself.

but the idea of karma and its balance of good and bad deeds makes a worthwhile lesson. It is hard to get to the bottom of a single event, as every life is affected by complex patterns of action and reaction and it is the soul that chooses the conditions into which it will be born each time. No other being directs the pattern of reincarnation.

SOULMATES

It is possible that long-lasting relationships can continue from one life to the next. When people describe having a "soulmate", in the true sense of the word, they mean a lover with whom they have journeyed through many lives. This is because true love is eternal and its bonds outlive the grave.

PAST-LIFE RECALL

If you are interested in exploring your own past lives, go about it sensibly, because it can be an unsettling

experience. It is vital to have a reliable companion, plenty of time, and to make detailed records. Do not take everything you learn for granted without checking

the facts – there are plenty of accurate historical accounts of most times and places, and the research can help confirm whether what you recall is valid and "real". However, even if it is just fantasy, your imagination may have something valid to show you about yourself.

A mirror spell to see who you have been

This will allow you to get a small glimpse of the past, on which you can work to gain more details.

1 Make a magical circle of protection and calmness by sprinkling blessed water around you. Become relaxed and focused.

2 At night, place a mirror on a stand and a single lit white candle on a table so that the light shines on your face. Also take a sheet of writing paper and a pen. Write clearly the following words, then carefully burn the writing in the candle flame:

I wish to see who I have been in a past life, at a time when all was going well. Reveal to me in this shining glass, I summon old "me" by this spell.

3 Just focus your vision on your eyes reflected in the mirror and after a while you may see the image change and become another face. It can seem a bit weird at first, but if you are patient and certain it is what you want, it will happen.

4 When your face returns to normal, say:
Thank you, me, whoever you seem, perhaps we will meet again in dream.

MAGICAL
CORRESPONDENCES

Magic is a vast and ancient subject and tables of correspondences have always been an important part of the magic-worker's tool kit. They provide a useful at-a-glance guide to some of the main properties of the various magical "ingredients" that are used in spells, ceremonies, rituals and all other kinds of magic. Once you start looking, you will find that there are literally hundreds of tables available – both ancient and modern – that can all be used to help you with your magical journey.

What is given here is a selection of some of the most useful correspondence charts to get you started, but as you become more experienced you will find the confidence to develop your own charts based on your own magical knowledge. This final chapter contains correspondence charts on the symbolism of crystals, birds and animals, trees, plants and herbs, incense and essential oils as well as colour. It also contains tables of the elements, of planetary associations, and a guide to some of the main gods, angels and spirit beings in magical use today. Remember that such information is not intended as a substitute for in-depth knowledge, but as a quick reference tool to help you when selecting the appropriate ingredients for use in your magic.

The symbolism of crystals

Amber	Good luck stone, draws out disease and clears negativity and depression
Agate	For inspiration from the spiritual realm
Amethyst	Peace, protection and spirituality; healing; release from addiction, help with meditation and peaceful sleep, eases transition between life and death
Angelite	Heals anger, restores harmony; helpful in telepathic communication, connecting with angels and spirits
Aquamarine	Helps in the expression of spiritual truths; aids dreaming to increase psychic power
Aventurine	Healing at all levels, dissolves blockages, balances the emotions; green aventurine attracts good fortune and increases perception; pink aventurine heals relationships
Azurite	Mental clarity and renewal, releases painful ideas from the subconscious; also known as 'the stone of heaven', can help attunement to the psychic world
Beryl	Enhances psychic ability
Black onyx	Protects against negative energy, helps emotional stability, encourages connection with reality
Blue lace agate	Symbolizes health and long life, grounding, brings inspiration and facilitates self-expression
Calcite	Balances male and female energies; allays fears and stress, assists with astral travel; orange calcite is particularly useful for shock or trauma
Carnelian	Aids creative flow, grounds in the present, inspires confidence, courage and motivation
Celestite	To link with angels and spirit guides, a bright moontime crystal
Chrysocolla	Soothes and calms, eases fear and guilt, attracts luck
Chrysoprase	Emotionally uplifting, attracts abundance and success, spiritual energy
Citrine	Prevents nightmares, enhances self-esteem and responsible use of power, brings abundance and material wellbeing; a crystal of the sun
Clear quartz	Amplifies energy, spiritually and emotionally healing, aids meditation; a bright moontime crystal
Diamond	Symbolizes power, purity, strength, trust, commitment and love; instils wisdom and confidence
Emerald	Physically healing and protective; lends insight and security in love
Fluorite	Gathers together different energies and assists in focus and concentration; aids communication with higher self; yellow fluorite promotes self-confidence
Garnet	Stimulates energy, aids expression, strengthens love

Crystals are a powerful magical tool.

	and friendship
Haematite	Aids concentration, reasoning, memory and self-discipline; healing and protective; grounding
Herkimer diamond	Releases energy blockages, helps with dream recall
Jade	Clarity, justice and wisdom; balances the emotions, promotes peaceful sleep; attracts prosperity
Jasper	Often referred to as a talisman; one of the most powerful healing stones
Jet	Calms the subtle bodies, clears a heavy head and helps lift depression, useful for clearing negativity; a dark moontime crystal
Kunzite	Redresses compulsive tendencies and restores balance; opens up the heart and connection to higher self
Kyanite	Balances emotional disturbances, promotes inner peace; helps intuition
Labradorite	Develops psychic ability
Lapis lazuli	Strengthens will, awareness, integrity in relationships; aids the release of emotional wounds
Malachite	Healing, absorbs negativity, stimulates creativity
Moonstone	Wishes, intuition and new beginnings; restores harmony in relationships, calms emotions and induces lucid dreaming; a bright moontime crystal
Moss agate	Connects with earth spirits, brings abundance and self-confidence
Obsidian	Protective and grounding, reduces escapism and dissolves anger and fear; snowflake obsidian has a softer effect, restores balance and clarity
Opal	Visionary, attracts inspiration and insight
Pearl	Enhances purity, clarity and grace; balances emotions, increases confidence in inner wisdom
Pyrites	Harnesses creative thinking and practicality
Red jasper	Connects with earth energy, emotionally calming
Rhodonite	Fosters patience, selflessness
Rose quartz	Heals emotional wounds, restores love
Ruby	Amplifies emotions, releases and dissolves anger, attracts loyalty, awakens passion and beauty
Sapphire	Symbolizes peace, gives protection and wisdom
Selenite	Mental focus, clarity and clairvoyance
Smoky quartz	Lightly grounding and balancing; fosters self-acceptance; absorbs negative vibrations
Sodalite	Calms troubled mind and emotions; promotes inner peace
Sugilite	Aids physical healing and purification of all body systems; strengthens will; aid to meditation
Tiger's eye	Creates order and harmony; attracts beauty
Topaz	Symbolizes light and warmth, heals and absorbs tension, attracts love and creativity
Tourmaline	Grounding, healing and protective, absorbs negativity and brings discernment and vitality
Turquoise	Healing and protection; blessing and partnership

The symbolism of birds and animals

Alligator/ crocodile	Guardian and fierce protector; stealth, ferocity; primal power
Antelope	Vision and foresight; speed and quick action; gentleness
Armadillo	Armour, boundaries and protection
Badger	Strength and perseverance; fighting for what you want, tenacity; prophesy and divination
Bat	Death and rebirth; initiation, transition, change
Bear	Receptive female energy; earth wisdom, introspection; lunar energies
Beaver	Industrious; flexibility and creativity
Blackbird	Gatekeeper
Bison (buffalo)	Wisdom of the elders; provider and protector; fertility, sexual vigour, power
Bull	Male sexual potency, strength; war
Cat	Independence, intuition; sacred to the Goddess, female medicine
Cow	Fertility and prosperity; motherhood, family life
Coyote	Childlike trust, innocence and playfulness; a trickster figure, mischievous and exposes pretensions in others
Crow/raven	Change; foresight and prediction; shape shifting; good and bad luck; all aspects of witchcraft and magic
Deer	Security and protection; male and female sexuality; keeper of wisdom, storyteller
Dog	Friendship, kindness, loyalty and protection, guardian of ancient secrets
Dolphin/porpoise	Understanding, wisdom; unconditional love; laughter, harmony and healing
Dove	Peace and love; marriage, spiritual harmony; purity and clear vision
Dragon	Mythical beast, symbol of good luck; energetic, fun-loving, confident
Duck	Love and harmony, domesticity, abundance; motherhood and children; new beginnings
Eagle	Divine and earthly power; freedom, fearlessness striving for higher goals; clarity, clairvoyance
Fish	Mystery, the depths of the subconscious, emotions; lunar magic
Fox	Trickery and guile, secrets; protection, family, maternal instincts
Frog	Cleansing, emotional healing; fertility; change and transformation
Goat	Relaxed and happy-go-lucky; ability to live in the present; creative, friendly; ambitious
Goose	Storytelling; protection, fertility; rebirth; links with the Great Mother
Hare	Quickness of thought; intuition, sensitivity; creativity; associated with the moon goddess, fertility

Hawk	The gift of foresight, perception, psychic powers; messenger from spirit world bringing knowledge and wisdom
Heron	Self-reliance
Horse	Freedom, swiftness, stamina and endurance; earthly and otherworldly power; strength and self-confidence
Jaguar (panther, leopard)	The gift of vision; prediction, prophesy and divination; intuition and psychic power
Lion	Strength, majesty; power and leadership
Lizard	Illusions, letting go; adaptability; change, transition
Magpie	Relationships
Moose (elk)	Strength and endurance; male and female sexuality; relationships
Monkey	Inquisitive, energetic, competitive; leadership; clever and sharp-witted
Mouse	Finely attuned sensitivity; messenger; abundance and fertility
Owl	Wisdom; understanding hidden truths; insight and telepathy; all forms of magic
Ox	Patience, kindness and responsibility; routine, order and discipline
Pig	Diplomacy, common sense; prone to greed
Pigeon	Messages
Rabbit	Fertility and love; fear and cowardice
Ram/sheep	Lust, fertility; action without forethought, youthful zest
Rat	Self-motivated, strong sense of self-preservation; cheerful, ability to bounce back
Robin	New beginnings; protection
Rooster	Flamboyant; a good communicator
Snake	Shedding of the old; transformation; philosophical, mysterious, shrewd, sensual; underworld guardian
Swan	Purity, serenity, peace; spirituality and dignity
Tiger	Rash, impulsive, dynamic; risk-taking, leadership
Turtle	Endurance; knowledge; Mother Earth, women
Wolf	Loyalty; freedom; independence; afterlife and rebirth; teacher
Woodpecker	Magic and prophecy; sacred cycles; rain, storms and thunder
Wren	Protection

The proud eagle symbolizes freedom and fearlessness

The wolf symbolizes loyalty and freedom.

The symbolism of trees, plants and herbs

Angelica	Burn dried leaves for protection and healing
Anise	Keeps away nightmares
Apple	For love and friendship; youth, beauty, innocence
Ash	The world tree; purification and cleansing
Basil	Gives protection, repels negativity, brings wealth
Bay	Guardian of the house, protects against illness; burn leaves to produce visions
Beech	Stability, flow of energy; protector of written wisdom, guardian of knowledge
Blessed thistle	Brings spiritual and financial blessing; fresh plant brings strengthening energy to a sickroom
Cabbage	Brings good luck
Carrot seed	Illuminating; use for visions and vision quests, journeying
Catnip	Encourages a psychic bond with cats; attracts luck and happiness
Chamomile	For meditation and relaxation; use in prosperity charms to attract money
Chickweed	For attracting love or maintaining a relationship
Chilli	Assures fidelity and love
Cinnamon	Aphrodisiac; draws money, protection and success
Clove	Banishes hostile or negative forces and helps to gain what is sought; use in spells to stop gossip
Clover	For love and fidelity
Coltsfoot	Brings love, wealth and peace
Comfrey	For safety when travelling
Cyclamen	For love and truth
Dandelion	Enhances dreams and prophetic power
Dogwood	Charm and finesse
Elm	Love, light and purification; death and rebirth;
Fennel	Protects from curses
Gardenia	For peace and healing
Garlic	For magical healing, protection and exorcism
Ginger	For success and empowerment
Grape	For fertility and garden magic, attracts money
Hawthorn	Marriage, fertility, happiness, protection of children; gateway to the otherworld
Hazel	Wisdom and fertility; used for wands, divining
Hibiscus	Attracts love, aids divination and dreams
Honeysuckle	Strengthens the memory, helps in letting go of the past
Holly	Strongest protective tree; dream magic, wisdom and courage; healing of subtle bodies
Hops	Improves health and induces sleep; goddess energy
Hyacinth	For love and protection

Clover is associated with love and fidelity.

Tobacco is a sacred herb in the Native American Indian tradition

Hyssop	Purification; dispel negativity
Jasmine	Induces lucid dreams; brings good fortune in love, friendship and wealth; raises self-esteem
Juniper	Calms and brings good health; berries ward off evil
Lavender	Purifying; brings peace and happiness, love; helps sweet dreams
Lemon	Attracts happiness, relieves stress
Lettuce	Induces sleep, assists in divination
Lily-of-the-valley	Brings peace, harmony and love
Lime	Increases energy, encourages loyalty
Lotus	Emblem of enlightenment, elevates and protects
Magnolia	Assures fidelity
Marigold	Enhances visions and dreams; renews energy
Mistletoe	For protection, love and visionary ability; hang on the bedpost for beautiful dreams
Mugwort	For clairvoyance, scrying and dream interpretation
Oak	Wisdom, strength and endurance; groves of oak trees associated with prophecy and divination;
Olive	Brings peace of mind and fidelity in love fruitfulness and security
Orange	Attracts peace, power and luck
Orris	Attracts love and romance
Passion flower	Fosters friendship, brings peace and understanding
Pennyroyal	Increases alertness, helps peace between partners
Pine	Grounding and cleansing, use for a fresh start; repels evil; cleansing and purifying
Rice	Attracts fertility and money
Rose	Blesses love, domestic peace, generosity and beauty
Rosemary	Protects the home, brings mental clarity and sharpens memory
Rowan	Protection against evil, enchantment and negative energies; development of psychic powers
Sage	Brings wisdom, fertility, healing and long life
Silver birch	New beginnings, healing; mysteries of the maiden
Strawberry	For love and luck
Sweet pea	For friendship and courage
Thyme	For courage and confidence
Tobacco	Introduces sacred spirit
Valerian	Brings love and harmony
Vervain	For inner strength and peace
Violet	Contentment and love
Willow	Love and regeneration; lunar and feminine rhythms; healing and to empower wishes
Yew	Immortality, transformation and inner wisdom

The symbolism of incense and essential oils

Acacia (gum arabic) Protection; develops psychic awareness

Agarwood (aloes) Protection, consecration; prosperity and success; connection with the upperworld

Amber Love and healing

Benzoin Aid to meditation; grounding, helps reconnect with inner self

Bergamot Attracts success and prosperity; use in rituals of initiation

Camphor Guardian of rebirth; assists in change and transformation; used in moon magic

Cajeput Spiritual expansion and freedom

Cedar Associated with magical power, vitality and immortality

Chamomile Peace, tranquillity and emotional stability; aid to sleep and dreaming

Clary sage Aphrodisiac; stimulates vivid dreams and encourages dream recall

Clove Clears the mind and assists in past life recall

Copal Protection, purification and banishing negativity; a fragrance of the gods and angels

Dragon's blood Neutralizes negative energies; cleansing and protecting

Eucalyptus Healing and purifying; use in space clearing

Frankincense Calms and quietens the mind; an aid to meditation; use in rituals of initiation and rites of passage

Galbanum Spells for endings and letting go; clears negativity

Geranium Balancing and adjusting; assists with new projects

Helichrysum Opens channel for healing, dreams and visions; spells for inspiration

Jasmin Imagination

Juniper Clearing negative energies

Lavender Psychic balance; brings emotions under control

Lemon grass Cleansing and purifying; releasing the past, forgiveness

Mandarin Inspiration; aid to communication, useful for harmony with friends and family

Mimosa Opens up channel of communication with higher self, angels and spirit beings

Melissa Strengthens connection with cosmic energies; love, harmony and happiness

The smoke of any incense will add the Air element to your ritual.

Musk For love and sexual attraction

Myrrh Helps connect with True Will, courage to follow the soul's path

Myrtle For spiritual love and immortality of the soul

Neroli For love and fertility; use in wedding ceremonies

Niaouli Clearing negative thoughts, expanding consciousness

Nutmeg Stimulating aphrodisiac; clairvoyance and psychic development

Olibanum Similar to frankincense, but with a lighter, more delicate fragrance. An incense of the sun

Palmarosa For letting go of the past and spiritual illumination

Patchouli Relaxing aphrodisiac; grounding, helps connection with earth energies

Peppermint For clarity and courage; increases perception and awareness in the dream state

Ravensara For spontaneity and determination; deepens meditation

Rose To honour the Goddess and strengthen a connection with all aspects of the feminine force

Rosewood For space clearing

Sandalwood Aphrodisiac (especially for men); comforts the dying and helps ease transition between the worlds; opens the gates to spirit guides

Storax Ancient incense burning substance with long tradition of use in magic and sacred ceremony; calming and relaxing, helps the mind unburden

Tea tree For space clearing and purification; a light in the darkness

Tobacco Sacred to native Americans, usually used for making offerings

Vanilla Aphrodisiac (especially for women); attracts love and romance

Vetivert Protection against negative energies; for over sensitivity to psychic impressions

Ylang ylang For love and sensuality

All kinds of incense can be bought in stick, cone or resin form.

The symbolism of colours

Red

Blood, passion, the life essence, power, physical energy, courage, bringing change in difficult circumstances. Associated with Mars, battle, the element of fire, the south, projective energy

Use red for a lack of enthusiasm and interest in life, low energy; inability to turn dreams into reality, feelings of insecurity, fear or anxiety; sex magic

Pink

Love and kindness, reconciliation, peace and harmony, compassion, gentle emotions. Associated with family, children and friendship, receptive energy

Use pink to bolster yourself up; in any aggressive or threatening situation; visualizing with pink can calm an angry mood and reduce tension. Magic for peace, love and romance

Orange

Abundance, fertility, health, joy, attraction, luck, friendship. Marks the boundary between self and others. Associated with the sun, projective energy

Use orange for feelings of boredom and bleakness; difficulty to adapt to change and let go of the past; over-seriousness and unable to enjoy life's humour; energy blocks. Magic associated with fire element

Yellow

Communication, the intellect, learning, concentration, also movement, travel and change. Associated with Mercury, the element of air, the east, projective energy

Use yellow for confusion and indecision; vague fears and anxieties; nervous exhaustion; poor memory, inability to study or concentrate, tendency to suffer 'winter blues'. Magic associated with the air element, storytelling spells

Green

The heart and emotions, love, also nature, gardens and growth, money and prosperity, employment. Associated with the earth element

Use green for feelings of being trapped or restricted, a need to break rigid patterns, a need for new ideas; fear of the unknown; a new state of balance; negative emotions such as jealousy, envy and greed. Fertility magic, spells for children, earth spells

Turquoise

Confidence, inner strength, positive self-esteem; allows expression of wishes

Use turquoise for protection against negativity, low energy and lack of interest in life, lack of courage to strike out and risk being different

Blue

Wisdom, patience, possibility, the healing of the spirit, idealism, truth and justice. Associated with the moon, the element of water, the west, reflective energy

Use blue for calming agitated, excitable or chaotic states; clear communication; peace, detachment, solitude and rest. Goddess magic; magic for dreams, past lives, and any associated with water element

Purple

Royal and priestly, a link with the higher dimension, wisdom, inspiration, magic, religion and spiritual strength. Associated with Osiris, the Egyptian god who judges the dead

Use purple for reflection, contemplation and deep meditation; be inspired by the bluish purple of the night sky. Magic for psychic development and divination

Use everyday objects, such as beads, to add colour to your magic work.

The colour purple is ideal for magic to connect with higher powers.

Add colour-symbolism by burning the right coloured candle.

Incense can be used for its colour association, as well as its scent.

Violet	Temperance, spirituality, repentance, transition from life to death	Use violet for rebalancing subtle energies; speeding up healing process; using the imagination in practical ways; integrating new skills into daily life; removing obstacles. Magic to connect with higher powers
Magenta	Letting go, change and transition; moving to a higher plane	Use magenta to take time out for healing, self-repair. Magic for change and transformation
Brown	Earth and earth spirits, instinctive wisdom, the natural world. Practical and financial matters, the home, stability, old people, animals. A protective force	Use brown when there is a need to blend or fit in; for grounding especially when overtaken by impractical and unrealistic ideas. Animal magic
Grey	Compromise and adaptability, psychic protection and secrecy	Use grey to project a cool, detached attitude and emotional stability. Magic for protection
White	Divinity, potential, the life-force, energy, purity, innocence. Contains all other colours. Associated with the sun	Use white for new beginnings, clear vision and originality; space clearing on all levels. Magic for purification and spirituality
Black	Death and regeneration. Conclusions that lead to new beginnings, marking a boundary with the past, banishing and releasing negativity, shedding guilt and regret	Use black to project mystery and self-control; to foster silence and a restful emptiness. Magic for protection and banishing
Gold	Worldly achievement, wealth, long life and ambition, confidence and understanding. Associated with solar deities	Use gold to relax and enjoy life; banish self-doubt. Magic for health, stamina and good fortune
Silver	Dreams, visions, intuition, hidden potential; cosmic intelligence. Associated with the moon and lunar deities	Use silver for development of psychic abilities, divination. Goddess and dream magic

The symbolism of gods and angels

Agni	Hindu god of fire
Amaterasu	Shinto sun goddess
Anubis	Egyptian god of the underworld, depicted with a jackal's head
Aphrodite	Greek goddess of love and beauty; known as Venus to the Romans
Apollo	Greek god of the sun, medicine and music, patron of the Muses
Arianrhod	Celtic mother goddess and keeper of time and fate
Artemis	Greek goddess of the waxing moon, protector of women; known as Diana to the Romans
Athene	Greek goddess of war, wisdom and the arts; known as Minerva to the Romans
Uriel	Archangel, earth
Bast	Egyptian cat goddess of love and fertility
Brigid	Celtic triple goddess, fire deity and patron of the hearth, healing, prophecy and inspiration
Cassiel	Archangel who assists with overcoming obstacles
Ceridwen	Celtic goddess of wisdom and death; her cauldron contained the brew of inspiration
Cerunnos	The celtic horned god, like Pan he is a fertility god; god of the witches
Cybele	Phrygian dark moon goddess who governs nature, wild beasts and dark magic
Demeter	Greek goddess of the earth, corn and vegetation; represents abundance and unconditional love; known as Ceres to the Romans
Dhagda	Celtic father god
Dionysus	Greek god of wine and ecstasy; known as Bacchus to the Romans
Epona	Celtic horse-goddess of fertility, abundance and healing

Pan, half man half goat, is the Greek personification of the horned god.

The huntress goddess Artemis was known as Diana to the Romans.

Freya	Norse mother goddess of love, marriage and fertility
Gabriel	Archangel of the moon, associated with the west
Gaia	Primeval Greek earth deity, prophetess of Delphi, goddess of dreams
Ganesha	Elephant-headed Hindu god of wisdom and literature, son of Parvati and Shiva, patron of business
Hades	Greek god of the underworld; known as Pluto to the Romans
Anael	Archangel of divine love and harmony, beauty and the creative arts
Hathor	Egyptian sky-deity, goddess of love, joy and dance, usually represented as a cow
Hecate	Greek triple goddess, rules magic, sorcery, death and the underworld; associated with crossroads
Hermes	Greek messenger god; represents communication, transition and exchange; associated with magic, healing and thieves; known as Mercury to the Romans
Hestia	Greek goddess of the hearth and stability

Horus	Egyptian sun god, depicted with a falcon's head
Indra	Hindu god of war; associated with weather and fertility
Ishtar	Mesopotamian goddess of sexual love, fertility and war
Isis	Egyptian mother-goddess, wife of Osiris and mother of Horus; represents life, loyalty, fertility and magic
Ixchel	Mayan goddess of storms and protector of women in childbirth
Janus	Roman guardian of the entrance and god of transition
Jizo	Japanese protector of children and travellers
Kali	Destructive aspect of the Hindu mother goddess
Kuanyin	Chinese goddess of compassion
Kwannon	Japanese goddess of compassion
Lakshmi	Hindu goddess of abundance, wealth and harmony
Lugh	Celtic sky god, associated with skills and the arts
Luna	Roman goddess of the full moon
Maat	Egyptian goddess of truth, justice and order
Mars	Roman god of war, lover of Venus
Manjushri	Buddhist bodhisattva of wisdom
Michael	Archangel of the sun, associated with rulership, marriage, music
Minerva	Roman goddess of wisdom
Mithras	Roman god of light
Morrigan	Celtic goddess of battlefields and death
Nephthys	Sister of Isis, the Egyptian mother goddess, guardian of the dead Osiris
Neptune	Roman god of the sea; known as Poseidon to the Greeks
Odin	Norse sky-father god and Master of the Runes
Osiris	Egyptian god of vegetation and judge of the dead, brother and husband of Isis; symbolizes regenerative power of nature
Pan	Greek horned god of wild things, half man, half animal
Parvati	Hindu mother goddess, consort of Shiva
Persephone Kore	Kore, Greek goddess of Spring was abducted by Hades and became Persephone, Queen of the underworld
Raphael	Archangel of the air element, associated with communication and business
Re	Egyptian sun god and creator
Sachiel	Archangel ruling justice and financial matters
Samael	Protective archangel, helps with matters that require courage or perseverance
Sekhmet	Egyptian goddess of destruction and healing, depicted with the head of a lioness
Selene	Greek goddess of the full moon
Shang Ti	Chinese supreme god
Shiva	Hindu creator god whose meditation sustains the world
Shu	Egyptian god of the air, creator of earth and sky

The majestic glory of archangels must be treated with the utmost respect.

Sif	Norse goddess of the grasslands, wife of Thor
Sophia	Greek goddess of divine knowledge and wisdom
Sul	Celtic goddess of healing
Sunna	Norse sun goddess
Surya	Hindu sun god
Tara	Tibetan goddess of wisdom and compassion
Thor	Norse god of thunder and industry, married to Sif
Thoth	Egyptian god of wisdom and the moon, scribe of Osiris
Tiamat	Mesopotamian creator goddess
Tsao-chun	Taoist kitchen god
Uriel	Archangel of high magic
Vesta	Roman goddess of the hearth
Vishnu	Hindu protector of the world
Zeus	Greek supreme god; known as Jupiter to the Romans

Table of the four elements

	Air	Fire	Water	Earth
Direction	East	South	West	North
Season	Spring	Summer	Autumn	Winter
Time of day	Dawn	Noon	Sunrise	Midnight
Moon phase	New	First quarter	Full	Dark
Planets	Sun, Mercury, Uranus	Mars, Pluto	Moon, Neptune, Venus	Earth, Saturn
Astrological signs	Gemini, Libra, Aquarius	Aries, Leo, Sagittarius	Cancer, Scorpio, Pisces	Taurus, Virgo, Capricorn
Magical tool	Dagger, athame, sword	Candles, lanterns, solar icons	Chalice, cauldron, mirror	Pentacle/stone, wand
Altar symbol	Incense	Lamp or candle	Chalice	Platter
Communion symbol	Scent	Heat	Wine/water	Bread/salt
Elemental symbol	▲	▲	▽	▽
Archangel	Raphael	Michael	Gabriel	Uriel
Polarity	Male positive	Male negative	Female negative	Female positive
Human sense	Hearing and smell	Sight	Taste	Touch
Art forms	Poetry/painting	Dance/drama	Music/song	Sculpture/embroidery
Creatures	Birds, bats, winged insects	Lizard, snake, lion, ram	Cat, frog, turtle, dolphin, whale, otter, seal, fish	Ox, dog, wolf, goat, stag
Elemental beings	Sylphs	Salamanders	Undines	Gnomes
Exhortation	To will	To dare	To know	To keep silent
Mythical beast	Winged horse	Dragon, phoenix	Sea serpent	Unicorn
Magical arts	Divinations	Ritual	Healing	Talismans
God forms	Sky/weather god	Sun/protector god	Moon/water goddess	Earth/underworld goddess
Meditation	Sky/clouds	Bonfires	The ocean/rivers	Fertile landscape
Colours	Yellow, blue, violet	Red and orange	Blue, turquoise, green	Russet, brown, black, olive-green, sometimes white
Instruments	Wind instruments/harp	Brass instruments	Strings/bells	Drums/percussion
Natural symbols	Feathers, incense smoke, fragrant flowers	Flame, lava	Shells, water, river plants, watercress	Fossils, stones, grains and seeds, salt, earth
Trees	Elder, eucalyptus	Oak, hawthorn	Willow, alder, ash	Cypress, pine
Herbs	Comfrey, lavender, mint	Basil, bay, garlic, hyssop, juniper, rosemary, rue	Chamomile, hops, lemon balm, orris, seaweeds, yarrow	Pennyroyal, lovage, sage
Incense	Sandalwood, lemon	Frankincense, cinnamon, basil	Jasmine, rose	Myrrh, patchouli
Minerals	Mercury, aventurine, topaz	Brass, gold, iron, fire opal, garnet, haematite, red jasper, sardonyx, flint, pearl, sapphire	Silver, copper, amethyst, aquamarine, turquoise, tourmaline, opal, jade, moonstone	Lead, emerald
Images and Themes	Mountain Tops, flying, sunrise, Wisdom and knowledge	Flames, Volcanoes, walking through fire, Sun at Noon	Lakes/pools, living under water, setting sun, Healing and calm	Caves/rocks, growing organically, moon/stars/night, Growth and life

Fire element can be added with heat and flame.   *Use smoke in your magic to add the Air element.*   *A bowl of water will bring the Water element.*

Table of planets

Planet	Moon	Mars	Mercury	Jupiter	Venus	Saturn	Sun	Earth
Day	Monday	Tuesday	Wednesday	Thursday	Friday	Saturday	Sunday	Any
Metal	Silver	Iron	Quicksilver	Tin	Copper	Lead	Gold	Any
Colours	White, silver, blue	Red	Yellow	Royal blue, violet, purple	Green	Black	Gold/orange	All, but especially earth shades (browns, russets)
Gemstones	Moonstone, pearl	Garnet, ruby, bloodstone, haematite	Opal, beryl, agate, carnelian	Amethyst, lapis lazuli, aquamarine	Emerald, peridot, jade	Jet, onyx, obsidian	Diamond, amber, topaz	Agate
Number	9	5	8	4	7	3	6	10
Angel	Gabriel	Zamael	Raphael	Sachiel	Anael	Cassiel	Michael	Sandalphon
Deities	Artemis, Luna, Selene	Mars, Samael, Anath	Hermes, Mercury, Athena	Zeus, Jupiter, Juno	Aphrodite, Venus	Cronos, Saturn, Kali	Helios, Sol, Apollo, Re	Gaia, Ceres
Trees	Aspen, willow, lemon, eucalyptus	Larch, hawthorn, dogwood	Ash, hazel	Almond, horse chestnut, oak	Apple, fig, magnolia, pear, elder, damson	Alder, beech, holly, elm, yew	Acacia, bay, birch, cedar, walnut, lime, orange, rowan, juniper	All
Plants and herbs	Jasmine, poppy, white lily, all aquatic plants	Anemone, tobacco, coriander, garlic	Impatiens, caraway, lavender, marjoram, dill	Honeysuckle, nutmeg, sage, star anise, cloves	Heather, hyacinth, rose, love-in-a-mist, iris, vervain, myrtle, yarrow	Ivy , evergreens, asafoetida	Mistletoe, marigold, bay laurel, benzoin gum, angelica, cinnamon, bay leaves	All
Incenses	Jasmine, sandalwood	Tobacco, pine	Mastic, lavender	Cedar, honeysuckle	Rose	Myrrh, cypress	Frankincense	Dittany of Crete patchouli
Magic for	Increasing intuition, psychic ability, fertility and all female issues	Improving strength, power and authority; banishing conflicts	All forms of travel and communication, including writing, teaching, speaking, learning, studying	Luck and prosperity; employment opportunities, travel, money, justice and wealth	Love, friendship, marriage, beauty and harmony creativity, artistic endeavours	Clearing obstacles and restrictions; patience	Good fortune in all areas of life; health, success and prosperity	Connecting with the Earth's mysteries, and the underworld

Saturn's influence in magic helps clear obstacles and remove restriction.

Use the moon's influence in magic to increase psychic ability and intuition.

Glossary

Adonai Hebrew name meaning Lord of Light.

Akashic Records Also known as the Book of Lives, a living archive helad on the astral planes, in which details of every life on earth, past, present and future, is detailed.

Altar A focal point for magical activity, symbolizing a gateway to the otherworld.

Amulet An object, often in the shape of an eye, worn to ward off harm.

Anael Angel of the planet Venus.

Angels Divine beings that act as messengers, protectors and guides.

Animism The belief that everything in the natural universe has a soul or vital essence.

Archetype A universal pattern, symbol or figure of primordial origins.

Astral planes the invisible, starry realms that are beyond space and time.

Astral travel Spiritual journeys, often during sleep, when the dreaming self leaves the physical body to visit the astral planes. Sometimes called 'out-of-the-body experiences'.

Athame (pronounced Ath-a-mey) A ritual dagger used by Wiccans.

Aura The energy patterns around living things, visible to witches and magicians.

Beltane Celtic May Day fertility festival to mark the beginning of summer.

Book of Shadows Originating in the Wiccan tradition, a personal record of spells, poems, rituals and other useful information collected by the magic worker.

Cabbala A form of Hebrew mysticism that uses the symbolism of the Tree of Life as a path to salvation. Also spelt Kabbalah and Qabalah.

Cassiel Angel of the planet Saturn.

Ceremonial magician Male or female, of any religious tradition, a ceremonial magician's knowledge is more philosophical and intellectual than it is religious. The different, ancient traditions of the Western Mysteries are important.

Chakra Sanskrit for 'wheel', one of seven energy centres running through the body.

Coven A group of 13 or fewer wiccans, led by a High Priestess and High Priest. Derives from the same word as 'convent'.

Deosil To move in a clockwise direction.

Devas A name for beings of the light.

Discarnate A spirit that does not inhabit a physical body (such as a ghost or angel) and so therefore not belonging to the earthly plane.

Divination The many arts of consulting the 'divinity'. reading Tarot cards, seeking water or consulting oracles such as the runes or the I Ching.

Dowsing From the old Cornish for 'to seek', especially water or buried treasure, using a Y-shaped hazel dowsing wand or a pendulum.

Druid A follower of a spiritual tradition based on veneration of the Earth and nature as a deity.

Elementals Spirit beings associated with the four elements: sylphs (air), salamanders (fire), undines (water), gnomes (earth).

Ephemeris A list of tables of positions of the planets, the Sun and Moon, used by astrologers.

Equinox One of two fixed points of the year, spring and autumn, when day and night are of equal duration.

Esbats Times of lunar celebration.

Ether The invisible fifth 'element' of spirit, from which we get the 'etheric' body, the subtle or spirit body.

Gabriel (pronounced Gabr-I-el) Archangel of the moon, whose name means 'the Strength of God'.

Geomancy The study of earth energies.

Goddess The Great Mother and source of all life and its cycles of birth, growth, death and rebirth.

Golden mean This is a ratio between the lengths of the sides of a rectangle which produce regular patterns. It occurs in nature in spiral snail shells and flower petals.

Hall of records The place where the Akashic Records, or Books of Lives, are held.

Hedgewitch Magic worker who practises alone and according to their own style and belief system.

Hermetic mysteries Hermes was the Greek God of wisdom, based on the Egyptian god Thoth, who gave the understanding of magic to humankind.

Higher self Also known as god-self, the spiritual part of you that seeks to align you to your True Will.

Holy or holey stones These are stones, sometimes fossil sponges, which have natural holes right through them, and are traditionally hung by red wool or ribbon to bring luck.

Imbolc Celtic festival marking spring.

Inner plane adepti These are otherworldly teachers: some are discarnate wise people; others are angels.

Invocation Used at the beginning of magic work to call upon the aid of spirits, angels and other spiritual beings.

Journeying The ability to visit the otherworld through an altered state of awareness.

Karma A Sanskrit word for fate or balance. Every action accrues spiritual profit or loss, and through a series of reincarnated lives, the balance must be worked out.

Kokab Hebrew name for sphere of Mercury.

Lammas Celtic festival of the harvest.

Levanah Hebrew name for the moon.

Lodge A group of magicians meet in a lodge, as do Freemasons. It is a term used for both the building or temple and the group itself.

Mabon In Welsh this means 'son' or 'boy' and is another name for the divine child born at midwinter.

Madim Hebrew name for the planet Mars.

Magic circle A sacred space 'between the worlds' used in magic work.

Mantra Repetition of a sacred sound to induce an altered state of consciousness.

Medicine wheel Originating in the native American tradition, a framework for understanding and experiencing life based on the four compass directions and their symbolic correspondences.

Medicines Another word for spells where natural magic is used to attract, repel, maintain or balance energies.

Michael (pronounced Mik-I-el) Archangel of the sun, the leading angel, whose name means 'Like unto God'.

Mote Old English word meaning 'may' or 'might'. Mysteries Occult or secret knowledge that can only be gained through experience; novices are usually initiated into a particular mystery path, such as the Western Mysteries.

Nogah Hebrew name for the planet Venus.

Och Healing spirit of the sun.

Otherworld The invisible spiritual world accessed by workers of magic.

Pagan One who follows a spiritual tradition that venerates the power of the Mother Goddess and the natural world.

Pentacle A five-sided shape (*penta* is Greek for five); as opposed to a pentagram, which has five points.

Psychometry To sense by touch the history of an object or information about its owner.

Raphael (pronounced Raph-I-el) Archangel of the planet Mercury, whose name means 'Healer of God'.

Rite of Abramelin This is a six-month-long magical retreat aimed at establishing

communication with a Holy Guardian Angel.

Ritual An activity following certain set procedures designed to focus attention on the otherworld.

Sabbat Derived from 'Sabbath', the holy day of the week, these are the eight important seasonal festivals of the wiccans.

Sachiel Angel of the planet Jupiter.

Samhain Celtic festival, also known as Halloween.

Scry Derived from the French *descrier*, to proclaim, scrying means divining by crystal-gazing. A scrying glass is a crystal ball, or other reflective surface such as a mirror or pool of water.

Shabbathai Hebrew name for the planet Saturn.

Shaman Through trance, drumming and using herbs, one who shape-shifts and journeys to the otherworld ; most types of magic have their roots in some kind of shamanic tradition.

Shemesh Hebrew name for the sun.

Sidereal Star time, used by many astrologers as the time frame from which they calculate the positions of the planets and stars in a horoscope. It differs slightly from 'clock' time.

Sigil A pictorial depiction of a name.

Smudging Cleansing, using the smoke of burning herbs, especially sage.

Solstice One of two fixed points of the year, marking midwinter and midsummer, when the sun's power is at its weakest and strongest respectively.

Talisman An object which draws on the power of magic, often using archaic writing, to bring about a single specific purpose.

Telepathy The ability to communicate thought-forms using other than the known senses.

Thought-forms Subtle vibrational patterns produced by the mind that make up an atmosphere.

Totem A symbol or emblem adopted by a magic worker as an ally or helper.

Tree of Life A diagram consisting of 10 spheres connected by 22 paths showing the spiritual evolution of creation. It is central to the Cabbala and is used by many western magicians as a kind of road map, showing where planetary or angelic powers may be located.

True Will Your divine purpose, the reason you are here on earth; when you are aligned with your True Will, your magic will be much more effective.

Tzedek Hebrew name for the planet Jupiter.

Underworld The hidden or occult realm through which all souls must journey on their passage into death and rebirth.

Upperworld The heavenly realm; associated with the higher self and spiritual transformation.

Uriel (pronounced Ur-I-el) Archangel of the north and Earth, whose name means 'Light of God'.

Waning The moon's decrease in influence.

Waxing The moon's increase in influence.

Wicca A modern form of witchcraft that venerates nature, based on the teachings of Gerald Gardner. Wiccans are initiated into a coven, where they are led in their seasonal rituals by a High Priestess and High Priest.

Widdershins To move anti-clockwise (counter-clockwise).

Witch A person, male or female, who uses the powers of Nature to work magic for healing or guidance. Witches may use ritual and celebrate the passing seasons but they are not necessarily pagans.

Wyrd An Anglo-Saxon term for the magical web of life, where everything in the universe is believed to be interconnected along fine energy pathways. This belief is at the heart of natural magic.

Yule A pagan festival to celebrate the rebirth of the sun at the midwinter solstice. The word 'yule' is derived from an old Norse word, written 'Jul', meaning 'wheel'. The festival lasts for 12 days and nights and is accompanied by feasting, and the enactment of ritual.

Zamael Archangel of the planet Mars.

Zen A Buddhist tradition based on the idea that spiritual perfection (nirvana) is attained when all is reduced to nothing.

BIBLIOGRAPHY

ANKARLOO, B. and CLARK, S. 1999. Witchcraft and Magic in Europe: Ancient Greece and Rome. Philadelphia University of Pennsylvania Press.

ANKARLOO, B. and HENNINGSEN, G., eds. 1993. Early Modern European Witchcraft: Centres and Peripheries. Oxford: Clarendon.

ARROWSMITH, N., 1977. A Field Guide to the Little People. London: Pan.

ASWYN, F., 1998. Northern Mysteries and Magick: Runes, Gods and Feminine Powers. St Paul, MN: Llewellyn.

BARING, A. and CASHFORD, J., 1993. The Myth of the Goddess. London: Arkana.

BATES, B., 1983. The Way of Wyrd. London: Century.

BATES, B., 1996. The Wisdom of the Wyrd. London: Rider.

BURTON RUSSELL, G., 1991. The historical Satan. In: J.T. Richardson, J. Best and D. Bromley, eds. The Satanism scare. New York: Aldine de Gruyter.

CAPRA, F., 1976. The Tao of Physics. London: Flamingo.

CAPRA, F., 1983. The Turning Point. London: Flamingo.

CARDOZO, A.R., 1990. A modern American witch-craze. In: M. Marwick, ed. Witchcraft and sorcery. London: Penguin.

CARR-GOMM, P., 1995. The Druid Tradition. Shaftesbury, Dorset: Element.

CARROLL, P., 1987. Liber Null and Psychonaut. York Beach, ME: Samuel Weiser.

CHAMBERLAIN, M., 1981. Old Wives Tales: their History, Remedies and Spells. London: Virago.

CLARK, E.E., 1953. Indian Legends of the Pacific Northwest. Berkeley and Los Angeles: University of California Press.

CLARK, S., 1999. Thinking with Demons. Oxford: Clarendon.

COHN, N., 1993. Europe's Inner Demons: the Demonization of Christians in Medieval Christendom. London: Pimlico.

CROWLEY, V., 1989. Wicca: the Old Religion in the New Age. Wellingborough: Aquarian.

CUNLIFFE, B., 1992. The Celtic World. London: Constable.

CUNLIFFE, B., 1997. Prehistoric Europe: an Illustrated Guide. Oxford: Open University Press.

DOUGLAS, A., 1974. The Tarot. London: Penguin.

ELIADE, M., 1974. Shamanism. Princeton: Princeton University Press.

ELIADE, M., 1975. Some observations on European witchcraft. History of Religions, 14, pp. 149–72.

EVANS-PRITCHARD, E., 1985. Witchcraft, Oracles and Magic Among the Azande. Oxford: Clarendon.

FARRAR, S. and FARRAR, J., 1991. A Witches' Bible Compleat. New York: Magickal Childe.

GARDNER, G., 1988. Witchcraft Today. New York: Magickal Childe.

GIJSWIJT-HOFSTRA, M., LEVACK, B. and PORTER, R., eds. 1999. History of Witchcraft and Magic in Europe: the Eighteenth and Nineteenth Centuries. London: Athlone Press.

GINZBURG, C., 1966. The Night Battles. Baltimore: The John Hopkins University Press.

GINZBURG, C., 1992. Deciphering the Witches' Sabbath. New York: Penguin.

GODBEER, R., 1992. The Devil's Dominion. Cambridge: Syndicate.

GRAVES, R., 1960. The Greek Myths. London: Penguin.

GRAVES, R., 1981. The White Goddess. London: Faber & Faber.

GREENWOOD, S., 2000. Magic, Witchcraft and the Otherworld. Oxford: Berg.

GUILEY, R., 1989. The Encyclopedia of Witches and Witchcraft. New York: Facts on File.

HARVEY, G., 1997. Listening People, Speaking Earth. London: Hurst & Co.

HENNINGSEN, G., 1993. The ladies from outside: an archaic pattern of the witches Sabbath. In: B. Ankarloo and G. Henninsen, eds. Early modern witchcraft. Oxford: Clarendon.

HILL, F., 1996. A Delusion of Satan: the full story of the Salem Witch Trials. London: Hamish Hamilton.

HINE, P., 1995. Condensed Chaos. Arizona: New Falcon Publications.

HINE, P., 1999. Prime Chaos. Arizona: New Falcon Publications.

HUTTON, R., 1991. The Pagan Religions of the Ancient British Isles. London: BCA.

HUTTON, R., 1996. The roots of modern paganism. In: G. Harvey and C. Hardman, eds. Paganism Today. London: Thorsons.

HUTTON, R., 1999. The Triumph of the Moon. Oxford: Oxford University Press.

JAMES, S., 1999. The Atlantic Celts: Ancient People or Modern Invention? London: British Museum Press.

JONES, P. and PENNICK, N., 1995. A History of Pagan Europe. London: Routledge.

KATZ, R., 1982. Boiling Energy: Community Healing among the Kalahari Kung. Cambridge, Ma: Harvard University Press.

KELLY, A., 1991. Crafting the Art of Magic: a History of Modern Witchcraft 1939-1964. St Paul, MN: Llewellyn.

KING, F., 1975. Magic: the Western Tradition. London: Thames & Hudson.

KING, F., 1990. Modern Ritual Magic. Bridport, Dorset: Prism.

KLANICZAY, G., 1993. Hungary: the accusations and the universe of popular magic. In: B. Ankarloo and G. Henningsen, eds. Early modern European witchcraft: centres and peripheries. Oxford: Clarendon.

KNAPPERT, J., 1995. African Mythology. London: Diamond.

La VEY, A., 1969. The Satanic Bible. New York: Avon Books.

LAMER, C., 1981. Enemies of God. London: Chatto & Windus.

LEVACK, B., 1995. The Witch-Hunt in Early Modern Europe. London: Longman.

LÉVI-STRAUSS, C., 1979. The effectiveness of symbols. In: W. Lessa and E. Vogt, eds. Reader in comparative religion: an anthropological approach. New York: Harper & Row.

LOW, M., 1999. Celtic Christianity and Nature: early Irish and Hebridean Traditions. Edinburgh: Polygon.

LUCE, J., 1973. The End of Atlantis. London: Book Club Associates.

LUCIUS APULEIUS, 1960. The Golden Ass. London: Folio Society.

LUHRMANN, T., 1989. Persuasions of the Witch's Craft. Oxford: Blackwell.

MACFARLANE, A., 1999. Witchcraft in Tudor and Stuart England: a Regional and Comparative Study. London: Routledge.

MacLELLAN, G., 1996. Dancing on the edge: shamanism in modern Britain. In: G. Harvey and C. Hardman, eds. Paganism Today. London: Thorsons.

MacLELLAN, G., 1999. Shamanism. London: Piatkus.

MACNULTY, W., 1991. Freemasonry. London: Thames & Hudson.

MAIR, L., 1969. Witchcraft. London: World University Library.

MARWICK, M., ed. 1990. Witchcraft and Sorcery. London: Penguin.

MBITI, J., 1982. African Religions and Philosophy. London: Heinemann.

McKIE, R., 2000. ApeMan: the Story of Human Evolution. London: BBC.

MORGAN, L. H., 1960. The league of the Iroquois. In: M. Mead and R. Bunzel, eds. The golden age of American anthropology. New York: George Braziller.

PENNICK, N., 1994. Practical Magic in the Northern Tradition. Loughborough: Thoth.

PIGGOT, S., 1989. The Druids. London: Thames & Hudson.

RASMUSSEN, K., 1979. A shaman's journey to the sea spirit. In: W. Lessa and E. Vogt, eds. Reader in comparative religion: an anthropological approach. New York: Harper & Row.

ROPER, L., 1994. Oedipus and the Devil: Witchcraft, Sexuality and Religion in Early Modern Europe. London: Routledge.

ROSEN, B., ed. 1969. Witchcraft. London: Edward Arnold.

SHALLCRASS, P., 1996. Druidry today. In: G. Harvey and C. Hardman, eds. Paganism Today. London: Thorsons.

SHARPE, J., 1996. Instruments of Darkness: Witchcraft in England 1550-1750. London: Penguin.

STANFORD, P., 1997. The Devil: a biography. London: Mandarin.

STARHAWK, 1982. Dreaming the Dark. Boston: Beacon.

STARHAWK, 1989. The Spiral Dance. San Francisco: Harper & Row.

STEVENS, A., 1991. On Jung. London: Penguin.

SULLIVAN, L., 1989. Hidden Truths: Magic, Alchemy and the Occult. New York: Macmillan.

SUN BEAR, WABUN WIND and CRYSALIS MULLIGAN, 1992. Dancing with the Wheel: the Medicine Wheel Workbook. New York: Fireside Books.

THOMAS, K., 1973. Religion and the Decline of Magic. London: Penguin.

TYLOR, E., 1970. Religion in Primitive Cultures. Gloucester, Ma: Peter Smith.

VALIENTE, D., 1985. Witchcraft for Tomorrow. London: Robert Hale.

WARNER, M., 1981. Joan of Arc: the Image of Female Heroism. London: Penguin.

WASHINGTON, P., 1993. Madame Blavatsky's Baboon. London: Secker & Warburg.

WILSON, C., 1989. Witches. Limpsfield: Dragon's World.

YORK, M., 1994. The Emerging Network: a Sociology of the New Age and Neo-Pagan Movements. Lanham, MD: Rowman & Littlefield.

SUGGESTED SOURCES FOR FURTHER READING

Human evolution:
C. STRINGER & R. McKIE African Exodus; the origins of modern humanity London: Pimlico 1997

The anthropological study of religion:
W. LESSA & E. VOGT Reader in Comparative Religion: an anthropological approach New York: Harper & Row 1979
B. MORRIS Anthropological Studies of Religion: an introductory text Cambridge: Cambridge University Press 1987

An anthropological study of ritual in Africa:
V. TURNER The Forest of Symbols: aspects of Ndembu ritual London: Cornell University Press 1972

Anthropological studies of spirit healing:
R. KATZ The Straight Path of the Spirit: ancestral wisdom and healing traditions in Fiji Vermont: Park Street Press
B. KAPFERER A Celebration of Demons; exorcism and aesthetics of healing in Sri Lanka 1991

Anthropological study of sorcery:
B. KAPFERER The Feast of the Sorcerer: practices of consciousness and power Chicago: University of Chicago Press 1997

Shamanism:
G. SAMUEL Civilized Shamans: Buddhism in Tibetan societies Washington: Smithsonian 1993
C. HUMPHREY with U. ONON Shamans & Elders: experience, knowledge & power among the Daur Mongols Oxford: Oxford University Press 1996

Psychological approaches to western shamanism:
S. LARSEN The Shaman's Doorway: opening imagination to power and myth Vermont: Inner Traditions International 1998
D. NOEL The Soul of Shamanism: western fantasies, imaginal realities New York: Continuum 1997

History of Western Magic:
C. SNYDER Exploring the World of King Arthur London: Thames & Hudson 2000
F. YATES Giordano Bruno & the hermetic tradition Chicago: University of Chicago Press 1991

Paganism:
S BILLINGTON & M. GREEN [eds] The Concept of the Goddess London: Routledge 1999
C. ALBANESE Nature Religion in America Chicago: University of Chicago Press 1991
S. SUTCLIFFE & M. BOWMAN [eds] Beyond the New Age: exploring alternative spirituality Edinburgh: Edinburgh University Press 2000
S. GREENWOOD Magic, Witchcraft and the Otherworld (from bibliography)
L. HUME Witchcraft and Paganism in Australia Melbourne: Melbourne University Press 1997

PICTURE ACKNOWLEDGEMENTS

AKG: p22T Evening in Aswan, Erich Lessing. p23T Osiris, Erich Lessing. p23B Day and night journey of the sun, Erich Lessing. p25B Hecate, William Blake. p27B Ossian, Francois Baron Gerard. p28T Odin. p29T Das Rheingold, Richard Wagner. p31T Zoroaster. p33BR The Sefirot Tree. p34BR Moghul Prince speaking to a Dervish. p35T Jalal ad-Din ar-Rumi. p35B Whirling Dervish, Lothar Peters. p40BR Agni, Irmgard Wagner. p41BR Pakhandi, Jean-Louis Nou. p42B Dancing Bayadere, VISIOARS. p42M Prince Siddhartha cuts off his hair, Gilles Mermet. p44T Shiva, Jean-Louis Nou. p45TM Indian Buddhist tantrist and magus, 721–c.790, Jean-Louis Nou. p45B Bhairava in the land of burning corpses, Jean-Louis Nou. p47R Figure of a goddess. p54T The Alchemists, Pietro Longhi. p57T Northern and Southern hemispheres. p56T Hipparchus. p57BR Christian-allegorical depiction of the world. Wolfgang Kilian. p58T Paracelsus. p58BL Hermes Trismegistos. Hermann tom Ring. p59TR An alchemist after staying up all night, Thomas Wijck. p65T Hansel and Gretel outside the gingerbread house, Ludwig Richter. p64T nymph, Arnold Böcklin. p66T Persephone and Hecate. p67TL Hecate, William Blake. p67B Sorceress Circe with the Companions of Odysseus that have been transformed into Animals, Alessandro Allori. p67TR Sorceress Circe, Giovanni Battista Luteri Dossi. p69T Medea with the Dagger, Anselm Feuerbach. p71T Hansel and Gretel outside the gingerbread house, Ludwig Richter. p76B Titania and Oberon. p80 The Fairytale Witch, Paula Modersohn-Becker. p81T Hobgoblins, Goya y Lucientes. p78T Persephone and Hecate. p100T. p101B Witches drawing milk from an axe handle. p107T Magic scene, Andrea Locatelli. p109B Three witches at the bedside of a sick woman. p111B Women in herb garden. p113T Witches' Kitchen, Hieronymus Francken the Elder, Erich Lessing. p114T Witch exercising her conjuration rituals. p117 Witches' Gathering, Frans Francken II, Erich Lessing. p122BR Devil conjured up from a magic circle. p123B British Library. p123T. Witches children are initiated into a Sabbath. p126B Burning witches on the market place in Guernsey. p127B A terrible story of three sorceresses of Derneburg. p129BR. p129L Satan and the birth of Sin, Johann Heinrich Füssli. p130TR Persecution of the Turlupins. p133T Knight Templars led into prison, British Library. p138T torture of suspected witch. p139T Jean Bodin. p141BR Essex Witches. p143BR Johann Calvin. p143BL Martin Luther, Lucas Cranach the Elder. p143TR Pope's selling of indulgences, Lucas Cranach the Elder. p144T Caricature of Luther's opponents. p144B Pope Alexander VI as devil. p145T In the Jaws of Hell. p145B Allegory on Luther's thesis against indulgences. p148BR Burning of witches, Paris. p149B Gilles de Rais. p151T Midwife assisting woman in labour. p151BL Affair with the devil, witches' balm…. p153B Catherine Cawches and her daughters, Guernsey. p162 Witches' dancing ground, Harz mountains, Robert Müller. p168B Socrates and disciples. p169T Atlantis. p178T Hypnotic session, Sven Richard Bergh. p184BL Knights of the Round Table. p187B Marching Infantry. p194T Pan. p196BR Artemis Ephesia, Erich Lessing. p197T Diana's Hunt, Luca Giordano. p198T Stag god Cerunnos, Erich Lessing. p238B Freyja. p239B Winter Solstice. **BRIDGEMAN ART LIBRARY:** p20B Medicine mask dance, Paul Kane. p24B The Return of Persephone, Frederic Leighton. p24T Aegeus consulting the Delphic Oracle. p25TL Circe, Wright Barker. p25TR Medea, Anthony Frederick Augustus Sandys. p27T Druid's Ceremony, Noel Halle. p29B Hermod, son of Odin, at the barred gates of Hel, pleading for the return of his brother. p30R The spirit of Samuel appearing to Saul at the house of the Witch of Endor, Salvatore Rosa. p31B Adam and Eve in Paradise, Jan Brueghel. p32T Jewish cabbalist holding a sephiroth. p32L Adam and Eve banished from Paradise, Tommaso Masaccio. p32BR Procession of the Bishop in front of the Church of S. Ambrogio, Cosimo Rosselli. p33T St Francis of Assisi, Bonaventura Berlinghieri. p37TR Taoist weather manual. p40T Indra, the Aryan God of War seated on an elephant. p40BL Varunani. p42T Padmasana Yoga. p45TR Illustration from 'Theosophica Practica' showing the seven Chakras. p57BL Signs of the Chinese Zodiac surrounding the symbol of Yin and Yang. p56B The God Thoth. p59TL Emblematic diagram of the alchemical processes for the production of the Philosopher's Stone. p63T Three Women and Three Wolves, Eugene Grasset. p63BR Scene of Witches, Salvator Rosa. p66B Medea, Giovanni Benedetto Castiglione. p68T Ulysses and the Sirens, Herbert James Draper. p68B The Golden Fleece, Herbert James Draper. p69T Circe Pouring Poison into a Vase and Awaiting the Arrival of Ulysses, Sir Edward Burne-Jones. p69 Justice and Divine Vengeance pursuing Crime, Pierre-Paul Prud'hon. p70B The Witches in Macbeth, Alexandre Gabriel Decamps. p70T Scene from Midsummer Night's Dream, Francis Danby. p71B Macbeth and the Witches, Theodore Chasseriau. p77T A Dance around the Moon, Charles Altamont Doyle. p77B Diana the Hunter, Orazio Gentileschi. p78L Morgan le Fay, Anthony Frederick Augustus Sandys. p79 Calling shapes and beckoning shadows dire, Arthur Rackham. p81B Dancing Fairies, August Malmstrom. p88T Divination board, Heini Schneebeli. p92B Native American Shaman, Dutch School. p99R Witches' Sabbath, Francisco Jose de Goya y Lucientes. p100B The Sermon, Walter Frederick Roofe Tyndale. p102T Old Cronies, George Henry Boughton. p106B The Sorceress, Lucien Levy-Dhurmer. p108 The Witch gives (advice) as to Sir Tristram's wounds, Walter Crane. p110T Administering medicinal herbs, Polish School. p110B Fennel. p111T Doctor visits patient; an apothecary. p116BL Scene of Sorcery, David Teniers the Elder. p119BL John Dee, English School. p120T Astrological chart with Signs of the Zodiac. p121TR James I and VI of Scotland, John Decritz the Younger. p121B High Commission Court and Star Chamber, English School. p127B Many poor women imprisoned and hanged for witches, English School. p128R The hero Gilgamesh. p129T Satan binds the eyes of the Jews, Ermengald de Bezieres. p130BL Victims tortured to decide on innocence or guilt. p132T Expulsion of Albigenses from Cerlesonne. p133T Looting of Jerusalem, 1099, Jean de Courcy. p134 Judge interrogating prisoners. p135B Mary Sutton, suspected witch, being 'swum', 1612, English School. p136 Good and Evil, Andre Jacques Victor Orsel. p137 The Story of Adam and Eve, Giovanni Boccaccio. p140B Matthew Hopkins, Witchfinder General, English School. p142T John Wycliffe, English School. p142B Wycliffe appearing before the Prelates at St Paul's, English School. p149T Joan of Arc being led to her death, Isidore Patrois. p158T Landing of Pilgrims at Plymouth. p161B The Witches' Sabbath, Francisco Jose de Goya y Lucientes. p161T Magic Circle, John William Waterhouse. p166T Buddha. p166B The Annunciation, Italian School. p167M 'H' in the form of two conjurors. p167TR Alchemy master. p174T Friedrich Anton Mesmer, French School. p196BL Persephone, Anthony Frederick Augustus Sandys. p198B Pan and Psyche, Sir Edward Burne-Jones. p212T Diana, Agostino di Duccio. p222B Days of Creation, Sir Edward Burne-Jones. p222T Annunciation, Fra Angelico. p223B Angel, Sir Edward Burne-Jones. p224R Beguiling of Merlin, Sir Edward Burne-Jones. p224L Bedivere returns Excalibur to the lake, Roman du Saint Graal. p225T Last Supper, Francesco Bassano. p225B King Arthur, Lancelot and the Lady, Roman de Tristan. p226T Stonehenge, Italian School. p226B Wicker Man, Italian School. p233B Fairy Tree, Richard Doyle. p235TL Pehriska-Ruhpa, Karl Bodmer (after). p234BL Mandan Medicine man, George Catlin. p238T Odin. p242B Sir Francis Dashwood, Bartolommeo Nazari. p243TL Francois Rabelais, Eugene Delacroix. p243TR Satan Arousing the Rebel Angels, William Blake. p248 Thanatos, Jacek Malczewski, p258T&B, p259B, p260, p261B, 263, 264T&B, 265, 272T&B, 273, 274, 275, 354, 484T, 484B, 485. **CAMERA PRESS:** p206BL Alex Sanders, John Drysdale. p207BL. John Drysdale. p207TL. John Drysdale. p207TR John Hedgecoe. **CHRISTINE OSBORNE PICTURES:** p194B Secret Wicca Ritual. p195T Sacred Goddess Altar. p205TL Goddess. p207BR Artefacts used in Wicca ceremonies. p215B Sacred rites: Goddess Festival, Glastonbury 2000. p216T Starhawk. p216B Sacred spiral dance. p217 'Black madonna'. p234T Drumming class. p235TR Dream rings. **COLLECTIONS:** p26T Castlerigg Stone Circle, Cumbria, Gary Smith. **CORBIS:** p16B Wolfgang Kaehler. p18T David Muench. p19BR The Purcell Team. p21BR Earl and Nazima Kowall. p39BL. p39BR Earl and Nazima Kowall. p43T & 43B Michael Freeman. p54L Sir James George Frazer. p62T Lindsay Hebberd. p62B Paul Almasy. p70T Robert Estall. p84T Peter Johnson. p94T. p163T & 163B Bettmann. p200B Raymond Gehman. p232T People dancing in the Findhorn Foundation, Sandro Vannini. p233T Musicians of the Paul Winter Consort, Roger Ressmeyer. p243B La Vey conducts a devilish service, Bettmann. p245B Charles Manson, Bettmann, 261. **E.T.ARCHIVE:** p20T Aaron's rod as serpent devouring rods or serpents of pharaoh's magicians to release Israelites. p21T Fresco, depicting a traveller and a sorceress. p21BL Fresco of Aztec priest praying. p28B Viking memorial picture stone. p36T Sakgamuni, Confucius and Lao Tzu. p59B The four elements, zodiac signs and alchemical symbols. p64B Centaur Chiron and Hermes, Saverio Altamura. p74T Men transformed into wolves in ferocious flying hunt. p102BL The Witch from Gravenbroch. p105T Magic circle of a witch. p107B Fairies and Elves on their nightly ritual dance. p112B Sorcerers and witches on Sabbath. p116BR Witches Sabbath, Frans

Francken. p128BL Gilgamesh between two demi gods. p138B Frontispiece from Compendium Maleficarum, Francesco Guazzo. p167TM Nostradamus. p168T Mosaic of Triumph of Poseidon and wife. p173T Candidate for Master, Freemasonry. p173B Frontispiece to History of Freemasonry. p182B King Of Woods, Frieda Harris. p185TL Quetzacoatl. p187T Inside the Temple of the Grail, W Hauschild. p212B French Diana Bathing, Francois Boucher. p240BR Rune stone. **FORTEAN PICTURE LIBRARY:** p26B St Beuno's Well, Janet and Colin Ford. p58BR Two alchemists at work. p65B Lucius witnesses a witch rubbing unguent on to her body in order to fly. p131T Torture to obtain a confession. p135T Ducking a Witch. p139B Instruments of torture. p140T Witches create a storm at sea. p147T North Berwick coven. p148T Witch Guillemette being stripped for torture. p151BR Torture of Herr Lirtzen. p152TR Mother Agnes Waterhouse. p153T Judith Philips. p170M Tarot cards: Waite pack. p170BL Eliphas Levi. p175TL Madame Blavatsky. p177R Samuel Liddell MacGregor Mathers. p183TR Blood on the Moon, Austin Osman Spare. p183TL Resurrection of Zoroaster, Austin Osman Spare. p190B White witchcraft altar, Kevin Carlyon. p192T Gerald Gardner, Raymond Buckland. p195BL Drawing down the moon. p200T Winter Solstice ritual, Kevin Carlyon. p201TL Kevin Carlyon binding new initiates, Kevin Carlyon. p205B Wiccan initiation, Raymond Buckland. p208T Raymond Buckland. p208B Priest enters the Temple, Raymond Buckland. p209T Samhain ceremony, Raymond Buckland. p209B Wiccan High Priest and High Priestess, Raymond Buckland. p211BR Title page of Leland's Aradia. p211T Cornish witches invoking the 'owlman', Anthony Shiels. p213T Cornish witch Cait Sidh. p213B Witches dancing at midnight. p227B Emma Restall-Orr, Kevin Carlyon. p229T Arch-Druid at Avebury, Clive Odinson. p229B Druids at Winter Solstice, Stonehenge, Clive Odinson. p230BR Edgar Cayce Foundation, Klaus Aarsleff. p231T Fountain International members, Paul Broadhurst. p231B Tourist doing Tai Chi, Klaus Aarsleff. p230BL Celtic music at Roughtor, Paul Broadhurst. p232BL Eileen Caddy, Dr Elmar R Gruber. p232BR Findhorn meditation room, Tony Healy. p236B Man meditating at Medicine Wheel, Arizona, Klaus Aarsleff. p241TL Rune stones, Klaus Aarsleff, 262T, 266, 267. **SUSAN GREENWOOD:** p199(all) owl mask, plaque and Bubo made by Maria Strutz, p237TR, p249(all). **HULTON PICTURE LIBRARY:** p94B Lewis H Morgan. p115B Mother Shipton's favourite mode of travelling. p170TR AE Waite. p174BL Helena Petrovna Blavatsky. p174BR Henry Steel Olcott. p175TR Anne Besant. p175B Krishnamurti with Annie Besant. p176BR Miss Horniman. p179TR Garb of the Golden Dawn, A Crowley. p179BL Alan Bennett. p180BM Aleister Crowley in robes of Golden Dawn. p180TR Aleister Crowley. p181BL Self-portrait-Aleister Crowley. p181TR Certificate acknowledging Crowley as member of High Order of Freemasons. p182T Aleister Crowley, Fosco Maraini. p193B Margaret Murray. p214T Jules Michelet. p244B Jayne Mansfield, Keystone Press Agency. p246BR Sex pistols. p246BL Austin Spare, Bert Hardy. **HUTCHISON LIBRARY:** p17T Shaman, Andrey Zvoznikov. p38T Shinto Priest, R Ian Lloyd. p41TL Holy Man Chanting a Mantra, Michael MacIntyre. p41TM Ancient Indian Coin depicting Goddess Kali, Goycoolea. p46BL Traditional Zulu diviner. p47L Witch doctor, Victoria Falls, Zimbabwe, Mary Jelliffe. p48BR Witch doctor with juju fetishes, Harvey. p49TR Casting out devils. p50B Ancestor worship ceremony, Michael MacIntyre. p51BR Fetishes for sale, Mary Jelliffe. p83TL Potent juju symbols. p85 Ritual cleansing by smoking of baby after birth, John Ryle. p86T Shaman diviner, John Ryle. p86B Tribal chief. p87T Shilluk people making thatched roof for mud hut. p87B Pende festival dancers, Michael MacIntyre. p88B Storytelling, Dinka tribe, Sarah Errington. p89B Dodoth women, Sarah Errington. p90T Traditional healer, Ingrid Hudson. p91T xylophone players, John Ryle. Images: p37L The Tai Chi symbol. p101T Curse doll. p111M Zodiac with plants and herbs. p114BR Mother Shipton casting a horoscope. p118T Hermaphrodite. p118B Macrocosmus Schema of Great World. p169ML Ya-uli. p169BR Atlantean Mystery Pyramid. p171B Tree of Life. p171TR Cabbala, Great Countenance. p178T Rosicrucian – reincarnation. p178B Rosicrucian Rosy Cross. p178BL Order of Pectoral. p178BM Pectoral Cross. p178BR Symbol used in Hermes Lodge of Stella Matutina. p210T Drawing down the moon. p235B Shamanistic drum. p242T Devils pact. p244T Anton La Vey. p245TR Woman devil. James Wood: p237BR Modern shaman. **MARK FIENNES:** p196T Diana, Frans Floris. **MARY EVANS PICTURE LIBRARY:** p46BR Female witch doctor of the Usumbura religion, of East Africa. p54BR Kaffir witch doctor discovers unfavourable signs. p55T Bronislaw Malinowski in the Trobriand Islands. p55B Swaziland witch-doctor goes round the village 'smelling' for the sorceror. p65T The Golden Ass. p72T Witches dine with the devil, dance round the gallows… . p72B Witches with their familiars. p73T A sabbat in the Basque country. p73B Mother Chattox rides to Pendle Hill. p104 Witch, accompanied by beggar and fool. p105B La sorciere des Vosges. p106T Jennet urges her cat, Tib, to attack her

victim. p109T French village wise woman. p114BL Mother Shipton with familiar. p115T Mother Shipton admonishes Cardinal Wolsey. p116T Isobel Gowdie tells how she and her companions were visited by 'Black John'. p146B La Murqui, witchfinder, indicates marks that prove a pact with Satan. p147B Justice Chamber, Valenciennes. p150BL The 'Malefitz Haus'. p150T Konrad von Marburg sends another victim to the torture chamber and stake. p154T Norwegian 'huldre'. p154B Scandinavian witches call up monsters. p155T Swedish witches. p155B Finnish witches sell favourable winds to sailors. p176T William Butler Yeats. p176BL Maud Gonne. p183B Symbolic painting for Crowley's Temple of the A.A, JFC Fuller. p185M Carl Gustav Jung. p184BR The Passing of Arthur. p214B Witchcraft in flight. p215T Susan B Anthony. p228T Druid priestess. p228B Druids of Anglesey. p245TL Ceremonial seal designed by A Crowley. **MICK SHARP PHOTOGRAPHY:** p190T Modern offerings at prehistoric rock carvings. p191T Tintagel Castle. p191B Madron Well. p203T Bethesda Woods. p230T Sunset from Snowdon summit. **NORMAN BANCROFT HUNT:** p92TR Portrait of Black Elk, Oglala Sioux. **PANOS PICTURES:** p14B Sunrise at Xakanaxa, inside Moremi Game Reserve on the Okavango Delta, Botswana, Pietro Cenini. p14T Victoria Falls, Zimbabwe, Neil Cooper. p15 South eastern wall of Cho-Oyu (8201m) Kumbu, Nepal, JC Callow. p19BL Tashiparkhel Tibetan camp, Wangchuck, Tibetan shaman wearing special ringer hat for trances, Alison Wright. p34T Faith healer tapes up toes and fingers to 'lock in' a djin which possesses the patient. JC Tordai. p34B Herbalist's souq in the old Medina. Jeremy Horner. p36B Pilgrims burning spirit money at the temple of the Spirits' retreat, Hangzhou, Sandrine Rousseau. p38B Shamanic ritual on a boat, Jean-Léo Dugast. p39T wooden good luck charms at a Shinto in Kyoto, J Holmes. p46T Ritual killing of a cow, Betty Press. p48BL Kikuyu witch doctor, Kenya. Stuart Hollis. p49TL Traditional healer's medicines, David Reed. p49B Traditional cure for migraine in Mali, Neil Cooper. p51T Zangbeto (village guardian) at voodoo festival, Caroline Penn. p51BL Voodoo initiates in 'kapame', Caroline Penn. p82L Traditional medicines, Giacomo Pirozzi. p82T Akodessewa market in Lome, Anders Gunnartz. p90B Circumcision dance, Ray Wood. p91B Fetish priest with attendants, Caroline Penn. **PAPILIO PHOTOGRAPHIC:** p19T Arctic Wolf. **PETER NEWARK'S AMERICAN PICTURES:** p93TL Native American Shaman of the Assiniboin tribe, Edward Curtis. p95B Shaman blows pollen over pueblo shrine. p158B Arresting a suspected witch, Howard Pyle. p159L Cotton Mather. p159T Salem. p159BR Girl 'bewitched' at trial. **PETER NEWARK'S HISTORICAL PICTURES:** p63L Witches brewing up a hailstorm, Ulrich Molitor. p74B Witches, cats and rats. p98L Sorcery, AB Frost. p98R Witches concocting flying ointment, Hans Baldung Grien. p112T Devil rides off with Witch. p113B Demon carrying off child. p119T Queen Elizabeth I, Isaac Oliver. p128M Satan gives images to witches to use as charms. p146T Bamberg witch trials, Bavaria. p152B Christian Bowman burned at the stake. p152TL English Witch Anne Turner. p157B Vlad the Impaler. p160B Faustus. Peter Newark's Military Pictures: p132B Expedition embarking for a crusade. p148BL Joan of Arc. p156 Maria Theresa. p157T Dracula. **PETER NEWARK'S PICTURES:** p122T Page of symbols. p122BL Page of symbols 'the seales of the earth'. p123TL Trick bodkins. p126T Man suspected of sorcery. p131BL Waldenses fleeing from their burning village. p131BR Early Papal Crusade against the Waldenses. p141TL Witch sits with devils. p160T Jane Wenham. RA Gilbert: W Wynn Westcott. p179BM Samuel and Mina Mathers. **REX FEATURES:** p188. p193T Wicker Man, Lesley Smith. p231TR James Lovelock. p240T May Day, N Ireland, Lesley Smith. **ROBERT ESTALL PHOTO LIBRARY:** p17B Bushman dancing, David Coulson. p89T Himba women, Namibia, Angela Fisher/Carol Beckwith. **SALLY GRIFFYN:** p204T Doreen Valiente. p221B. **SCALA:** p93B Interior view of the Medicine Lodge, George Catlin. p103 Rissa di giocatori, Pieter il Giovane Bruegel. **SOCIETY OF THE INNER LIGHT:** p184T Dion Fortune. p188B Dion Fortune. **TONY STONE IMAGES:** p202T Water droplet on pink marble, Charles Krebs. **WELLCOME LIBRARY:** p52B A shaman or medicine man with extensive body painting. **WERNER FORMAN ARCHIVE:** p16T. p18BL. p18BR. p22B Detail from coffin of Nespawershepi. p30L Darius I hunts lions from his chariot in a conventional southern Mesopotamian landscape. p37BR An 'immortal' playing a flute in the Tao paradise. p44BR Shiva and Shakti. p44BL Linga, a phallus, symbol of the god Lord Shiva. p48T Senufo kunugbaha mask used in anti-witchcraft rites. p50T A Fon bocio figure. p52TL Bark painting depicting a Wandjina. p52TR A churinga. p53T Petroglyph incised in the rock at an Aboriginal sacred site. p53BL Bark painting depicting three spirit figures. p53BR Aboriginal bark painting of two crocodiles. p83B Shrine of an Ashanti spirit medium. p83TR Stool shrine. p84B Western Pende divination instrument, 'Gulukoshi'. p92M Medicine pipe. p93TR Sun Dance effigi doll. p95T Chest lid. p120BL Crystal ball of Dr John Dee. p120BM Obsidian mirror once belonging to Dr Dee. p202–203B Ring Of Brodgar. p239T Tapestry detail.

Notes

These references give the sources for direct and indirect quotes within the text.

p 27 CUNLIFFE, B., 1992. The Celtic World. London: Constable.

p 33 SORRELL, R., 1988. St Francis of Assisi and Nature. Oxford: OUP.

p 35 HUXLEY, A., 1994. The Perennial Philosophy. London: Flamingo.

p 37 PALMER, M., 1996. The Book of Chuang Tzu. London: Penguin.

pp 38–39 KENDALL, L., 1988. The Life and Hard Times of a Korean Shaman. Honolulu: University of Hawaii Press.

p 47 KNAPPERT, J., 1995. African Mythology. London: Diamond.

p 53 BOURKE, JOHNSON and WHITE, 1980. Before the Invasion: Aboriginal Life to 1788. Oxford: OUP.

p 58 GOODRICK-CLARKE, N., 1990. Paracelsus: essential readings. Wellingborough: Aquarian.

p 69 COHN, N., 1993. Europe's Inner Demons: the Demonization of Christians in Medieval Christendom. London: Pimlico.

pp 72–73 ARROWSMITH, N., 1977. A Field Guide to the Little People. London: Pan.

p 74 HENNINGSEN, G., 1993. The ladies from outside: an archaic pattern of the witches Sabbath. In: B. Ankarloo and G. Henningsen, eds. Early Modern European Witchcraft: Oxford: Clarendon.

p 77 LUCIUS APULEIUS, 1960. The Golden Ass. London: Folio Society.

p 81 BARING, A. and CASHFORD, J., 1993. The Myth of the Goddess. London: Arkana.

p 89 EVANS-PRITCHARD, E., 1985. Witchcraft, Oracles and Magic Among the Azande. Oxford: Clarendon.

p 92 NEIHARDT, J.G., 1995. Black Elk Speaks: being the Life Story of a Holy Man of the Oglala Sioux. Lincoln, NE: University of Nebraska Press.

p 101 MACFARLANE, A., 1999. Witchcraft in Tudor and Stuart England: a Regional and Comparative Study. London: Routledge.

p103 MACFARLANE, A., 1999. Witchcraft in Tudor and Stuart England: a Regional and Comparative Study. London: Routledge.

p 109 CHAMBERLAIN, M., 1981. Old Wives Tales: their History, Remedies and Spells. London: Virago.

p 110 CHAMBERLAIN, M., 1981. Old Wives Tales: their History, Remedies and Spells. London: Virago.

p 111 CHAMBERLAIN, M., 1981. Old Wives Tales: their History, Remedies and Spells. London: Virago.

pp 120–121 ROSEN, B., ed. 1969. Witchcraft. London: Edward Arnold.

pp 122–123 ROSEN, B., ed. 1969. Witchcraft. London: Edward Arnold.

p 128 SANDARS, N.K., ed. 1960. The Epic of Gilgamesh. London: Penguin.

p 130 COHN, N., 1993. Europe's Inner Demons: the Demonization of Christians in Medieval Christendom. London: Pimlico.

p 134 CLARK, S., 1999. Thinking with Demons. Oxford: Clarendon.

p 137 KRAMER, H. and SPRENGER, J., 1971. Malleus Maleficarum. Transl. by Montague Summers c.1486. New York: Dover.

p 151 ROPER, L., 1994. Oedipus and the Devil: Witchcraft, Sexuality and Religion in Early Modern Europe. London: Routledge.

p 153 ROSEN, B., ed. 1969. Witchcraft. London: Edward Arnold.

p 153 LAMER, C., 1981. Enemies of God. London: Chatto & Windus.

p 157 ANKARLOO, B. and HENNINGSEN, G., eds. 1993. Early Modern European Witchcraft: Centres and Peripheries. Oxford: Clarendon.

pp 158–159 GODBEER, R., 1992. The Devil's Dominion. Cambridge: Syndicate.

p 169 LUCE, J., 1973. The End of Atlantis. London: Book Club Associates.

p 171 WANG, R., 1983. The Qabalistic Tarot. York Beach, Maine: Samuel Weiser.

p 172 KING, F., 1990. Modern Ritual Magic. Bridport, Dorset: Prism.

p 182 CROWLEY, A., 1991. Magick in Theory and Practice. Secaucus, NJ: Castle.

p 187 FORTUNE, D., 1989. The Sea Priestess. Wellingborough: Aquarian.

p 194 GARDNER, G., 1988. Witchcraft Today. New York: Magickal Childe.

p 198 GADON, E., 1990. The Once and Future Goddess. Wellingborough: Aquarian.

p 205 KELLY, A., 1991. Crafting the Art of Magic: a History of Modern Witchcraft 1939–1964. St Paul, MN: Llewellyn.

p 209 BUCKLAND, R., 1989. The Complete Book of Saxon Witchcraft. York Beach, Maine: Samuel Weiser.

p 240 WILLIS, T., 1986. Discover Runes. London: Harper Collins.

p 241 PENNICK, N., 1994. Practical Magic in the Northern Tradition. Loughborough: Thoth.

p 244 La VEY, A., 1969. The Satanic Bible. New York: Avon Books.

p 248 HINE, P., 1995. Condensed Chaos. Arizona: New Falcon Publications.

p 248 CARROLL, P., 1987. Liber Null and Psychonaut. York Beach, ME: Samuel Weiser.

INDEX

Italics refer to picture captions.

aboriginals 268
Aborigines, 52–3, 268
abstract symbols 304–5, 410–11
abundance 417, 432–3
Adeline, Guillaume, 148
affirmations 432
Africa, 17, 46–51, 62, 82–91
African traditions 261, 265
alchemy, 58–9, 118, 119, 166–7, 221;
    and cabbala, 171; and
    Rosicrucianism, 172, 173
Alexandrian witchcraft, 206–7,
    209, 216
aligning with nature 308–9, 328
altars 279, 280–1, 401
    abundance 432, 433
    angels 381
    autumn 336
    children 413
    family 428–9
    inspiration 419
    outdoors 414–15
    personal 410–11
    positioning 412–13
    spring 334
    summer 335
    winter 337
    workplace 409
Amaterasu, 38
America, 15, 62, 162–3, 191, 226,
    234; *see also* Canada; Native
    Americans; New England
ancestors, 186; spirits of, 46, 48,
    49, 107, 226; worship of, 15, 38,
    39, 50
amulets 302
    strengthening willpower 387
Anderson, Victor, 216, 217
angels, 32, 50, 72, 105, 119, 223,
    257, 274–5, 343, 361, 381, 465,
    484–5
    fallen, 34, 129, 132
    symbolism 496–7
Anglo-Saxons, 29, 107, 224, 228,
    238, 241
animals 56, 111, 136, 279, 300–1, 491
    as disguise, 62, 73, 94, 131;
    owls, 65, 82, 199;
    sacrifice of, 47, 50, 68, 112, 113,
    243;
    in shamanism, 16, 18, 27, 74, 92,
    107, 234;
    snakes, 58, 84, 247;
    see also familiars
animism, 14, 15, 33, 43, 99, 227, 269
Anthony, Susan B., 215, 216
aphrodisiacs 337
apocalypse, 129, 230
Apuleius, Lucius, 25, 64, 65

Aradia, 80, 213; *see also* Herodias
Aradia (by Charles Leland), 194,
    204, 210, 211
aristocracy, 112, 113, 118–21, 147,
    162
Aristotle, 129
Armenia, 130
aromatics 290–1
Artemis, *see* Diana
Arthurian legends, 27, *78*, 184, 187,
    222, 223–5, 262–3, 275
asceticism, 42
ash trees, 110
astral travel 465, 474–5
astrology, 56–7, 118, 119, 120, 140,
    312–13, 437, 442–5
    and alchemy, 167;
    and Cabbala, 171;
    in Chinese magic, 36;
    in Islam, 34;
    in shamanism, 39;
    in spirit cults, 43;
    and tarot, 170
astronomy 328
Atlantis, 168–9, 184, 186, *222*, 226,
    263
atmospheres 293
    changing 371, 404–5
auras, 166, 465, 472–3
    aura of confidence 387
Australia, 52–3, 191
Austria, 42, 238
autumn 333, 336–7
Azande (African tribe), 55, 63, 85–9,
    90, 99
Aztecs, 215, 230

Babylonia, 56, 129
Banishing Ritual 360–1
Bates, Brian, 200, 239
bedrooms 413
beginnings 372–3, 431
Beltane 333, 335
benandanti, 72, 74, 76
Besant, Annie, 175
Bible, 132, 149, 172, 211;
    view of the Devil, 128;

reference to tarot, 171;
    references to witchcraft, 30–1,
    139, 158
bilocation 475
black magic, 49, 71, 180, 206, 243,
    247
Blavatsky, Helena, 174, 178
blessing 370–1, 429
blessing equipment 351
Bloom, William, 231
blue moon 330
Bodin, Jean, 136, 139, 141
Bonnevaux, Jean de, 134
Book of Shadows 377, 379, 477
breathing exercise 349
Britain, 152–3, 184, 187, 226;
    Freemasonry in, 173;
    Golden Dawn in, 177;
    Northern Tradition in, 238;
    alleged Satanic abuse in, 163,
    244–5;
    shamanism in, 236–7;
    see also England; Scotland; Wales
broomsticks 279, 284
Bruno, Giordano, 32, 260
Buckland, Raymond, 208–9
Budapest, Zsuzsanna, 215, 216
Buddha, 42, 175, 184
Buddhism, 38, 42–3, 44, 182, 192,
    314, 366–7
business, improving 389

Cabbala, 31–2, 33, 167, 170, 171,
    185, 260, 360–1
    use in Gardnerian witchcraft, 193;
    use in secret societies, 172, 173,
    176;
    use in Western Mystery Tradition,
    223
cairns, making 415
calm 366–7
Calvin, John, 143, 145
camomile 423
Canada, 95
Candlemas 288, 332
candles 279, 288–9
cannibalism, 93, 130, 131, 244;
    and witch stereotype, *63*, 75,
    126, 133, 134, 136
Canon Episcopi, 75
carnelian 383
Carroll, Peter, 247, 248
casket, magic 283
Castaneda, Carlos, 234
Catholicism, 142, 143, 144, 154,
    167
cats 301
cauldrons 279, 284
cauls, 18, 72, 73, 108
Cayce, Edgar, 169, 230
Celts, 26–7, 77, 227, 228, 236;
    and druidry, 226, 229
ceremonial magic 267, 302

magic symbols 285
chakras, 45, 269, 286, 424, 473
change 417, 430–1
    changing oneself 403
chaos magic, 219, 246–9
charms 279, 302
China, 36–7, 57, 58–9, 170, 215, 226
Christianity, 25, 30–3, 64, 165, 210,
    260, 264, 280, 288, 304, 314
    and alchemy, 167;
    and Alexandrian witchcraft, 206,
    207;
    and anthropology, 15;
    and class war, 214;
    co-existence with magical
        beliefs, 100, 108, 109, 118;
    and feminism, 198, 214;
    and the Golden Dawn, 1784, 181;
    connection with Islam, 34;
    connection with Korean
        shamanism, 38;
    mystical, 184, 222;
    and the New Age, 230, 233;
    origins of, 129, 130, 194;
    and patriarchal attitudes, 194, 196;
    views on primitive spirituality,
        235;
    and the Reformation, 142–5;
    renunciation of, 73, 112, 113, 116,
        133, 180;
    and Satanism, 242;
    connection with voodoo, 50;
    see also Church; Inquisition, the
Church, 26, 27, 57, 123;
    creates fear of witchcraft, 98, 101,
        125, 147, 161, 199;
    role in persecution of witches,
        135, 141, 156, 162;
    12th century views on witchcraft,
        126–33;
    15th–18th century views on
        witchcraft, 62, 63, 70, 107, 134,
        148;
    see also Christianity; Inquisition,
        the
Circe, 24, 66, 67–9